T0189291

# IFIP Advances in Information and Communication Technology 397

# IFIP – The International Federation for Information Processing

IFIP was founded in 1960 under the auspices of UNESCO, following the First World Computer Congress held in Paris the previous year. An umbrella organization for societies working in information processing, IFIP's aim is two-fold: to support information processing within its member countries and to encourage technology transfer to developing nations. As its mission statement clearly states,

> IFIP's mission is to be the leading, truly international, apolitical organization which encourages and assists in the development, exploitation and application of information technology for the benefit of all people.

IFIP is a non-profitmaking organization, run almost solely by 2500 volunteers. It operates through a number of technical committees, which organize events and publications. IFIP's events range from an international congress to local seminars, but the most important are:

- The IFIP World Computer Congress, held every second year;
- Open conferences;
- Working conferences.

The flagship event is the IFIP World Computer Congress, at which both invited and contributed papers are presented. Contributed papers are rigorously refereed and the rejection rate is high.

As with the Congress, participation in the open conferences is open to all and papers may be invited or submitted. Again, submitted papers are stringently refereed.

The working conferences are structured differently. They are usually run by a working group and attendance is small and by invitation only. Their purpose is to create an atmosphere conducive to innovation and development. Refereeing is also rigorous and papers are subjected to extensive group discussion.

Publications arising from IFIP events vary. The papers presented at the IFIP World Computer Congress and at open conferences are published as conference proceedings, while the results of the working conferences are often published as collections of selected and edited papers.

Any national society whose primary activity is about information processing may apply to become a full member of IFIP, although full membership is restricted to one society per country. Full members are entitled to vote at the annual General Assembly, National societies preferring a less committed involvement may apply for associate or corresponding membership. Associate members enjoy the same benefits as full members, but without voting rights. Corresponding members are not represented in IFIP bodies. Affiliated membership is open to non-national societies, and individual and honorary membership schemes are also offered.

Christos Emmanouilidis   Marco Taisch
Dimitris Kiritsis (Eds.)

# Advances in Production Management Systems

Competitive Manufacturing
for Innovative Products and Services

IFIP WG 5.7 International Conference, APMS 2012
Rhodes, Greece, September 24-26, 2012
Revised Selected Papers, Part I

 Springer

Volume Editors

Christos Emmanouilidis
ATHENA Research and Innovation Centre
in Information Communication and Knowledge Technologies
ATHENA RIC Building, University Campus, Kimeria, 67100 Xanthi, Greece
E-mail: chrisem@ceti.athena-innovation.gr

Marco Taisch
Politecnico di Milano
Department of Management, Economics, and Industrial Engineering
Piazza Leonardo da Vinci, 32, 20133 Milano, Italy
E-mail: marco.taisch@polimi.it

Dimitris Kiritsis
École Polytechnique Fédérale de Lausanne (EPFL)
STI-IGM-LICP, ME A1 396, Station 9, 1015 Lausanne, Switzerland
E-mail: dimitris.kiritsis@epfl.ch

ISSN 1868-4238  ISSN 1868-422X
ISBN 978-3-642-44242-1  ISBN 978-3-642-40352-1 (eBook)
DOI 10.1007/978-3-642-40352-1
Springer Heidelberg Dordrecht London New York

CR Subject Classification (1998): J.1, J.7, I.2, H.1, H.4, C.2, K.4.3

*Typesetting:* Camera-ready by author, data conversion by Scientific Publishing Services, Chennai, India

Printed on acid-free paper

Springer is part of Springer Science+Business Media (www.springer.com)

# Preface

Since the first conference that took place in Helsinki back in 1990, APMS is one of the major events and the official conference of the IFIP Working Group 5.7 on Advances in Production Management Systems. Recently, APMS successfully took place in Washington (USA, 2005), Wroclaw (Poland, 2006), Linköping (Sweden, 2007), Espoo (Finland, 2008), Bordeaux (France, 2009), Cernobbio (Italy, 2010), and Stavanger (Norway 2011).

APMS 2012 was sponsored by the IFIP WG 5.7 and co-sponsored by the ATHENA Research & Innovation Centre and the Hellenic Maintenance Society in Greece. In an era of increased globalization and ever-pressing needs for improved efficiency, the APMS 2012 theme was "Competitive Manufacturing for Innovative Products and Services." In this setting, among the key elements of success in modern manufacturing and production management are:

- **Resource Efficiency**: the ability to perform in a resource-efficient manner throughout the lifecycle of a production process, product use or offered services.
- **Key Enabling Technologies**: the exploitation of the latest materials, manufacturing and production control technologies to support competitive and sustainable production.
- **Networked Enterprise and Global Manufacturing and Supply Chains**: the ability to operate as a globally interconnected organization and perform at a global scale, both at an intra- and inter-organizational scale.
- **Knowledge Intensity and Exploitation**: the efficient use of enterprise and human resources tangible and intangible knowledge, including efficient knowledge lifecycle management.
- **Innovation**: the ability to efficiently port R&D results into competitive new forms of production, products or services.

The APMS 2012 conference brought together leading experts from industry, academia and governmental organizations. They presented the latest developments in production management systems and debated how to shape up the future of competitive manufacturing. It comprised seven keynote talks and 36 sessions, including a dedicated Industry Panel Session, to offer the practitioners' view on linking research to industry, thus efficiently supporting the innovation process. The keynotes offered insight into cutting-edge issues of production management and its future, comprising the following talks:

- "A Business Perspective for Manufacturing Research," Jochen Rode, SAP
- "ICT-Driven Innovation in the Factories of the Future," Rolf Riemenschneider, European Commission
- "Sustainable Manufacturing: Towards a Competitive Industrial Base in Europe," Filip Geerts, CECIMO

- "ICT Integration Challenges in Manufacturing: From the Device to the Enterprise Level," Thilo Sauter, Austrian Academy of Sciences
- "The IMS Global Platform Services for Manufacturing Research and Innovation," Dan Nagy, IMS
- "Energy Management Operations in Shipping Industry," Takis Varelas, DANAOS
- "The FoF PPP Call in WP2013 and Future Opportunities for Manufacturing R&I in Horizon2020," Andrea Gentili, European Commission

Industry and academia converged in a stimulating Industry Panel Session, organized by Prof. Hermann Loedding and Dr. Gregor Alexander von Cieminski. The session theme was "Linking Research to Industry: The Practitioner's view on Competitive Manufacturing for Innovative Products and Services." The following panellist talks introduced the session discussion:

- "Leadership in Electronics Operations @Continental," Wolfgang Menzel, Continental
- "Integrating Industrial Needs with Academic Perspectives — Concept and Realization of the RWTH Aachen High Tech Campus," Volker Stich, RWTH Aachen

Wolfgang Menzel and Volker Stich were joined in the panel by Paul Schönsleben (ETH), Dan Nagy, IMS and Filip Geerts, CECIMO and debated about the crucial linkage between research and industry in order to shed light on what constitutes successful practices in bringing forward R&D from the lab to industry-relevant innovation. The panel argued that higher education institutions should offer opportunities to students to undertake part of their studies in industry, with this being acknowledged and recognized as a formal part of education. Furthermore, industry could have more active presence within public research and educational campuses and FIR-RWTH Aachen was presented as an example of such an endeavor. Emphasis was placed on the industrial relevance of research, which would depart from theoretical solutions for "non-relevant" problems to conducting "relevant" research offering pragmatic and innovative solutions to industry.

Several special sessions were organized and ongoing research initiatives and projects presented their progress and results. A PhD Workshop was held prior to the conference, chaired by Sergio Cavalieri (University of Bergamo) and offered the opportunity to PhD researchers to present their research plans, objectives, and results to scientific discussants and gain valuable feedback to strengthen their research plan and activities.

At the conclusion of the conference, following the APMS tradition, the conference offered the following awards:

- Burbidge award for best paper to Dimitris Mourtzis (University of Patras)
- Burbidge award for best presentation to Morten Lund (University of Aalborg)

– Best PhD workshop paper award to Elzbieta Pawlik (University of Strathclyde)

Approximately 240 academics, researchers, practitioners and scientists from 31 countries joined the APMS 2012 conference, sharing their expertise and providing insight into what constitutes the currently best practice in manufacturing and production management, while also projecting into the future of competitive manufacturing for innovative products and services. The conference involved a high-quality International Steering and a Scientific Committee of acknowledged excellence, while the review process involved 73 experts, all making key contributions to the conference success. The conference program included 196 regular presentations and 11 PhD workshop presentations. The review process involved pre-conference extended abstracts reviews and a post-conference full paper review process, followed by a final paper submission by the authors, addressing the review comments. The result of this process is the present two-volume edited proceedings, comprising 182 full papers, organized under the following sections:

– Part I, Sustainability, including Energy Efficient Manufacturing, Sustainable Value Creation, Business Models and Strategies
– Part II, Design, Manufacturing and Production Management, including Mass Customization, Products of the Future and Manufacturing Systems Design, Advanced Design, Manufacturing and Production Management, as well as Robotics in Manufacturing
– Part III, Human Factors, Learning and Innovation, including Modern Learning in Manufacturing and Production Systems, Human Factors, Quality and Knowledge Management, as well as Innovation in Products and Services in Developing Countries
– Part IV, ICT and Emerging Technologies in Production Management, including Emerging Technologies in Production and the Lifecycle Management of Products and Assets, Enterprise Integration and Interoperability, as well as ICT for Manufacturing, Services and Production Management
– Part V, Product and Asset Lifecycle Management, including Product Lifecycle Management, Asset Lifecycle Management, as well as Performance and Risk Management
– Part VI, Services, Supply Chains and Operations, including Services, Managing International Operations, Supply Networks and Supply Chain Management, as well as Production Management, Operations and Logistics

We wish to acknowledge the support of **Intelligent Manufacturing Systems (IMS)** for the USB sticks and Lanyards for badges, as well as **Prisma Electronics SA** for sponsoring the APMS 2012 Welcome Reception.

We wish to thank the active members of the IFIP WG 5.7 community for their contribution and support of the conference, their support in the papers review process and the promotion of APMS 2012 through their networks and collaborating partners. Particular thanks are due to the **ATHENA Research and Innovation Centre** and the **Hellenic Maintenance Society** in Greece for co-sponsoring and supporting the conference and Zita Congress SA for their professional conference management services.

The conference was hosted on the island of Rhodes, Greece, a world-class destination, boasting a unique mixture of ancient and modern with holiday attractions and a continuing history of well over three millennia. According to mythology, Rhodes was created by the union of Helios, the Titan personalizing the sun, and the nymph Rhode. The ancient city of Rhodes hosted one of the ancient wonders of the world, the Colossus of Rhodes, a giant statute of Helios. Manufacturing and production management have made giant strides and continue to contribute toward a world of smart, sustainable and inclusive growth, but much more needs to be done and a global effort is needed to continue pushing toward such ends. The APMS 2012 conference constituted a focused effort and contribution in supporting such aims. We hope that the present two-volume set will be of interest to the industrial and academic communities working in the area of manufacturing and production management and the associated enabling technologies.

February 2013                                      Christos Emmanouilidis
                                                        Marco Taisch
                                                      Dimitris Kiritsis

# Organization

**The APMS 2012 conference was** sponsored by the IFIP WG 5.7 Advances in Production Management Systems, co-sponsored by the ATHENA Research & Innovation Centre, in Information, Communication and Knowledge Technologies, Greece, and co-sponsored by the Hellenic Maintenance Society (HMS), Greece.

## Conference Chair

Christos Emmanouilidis      ATHENA Research & Innovation Centre, Greece

## Conference Co-chairs

Marco Taisch      Politecnico di Milano, Italy
Dimitris Kiritsis      Ecole Polytechnique Fédérale de Lausanne, Switzerland

## APMS 2012 International Advisory Board

| | |
|---|---|
| Christos Emmanouilidis | ATHENA R.I.C., Greece |
| Jan Frick | University of Stavanger, Norway |
| Dimitris Kiritsis | EPFL, Switzerland |
| Vidosav Majstorovich | University of Belgrade, Serbia |
| Riitta Smeds | Aalto University, Finland |
| Volker Stich | FIR - RWTH Aachen, Germany |
| Marco Taisch | Politecnico di Milano, Italy |
| Bruno Vallespir | University of Bordeaux, France |

## APMS 2012 Doctoral Workshop Chair

Sergio Cavalieri      University of Bergamo, Italy

## APMS 2012 Local Organizing Committee

| | |
|---|---|
| Christos Emmanouilidis | ATHENA R.I.C, Greece |
| Athanassios Kalogeras | ATHENA R.I.C, Greece |
| Zacharias Kaplanidis | Zita Congress, Greece |
| Irini Katti | Zita Congress, Greece |
| Christos Koulamas | ATHENA R.I.C, Greece |
| Dimitris Karampatzakis | ATHENA R.I.C, Greece |
| Nikos Papathanasiou | ATHENA R.I.C, Greece |
| Petros Pistofidis | ATHENA R.I.C, Greece |

# APMS 2012 Conference Secretariat

Zita Congress SA             Attica, Greece

# International Scientific Committee

| | |
|---|---|
| Bjørn Andersen | Norwegian University of Science and Technology, Norway |
| Abdelaziz Bouras | University of Lyon, France |
| Luis M. Camarinha-Matos | New University of Lisbon, Portugal |
| Sergio Cavalieri | University of Bergamo, Italy |
| Stephen Childe | University of Exeter, UK |
| Alexandre Dolgui | Ecole des Mines de Saint-Etienne, France |
| Guy Doumeingts | University Bordeaux, France |
| Heidi C. Dreyer | Norwegian University of Technology and Science, Norway |
| Christos Emmanouilidis | ATHENA Research & Innovation Centre, Greece |
| Peter Falster | Technical University of Denmark, Denmark |
| Rosanna Fornasiero | ITIA-CNR, Italy |
| Jan Frick | University of Stavanger, Norway |
| Susumu Fujii | Sophia University, Japan |
| Marco Garetti | Politecnico di Milano, Italy |
| Antonios Gasteratos | Democritus University of Thrace, Greece |
| Bernard Grabot | Ecole Nationale d'Ingénieurs de TARBES, France |
| Robert W. Grubbström | Linköping Institute of Technology, Sweden |
| Thomas Gulledge | George Mason University, USA |
| Hans-Henrik Hvolby | University of Aalborg, Denmark |
| Harinder Jagdev | National University of Ireland, Ireland |
| Athanassios Kalogeras | ATHENA Research & Innovation Centre, Greece |
| Dimitris Kiritsis | EPFL, Switzerland |
| Christos Koulamas | ATHENA Research & Innovation Centre, Greece |
| Andrew Kusiak | University of Iowa, USA |
| Lenka Landryova | VSB Technical University Ostrava, Czech Republic |
| Ming Lim | Aston University, UK |
| Hermann Lödding | Technical University of Hamburg, Germany |
| Vidoslav D. Majstorovic | University of Belgrade, Serbia |
| Kepa Mendibil | University of Stratchclyde, UK |
| Kai Mertins | Fraunhofer IPK, Germany |
| Hajime Mizuyama | Kyoto University, Japan |
| Irenilza Nääs | Universidade Paulista, Brazil |
| Gilles Neubert | ESC Saint-Etienne, France |

| Jan Olhager | Linköping University, Sweden |
| Jens Ove Riis | University of Alborg, Denmark |
| Henk Jan Pels | Eindhoven University of Technology, Netherlands |
| Selwyn Piramuthu | University of Florida, USA |
| Alberto Portioli | Politecnico di Milano, Italy |
| Asbjorn Rolstadas | Norwegian University of Science and Technology, Norway |
| Paul Schoensleben | ETH Zurich, Switzerland |
| Dan L. Shunk | Arizona State University, USA |
| Riitta Smeds | Aalto University, Finland |
| Vijay Srinivasan | National Institute of Standards and Technology, USA |
| Kenn Steger-Jensen | Aalborg University, Denmark |
| Kathryn E. Stecke | University of Texas, USA |
| Volker Stich | FIR RWTH Aachen, Germany |
| Richard Lee Storch | University of Washington, USA |
| Jan Ola Strandhagen | SINTEF, Norway |
| Stanisław Strzelczak | Warsaw University of Technology, Poland |
| Marco Taisch | Politecnico di Milano, Italy |
| Ilias Tatsiopoulos | National Technical University of Athens, Greece |
| Sergio Terzi | University of Bergamo, Italy |
| Klaus-Dieter Thoben | University of Bremen/BIBA, Germany |
| Mario Tucci | University of Florence, Italy |
| Bruno Vallespir | University of Bordeaux, France |
| Agostino Villa | Politecnico di Torino, Italy |
| Gregor Alexander von Cieminski | ZF Friedrichshafen AG, Germany |
| Dan Wang | Harbin Institute of Technology, China |
| J.C. Wortmann | University of Groningen, The Netherlands |
| Iveta Zolotová | Technical University of Košice, Slovakia |

## External Reviewers

| Alexander von Cieminski, Gregor | ZF Friedrichshafen AG, Germany |
| Andersen Bjorn | Norwegian University of Science and Technology, Norway |
| Battaïa Olga | EMSE, France |
| Bouras Abdelaziz | Lumière University Lyon 2, France |
| Camarinha-Matos Luis M. | New University of Lisbon, Portugal |
| Cavalieri Sergio | University of Bergamo, Italy |
| Childe Stephen | University of Exeter, UK |
| Corti Donatella | Politecnico di Milano, Italy |
| Dolgui Alexandre | Ecole des Mines de Saint-Etienne, France |

| | |
|---|---|
| Dreyer Heidi C. | Norwegian University of Technology and Science (NTNU), Norway |
| Emmanouilidis Christos | ATHENA Research & Innovation Centre, Greece |
| Errasti Ander | TECNUN University of Navarra, Spain |
| Evans Steve | University of Cambridge, UK |
| Eynard Benoit | Université de Technologie de Compiègne, France |
| Falster Peter | Technical University of Denmark, Denmark |
| Fornasiero Rosanna | ITIA-cnr, Italy |
| Frick Jan | University of Stavanger, Norway |
| Garetti Marco | Politecnico di Milano, Italy |
| Gasteratos Antonios | Democritus University of Thrace, Greece |
| Grabot Bernard | Ecole Nationale d'Ingenieurs de TARBES, France |
| Grubbstrom Robert W. | Linkoping Institute of Technology, Sweden |
| Hvolby Hans-Henrik | Aalborg University, Denmark |
| Jagdev Harinder | National University of Ireland, Galway, Ireland |
| Kaihara Toshiya | Kobe University, Japan |
| Kalogeras Athanasios | ATHENA Research & Innovation Centre, Greece |
| Karampatzakis Dimitris | ATHENA Research & Innovation Centre, Greece |
| Kiritsis Dimitris | EPFL, Switzerland |
| Koulamas Christos | ATHENA Research & Innovation Centre, Greece |
| Krüger Volker | Aalborg University, Denmark |
| Landryova Lenka | VSB - Technical University of Ostrava, Czech Republic |
| Lim Ming | University of Derby, UK |
| Loedding Hermann | Technical University of Hamburg, Germany |
| Macchi Marco | Politecnico di Milano, Italy |
| Majstorovic Vidosav D. | University of Belgrade, MEF, Serbia |
| Mandic Vesna | University of Kragujevac, Serbia |
| May Gökan | Politecnico di Milano, Italy |
| Mendibil Kepa | University of Strathclyde, UK |
| Mertins Kai | Fraunhofer IPK/TU Berlin, Germany |
| Mizuyama Hajime | Aoyama Gakuin University, Japan |
| Nääs Irenilza | Paulista University-UNIP, Brazil |
| Netland Torbjoern H. | Norwegian University of Science and Technology, Norway |
| Neubert Gilles | Ecole Supérieure de Commerce, France |
| Olhager Jan | Lund University, Sweden |
| Oliveira Manuel F. | SINTEF, Norway |

# Table of Contents – Part I

## Part I: Sustainability

### Energy Efficient Manufacturing

## Sustainable Value Creation, Business Models and Strategies

## Part II: Design, Manufacturing and Production Management

### Mass Customization

## Products of the Future and Manufacturing Systems Design

## Advanced Design, Manufacturing and Production Management

## Robotics in Manufacturing

# Part III: Human Factors, Learning and Innovation

## Modern Learning in Manufacturing and Production Systems

## Human Factors, Quality and Knowledge Management

## Innovation in Products and Services in Developing Countries

# Table of Contents – Part II

## ICT for Manufacturing, Services and Production Management

# Part V: Product and Asset Lifecycle Management

## Product Lifecycle Management

## Asset Lifecycle Management

# Performance and Risk Management

# Part VI: Services, Supply Chains and Operations

## Services

## Managing International Operations

## Supply Networks and Supply Chain Management

## Production Management, Operations and Logistics

# Toward Energy Efficient Manufacturing:
# A Study on Practices and Viewpoint of the Industry

Gökan May, Marco Taisch, Bojan Stahl, and Vahid Sadr

Politecnico di Milano, Department of Management, Economics and Industrial Engineering,
Piazza Leonardo da Vinci 32, Milano, 20133, Italy
{goekan.may,vahid.sadr}@mail.polimi.it,
{marco.taisch,bojan.stahl}@polimi.it

**Abstract.** The main objective of this study is to assess current situation and applications in the industry with respect to energy efficiency. From literature, a four pillar framework (strategy, tool, process, technology) has been developed, outlining the essential elements to successfully integrate energy efficiency in manufacturing. Based on the framework, a questionnaire is developed to assess manufacturing companies in Europe. How and what companies are doing currently to integrate energy efficiency in their manufacturing is under investigation through surveys and complementary case studies. This paper presents a fact finding study, aimed to understand the main motivations, limitations, and effectiveness of integrating energy efficiency in manufacturing. Hence, this study intends to establish a basis for the companies and academia to have a holistic understanding on energy efficient practices as a first step on the way to integrate energy efficiency in manufacturing. Consequently, the gaps between theory and practice are revealed.

**Keywords:** Energy efficient manufacturing, energy management, industrial viewpoint, manufacturing plant, sustainability.

## 1    Introduction

Manufacturing has changed its focus and approaches from pure cost to quality, productivity and delivery performance in the last couple of decades [1]. Currently, the new topic of interest that has gained significant attention from both academia and the industry is energy efficiency due to the significant environmental and economic impacts associated with consumption of energy. The change of approach in the industrial world stemmed from the global drivers for improving energy efficiency such as climate change, scarcity of resources and energy supply as well as the industrial drivers including rising energy prices, ever-stricter becoming legislations, customer demand and awareness along with competitiveness have pushed energy efficient manufacturing to the top of the agenda for both governments and companies.

Companies have been feeling the pressure and urge to examine how their processes, methods and structures could become more energy-efficient considering global and industrial drivers forcing them to do so. Since energy consumption

C. Emmanouilidis, M. Taisch, D. Kiritsis (Eds.): APMS 2012, Part I, IFIP AICT 397, pp. 1–8, 2013.

advances in having paramount importance for manufacturing companies, continuous improvement in energy management is now integrated into strategies of companies. In this regard, taking action (e.g. adopting energy management standards such as ISO 50001) to build a continuous improvement process to use energy resources more efficiently becomes essential [2].

In this manner, this research is based on a fact finding study, aimed to understand the main motivations, limitations, and effectiveness of integrating energy efficiency in manufacturing. In this vein, we investigate the current practices and approaches of the companies regarding energy efficiency where we suggest an evaluation framework in order to successfully integrate Energy Efficiency (EE) in manufacturing in a systematic way, with the aim of gaining insight into energy efficiency in manufacturing and finding out the gaps between theory and practice.

Thus, the main objective of the study is to assess current situation and applications in the industry with respect to energy efficiency improvement measures using the proposed framework to help companies to integrate energy efficiency in manufacturing. How and what companies are doing currently to integrate energy efficiency in their manufacturing is investigated through surveys and case studies.

Hence, this study intends to establish a basis for the companies and academia to have a holistic understanding on energy efficient practices as a first step on the way to integrate energy efficiency in manufacturing. In this context, we identify the main objectives as below:

- Understand how and what companies are doing currently to integrate energy efficiency in their manufacturing
- Determine the priorities of companies and stimuli for energy efficient manufacturing
- Understand the level of consideration given to integration of energy efficiency in manufacturing on the industry side
- Develop insight into the use of ICT and other supporting tools/methodologies for improving energy efficiency
- Identify the gap between the theory and the practice

## 2    State of the Art

Nowadays, energy consumption is considered as one of the key item for sustainable development due to its environmental, economic and social impacts. Brundtland Commission [3] defines sustainable development as "a development that meets the needs of the present without compromising the ability of future generations to meet their own needs". In this regard, IEA [4] considers energy efficiency improvements as a principal component for sustainable development. Thus, energy efficiency becomes a core issue for policy-makers, industries, and society. Indeed, improving EE has been mentioned as paramount by several communities of research, industry and policy-making in order to overcome the challenges of today stemmed from both global and industrial drivers of energy efficiency (e.g. [5]). Aligned with 3 pillars of sustainability, improving EE provides benefits in environmental (e.g. reduced GHG emissions), economic (e.g. reduced costs, improved competitiveness) and social (e.g. increased security of energy supply) dimensions. Hence, above mentioned gains prove powerful interdependence between energy efficiency and sustainable development [6].

Energy efficiency is a key target for the factory of the future stemmed from both global and industrial drivers and hence many studies have been carried out in the field of industrial energy efficiency. In fact, Chow et al. [7] points EE as the "lifeblood of technical and economic development".

Based on the critical review of the literature, the studies on energy efficient manufacturing can be grouped in six main dimensions which are essential to integrate energy efficiency in manufacturing.

- **Drivers/Barriers:** As the name implies, these are the stimuli/drivers for energy efficient manufacturing which are the main reasons for the industrial companies to implement energy efficiency measures in manufacturing.
- **Strategic approach:** The main issue here is the alignment of energy efficiency in manufacturing with corporate goals. Commitment of top management is a crucial part for implementation of any kind of measures in the industry and establishes the base for strategic focus. The concepts under scrutiny regarding the strategic focus of the companies are e.g. policies & standardization; strategic decisions (e.g. buy-sell, demand management, location decisions, etc.); technology selection, development and deployment; Investments on R&D and innovation; and eventually voluntary initiatives (e.g. CSR, etc.).
- **Information and Communication Technologies:** ICT has the potential to play a very significant role in improving energy efficiency in manufacturing and its share and importance has been growing during recent years. Hence, ICT as a supporting tool and an enabler for achieving energy efficiency in manufacturing needs a further consideration.
- **Supporting tools and methodologies:** This part comprises the methods and tools available which mostly provide support in making energy related analysis and decisions in manufacturing environment. Examples to this dimension could be modeling and analysis (e.g. simulation, DEA modeling, etc.), energy assessment tools, sustainability tools (e.g. LCA), emission calculation tools and benchmarking tools & techniques.
- **Manufacturing Process Paradigms:** To manufacture any product, some set of processes should be followed and types of processes depend on the type of products as well as companies' considerations of different aspects and related decisions in manufacturing. Manufacturing technologies (e.g. development of technologies & materials), manufacturing process management (MPM), process design & optimization, switching energy modes of machines (i.e. on, off, stand-by, etc.) and scheduling are examples to paradigms to be considered.
- **Manufacturing Performances:** Traditional performance measures considered in manufacturing include factors such as quality, cost, delivery time and safety. Thus, it is essential to investigate the impacts of integrating energy efficiency as another performance dimension in manufacturing on traditional performances.

## 3     Research Design and Framework

Taking the concepts to support and foster energy management in manufacturing such as processes, methods along with standardization and combining them with the significant role of ICT also stressed out in the literature as mentioned before, we come up with a 4-pillar framework comprised by the enablers for energy efficient manufacturing (i.e. Strategic approach, manufacturing process paradigms, supporting tools/methodologies and ICT). Integrated with the drivers/barriers on one side and attained manufacturing performances on the other side, we propose the framework (see Figure 1) for successfully integrating energy efficiency in manufacturing that can also be of use for assessing the current practices in the industry with the aim of finding out the gaps between the concepts in theory and industrial practices in the area.

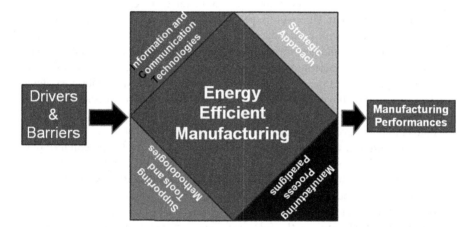

**Fig. 1.** Framework for successfully integrating energy efficiency in manufacturing

The framework provides a holistic view on all the aspects to be considered for implementing energy efficiency measures in manufacturing. The model can as well be of use for assessing the current practices of the industrial companies from an energy efficiency perspective and for understanding how and what companies are doing currently to integrate energy efficiency into their manufacturing processes. Thus, it provides support in identifying the gaps between the available solutions in theory and companies' current actual practices.

Utilizing the proposed framework, it is possible to gain a profound insight into current practices in the industry that might reveal the gap with theory as well as into overall integration of energy efficiency in manufacturing. Besides, we investigate the importance of ICT as an enabler for energy efficient manufacturing along with the non-energy benefits associated with energy improvement measures. Further, the impact of energy efficient way of thinking and implementation on traditional manufacturing performances is highlighted.

# 4    Research Methodology

To pursue the objectives of the study, an explorative research is carried out through the development and use of an on-line survey in order to assess manufacturing companies operating in Europe and is further supported by complementary case studies.

Survey method is mainly followed in the study to assess the energy efficiency related practices in the industry with the aim of gaining insight using the developed framework. Based on the research objectives and framework described previously, a questionnaire of 10 comprehensive questions has been developed to assess the companies. This survey was composed of questions about company characteristics, energy efficient strategies and applications of the company, supporting tools and relevant manufacturing processes.

Questionnaire is thus based on the main components of the framework which comprises four enablers for energy efficient manufacturing, drivers/barriers and attained manufacturing performances. So, questions are identified related to these sub-points. On-line version of the questionnaire has been created using Survey Monkey and was sent to companies via the following link: http://www.surveymonkey.com/s/Y59Y36C.

Questionnaire was sent to a combination of large companies and SMEs. Sample firms were selected from manufacturing companies operating in Europe in mechanical, electric and automotive sectors. The respondents were all relatively large companies. This survey includes questions about company characteristics, energy efficient strategies and applications of the company, supporting tools and relevant manufacturing processes.

Furthermore, case study methodology is used as complementary to surveys to further analyze and validate the gathered data. The principal way of data gathering through the case study is conducting interviews and analyzing sustainability related reports.

# 5    Results and Discussion

As explained in Part 4, the questions are organized in three parts (i.e. drivers/barriers; enablers; manufacturing performances in trade-off). The discussions of the results are also presented in this structure:

## 5.1    Drivers and Barriers

Companies considering energy efficiency performance measures in manufacturing could have many reasons or drivers to do so. Among them, reduction of costs, reduction of the environmental impact (commitment to reduce the environmental impact), image improvement due to enhanced reputation and achieving sustainability targets are the most important reasons provided by companies interviewed. Changes in customer behavior and compliance with legislations are considered relatively less forcing factors whilst reducing carbon footprint is not considered as a driver in most of the companies. However, companies' responds regarding their commitment to reduce environmental impact here might not reflect the reality as they tend to show/think their companies more committed than they actually are. In reality, most of the decisions and interest depend on either costs or long term plans like image improvement.

From the study it has been found that companies are feeling responsible for considering energy efficiency as a new performance target area in manufacturing. However, insufficient investment paybacks (e.g. ROI), the lack of fund to pay for improvements and insufficient government incentives are considered by them as the most important barriers to implementing energy efficiency in manufacturing. Some companies mention the weakness of current legislations and policies on forcing the industry to become more energy efficient since they are mostly easy to tackle and not challenging enough especially for large enterprises. In this manner, manufacturing firms do not aim toward energy efficiency by considering it as one of the key target areas unless they find strong financial motivation in doing so.

## 5.2    Enablers for Energy Efficient Manufacturing

Most of the companies interviewed have high level sustainability and energy related initiatives such as CSR (corporate social responsibility) strategic scheme, ISO14001 (Environmental management system) and ISO 50001 (Energy Management System). This shows that top managements are also committed for overall sustainability and energy efficiency in the industry. However, when it comes to the ground level, as of manufacturing, there is not enough evidence that energy efficiency is properly integrated in top-down approach.

To better understand if top managements have genuinely cascaded energy efficiency into manufacturing, other questions have been asked such as the way they integrate energy efficiency in manufacturing, level of investments, and implementation of different options for improvements in energy efficiency, how tradeoffs between traditional performances (cost, quality, delivery and functionality) are considered and finally the type of methods they follow.

The significance of different methods and ways in integrating energy efficiency in manufacturing was one of the key concerns of the study. In this context, companies reported "optimization of current production processes" and "aligning production planning with energy efficiency practices (e.g. switching energy states of the equipment)" as two key factors to be followed effectively. "Integrating energy efficiency in product and process design" along with "combining energy efficiency with manufacturing strategies (e.g. resource planning)" are considered as important however with a less impact compared to former ones.

The companies were interviewed also for the activities they have been following to improve energy efficiency in their manufacturing plants. They mentioned energy monitoring and control, use of new technologies and consultancy with energy experts among the mostly adopted ways in their company. Energy recovery and renewable energy use, on the other hand, are not considered and do not take place in most of the firms. In fact, these are the two areas for energy improvement in manufacturing facilities which have been somehow ignored to date but are considered as two important future streams both for academia and industry as far as energy efficiency in manufacturing is concerned.

When companies were asked to rate the importance of different ways for improving energy efficiency regardless of they have been following or not, the most important activities highlighted were "more efficient equipment and technologies for improving production processes", "optimizing the plant level activities by using technical services (e.g. HVAC control system), "enhanced monitoring and control of energy consumption" and "use of energy related performance indicators". Above mentioned activities are indeed aligned with the two ways for reducing energy consumption as defined by Rahimifard [11]. The latter two are in fact the main essential elements for an effective energy management in a manufacturing plant. On the other hand, ICT support on energy efficient manufacturing and consideration of energy efficiency in long term decisions are not considered as essential and important by contacted companies. Taking into account the importance of ICT related stream for research in energy efficiency and so for academia, we might say that the viewpoint of the industry is not aligned with academia at this point. However, this might be due to the fact that industrial contacts might have thought regarding the current practices and needs whereas academia is more into potential solutions for future aligned with the vision for Factories of the Future.

With regards to ICT support for enhanced energy management, "improving the reliability of the data" and "evaluation software for process performance with respect to energy efficiency" are the main aspects companies stressed out. Especially, the latter one is of good use since it helps evaluating the trade-off between traditional performances in manufacturing such as cost, quality, delivery and flexibility and improvements in energy efficiency as well.

Besides, there are several tools used in manufacturing to support decision making with regards to energy efficiency, as also mentioned in part 3. Companies interviewed mostly use energy assessment tools and cost calculation & energy tracking tools whilst benchmarking and simulation tools are used relatively less compared to former mentioned ones. However, carbon footprint measurement tools and sustainability assessment tools such as LCA are not adopted by majority of the companies for energy related decision making.

## 5.3    Manufacturing Performances

Till now, the main drivers and barriers for companies towards improving energy efficient manufacturing then the main enablers to integrate energy efficiency in manufacturing have been discussed. Now, in this section the impacts of integrating energy related issues on traditional performances are investigated. This is a crucial issue, since it is seldom that companies worry about energy efficiency issues if the traditional manufacturing performances such as cost, quality, delivery and flexibility are jeopardized.

Companies interviewed stressed that fully integrating energy efficiency in manufacturing might sometimes cost more than the gained they could have achieved.

Moreover, quality could be affected due to some strategies towards energy efficiency (e.g. shutting down the equipment to reduce energy consumption).

But, they also stress that non-financial gains have been achieved such as improved company image, new skills and competences, increased customer acceptance and raised overall sensitivity towards environmental impacts inside the company. Therefore, the main challenge here is how to structure manufacturing strategy, tools, processes and information systems in such a way those traditional manufacturing performances are either unaffected or even improved.

To sum up, the developed framework can easily be used to evaluate how energy efficiency is effectively addressed in manufacturing industries. As also highlighted with the key findings of the study, the consideration of energy efficiency is not matured enough to attain the general energy performance goals expected by multiple stakeholders. In that vein, academia should not only focus on developing solutions for key aspects (i.e. 4 enablers) in a disparate manner but also on need to investigate new way of holistic and integrative design of manufacturing systems, better aligning strategy objectives with energy improvement goals.

# 6    Conclusion

In this research, we investigated practices and viewpoint of the manufacturing industry with regards to energy efficiency. The findings revealed that although there has been a consistent progress in the industry toward energy efficiency, the implementation of the concept is still not mature enough. There is no sign of strong evidence regarding the integration of energy efficiency in manufacturing as a new performance target area.

## References

1. Hon, K.K.B.: Performance and evaluation of manufacturing systems. CIRP Annals – Manufacturing Technology 54(2), 139–154 (2005)
2. Fraunhofer IPA, Designing Energy-Efficient Production Processes (2011), http://www.ipa.fraunhofer.de/index.php?id=188&L=2
3. Brundtland, Report at world commission on environment and development. Technical report, United Nations (1987)
4. IEA: Worldwide Trends in Energy Use and Efficiency, Key Insights from IEA Indicator Analysis. (2008), http://www.iea.org/Textbase/Papers/2008/indicators_2008.pdf
5. ICC: Energy efficiency: a world business perspective. International Chamber of Commerce (2007)
6. Eurostat, Measuring progress towards a more sustainable europe. Technical report, European Commission Eurostat (2007)
7. Chow, J., et al.: Energy Resources and Global Development. Science 302(5650), 1528–1531 (2003)

# Energy Efficient Production through a Modified –Green–PPC and a Communication Framework for the Energy Supply Chain to Manage Energy Consumption and Information

Ulrich Brandenburg, Sebastian Kropp, Jorge Sunyer, and Daniel Batalla-Navarro

Institute for Industrial Management at RWTH Aachen University,
Pontdriesch 14/16, 52062 Aachen, Germany
{Ulrich.Brandenburg,Sebastian.Kropp}@fir.rwth-aachen.de

**Abstract.** This paper presents a definition of an energy product model through a holistic approach of energy management that recognizes both the side of the energy provider and energy consumer. Therefore, it is needed to design a model for a "Green PPC" that uses energy consumption as an additional planning and control criterion to enable a producing company to optimise and forecast its energy consumption. Furthermore, an inter-organisational information system will be described that allows an information exchange with the energy supplier to include the energy use in production planning.

**Keywords:** Production planning and control, energy efficiency, energy management systems, inter-organisational information systems.

## 1    Introduction

The implementation of energy management processes and tools is growing in importance for today's organisations. Especially within the manufacturing industries which are more and more reliant on the availability and efficient management of the scarce resource energy, the sensibility for this topic is heightened also on the decision making level. The decisive factors for this development are the increasing costs of energy, aspects of sustainability and an increasingly tightened regulative environment.

Increasing demand for energy coupled with a decreasing supply on the world markets results in continuously increasing prices for energy. This general development as well as the dynamics in price setting creates uncertainty for organisations with respect to accurately calculated energy costs [1]. This demand for energy efficient production is intensified by the demand of customers for sustainable products. Due to this increasing demand, organisations which are successfully able to produce efficiently can differentiate themselves from the competition. Finally organisations are forced by the developments within the regulative environment to adhere to higher standards of efficient production and introduce energy management programs. Within the regulative environment and market a shift from the individual organization

C. Emmanouilidis, M. Taisch, and D. Kiritsis (Eds.): APMS 2012, Part I, IFIP AICT 397, pp. 9–16, 2013.

towards its supply chain can be observed. Consequently, transparency with respect to all aspects of energy management is of the utmost importance.

On the basis of these developments it becomes clear that any activities that are carried out in isolation from relevant third parties or complementary activities with the overall goal to achieve efficiency are likely to fail or lead to suboptimal results. In alignment with [13] it must be recognized that improvements in productivity and reduction of energy consumed in the various manufacturing applications and activities may only be reached by an approach that allows for consideration of multiple activities and the involvement of relevant third parties. To allow for this flexibility and to be able to incorporate a variety of approaches, the concept of product modelling is utilized.

## 2      Energy Product Model

The aim of the energy product model is to provide the means to a holistic approach of energy management and hence induce a more efficient and effective utilization of energy. Essential within the context of energy and energy management is information about such (for example: prices, generation etc.). In the future energy as a product can be described through the information attached to it. In that sense the energy product model aims at capturing the necessary information and its streams along the energy supply chain and within the single company with the overall focus to utilize this information to improve overall energy efficiency. To provide a holistic approach that is able

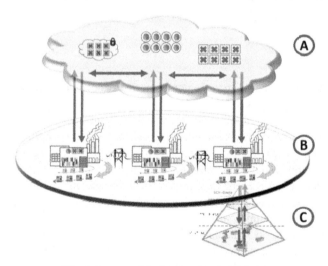

**Fig. 1.** Layers of the Energy Product Model

to carter to the problems identified above the model recognizes both the side of the energy provider and energy consumer. The following paragraphs review the three levels of production, company and supply chain that encompasses the model (cf. Fig. 1).

On the production level (C) the critical variables of production planning and control are analysed. The model to be built on this level is based on the acknowledged Aachen PPC-Model [2] and extends the four reference views of the model to incorporate the aspects of energy efficient production planning and control. On the basis of the EnergyBlocks [3] concept every process will include its energy consumption information. This is necessary to be able to forecast the energy consumption of the planned processes and identify power peaking situations. In a second step the remaining power-consumption peaks caused by overlapping processes have to be timed in a way that they will not overlap anymore and thus achieve a smoother energy consumption curve resulting in overall savings of costly maximum load energy [4].

On the company level (B) the energy flows within an organization are combined with its information flows. The goal is the recording and assessment of all relevant information and energy flows from the surrounding area (Heating, Ventilation and Air condition, etc.) to the production level. In this context, energy is not perceived anymore as an overhead cost but as one that is directly linked to the single product and production phase and needs to be managed accordingly, as well as all other resources. Finally, the data that is collected within the individual organisations can be aggregated on an overarching level (A) and hence provides a connection to the energy supply chain the organization is enclosed.

## 3    Intra-company Communication Framework

Although it can be easily argued that manufacturing companies have a strong necessity to be more efficient in their usage of energy it is nonetheless at the moment quite complicated for any company to assess how their processes are performing in terms of energy efficiency. [5] underline this by establishing that until now it is not possible to classify manufacturing processes or machine tools into standards based on their energy efficiency. Considering that both operations and possible improvement measures are usually implemented at the single process level [6], the calculation of energy efficiency must be integrated in the bottom layer and then transferred to the upper levels throughout the IT-systems.

Fig. 2 gives an overview over the necessary information flows through the different layers of IT-Systems. The main reason to base the model in the Aachener PPC [2] is its vertical vision of the manufacturing companies. Consequently the proposed model represents an application and extension of the Aachener PPC model, taking energy consumption at the moment of planning the production processes into consideration.

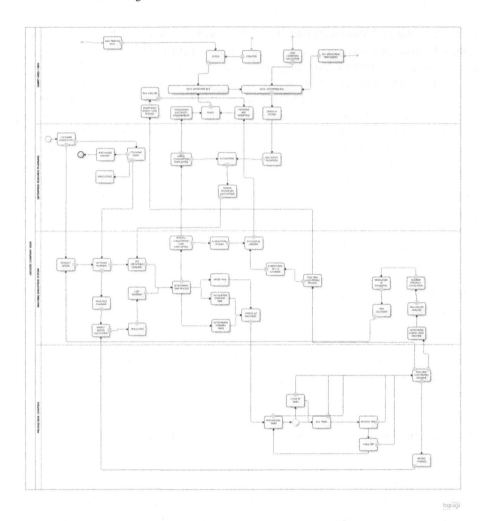

**Fig. 2.** Holistic Company Information View

## 3.1   Connecting the Layers – Enterprise Resource Planning and Smart Grid EMS

ERP systems need to be prepared to face and anticipate the challenge of the coming "intelligent energy delivery", which will be fully implemented based on smart grid technologies in 2020 [10].The main task concerning energy management is to define which impacts different decisions concerning energy efficiency have on the other functions of the company (e.g. Finance and Accounting) as well as production planning. In that regard a focus is put on the analysis of the costs involved with respect to energy consumption in the production plan. Additionally, a focus is placed on real-time information flows because of the rising dominance of e-business tools, which have added a higher degree of velocity within all the activities of the industry, having a huge impact on all the systems related with production processes, such as Customer Relations Management (CRM), Machine Execution Systems (MES) and of course the Enterprise Resource Planning (ERP) systems [11].

Overall in contrast to the Aachener PPC model [2], in the model proposed within this paper an extra layer is added corresponding to the Smart Grid systems as the communications with the energy providers are not part of the products and goods supply chain.

# 4     Communication Framework for the Energy Supply Chain

On a very basic level energy related problems can be currently categorized within either the realm of forecasting or traceability of energy consumption. The issue of forecasting encompasses the current problem that the various energy providers face with respect to accurate forecasts of energy consumption of their customers. Currently energy providers almost solely base their forecasts on data of energy consumption from the previous year. Naturally this method is rather inaccurate as energy consumption of business fluctuates for a variety of reasons and not all of these factors are stable across time. With a cloud-based service, forecasting can tremendously be improved and the single organisations that are members can feed data into it in real- time and the energy providers can then aggregate it. Basically, cloud computing describes different types of services in a layer model (infrastructure, platform, software) and distinguishes private, public, community and hybrid clouds depending on the exclusiveness of the service model [12]. Because of its abilities to facilitate data exchange between even physically and structurally different parties the cloud computing concept can play a fundamental role to solve energy related problems within the realm of both B2B and B2C related issues.

## 4.1     The Communication Model

The communication within the cloud is based on interconnections between the different actors. In order to provide a good balance of energy, it is mandatory to have an accurate and reliable forecast. Communication plays a fundamental role in accomplishing this objective and must therefore be carried out with a high level of speed and reliability. Having a cloud system running the communications allows the Transmission System Operator (TSO) to better forecast energy consumption since each industry will be able to report how much energy is going to be needed in advance. Therefore, real-time usage and generation of the electricity will be monitored.

The following information model (Fig. 3) contains all the interconnections of the main actors to provide a good balance of the electricity. Renewable generators with knowledge of the weather conditions for the following days can make a first estimation of how much electricity they can provide. Based on the maximum power capability, a calculation is made by the renewable generators and forwarded to the TSO. This information will also be accessible to industries. The same procedure is carried out by non-renewable power plants that do not rely on weather conditions to make their forecast. The industries are able to access information on forecasted energy generation through the public cloud, and, given this data, they can forecast their own energy requirements.

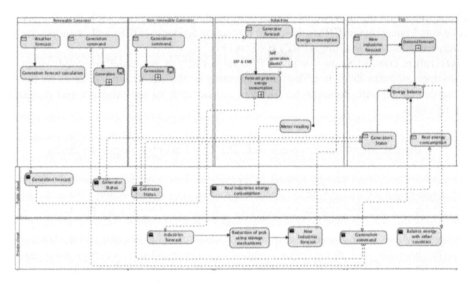

**Fig. 3.** Energy Supply Chain Information Model

The model offers the possibility to introduce self-generation devices to the industries. The only difference between renewable generators and the industries lies in the information; the information is kept in a private cloud and the industries can determine whether or not to use it. Before the industry forecast is sent to the TSO, the possibility to change the forecast using storage mechanisms is offered. This model also offers the possibility of making an alliance between different industries in the same physical area.

Once the TSO has all of the forecast consumption reports from the industries and the generation forecast reports, it is able to make a prediction for balancing the electricity more accurately. In order to balance the electricity load, the most important information is the quarter-hourly data regarding how much electricity is being consumed in each industry. With these three sets of reports, the TSO can better balance the electrical grid and give more accurate orders to the generators. This kind of communication system automatically results in a more efficient generation-consumption relationship.

## 4.2    Balance in the Cloud

To provide a good balance and performance of the needs and usage of the electrical grid, the TSO needs to use different EMS systems to perform the calculations. Most of this data that the different EMS systems need is pushed through the cloud. All the EMS systems being set-up in the cloud have many interconnections and different functions, but the most important interconnections and the main utilities that will be in use can be set up in a unique model map (Fig. 4).

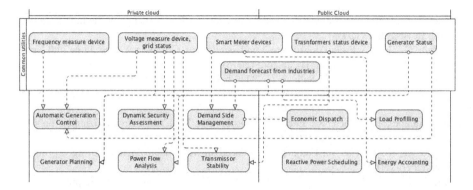

**Fig. 4.** EMS and Utilities

Furthermore, in the Communication Model Web-posted services are also considered. In order to provide good information of the electrical network, some data should be posted to provide clear and transparent information about the electricity or facilities. Some of these reports are mandatory by the European Union, such as Real-time demand, Forecasted demand or Real-time generation. These reports will also gather the information from the different devices used to measure or to control the demand and the status of the network.

# 5    Conclusions and Outlook

The approach to create an energy product model that gives an overall view on the intra-company and corporate information flows concerning energy efficiency is the first step towards an energy-efficient PPC. It enables an energy-efficient manufacturing by reducing costly power peaks through on optimized PPC and a more transparent consumption forecast that allows operating at a more efficient operation point. The accumulated real-time consumption-data and the consumption-forecast that are processed through the company`s system and shared with the TSO allows a network load of higher accuracy.

Further steps towards an energy-efficient production planning is the inclusion of energy-efficiency within existing target systems for production planning and control. Hence, the interdependencies between variables affecting economic efficiency and energy efficiency have to be analysed. Based on that it will be possible to define settings of parameters (e.g. order-release, lot sizes etc.) that increase the overall energy-efficiency of a production system while assuring a favourable degree of economic efficiency. These settings will be highly company-dependent and have to be defined for each company individually.

# References

1. Jucker, B., Leupp, P., Sjökvist, T.: Electrical energy - The challenge of the next decades. Abb Review, 8-13 (2008)
2. Schuh, G., (Hrsg.): Produktionsplanung und –steuerung. Grundlagen, Gestaltung und Konzepte. Aufl., vol. 3. Springer, Heidelberg (2006)
3. Weinert, N.; Chiotellis, S.; Seliger, G.: Methodology for planning and operating energy-efficient production systems. CIRP Annals – Manufacturing Technology 60(1), S.41–S.44 (2011)
4. Westkämper, E., Erlach, K.: Energiewertstrom. Der Weg zur energieeffizienten Fabrik. Fraunhofer-Verlag, Stuttgart (2009)
5. Schlosser, R., Klocke, F., Lung, D.: Advanced in Sustainable Manufacturing. Springer, Heidelberg (2011)
6. Li, W., Winter, M., Kara, S., Hermann, C.: Eco-efficiency of manufacturing processes: A grinding case. In: CIRP Annals – Manufacturing Technology 61(1), S. 59–S.62 (2012)
7. Putnam, B.: ISO 14031: Environmental Performance Evaluation (2002)
8. DIN EN ISO 50001: Energy management systems - Requirements with guidance for use (2011)
9. Herrmann, C., Thiede, S., Kara, S., Hesselbach, J.: Energy oriented simulation of manufacturing systems – Concept and application. CIRP Annals – Manufacturing Technology 60(1), S.45–S.48 (2011)
10. California ISO: SMART GRID – Roadmap and Architecture (2010)
11. Lee, J.: E.-manufacturing. Robotics and Computer-Integrated Manufacturing 19(6), S.501–S.507 (2003)
12. Schubert, P., Adisa, F.: Cloud Computing for standard ERP systems: Reference framework. Supply Chain Management: An International Journal (2011)
13. Rahimifard, S., Seow, Y., Childs, T.: Minimising Embodied Product Energy to support energy efficient manufacturing. CIRP Annals - Manufacturing Technology 59(1), 25–28 (2010)

# Energy-Efficient Machining via Energy Data Integration

Tao Peng[1], Xun Xu[1], and Juhani Heilala[2]

[1] Department of Mechanical Engineering, University of Auckland, New Zealand
tpen024@auckduni.ac.nz, xun.xu@auckland.ac.nz
[2] VTT Technical Research Centre of Finland, Finland
juhani.heilala@vtt.fi

**Abstract.** Energy-efficient machining strategies are required to be implemented in daily practice to advance the competitiveness of the enterprises on global scale. Energy information, which currently not considered as an integral part of production data, is studied. A need is identified to integrate energy information into production program and solidify the knowledge for extensive reference. To effectively represent and share the data, standardized format is regarded as one promising approach, thus STEP-NC is adopted. The proposed data models are grouped into four, i.e. automated energy monitoring and recording, energy estimation and labeling, energy optimization, and machine tool energy performance. The developed schema is compliant and harmonized with other parts in STEP-NC standards. A case study is presented to add energy information to STEP-NC file. It can be concluded that standardized data format enables the integration of energy information into the production process and enhances its sustainable performance.

**Keywords:** Energy efficiency, STEP-NC, Data integration, CNC Machining.

## 1 Introduction

The world is well-connected and better-informed nowadays than ever before. It is also true to manufacturing domain. New requirements of modern manufacturing industry are placed, such as sustainable performance, minimum supply chain management cost, and optimal product lifecycle performance. Energy-efficient machining system is focused in this study, as it is the key area in metalworking industry for the future. To keep energy efficiently used, energy information from machining process shall be available to assist process planning or lifecycle analysis [1]. A series of simulation-based analysis and decision making systems are developed, focusing on energy usage and performance on product lifecycle level [2]. However, the ways to actually improve the daily practice in factories is still lacking.

The separated parties along the production chain desire to seamlessly share energy knowledge and data in a systematic manner. Data representation and exchange activities demand to be universal and consistent. This also contributes to significant savings on supply chain management cost, which is considered as the top priority of the enterprises for the next decade. With the rapid development in CAx, data communication problem exists between different activities, known as "Island of Automation".

C. Emmanouilidis, M. Taisch, D. Kiritsis (Eds.): APMS 2012, Part I, IFIP AICT 397, pp. 17–24, 2013.

Even within each activity, the data exchange between different applications cannot be done without sacrificing accuracy or completeness. Energy-efficient machining system inherits the same problem. Therefore, how to standardize the energy consumption data and make it accessible and interoperable to different parties is focused in this research. ISO 14955 envisions establishing a method to evaluate environmental impact of machine tools, including eco-design and testing on metal cutting machines [3]. ISO 20140 aims to standardize evaluation procedure and data model for environmental performance of manufacturing systems [4]. Though both standards are still at the draft stage, it can be seen that standards are regarded as a good solution to remedy this problem. In this paper, existing STandard for Exchange of Produce model data (STEP [5]) is adopted to connect energy data model developed. The proposed data models are likewise open to be integrated with ISO 14955/20140 if it fits better.

## 2     Literature Review

Energy-efficient machining covers the principle metalworking operations, e.g. milling, turning, and drilling. Computerized numerical control (CNC) machines, as the key players, are designed and widely adopted to perform these types of operation. Up till now, more than 70% of the jobs are done using CNC machines world-wide. Over the years, researchers in this area endeavor to figure out how energy consumption behaves in machining, and what are the influential factors. Energy modeling research started with examining cutter-workpiece interaction [6]. The theoretical analysis discovered some critical factors that affect the energy consumption, such as tool properties, materials [7]. Later, with the development of computing technology, statistic modeling based on rich data became popular [8]. These so-called empirical models use the production data to establish the relationship between the main variables and the energy usage. It allows the analysts to select only the interested/controllable factors. More factors yield to have impact on energy consumption, e.g. machining environment [9]. The factors that influence energy consumption are summarized in [10].

However, the studies are focused on one part of energy usage, i.e. cutting energy. Researchers dealing with sophisticated CNC machine tools nowadays realize the actual cutting energy is only account for 15%-25% of the total energy consumed [11]. Thus, discrete event modeling is introduced to model energy usage [12]. More components are being considered in this new approach, so a more complete energy profile can be obtained.

Moreover, advanced energy signal monitoring system is requested to collect and record data of influential factors. It is crucial to create adequate awareness of the energy efficiency information, but available system is still lacking. One application of energy efficiency monitoring and optimization system was reported in [13]. Automated monitoring process enables online energy optimization for a process. To apply the energy information collected during machining to other applications, data model should be able to hold the basic energy information and detailed energy report for reference. Databases are essential to sustain the analysis, as energy is related to diverse factors. A well-organized database should contain energy reference. Even the representative data from previous operations can help. All these aspects mentioned should be well considered to make the energy data integration successful. Figure 1 shows the IDEF0 diagram on how energy information acts to enhance energy-efficient machining processes.

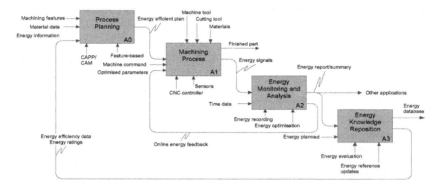

**Fig. 1.** IDEF0 diagram of integrating energy information into machining processes

## 3    Energy Data Model Development

STandard for Exchange of Produce model data (STEP) is standardized as ISO 10303 [5], which is a family of standards defining methodology for describing product data throughout the lifecycle of a product. STEP-compliant Numerical Control (STEP-NC) is designed for machining industry. It is task-oriented and enables bi-directional in-formation flow. It is standardized in ISO 14649 [14] and ISO 10303-238 [15]. ISO 14649 is used in this research for data modeling purposes, considering its straightfor-ward data structure and adequate manufacturing data. The proposed energy data models are developed using EXPRESS language (standardized in Part 11 of STEP standard [16]) and presented using EXPRESS-G (graphical representation of EXPRESS) in a more understandable manner.

Four groups of data models are proposed to hold energy information, i.e. data models for automated energy monitoring and recording, energy estimation and labe-ling, energy optimization, and machine tool energy performance. The suggested data model is connected to and harmonized with other parts in ISO 14649. Detailed dia-grams are omitted due to page limits.

### 3.1    Automated Energy Monitoring and Recording

Before the actual machining happens, energy data collection can be planned. Inspired by the traceability data model developed by Campos et al. [17], new functions are modeled and connected to nc_function in Part 10 to automate the monitoring process. A holistic view of this group is illustrated in Figure 2, with proposed nc_functions. All the entities can be Sub-Grouped (SG) into three. SG I functions are designed to hold information of current system, including Obtain_time, obtain_sensor_data, and obtain_machine_tool_data. SG II functions aim for holding energy monitoring data. They can be inserted in the NC program, and enables appropriate data acquisition automatically.    Start_energy_monitoring_sensor_data,    stop_energy_monitoring_sensor_ data, and signal_source_identified belong to this group. SG III defines the data structure of energy report for reviewing or auditing. Enable_energy_report, energy_report_format, and data_for_generate_energy_report are core functions.

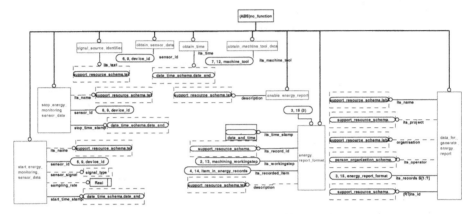

**Fig. 2.** Data models for automated energy monitoring and recording

## 3.2    Energy Estimation and Labeling

The influential factors are considered to develop this part of data model. Figure 3 illustrated the major entities proposed. As one attribute of ENTITY energy_usage_label, ENTITY machining_energy_model is abstract supertype of machine_tool_energy_model and main_cutting_energy_model. The former is used for systematic energy profile, while the latter is focused on actual cutting energy. Attach the estimated energy usage to NC program is called energy labeling. The main purpose is to indicate the energy used for the current project and its constituent elements, offering a brief view to the process reviewer or process planner.

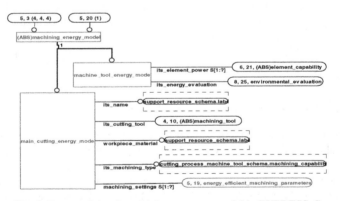

**Fig. 3.** Data models of machining_energy_model in EXPRESS-G

Utilizing the proposed data model, energy labeling can be done in two ways, i.e. energy estimation for selected workplan/workingstep and energy summary for the project.

### 3.3    Energy Optimization

Currently, energy optimization is not regarded as major or even one concern of most machining. Online energy optimization is rarely supported. Realizing the need, energy_optimization_data is proposed to hold data for machining. It allows the controller to adapt the settings autonomously for following steps based on specified energy model within the max value permitted and other availability at the shop floor. It enhances the smart controller performance in an energy-efficient fashion.

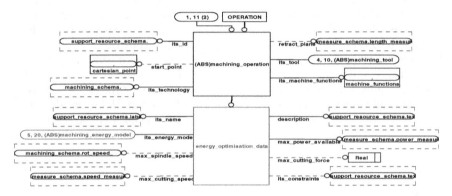

**Fig. 4.** Proposed energy_optimization_data and its relationship with machining_operation

### 3.4    Machine Tool Energy Performance

A well-organized database is critical for a comprehensive energy analysis. It should contain energy reference as a part of machine tool performance. To include this piece of information, it is best to attach it to machine tool database. This is because generally energy performance of a machining process is related to the machine tool in use, its structure, capability and condition. Produce the same part on different machine tools often results in different energy usage pattern. Hence, we proposed ENTITY energy_performance_reference (Figure 5) to store the energy history of the machine tool, connected to standard_machining_process of machine tool data model.

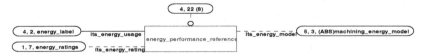

**Fig. 5.** ENTITY energy_performance_reference

A machining energy model will be specified for an energy performance record, as well as its ratings. How to quantify the energy efficiency index in a meaningful and standardized manner can be further explored incorporate with ISO 20140. This is included as future research work.

To sum up, tighter data flow and integration is highly required. The energy information data model proposed in this section enhances data integration for energy-efficient CNC machining processes, and fully harmonized with existing parts in STEP-NC standards. The EXPRESS-G diagrams are developed using ST-Developer version 14, STEP Tools. Inc., USA.

# 4    A Case Study

A case study is conducted to demonstrate the use of energy data model in Example 1 of ISO 14649-11 [18]. To produce this part, five workingsteps are required, i.e. planar face finishing, hole drilling, hole reaming, pocket roughing, and pocket finishing. Originally, there is no energy information in the sample NC program.

We implement the developed data models in section 3.2 to modify sample STEP-NC file. Energy information is added. The calculated energy summary of the production project is attached at the end of the file. It estimates how much energy is expected to be consumed before it happens. Segments of modified part 21 file are shown below. One can easily locate the basic energy consumption summary at line #200.

```
ISO-10303-21;
HEADER;
FILE_DESCRIPTION(('EXP1 WITH ENERGY INFORMATION'),'1');
FILE_NAME('EXP1_E.STP','25-06-2012',('TAO PENG'),('UoA'),'','','');
FILE_SCHEMA((('COMBINED_SCHEMA','ENERGY_INFO_FOR_MACHINING_SCHEMA')));
ENDSEC;
DATA;
...
#43=PLANAR_FACE('PLANAR FACE1',#18,(#27),#31,#36,#40,#42,$,());
#44=MACHINING_WORKINGSTEP('WS FINISH PLANAR FACE1',#5,#43,#27,$,#198);
...
#108=WORKPLAN('MAIN WORKPLAN',(#44,#64,#65,#93,#94),$,#107,$,#199);
#109=PROJECT('EXECUTE EXAMPLE1',#108,(#18),$,$,$,#200);
...
#194=CUTTING_FORCE(0.04000000, 12.00000000, 2.50000000, 20.00000000, $);
#195=MAIN_CUTTING_POWER(#194, $);
#196=ENERGY_EFFICIENT_MACHINING_PARAMETERS(#195,100.00000000,"DRY");
#197=MAIN_CUTTING_ENERGY_MODEL('ENERGY WS FINISH PLANAR
FACE1',#20,'STEEL',.MILLING_CAPABILITY.,#196);
#198=ENERGY_USAGE_LABEL(2789.500000000, #197);
#199=ENERGY_USAGE_LABEL(8425.00000000, $);
#200=BASIC_ENERGY_CONSUMPTION_DATA($,
8425.00000,(2789.500000,$,$,3975.500000,1660.00000),$,'REPORT EXP1',$);
ENDSEC;
END-ISO-10303-21;
```

## 5     Discussion and Future Work

The drive for increased competitiveness, reduced energy consumption and overall cost, pushes for energy-efficient machining operations. It has become evident that machine tool vendors and CNC users are making great efforts to improve the energy efficiency, both on machine tool itself and operation strategies. However, it is observed that insufficient energy data interoperability from CNC machining to other applications remains as one of the key issues in limiting energy-efficient machining processes. Thus it yields a necessary and crucial step to include energy information into the data sharing. The proposed data models for covering energy information purposes, augments the existing STEP-NC data model. It is important to collaborative machining environment in which energy monitoring, analysis and optimization can be exercised based on the developed data model.

For the next generation of intelligent CNC machines. The possible applications enabled by this data model are beyond the case study. For example, automated energy monitoring can be achieved by inserting standardized energy monitoring functions into the production file, and while executing the file, the STEP-compliant smart CNC controller can automatically activate requisite sensor to capture the data, and store the data in a consistent manner. The planning system can select the most satisfactory signal and effective sensor if there is more than one sensor on the CNC. The recorded energy profile can be recorded in a separate file, which is ready for post machining analysis. With the energy footprint, one can re-evaluate the energy consumption planned at the beginning, and update the energy pattern. Other areas that may benefit from the energy information data model includes but not limited to,

- Design for manufacturing
- Energy-efficient process and production planning
- Resource management
- Enterprise investment guidance

Though attentions are drawn in this field, research results are relatively preliminary. Future work will focus on optimizing energy consumption for machining practices, and explore the possible approach to control the CNC machines adaptively based on the data model. Development of software tools in assisting energy data monitoring, analysis and optimization is another useful work planned in the near future.

## References

1. Heilala, J., Klobut, K., Salonen, T., Järvinen, P., Siltanen, P., Shemeikka, J.: Energy efficient enhancement in discrete manufacturing with energy use parameters. In: International Conference on Advances in Production Management Systems, Cernobbio-Como, Italy (2010)
2. Heilala, J., Vatanen, S., Tonteri, H., Montonen, J., Lind, S., Johansson, B., Stahre, J.: Simulation-based sustainable manufacturing system design. In: Winter Simulation Conference, Miami, USA, pp. 1922–1930 (2008)

3. International Organisation for Standardisation: ISO/DIS 14955-1, Machine tools - Environmental evaluation of machine tools - Part 1: Design methodology for energy-efficient machine tools. Geneva, Switzerland (2012)
4. International Organisation for Standardisation: ISO/DIS 20140-1, Automation systems and integration - Evaluating energy efficiency and other factors of manufacturing systems that influence the environment - Part 1: Overview and general principles. Geneva, Switzerland (2012)
5. International Organisation for Standardisation: ISO 10303-1, Industrial Automation Systems and Integration - Product Data Representation and Exchange - Part 1: Overview and Fundamental Principles. Geneva, Switzerland (1994)
6. Munoz, A.A., Sheng, P.: An analytical approach for determining the environmental impact of machining processes. J. Mater. Process. Tech. 53(3-4), 736–758 (1995)
7. Shao, H., Wang, H.L., Zhao, X.M.: A cutting power model for tool wear monitoring in milling. Int. J. Mach. Tool. Manu. 44(14), 1503–1509 (2004)
8. Draganescu, F., Gheorghe, M., Doicin, C.V.: Models of machine tool efficiency and specific consumed energy. J. Mater. Process. Tech. 141(1), 9–15 (2003)
9. Aggarwal, A., Singh, H., Kumar, P., Singh, M.: Optimizing power consumption for CNC turned parts using response surface methodology and Taguchi's technique-A comparative analysis. J. Mater. Process. Tech. 200(1-3), 373–384 (2008)
10. Peng, T., Xu, X.: The state of the art in energy consumption model - the key to sustainable machining. Appl. Mech. Mater. 232, 592–599 (2012)
11. Dahmus, J.B., Gutowski, T.G.: An environmental analysis of machining. In: International Mechanical Engineering Congress and RD&D Expo, Anaheim, California, USA, pp. 643–652 (2004)
12. Dietmair, A., Verl, A.: A generic energy consumption model for decision making and energy efficiency optimisation in manufacturing. Int. J. Sustain. Eng. 2(2), 123–133 (2009)
13. Heilala, J., Klobut, K., Salonen, T., Siltanen, P., Ruusu, R., Armijo, A., Sorli, M., Urosevic, L., Reimer, P., Fatur, T., Gantar, Z., Jung, A.: Ambient Intelligence based monitoring and energy efficiency optimisation system. In: IEEE International Symposium on Assembly and Manufacturing, Tampere, Finland (2011)
14. International Organisation for Standardisation: ISO 14649-1, Data Model for Computerized Numerical Controllers - Part 1: Overview and Fundamental Principles. Geneva, Switzerland (2003)
15. International Organisation for Standardisation: ISO 10303-238, Industrial Automation Systems and Integration - Product Data Representation and Exchange - Part 238: Application Protocal: Application Interpreted Model For Computerized Numerical Controllers. Geneva, Switzerland (2007)
16. International Organisation for Standardisation: ISO 10303-11, Industrial Automation Systems and Integration - Product Data Representation and Exchange - Part 11: Description Methods: The EXPRESS Language Reference Manual. Geneva, Switzerland (1994)
17. Campos, J.G., Miguez, L.R.: Standard process monitoring and traceability programming in collaborative CAD/CAM/CNC manufacturing scenarios. Comput. Ind. 62, 311–322 (2011)
18. International Organisation for Standardisation: ISO 14649-11, Data Model for Computerized Numerical Controllers - Part 11: Process Data for Milling. Geneva, Switzerland (2004)

# An ICT Supported Holistic Approach
# for Qualitative and Quantitative Energy Efficiency
# Evaluation in Manufacturing Company

Hendro Wicaksono[1,*], Kiril Aleksandrov[1], Sven Rogalski[2], and Jivka Ovtcharova[2]

[1] Intelligent Systems and Production Engineering/ Process
and Data Management in Engineering FZI Research Center for Information Technology,
Karlsruhe, Germany
{wicaksono,aleksandrov}@fzi.de
[2] Institute for Information Management in Engineering, Karlsruhe Institute of Technology,
Karlsruhe, Germany
{sven.rogalski,jivka.ovtcharova}@kit.edu

**Abstract.** The global climate change and the rising of energy prices force man-ufacturing companies to regulate their energy usage. A suitable step to achieve that is the introduction of energy management. This paper presents an ICT based holistic approach to help manufacturing companies in the implementation of energy management system. It consists of methods to support quantitative and qualitative energy efficiency evaluation of their operations. The approach uses an ontological knowledge base containing the structures and rules representing best practices as reference of energy efficiency to support the qualitative evaluation. In the approach, we also develop measurement figures called Energy Performance Indices (EPI) to determine the energy efficiency degrees in different organizational parts of the company. The paper also describes the application of the approach in a small medium sized manufacturer.

## 1 Introduction

The global climate change and the rapid growth of industrialization, have led to a significant increase of energy demand that results to constantly increasing of electricity, gas, and oil prices. Meanwhile, the changes of social, technical, and economic conditions in the market have challenged manufacturers to deal with the requirements for various and complex products. Hence, energy efficiency in accordance with the economization of production costs is an important competitive factor in the energy-intensive industry. A common solution to achieve this is through a corporate energy management. Energy management defines the sum of all processes and measures to ensure minimal energy consumption by a given demand including the implementation of organization, information structure, and tools [1]. The standard ISO 50001 describes the requirements for energy management systems in industrial companies.

---

* Corresponding author.

C. Emmanouilidis, M. Taisch, D. Kiritsis (Eds.): APMS 2012, Part I, IFIP AICT 397, pp. 25–32, 2013.
© IFIP International Federation for Information Processing 2013

However, most of the manufacturing companies face problems in implementing the energy management standards, due to the distributed and unstructured energy related information within the company. The information is difficult to be accessed by all stakeholders in the company. Best practices to avoid energy wasting are only known by some employees. This is due to the knowledge gap and insufficient access methods to the knowledge.

To overcome this problem, this paper introduces an approach utilizing information and communication technology that supports a holistic evaluation of energy efficiency both qualitatively and quantitatively. Qualitative evaluation focuses on the criteria that can be observed but not measured using figures, such as energy wasting situations, or energy efficient best practices. The qualitative evaluation is performed by employing a knowledge base, which is accessible by all of personals and systems in the company. The best practices and knowledge about energy efficient and energy wasting activities are standardized, formalized and stored in the knowledge base. Researchers have been applying ontologies as knowledge representation in various domains to solve the shared understanding problems among people and even software. In this paper, the knowledge base is represented with OWL (Web Ontology Language)[1] combined with SWRL[2]. Quantitative evaluation evaluates energy efficiency using measurement figures. Therefore it is possible to determine the energy efficiency degree in different organizational parts or processes in company. The figure is called Energy Performance Indices (EPI). In this paper, energy performance indicators that are able to measure the energy efficiency in different level of company organizations, is proposed.

## 2     Literature Overview

Researchers have developed knowledge based approach since end of 80s to manage information from different sources to support the decision making, in order to improve the efficiency, flexibility, and reliability of manufacturing processes [2][3]. Knowledge and communication models were developed to relate different aspects in manufacturing and to allow coordination of different components in the manufacturing organization [4] [5]. For the last ten years, researchers have been applying ontologies as knowledge representation in various domains, including manufacturing. Ontology has been used as a solution to the shared understanding problems among people and even software [6]. It has also been proven to harmonize the knowledge gap between customers and manufacturers during the requirement elicitation phase [7] and to solve the semantic ambiguities [8]. Different approaches to create ontologies in manufacturing domain were developed to model the processes, product, and resources as well as their relation in production [9] [10]. In energy management domain, to improve the energy efficiency especially in households, analysis of energy consumption of different appliances from various manufacturers and technologies is performed with the help of ontology as the integration model [11] [12]. Furthermore,

---

[1]  http://www.w3.org/TR/2004/REC-owl-ref-20040210/
[2]  http://www.daml.org/rules/proposal/

ontology combined with rules is also used to represent the knowledge base of an intelligent energy management system that monitors and controls the energy consumption in a household [13]. Until now, there is still a lack of knowledge based approach to support the evaluation tasks of energy management in manufacturing. This paper introduces a novel method using ontology and rules represented knowledge to formalize and to structure the knowledge and the best practices as references to regulate the energy consumption in manufacturing.

By using metrics as the performance indicators, an assessment for the state and condition of complex systems is easier and faster, due to their simple representations. The figures to measure energy efficiency are classified into different categories, such as absolute, relative, classification, and relational figures [14]. This paper focuses on relational figures, since they describe the energy consumption based on cause-effect relation, for instance, energy consumption per a produced product piece. German Engineer Association (VDI) introduces different technical figures related to energy evaluation [15]. The energy requirements relative to the amount of products depend very much on the type and quality of the products. An approach to fix this problem is by converting the output product values into a particular unit [16]. Some metric systems have been developed to evaluate the energy efficiency for entire industry sectors, such as EPI from Energy Star and ODEX [17] [18] [19]. However, there is still lack of figures that are able to measure energy efficiency of different organization levels in a single manufacturing company, such as of a machine, of a production line, and of the whole factory. This paper proposes a method that addresses this problem.

## 3    Overview of the Solution

In this paper, we propose an ICT framework that supports the implementation of energy management in manufacturing companies consisting of both tools for quantitative and qualitative energy efficiency evaluation. Fig. 1 illustrates the overview of the framework. The information about products, production processes, and resources are collected from different IT systems of the company, such as ERP, MES (Manufacturing Execution System). The energy related data are gathered from Energy Monitoring and Data Acquisition (EMDA) System. Those different data are aggregated and analyzed, in order to have the relation between products, production processes, and resources e.g., machines, surrounding factors (i.e., temperatures), and energy consumptions.

The data analysis to create the relations could be done semi-automatically with the help of algorithms, such as data mining. Rules representing the energy usage patterns are deduced from the data mining result. The rules allow the identification of energy usage anomalies or inefficiencies. Knowledge engineer of the company could also models the common best practices of energy management with rules. These rules are stored in the form of a knowledge base as a reference of energy efficiency qualitative evaluations. The collected data are used to assign the values of the mathematical model that calculates the EPI. The simulation and optimization module is responsible to help the production planners to perform production planning that consider not only the costs but also energy efficiency. The module contains an optimization algorithm for finding the optimal production schedule that takes the rules as the constraints and the maximum EPI as the objective function.

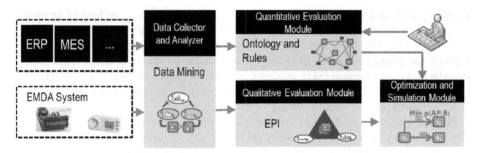

**Fig. 1.** Overview of the approach

# 4    Qualitative Evaluation using Knowledge Base

In our work, we develop OWL ontology for manufacturing energy management. There exists PLM ontology that models the structure and relationships among products, processes, and resources [9] [20]. In our work, we consider knowledge elements representing the energy management with an additional related knowledge, such as ancillary, transport or intra-logistics and energy conversion facilities. Equation (1) gives an example of a SWRL rule that models energy wasting practice in a stainless steel manufacturer. It describes, if an oven is active during a heat treatment process and the heating system is located in the same zone is still turned on, then it is considered as an energy inefficiency condition. The rule is created manually, since it represents the common knowledge.

$$
\begin{aligned}
&Oven(?o) \wedge HeatTreatment(?ht) \wedge operates(?o,?ht) \wedge isActive(?ht, true) \wedge \\
&HeatingSystem(?hs) \wedge hasState(?hs, true) \wedge Zone(?z) \wedge isLocate- \\
&dIn(?o,?z) \wedge isLocatedIn(?hs,?z) \rightarrow AncillaryFacilityEnergyWasting(?hs)
\end{aligned} \tag{1}
$$

Fig. 2 illustrates a decision tree resulted from the data mining that extracts the relation between product properties and the energy consumption in forging process. The tree represents the common and normal situation that the forging process of products, having material type M1 and outer diameter greater than 115 cm, consumes energy between 175 and 268 kW. The tree is then transformed into SWRL rules, for example into rule (2), to detect the energy inefficiency or anomaly states. The rule implies, if the forging process on presser machine consumes energy more than 268 kW, then there is something wrong in the process causing energy inefficiency.

$$
\begin{aligned}
&Product(?p) \wedge hasMaterialType(?p, "M1") \wedge hasOuterDimeter(?p,?od) \wedge \\
&swrlb:greaterThan(?od,115) \wedge Presser3000T(?ps) \wedge Forging(?f) \wedge op- \\
&erates(?ps,?f) \wedge produces(?o,?p) \wedge hasEnergyConsumption(?ps,?e) \wedge \\
&swrlb:greaterThan(?ps,268) \rightarrow ProductionFacilityEnergyWasting(?ps)
\end{aligned} \tag{2}
$$

By using the knowledge, the energy wasting can be detected, hence energy efficiency can be evaluated. By assigning the variables with current states in the company, running a rule engine on the SWRL rules and using SQWRL[3] to query the knowledge base as shown in (3), the inferred information can be retrieved from

---

[3]  http://protege.cim3.net/cgi-bin/wiki.pl?SQWRL

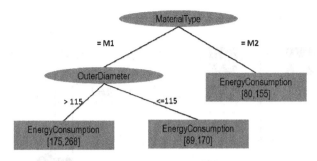

**Fig. 2.** Decision tree of data mining result

the rules. The retrieved information can be further processed by using the company's messaging or alerting system.

$$AncillaryFacilityEnergyWasting(?h) \rightarrow sqwrl:select(?h)$$ (3)
$$ProductionFacilityEnergyWasting\ (?h) \rightarrow sqwrl:select(?h)$$

## 5     Energy Performance Indices (EPI) for the Quantitative Evaluation

To develop energy efficiency metric for a single manufacturing company, first, it is important to define the system boundaries and a model that covers the different organization levels of production. In our work we develop UPNT, which is based on UPN model [21], and considers the machine, production line and factory level. The basic elements of the UPNT model are energy conversion (U), production (P), ancillary (N), and transport (T) facilities. The production and transport facilities are modeled as subclasses of ontological class `ManufacturingResource`, the energy conversion as `EnergySource`, and ancillary facility as `BuildingElement` in ontology. Fig. 3 illustrates the boundaries of different manufacturing organization levels. It can be seen, that the inputs of a production facilities are made up from direct and an indirect ones. The direct inputs are from utility companies or conversion facilities. The indirect inputs are provided due to the fact that the production facility receives the outputs of ancillary and transportation facility. Therefore the energy cost of a production facility is also ascribed with the output of the connected ancillary and transport facilities. Equation (2) calculates the EPI for factory level. The calculations for the machine and production line levels are also performed similarly.

$$EPI_l = \frac{V_l}{\sum_k^p P_k + \sum_{i=1}^m \alpha_i A_i + \sum_{j=1}^n T_j + \sum_v^q A_v}$$ (4)

where   $V_l$   =   output value generated by production line $l$ [€]

        $P_k$   =   input of production facility $k$ [€]

        $\alpha_i$   =   ratio of use input ancillary facility = [0,1]

        $A_i$   =   input ancillary facility $i$ to each production facility [€]

        $T_j$   =   used transport facility $j$ [€]

        $A_v$   =   input ancillary facility $v$ for the whole production line [€]

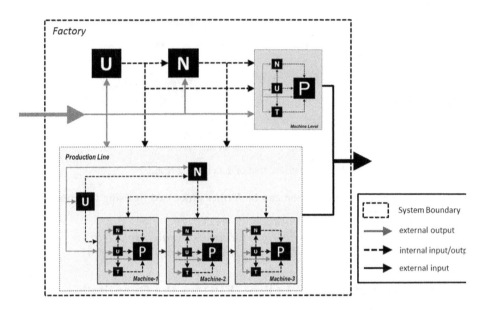

**Fig. 3.** Energy flows and system boundaries for EPI calculation

The calculation method is applied in a stainless steel manufacturer. Table 1 shows examples of the calculation results in machine and production line levels. Theoretically, the EPI values should be positive rational numbers. Less than one value means that energy costs exceed the supply and therefore should not occur. Otherwise, it would be an alarm signal, because the process is extremely inefficient. Higher values are conceivable when a process generates a lot of values and /or require very little energy. A value greater than one does not automatically make a positive contribution margin, as there are other costs in addition to the energy costs that must be met. However, this is not the objective of the EPIs. Rather, they should provide a comparison of different alternatives in the choice of equipment to be used.

**Table 1.** EPI calculation results in stainless steel production

| Description | EPI |
|---|---|
| M: Oven | 21,0 — 30,3 – 49,6 |
| M: Presser (1x) and Drop hammer (2x) | 11,4 - 21,0 – 21,9 |
| M: Turning machine (3x) | 10,5 – 20,9 – 32,6 |
| M: Boring Machine, CNC machine (1x) | 15,7- 17,7 |
| M: Ring roller(2x) | 15,5 – 18,9 |
| L1: Oven (EPI = 21,0), Drop hammer (EPI = 21,9), Ring-rolling (EPI = 15,5) | 19,5 |
| L2: Oven (EPI = 49,6), Presser (EPI = 11,4), Ring-roller (EPI = 18,9), Rolling- machine (EPI = 21,7) | 19,3 |
| L3: Oven (EPI = 30, 3), Drop hammer (EPI = 21,0), Rolling machine (EPI = 20,9), | 21,3 |

# 6    Summary

This paper presents an approach that employs ICT method to support the holistic evaluation of energy efficiency in the manufacturing on both quantitative and qualitative ways. The knowledge base provides the structured and formalized knowledge as references of best practices in the company related to energy efficiency. By using the data mining, the previously unknown relations among products, manufacturing processes, facilities, resources and energy consumption are revealed and incorporated into knowledge base. The ontology represented knowledge base provides formalized knowledge that allows common understanding among employees and software in the company.    By using developed EPI, the energy consumption's performance of different production facilities and production lines is measured quantitatively. Therefore, it helps the managers and production planners to plan their production not only by considering the costs, but also by considering the energy efficiency. Manufacturers can benefit from this approach by receiving an evaluation tool that enables them, despite the ever-intensifying competition with higher energy costs and scarce natural resource and an increase of production of complexity, to compete with competitors. The approach also improves the awareness of the stakeholders to make decision by strongly taking considerations whether their decision affects the energy efficiency in the company.

# References

1. Kahlenborn, W., Kabisch, S., Klein, J., Richter, I., Schürmann, S.: DIN EN 16001: Energy Management Systems in Practice - A Guide for Companies and Organisations. In: Bundesministerium für Umwelt, Naturschutz und Reaktorsicherheit, Berlin, Germany (2010)
2. Hsu, C., Skevington, C.: Integration of data and knowledge in manufacturing enterprises: A conceptual framework. Journal of Manufacturing Systems 6(4), 277–285 (1987)
3. Weber, D., Moodie, C.: A knowledge-based system for information management in an automated and integrated manufacturing system. Robotics and Computer-Integrated Manufacturing 4(3-4), 601–617 (1988)
4. Guerra-Zubiaga, D., Young, R.: A manufacturing model to enable knowledge maintenance in decision support systems. Journal of Manufacturing Systems 25(22), 122–136 (2006)
5. Oztemel, E., Tekez, E.: Integrating manufacturing systems through knowledge exchange protocols within an agent-based Knowledge Network. Robotics and Computer-Integrated Manufacturing 25(1), 235–245 (2009)
6. Noy, N., McGuinness, D.: Ontology Development 101: A Guide to Creating Your First Ontology (2001), http://www.ksl.stanford.edu/people/dlm/papers/ontology101/ontology101-noy-mcguinness.html (accessed on July 10, 2012)
7. Wicaksono, H., Schubert, V., Rogalski, S., Ait Laydi, Y., Ovtcharova, J.: Ontology-driven Requirements Elicitation in Product Configuration Systems. In: Enabling Manufacturing Competitiveness and Economic Sustainability, pp. 63–67. Springer, Heidelberg (2012)
8. Valiente, M.C., Garcia-Barriocanal, E., Sicilia, M.A.: Applying an ontology approach to IT service management for business-IT integration. In: Knowledge-Based Systems, vol. 28, pp. 76–87. Elsevier Science Publishers, Amsterdam (2012)

9. Lemaignan, S., Siadat, A., Dantan, J.Y., Semenenko, A.: MASON: A Proposal For An Ontology of Manufacturing Domain. In: Proc. Workshop on Distributed Intelligent Systems: Collective Intelligence and Its Applications, pp. 195–200. IEEE Computer Society, Washington (2006)
10. Panetto, H., Dassisti, M., Tursi, A.: ONTO-PDM: Product-driven ONTOlogy for Product Data Management interoperability within manufacturing process environment. Advanced Engineering Informatics (26), 334–348 (2012)
11. Shah, N., Chao, K.-M., Zlamaniec, T., Matei, A.: Ontology for Home Energy Management Domain. In: Cherifi, H., Zain, J.M., El-Qawasmeh, E. (eds.) DICTAP 2011 Part II. CCIS, vol. 167, pp. 337–347. Springer, Heidelberg (2011)
12. Rossello-Busquet, A., Brewka, L., Soler, J., Dittmann, L.: OWL Ontologies and SWRL Rules Applied to Energy Management. In: Proc. 13th International Conference on Modelling and Simulation, pp. 446–450. IEEE Computer Society, Washington DC (2011)
13. Wicaksono, H., Rogalski, S., Kusnady, E.: Knowledge-based Intelligent Energy Management Using Building Automation System. In: Proceeding of the 9th International Power and Energy Conference, pp. 1140–1145. IEEE Computer Society, Washington (2010)
14. Kals, J.: Betriebliches Energiemanagement - Eine Einführung. Verlag W. Kohlhammer, Stuttgart (2010)
15. Verein Deutscher Ingenieure (VDI): Energetic characteristics: definitions – terms – methodology. Beuth Verlag GmbH, Düsseldorf (2003)
16. Müller, E., Engelmann, J., Löffler, T., Strauch, J.: Energieeffiziente Fabriken planen und betreiben. Springer (2009)
17. Boyd, G., Zhang, G.: Measuring Improvement in the Energy Performance of the U.S. Cement Industry. In: Technical Report, Duke University, Durham, North Carolina (2011)
18. European Energy Efficiency: Analysis of ODYSSEE indicators. In: Technical Report. Department of Energy & Climate Change, London (2012)
19. Tanaka, K.: Assessing Measures of Energy Efficiency Performance and their Application in Industry. In: Technical Report, International Energy Agency (IEA), Paris, France (2008)
20. Raza, M.B., Harrison, R.: Ontological Knowledge Based System for Product, Process and Resource Relationships in Automotive Industry. In: Proc. International Workshop on Ontology and Semantic Web for Manufacturing, Heraklion, Crete, Greece (2011)
21. Fünfgeld, C.: Energiekosten im Betrieb. Solar Promotion GmbH-Verlag, Munich (2000)

# How Energy Recovery Can Reshape Storage Assignment in Automated Warehouses

Antonella Meneghetti and Luca Monti

DIEG – Dipartimento di Ingegneria Elettrica, Gestionale e Meccanica,
University of Udine, Via delle Scienze 208, 33100 Udine, Italy
{meneghetti,luca.monti}@uniud.it

**Abstract.** In automated storage and retrieval systems energy in descending and deceleration phases of cranes can be recovered into the power supply system instead of being dissipated as waste heat. Such technological opportunity should be exploited by properly modifying control policies in order to improve energy efficiency of warehousing operations. In this paper the impact of energy recovery on the storage assignment process is analysed. A model of energy consumption with recovery is proposed so that each location within a rack can be associated with energy required to be served in a storage or a retrieval cycle. Shape and distribution of zone for energy-based dedicated strategies are analysed. Energy and picking time performances of different storage policies when AS/RSs machines are equipped for energy recovery are analysed and compared.

**Keywords:** energy efficiency, energy recovery, automated storage and retrieval systems, storage location assignment, picking time.

## 1 Introduction

While in the process industry energy efficiency has been pursued for several decades due to its energy-intensive nature, in the discrete one the current level of control in energy use is very poor or absent [1]. However, the growing of green consciousness from one hand and energy resource scarcity from the other are inducing all manufacturing firms to pay attention to energy efficiency as a way to pursue sustainability in all its components. This trend is confirmed by results of the 2011 Material Handling Association of America survey on sustainability in warehousing, distribution and manufacturing [2], which have highlighted how for more than 60% of respondents the greatest accomplishment is becoming energy efficient. As asserted by Elkington [3] in his triple bottom line model, in facts, at the intersection of social, environmental, and economic performance, there are activities that organizations can engage which not only positively affect the natural environment and society, but which also result in long-term economic benefits and competitive advantage for the firm. Reducing energy consumption is one of such activities, since it allows to mitigate greenhouse gas emissions related to energy generation, to reduce natural resource exploitation, and to reduce energy supply costs. Moreover it can be associated with a green imagine of enterprise that can attract and consolidate client fidelity.

C. Emmanouilidis, M. Taisch, D. Kiritsis (Eds.): APMS 2012, Part I, IFIP AICT 397, pp. 33–40, 2013.

Automated warehouses have been seen as intrinsically energy efficient solutions for warehousing. The ability of automated storage systems to store inventory more densely eliminates, in fact, the need for energy to heat, cool, light and ventilate excess square footage [4]. However, automated storage and retrieval systems (AS/RSs) require energy for movements of their cranes to serve locations within racks. Therefore, new attention is claimed to be paid to control policies of AS/RSs in order to minimize energy requirements also for their storage and retrieval operations, so that the sustainable perspective can be fully embraced.

Storage assignment is the control policy that can more strongly affect picking time, which has been the primary performance traditionally pursued in warehouse management for decades, since it is directly linked to service level perceived by customers (see [5], [6], and [7] for comprehensive literature reviews on warehousing). Recent studies have highlighted how it can affect also energy consumption for crane movements and therefore belongs to such activities that can foster sustainability. In particular, when adopting the energy-based full turnover strategy [8], thus allocating more frequently moved items to convenient locations in order to optimize energy requirements for storage and retrieval operations, the shape of dedicated zones changes from the well known time-based rectangular or L shape [9] to a step-wise one, with vertical positions becoming more attractive to exploit gravity in descending phases. These results are based on the assumption of fully dissipating energy when torque becomes negative during descending or deceleration phases and energy flows from the AS/RS machine to motors and is converted into waste heat.

Manufacturers are offering the option of equipping cranes with energy-recovery modules so that energy otherwise dissipated can be re-generated into the power supply system. This technological opportunity should be fully exploited by properly modifying AS/RSs control policies in order to minimize net energy requirements. The challenge becomes to adequate operations management to technological development so that they can enforce each other towards higher and higher sustainability levels. As regards storage assignment, energy recovery can change the relative convenience of each location within a rack, in particular higher locations can become even more attractive, since their gravitational energy can lead to higher electrical energy flows to be supplied to the grid.

Thus, the first question to be answered is if and how energy recovery can change the shape of dedicated zones in comparison to both the traditional time-based zones and the energy-based ones with full dissipation. The second question is how much energy saving can be achieved with the energy-based full turnover strategy associated with energy recovery in comparison to the same storage policy with full dissipation. Furthermore, comparisons with the time-based full turnover policy, where the most frequently moved items are assigned to locations requiring the least picking time, and with other common storage assignment strategies as the random one, can give insight on how much energy can be saved by properly changing the assignment process.

The paper is organized as follows: in sect. 2 the energy model adopted to associate energy consumption to each location in a rack is described, while the shared storage policy is analysed in sect. 3. Zone distributions are analysed in sect. 4, and simulation experiments among different dedicated storage policies are reported in sect. 5.

## 2   The Energy Model with Recovery

To adopt an energy based storage assignment, energy related to crane movements along vertical and horizontal axes must be evaluated. Movements along z axis to pick up and drop off loads are independent from locations in the racks and therefore they can be ignored.

AS/RS machines are equipped by a different A.C. 3-phase inverter duty motor per axis; the energy required to reach a given location is the sum of energy provided for the x-axis and the energy provided for the y-axis (time, instead, is calculated as the maximum of the values along the two axes due to simultaneity of movements).

Assuming that crane movements can be described as a rectilinear motion with constant acceleration, speed profile for both horizontal and vertical axes can be either triangular, if maximum allowed speed isn't reached due to limited shifts, or a trapezium one if an acceleration phase, a constant speed phase, and a deceleration phase must be considered in sequence [10].

Being torque C constant during the acceleration phase of the crane due to the inverter duty motor type, mechanical energy provided by motors can be calculated by integrating the product of the torque and the angular speed at the shaft over time. The torque provided by each motor has to counterbalance inertia of motor and masses to be moved (crane and unit load), friction and gravity (vertical motion). These forces strictly depend on design specifications, maximum speed and acceleration of the AS/RS machine, so we used actual data provided by System Logistics S.p.A., to compute energy values for a given AS/RS configuration.

New generation cranes are controlled so that horizontal and vertical movements end simultaneously, differing from traditional cranes where an additional torque must be applied to keep in position the load while completing the slowest movement. This means that speed profile of the fastest motion should be modified in order to complete the required shift along the rack in a time as long as the other axis one. We suppose to travel with nominal acceleration until a speed lower than the maximum one is reached and extend the constant phase in order to complete the shift in the same time of the slowest motion. By recalculating for each location the new acceleration/deceleration time and the constant speed time of the fastest motion, it is possible to evaluate the actual energy required to perform a storage or a retrieval cycle in a given position within the rack (energy differs since load is on board during different shifts).

The I/O point is co-located at the lower left corner of the rack, which represents also the optimal dwell point location (i.e. the optimal location where the crane should wait when idle) from the energy perspective, as shown in [8].

We suppose that the y-motor is equipped for energy recovery in order to exploit gravitational energy. An energy recovery factor is introduced whenever the torque becomes negative, generating negative energy flows that partially balance the positive ones related to the other shifts of each single command cycle. Based on actual data from manufacturers, we assume a prudential overall recovery factor of 26% on the energy otherwise dissipated.

# 3    Energy Savings with Shared Storage Policies

We can evaluate energy savings associated with shared storage policies when energy recovery is performed by analysing the rack energy potentials.

The rack energy potential (REP) can be defined as the sum of the energy values required to complete a single storage plus a single retrieval cycle for all the locations in the rack, i.e. 2 idle travels and 2 travels with load on board per location [8].

Multiplying REP by the overall turnover (total demand divided by rack storage capacity), we obtain a measure of the energy requirement for a given time horizon, when the random storage policy is adopted and every location has equal probability of being visited. Therefore, given a rack storage capacity, energy requirements are proportional to REPs, so we can compare REPs among different rack shapes and different unit load weights to get insight on potential energy savings with shared allocation.

In Table 1 rack energy potentials for a rack storage capacity of 990 unit load locations are reported. We considered two alternative configurations: a 22 levels and 45 columns rack (22×45) and a 10 levels and 99 columns rack (10×99). Since energy recovery depends mainly on gravitational energy, which is related to location height from floor, the rationale is to evaluate the impact that vertical development of the rack can have on energy recovery with respect to horizontal development.

Energy values were evaluated by associating the proper crane specifications with each configuration as suggested by manufacturers.

Unit load weights of 1000 kg, 600 kg and 200 kg were considered in order to evaluate energy savings associated with different classes of product weight.

**Table 1.** Rack Energy Potentials

| Rack | Unit load [kg] | REP [MJ] | Recov. REP [MJ] | Δrel % |
|------|------|------|------|------|
| 22×45 | 1000 | 1,262 | 1,089 | 13.76 |
| 10×99 | 1000 | 1,265 | 1,189 | 6.03 |
| 22×45 | 600 | 1,189 | 1,033 | 13.15 |
| 10×99 | 600 | 1,219 | 1,150 | 5.65 |
| 22×45 | 200 | 1,115 | 976 | 12.46 |
| 10×99 | 200 | 1,173 | 1,112 | 5.23 |

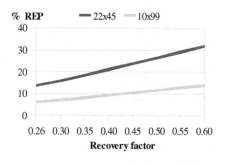

**Fig. 1.** Relative % decrease of Rack Energy Potentials for different energy recovery factor

Energy saving for a 1000 kg unit load is 13.76% when energy recovery is performed in the 22×45 rack, while it is 6.03% for the 10×99 one. In the more horizontally laid rack, in fact, less energy can be generated during descending phases and recovered into the power supply system. This is enforced when the energy recovery factor grows as shown in Fig. 1, where the curves diverge. As also expected, for a given rack configuration, energy saving grows with increasing unit load weight.

From the design perspective, it comes that the benefit of AS/RSs of allowing better use of vertical space can be further exploited for energy recovery during operations, thus leading to more energy efficient facilities.

## 4    Dedicated Zones Shape and Distribution

When a dedicated storage policy is adopted, each item is associated with a given number of fixed locations within the rack. The full turnover policy consists in assigning the most convenient locations to items sorted by their turnover frequency (number of visits per unit load location in the planning horizon) in decreasing order.

If the traditional time-based turnover policy is adopted, the most frequently moved unit loads are assigned to locations requiring the least picking time to be served, so that response time to clients can be minimized. In this case, it is a well-known analytical result [9] that dedicated zones have a rectangular or L shape (see Fig. 2).

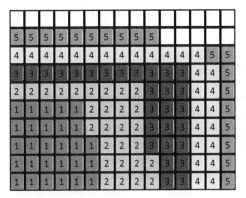

**Fig. 2.** Dedicated zones for the time-based full turnover policy for the first part of the 22×45 rack.

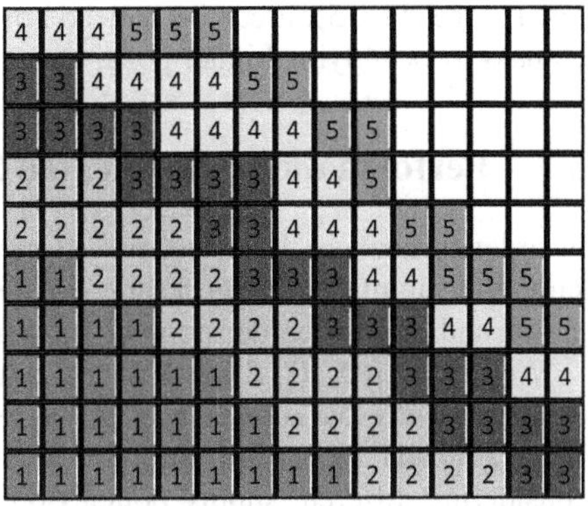

**Fig. 3.** Dedicated zones for the energy-based full turnover policy with 1000 kg unit loads and full dissipation ( 22×45 rack, first part)

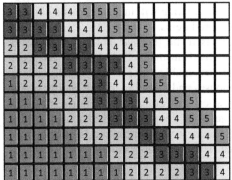

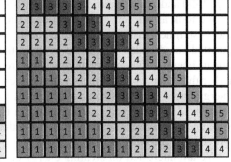

**Fig. 4.** Dedicated zones for the energy-based full turnover policy with 1000 kg unit loads and energy recovery (22×45 rack, first part)

**Fig. 5.** Dedicated zones for the energy-based full turnover policy with 600 kg unit loads and energy recovery ( 22×45 rack, first part)

When the energy-based turnover policy is adopted, instead, the most frequently moved items are associated with locations requiring the least energy to be served for a complete storage plus retrieval single command cycle. For full dissipation, dedicated zone shape is step-wise, as shown in Fig. 3.

Thus, we wonder about the impact of energy recovery on both shape and positions of dedicated zones. Energy recovered during descending phases is subtracted to the total amount of energy required to complete a storage plus a retrieval single command cycle, and the net value for each location is used for storage assignment.

Results for the first part of the 22×45 rack are shown in Fig. 4. The step-wise shape is confirmed to be a peculiarity of energy-based assignment. The shift towards higher positions from the time-based to the energy-based allocation is even more marked when energy recovery is performed (compare Fig. 2-4). The most convenient positions occupy, in facts, higher and higher levels which assure a favourable net balance of energy requirements and energy recovery.

If dedicated zone distribution for the 1000 kg unit load (Fig. 4) is compared to the 600 kg one (Fig. 5), it can be noticed how lighter items tend to compensate their lower mass by occupying higher positions in order to enhance energy recovery.

## 5    Performance of Dedicated Storage Assignment Policies

In order to analyse the effect of different dedicated energy policies on energy consumption, simulations over 5 time windows for a total amount of 53090 retrievals per period and related reorder point based storage operations were performed.

We considered 100 different items with strictly decreasing demand. As in the fundamental study by Hausman et al. [9] we adopted a reorder point policy based on EOQ. An equal ratio of inventory to order costs was selected for all products, to avoid considering different supply policies other then demand rates when establishing the number of locations to be dedicated to each item. Since REPs have highlighted how the shape of the rack significantly affects energy performance we considered both the vertically laid 22×45 rack and the horizontally laid 99×10 one in our simulations. Moreover, to study how a different distribution of items among aisles affects energy saving, we considered also the ABC demand distribution within a single aisle comparing 20-50 and 20-80 distributions of the 100 stored items.

We took as reference the traditional time-based full turnover policy which assure the best time performance as demonstrated by Hausman et al. [9] and has been adopted for decades. Then, we adopted the sustainable perspective, which leads to pursue energy efficiency in automated warehouses and therefore to take energy saving rather than time as the primary performance when dedicating zones within a rack. The energy-based full turnover strategy was therefore adopted. We computed performances of the analysed configurations in two cases: when the crane is not provided with energy recovery and when it is, so that benefits of upgrading AS/RS machines with energy recovery can be assessed.

We are interested on creating energy efficient facilities and processes, but we cannot neglect the importance of time performance in warehousing for its direct link with the service level perceived by clients. This is the reason why we computed picking time other than energy requirements for each simulation run, in order to get insight into potential trade-off between time and energy performances.

Results in Table 2 and Table 3 show how relative variations in time and energy performance when moving from the time-based allocation to the energy-based one are of the same magnitude, since energy is the integral of power over time. Therefore a trade-off between picking time and energy consumption arises and a firm should choose what

performance leads to major competitive advantage in order to apply the proper allocation policy. However, it should be noticed how in the presence of energy recovery, even
the time-based allocation gains energy saving with respect to both time-based and energy-based turnover policies with full dissipation (12.7% for the 22×45 rack and 20-50
demand curve). This means that the energy recovery option can trigger hybrid approaches as a good compromise between time and energy performances, such that of
allocating by a time-based policy in order to optimize service level, while still pursuing
energy efficiency due to re-generation into the power supply system.

Table 4 allows to analyse, instead, the effect of a radical change of perspective,
from the traditional time-based approach associated to time-based assignment with
full dissipation to the sustainable perspective of energy-based assignment enforced by
energy recovery. In this case improvements on energy efficiency is significantly higher than worsening on time-performance, reaching 16% of energy saving for the 22×45
rack and the 20-50 curve with picking time worsening of 3.5%.

**Table 2.** Time and energy performances of the time-based full turnover strategy (TB) and the
energy-based one (EB) with full dissipation

| Rack | Demand curve | Time TB [h] | Time EB [h] | Energy TB [MJ] | Energy EB [MJ] | Δ rel Time | Δ rel Energy |
|------|------|------|------|------|------|------|------|
| 10×99 | 20-50 | 1019.7 | 1033.9 | 59036.8 | 58340.8 | -1.39% | 1.18% |
|       | 20-80 | 949.7 | 970.7 | 55801.9 | 54878.5 | -2.21% | 1.65% |
| 22×45 | 20-50 | 1136.8 | 1164.4 | 59779.6 | 58194.4 | -2.42% | 2.65% |
|       | 20-80 | 1084.1 | 1123.5 | 57057.6 | 54779.4 | -3.63% | 3.95% |

**Table 3.** Time and energy performances of the time-based full turnover strategy (TB) and the
energy-based one (EB) with energy recovery

| Rack | Demand curve | Time TB [h] | Time EB [h] | Energy TB [MJ] | Energy EB [MJ] | Δ rel Time | Δ rel Energy |
|------|------|------|------|------|------|------|------|
| 10×99 | 20-50 | 1019.7 | 1028.6 | 54982.9 | 54552.1 | -0.87% | 0.78% |
|       | 20-80 | 949.7 | 962.5 | 51744.2 | 51202.1 | -1.35% | 1.05% |
| 22×45 | 20-50 | 1136.8 | 1176.2 | 52196.5 | 50220.2 | -3.47% | 3.79% |
|       | 20-80 | 1084.1 | 1143.6 | 50121.7 | 47289.6 | -5.48% | 5.65% |

More insight on energy recovery can be gained by performing a $2^3$ factorial design
of experiments, which is obtained by considering the rack shape (99×10 as low level,
22×45 as high level), the ABC demand curve (20-50 as the low level, 20-80 as the
high one), and the full turnover policy (the time-based one as the low level, the energy-based one as the high level). Main and interaction effects are reported in Fig. 6 as
relative percentage with respect to the basic solution with lower levels. It can be noticed how the rack shape becomes the major factor in the presence of energy recovery,
overcoming the demand distribution which was highlighted as gaining the major effect for cranes with full dissipation [8]. Rack shape effect is even enforced by the
adoption of the energy-based storage policy, as the significant related interaction effect underlines.

From a design point of view, results suggest that exploiting vertical space when
building automated warehouses together with energy recovery option for cranes
should become the preferred practice to enhance sustainability. Attention should be

paid also to distribute items among racks so that skewed demand curve can be obtained and therefore advantages related to dedicated policies can be maximized.

Finally, from the control point of view, we underline the energy saving achievable by dedicated policies with respect to the common random policy. If energy recovery is performed, for the 22×45 rack and 20-50 curve 22% of relative decrease in energy consumption is gained by the energy-based full turnover policy, reaching 26% for the 20-80 demand curve.

**Table 4.** Time and energy variation (relative %) from no-recovery time-based allocation to energy recovery based one.

| Rack | Demand curve | Δ % Time | Δ % Energy |
|------|------|------|------|
| 10×99 | 20-50 | -0.87 | 7.60 |
| | 20-80 | -1.35 | 8.24 |
| 22×45 | 20-50 | -3.47 | 15.99 |
| | 20-80 | -5.48 | 17.12 |

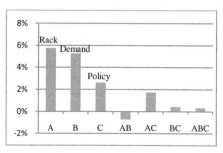

**Fig. 6.** Main and interaction effects on energy requirements of the rack shape (A), demand curve (B), and the full turnover policy (C)

## References

1. Garetti, M., Taisch, M.: Sustainable manufacturing: trends and research challenges. Prod. Plan. Control. 23(2-3), 83–104 (2012)
2. MHIA, Sustainability in warehousing, distribution & manufacturing, Promat (2011), http://www.mhia.org/news/mhia/10621/mhia-releases-results-of-sustainability-study-during-promat-2011 (last access February 2012)
3. Elkington, J.: Cannibals with Forks: The Triple Bottom Line of the 21st Century. New Society Publishers, Stoney Creek (1998)
4. MHIA, Automated Storage Systems Make a Play for Sustainability, quarterly report fall (2009), http://www.mhia.org/news/industry/9141/as-rs-industry-group-releases-fall-2009-quarterly-report (last access December 2011)
5. de Koster, R., Le-Duc, T., Roodbergen, K.J.: Design and control of warehouse order picking: A literature review. Eur. J. Oper. Res. 182, 481–501 (2007)
6. Gu, J., Goetschalckx, M., McGinnis, L.F.: Research on warehouse design and performance evaluation: a comprehensive review. Eur. J. Oper. Res. 203, 539–549 (2010)
7. Roodbergen, K.J., Vis, I.F.A.: A survey of literature on automated storage and retrieval systems. Eur. J. Oper. Res. 194, 343–362 (2009)
8. Meneghetti, A., Monti, L.: Sustainable storage assignment and dwell-point policies for automated storage and retrieval systems. Prod. Plan. Control, iFirst (December 15, 2011)
9. Hausman, W.H., Schwarz, L.B., Graves, S.C.: Optimal Storage Assignment in Automatic Warehousing Systems. Management Science 22(6), 629–638 (1976)
10. Hwang, H., Lee, S.B.: Travel-time models considering the operating characteristics of the storage and retrieval machine. Int. J. Prod. Res. 28(10), 1779–1789 (1990)

# Modeling Green Fabs – A Queuing Theory Approach for Evaluating Energy Performance

Hyun Woo Jeon and Vittaldas V. Prabhu

Harold and Inge Marcus Department of Industrial and Manufacturing Engineering,
Pennsylvania State University, University Park, PA 16802 USA
albert.jeon@psu.edu, prabhu@engr.psu.edu

**Abstract.** More than 30% of the total energy consumed in the U.S. is attributed
to industrial sector which motivated improvements in energy efficiency of
manufacturing processes and entire factories. Semiconductor fabrication (fab)
represents an interesting challenge for energy efficiency because of their relatively high energy consumption to process a unit mass of material. The focus of
this paper is to develop an energy-aware analytical model based on queuing
theory that has re-entrant network structure commonly found in fabs to analyze
the impact of reducing idle power consumption in individual equipment.
The proposed analytical model based on BCMP network for re-entrant lines has
the same mathematical form as serial lines and is tested for using detailed simulation of a generic CMOS fab with three processing steps. Results show that the
energy consumption predicted by the analytical model differs from simulation
typically within 10% and worst case of 14%, in the tested cases.

**Keywords:** Sustainability, Queueing Network, Re-entrant Networks, Semiconductor Manufacturing, Energy-aware Model.

## 1    Introduction

Faced with a growing trend of increasing energy consumption worldwide, various organizations are trying to be more energy efficient [1]. Especially there is a particular need for
the U.S., as one of the largest energy consumers among nations, to increase energy efficiency across all segments of the economy as the American industrial segment accounts
for 31% of its total energy consumption [2]. Two benefits that can be expected from
improved energy efficiency in the industry segment are direct cost savings and indirect
environmental benefit, both stemming from reduced energy consumption. Consequently
there has been increasing research on understanding energy consumption of various
manufacturing processes and associated equipment [3]. This prior research has found that
semiconductor manufacturing processes is among the highest energy consumption per
unit mass in the manufacturing industry. For example, the oxidation process in fabs typically consumes 1.E+13 – 14 J/kg compared to milling steel which consumes about
1.E+05 J/kg. Moreover, idling manufacturing machines typically consume as much as 40
to 60% of the power when they are busy for processing parts [4]. A logical progression of
research effort is to build on the energy consumption models of unit processes to higher

C. Emmanouilidis, M. Taisch, D. Kiritsis (Eds.): APMS 2012, Part I, IFIP AICT 397, pp. 41–48, 2013.

levels such as the factory level and the supply chain level. For analyzing busy/idle states of a system consisting of many machines, simulation and queuing modeling are attractive approaches. Good insights can be acquired when both approaches are used, including testing and validation of each other judiciously [5].

Our recent efforts in this direction include developing hybrid simulation models consisting of continuous and discrete process for predicting energy consumption in discrete manufacturing [6]. We have also proposed queuing models to predict energy savings in serial production lines when idling machines are switched to a lower power state in serial production lines consisting of machines with Poisson arrival and exponential service time [7].

This paper builds on our previous work [7] to extend and generalize the energy-aware queuing model to a re-entrant structure which is applied to model semiconductor fabs. Section 2 reviews the prior analytical model along with its parameters and limitations. In Section 3 a model for re-entrant lines is introduced and energy performance characteristics are derived. In Section 4 a generic semiconductor production system is used for comparing results predicted by the analytical model with those by detailed simulation. Section 5 summarizes this paper with possible future research directions.

## 2    Energy-Aware Queuing Model

Our recently proposed approach for improving energy efficiency in manufacturing system is to use energy control policies that switch machines to a lower power consumption state when a machine is anticipated to be idle for longer than some threshold, $\tau$ [6, 7]. In order to predict the efficiency gained by using such energy control policies, the state transitions between the various energy consumption states and production states of the machines need to be modeled. Without any energy control policy ($EC_0$) the machine power consumption in its idle state will be $W_1$, the nominal power for idling. When energy control policy is used ($EC_1$), energy state will be switched to the low power idling of $W_0$ if the idle time duration is anticipated to be longer than $\tau$; otherwise it will be $W_1$. In the busy state the power consumption will be $W_p$ regardless of whether $EC_0$ or $EC_1$ used.

For an M/M/1 queue with an arrival rate of $\lambda$ and a service rate $\mu$, the probability that a new arrival arrives after the time threshold $\tau$ is given by

$$P(x > \tau) = \int_{\tau}^{\infty} \lambda e^{-\lambda x} dx = e^{-\lambda \tau} \tag{1}$$

Based on this, the total energy consumption with $EC_0$ and $EC_1$ over time $T$ can be modeled as follows

$$E_{EC0} = \{W_p \rho + W_1(1 - \rho)\} T \tag{2}$$

$$E_{EC1} = \{W_p \rho + W_1(1 - \rho)(1 - e^{-\lambda \tau}) + W_0(1 - \rho)e^{-\lambda \tau}\} T \tag{3}$$

In Equations 2 and 3 $\rho$ is the machine utilization. Therefore the total energy saving can be expressed as

$$E_{total\ energy\ saved} = (W_1 - W_0)(1 - \rho)e^{-\lambda \tau} T \tag{4}$$

It should be noted from Equation 4 that energy saving can be increased by decreasing $W_0$ and $\tau$ for a given $\rho$. The above model for a single queue can be extended to serial production lines [7].

# 3    Re-entrant System Modeling

## 3.1    Queueing Model for Re-entrant System

Semiconductor fabs are markedly different from serial production lines or job shops [8, 9]. A typical semiconductor fab has a re-entrant structure in which the products flow through a fixed route visiting a machine multiple times [10, 11]. Semiconductor fabs can be modeled as an open queuing network in which parts visit a machine multiple times. It should be pointed out that because the route in semiconductor fab is deterministic such systems cannot be modeled as Jackson networks [12]. Therefore in this paper we will model semiconductor fabs as a BCMP network, which is also the approach taken by several other researchers [9, 11, 13]. The main parameters and assumptions in modeling a semiconductor fab as a BCMP queuing network are as follows

- Arrival rate from outside is $\lambda$ and $V_m$ is the number of visits to machine $m$ before a part exits the system.
- Arrival process is Poisson and mean service time follows exponential distribution with rates of $\lambda_m$ and $\mu_m$, respectively.
- Queueing discipline is FCFS (first come first serve) and parts are served regardless of buffer in which the part is located.
- Service rate $\mu_m$ is same for all parts in any buffer of the machine.
- Route of each part is fixed and deterministic.
- Idle time threshold for $EC_1$ is $\tau_m$ for machine $m$.

Based on the above model, the arrival rate at machine $m$ can be expressed as

$$\lambda_m = V_m \lambda \tag{5}$$

The utilization of machine $m$ can be also defined as

$$\rho_m = \lambda_m/\mu_m = V_m\lambda/\mu_m \tag{6}$$

The long run probability that there are n parts at a machine $m$ is therefore given by

$$\pi_n(m) = (1 - \rho_m)\rho_m^n \tag{7}$$

From (6), (7) the probability of machine $m$ is busy, $P_B(m)$ can be expressed as

$$P_B(m) = \rho_m \tag{8}$$

The re-entrant structure of the model gives rise to multiple arrival streams at a machine that may not be independent of each other. Furthermore, summing these arrivals may not be an exact model for a composite Poisson process with an exponentially distributed inter-arrival time [14]. However treating the composite arrivals as a Poisson process can be a reasonable approximation [15], which we adopt for modeling the probability of a machine being in nominal power idling $(P_N)$ and low-power idling $(P_L)$ states when $EC_1$ is used. These probabilities for machine $m$ are

$$P_N(m) \approx (1 - \rho_m)\left(1 - e^{-\lambda_m \tau_m}\right) \tag{9}$$

$$P_L(m) \approx (1 - \rho_m)e^{-\lambda_m \tau_m} \tag{10}$$

From (8)-(10), the energy consumption for machine $m$ of a re-entrant system for time period $T$ can be modeled as

$$E_{ECO}(m) \approx \left\{W_p(m)\rho_m + W_1(m)(1 - \rho_m)\right\}T \tag{11}$$

$$E_{EC1}(m) \approx \left\{ \begin{matrix} W_p(m)\rho_m + W_1(m)(1 - \rho_m)\left(1 - e^{-\lambda_m \tau_m}\right) \\ + W_0(m)(1 - \rho_m)e^{-\lambda_m \tau_m} \end{matrix} \right\}T \tag{12}$$

where $W_p(m)$, $W_1(m)$, and $W_0(m)$ are power consumption levels of machine $m$ for busy, nominal power idling, and low power idling states respectively. It should be emphasized that this energy model for a re-entrant line has the same mathematical structure as the M/M/1 model reviewed in the previous section. Therefore the total spent energy in the entire re-entrant system can be modeled as

$$E_{Total(ECO)} \approx \sum_{m=1}^{n} E_{ECO}(m) \tag{13}$$

$$E_{Total(EC1)} \approx \sum_{m=1}^{n} E_{EC1}(m) \tag{14}$$

In the next section the energy consumption predicted by this analytical model is compared with a detailed simulation model to the efficacy of the model.

## 3.2    Simulation Experiments

Figure 1 illustrates a generic CMOS (Complementary Metal Oxide Semiconductor) fab with Deposition (D), Lithography (L), and Etching (E) processes and a re-entrant structure that follows an overall processing sequence indicated by the numerical values on the arrowed lines. The power consumption levels in these processes are hypothesized based on published data [16] and shown in Table 1 along with other parameters used to simulate three different scenarios with varying arrival rates into the system.

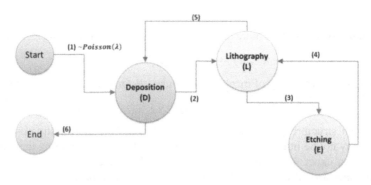

**Fig. 1.** Example re-entrant system for CMOS

The simulation model was implemented by using the SIMIO simulation software package. For each scenario, $P_B$, $P_N$, and $P_L$ are estimated by fraction of the time a machine is in the corresponding state during a simulation run of 10,000 time units and averaged over 30 replications which is then used to compute the results in Tables 2 and 3.

**Table 1.** Simulation parameters

| Parameters for each Simulation Scenario | | | | | | | | | |
|---|---|---|---|---|---|---|---|---|---|
| Scenario | 1 | | | 2 | | | 3 | | |
| Process | D | L | E | D | L | E | D | L | E |
| $\lambda$ | 0.050 | 0.050 | 0.025 | 0.040 | 0.040 | 0.020 | 0.030 | 0.030 | 0.015 |
| $\mu$ | 0.100 | 0.067 | 0.029 | 0.100 | 0.067 | 0.029 | 0.100 | 0.067 | 0.029 |
| $\rho$ | 0.500 | 0.750 | 0.875 | 0.400 | 0.600 | 0.700 | 0.300 | 0.450 | 0.525 |
| $\tau$ | 8.00 | 10.00 | 24.00 | 10.00 | 12.50 | 30.00 | 13.33 | 16.67 | 40.00 |
| $\lambda\tau$ | 0.40 | 0.50 | 0.60 | 0.40 | 0.50 | 0.60 | 0.40 | 0.50 | 0.60 |
| $W_p$ | 24857 | 9140 | 12238 | 24857 | 9140 | 12238 | 24857 | 9140 | 12238 |
| $W_1$ | 8286 | 3047 | 4079 | 8286 | 3047 | 4079 | 8286 | 3047 | 4079 |
| $W_0$ | 1657 | 609.3 | 815.9 | 1657 | 609.3 | 815.9 | 1657 | 609.3 | 815.9 |
| Replication | 30 | | | 30 | | | 30 | | |

The Figure 2 illustrates energy consumed with $EC_0$ and $EC_1$ of each of the deposition process in scenario 1. As expected, energy savings in all three processes increases with time. Figure 3 shows the power consumption for the deposition processing step with $EC_0$ and $EC_1$ in scenario 1.

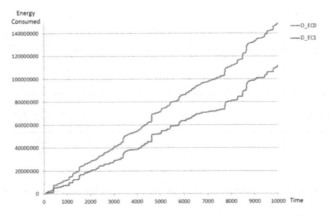

**Fig. 2.** Energy consumed in the deposition process in scenario 1

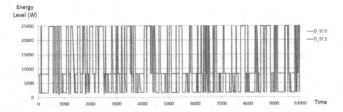

**Fig. 3.** Power consumption level for deposition process in scenario 1

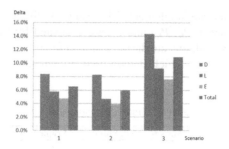

**Fig. 4.** Model difference with $EC_1$

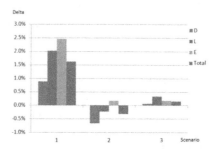

**Fig. 5.** Model difference with $EC_0$

**Table 2.** Comparison of Simulation and Analytical Models with $EC_1$

| Scenario | Simulation | | | | Analytical Approximation | | | | Delta = (A-S)/S | | | |
|---|---|---|---|---|---|---|---|---|---|---|---|---|
| | D | L | E | Total | D | L | E | Total | D | L | E | Total |
| 1 | 13245 | 6850 | 10494 | 30590 | 14350 | 7247 | 10994 | 32591 | 8.3% | 5.8% | 4.8% | 6.5% |
| 2 | 11315 | 5837 | 8903 | 26054 | 12248 | 6111 | 9253 | 27613 | 8.2% | 4.7% | 3.9% | 6.0% |
| 3 | 8876 | 4556 | 6982 | 20414 | 10147 | 4976 | 7512 | 22634 | 14.3% | 9.2% | 7.6% | 10.9% |

**Table 3.** Comparison of Simulation and Analytical Models with $EC_0$

| Scenario | Simulation | | | | Analytical Approximation | | | | Delta = (A-S)/S | | | |
|---|---|---|---|---|---|---|---|---|---|---|---|---|
| | D | L | E | Total | D | L | E | Total | D | L | E | Total |
| 1 | 16425 | 7465 | 10949 | 34839 | 16571 | 7617 | 11218 | 35406 | 0.9% | 2.0% | 2.5% | 1.6% |
| 2 | 15013 | 6717 | 9774 | 31504 | 14914 | 6703 | 9790 | 31407 | -0.7% | -0.2% | 0.2% | -0.3% |
| 3 | 13248 | 5769 | 8348 | 27365 | 13257 | 5789 | 8363 | 27408 | 0.1% | 0.3% | 0.2% | 0.2% |

From Table 2 and 3, it can be observed that analytical and simulation estimate of total energy consumed typically differ within 10% with the worst case being 14.3%. Figures 4 and 5 graphically illustrate the difference between analytical and simulation models (delta) presented in Tables 2 and 3. The difference is much less with $EC_0$ compared to $EC_1$ and delta decreases as utilization $\rho$ increases. We conjecture that the exponential distribution assumption for the composite inter-arrival times used in the analytical model underestimates the probability of being in low-power idling states, therefore overestimating the energy consumption. From energy efficiency perspective, $EC_1$ consumes less energy than $EC_0$ as expected. Energy savings $(EC_0 - EC_1)$ decrease as $\rho$ increases because there is lesser opportunity for $EC_1$ as machines get busier. Moreover, for a given $\rho$, smaller $\tau$ will make $EC_1$ more energy efficient. In practice, the choice of $\tau$ will be constrained by the physics and economics of the process.

# 4    Conclusions

An energy-aware analytical model based on BCMP network is proposed in this paper for semiconductor fabs with re-entrant structure commonly. Focus of the analysis is to assess the energy efficiency gained by reducing idle power consumption by switching machines to a lower power state when idling. Simulation tests indicate that the energy consumption predicted by the analytical models are typically differ within 10% from detailed simulations with worst case being about 14%, which makes the approach promising for rapid evaluation of candidate energy control strategies. Future work could focus on analyzing the factors that can influence the accuracy of the analytical model including the composite inter-arrival distribution model. Another potential future direction is to generalize the queuing networks to include G/G/1 and GI/G/1 systems [17, 18].

# References

1. The U.S. Energy Information Administration: International Energy Outlook 2011, DOE/EIA-0484(2011) (2011), http://www.eia.gov/forecasts/ieo/
2. The U.S. Department of Energy: Annual Energy Review 2010, DOE/EIA-0384 (2010), http://www.eia.gov/totalenergy/data/annual/index.cfm
3. Gutowski, T.G., Branham, M.S., Dahmus, J.B., Jones, A.J., Thiriez, A., Sekulic, D.P.: Thermodynamic analysis of resources used in manufacturing processes. Environ. Sci. and Technol. 43, 1584–1590 (2009)
4. Diaz, N., Redelsheimer, E., Dornfeld, D.: Energy Consumption Characterization and Reduction Strategies for Milling Machine Tool Use. In: Glocalized Solutions for Sustainability in Manufacturing 2011, pp. 263–267 (2011)
5. Connors, D.P., Feigin, G.E., Tao, D.D.: A Queueing Network Model for Semiconductor Manufacturing. IEEE Transactions on Semiconductor Manufacturing 9(3) (1996)
6. Prabhu, V., Taisch, M.: Simulation Modeling of Energy Dynamics in Discrete Manufacturing Systems. In: Proceedings of 14th IFAC Symposium on Information Control Problems in Manufacturing (INCOM 2012), Bucharest, Romania, May 23-25 (2012)
7. Prabhu, V., Jeon, H.W., Taisch, M.: Modeling Green Factory Physics – An Analytical Approach. In: Proceedings of IEEE CASE 2012 (2012)
8. Graves, S.C.: A review of production scheduling. Operations Research 29, 646–675 (1981)
9. Kumar, P.R.: Re-entrant lines. Queueing Systems 13, 87–110 (1993)
10. Jaeger, R.C.: Introduction to Microelectronic Fabrication, 2nd edn., vol. V. Prentice Hall (2002) ISBN 0-201-44494-7
11. Kumar, S., Kumar, P.R.: Queueing Network Models in the Design and Analysis of Semiconductor Wafer Fabs. IEEE Transactions on Robotics and Automation 17(5), 548–561 (2001)
12. Jackson, J.R.: Networks of waiting lines. Operations Research 5(4) (1957)

13. Baskett, F., Chandy, K.M., Muntz, R.R., Palacios, F.G.: Open, Closed, and Mixed Networks of Queues with Different Classes of Customers. Journal of the Association for Computing Machinery 22(2), 248–260 (1975)
14. Wolff, R.W.: Stochastic Modeling and the Theory of Queues, 1st edn., pp. 321–322. Prentice Hall (1989)
15. Kuehn, P.J.: Approximate Analysis of General Queueing Networks by Decomposition. IEEE Transactions on Communications Com. 27(1) (1979)
16. Hu, S.-C., Chuah, Y.K.: Power consumption of semiconductor fabs in Taiwan. Energy 28(8), 895–907 (2003)
17. Whitt, W.: The Queueing Network Analyzer. The Bell System Technical Journal 62(9) (1983)
18. Daley, D.J.: Queueing Output Processes. Adv. Appl. Prob. 8, 295–415 (1976)

# Analyzing Energy Consumption for Factory and Logistics Planning Processes

Egon Müller, Hendrik Hopf, and Manuela Krones

Department of Factory Planning and Factory Management
Institute of Industrial Sciences and Factory Systems
Chemnitz University of Technology
Chemnitz, Germany
`{egon.mueller,hendrik.hopf,manuela.krones}@mb.tu-chemnitz.de`

**Abstract.** Energy efficiency increasingly becomes a relevant objective in industry. Factory planning plays an important role for energy-efficient factory, production and logistics systems. The design of systems and processes in intralogistics, as an essential part of factory planning, is in the focus of this paper. Existing approaches for energy efficiency-oriented planning of logistics systems are either empirical or theoretical. The paper describes an approach combining both aspects. With the presented approach, the energy consumption of a system in a factory can be determined and evaluated systematically. As a result, energy efficiency measures are deduced and generalized. The approach provides energy data and knowledge to support analyzing and optimization activities in planning processes.

**Keywords:** Energy Efficiency, Analysis of Energy Consumption, Factory Planning, Logistics Planning.

## 1 Introduction

Energy efficiency becomes a more and more important objective for industrial companies due to several factors, e.g. rising energy prices, growing environmental awareness and energy policy conditions. The EU member states agreed on the principle of "20/20/20 by 2020", i.e. a 20 % reduction in greenhouse gases, a 20 % share of renewable energies and a 20 % increase in energy efficiency by the year 2020 compared to 1990 [1]. The national implementation differs between the countries. For example, Germany wants to take a pioneering role and therefore adopted the "Energy Concept 2050", which staggers the achievement of goals in different phases. The greenhouse gas emissions should be reduced by 40 % until 2020, by 55 % until 2030 and by at least 80 % until 2050 [2].

Industrial companies have recognized this trend and implement corporate strategies for improving sustainability and energy efficiency. The energy efficiency of the entire factory system does not result directly from the sum of individual parts or actions, i.e. individual actions can affect each other positively or negatively. Only through a holistic view of the complex coherences and interactions of individual resources, processes

C. Emmanouilidis, M. Taisch, D. Kiritsis (Eds.): APMS 2012, Part I, IFIP AICT 397, pp. 49–56, 2013.

and structures of a factory, energy optimization potentials of the overall process or the total system can be exploited [3].

Therefore, factory planning plays a significant role for energy efficiency of factory, production and logistics systems. Despite of this importance, there is still a demand on tools and methods to integrate energy efficiency in planning processes systematically.

In the Cluster of Excellence eniPROD®, which is a collaboration of Chemnitz University of Technology and Fraunhofer Institute for Machine Tools and Forming Technology, the research is focused on "Energy-Efficient Product and Process Innovations in Production Engineering". An objective of eniPROD® is a national and international visible contribution to realizing the vision of an almost emission-free production while simultaneously reducing the demand for energy as well as increasing the efficiency of resources [4]. One of the specific issues is "Energy-Efficient Systems and Processes in Logistics and Factory Planning".

The contribution of logistics to energy efficiency is often neglected by practitioners. But it is estimated that 40% of the energy consumption in production are caused by production surroundings which have their greatest share in logistics processes [5]. Especially in the field of intralogistics, there are only few scientific publications to support energy efficiency-oriented planning [6]. The presented approach for analysis and evaluation of energy consumption has been developed within eniPROD® to meet these deficits.

The remainder of the paper is organized as follows: In section 2, the basics of energy efficiency in logistics systems are presented. Section 3 contains the developed approach, which is applied to a use case in section 4. A short discussion and an outlook on further research are given in section 5.

## 2     Energy Efficiency in Logistics Systems

Energy efficiency, in general, is defined by the ratio of useful process output and energy input [7]. Possibilities to reduce energy consumption are either technological (e.g. reducing friction) or organizational (e.g. reducing transport effort or switching off components when they are currently not used). Technological measures often lead to a change of construction and cause additional costs. Organizational measures can often be realized without additional costs.

Scientific problems in the field of energy efficiency are highly diversified. A main problem to raise energy efficiency consists in the understanding and modeling of the relationship between energy consumption and its causes. Methods that have been developed for this problem are mostly found in the field of machine tools and can be divided into empirical and theoretical approaches (figure 1). Empirical methods focus on the collection and comparison of energy data for different states of operating. Afterwards, these data can be used for simulation studies [8], [9]. Theoretical approaches use models to describe the influence of different variables on energy consumption [10], [11].

A transfer of the fore-mentioned methods to logistics systems is hardly possible, because their structure and functions are very heterogeneous (e.g. transport, storage, picking and packaging). There are only few scientific publications considering systematic approaches to increase energy efficiency in logistics systems. For instance, an empirical approach is presented by Prasse et al. [12]. A theoretical analysis on energy efficiency improvement based on a physical model is performed by Zhang et al. [13], but there is no verification of the theoretical findings with empirical studies.

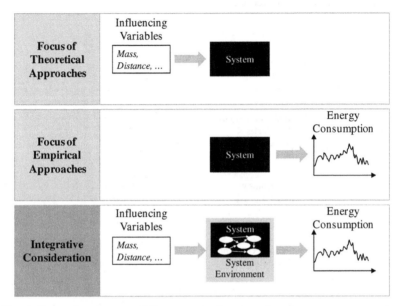

**Fig. 1.** Comparison between different approaches to analyze the energy consumption

# 3    Approach for Analysis and Evaluation of Energy Consumption

The presented approach uses an integrative consideration of theoretical and empirical methods (figure 1). The goal is to determine and evaluate the energy consumption of a system and to deduce energy efficiency measures based on this. The approach is divided into seven steps (figure 2).

In the first step, "Definition of Target Figures", the considered system is chosen as object of investigation and the goal of the analysis as well as the target figures are defined. A typical goal of the analysis is to determine the energy consumption depending on different operating states of the system. In this case, electrical power and electrical work can be defined as target figures. In the further procedure, possible influencing variables need to be identified and evaluated regarding their quantitative effect.

Then, the system is described in detail and available data is collected in the step "Definition of System Boundaries & Data Acquisition". The analyzed system is separated into subsystems, elements, structures and processes to define the system boundaries. Different description models can be used for this task (e.g. hierarchical or peripheral order). A system is gradually divided into subsystems with the hierarchical order. The peripheral order structures a system according to the dependence on the master production schedule [14]. Thus, the energy consumption can be traced to its origin. After that, required information about energy carriers, processes or materials etc. is gathered. If the system is similar to other systems, the results of the analysis could be transferred in order to reduce effort.

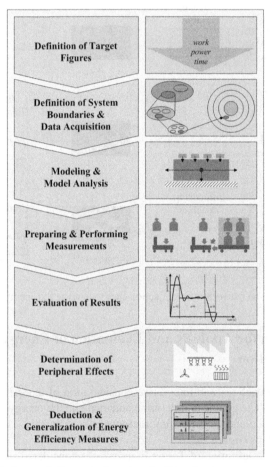

**Fig. 2.** Approach for analysis and evaluation of energy consumption

A central step is the "Modeling & Model Analysis", which comprises creating a model of the system and identifying influencing variables on energy efficiency. Physical principles in the model describe how the defined target figures (see step 1) depend on the influencing variables. According to the system boundaries (see step 2), the influencing variables are divided into control and disturbance variables. Control variables can be changed within the system boundaries, whereas disturbance variables cannot be influenced. After modeling, the effects of changing control variables are analyzed. Two advantages can be achieved with this theoretical consideration: Firstly, the effects of energy efficiency measures can be estimated without affecting the real system in its operation. Secondly, the operating states can be specified for the preparation of the practical examination.

In the next step, "Preparing & Performing Measurements", the energy consumption of the system is measured in order to test the theoretical findings practically. The measuring variables, points and instruments are defined on the basis of the target figures and influencing variables (see step 3). Possible measuring points are the main connection (e.g. control cabinet) or the connections of the components (e.g. drive motors). Batteries or their charging stations can be used as measuring points for material handling vehicles. Measuring instruments can be stationary or mobile. Special attention should be paid to the acquisition of process data in addition to energy data in order to link this data.

Theoretical and practical results are compared in the step "Evaluation of Results". The measured values can be summarized with the use of statistical metrics according to the required accuracy. Key figures, e.g. specific energy consumption, are calculated to compare different planning or operation alternatives. Depending on the system complexity, visualization in form of energy flow charts or diagrams is helpful for better understanding.

The sixth step, "Determination of Peripheral Effects", is very important for energy efficiency-oriented factory and logistics planning. The energy consumption depends on the design and operation of a system. Energy measurements often focus just on this direct consumption. But in addition, indirect energy consumption is caused by the area taken up within a superior system (e.g. energy demand for HVAC and lighting). Intralogistics systems, e.g. transport systems, typically take up a great share of the floor space, so the indirect energy consumption should not be disregarded.

The last step consists of the "Deduction and Generalization of Energy Efficiency Measures". Based on the findings of theoretical and practical analysis, influencing variables and optimization opportunities are pointed out. Recommendations for energy efficiency-oriented planning and energy-efficient operation of the system are generalized.

## 4    Use Case "Automated Guided Vehicle"

The application of the approach is presented on an example in the "Experimental and Digital Factory" of the Department of Factory Planning and Factory Management [15]. Further practical case studies were performed in an industrial environment [16]. The automated guided vehicle "MOVE" of Trilogiq was selected to analyze electrical power and electrical energy consumption depending on the transport task (figure 3). The investigation focuses on the vehicle operation, not on the construction. Therefore, it is not further separated into its components (e.g. drive, control system), although this would be possible for analyzing the dependence between the energy consumption and the vehicle's construction. The points for material transfer and battery charging stations belong to the system environment.

The only needed energy form is electrical power, which is provided by two lead batteries with each 12 V voltage and 120 Ah capacity. The vehicle uses magnetic navigation with a passive guide line and passive ground markers to follow a programmed route.

The physical model is build in order to deduce the influencing variables on energy consumption. It bases on the planar motion of a particle. The energy consumption of electrical components is not considered at this point. The mechanical work is calculated as target figure by adding the forces due to rolling and acceleration resistance. The influencing variables are divided into control and disturbance variables. As only the vehicle operation is analyzed, the control variables are the mass of the transported goods, the number of acceleration processes, the distance and the velocity. A sensitivity analysis is used to order the variables according to their predicted influence. The ratio between energy consumption and transport effort (specific energy consumption) is calculated as key figure.

Afterwards, the practical measurement was performed by absolving a driving cycle with different transport loads and different velocities. The insights of the analysis of the physical model were tested. The energy consumption was recorded by the battery controller "WI-iQ®" from EnerSys/Hawker, which transfers the data of the current power consumption to a laptop by wireless communication. It is important to log the position of the vehicle and its driving time in order to connect energy and process data, i.e. to assign the energy consumption to different parts of the driving cycle.

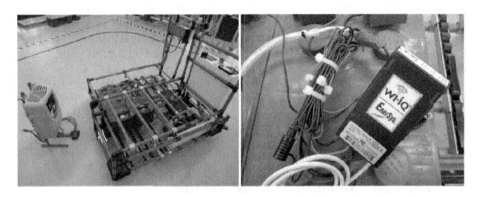

**Fig. 3.** Analyzed automated guided vehicle (left) and battery controller (right)

When the measured results were evaluated, there were, at first, differences between the model and the real energy consumption. This means, the mechanical energy used for the movement, which is calculated with the physical model, represents only a part of the consumed electrical energy. However, the important influencing variables were identified before the measurements. As one measured result, less acceleration processes led to reduced energy consumption. Whereas, the reduction of velocity led to a reverse effect: Although the electrical power was reduced, the time for the driving cycle increased and therefore, energy consumption increased, too. The specific energy consumption was calculated again from the measured values. Increasing transport load led to the decrease of the specific energy consumption i.e. makes the transport more efficient. In general, this depends on the relation between the mass of the transported goods and the mass of the vehicle.

After performing the measurements, the peripheral effects were analyzed. The automated guided vehicle needs area for transportation as well as for loading and unloading (about 28 % of the floor space), so indirect energy consumption is caused. Additionally, the battery charging stations need air-conditioning. If the energy consumption of the vehicle is reduced, the battery needs to be charged less often and therefore, the charging components could be smaller sized.

In the last step, energy efficiency measures are generalized. As already mentioned, transport distance has a great influence on energy consumption and should therefore be reduced. If the transport route cannot be modified, distance can be reduced by summarizing transports, which leads to increasing transport loads. The effect of aggregating two transports was analyzed with the physical model as well as with another measurement and led to 30 % energy savings.

# 5    Conclusions

It was shown that energy efficiency becomes more and more important for industrial systems and processes. Hence, there is a demand on energy efficiency-oriented tools and methods.

A systematic approach for analysis and evaluation of energy consumption was presented and exemplarily applied. The approach describes the collection and the interpretation of energy data in order to analyze energy consumption of logistics systems. Based on this, energy efficiency measures are deduced and generalized. The approach was demonstrated on the example of an automated guided vehicle. The structured procedure helped to predict the effects of energy efficiency measures and moreover, to prepare and perform measurements systematically and with less effort.

The measured values can be applied for process modeling and simulation. Different planning or operation alternatives can be compared regarding their energy efficiency. Besides the scientific application, industrial companies are able to realize energy-efficient processes with the help of this approach.

**Acknowledgements.** The Cluster of Excellence "Energy-Efficient Product and Process Innovation in Production Engineering" (eniPROD®) is funded by the European Union (European Regional Development Fund) and the Free State of Saxony.

# References

1. Council of the European Union, http://register.consilium.europa.eu/pdf/en/07/st07/st07224-re01.en07.pdf
2. Federal Ministry of Economics and Technology: Energy Concept for an Environmentally Sound, Reliable and Affordable Energy Supply, http://www.bmu.de/files/english/pdf/application/pdf/energiekonzept_bundesregierung_en.pdf
3. Müller, E., Löffler, T.: Energy Efficiency at Manufacturing Plants – A Planning Approach. In: 43rd CIRP International Conference on Manufacturing Systems, Vienna, pp. 787–794 (2010)
4. Neugebauer, R.: Energy-Efficient Product and Process Innovation in Production Engineering – 1st International Colloquium of the Cluster of Excellence eniPROD. Wissenschaftliche Scripten, Chemnitz (2010)
5. Hellingrath, B., Schürrer, S.: Software in der Logistik – Klimaschutz im Fokus. In: ten Hompel, M. (ed.) Energieeffizienz und Umweltbilanz von Supply Chains, pp. 16–21. Huss, Munich (2009)
6. Schmidt, T., Schulze, F.: Simulationsbasierte Entwicklung energieeffizienter Steuerungsstrategien für Materialflusssysteme. In: Vojdani, N. (ed.) 7th Colloquium of the Scientific Association for Technical Logistics (WGTL), pp. 150–159. Praxiswissen Service, Dortmund (2011)
7. Müller, E., Engelmann, J., Löffler, T., Strauch, J.: Energieeffiziente Fabriken planen und betreiben. Springer, Heidelberg (2009)
8. Herrmann, C., Thiede, S.: Process Chain Simulation to Foster Energy Efficiency in Manufacturing. CIRP J. Manuf. Sci. Technol. 1, 221–229 (2009)
9. Larek, R., Brinksmeier, E., Meyer, D., Pawletta, T., Hagendorf, O.: A Discrete-Event Simulation Approach to Predict Power Consumption in Machining Processes. Prod. Engineer. 5, 575–579 (2011)
10. Dietmair, A., Verl, A., Eberspaecher, P.: Model-Based Energy Consumption Optimization in Manufacturing System and Machine Control. Int. J. Manuf. Res. 6, 380–401 (2011)
11. Seow, Y., Rahimifard, S.: A Framework for Modeling Energy Consumption within Manufacturing Systems. CIRP J. Manuf. Sci. Technol. 4, 258–264 (2011)
12. Prasse, C., Kamagaew, A., Gruber, S., Kalischewski, K., Soter, S., ten Hompel, M.: Survey on Energy Efficiency Measurements in Heterogeneous Facility Logistics Systems. In: IEEE International Conference on Industrial Engineering and Engineering Management, Singapore, pp. 1140–1144 (2011)
13. Zhang, S., Xia, X.: Modeling and Energy Efficiency Optimization of Belt Conveyors. Appl. Energ. 88, 3061–3071 (2011)
14. Schenk, M., Wirth, S., Müller, E.: Factory Planning Manual – Situation-Driven Production Facility Planning. Springer, Heidelberg (2009)
15. Horbach, S., Ackermann, J., Müller, E., Schütze, J.: Building Blocks for Adaptable Factory Systems. Robot. Cim.-Int. Manuf. 27, 735–740 (2011)
16. Veit, T., Fischer, S., Strauch, J., Krause, A.: Umsetzung logistischer Strategien unter Berücksichtigung der Energieeffizienz. In: Müller, E., Spanner-Ulmer, B. (eds.) Tagungsband 4. Symposium Wissenschaft und Praxis & 8. Fachtagung Vernetzt Planen und Produzieren – VPP 2010, pp. 167–181. Wissenschaftliche Schriftenreihe des IBF, Chemnitz (2010)

# Energy Implications in the Single-Vendor Single-Buyer Integrated Production Inventory Model

Simone Zanoni[1], Laura Bettoni[1], and Christoph H. Glock[2]

[1] Department of Mechanical and Industrial Engineering
Università degli Studi di Brescia, Via Branze, 38, I-25123, Brescia, Italy
{simone.zanoni,laura.bettoni}@ing.unibs.it
[2] Carlo and Karin Giersch Endowed Chair "Business Management: Industrial Management",
Technische Universität Darmstadt, Hochschulstr. 1, 64289 Darmstadt, Germany
glock@bwl.tu-darmstadt.de

**Abstract.** Increasing energy efficiency is one of the main objectives of the Directive 2009/28/EC of the European Commission (called 20-20-20), which aims at decreasing greenhouse gas emissions by jointly increasing the use of renewable energy and improving energy efficiency, all by 20% until 2020. To reduce energy consumption in producing and distributing products, it is of major importance to consider energy consumption in the whole supply chain and for all activities associated with production and distribution. For this reason, this paper studies a single-vendor single-buyer integrated production-inventory system and explicitly takes account of energy consumption. The use of energy is weighted with a cost factor and evaluated together with classical production-inventory costs. We find that if energy costs are considered together with traditional cost components, then the inventory costs of the system increase slightly in the optimum, but the total costs of the system decrease and we observe great energy savings.

**Keywords:** JELS, joint economic lot size model, energy efficiency, energy consumption, single-vendor single-buyer, lot sizing.

## 1 Introduction

Reducing energy consumption is an important measure for firms to lower costs and increase competitiveness, especially in energy-intensive sectors. In trying to reduce the use of energy in industry, a coordinated approach of multiple stages of the supply chain is more promising than individual, uncoordinated actions taken by the members of the chain.

The benefits of coordinated production and replenishment decisions have frequently been studied in the past. So-called joint economic lot size models [1] extend the classical EOQ model to take account of additional cost factors, such as the costs of backorders and lost sales or quality-related costs. Costs associated with the use of energy have, to the best of the authors' knowledge, not been considered in supply chain models before, apart from a preliminary investigation reported in [2].

C. Emmanouilidis, M. Taisch, D. Kiritsis (Eds.): APMS 2012, Part I, IFIP AICT 397, pp. 57–64, 2013.

In many industries, energy is one of the most important resources. Preserving energy is the best way to ensure a reliable and sustainable energy supply and to reduce greenhouse gas emissions. Energy can be saved by introducing higher levels of energy efficiency throughout the supply chain, which includes the generation of energy, its transmission and distribution as well as an efficient end use.

This work aims at integrating the use of energy in the classical production-inventory costs of a single-vendor single-buyer supply chain. The intention is to investigate the behavior of the main decision variables in the presence of energy costs. The developed model helps managers in the tactical decision for how to coordinate production, distribution and storage in a supply chain to meet economic and environmental (strictly linked to the total energy spent) targets.

## 2    The System

This study considers an integrated production and inventory system with a single-vendor and a single-buyer, as illustrated in Figure 1.

In this paper, we assume that energy consumption in the supply chain can be influenced by changing the production rates of the vendor and by determining the size of the warehouses used at both parties. Both decisions influence the use of energy in the supply chain by determining how much energy the machines of the vendor require for processing a product, and how much energy is used for operating the warehouse. The use of energy in production has been studied by [3], who showed that different production rates result in different levels of energy consumption. In warehousing, especially for products that need particular conditions for proper storage (e.g. food or perishable items), the dimensions of a warehouse directly impact the use of energy, e.g. due to the need to light or cool the facility [4]. Thus, the consumption of energy is influenced by the lot size decision, and it can be weighted with a cost factor and added to the traditional production-inventory costs.

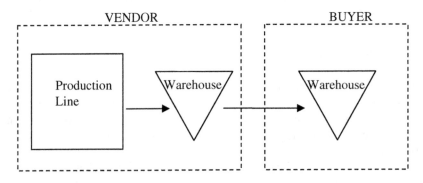

**Fig. 1.** System considered in the analysis

The following notation will be used throughout the paper:

$A_1$: setup cost of the vendor [€/lot]

$A_2$: order cost of the buyer [€/order]

$h_1$: inventory holding cost of the vendor [€/unit/time unit]

$h_2$: inventory holding cost of the buyer [€/unit/time unit]

$p$: production rate [unit/time unit]

$D$: demand rate[unit/time unit]

$n$: number of shipments per production lot [delivery/lot]

$q$: quantity transported per delivery [unit/delivery]

$q_{max,v}$: maximum level of stock of the vendor that can be kept, which is subject to the dimensions of the warehouse

$q_{max,b}$: maximum level of stock of the buyer that can be kept, which is subject to the dimensions of the warehouse

$Q$: lot size [unit/lot] $= n \cdot q$

$e$: energy cost [€/kWh]

$a$, $b$: coefficients that depend on the specific production system (machine) of the vendor

$\alpha$, $\beta$: coefficients that depend on the vendor's warehouse characteristics

$\gamma$, $\delta$: coefficients that depend on the buyer's warehouse characteristics

$TrC$: traditional total cost (cost per time unit [€/time unit], a function of $n$ and $q$)

$EC$: energy costs (cost per time unit [€/time unit], a function of $n$ and $q$)

$TC$: total costs considering ($TC=TrC+EC$).

Moreover, we assume that $p>D$, i.e. the production rate is higher than the demand rate and stock-outs or shortages are not allowed.

## 3    Model

In the following, we develop a model that considers the total costs of producing and distributing a product in a single-vendor single-buyer supply chain and that explicitly takes account of energy costs. We then compare the traditional single-vendor single-buyer system to the system that takes account of energy consumption. The total costs of the traditional single-vendor single-buyer system are formulated as the sum of setup costs, order costs and inventory holding costs for the vendor and the buyer.

In the traditional model, the total inventory costs ($TrC(q,n)$) are a function of the lot size and the number of shipments, and they are calculated as follows [5].

$$TrC(q,n) = (A_1 + n \cdot A_2) \cdot \frac{D}{n \cdot q} + h_1 \cdot \left( \frac{D \cdot q}{p} + \frac{(p-D) \cdot n \cdot q}{2 \cdot p} \right) + (h_2 - h_1) \cdot \frac{q}{2}. \quad (1)$$

Energy costs are formulated as the sum of energy costs during production at the vendor and energy costs caused by storing the products in warehouses at the vendor and the buyer.

As was shown by [3], energy consumption during production can be divided into fixed energy consumption (costs), which is independent of the production rate, and variable consumption (costs). Fixed energy costs are caused by auxiliary tools of machines which are switched on during standby and which consume energy although the machine is not producing. Variable energy costs, in turn, depend on the production volume that is processed per unit of time. Both types of energy consumption are illustrated in Figure 2. The fixed component is not affected by a change in the production rate or an increase in the volume of the warehouse, while the variable component increases as the production rate of the machine is increased.

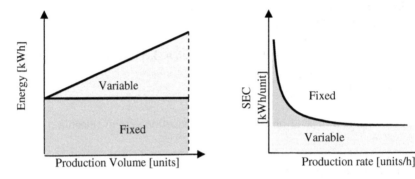

**Fig. 2.** Energy consumption as a function of the production volume

**Fig. 3.** Specific Energy Consumption as a function of the production rate

Figure 3 illustrates how energy consumption per unit of the product develops in the production rate. It can be seen that if we consider the Specific Energy Consumption (SEC) [kWh/kg], the variable component remains constant for different production rates, while the fraction of the fixed component that is assigned to one unit of the product decreases as the production rate is increased.

A number of studies have been carried out to benchmark energy uses in warehouses [4]. Based on this empirical evidence, especially for refrigerated warehouses, the relationship between SEC and the volume of the warehouse can be modeled as in Figure 4. Thus, the SEC decreases both in the production rate as well as in the size of the warehouse.

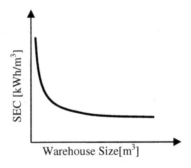

**Fig. 4.** Specific Energy Consumption as a function of the warehouse size

In this work, the energy consumption of the production process and the warehouse are formulated with the help of the SEC, which is a well-accepted variable for measuring energy consumption and energy costs. All types of energy consumption, named $SEC_{Vp}$ for the Specific Energy Consumption at the production line of the vendor, $SEC_{Vw}$ for the Specific Energy Consumption at the warehouse of the vendor and $SEC_{Bw}$ for the Specific Energy Consumption at the warehouse of the buyer, are modeled as follows:

$$SEC_{Vp} = a \cdot (p)^{-b} \tag{2}$$

$$SEC_{Vw} = \alpha \cdot (q_{max,v}(q,n))^{-\beta} \tag{3}$$

$$SEC_{Bw} = \gamma \cdot (q_{max,b}(q))^{-\delta} \tag{4}$$

The maximum inventory at the vendor is $q_{max,v}(q,n) = q \cdot n \cdot \left(1 - \frac{D}{p}\right)$, while the maximum inventory at the buyer equals $q_{max,b}(q) = q$.

Energy costs are calculated as the energy consumption of the production process, i.e. the Specific Energy Consumption multiplied with the demand and the energy cost ($EC_{Vp}$), and the energy consumption of the warehouses, calculated as the Specific Energy Consumption multiplied with the maximum size of the warehouse and the energy cost ($EC_{Vw}$, $EC_{Bw}$), as in the following formula:

$$EC_{Vp} = SEC_{Vp} \cdot D \cdot e \tag{5}$$

$$EC_{Vw} = SEC_{Vw} \cdot q_{max,v}(q,n) \cdot e \tag{6}$$

$$EC_{Bw} = SEC_{Bw} \cdot q_{max,b}(q) \cdot e \tag{7}$$

The total energy cost is the sum of the three components given in Eqs. (5) to (7):

$$EC(q,n) = EC_{Vp} + EC_{Vw} + EC_{Bw} \tag{8}$$

If energy costs are considered in addition, the total costs are a function of the lot size and the number of shipments, and they are calculated as:

$$TC(q,n) = (A_1 + n \cdot A_2) \cdot \frac{D}{n \cdot q} + h_1 \cdot \left(\frac{D \cdot q}{p} + \frac{(p-D) \cdot n \cdot q}{2 \cdot p}\right) + (h_2 - h_1) \cdot \frac{q}{2} + a$$
$$\cdot p^{-b} \cdot D \cdot e + \alpha \cdot \left(Q \cdot \left(1 - \frac{D}{p}\right)\right)^{-\beta+1} \cdot e + \gamma \cdot (q)^{-\delta+1} \cdot e. \tag{9}$$

The optimal values that minimize $TrC(q,n)$ are $(q^*, n^*)$, while the optimal parameters that minimize $TC(q,n,)$ are $(q^{**}, n^{**})$. Since it is not possible to use the first order conditions to minimize Eq. (9), a numerical analysis is necessary to investigate the behavior of the system.

## 4    Numerical Analysis

To study the behavior of the model, we performed a numerical analysis to investigate how the model parameters influence the optimal solution of the energy model.

We performed the numerical analysis for a company in the dairy sector of Parmesan production and aging. The high energy consumption in this sector is due to the conditioning of the warehouse, in which milk and cheese are stocked.

Table 1 summarizes the data that was used in the analysis.

**Table 1.** Data used in the numerical analysis

| Milk necessary | 14 | [l/kg cheese] | $h_2=$ | 0.15 | [€/ton year] |
| Weight | 8 | [kg/Cheese round] | $a=$ | 392.15 | |
| Volume occupied | 30 | [Cheese round/m³] | $\beta=$ | 0.256 | |
| $p=$ | $2 \div 50 \cdot 10^6$ | [l/year] | $\gamma=$ | 392.15 | |
| $D=$ | $2 \cdot 10^6$ | [l/year] | $\delta=$ | 0.256 | |
| $A_1=$ | 2,000 | [€/set-up] | $a=$ | 25.354 | |
| $A_2=$ | 400 | [€/order] | $b=$ | 0.29 | |
| $h_1=$ | 0.1 | [€/ton year] | $e=$ | 0.12 | [€/kWh] |

The results of traditional model (minimizing Eq. (1)) and the energy model (minimizing Eq. (9)) are summarized in Table 2.

**Table 2.** Results of the numerical analysis

| | Q [kg cheese] | TC [€/year] | TrC [€/year] | EC [€/year] | Energy storage [TOE/ton] | Energy production [TOE/ton] | Total TOE/ton |
|---|---|---|---|---|---|---|---|
| **Min *TrC*** | 21,381 | 840,682 | 36,757 | 803,924 | 3.70 | 0.33 | 4.03 |
| **Min *TC*** | 3,506 | 370,629 | 132,989 | 237,640 | 0.86 | 0.33 | 1.19 |

The results illustrate that the proposed energy model leads to a higher profit than the traditional model which does not consider energy costs. The total costs and the energy costs are lower in the energy model than in the traditional model, even if inventory carrying costs are higher. Figure 5 illustrates the trends of the total costs and its two main components as functions of the lot size Q.

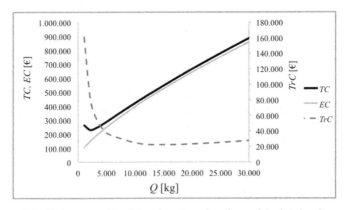

**Fig. 5.** Energy and traditional costs as functions of the lot size Q

Figure 6 illustrates the behavior of the two main cost components for varying production rates. As can be seen, the result is that both cost components ($EC$ and $TrC$) increase in the production rate, but that the increase in $TrC$ costs (difference between dashed black line and dashed gray line) for the case where the optimal parameters considering energy consumption ($q^{**}$, $n^{**}$) are used is much less than the decrease in $EC$ (difference between continuous black line and continuous gray line) while adopting the same parameters.

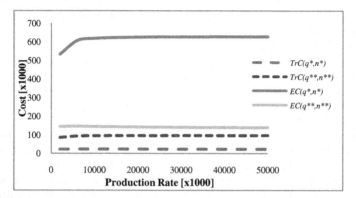

**Fig. 6.** Energy and inventory costs for the cases where the optimal parameters of the traditional model and the optimal parameters of the proposed energy model are adopted

Figure 7 illustrates the trend of the total Specific Energy Consumption, the specific consumption of energy by the warehouse and the Specific Energy Consumption of production as functions of the ratio of the demand and the production rate ($D/P$).

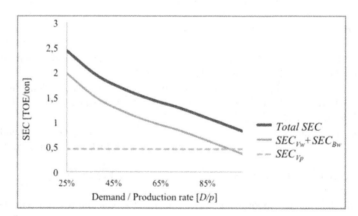

**Fig. 7.** Specific Energy Consumptions as functions of the ratio of the demand and the production rate

# 5    Conclusion

This study proposed a variation of the traditional single-vendor single-buyer production inventory model by considering energy cost components for production and for warehousing of items (at the vendor and at the buyer). To model these cost components, we used specific relationships that were found in empirical studies. In particular, the production rate mainly affects the specific energy consumed during the production process, while the size of the warehouse (which is a result of the batch sizing policy) mainly affects the specific energy consumed for properly storing the items at the vendor and at the buyer.

The main finding of the study is that it is possible to reduce total costs while accounting for energy components and to obtain consistent saving in energy components, while only a small increase in traditional inventory carrying costs has to be accepted. Moreover, the results of this study are particularly important for energy-intensive production processes in which the production rate may be set to a particularly high value.

This study has several limitations. First, it considered a very specific functional relationship to model the impact of the production rate on energy consumption. Other studies have shown that a varying production rate leads to a different pattern of resource consumption [6-7], and this may be valid for energy consumption as well. It is obvious that if a different functional relationship is assumed, the results of the model may change. Secondly, this study did not take account of all processes in a supply chain that consume energy (e.g. in [8] the effect on lot sizing decisions of different temperature settings in a cold supply chain is studied). Accomplishing these two and other aspects in an extension of this paper would be helpful to further our understanding of the impact of energy consumption and energy costs on the production and distribution policies of supply chains.

# References

1. Glock, C.H.: The joint economic lot size problem: A review. International Journal of Production Economics 135, 671–686 (2012)
2. Bettoni, L., Zanoni, S.: Energy implications of production planning decisions. In: Frick, J., Laugen, B.T. (eds.) Advances in Production Management Systems. IFIP AICT, vol. 384, pp. 9–17. Springer, Heidelberg (2012)
3. Gutowski, T., Dahmus, J., Thiriez, A.: Electrical Energy Requirements for Manufacturing Processes. In: 13th CIRP International Conference on Life Cycle Engineering, Leuven (2006)
4. DEFRA, Greenhouse Gas Impacts of Food Retailing: Final Report (2008), http://statistics.defra.gov.uk/esg/reports/
5. Hill, R.M.: The single-vendor single-buyer integrated production-inventory model with a generalised policy. European Journal of Operational Research 97, 493–499 (1997)
6. Glock, C.H.: Batch sizing with controllable production rates. International Journal of Production Research 48, 5925–5942 (2010)
7. Glock, C.H.: Batch sizing with controllable production rates in a multi-stage production system. International Journal of Production Research 49, 6071–6039 (2011)
8. Zanoni, S., Zavanella, L.: Chilled or frozen? Decision strategies for sustainable food supply chains. International Journal of Production Economics 140(2), 731–736 (2012)

# An Extended Energy Value Stream Approach Applied on the Electronics Industry

Gerrit Bogdanski, Malte Schönemann, Sebastian Thiede, Stefan Andrew, and Christoph Herrmann

Technische Universität Braunschweig, Institute for Machine Tools and Production Technology, Product- and Life-Cycle-Management Research Group, Braunschweig, Germany
{g.bogdanski,m.schoenemann,s.thiede,s.andrew,
c.herrmann}@tu-braunschweig.de

**Abstract.** In today's manufacturing companies lean production systems are widely established in order to address the traditional production objectives such as quality, cost, time and flexibility. Beyond those objectives, objectives such as energy consumption and related $CO_2$ emissions gained relevance due to rising energy costs and environmental concerns. Existing energy value stream methods allow the consideration of traditional and energy related variables. However, current approaches only take the energy consumptions of the actual manufacturing process and set-up times into account neglecting non-productive operational states and technical building services related consumption. Therefore, an extended energy value stream approach will be presented that provides the necessary degree of transparency to enable improvements of the energy value stream of a product considering also the influence of product design parameters.

**Keywords:** energy value stream mapping, sustainable manufacturing.

## 1    Introduction

The rising environmental awareness in society as well as worldwide increasing prices for natural resources and energy impose higher pressure on the manufacturer of goods than ever before. During the last 20 years an increase in energy prices of up to 100% has been recorded in Germany [1]. To cope with these cost advantages, companies have to identify measures to lower their energy consumption while maintaining their throughput. To accomplish the challenge of identifying and reducing the energy consumption within the production environment, the principles of the lean management have been adapted and extended towards this topic and a "lean and green" philosophy has been developed. From a methodological perspective the value stream mapping has been extended in order to identify the main energy consumers in a production line – the energy value stream mapping [2], [3]. In this paper the printed circuit board (PCB) manufacturing will be used as a case study for the methodological developments. PCBs are used in most electronic devices. The manufacturing of PCBs is a complex and energy intensive process. As about 88% of the worlds PCBs production is situated in Asian countries and only approximately 5% of the production located in Europe [4], this imposes a high cost pressure on the PCB producers in Europe.

C. Emmanouilidis, M. Taisch, D. Kiritsis (Eds.): APMS 2012, Part I, IFIP AICT 397, pp. 65–72, 2013.

A possible cost reduction can be achieved by reducing the energy demand of the production system. While there has already been done a comprehensive research work on recycling of PCBs [5], [6] as well as in terms of life cycle assessment for PCBs and PCB using products [7], [8] the energy consumption aspects in the PCB manufacturing have not been addressed so far.

## 2    Background

Manufacturing processes transform inputs into value-added outputs. Energy consumption is a physical necessity to perform that transformation. Gutowski et al. have shown in early studies that the actual consumed energy for machining processes is exceeded by the energy demand for related auxiliary processes like coolant pumps, lubrication supply and technical air ventilation [9], not mentioning the indirect energy drawn by technical building services such as heating, air conditioning or air suction. Additionally, Devoldere et al. are stating that in energy assessments of manufacturing processes the time aspect cannot be neglected. Specific time studies have shown that less than 13% of energy expenditures have been utilized for productive operations [10]. This clearly indicates the need to approach the assessment of energy demand of production systems by considering also the dynamic behaviour of machines. As depicted in Fig. 1, the dynamic load profile of a manufacturing process can be broken down over time by energy analysis, clearly stating, that all defined operating states of the given process are varying in their mean power demand, timing and therefore also in their energy amounts (indicated by the shaded areas).

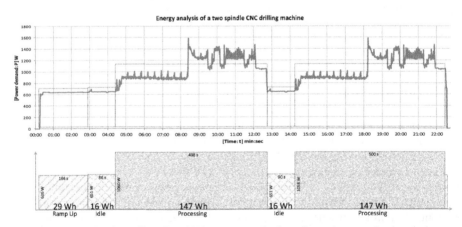

**Fig. 1.** Electrical load profile of a drilling process broken down into productive and non-productive energy shares

To cope with these dynamic energy demands, a suitable assessment of energy performance can be applied as proposed by Zein [11]. And feedback using key performance indicators (KPI) can be given. One effective way to assess the energy demand of production lines is a tool adapted from lean production. The *energy value stream mapping* (EVSM) is an extension of the lean production tool *value stream mapping* (VSM). VSM is utilized to analyse and prioritize sources of waste as listed by Womak and Jones [12] in order to enable future process improvement efforts through eliminating them by a continuous improvement processes. Extending methods for *value stream mapping* are presented by several authors. The U.S. Environmental Protection Agency (EPA) has given a recommendation to enhance the widely known lean process data by process specific energy use data [13]. Erlach and Westkämper are proposing a rather more detailed assessment of process energy. Next to the lean process variables the calculated energy intensity (EI) of the specific process [2] is displayed. In terms of lean KPI, both methods are using similar syntax and structure. While, the EPA is giving recommendations to include energy usage data without clearly stating how to ascertain the energy intensity KPI, Erlach and Westkämper are clearly allocating the mean energy demands of the processing state to the main energy carriers of production environments (electrical power, compressed air volume flow and gas volume flow) and giving them a common physical unit of measurement (kW) in order to allow an easier comparison. The common KPI for energy intensity (EI) is calculated by Erlach and Westkämper by summing up all mean power demands of the process specific energy carriers and multiplying this sum with the specific customer takt time and the number of resources [2]. The idle time of the processes is considered indirectly in the EI indicator. A drawback of this is the lack of visibility of the impact of the unproductive and productive time shares in matter of energy intensity as well as the influence of supporting processes from technical building services side. As shown earlier in Fig. 1, the power demand for idle states (non-productive) and processing (productive) can differ significantly. Additionally, the influences of product design parameters on the process design and scheduling are not represented in current approaches, as they represent the basis for a truly co-evolving energy-aware product and process design. Therefore, an approach is needed that is able to differentiate between different states of a production process and is able to indicate influences from product design perspective in order to truly derive hot spots of energy intensity and trigger improvement measures into the right direction.

## 3     Concept

Fig. 2 shows the conceptual framework of the extended energy value stream mapping approach. In a first step, the basic procedure is similar to the (energy) value stream mapping approaches mentioned above - from the perspective of one product (family), it is necessary to identify related processes and collect relevant data on time and energy related indicators. However, three innovative characteristics are introduced here:

**Dynamics of Energy Consumption (A)**
As indicated above, the pure consideration of single (average or nominal) values in energy value stream mapping impedes a closer look into composition of consumption and, thus, the derivation of improvement potentials for all relevant forms of energy. Therefore, the proposed approach distinguishes between three different machine states: ramp-up, processing and idle. The necessary data is being obtained through power measurements which provide power (P) profiles of the considered processes, respectively machines as shown in Fig. 1 exemplarily for a drilling process. Besides the power for ramp-up, idle and processing also the necessary time (t) values can be directly derived from the measurement as shown. The proposed method takes into account a specific production scenario in order to derive the necessary time values.

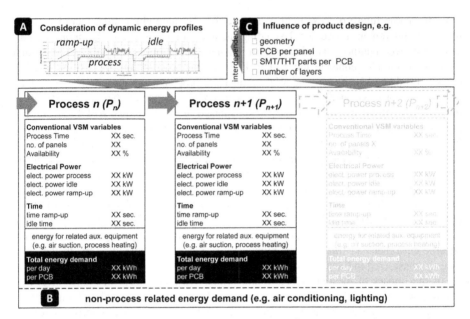

**Fig. 2.** Conceptual framework of the extended energy value stream mapping approach

As indicated in equation (1) the base is an available production time (e.g. per day) in which the machine can basically be used for production.

Through subtracting the calculated daily ramp-up time (number of ramp-ups per day multiplied by single ramp-up time, see equation) and processing time values (number of products multiplied by single processing time, see equation), a good estimation of idle time per day can be derived.

$$t_{idle} = t_{day} - t_{rampup} \times n_{rampup,day} - t_{process} \times n_{products,day} \qquad (1)$$

**Integration of Further Relevant Consumption Portions (B)**

In general, manufacturing process chains are embedded within a factory system which includes technical building services (TBS). TBS are not value adding in itself but provide necessary forms of energy and media (e.g. compressed air generation, coolants) and conditions (e.g. lighting) for enabling production [14], [15]. They can sum up to a significant share on energy demand of manufacturing companies, but were not considered in energy value stream mapping so far. Within the proposed extended EVSM approach TBS related energy demand can be either considered as

- related to specific processes respectively machines (e.g. air suction), or as an
- energy overhead with relevance for the whole process chain.

This distinction is made based on the technical circumstances but also depending on data availability while often a process specific breakdown is simply not available with reasonable effort. For the first case this indirect energy demand is directly added to the energy demand of the specific processes (TBS*). In the second case the energy demand of the TBS is equally distributed over all products within the considered time frame. The necessary energy demand rate and the time value for the specific TBS system is obtained through measurements or estimations. According to all those influences, e Conceptual framework of the extended energy value stream mapping approach quation (2) shows the calculation of the energy demand for the defined period of time. For the specific energy consumption, this value is divided by the amount of produced units within this timeframe.

$$
\begin{aligned}
E_{products,day} = \sum_{all,energies} & \left( P_{TBS} \times t_{TBS,day} \right. \\
+ \sum_{all,processes} & \left( P_{process} \times t_{process,day} + P_{rampup} \times t_{rampup,day} \right. \\
& \left. + P_{idle} \times t_{idle,day} + P_{TBS^*} \times t_{TBS^*,day} \right) \Big)
\end{aligned} \tag{2}
$$

**Consideration of Product Characteristics (C)**
Product design may have significant influence on manufacturing energy demand since already in the design phase necessary processes and partly also process parameters are determined. However, besides few publications for the case of metal machining (e.g. [16], [17], [18], [19]) just little work has been done to systematically address those interdependencies so far. Some tools provide environmentally related information to product designers already, but this information is mostly related to, e.g. used materials or recycling issues. Against this background, the proposed approach consciously integrates product related issues in energy value stream mapping. Therefore, for each process it is questioned to which extend the energy demand is influenced by product design characteristics. This paper specifically focuses on printed circuit boards (PCB) - in this case the amount of PCB layers (single-sided, double-sided or multi-layered), the PCB geometry in terms of size (how many PCB fit in one panel) and the number of electronic parts (separated according to SMD and THT parts) are relevant product related parameters. Whereas design parameters are mainly related to later functionalities of the product, the proposed approach provides manufacturing related information to the designer in order to create cost- and eco-efficient product designs.

# 4    Application

The extended EVSM method was applied exemplarily for the real case of a PCB value chain consisting of a PCB manufacturing and PCB assembly company, covering 46 sequential processes. In the selected scenario, the available production time per day is ten hours, the availability is assumed to be 100% and only one product type is produced. The maximum number of panels (products) per day is limited by the capacity of the bottle neck process. Since some processes can handle several panels at once, the bottle neck is not necessarily the process with the longest processing time. It is further assumed that no parallel process equipment is available and that the production system is in steady state. For each process, energy and time related parameters were determined and the energy demand was calculated. The process related indirect energy demand for air suction and compressed air and light was added to the process' energy demand if allocation was possible. Otherwise the indirect energy demand is summed up to the energy overhead of the process chain. In Fig. 3, the approach is exemplarily shown for the processes drilling and reflow soldering (the load profiles of

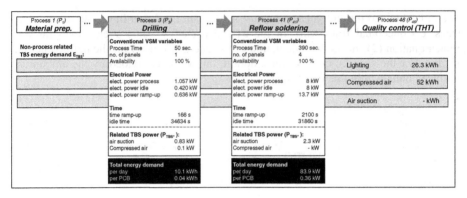

**Fig. 3.** Exemplary Extended Energy Value Stream Mapping for drilling and reflow soldering

the drilling process is shown in Fig. 1) for the fabrication of single-sided PCB with 50 SMT and 50 THT parts.

Drilling has a processing time of 50 seconds for one panel and reflow soldering requires 390 seconds for four panels, hence 97.5 seconds per panel. The total energy demands of the drilling process and reflow soldering process for one PCB are 0.04 and 0.36 kWh respectively. However, the energy consumption characteristics of these processes differ. While the power demand of the CNC drill is 1.06 kW during processing and 0.42 kW during idle, the reflow oven demands 8 kW constantly. Further indirect energy usage for air suction and compressed air is caused by the drilling process while 2.3 kW of energy demand for air suction is related to the reflow soldering process. Knowledge about these differences in energy consumption of production processes is important for the derivation of improvement measures. Therefore Fig. 4 presents the energy demand for each operational state of all 46 processes as well as for related TBS. It shows that several processes cause high energy consumption during idle mode. These processes with long idle times and high power demand during idle mode should be subject for production management, e.g. the energy consumption could be reduced by different scheduling strategies such as batch production.

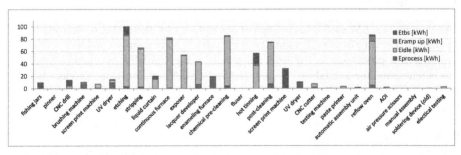

**Fig. 4.** Energy demand of each operational state and TBS of all 46 manufacturing processes

Besides specific energy consumption profiles of the processes, the influence of product properties on energy consumption is considered. For double-sided or multi-layered PCBs extra processes are required compared to single-sided PCBs; some of

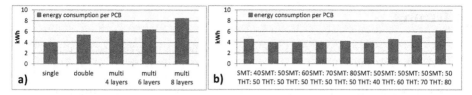

**Fig. 5.** Energy demand for one PCB for single-sided, double-sided and multi-layered boards with four, six and eight layers (a) and for different numbers of SMT and THT parts (b)

them also need to be repeated for each additional two layers. Thus the utilization of these processes as well as the energy consumption increases with the number of layers. The energy demand per PCB for different types of PCBs is shown Fig. 5a).

Further, the process times for the assembly of SMT and THT parts on the board increase with the number of parts. While the SMT assembly is performed by a machine the THT parts are manually mounted. The analysis shows that the total energy consumption is not increasing significantly with an increasing number of SMT or THT parts due to the low energy demand of assembly equipment. However, with a higher number of THT parts the THT assembly becomes the bottle neck process and the energy consumption per PCB increase due to a reduced output of PCB, as shown in Fig. 5b). The energy demand per PCB also depends on the number of PCBs per panel (ranging from 3.8 to 6.2 kWh), which is restricted by the geometry and size of each single board.

# 5    Summary and Outlook

Altogether the extended energy value stream is a powerful method which takes into account more realistic circumstances and provides valuable information for both manufacturing engineers and product designers. It gives very clear indications about the composition of energy demand according to all relevant subsystems of the factory and the different operation states of involved equipment. Based on this detailed analysis, a specific derivation of technical and organizational improvement measures becomes possible. The application of the approach further shows the influence of certain product properties on the energy demand of the production system. This information can be used during product development in order to evaluate design options regarding the trade of between higher production cost (due to energy consumption) and development effort. It is also the ideal base for product related cost or carbon footprint calculations. Future work will focus on the validation of the method on different production scenarios in other industries. Moreover the results of the case study indicate the importance of the co-evolutional development of product design and production system. Therefore the relevant dependencies have to be investigated and new ways and tools for the coordination and communication need to be established.

**Acknowledgements.** The introduced methodology was developed within the research project EnHiPro (Energy and auxiliary material efficiency in production) funded by the German Federal Ministry of Education and Research (BMBF) within the framework concept "Research for Tomorrow's Production" (02PO21201) and managed by the Project Management Agency Karlsruhe (PTKA).

72    G. Bogdanski et al.

# References

1. http://www.bmwi.de/BMWi/Navigation/Energie/Statistik-und-Prognosen/Energiedaten/energiepreise-energiekosten.html# (last access: July 03, 2012)
2. Erlach, K., Westkämper, E.: Energiewertstrom – Der Weg zur energieeffizienten Fabrik. Fraunhofer Verlag, Stuttgart (2009) ISBN: 978-3-8396-0010-8
3. Shahrbabaki, S.A.D.: Green and Lean Production Visualization Tools - A Case Study exploring EVSM. Master thesis work, Mälardalen University (2010)
4. World PCB Production Report for the Year (2010) ISBN: 978-1-61193-500-4
5. Wang, X., Gaustad, G.: Prioritizing material recovery for end-of-life printed circuit boards Original Research Article. Waste Management (2012) (in Press)
6. Guo, J., Xu, Z.: Recycling of non-metallic fractions from waste printed circuit boards: A review. Journal of Hazardous Materials 168(2-3, 15), 567–590 (2009)
7. Taiariol, F., Fea, P., Papuzza, C., Raffaella Casalino, R., Galbiati, E., Zappa, S.: Life Cycle assessment of an integrated circuit product. In: Proceedings of the 2001 IEEE International Symposium on Electronics and the Environment, pp. 128–133 (2001)
8. Kanth, R.K., Wan, Q., Liljeberg, P., Zheng, L., Tenhunen, H.: Comparative Study for Environmental Assessment of Printed and PCB Technologies, Joukahaisenkatu. TUCS General Publication Series, pp. 978–952 (2010) ISBN: 978-952-12-2497-3
9. Gutowski, T., Murphy, C., et al.: Environmentally benign manufacturing: Observations from Japan, Europe and the United States. Journal of Cleaner Production 13(1), 1–17 (2005)
10. Devoldere, T., Dewulf, W., Deprez, W., Willems, B., Duflou, J.: Improvement Potential for Energy Consumption in Discrete Part Production Machines. In: Proceedings of 14th CIRP Conf. on LCE, pp. 311–316 (2007)
11. Zein, A.: Transition towards Energy Efficient Machine Tools. Springer Verlag, Heidelberg (2012) (pending for publication) ISBN 978-3-642-32246-4
12. Womack, J.P., Jones, D.T.: Lean Thinking: Banish Waste and Create Wealth in Your Cooperation. Harper Business (2003) ISBN 0-7432-4927-5
13. US EPA: Lean, Energy & Climate Toolkit: Achieving Process Excellence Through Energy Efficiency and Greenhouse Gas Reduction, EPA-100-K-07-003 (2007)
14. Hesselbach, J., Herrmann, C., Detzer, R., Martin, L., Thiede, S., Lüdemann, B.: Energy Efficiency through optimized coordination of production and technical building services. In: 15th CIRP International Conference on Life Cycle Engineering, Sydney, pp. 624–629 (2008) ISBN 978-1-877040-67-2
15. Seow, Y., Rahimifard, S.: A framework for modelling energy consumption within manufacturing systems. CIRP Journal of Manufacturing Science and Technology 4(3), 258–264 (2011)
16. Narita, H., Fujimoto, H.: Environmental burden analysis due to high speed milling. Presented at the 19th International Conference on Production Research (2007)
17. Nawata, S., Aoyama, T.: Life-cycle design system for machined parts - linkage of LCI data to CAD/CAM data. Presented at the Second International Symposium on Environmentally Conscious Design and Inverse Manufacturing, pp. 299–302. IEEE Comput. Soc., Tokyo (2001)
18. Seow, Y., Rahimifard, S.: Improving Product Design based on Energy Considerations. In: Hesselbach, J., Herrmann, C. (eds.) Glocalized Solutions for Sustainability in Manufacturing, pp. 154–159. Springer, Heidelberg (2011)
19. Thiede, S.: Energy Efficiency in Manufacturing Systems. Springer, Heidelberg (2012)

# An Approach for Energy Saving in the Compound Feed Production

Marc Allan Redecker and Klaus-Dieter Thoben

BIK Bremer Institut für integrierte Produktentwicklung, Badgasteiner Straße 1,
28359 Bremen, Germany
{red,tho}@biba.uni-bremen.de

**Abstract.** The importance of energy efficiency has increased significantly in recent years. By rising commodity prices and energy costs for electric and thermal energy the compound feed plants are forced to improve their processes. Significant savings are expected in the material changing refining stages. This paper, at first, gives an overview about the characteristics in the compound feed production, followed by the analysis of high energy consumption. There after followed a description of the uncertainties in the compound feed production. The next chapter demonstrates the efficient control of the compound feed production process.

**Keywords:** raw material, uncertainty, agricultural commodities, expert system, manufacturing processes, quality.

## 1 Introduction

The dynamics of price developments in recent years for raw materials and energy will tend to persist. The global competition for resources and the legally mandated emission limits placed will determine the conditions of stronger companies. The competitiveness of an increasing productivity can be achieved only if the available resources such as energy, materials and personnel will be handled efficiently. The resulting gaps have to be closed by increasing efficiency [1].

Effectiveness and efficiency are to be distinguished from each other. The effectiveness generally referred to the Ratio of the achieved to a defined target. The efficiency in turn describes the performance and economic efficiency. Efficiency is thus understood as the ratio between a defined input and a fixed size of an output. Energy efficiency means reducing energy consumption in a system to providing a service [2]. The European Union defines energy efficiency as the ratio of the return of performance, services, goods or energy to use of energy [3].

The significant energy cost increases in recent years have been creating high economic incentives for rational energy budgets in the compound feed industry [4]. In Germany the annual production output of the compound feed production exceeding approximately by 22,500,000 tons in 319 factories [5]. The total yearly electricity consumption of this branch of industry lies at 1.65 billion kWh per annum [6]. Our case study is the production of compound feed in a commercial feed processing plant in Northern Germany. The energy consumption accounts up to 4-6 GWh per annum by

C. Emmanouilidis, M. Taisch, D. Kiritsis (Eds.): APMS 2012, Part I, IFIP AICT 397, pp. 73–79, 2013.

an annual production output up to 240,000 tons of feed. The biggest part represents the pig feed with 80 %, followed by chicken feed with 15 % and 5 % bovine animal feed. For various costumers the plant is producing 200 different feed recipes with over 60 different ingredients. All these recipes are produced batchwise on one single plant.

## 2     Characteristics in the Compound Feed Production

The industrial feed compounding is focused on the refining of natural resources like grains. Feed recipes are consisted of up to 40 different natural resources, for example wheat, barley, corn, soy, molasses, limestone and micro components like vitamins and enzymes. The composition of feed recipes depends on the animal species as well as the period of growth and is currently adjusted for example by availability and market price of raw materials.

In the compound feed production the demands of customer are at the forefront and the lead-time of the order of feed are only few hours. In our case study the production plant has to produce 200 different composites in short-term.

The compound feed production process could be divided into four process steps. At first the feed processing starts with the incoming of different natural resources like wheat, barley, rye and so on which are delivered by trucks, discharged into collecting vessels and short-term stored in silo compartments.

On the respective feed recipes the components could mixed automatically. All recipes are registered in a control system. If the process is starting, the refinement begins with the transportation of the raw materials to the following process step to weigh and to mix the natural resources. The next step includes the comminution of the grainy raw materials by the use of hammer mills or roller mills. Every time it is necessary to aspirate the dust, which comes out by hurrying the materials. After the milling process the mealy material gets an admixture of molasses, linoleic acid and other ingredients. To produce the final product the raw materials have to be pressed to pellets. Thus the mealy material with the admixture has to be transported to the pelletizing process [7].

The pelletizing process comprised the pressure grouting of the mealy material. Before the mealy material could be pressed the floury texture will be added with steam and grease in the conditioner. The next step includes the compactor process. This step manufactured the pellets with high quality performance and physical impacts against pressure, abrasion and critical strength. The quality of a pellet must have an uniform length, hardness and has to be resistant against all strains. Pelleting in combination with short-term conditioning is most common as hydrothermal treatment in feed mills. After the pelletizing process the material has to be cooled and as a last process step transported in the corresponding silo compartments.

## 3     Analysis of High Energy Consumption

Among the most important forms of energy in a compound feed production process are the thermal energy, mechanical energy and electrical energy. Figure 1 shows the percentage of the consumption of electricity of the compound feed production in the case study.

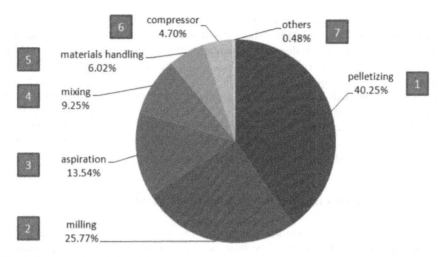

**Fig. 1.** Consumption of electricity in percentage of compound feed production in the case study

The pelletizing process provides the highest energy consumption in front of the milling process. These two processes have a total electricity consumption by more than 60 %. Figure 2 gives an overview of the process steps in the feed industry as well as an allocation of the current energy consumption of the individual process steps. It is necessary to have a closer look at the process step pelletizing and milling in order to ensure a more efficient production.

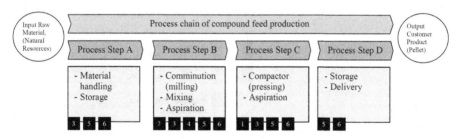

**Fig. 2.** Process chain of compound feed production

To actuate a hammer mill more energy-efficient it must be known the texture about the raw materials. In connection with the conclusion of milling it concerns the elastic force and the strength of the mill material. By increasing influence on the elastic force and the strength, the product moisture and the energy consumption are rising. Therefor it is important that the output data are known for the humidity and the bulk weight.

A pelletizing process should have a high throughput rate and low energy consumption. The quality and the efficiency of the compactor process will be influenced by the physical quality of the pellets and the specific energy demand (kW/t). These requirements are difficult to reach. The manufacturing of hard pressed pellets demanded high pressure and therefore high energy consumption as soft pressed pellets. Depending on the composition of the raw materials the energy consumption fluctuates between 10 up to 25 kWh/t by pressing pellets based on the ratio of moisture and quality [8].

Essential for the energy consumption and the product quality is in addition to time, the temperature and the moisture. The temperature is determined by adding steam. The temperature rising by 10 degrees by increasing the raw material from 0.6 to 0.7 of the moisture. On account of this it has to be detected the optimum between the quantity of steam and product quality to reduce the energy consumption.

For example industrial products (like automobile, aircraft, etc.) can be constructed by reducing the weight without loosing quality properties. But in the food and feed processing industry reducing weight means that we put the animals on diet. The research focus therefore must be placed on the investigation of energy efficiency of the production process without changing the end-product quality.

# 4     Uncertainties in the Compound Feed Production

The uncertainties in the compound feed production can be divided into two parts, on the one hand in properties that can be influenced and on the other hand in properties that cannot be influenced. Figure 3 shows graphically the general connection between the product quality and the uncertainty of the process steps compacting (pressing), comminution (milling) and adding steam (conditioning). The bars in the chart show that fluctuations of the product properties are available. Mainly for example the water content of raw materials for the compound feed production can changed by a controlled steam entry.

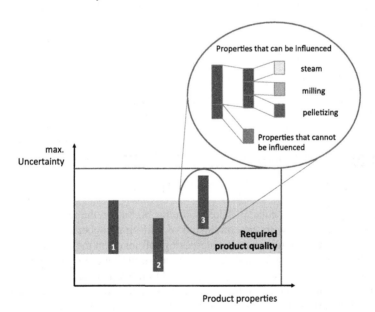

**Fig. 3.** Uncertainties of product properties

For example different natural resources will trigger different grinding characteristics and will reveal different particle size distributions.

## 5    Efficient Control of the Compound Feed Production Process

In the case study, the product quality will be considered only at the end of the process chain. To save the energy it is important to analyse the different ingredients in different process steps, which does not exist in the current compound feed production. For example, information is needed about the particle sizes during milling process. The same applies to the moisture content of raw materials before the pelletizing process is starting.

One possibility is to detect the uncertainties during the production process with measurement instruments. For Example the analysis of the grain sizes during the production process could be done with computerized particle analyser (CPA) which could be integrated in the milling process step to analyse the grain size at the beginning of the manufacturing process. They, in turn, support information about how the parameters must be set in the milling process in order to the optimal size of the raw material before passing into the pressing process and thus provide information on how the machine settings must be made so that energy efficiency works. CPA-Measuring instruments used to perform particle size and particle shape analysis of dry and non-agglomerated particles in ranges from 0.010 mm to 400. The systems can also be used as particle counters. CPA measuring instruments are used for digital image processing for analyzing the particles. A CPA measuring device is connected after a comminution unit to monitor the particle size distribution of the comminuted material. In strong or less comminution the measuring device can guide them on the desired particle size distribution. However, this requires a good calibration of the instrument and to be determined at the beginning experience on the process parameters. Furthermore a pre-sieve should be installed to separate fines before grinding in order to unload the milling process and reduce its energy consumption.

The diode array base spectrometer (NIR) is used for the ingredients description and causes the optimized control of the conditioning and compacting process steps. The sample material is irradiated with light in the range of the near-infrared wavelength range. The reflected light is read out by a diode array spectrometer. The reflections vary depending on which of the parameters of concentration in the raw materials and feed mixtures and provide information on the material composition of sample materials. With this device single samples can be measured. In addition to product moisture is usually the protein, fat and crude fiber and starch content can be determined. In addition to product moisture content of protein, fat and fiber content of the starch content and can be determined.

Figure 4 shows a possible process control in real time to get high quality products with low energy consumption. The system receives information during the production process about the grain size and moisture content and is directly put in a position to influence the machine parameters.

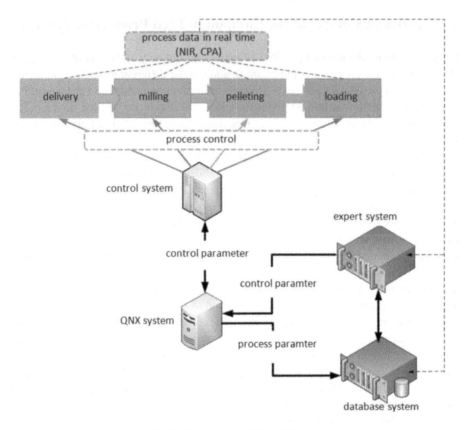

**Fig. 4.** Process control in real time

## 6    Conclusion

The integration of these instruments within the process can provide information on the uncertainties and allow a process control. The development of the control system of the production process is performed according to uncertainty management. Uncertainties are present at any time in the process and has therefore taken into account during the decision making process. The uncertainties are formed into fuzzy rules and are implemented as a new software tool that supports the process control. It will be possible to simulate the production process with varying parameters to evaluate the result of the simulation.

**Acknowledgement.** The authors thanks the German Ministry of Economy and Technology and the Project Management Jülich for funding the project in the compound feed production.

# References

1. Neugebauer, R.: Energieeffizienz in der Produktion - Untersuchung zum Handlungs- und Forschungsbedarf, Fraunhofer Gesellschaft, Chemnitz, Germany (2011)
2. Pehnt, M.: Energieeffizienz: Ein Lehr- und Handbuch. Springer, Heidelberg (2010)
3. EU: Richtlinie 2006/32/EG des europäischen Parlaments und des Rates vom 5. April 2006 über Endenergieeffizienz und Energiedienstleistungen und zur Aufhebung der Richtlinie 93/76/ (2006), http://europa.eu
4. Stelling, M.: Notwendige Schritte zur Implementierung eines Energiemanagementsystems in Mischfutterwerken. In: Mühle + Mischfutter, vol. 149(9), pp. 266–270. Verlag Moritz Schäfer, Detmold (2012)
5. Kunkel, S., Platz, U.: Struktur der Mischfutterhersteller in Deutschland - Wirtschaftsjahr 2009/10. Bundesministerium für Ernährung. Landwirtschaft und Verbraucherschutz (BMELV), Bonn, Germany (2011)
6. Heidenreich, E.: Gestaltung der Zukunft durch Schüren von Ängsten? In: Mühle + Mischfutter, vol. 149, pp. 266–270. Verlag Moritz Schäfer, Detmold (2007)
7. Kirchner, A., et al.: Manufacturing with minimal energy consumption – a product perspective, Braunschweig, pp. 4–5 (2012) (to be published)
8. Kersten, J., Rohde, H., Nef, E.: Mischfutterherstellung. Agrimedia, Bergen (2003)

# Bridging the Gap between Energy Management Systems and Machine Tools – Embedded Energy Efficiency in Production Planning and Control

Manuel Rippel[*], Olga Willner, Johannes Plehn, and Paul Schönsleben

ETH Zurich, BWI Center for Industrial Management, Zurich, Switzerland
mrippel@ethz.ch

**Abstract.** Global environmental challenges lead to a rising importance of resource efficiency in industry. The strong environmental impact of manufacturing processes necessitates a significant reduction of the amount of employed resources. Therefore, the potential of production planning and control (PPC) systems is analyzed from a top-down and bottom-up perspective in terms of increasing the energy efficiency of manufacturing processes. A conceptual approach is developed to embed energy efficiency in a PPC-logic in order to link managerial targets with machine tools located on the shop-floor.

**Keywords:** PPC, Process Chain, Energy Efficiency, Energy profile.

## 1    Motivation and Purpose

Scarcity of resources and rising energy prices caused by an increasing primary energy demand started to change society and business values. Today, companies have to tackle three essential challenges related to global environmental issues: (1) legislation and governmental regulations, (2) consumer and public awareness, (3) resource and energy prices and $CO_2$-costs [1]. These challenges lead to an increasing importance of resource efficiency and in particular energy efficiency in European manufacturing industry. Manufacturing is directly connected to natural resources, since this sector is responsible for about 33% of the primary energy use and for 38% of the $CO_2$ emissions [2].

The efficient use of energy in manufacturing is seen as an effective approach to decrease the energy needs and the associated $CO_2$ emissions [1]. Moreover, it is, and will be even more in future, a central competitive factor, since resource efficiency is gaining importance next to economic objectives. The challenge for manufacturing companies is to tackle the assumed dichotomy between competitive and environmental friendly operations.

The significance of this field can be illustrated by looking at the German industry, which accounts for around 46% of the country's overall energy consumption [3]. Experts estimate that 10-15% of this amount is consumed by machine tools for

---

[*] Corresponding author.

C. Emmanouilidis, M. Taisch, D. Kiritsis (Eds.): APMS 2012, Part I, IFIP AICT 397, pp. 80–87, 2013.

machining operations [3]. Since 99% of the environmental impacts of machine tools are due to the consumption of electrical energy, the energy consumption is solely considered in this paper [4].

The Smart Manufacturing Consultation Group of the European Commission for energy efficiency declares that "it is necessary to develop tools and relevant algorithms which will be able to take energy efficiency into account as a significant parameter of the process, and to calculate best energy performance results along with other desired process results" [5]. Hence, the objective is to identify and analyze the potential of production planning and control (PPC) systems, in order to increase the energy efficiency in manufacturing processes.

## 2    Methodological Approach

This paper is mainly based on qualitative research. A literature analysis is conducted with a focus on energy efficiency in the manufacturing industry both from a managerial and a technical background. A "Top-down/Bottom-up" process is used as a hierarchical analysis, in order to assure a structured approach. As depicted in Figure 1, this paper conceptually and methodologically systematizes existing concepts from Energy Management Systems (EMS) as top-down perspective and from process chain level respectively machine tools as bottom-up perspective. The process for achieving energy efficiency in production systems is categorized in four steps: data collection, data visualization, evaluation and improvement measures. The key elements for embedding energy efficiency in a PPC-logic are reviewed and allocated to four overlaying levels of analysis: data, model, system and logic.

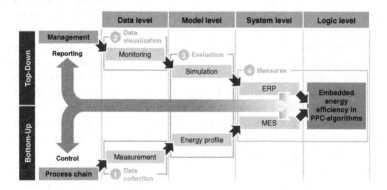

**Fig. 1.** Top-down and bottom-up analysis process

## 3    Findings

This section presents the findings by identifying essential elements for increasing energy efficiency in production systems as a combination of superior management perspective and the technical entities within the process chain.

## 3.1    Bottom-Up Perspective: Process Chain

Manufacturing companies underestimate their potential to save energy and reduce related costs. For example, studies have shown saving potential of 25-30% in production [6]. Due to this promising impact, the focus of the bottom-up perspective is mainly on ongoing research to improve the energy efficiency of machine tools as operating elements of process chains.

Most machine tool suppliers and end users lack knowledge about time-dependent energy demand during operation [7]. Significant improvement potential is expected by enhancing transparency of energy consumption of machine tools and its components [6]. The measurement of machine tools with regard to energy used and material consumed is seen as the first step in order to understand, characterize and improve environmental impact and energy consumption of manufacturing processes [3] [8].

Energy demand of machine tools is primarily considered as an estimated value under either nominal or extreme conditions [11]. However, energy consumption is distinctly dynamic due to the temporal power demand throughout a machining process. It significantly depends on the operating states, like e.g. turn-off, start-up, warm-up, stand-by, processing or stopping [9] [10]. Furthermore, power demand while processing depends on several further factors, e.g. process design, selected machine tool, machine dynamics and process parameters [11] [7]. Taking into account these characteristics, it is not sufficient to consider energy consumption on average, but to provide time-dependent energy profiles for further evaluation. It is detected that the energy demand of machine tools consists of the fixed power as base load, which sets the process-time depending share of required energy for the machining of the work piece, and the variable power, which depends on the process [9].

The metering and monitoring of energy consumption of single machinery is time consuming and expensive. Furthermore, it is not feasible to measure energy demands considering all potential influencing factors among all machines in a factory [11]. Therefore, it is intended to define standards for the measurement considering operating state, consumer and exemplary processes and to formalize the results in appropriate models supporting the case-specific quantification [9]. Thereby, it is at least possible to rate and evaluate the scale of the consumption ex-ante or ex-post. Upcoming new sensor technologies within Information & Communication Technologies (ICT) enable to perform in-process measurement, which will provide more accurate information about temporal energy demands [12]. Thereby, the energy-oriented evaluation can be conducted continuously based on real-time data and decision makers can react instantaneously by taking dynamic measures.

Furthermore, ongoing research activities are analyzing when and under which conditions components can be deactivated or at least reduced in non-productive situations. However, the optimization is limited to single machines. There is no technological approach pursued in machine tool industry to aim at a dynamic energetic optimum for the whole process chain.

## 3.2    Top-Down Perspective: Energy Management Systems

Up to now, solely one third of all companies have a systematic evaluation and optimizing approach for their energy consumption [6]. Mostly, they just have an overall recording of data referring to their energy consumption, whereby they are not aware of their specific energy use and loss within production [6]. Several tools and methods are presently developed in this research area.

Monitoring and simulation are seen as essential elements of energy management [1]. Key Performance Indicators (KPIs) are developed to evaluate if changes in the process for increasing energy efficiency have a verifiable benefit [13]. Their monitoring supports assessment of optimization potentials and visualization of benefits from improvement measures. There exist various structural and explanatory indicators, since the variety and complexity of industrial processes set different requirements [1].

The evaluation of energy costs, environmental impacts and technical performance are of major importance in order to achieve a holistic image of the factory [14]. Different analytical techniques can be consulted for evaluating energy efficiency improvements in terms of economic impact, e.g. net present value method (NPV), the method of annualized value, the method of internal rate of return or payback period. However, it is difficult to quantify potential benefits in monetary terms for an economic evaluation [13].

Simulation can support to analyze the dynamic energy consumption behavior, operational data and interdependencies of machine tools and other technical equipment involved. It can be used to provide an overview of the system's performance on a realistic base. Simulation tools enable decision making to assess the expected effects of measures for improving the environmental performance both on process chain or machine level [15] [16].

However, a comprehensive portfolio of measures is still missing. The range of energy efficiency measures is limited to static approaches such as replacement of components, acquisition of new machinery or installation of fixed equipment. Dynamic approaches for reacting on short-term changes of the system's energy state are missing or are not fully developed.

### 3.3    Synthetic Link: Embedded Energy Efficiency in PPC

The above mentioned data and concepts from each perspective have to be utilized and adjusted with regard to a multi-object approach. Bunse et al. proposed to extend the scope of MES, ERP and simulation software to optimize processes throughout the whole production in terms of energy efficiency [1]. In the following, an integral PPC-concept is outlined, since PPC can exploit existing configuration flexibility within economic optimization of production systems for embedding also energy efficiency as optimization criteria.

PPC will not solely be used as information source for the economic values for monitoring of KPIs anymore. Therefore, the defined and monitored KPIs in EMS will be split into operational variables. Prior PPC algorithms solely focused on direct economic and technical aspects. They have to be extended for environmental aspects. By doing so, both energy-related costs and environmental footprint of the products can be enhanced. The extended PPC-logic provides the organizational conditions for exploiting several characteristics and technological developments of machine tools for increasing energy efficiency as follows:

First, the above mentioned characteristic of the energy profiles of time-dependent energy consumption consisting of fixed and variable power can be exploited. It is possible to reduce energy consumption per part by enhancing the productivity of the machine tool respectively the capacity utilization [8]. The resulting shorter production time enables savings of fixed power of the machine's base load. This saving is higher than the additional consumption within the process-dependent variable power [17]. PPC-algorithms have to consider within machine scheduling that the material removal rate (MRR) can be maximized in order to reduce the impact of fixed power share. Furthermore, the machine tool consumes a fixed amount of energy during non-value adding tasks (e.g. setting-up, handling) [18]. Those tasks have to be avoided as far as possible or the time required needs to be reduced by energy-oriented process and production planning, since the energy is wasted without adding value on the product.

Second, stand-by strategies for machine tools should be integrated in production scheduling in order to reduce energy consumption within the remaining non-productive times [7]. For example, to switch off a machine tool if stand-by time is long enough [8]. PPC should use existing flexibility in machine schedule to stop, postpone or bring forward different process steps for implementing such stand-by strategies of machine tools. The Consultation Group of the European Commission estimates the saving potential of the optimization of waiting/start-up times at 10-25% [5]. However, the task of an appropriate PPC-algorithm is to evaluate if shut-down and a start-up of a machine tool and its components is reasonable from the perspective of the whole production system and underlying process chain, since several important aspects have to be considered for the implementation of those strategies. For example, specific time and energy demand (e.g. maximum instantaneous peak power requirement, total energy consumption for start-up) is required both for start-up and power-off stage [11]. Therefore, non-productive times have to be distributed appropriately in order to realize stand-by concepts [9]. Furthermore, intervals need to be long enough, e.g. in order to ensure thermal stability of machine tools by sufficient lead times [9]. PPC has to determine the holistic optimum: On the one hand it has to examine total energetic benefit including multiple machines, which might be affected by a redistribution of orders. On the other the PPC has to assess further organizational consequences, e.g. additional changeover time, operational readiness of the machine (since the gained energy saving should not sacrifice the process stability) product quality or machine tool availability [11] [9].

Third, Brecher et al. indicate that current control systems of machine tools should be extended, e.g. by systems for forecasting load detecting and visualization [9]. Based on information derived from the above mentioned measurement of energy consumption on component level, abilities of machine's path planning simulations can be enhanced, since the cumulative energy consumption can be calculated by the iterative summation of all individual cuts [7]. Those results should be linked with PPC so that the technical potential of machine tools can be used by providing them conditions for operating in their optimal range of efficiency.

To conclude, to equip PPC with advanced algorithms is a measure for achieving energy efficiency performance on a high scale. Benefits will be as follows: PPC works as leverage for EMS by putting findings from monitoring and simulation tasks into action. It also is in an enabler to use effectively the potential of energy optimized machine tools. PPC is a cost-effective instrument for using the given configuration of machine tool infrastructure in regard to energy efficiency as best as possible. Besides, it is a tool to detect the energy efficiency boundaries and to determine promising improvement potential at shop-floor level. Finally, it takes over the dynamic optimization in continuation of static improvement measures like investments in single components of machine tool or the new acquisition of whole machine tools with less energy consumption.

# 4 Limitations and Practical Implications

The elaborated concept is restricted to an outline for embedding energy efficiency in the planning and control logic of a conventional PPC. The conducted analysis focuses on creating the conceptual basis as well as the influencing factors and interconnected elements for further research. The conceptual integration of environmental-oriented optimization targets in existing PPC-algorithms will be conducted in a next step. The principles will be transferred to other processes than machining, e.g. milling and turning. The final concept has to be tested and validated within a manufacturing company. Due to the high significance of the energy consumption of machine tools, energy consumption is solely considered in this concept [5]. After validating energy-oriented PPC-logic variables should be supplemented by the consideration of other environmental factors, e.g. compressed air, coolant and lubricants.

The impact of the embedded energy efficiency PPC consists in achieving energy efficiency in interconnected processes and in particular beyond individual entities. This will result in a decrease of the environmental impact of the production site, saving of resources and reduction of costs: Total energy consumption will be reduced by exploiting load characteristics of machine tools as useful potential and embed them in the scheduling algorithms. Besides, production schedule can be aligned to advantageous time periods, e.g. when renewable energy is available or day-time dependent prices for electricity are low [10]. Furthermore, PPC can distribute machining tasks so that undesirable, high impact marginal energy peak loads can be avoided, which reduces energy costs and the environmental footprint of a production site [5]. A prospective, schematic application example for a scheduling approach considering peak power demands is given in Figure 2.

Furthermore, the adapted PPC will improve Life-Cycle-Assessments (LCA) by supporting the calculation and evaluation of the employed resources on individual product and process level. The PPC will deliver detailed information to enhance transparency and validity of product-specific environmental footprints.

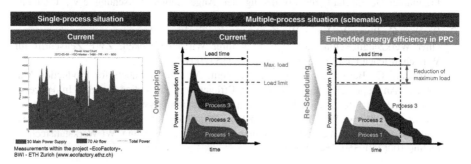

**Fig. 2.** Schematic example for scheduling considering peak power demands

## 5    Conclusion

Existing conceptual elements from a top-down and bottom-up perspective are analyzed and systemized in regards to their contribution to embed energy efficiency in PPC. The integration of energy efficiency criteria in PPC will enable to achieve an economic and environmental performance optimum while fundamental technical and organizational requirements are assured at once. As automated, integrated solution it provides the ability of responsiveness of EMS by taking appropriate situation-depending, dynamic improvement measures. Hence, the value proposition of embedded energy efficiency in a PPC is the ability to link managerial targets with technical entities on the shop-floor by balancing and combining organizational prerequisites with technical capabilities.

## References

1. Bunse, K., Vodicka, M., Schönsleben, P., Brülhart, M., Ernst, F.O.: Integrating energy efficiency performance in production management - gap analysis between industrial needs and scientific literature. Journal of Cleaner Production 19(6-7), 667–679 (2011)
2. International Energy Agency (IEA): Worldwide Trends in Energy Use and Efficiency, Key Insights from IEA Indicator Analysis (2008), http://www.iea.org/Textbase/Papers/2008/indicators_2008.pdf (accessed May 14, 2012)
3. König, J.: Energieeffiziente Produktherstellung. In: Uhlmann, E. (ed.) FUTUR - Produktionstechnik für die Zukunft, vol. 12(2), pp. 12–13 (2010)
4. CECIMO: Concept Description for CECIMO's Self-Regulatory Initiative (SRI) for the Sector Specific Implementation of the Directive 2005/32/EC (2009), http://www.eup-network.de/fileadmin/user_upload/Produktgruppen/Lots/Working_Documents/Lot_ENTR_05_machine_tools/draft_self_regulation_machine_tools_2009-10.pdf (acessed May 14, 2012)
5. European Commission: ICT and Energy Efficiency in the Case for Manufacturing. Recommendations of the Consultation Group (2009), http://ec.europa.eu/information_society/events/ict4ee/2009/docs/files/ec/ec/infso/g2/SmartManufacturing.pdf (accessed July 10, 2012)
6. Neugebauer, H., Westkämper, E., Klocke, F., Kuhn, A., Schenk, M., Michaelis, A., Spath, D., Weidner, E.: Abschlussbericht – Untersuchung zur Energieeffizienz in der Produktion. Fraunhofer-Gesellschaft zur Förderung der Angewandten Forschung e.V., Chemnitz (2008)
7. Brecher, C., Boos, W., Klein, W., Kuhlmann, K., Triebs, J.: Ressourceneffizienzbewertung einer Werkzeugmaschine zur Steigerung ihrer Wirtschaftlichkeit. ZWF Zeitschrift für Wirtschaftlichen Fabrikbetrieb 104(9), 711–715 (2009)
8. Herrmann, C., Bergmann, L., Thiede, S., Zein, A.: Energy Labels for Production Machines – An Approach to Facilitate Energy Efficiency in Production Systems. In: Proceedings of 40th CIRP International Seminar on Manufacturing Systems Location (2007)
9. Brecher, C., Herfs, W., Heyers, C., Klein, W., Triebs, J., Beck, E., Dorn, T.: Ressourceneffizienz von Werkzeugmaschinen im Fokus der Forschung. Wt Werkstattstechnik Online 100(7/8), 559–564 (2010)

10. Weinert, N., Chiotellis, S., Seliger, G.: Methodology for planning and operating energy-efficient production systems. CIRP Annals – Manufacturing Technology 60(1), 41–44 (2011)

11. Li, W., Zein, A., Kara, S., Herrmann, C.: An Investigation into Fixed Energy Consumption of Machine Tools. In: Hesselbach, J., Herrmann, C. (eds.) Glocalized Solutions for Sustainability in Manufacturing: Proceedings of the 18th CIRP International Conference on Life Cycle Engineering, Braunschweig, pp. 268–273. Springer, Heidelberg (2011)

12. Karnouskos, S., Colombo, A.W., Martinez Lastra, J.L., Popescu, C.: Towards the energy efficient future Factory. In: Institute of Electrical and Electronics Engineers, 7th IEEE International Conference on Industrial Informatics (INDIN 2009), pp. 367–371. IEEE, Piscataway (2009)

13. Bunse, K., Sachs, J., Vodicka, M.: Evaluating Energy Efficiency Improvements in Manufacturing Processes. In: Vallespir, B., Alix, T. (eds.) APMS 2009. IFIP AICT, vol. 338, pp. 19–26. Springer, Heidelberg (2010)

14. Herrmann, C., Thiede, S., Kara, S., Hesselbach, J.: Energy oriented simulation of manufacturing systems - Concept and application. CIRP Annals – Manufacturing Technology 60, 45–48 (2011)

15. Vijayaraghavan, A., Dornfeld, D.: Automated energy monitoring of machine tools. CIRP Annals – Manufacturing Technology 59, 21–24 (2010)

16. Hermann, C., Thiede, S., Heinemann, T.: A Holistic Framework for Increasing Energy and Resource Efficiency in Manufacturing. In: Seliger, G., et al. (eds.) Advances in Sustainable Manufacturing: Proceedings of the 8th Global Conference on Sustainable Manufacturing, pp. 265–271. Springer, Heidelberg (2011)

17. Brecher, C., Bäumler, S., Bode, H., Breitbach, T., Hansch, S., Hennes, N., Prust, D., Tannert, M., Thoma, C., Wagner, P., Witt, S., Würz, T.: Ressourceneffizienz im Werkzeugmaschinenbau. In: Brecher, C., Klocke, F., Schmitt, R., Schuh, G. (eds.) Proceedings of Aachener Werkzeugmaschinenkolloquium (AWK) 2011 - Wettbewerbsfaktor Produktionstechnik: Aachener Perspektiven, Shaker Verlag, Aachen (2011)

18. Zein, A., Li, W., Herrmann, C., Kara, S.: Energy Efficiency Measures for the Design and Operation of Machine Tools: An Axiomatic Approach. In: Hesselbach, J., Herrmann, C. (eds.) Glocalized Solutions for Sustainability in Manufacturing: Proceedings of the 18th CIRP International Conference on Life Cycle Engineering, Braunschweig, Braunschweig, pp. 274–279. Springer, Heidelberg (2011)

# Energy Efficient Production Planning

## A Joint Cognitive Systems Approach

Connor Upton[1], Fergus Quilligan[2], Carlos García-Santiago[3],
and Asier González-González[3]

[1] Intel Labs Europe, Intel Ireland, Leixlip, Co Kildare, Ireland
connor.upton@intel.com
[2] Irish Centre for Manufacturing Research, Collinstown Ind. Estate, Leixlip, Co Kildare, Ireland
fergus.quilligan@icmr.ie
[3] Tecnalia, Optima Unit, Parque Tecnológico de Álava, Miñano, Spain
{carlosalberto.garcia,asier.gonzalez}@tecnalia.com

**Abstract.** The introduction of energy efficiency as a new goal into already complex production plans is a difficult challenge. Decision support systems can help with this problem but these systems are often resisted by end users who ultimately bear the responsibility for production outputs. This paper describes the design of a decision support tool that aims to increase the interpretability of decision support outputs. The concept of 'grey box' optimisation is introduced, where aspects of the optimisation engine are communicated to, and configurable by, the end user. A multi-objective optimisation algorithm is combined with an interactive visualisation to improve system observability and increase trust.

**Keywords:** visualisation, optimisation, energy efficiency, manufacturing.

## 1 Introduction

Energy efficient manufacturing is a key research challenge for both industry and academia. Systemic energy waste is closely tied to strategic production decisions and therefore poses a complex operations-research problem. An example of this involves switching idle machine into a low-power mode. While this strategy is an effective way to save energy, it is not a straightforward task in many industrial environments. Energy savings are often subservient to production targets and decisions about changing machine states involve weighing up a complex set of goals and constraints. These include hard metrics such as production capacity, predicted inventory and product priorities as well as soft constraints such as technician skill level, engineering requests and machine recovery risks. Operations managers currently apply human expertise to cope with this complexity. In high product mix factories this problem can become very challenging and even before energy-saving is considered. Optimisation algorithms can be applied to reduce the problem space associated with this decision and to highlight energy saving opportunities; however an algorithmic approach is challenged by soft constraints and unpredictable changes in goals. In addition operations managers tend to be wary of decision support tools due to their perceived brittleness and lack of transparency [1].

C. Emmanouilidis, M. Taisch, D. Kiritsis (Eds.): APMS 2012, Part I, IFIP AICT 397, pp. 88–95, 2013.

A potential solution to this is to treat the human operators and automated systems not as autonomous agents but as team members in a joint-cognitive system [2]. Joint cognitive systems, where responsibility for control is shared between human and machine 'intelligence', are becoming increasingly important in all modern workplaces. System *observability* plays a critical role in the success of joint cognitive control as it ensures that human and automated agents can co-ordinate their actions and collaborate effectively [3]. This paper describes the design of a Decision Support System (DSS) using "grey box" optimisation and an interactive visualisation to ensure observability. This approach aims to expose aspects of an optimisation engine to increase flexibility in terms of goal and constraint settings and to communicate outputs in a manner that are easily interpretable to the end user. In this manner end user trust and the overall effectiveness of the system will be improved.

## 2    Applied Use Case

An individual operation within a manufacturing production process was selected for this research. This operation supports multiple products and involves a large fleet of parallel machines. Each machine requires a manual product configuration (a set-up) before processing can occur. This means that the production capacity for each product can be changed in response to demand. As well as set-ups and processing, machines may be in idle, maintenance, engineering, down or powersave states. The optimisation problem investigated here involves allocating machines to states over time under multiple constraints.

Some constraints are hard e.g. meeting production targets by specified date, while others are soft, e.g. technician skill level. An adaptation of the Cognitive Work Analysis framework [4] was used as a requirements engineering technique to understand how operations managers currently access information, prioritise goals and communicate decisions. Initially the supervisors answered questionnaires, followed by interviews and observations. Additional questionnaires were provided to further analyse the work flow and to complete task analyses. Supervisors decision making strategies were analysed using the think-aloud protocol [5] and the supervisors actions and thoughts were saved for extended analysis using audio and screen capture software. During interviews and observations three critical requirements of the solution were identified.

1. Trust

   A key challenge with any automated support system is that the final responsibility lies with the human agent. As a result an end user may not respond to a suggestion that they do not fully understand if the possible consequences are severe. Trust in automated systems is a well-known challenge in DSS and observability of system constraints is of key importance to increase user's confidence in the system. The representation of optimisation outputs in a relevant, interpretable format will be critical. In addition, to overcome the perceived brittleness of optimisation engines it is important that the end user can view, assess and edit goals, constraints and rules that act as inputs to the system.

2. Speed

Responsiveness is another key factor [6]. If a user is to interact and modifying goals and constraints it is important that they can get feedback on the impact of these changes without a prolonged waiting period. Furthermore, as this tool aims to optimise a current schedule it is critical that responses are provided before the current state changes.

3. Accuracy

The nature of this dynamic scheduling problem favours a satisficing [7] approach over maximal optimisation. On top of the speed requirement, it is important to realise that goals can change, different scheduling strategies can be used to arrive at the same outputs and some constraints may not be available to the system and will require adjustments by the end user.

At a high level the main objectives are to optimise energy efficiency by maximising the time that machines can remain in power-save state, without compromising production goals. The impact of the system will be to optimise for these key performance indicators resulting in maximised output, minimised cost and increased machine utilisation.

# 3    Optimisation Approach

## 3.1    Optimisation Engine Design and User Interaction

The optimisation engine has been designed to allow for a close integration with the final user. The visualisation and user interaction requirements have heavily affected the design approach taken for the optimisation engine.

One of these main requirements is increasing the trust from the user in the results obtained from the optimisation engine. This has been addressed in two different ways, affecting several basic components of the optimiser. First, the user is able to influence the solution selection by inputting his preferences, because depending on the dynamic situation at the plant the user will prefer different alternatives. To provide these options, the optimisation engine follows 2 different algorithms. In the first one the user provides his preferences "a priori", before the optimisation starts. This input will then be used by the algorithms as parameters that will guide the search for the optimum solution that best uses it.

The second approach does not need this prior info. In this case the optimisation algorithm will search for different solutions, together forming what is known as a "Pareto front" (the set of all solutions that are nondominated with respect to each other [8]). In this set of solutions, no one can be selected as better than another until the user selects one of them, based on his current preferences. This selection involves a certain amount of decrease in optimality in one objective to achieve a gain in another. The maximum number of solutions presented should be limited so as not to overload the supervisor and allow him to concentrate on a few possibilities. The user interview has shown that a maximum of 3 options is needed. The optimisation engine uses this requirement to select 3 solutions among the whole Pareto front that are different enough to provide a significant diversity of options to the user. The algorithm being currently under testing is the NSGA-II [9] which uses an elitist, non-domination approach, together with a crowded-comparison operator. There are plans to test other algorithms in the future, like for example Harmony Search.

The other design decision to increase trust has been using a simulation-based optimisation so the user gets detailed info on all the consequences/implications of the proposed solution. For example, machine utilisation, energy savings per machine, % of committed production in time, utilisation of tools in machines, etc. A discrete-event simulation is used, which provides a descriptive environment for such high-complexity systems as the one under study [10]. In this way the system observability and transparency is greatly increased. Figure 1 shows a high-level abstraction scheme of the DSS.

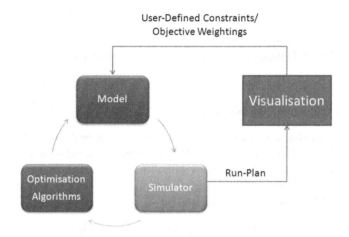

**Fig. 1.** Optimisation Engine - Visualisation Relation

This simulation design approach also opens the possibility to use this run-plan as a base for the introduction of new user-defined constraints directly over it. The user can introduce particular changes by using drag and drop or he can introduce them as general rules. For example, the user may want to select any machine to do some engineering work, but does not care which one. Then the optimisation engine will decide which machine to select.

The main features of the proposed optimisation engine are as follows:

- Multi-Objective. In a realistic manufacturing environment the final user has to balance different, often conflicting goals. This issue is explained below in more detail.
- Use of meta-heuristic algorithms e.g. simulated annealing and genetic algorithms. These types of techniques are approximated, meaning that they are not able to always produce the optimal solution, but have the potential to produce good solutions in a short time.
- Simulation-based: the optimisation algorithm relies on a simulation of the process to provide the fitness values for each solution. An advantage of this approach is

that it makes possible to provide the final user with increased environment descriptiveness, increasing the trust.

- Integration of PPIs (Production Performance Indicators) that act as goals and evaluation criteria for both the optimisation engine and the end user. PPIs are contextual information that provides common ground for human and automated agents.
- The user–defined constraints pose a problem of dynamic rescheduling, with the added difficulty that the time to get a solution adapted to the new scenario is limited.

To provide a solution to the new problem, the initial solution used for the rescheduling problem is obtained from the last solution generated for the old problem. This new starting solution must be first updated to the new problem, by deleting the operations already started. Starting with an already "good" solution, together with the reduction in the search space, will decrease the runtime needed to provide the new solution [11]. It is also necessary to adjust different algorithm parameters, like for example crossover operator and mutation rate in the case of genetic algorithms, to adapt to the new situation.

## 3.2    Multi-Objective Optimisation

This problem is defined as a multi-objective optimisation problem (MOO). There is no single global optimum solution in MOO problems. Instead of a single solution, there are a set of optimal valid solutions with different objectives magnitudes (fitness values) [12].

A general MOO problem can be defined as:

$$\text{Minimise:} \quad F(x) = [f_1(x), f_2(x) ... f_n(x)]$$

$$\text{Subject to:} \quad G_j(x) \leq 0, j = 1, 2 ... m$$

where $F(x)$ is the set of n objective functions, x is the vector of decision variables and $G_j$ are the m independent constraints.

In this use case the two following objectives are considered:

- Maximise duration in power saving state.
- Minimise the number of machine setups.

Multiple constraints are present in the model. Among the most important we can list the following:

- Meet production target. This is the hardest constraint in the model, involving a given number of different product types at a predefined time.
- Inventory arrival time.
- Machine setups require product-specific collateral equipment, of which there is a limited amount.
- User-Defined constraints: the user is able to change constraints online through the visualisation, such as fixing the state of a machine in a specified time.

The constraints impose limits in what is called the "feasible space", or the set of valid solutions that meet all constraints. The optimisation algorithms then try to find the Pareto front that optimises all objectives subject to those constraints.

In addition, the optimisation engine should be able to suggest maintenance timing within a defined window.

## 4    Visualisation Approach

The output of the optimisation algorithm is a schedule of machines transitioning between states across a production period. This schedule is presented to the user in the form of a run-plan (outline shown in Figure 1). Different machine are listed top to bottom on the left of the display. Machine states are shown over time from left to right and are colour coded so that idle states are highly salient and demand attention. The user can zoom into different time periods to assess production schedules across a shift, a day or an entire week. The current time is clearly marked and past events are shaded out to indicate that they are non-editable. On loading the screen, the user is presented with the current schedule but this may be manually edited or re-optimised by clicking on the appropriate function buttons located above and below the runplan. User defined rules may be generated based on an expert users knowledge. For example a user may wish to spread out machine setups due to an unexpected resource constraint. This is achieved by simply dragging the setup event forward or backward

**Fig. 2.** Run plan Visualisation

in time. Similar actions can also be carried out to input or modify maintenance or power saving states. The panels on the right of the run-plan communicate important production performance indicators. These are updated as the user modifies the run plan in order to allow them to assess the impact of their actions. Following updates the end user can commit the run plan or may choose to re-optimise with their newly defined constraints. The tabbed menu at the top of the screen allows the user to try out multiple runplans to assess which strategy best suits their needs.

# 5 Conclusions

This paper describes a decision support system (DSS) for improving the energy efficiency of production plans. The research aims to improve trust in DSS, and in turn its overall effectiveness, by combining an optimisation engine with a dynamic visualisation that:

- Communicates the rules and results of an optimisation engine in an intuitive manner
- Allows end-users to generate dynamic constraints using simple drag and drop actions
- Supports experimentation using what-if scenario planning
- Generates a production plan incorporating energy saving opportunities

This concept applies principles from joint cognitive system research to support complex decision making through the combination of human flexibility with computational power. A functional prototype has been developed and future work will focus of improving the performance of the algorithms, integration with a live production system and evaluation with end users.

**Acknowledgements.** The presented work has been funded by the European Union FP7 "Factories of the Future" research project "KAP: Knowledge, Awareness and Prediction". The authors would like to acknowledge the support and contributions of KAP industrial and academic partners in the development of this work. We also extend our thanks to the Irish Centre for Manufacturing Research (www.icmr.ie) which is supported by Enterprise Ireland and the Industrial Development Authority of Ireland.

# References

1. Carlsson, C., Turban, E.: Introduction: DSS: Directions for the next decade. Decision Support Systems 33(2), 105–110 (2002)
2. Hollnagel, E., Woods, D.D.: Joint cognitive systems: Foundations of cognitive systems engineering. Taylor and Francis, Boca Raton (2005)
3. Christoffersen, K., Woods, D.: How to make automated systems team players. Advances in Human Performance and Cognitive Engineering Research 2(1), 12 (2002)

4. Vicente, K.J.: Cognitive Work Analysis: Toward Safe, Productive, and Healthy Computer-Based Work. Erlbaum and Associates, Mahwah (1999)
5. Lewis, C.: Using the 'thinking-aloud' method in cognitive interface design, IBM Research Report RC 9265, 2/17/82 IBM T. J. Watson Research Center, Yorktown Heights, NY (1982)
6. Shneiderman, B.: Computing Surveys, vol. 16(3) (1984)
7. Simon, H.A.: Rational choice and the structure of the environment. Psychological Review 63(2), 129–138 (1956)
8. Martínez-Iranzo, M., Herrero, J.M., Sanchis, J., Blasco, X., García-Nieto, S.: Applied Pareto multi-objective optimization by stochastic solvers. Engineering Applications of Artificial Intelligence 22, 455–465 (2009)
9. Deb, K., Pratap, A., Agarwal, S., Meyarivan, T.: A fast and elitist multiobjective genetic algorithm: NSGA-II. IEEE Transactions on Evolutionary Computation 6, 182–197 (2002)
10. C.B., Beham, A., Heavey, C.: A comparative study of genetic algorithm components in simulation-based optimisation. In: Winter Simulation Conference 2008, pp. 1829–1837 (2008)
11. Bierwirth, C., Mattfeld, D.C.: Production scheduling and rescheduling with genetic algorithms. Evolutionary Computation 7, 1–17 (1999)
12. Marler, R.T., Arora, J.S.: Survey of multi-objective optimization methods for engineering. Structural and Multidisciplinary Optimization 26(6), 369–395 (2004)

# Using Internet of Things to Improve Eco-efficiency in Manufacturing: A Review on Available Knowledge and a Framework for IoT Adoption

Giovanni Miragliotta and Fadi Shrouf

Department of Management, Economics and Industrial Engineering,
Politecnico di Milano, Italy
{giovanni.miragliotta,fadi.shrouf}@polimi.it

**Abstract.** Green manufacturing and eco-efficiency are among the highest priorities of decision makers in today's manufacturing scenario. Reducing the energy consumption of production processes can significantly improve the environmental performance of the human activity. This paper aims at investigating, according to currently available technologies and to their short-term feasible evolution paths, how the Internet of Things (IoT) paradigm could actually be implemented to increase efficiency in energy consumption, and reducing energy consumption cost.

**Keywords:** Internet of Things, eco-efficiency, framework.

## 1 Introduction

The manufacturing sector is one of the largest energy consumer, estimated at more than 31% of global energy consumption [1]. Relevant energy savings are expected to be achievable both from increasing the energy efficiency of production and logistic processes as well as in innovative energy monitoring and management approaches [2]. In this scenario, emerging technologies such as IoT paradigm are believed to play a lead role in increasing energy efficiency, working at different levels. More specifically, IoT could play such a role first by increasing the awareness of energy consumption patterns (real time data acquisition level), and then by improving local (single machine) or global efficiency (multiple machines) by decentralizing data elaboration or even actuation decisions. In this regard, the paper is arranged in two sections. The first section is dedicated to a literature review covering energy efficient management, and IoT paradigm. Relying on this knowledge, the second section is devoted to present a framework for IoT adoption when pursuing energy efficiency targets in manufacturing. Some concluding remarks are drawn to address future research.

## 2 Literature Review

### 2.1 Energy Management and Monitoring

Many methods and tools have been used for reducing energy consumption, such as energy monitoring tools, process modeling, simulation and optimization tools, process

C. Emmanouilidis, M. Taisch, D. Kiritsis (Eds.): APMS 2012, Part I, IFIP AICT 397, pp. 96–102, 2013.

integration, energy analysis, and decision support tools, etc. [3]. Often energy reduction approaches in industry are related to lean manufacturing concepts, and rely on empirical observation as in [4]. The adoption of eco-efficiency needs to be included at all levels of production process, including the machinery [5]. Energy consumption of a machine is not strongly related to the production rate; conversely, the amount of consumed energy is mostly related to the time spent in specific operative states [6]; according to [7] the potential energy savings from reduction of waiting time or in the start-up mode are estimated around 10-25%.

Real time data from energy monitoring systems is necessary for improving energy efficiency on manufacturing [8]. For optimizing energy consumption of manufacturing processes, energy consumption awareness should be achieved first [9]. Monitoring and analysis of the energy consumption of machines are major steps towards increasing energy efficiency [10]. Some conventional production systems are not able to collect data on the amount of energy consumed in production processes [11]. In this regard, IoT based solutions can be very useful to drive energy efficient applications: smart metering is an example to show the importance of the IoT in the energy area; in addition to providing real-time data, it could make decisions depending on their capabilities and collaboration with other services, as mentioned in [12].

## 2.2    Internet of Things

Actually IoT technologies consist of an integration of several technologies, as identification, sensing and communication technologies, which consist of RFID, sensor, actuators, and wireless information network [13]. The IoT paradigm has opened new possibilities in terms of data acquisition, decentralized data elaboration/ decision making and actuation. The real time monitoring system enables continually monitoring production processes and machine status [14], and covering the disturbances through production line, such as machine failures, production errors, etc. as in [15]. Adoption of IoT technologies in manufacturing processes have been investigated in some researches, as shown in table 1. Few researches have investigated how and when IoT is useful for improving energy efficiency at the shop floor.

**Table 1.** Research on RFId and IoT application domains in manufacturing

| Manage and control inventory and material (trace and track) | | Monitoring shop floor | planning and control shop floor | Monitor and control the production process /machine status |
|---|---|---|---|---|
| Author | Year | | | |
| Meyer [15] | 2011 | x | x | x | x |
| Poon [16] | 2011 | x | | | x |
| Meyer [17] | 2009 | x | | | x |
| Zhang [18] | 2011 | x | x | x | |
| Zhou [19] | 2007 | x | | | x |
| Huang [20] | 2008 | x | | x | |
| Chen [21] | 2009 | x | | | x |
| Hameed [22] | 2010 | | | | X |
| Wang [23] | 2011 | | | x | X |

## 3    A Framework for IoT Adoption, and Managerial Impact

Stemming from the literature review, and focusing on discrete manufacturing systems, a framework for IoT adoption has been conceived, which considers the following factors:

- Type of energy fee structure. Two types of energy fee structure have been considered, fixed price, and variable energy price [24].
- Eco-efficiency targets (awareness, improvement, optimization).
- Existing IT infrastructure; Rely on the American national standard framework as in [25], which specifies 4 levels as listed below. For each of these levels, depending on the current state of IT adopted by the factory, different IoT applications may be conceived.

    — Level 1 defines the activities involved in sensing.
    — Level 2 defines the activities of monitoring and controlling processes.
    — Level 3 defines the activities of the work flow to produce the end products
    — Level 4 defines activities include plant schedule, inventory levels materials movements. Information from level 3 is critical for level 4 activities.

By combining the aspects above, the framework in Figure 1 points out a set of feasible application domains, covering some of the existing possibilities. For each feasible domain (i.e. energy fee structure, existing IT infrastructure and eco-efficiency targets)

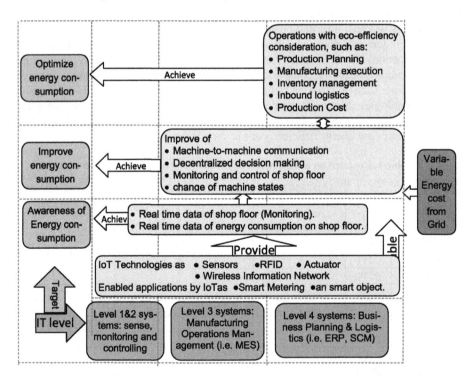

**Fig. 1.** Framework of adapting IoT for eco-efficiency at shop floor

the paper qualitatively discusses the current applicability of the IoT paradigm and points out which specific functionalities could be entrusted to such solutions (measurement, sensing and actuation).

Real time data from IoT including data from smart metering will be used to increase the awareness of energy consumption of each processes and machines, and providing new measures. Taking energy consumption in consideration during planning processes will lead to improve and optimize energy consumption, which requires more flexibility in planning and control, enable machine to machine communication, and adopting of decentralized decision making at shop floor. With adopting variable energy cost, the way of improving and optimizing energy consumption will be different, compared with fixed energy cost. IoT applications and real time data will play an important role in configuring, schedule, changing machine states, defining of current energy consumption during each process, monitoring, planning and control of the production processes at shop floor. IoT can feed MES with real time data from shop floor, and inventory movements, etc.; then, an efficient decision can be made. In this regards, adopting of decentralized decision making is important, whether decision will be made by shop floor supervisor, an employee, or by the machines. Examples of these decisions are: change the priority of production processes, change machine status, reschedule the production process, and inventory movement at shop floor.

Actually many scenarios can be applied in real world depending on the framework. In Table 2, three scenarios are discussed to explain the framework, encompassing both fixed and variable energy cost structure. The first scenario assumes the available IT in a factory is level 1 and 2; the target is increasing the awareness of energy consumption. The second scenario assumes the available IT in a factory is level 3; and the target is improving energy consumption. The third scenario supposes the available IT in a factory is level 4; and the target is optimizing energy consumption.

| Scenarios | Fixed Energy cost structure | Variable Energy cost structure |
|---|---|---|
| 1 | Adoption of IoT Technologies with its applications, such as Smart Metering (smart object) increase awareness of energy consumption, by providing detailed energy consumption data for specific machine, process, product and shift. | Integration of variable energy cost with real time data increases the awareness by providing real energy cost for specific process, machine, product, and shift. Accordingly, decision maker, etc. can take the proper decision depending on the new available data on short and long term. |
| 2 | Integrating of real time data from shop floor with manufacturing systems (e.g. MES) leads to improve energy consumptions by increasing monitoring and control of shop floor, enabling machine-to-machine communication, and by adopting decentralized decision making to make the proper decision depending on current production process. | Considering variable energy cost during production process will help to minimize energy consumption cost, for example, by changing machine states to reduce cost and wastage of energy consumption; this means the decision making will be depending on changeable energy price, and energy consumption data from IoT technologies for current production process. |

| 3 | The integration of real time data from smart metering on energy consumption (per machine and per process), real time data on inventory, production status, and other real time data from the field on production process, will be useful for optimizing energy consumptions. This data can be also useful for production schedule etc., Acquired data on energy should be feed to ERP systems to be considered during next production planning and during configuring of production systems, etc. | The integrations of variable energy cost information, with other information from MES, and ERP Systems, will be useful for optimize energy consumptions. Some alternatives will be offered for decision making, such as, changing machine statues, and reschedule production process (when it is possible, and depend on the energy cost). This means production planning is required to be more flexible to fit with energy price. Acquired data form IoT on energy consumption will effect on future production processes. |

## 4    Conclusions

Adopting of IoT technology (as smart metering) is able to provide high level of awareness of energy consumption at all factories level. The awareness leads to find available energy saving opportunities in production process, this lead to reduce energy consumption. Also, IoT technologies may provide new opportunities for improved monitoring of the inventory, and traceability and visibility of manufacturing process, which lead to improve the processes at shop floor, accordingly reduce of energy consumption. Integration of the collected real time data with manufacturing systems, such as ERP and MES help the decision makers to make decisions with considerations of energy consumption. Variable energy cost structure effect on the way of achieving awareness, improving, and optimizing of energy consumption at manufacturing plant. More investigated is needed; in how effectively connect IoT technologies (i.e. sensor) to machines, connected to interconnect sensors and collect data in a business sustainable as (costs, flexibility, etc.). And how to insert the energy perspective in current manufacturing's planning and control, and decision making.

**Acknowledgement.** This paper is produced as part of the EMJD Programme European Doctorate in Industrial Management (EDIM) funded by the European Commission, Erasmus Mundus Action 1.

## References

1. EIA: Annual Energy Review (2010)
2. Weinert, N., Chiotellis, S., Seliger, G.: Methodology for planning and operating energy-efficient production systems. CIRP Annals - Manufacturing Technology 60, 41–44 (2011)
3. Muller, D.C.A., Marechal, F.M.A., Wolewinski, T., Roux, P.J.: An energy management method for the food industry. Applied Thermal Engineering 27, 2677–2686 (2007)

4. Michaloski, J.L., Shao, G., Arinez, J., Lyons, K., Leong, S., Riddick, F.: Analysis of Sustainable Manufacturing Using Simulation for Integration of Production and Building Service. Compressed Air., 93–101 (2011)
5. Reich-Weiser, C., Vijayaraghavan, A., Dornfeld, D.: Appropriate use of Green Manufacturing Frameworks. Laboratory for Manufacturing and Sustainability (2010)
6. Gutowski, T., Dahmus, J., Thiriez, A.: Electrical Energy Requirements for Manufacturing Processes. 13th CIRP International Conference on Life Cycle Engineering (2006)
7. Park, C., Kwon, K., Kim, W., Min, B., Park, S., Sung, I., Yoon, Y.S., Lee, K., Lee, J., Seok, J.: Energy Consumption Reduction Technology in Manufacturing – A Selective Review of Policies, Standards, and Research. Precision Engineering and Manufacturing 10, 151–173 (2009)
8. Vijayaraghavan, A., Dornfeld, D.: Automated energy monitoring of machine tools. CIRP Annals - Manufacturing Technology 59, 21–24 (2010)
9. Karnouskos, S., Colombo, A.W., Martinez Lastra, J.L., Popescu, C.: Towards the energy efficient future factory. In: 2009 7th IEEE International Conference on Industrial Informatics, pp. 367–371 (2009)
10. Bunse, K., Vodicka, M., Schönsleben, P., Brülhart, M., Ernst, F.O.: Integrating energy efficiency performance in production management – gap analysis between industrial needs and scientific literature. Journal of Cleaner Production 19, 667–679 (2011)
11. Ikeyama, T., Watanabe, H., Isobe, S., Takahashi, H.: An Approach to Optimize Energy Use in Food Plants. In: SICE Annual Conference, pp. 1574–1579. Waseda University, Tokyo (2011)
12. Haller, S., Karnouskos, S., Schroth, C.: The Internet of Things in an Enterprise Context. In: Domingue, J., Fensel, D., Traverso, P. (eds.) FIS 2008. LNCS, vol. 5468, pp. 14–28. Springer, Heidelberg (2009)
13. Atzori, L., Iera, A., Morabito, G.: The Internet of Things: A survey. Computer Networks 54, 2787–2805 (2010)
14. Subramaniam, S.K., Husin, S.H., Singh, R.S.S., Hamidon, A.H.: Production Monitoring System for Monitoring the Industrial Shop Floor Performance. Int. J. of Systems Applications, Engineering & Development 3, 28–35 (2009)
15. Meyer, G.G., Wortmann, J.C., Szirbik, N.B.: Production monitoring and control with intelligent products. International Journal of Production Research 49, 1303–1317 (2011)
16. Poon, T.C., Choy, K.L., Chan, F.T.S., Lau, H.C.W.: A real-time production operations decision support system for solving stochastic production material demand problems. Expert Systems with Applications 38, 4829–4838 (2011)
17. Meyer, G.G., Främling, K., Holmström, J.: Intelligent Products: A survey. Computers in Industry 60, 137–148 (2009)
18. Zhang, Y., Qu, T., Ho, O., Huang, G.Q.: Real-time work-in-progress management for smart object-enabled ubiquitous shop-floor environment. International Journal of Computer Integrated Manufacturing 24, 431–445 (2011)
19. Zhou, S., Ling, W., Peng, Z.: An RFID-based remote monitoring system for enterprise internal production management. The International Journal of Advanced Manufacturing Technology 33, 837–844 (2007)
20. Huang, G.Q., Zhang, Y.F., Chen, X., Newman, S.T.: RFID-enabled real-time wireless manufacturing for adaptive assembly planning and control. Journal of Intelligent Manufacturing 19, 701–713 (2008)
21. Chen, R.-S., Tu, M. (Arthur): Development of an agent-based system for manufacturing control and coordination with ontology and RFID technology. Expert Systems with Applications 36, 7581–7593 (2009)

22. Hameed, B., Khan, I., Durr, F., Rothermel, K.: An RFID based consistency management framework for production monitoring in a smart real-time factory. In: 2010 Internet of Things (IOT), pp. 1–8 (2010)
23. Wang, B., Cao, Z., Yan, Y., Liu, W., Wang, Z.: Fundamental technology for RFID-based supervisory control of shop floor production system. The International Journal of Advanced Manufacturing Technology 57, 1123–1141 (2011)
24. Mercatoelettrico.org,
    http://www.mercatoelettrico.org/En/Default.aspx
25. ANSI/ ISA: Enterprise-Control System Integration Part 3: Activity Models of Manufacturing Operations Management (2005)

# An Investigation into Minimising Total Energy Consumption, Total Energy Cost and Total Tardiness Based on a Rolling Blackout Policy in a Job Shop

Ying Liu[1], Niels Lohse[1], Sanja Petrovic[2], and Nabil Gindy[3]

[1] University of Nottingham, Department of Mechanical,
Material and Manufacturing Engineering, Nottingham, United Kingdom
{epxyl9,niels.lohse}@nottingham.ac.uk
[2] University of Nottingham, Department of Computer Science, Nottingham, United Kingdom
sanja.petrovic@nottingham.ac.uk
[3] University of Nottingham Ningbo China, Division of Engineering, Ningbo, China
nabil.gindy@nottingham.edu.cn

**Abstract.** Manufacturing enterprises nowadays face the challenge of increasing energy price and emission reduction requirements. An approach to reduce energy cost and become environmental friendly is to incorporate energy consumption into consideration while making the scheduling plans. The research presented by this paper is set in a classical job shop circumstance, the model for the triple objectives problem that minimise total electricity cost, total electricity consumption and total tardiness when the Rolling Blackout policy is applied. A case study based on a 3*3 job shop is presented to show how scheduling plans affect electricity consumption and its related cost, and to prove the feasibility of the model.

**Keywords:** Energy efficient production planning, sustainable manufacturing, job shop scheduling.

## 1 Introduction

Manufacturing industry is one of the most important energy consumers and carbon emitters in the world. For instance, every year in China, manufacturing generates at least 26% of the total carbon dioxide emission [1]. In order to reduce the carbon emission and balance the time-based unevenness of electricity demand, some countries, like China had promulgated corresponding electricity usage control policies and tariffs (EPTs), such as the Rolling Blackout policy for industry electricity supply, which means the government electricity will be cut off several days in every week resulting in manufacturing companies illegally starting their own diesel generators to maintain production. However, the private diesel electricity is more polluting and costly than the government supplied resource. Thus, the increasing price of energy and the current trend of sustainability have exerted new pressure on manufacturing enterprises, therefore they have to reduce energy consumption for cost saving and to become more environmentally friendly. As a result, employing operational methods to reduce the

C. Emmanouilidis, M. Taisch, D. Kiritsis (Eds.): APMS 2012, Part I, IFIP AICT 397, pp. 103–110, 2013.

energy consumption and its related cost can be a feasible and effective approach for manufacturing enterprises [2]. The modelling method proposed in this paper can be applied to discrete event machining production system and may save significant amounts of energy and cost as well as keeping a good performance on classical scheduling objectives. The term "machining" will refer to processes such as milling, turning, drilling, and sawing [3]. In following content, the research problem will be raised after the research background and motivation; then the model will be presented, followed by a case study to demonstrate how scheduling plans affect the electricity consumption and its related cost in a job shop.

## 2      Background and Motivation

A considerable amount of research has been conducted in the area of sustainable machining. A detailed process model that can be used to determine the environmental impacts resulting from the machining of a particular part had been presented in [4]. The authors of [3] and [5] developed a system level research which not only includes energy requirement for material removal process itself, but also associated processes such as axis feed. The approach which breaks the total energy use of machining processes will be employed as the base for modelling electricity consumption of machine tools in this research.

Several operational methods, such as genetic algorithm, to minimise the electricity consumption and classical scheduling objectives on a single machine and parallel machines had been proposed in [6] and [7]. These methods are based upon the realization that in manufacturing environment, large quantities of energy are consumed by non-bottleneck machines as they lay idle. The Turn Off/On method developed in the above approach will be applied in this research. However, the applicable range of these works limits in single machine and parallel-machines circumstance. A modelling method for minimising energy consumption of manufacturing processes had been developed in [8], nevertheless, this research is based on the assumption that alternative routes with different energy consumption amounts exist for jobs in the manufacturing system. Therefore, the model is not applicable for workshops without, or having identical alternatives routes for jobs. What had been discussed above provides the motivation for this research from an academic aspect, i.e. that employing operational methods to reduce the electricity consumption in a typical job shop still has not been explored very well.

More importantly, from a practical aspect, the application of EPTs further complicate the aforementioned scheduling problem, since a scheduling plan that leads to reduction in electricity consumption does not necessarily lead to reduction in electricity cost in this situation. However, currently very little research focuses on this problem, even though it is important to deliver a trade-off between electricity consumption reduction and cost saving. Only [9] considered an instantaneous power limit in a case study. In this case the authors tried to use a discrete event simulation method to find a favourable solution. However, the solution quality could have been much improved if the intelligent search algorithms were applied.

Therefore, the new problem can be raised as: The Multi-objective Total Electricity Cost, Total Electricity Consumption and Total Tardiness Job Shop Scheduling problem based on Rolling Blackout policy (EC2T). The modelling method for this problem will be presented below.

# 3    Models and Case Study

In this section, models for EC2T will be defined. A case study of 3\*3 job shop will be presented to show how scheduling plans affect the objectives of Total Tardiness, Total Electricity Consumption and Total Electricity Cost.

## 3.1    Job Shop Model

Referring to [10] and [11] , in the job shop scheduling problem, $J = \{J_i\}_{i=1}^n$, a finite set of $n$ jobs are to be processed on $M = \{M_k\}_{k=1}^m$, a finite set of $m$ machines following a predefined order.; $O_{ik} = \{O_{ik}^l\}_{l=1}^{u_i}$ is a finite set of $u_i$ ordered operations of $J_i$; $O_{ik}^l$ is the $l$-th operation of $J_i$ processed on $M_k$ and it requires a processing time denoted $p_{ik}^l$. $S_{ik}^l$ indicates the time that $O_{ik}^l$ begins to be processed on $M_k$, while $C_{ik}^l$ is the corresponding completion time of that process. $Y_{ii'k}^{ll'}$ is a decision variable that $Y_{ii'k}^{ll'} = 1$ if $O_{ik}^l$ precedes $O_{i'k}^{l'}$ on $M_k$, 0 otherwise. Each $J_i$ has a release time into the system $r_i$ and a due date $d_i$. $w_i$ is the weight associated with $J_i$.

Constraints:

$$S_{ik}^l \geq r_i \tag{1}$$

$$C_{ik}^{l+1} - C_{ik'}^l \geq p_{ik}^{l+1}; \ S_{ik}^{l+1} - C_{ik'}^l \geq 0 \tag{2}$$

$$C_{i'k}^{l'} - C_{ik}^l \geq p_{i'k}^{l'} \ Y_{ii'}^{ll'} = 1 \tag{3}$$

Where

$Y_{ii'k}^{ll'} \in \{0,1\}; \ S_{ik}^l \geq 0; \ C_{ik}^l \geq 0; \ C_{ik'}^l \geq 0; \ k \neq k'; \ i \neq i'; \ 1 \leq l \leq u_i$

$\forall J_i, J_{i'} \in J; \ \forall O_{ik}^l, O_{ik}^{l+1}, O_{ik'}^l \in O_{ik}; \ \forall O_{i'k}^{l'} \in O_{i'k}; \ \forall M_k, M_{k'} \in M$

Constraint (1) makes sure that the starting time of any job must greater than its release time. Constraint (2) ensures that the precedence relationships between the operations of a job are not violated, i.e. the $O_{ik}^{l+1}$ is not started before the $O_{ik'}^l$ had been completed, and no job can be processed by more than one machine at a time. Constraint (3) takes care of the requirement that no machine can process more than one operation at a time, i.e. no pre-emption is allowed. A schedule $s$ that complies with constraints (1) to (3) is said to be a feasible schedule. $S$ is a finite set of all feasible schedules that $s \in S$. Given a feasible schedule $s$, let $C_i(s)$ indicate the completion time of $J_i$ in schedule $s$. The tardiness of $J_i$ can be denoted as $T_i(s) = max\{0, C_i(s) - d_i\}$. The objective is to minimise the total weighted tardiness of all jobs.

$$minimise\left(\sum_{i=1}^n w_i \times T_i(s)\right) \tag{4}$$

## 3.2    Electricity Consumption Model

Based on existing research work on environmental analysis of machining [5], [12], [13], [14], the simplified power input model of $M_k$ when it is working on $O_{ik}^l$ is shown in Fig. 1.

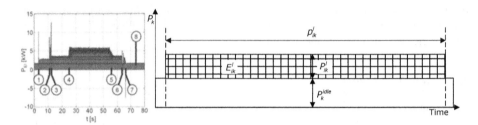

**Fig. 1.** Actual power input at machine tool main connection over time and its simplified model when it is working on one operation (based on [12])

$P_k^{idle}$ refers to the idle power of $M_k$, $P_{ik}^{lruntime}$ and $E_{ik}^{lruntime}$ represent the power and energy consumed by $M_k$ when it executes the runtime operations for processing $O_{ik}^l$ that $E_{ik}^{lruntime} = P_{ik}^{lruntime} \times p_{ik}^l$. $p_{ik}^l$ is defined as the time interval between coolant switching on and off. $P_{ik}^{lcutting}$ and $E_{ik}^{lcutting}$ are the power and energy consume by $M_k$ when it actually executes cutting for $O_{ik}^l$, $E_{ik}^{lcutting} = P_{ik}^{lcutting} \times t_{ik}^{lcutting}$. $t_{ik}^{lcutting}$ is the corresponding cutting time. $P_k = P_k^{idle} + P_{ik}^{lruntime} + P_{ik}^{lcutting}$. $E_{ik}^{lruntime}$, $E_{ik}^{lcutting}$ and $P_k^{idle}$ can be seen as constants when both of the product's and machine tool's characteristics are known. Thus, define $E_{ik}^l$ as energy consumed by runtime operations and cutting of $O_{ik}^l$ on $M_k$, that $E_{ik}^l = E_{ik}^{lruntime} + E_{ik}^{lcutting}$. $E_{ik}^l$ can be seen as a constant. To simplify the power input model, it is supposed that all the runtime operations and the actual cutting share the same starting and ending time. Therefore, define $P_{ik}^l$ as the average power input of $M_k$ during $p_{ik}^l$, $P_{ik}^l = E_{ik}^l / p_{ik}^l$, $P_k = P_k^{idle} + P_{ik}^l$. This model will simplify the calculation of total electricity consumption and electricity cost of the job shop, as well as guarantee the necessary accuracy for EC2T problem. Based on the model discussed above, it is easy to see that $E_{ik}^l$ is the processing related energy consumption, and $\sum E_{ik}^l$ will not be affected by different scheduling plans. Thus, the objective to reduce total electricity consumption of a job shop can be converted to reduce total non-processing electricity consumption which includes idle and Turn Off/On electricity consumption of machine tools [7]. The objective function can be set as:

$$mimise\left(\sum_{k=1}^{m} TEM_k^{np}\right) \tag{5}$$

$TEM_k^{np}$ is the non-processing electricity consumption of $M_k$. $M_k' = \{m_k^r\}_{r=1}^{\sum_{i=1}^{n}\sum_{l=1}^{u_i}\gamma_{ik}^l}$ is a finite set of operations processed on $M_k$. $\gamma_{ik}^l$ is a decision variable that $\gamma_{ik}^l = 1$ if the $l$-th operation of $J_i$ processed on $M_k$, 0 otherwise. $S_k^r$ and $C_k^r$ respectively indicate the start and completion time of $m_k^r$ on $M_k$. A schedule $s$ can be graphically expressed as a Gantt Chart, the calculation of the total non-processing electricity consumption will be based on it. Fig. 2 is an example for the calculation. $O_{i_1k}^{l_1}$, $O_{i_2k}^{l_2}$, $O_{i_3k}^{l_3}$, and $O_{i_4k}^{l_4}$ are processed by $M_k$. The Turn Off/On method suggested by [6] is allowed, then:

$$TEM_k^{np} = P_k^{idle} \times \left[ max\left(C_k^r\right) - \Sigma_r(C_k^r - S_k^r) - \Sigma_r(S_k^{r+1} - C_k^r) \times Z_k^r \right] + E_k^{turn} \times \Sigma_r Z_k^r \quad (6)$$

According to [6], $E_k^{turn}$ is the the energy consumed by Turn Off/On; $B_k$ is the break-even duration of machine for which Turn Off/On is economically justifiable instead of running the machine idle, $B_k = E_k^{turn}/P_k^{idle}$. $t_k^{OFF}$ is the time required to turn off then turn on $M_k$; $Z_k^r$ is a decision variable that $Z_k^r = 1$ if $S_k^{r+1} - C_k^r \geq max(B_k, t_k^{OFF})$, 0 otherwise.

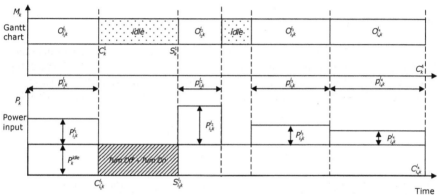

**Fig. 2.** Gantt chart of $M_k$ and its corresponding power profile

### 3.3    Electricity Cost Model (Based on the Rolling Blackout Policy)

The objective function for electricity cost of a job shop is:

$$minimise(TEC(s)) \quad (7)$$

$$TEC = \Sigma_{k=1}^m TEC_k(s) \quad (8)$$

$$TEC_k(s) = p^e \times \int_0^{max(C_k^r)} P_k \quad p^e = \begin{cases} \beta_1, & t \in [(n-1)T, \ (n-1)T + t_s) \\ \beta_2, & t \in ((n-1)T + t_s, nT] \end{cases} \quad (9)$$

As seen in Fig. 3, $TEC(s)$ and $TEC_k(s)$ respectively refer to the total electricity cost of the job shop and $M_k$ in a feasible schedule $s$; $p^e$ represents the electricity price that $p^e = \beta_1$ $Pounds/Kwh$ if it is government electricity supply, while $p^e = \beta_2$ $Pounds/Kwh$ if it is private diesel electricity supply. $T$ denotes the cycle period of Rolling Blackout policy. $t_s$ has separated $T$ to $\Delta t_s$ and $\Delta t_o$ that indicate the period of government and private electricity supply respectively. In this model, $n$ is the natural numbers starting from 1; $t$ indicates the time. Referring to [15], the objective function of EC2T can be expressed as:

$$minimise\ F(s) = \big(f_1(s), f_2(s), f_3(s)\big)\ s \in S$$

$$f_1(s) = \sum_{i=1}^{n} w_i \times T_i(s);\ f_2(s) = \sum_{k=1}^{m} TEM_k^{np};\ f_3(s) = TEC(s) \qquad (10)$$

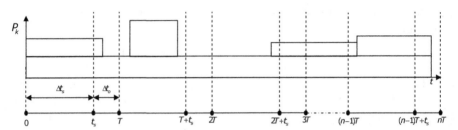

**Fig. 3.** The timeline for TOU tariff and the power input profile of machine tool

## 3.4    Case Study

Parameters of the 3*3 job shop [16] is given in Table 1, numbers in the brackets are the values of $p_{ik}^l$ . The values for the parameters are assumed, based on experiments of [17] in Table 2. Fig. 4 shows a comparison between two feasible schedules. The reasonable Turn Off/On plans for each of them are developed. The values of the three objectives of the two plans are shown in Table 3.

**Table 1.** The 3*3 job shop

| $O_{ik}^l$  $J_i$ | $O_{ik}^1$ | $O_{ik}^2$ | $O_{ik}^3$ | Release time | Due date |
|---|---|---|---|---|---|
| $J_1$ | $M_1(2)$ | $M_2(2)$ | $M_3(3)$ | 0 | The 10$^{th}$ time unit |
| $J_2$ | $M_3(3)$ | $M_2(1)$ | $M_1(4)$ | 0 | The 10$^{th}$ time unit |
| $J_3$ | $M_2(1)$ | $M_1(3)$ | $M_3(2)$ | 0 | The 10$^{th}$ time unit |

**Table 2.** Values for other parameters

| | |
|---|---|
| $P_{ik}^l = 1\ (power\ unit)$ | $P_k^{idle} = 0.3\ (power\ unit)$ |
| $E_k^{turn} = 0.2\ (energy\ unit)$ | $t_k^{OFF} = 1.5\ (time\ unit)$ |
| $p^e = \begin{cases} 1\ (money\ unit), & t \in [0, t_s] \\ 1.5\ (money\ unit), & t \in (t_s, T] \end{cases}$ | $w_i = 1$ <br> $t_s = 6\ (time\ units)$ <br> $T = 12\ (time\ units)$ |
| $i \in \{1,2,3\}; k \in \{1,2,3\}; l \in \{1,2,3\}$ | |

**Table 3.** Values of three objectives for two scheduling plans

| $f(s)$ s | Total weighted tardiness | Total non-processing electricity consumption | Total electricity cost |
|---|---|---|---|
| $s_1$ | 0 | 0.5 energy unit | 32.35 money units |
| $s_2$ | 1 | 0.4 energy unit | 32.90 money units |

$s_1$ outperforms on minimising total tardiness, while $s_2$ outperforms on minimising total non-processing electricity consumption. However, when applying the Rolling Blackout policy, the comparison between the two schedules on minimising total electricity cost demonstrates that scheduling plan ($s_2$) that reduces electricity consumption does not necessarily reduce electricity cost. This simple case could demonstrate the feasibility of the aforementioned model. The complexity of the problem will increase along with the increasing numbers of jobs and machines, various energy characteristic of machine tools and the application of different electricity control policies and tariffs.

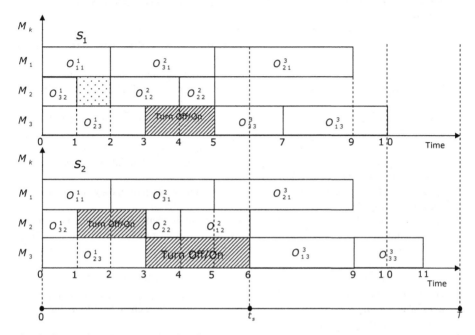

**Fig. 4.** Comparison between two feasible schedules on total electricity consumption and total tardiness

## 4    Conclusion and Future Work

Reducing electricity consumption and its related cost as well as keeping good performance in classical job shop scheduling objectives is a difficult problem that can take a large amount of time if optimally solved. The model for EC2T had been developed in this paper. A case study had been presented to show how scheduling plans affect the objectives of total tardiness, total non-processing electricity consumption and total electricity cost. Obviously, the differences in electricity consumption and its related cost among different scheduling plans will increase along with the increasing units in each job. This provides new insight for managers that optimisation in scheduling is not only a factory performance improvement approach, but also a route that leads to sustainability. In future work, more complicated job shop instance will be studied based on the aforementioned model. The Non-dominated Sorting Genetic Algorithm (NSGA-II) had been selected as the problem solving approach. For more information refer to [18]. In addition, various situations about job arrival patterns will also be taken into consideration in the future work.

# References

1. Tang, D., Li, L., Du, K.: On the Developmental Path of Chinese Manufac-turing Industry Based on Resource Restraint. Jiangsu Social Sciences 4, 51–58 (2006)
2. Mouzon, G., Yildirim, M.B.: A framework to minimize total energy con-sumption and total tardiness on a single machine. In: Proceedings of 4th Annual GRASP Symposium, vol. 1(2), pp. 105–116 (2008)
3. Dahmus, J.B., Gutowski, T.G.: An environmental analysis of machining. In: Proceedings of ASME International Mechanical Engineering Congress and RD&D Expo 2004, pp. 1–10 (2004)
4. Munoz, A.A., Sheng, P.: An analytical approach for determining the envi-ronmental impact of machining processes. Journal of Materials Processing Technology 53, 736–758 (1995)
5. Kordonowy, D.: A power assessment of machining tools. Massachusetts Institue of Technology (2003)
6. Mouzon, G., Yildirim, M.B., Twomey, J.: Operational methods for mini-mization of energy consumption of manufacturing equipment. Interna-tional Journal of Production Research 45(18-19), 4247–4271 (2007)
7. Mouzon, G.: Operational methods and models for minimization of energy consumption in a manufacturing environment. Wichita State University (2008)
8. He, Y., Liu, B., Zhang, X., Gao, H., Liu, X.: A modeling method of task-oriented energy consumption for machining manufacturing system. Journal of Cleaner Production 23(1), 167–174 (2012)
9. Herrmann, C., Thiede, S.: Process chain simulation to foster energy effi-ciency in manufacturing. CIRP Journal of Manufacturing Science and Technology 1, 221–229 (2009)
10. Özgüven, C., Özbakır, L., Yavuz, Y.: Mathematical models for job-shop scheduling problems with routing and process plan flexibility. Applied Mathematical Modelling 34(6), 1539–1548 (2010)
11. Antonio, J., Petrovic, V.S.: A new dispatching rule based genetic algorithm for the multi-objective job shop problem. Journal of Heuristics, 771–793 (2010)
12. Dietmair, A., Verl, A.: Energy Consumption Forecasting and Optimisation for Tool Machines. Energy, 63–67 (2009)
13. Diaz, N., et al.: Machine Tool Design and Operation Strategies for Green Manufacturing. In: Proceedings of 4th CIRP Internatinal Conference on High Performance Cutting, pp. 1–6 (2010)
14. Avram, I.O.: Machine Tool Use Phase: Modeling and Analysis with Environmental Considerations," ÉCOLE POLYTECHNIQUE FÉDÉRALE DE LAUSANNE (2010)
15. Vázquez-Rodríguez, J.A., Petrovic, S.: A new dispatching rule based genetic algorithm for the multi-objective job shop problem. Journal of Heuristics 16(6), 771–793 (2009)
16. Liu, M., Wu, C.: Intelligent Optimization Scheduling Algorithms for Manufacturing Process and Their Applications, p. 334. National Defense Industry Press (2008)
17. Lv, J.X., Tang, R.Z., Jia, S.: Research on energy consumption modeling of CNC machine tool for non-cutting operations, no. 51175464 (2012)
18. Deb, K., Pratap, A., Agarwal, S., Meyarivan, T.: A Fast and Elitist Multiobjective Genetic Algorithm: NSGA-II 6(2), 182–197 (2002)

# Requirements Analysis and Definition for Eco-factories: The Case of EMC2

Marco Taisch and Bojan Stahl

Politecnico di Milano, Department of Management,
Economics and Industrial Engineering, Milan, Italy
{marco.taisch,bojan.stahl}@polimi.it

**Abstract.** Climate change mitigation and the EU2020 strategy foster energy efficiency in Europe's future manufacturing landscape. These challenges make high demands to SMEs as well to MNCs. The paper gives insight to an approach on Eco-factories based on the EU-funded FP7 project EMC2. Eco-factories will enable the quantum leap in integrating environmental issues in brownfield and greenfield factory planning and factory operation. The paper focuses on the identification, structuring and definition of requirements for Eco-factory simulation approaches. Requirements for developing a simulation environment for integrating energy and material flows for detailed analysis but also wide user spectrum is presented. The paper shows that demands are twofold requesting integrated, modular and detailed simulation solutions as well as emphasize on user-friendliness and low complexity.

**Keywords:** eco-factory, energy efficiency, sustainable manufacturing, simulation requirements, energy flow.

## 1    Introduction

Climate change mitigation and security of supply are the major drivers for raising, keeping and enhancing the attention towards energy consumption on European level, addressing policy-makers, industry and society in the same way [1]. Energy consumption implies severe ecological consequences such as global warming and resource depletion on the one hand, and being dependent of supply from non-European countries may lead to potential economic and social risks.

Industry is facing a strong economic pressure which might endanger the global competiveness. Energy and raw material prices are steadily increasing in the last years, and the public awareness for green products is steadily rising with more enlightened customers. Consequently, awareness towards energy efficiency is strongly addressed by European policy-makers [2]. The European 2020 strategy defined several eco-targets to be reached by 2020, i.e. the reduction of emissions by 20%, and the reduction in primary energy of 20% to be achieved by improving energy efficiency, while securing the competitiveness of European companies at the same time.

C. Emmanouilidis, M. Taisch, D. Kiritsis (Eds.): APMS 2012, Part I, IFIP AICT 397, pp. 111–118, 2013.

Production processes are the backbone of the industry in Europe regarding economic success but also regarding environmental and social impact. Resources and energy are the major inputs for the transformation processes to create value. However, creating value by the input of resources and energy leads also wastes in terms of losses, heat, and emissions.

Together with households, commercial and transportation in the domain of energy consumption, manufacturing is considered as a main contributor, with being responsible for approximately 37% of primary energy consumption on global scale. At European level, industry is responsible for about 40% of the electricity consumption [3]. Future manufacturing paradigm should therefore be built on two pillars: avoiding material and energy waste through increased efficient production and avoiding energy and material consumption with harmful impact on the environment.

Diverse studies have been carried out to highlight the improvement potential within industry. The international Energy Agency has stated in their Energy Efficiency Policy Recommendation that potential savings sum up to 18.9 EJ/year and 1.6Gt CO2/year by 2030 [4]. A German-lead consortium of the Fraunhofer Gesellschaft highlights the major potential of increased production process efficiency to optimize the environmental as well as economic performance of companies [5]. A consultation group operating on European level has identified saving potentials of 10-40% in manufacturing in their "Smart Manufacturing" report [6]. A similar study carried out on country level in Germany has likewise identified a saving potential of 10-30% on energy consumption [7].

Production system simulation incorporating environmental perspectives is seen as one appropriate tool in the design and optimization of manufacturing systems towards energy efficiency. The paper presents an approach for defining requirements on such simulation approaches by applying a requirements engineering approach. The aim is to gain a detailed insight into what developers, stakeholders and users see as main features to be implemented in order to support the successful application in industry and research.

## 2    Methodology

A requirement can be defined as a need that a specific product shows by attributes, characteristics or specific qualities that the end product should possess [8]. According to [9], requirements engineering regards establishing and documenting software requirements. Through this process it is possible defining what the system should be able to do and the constraints in which it needs to operate. This process consists of four major steps: elicitation, analysis, specification, verification and management. The requirements management is represented by the planning and controlling of the other steps of the requirements engineering phase.

In the elicitation phase the problem to be solved is defined through the identification of the boundaries and the stakeholders' and goals' definition. It is the first step of the requirements engineering. The information gathered in this phase need to be interpreted, analysed and validated [10]. Different techniques exist to perform the elicitation phase, e.g. interviews, scenarios creation, prototypes, meetings and observation.

The second phase, analysis, potential conflict by different requirements sources could imply need to be solved. Consequently this step deals with the requirements' conflicts detection and resolution. The conflict resolution is lead by negotiation. Furthermore, this is the phase in which the system bounds are discovered together with the interactions with the environment [8].

In the documentation phase the requirements identified are specified and formalized. It is important that the requirements can be traced in order to be easy to read, understood and navigated [10]. The output of this process is a requirements document.

Finally, in the validation the requirements are checked in order to find out further omissions and conflicts. In this phase it is checked if the requirements document created is consistent and complete and requirements priorities are attributed. This is the step into which the quality of the model developed is validated [8].

In order to be complete, the process of requirements engineering should consider all the important sources of requirements from which the requirements are gained. These sources can be in conflict among them and part of the requirements engineering is, for this reason, represented by negotiation and prioritization activities. Each step is described in detail in the subsequent sections.

## 3    Elicitation

In this step of the simulation requirements engineering, the requirements are collected from different sources and different stakeholders. It is the first phase of the requirements engineering and it helps the developers of the product in understanding the problem. The stakeholders from which the requirements are developed may belong to different categories. They can be end-users, customers, regulators, developers, neighbouring systems and domain experts. In this case the requirements have been collected from three sources. The first one is represented by a classical literature review of papers dealing with simulation of energy in manufacturing, in order to take into account from them the general simulation requirements to be used in the model development. The second type of source is represented by the opinions of experts, stakeholders and users, represented by the partners and consortium of the EMC2-Factory project. The last source is represented by the developers themselves by having a visionary idea of building a holistic simulation model for combining energy and material flow simulation.

Different works available in the literature have been reviewed according to their postulations of requirements for "integrating energy, material and building simulation which resulted in total in 52 requirements [12]-[31]. 42 requirements have been identified by the partners and consortium members. For this reason questionnaires were provided to the stakeholders in order to capture their opinion. The developers themselves provided 17 more requirements.

Summarized, 111 requirements have been identified in total from the literature review, the stakeholder consultation and the internal development team. The requirements present overlaps and conflicts which need to be managed in order to avoid repetitions and contradictions for the final requirements which is done in the next step.

# 4     Analysis

In the second step of the requirements methodology applied, two main activities are performed: the requirements classification and the requirements negotiation. In the classification of the requirements, they are divided into distinguishable categories while in the negotiation the resolution of the conflicts has been conducted.

The following paragraph identifies the categories in which the requirements are classified and divided. The simulation requirements were divided in four categories: general, functional, non-functional and implementation requirements. General requirements are high level conceptual requirements. Implementation requirements focus on the system-side conceptualization of the simulator. Functional requirements define what the simulator should be able to perform. Non-functional requirements describe characteristics linked to the way in which the simulator performs its functions.

According to the mentioned categories, the requirements listed in the requirements elicitation step have been divided and categorised, each one in one of the above mentioned categories. Hence, the requirements with the same or similar meaning and scope have been joined together and the ones in conflicts have been resolved. Starting from the 111 requirements identified in the elicitation phase it has been possible to group and merge them according to the scope and the meaning they presented and to arrive until 33 final requirements. The meaning and the scope of each requirement has been identified by checking how each requirement fit with the simulation purpose. The set of requirements obtained at the end of the analysis process are listed and explained in the documentation phase in which all the requirements identified are explained and classified.

# 5     Documentation and Validation

Documenting the requirements is the fundamental condition to the requirements handling. In this phase the structure of the requirements document is developed. The two tables below provide a short excerpt of the documentation of the requirements defined in the analysis step.

The last phase of the requirements engineering is represented by the validation. This steps deals with the analysis of the document produce in the documentation phase in order to be sure that it represents the right requirements in the most complete way. In this phase the focus is on looking for mistakes, errors or lack of clarity. According to [11], the requirements validation needs to be performed in order to be sure that the requirements are: unambiguous, allowing only a single interpretation; concise; finite; measurable; feasible to be implemented with the available technologies; traceable. This phase has been performed, however results are not explicitly mentioned here.

**Table 1.** Functional Requirements

| Requirements | Description |
|---|---|
| Assessing different kind of KPIs | The KPIs' framework should include the evaluation of production, energy and environmental KPIs both real-time and post-processing in order to allow timely decisions oriented to the reduction of the energy costs and to the decrease of the environmental impact. |
| Considering production assets and technical building services | It means modeling and simulating not only the energy consumption of the production-related assets but also of the non-productive equipments, like the central TBS and the periphery systems, supporting their dimensioning and optimization. |
| Supporting the dynamic connections of elements and interrelations | Representing in the simulation the dynamic connections existing among production assets, periphery systems and central technical building services. |
| Bringing inside the states based energy consumption calculations | It underlines the importance of implementing energy calculations during the simulation running basing them on the energy consumption associated to entities' states; representing the basis for non-productive states energy consumption reduction. |
| Interfacing with production control policies | It means supporting the connection of the simulation with production control policies at machines' coordination level, oriented toward the energy consumption reduction and able to influence the equipments' states. |
| Preventing energy peaks | It underlines the important of intervening real time on the manufacturing through control policies when the energy consumption shows rapidly increases. |
| Including multi-product perspective | Including product type control policies and supporting the different product type's identification during the simulation. |
| Supporting green oriented perspectives | Enabling green oriented decisions in terms of scheduling, production configurations. |
| Allowing different levels of energy consumption calculations | It underlines the importance for the simulation model to calculate energy consumptions starting from the machine level and arriving till the factory one. |
| Considering different energy carriers and supply systems | It stresses the high contribution to the holistic perspective given by the consideration of different energy carriers and different periphery systems. |

**Table 2.** Non-functional requirements

| Requirements | Description |
|---|---|
| Creating a simple and controllable solution | It underlines the need of a manageable solution, easy to be controlled and customized. |
| Integrated solutions | It means integrating different tools together in order to develop an interoperable simulation approach. |
| Activating Plug-ins functions | It sets the need to have functions which can be activated through plug-ins. |
| Using graphical interface | The functionalities of the simulation model are shown in a graphical interface. |
| Optimizing ease of use | The requirement stresses the relevance of having a tool easy to be used. |
| Increasing speed | It refers to the required increase of speed in the simulation running. |
| Increasing the user-friendliness | High user friendliness makes the model easier to be used and more attractive. |
| Supporting step-by-step guiding procedures | It underlines the importance for the model to be equipped with exhaustive descriptions. |
| Including stochastic inputs and unpredictable events | The model should allow the possibility to insert input data which are not deterministic. |
| Increasing the level of data detail | The model should support the highest possible level of data detail. |

## 6    Summary and Outlook

The definition of functional requirements for simulation of eco-factories is a first step to guide the way from traditional factory design and operations to eco-enabled competitive factories. The functional requirements build the backbone of the definition of a holistic reference model for eco-factories which serves on the one hand as a meta-model for future activities in the project itself and on the other hand as an enabler for a comprehensive guide or toolkit to support industrial implementation by hands on suggestions. The functional requirements need to be implemented into a discrete event simulator.

This paper presented the requirement engineering process as an initial step before the development of a discrete event simulation environment which combines energy and material flow simulation. Analyzing the requirements leads to the following conclusions. There is an increasing demand in adapting simulation applications to a larger user group, hence giving support by pre-defined objects and decreasing the modelling complexity. It is demanded to increase user-friendliness and keep solutions easy and simple. On the other side the integration of different tools and increase of level of detail of data are requirements which may result in a stress-field in accomplishment. The functional requirements are widely focused on the increase of detail concerning energy considerations and widening the scope of traditional production asset simulations taking into account periphery systems and central technical building services.

Finally it can be summarized that literature and stakeholders see an increasing interest in making energy simulations in manufacturing more comprehensive, detailed, but also simple. The requirement engineering process served as an initial step of a simulation environment development approach. The next major phase includes the conceptual design of a simulation environment which combines material flow and energy flow in production systems taking into account production assets as well as technical building service and being applicable on different scales in the factory.

**Acknowledgements.** The introduced requirements and results were developed within the research project EMC2 (Eco Manufactured transportation means from Clean and Competitive Factory) funded by the European Commission within FP7 (285363).

# References

1. Eurostat. Measuring progress towards a more sustainable Europe. European Commission, http://epp.eurostat.ec.europa.eu/cache/ITY_OFFPUB/KS-77-07-115/EN/KS-77-07-115-EN.PDF
2. European Commission: EUROPE 2020 A strategy for smart, sustainable and inclusive growth (2010)
3. European Environmental Agency, http://www.eea.europa.eu/
4. International Energy Agency: Energy Efficiency Policy Recommendations Worldwide Implementation (2008)
5. Fraunhofer Gesellschaft: Energieeffizienz in der Produktion - Untersuchung zum Handlungs- und Forschungsbedarf (2008)
6. ICT and Energy Efficiency - Consultation Group on Smart Manufacturing: Report: Energy Efficiency in Manufacturing - The Role of ICT (2008)
7. Seefeldt, F., Wünsch, M.: Potenziale für Energieeinsparung und Energieeffizienz im Lichte aktueller Preisentwicklungen, Prognos AG (2007)
8. Sawyer, P., Kotonya, G.: Software Requirements. SWEBOK (2001)
9. Thayer, R., Dorfman, M.: Software Requirements Engineering, 2nd edn. IEEE Computer Society Press, Los Alamitos (1997)
10. Nuseibeh, B., Easterbrook, S.: Requirements Engineering: A Roadmap. In: ICSE 2000 Proceedings of the Conference on the Future of Software Engineering, pp. 35–46 (2000)
11. Westfall, L.: Software Requirements Engineering: What, Why, Who, When, and How (2006)
12. Thiede, S.: Energy Efficiency in Manufacturing Systems. Springer, Berlin (2012)
13. Heilala, J., et al.: Simulation-based sustainable manufacturing system design. In: Winter Simulation Conference, pp. 1922–1930 (2008)
14. Seow, Y., Rahimifard, S.: A framework for modelling energy consumption within manufacturing systems. CIRP Journal of Manufacturing Science and Technology 4(3), 258–264 (2011)
15. Rahimifard, S., Seow, Y., Childs, T.: Minimising Embodied Product Energy to support energy efficient manufacturing. CIRP Annals - Manufacturing Technology 59(1), 25–28 (2010)

16. Solding, P., Petku, D.: Applying Energy Aspects on Simulation of Energy-Intensive Production Systems. In: Proceedings of the 2005 Winter Simulation Conference, pp. 1428–1432 (2005)
17. Solding, P., Thollander, P.: Increased energy efficiency in a swedish iron foundry through use of discrete event simulation. In: Proceedings of the 2006 Winter Simulation Conference, pp. 1971–1976 (2006)
18. Solding, P., Petku, D., Mardan, N.: Using simulation for more sustainable production systems – methodologies and case studies. International Journal of Sustainable Engineering 2(2), 111–122 (2009)
19. Weinert, N., Chiotellis, S., Seliger, G.: Methodology for planning and operating energy-efficient production systems. CIRP Annals - Manufacturing Technology 60, 41–44 (2011)
20. Hesselbach, J., et al.: Energy Efficiency through optimized coordination of production and technical building services. In: LCE 2008 - 15th CIRP International Conference on Life Cycle Engineering, Sydney, pp. 17–19 (2008)
21. Löfgren, B., Tillman, A.-M.: Relating manufacturing system configuration to life-cycle environmental performance: discrete-event simulation supplemented with LCA. Journal of Cleaner Production 19(17-18), 2015–2024 (2011)
22. Johansson, B., et al.: Discrete event simulation to generate requirements specification for sustainable manufacturing systems design. In: Proceedings of the 9th Workshop on Performance Metrics for Intelligent Systems - PerMIS 2009, pp. 38–42. ACM Press, New York (2009)
23. Dietmair, A., Verl, A.: A generic energy consumption model for decision making and energy efficiency optimisation in manufacturing. International Journal of Sustainable Engineering 2(2), 123–133 (2009)
24. Dietmair, A., Verl, A., Eberspaecher, P.: Predictive Simulation for Model Based Energy Consumption Optimisation in Manufacturing System and Machine Control. In: Flexible Automation and Intelligent Manufacturing (FAIM), pp. 226–233 (2009)
25. Wohlgemuth, V., Page, B., Kreutzer, W.: Combining Discrete Event Simulation and Material Flow Analysis based on a Component-Oriented Approach to Industrial Environmental Protection. Environmental Modeling and Software 21, 1607–1617 (2006)
26. Cannata, A.: A Methodology to enhance Energy Efficiency at Factory Level: Improvements for sustainable Manufacturing. Dissertation, Politecnico di Milano (2011)
27. Cannata, A., Karnouskos, S., Taisch, M.: Energy efficiency driven process analysis and optimization in discrete manufacturing. In: 2009 35th Annual Conference of IEEE Industrial Electronics (2009)
28. Cannata, A., Taisch, M.: Introducing Energy Performances in Production Management: Towards Energy Efficient Manufacturing. In: Vallespir, B., Alix, T. (eds.) APMS 2010. IFIP AICT, vol. 338, pp. 168–175. Springer, Heidelberg (2010)
29. Shao, G., Bengtsson, N., Johansson, B.: Interoperability for Simulation of Sustainable Manufacturing. In: Proceedings of the 2010 Spring Simulation Multi-Conference (SpringSim 2010), pp. 1–8 (2010)
30. Shao, G., Kibira, D., Lyons, K.: A virtual Machining Model for Sustainability Analysis. In: Proceedings of the ASME 2010 International Design Engineering Technical Conference & Computers and Information in Engineering Conference, pp. 1–9 (2010)
31. Prabhu, V.V., Cannata, A., Taisch, M.: Simulation Modeling of Energy Dynamics in Discrete Manufacturing Systems. In: Borangiu, T., et al. (eds.) 14th IFAC Symposium on Information Control Problems in Manufacturing (INCOM), Bucharest (2012)
32. Prabhu, V.V., Jeon, H.W., Taisch, M.: Modeling Green Factory Physics – An Analytical Approach. In: 2012 IEEE International Conference on Automation Science and Engineering (CASE), pp. 46–51 (2012)

# Energy Efficient Process Planning System – The ENEPLAN Project

Paolo Calefati[1], John Pandremenos[2], Apostolos Fysikopoulos[2],
and George Chryssolouris[2,*]

[1] PRIMA INDUSTRIE S.p.A., Via Antonelli 32, 10097 Collegno (TO), Italy
paolo.calefati@primapower.com
[2] Laboratory for Manufacturing Systems and Automation,
University of Patras, Rio, Patras 26500, Greece
{jpandrem,afysiko,xrisol}@lms.mech.upatras.gr

**Abstract.** The key factor to success, towards a competitive energy consumption reduction, is the effective involvement of SMEs both in the use of more efficient machines and in the Design of an Environment for new products. A specific product can be manufactured in different ways, based on cost optimization rather than on production flexibility and energy efficiency with the involvement of different suppliers. The ENEPLAN project aims at the development of a digital and real, energy-efficient, multi-process, networked, manufacturing system, adapted to the functional specifications of metal formed or machined parts for automotive, aeronautic and domestic appliances. Seventeen partners, coming from seven European countries and the participation of OEMs, SMEs, RTD and technology providers, who work jointly to deliver through ENEPLAN a manufacturing planning decision support tool (meta-CAM tool), for the optimization of the plant operation. This tool will be used from the conceptual phase of the product (final blueprints) to its final dispatch to the customer. This paper will provide a short overview of the ENEPLAN project and its ongoing developments, while the existing results will be presented and discussed and the next steps will be described.

**Keywords:** Energy efficiency, process planning, Meta-CAM tool, process optimization.

## 1    Introduction

Today's manufacturing plants provide a number of different processing possibilities for the manufacturing of a specific product. Each one of these processing possibilities poses different advantages and limitations that are functions of both the geometry and the lot size of the part to be manufactured. However, one of the main driving forces in today's production, as shown below, is the environmental friendliness and the energy efficiency of the production itself. Additionally, the manufacturing processes are required for quickly enabling the shifting between diverse manufacturing operations with short transfer, program and set-up times without compromises to quality, reliability and life-cycle costs.

---

* Corresponding author.

C. Emmanouilidis, M. Taisch, D. Kiritsis (Eds.): APMS 2012, Part I, IFIP AICT 397, pp. 119–126, 2013.

The machine tools sector is one of the most relevant in Europe in terms of GDP (180 billion € of new orders before the crisis, 74 billion €/y in Q2 2010) [1], the sector mainly comprises SMEs (among machine users: 99.7% by number, 78.2% by GDP, 82.8 by persons employed among machine manufacturers: 98.7% by number, 49.7 by GDP, 56.5 by persons employed) [2]. In the same way the relevance of the sector in terms of energy consumption is high (>10,000 PJ/y) [3] and consequently, the financial pressure is high due to the unbalanced demand/offer of energy, which results in increasing the energy price (as in 2007-2008). Additionally, the recent developments in manufacturing production technologies brought about machines and processes of higher performance and higher energy utilization, in order for the productivity and reliability of the process to be increased. Besides, the growing environmental awareness of people worldwide has led to legislative pressure (EuP Directive) [4] and it is highly probable that tool machines will be subjected to energy efficiency regulations and classification in the years to come [5]. The potential of energy savings in the machine tool sector is high (e.g. low power factor of 0.7-0.8), as the potential efficiency increases by exploiting the Design for Environment strategies (e.g. reduction of mass, materials used, extension of tool lifetime, optimised PWB, CPU, monitor) [3]. Recent studies have shown that there is heavy unnecessary energy use in the industrial sector; typical figures for machining equipment are in the range of 20%-50%.

Today's European market has to deal, more than ever before, with highly demanding customers. In order for these advanced needs to be addressed, a large number of alternative products are being produced from the same production line within the industry. Additionally, the products are characterized by a short lifecycle since they are quickly depreciated. Thus, flexible manufacturing processes should enable the immediate shifting between diverse manufacturing operations with short transfer, program and set-up times as required, without compromises to quality, reliability and life-cycle costs.

Today's process planning [6] approach is based on expert systems that are able to propose alternative process plans for the manufacturing of a specific product. Additionally, there are tools that can simulate the operation of each machine station both from technological (process parameters, energy efficiency, etc) and economical point of view. All of the systems available though, can cover only portion of the production, requiring the exchange of data between different systems and thus, making the overall optimization of the plant operation a hard task.

ENEPLAN Project [7], as an NMP (Nanotechnology and nanosciences, knowledge-based multifunctional materials and new production processes and devices), is the Third Thematic Priority of the Focusing and Integrating research part of the Sixth Framework Programme aiming at Industrial research - which remains a key objective of FP6 in an evolutionary world. ENEPLAN is co-ordinated by the PRIMA INDUSTRIE Group and is initiated and managed by the Laboratory for Manufacturing Systems and Automation of the University of Patras. This project aims at delivering a manufacturing planning decision support tool for the optimization of the plant operation that will be able to be used from the conceptual phase of the product up to its final dispatch to the customer. The ENEPLAN consortium consists of 17 partners:

- two top-level OEMs from two different industrial sectors (CRF and GORENJE)
- one aeronautics sector supplier (NEW)
- four metal forming machine builders (PRIMA, FINNPOWER, GIZELIS and GIGANT)
- three users of those machines and suppliers of metal formed components to the above mentioned OEMS (TEKS, IAM and EXALCO)
- four high-ranked European university Labs (LMS, VTT, ITIA-CNR and AMRC)
- three "knowledge intensive" companies as RTD providers (CADCAMATION, CASP and IDEKO).

## 2 ENEPLAN's View Beyond the State of the Art

ENEPLAN aims at minimizing the inactivity time and waste streams, parameters that cover more than 30% percent of the energy used by machine tools. By using LCA methods and taking into consideration the consumption of natural resources, the waste streams will be accurately estimated and their environmental impact is to become clear. Furthermore, reliable and flexible process monitoring and controlling systems, for both conventional and non-conventional production technologies, will be developed. Finally, the introduction of novel simulation systems will result in reducing the required pre-production setup experimentation effort and subsequently increase the energy efficiency of the processes and the relevant machine tools.

The problem of energy management is solved by Load Management Systems; when a peak occurs, usually the system reactively reduces the power, instead of suggesting a better production planning [8-10]. Within ENEPLAN, a set of developments such as the identification of product's unique signature (CAD model, engineering requirements etc.), the monitoring systems and the multi-objective simulation techniques, will be all embedded into a Meta-CAM tool in order to be utilized for the optimization of the production planning, in terms of energy efficiency and other defined aspects. The existing systems are not capable of addressing the simultaneous consideration of many parameters, during optimization.

Since simulation engineering has since long been believed to be an enabling technology for life-cycle decision support [11-13], ENEPLAN will introduce a breakthrough to the current problem of optimization and decision making with simulation. Novel multi-objective simulation techniques will be introduced, with integrated techno-economical parameters and the assessment of different automation options will be applied to the evaluation of the process plans and the optimization of the production planning. In order for the process plan to be accurately evaluated, special attention will be paid towards the precise estimation of demand and production requirements throughout the product's life cycle. By utilizing analytical and numerical models on macro and micro/nano-scales, new reliable, production oriented process models, based on process parameters and particular process conditions, will be developed. Furthermore, models, either analytical and computational, or empirical, will also be developed for the analytical description of conventional and non-conventional processes.

Taking into consideration the state of the art [14-17], the proposed research work will aim at the development of a simple, nonetheless, an effective method that will guide the process engineer in constructing generic process plans adaptable to all possible different scenarios that market needs. Therefore, shortcomings might be revealed in the design of the product and alternative approaches will be assessed for the production of the product (such as use of alternative equipment, resources, or even subcontracting).

During the development of the meta-CAM tool modules, various optimization algorithms and methodologies will be evaluated and compared by their applicability and efficiency. In particular, heuristic methods, specific for energy efficiency optimization, will be used, in conjunction with Pareto-optimal based multi-objective optimization in order for the optimization efficiency to be enhanced. The meta-CAM tool, integrating the output of ENEPLAN RTD efforts, will offer multi-disciplinary and multi-level simulation, optimization and information modeling components. In addition, in order for the integration of them to be supported, a common/open source integration architecture will be used offering extensive compatibility with various production related software.

# 3    The ENEPLAN Project

The current industrial status indicates that the key factor to success, in a competitive energy consumption reduction, is the effective involvement of SMEs both in a more efficient use of more efficient machines and in the Design for Environment of new products. In the ENEPLAN project, the main objective is the development of manufacturing systems that will be highly flexible, and at the same time, are closely adapted to the single product. These manufacturing systems need an engineering tool that can cover the entire plant operation, from the overall planning of the plant operation (such as the routes that the product follow within the plant and the scheduling of the production) down to the individual process programming. Today's process planning approach is based on expert systems capable of proposing alternative process plans for the manufacturing of a specific product. Additionally, there are tools able to simulate the operation of each machine station techno-economically. All of the systems available though, can cover only part of the production, requiring the exchange of data between different systems and thus, rendering the overall optimization of the plant operation a hard task. The ENEPLAN project will deliver a manufacturing planning decision support tool for the optimization of the plant operation to be used from the conceptual phase of the product up to its final dispatch to the customer.

## 3.1    The Concept

A specific product, based on the cost optimization rather than on production flexibility and energy efficiency, can be manufactured in different ways and by

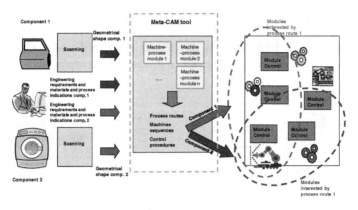

**Fig. 1.** ENEPLAN Concept

different suppliers. ENEPLAN aims at the development of a digital and real, energy-efficient, multi-process, networked, manufacturing system adapted to the functional specifications of metal formed or machined parts for automotive, aeronautic and domestic appliances:

- **digital and real:** a new CAPP-CAM digital platform will be developed with a DSS that would allow choosing among alternative processing cycles, based on the best compromise between energy and cost efficiency.
- **energy-efficient:** a new optimization strategy will be implemented on the digital platform to minimize lifecycle energy consumption of the selected process. In this optimization materials, process technologies and machine cycles will be taken into account. Furthermore, all the end-users involved will evaluate the substitution of the existing machines with more efficient ones of the next generation.
- **multi-process:** on the digital platform, alternative processes will be considered for the same product emphasizing a breakthrough potential for energy reduction through the introduction of  new technologies in the process (e.g. cutting and forming as alternative to machining).
- **networked:** optimization focus will be given to the manufacturing processes involving both multiple steps and companies along the supply chain, as well as SMEs. The involvement of SMEs is one of the pillars of ENEPLAN and, as a matter of fact, the SMEs partners in ENEPLAN account for more than 40% in number and 25% in budget.

The ENEPLAN's Meta CAM tool functions will perform the following:

- Process CAD data inserted either from a mathematical model or from shape acquisition of physical models through scanning
- Accept engineering requirements and material from a human operator
- On-line (or short-time) configuration of the manufacturing system
- Simulation of an overall manufacturing system, optimization and tuning for top production efficiency and minimum environmental impact
- Determine material selection, work sequences, cycles and process routes

## 3.2    The Main ENEPLAN Objectives and Targets

The main objective of ENEPLAN is the development of the Meta-CAM tool for optimum process planning from a given set of production requirements.

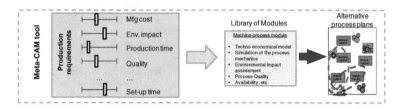

**Fig. 2.** The Meta-CAM tool

This system and its related technologies will enable the:

- Environmental footprint reduction for a metal formed component by selecting a more energy efficient combination of processes among those available in the already existing supply chain
  - Target: -40% of the lifecycle energy consumption (from cradle to grave), estimated 8 MJ per component, 14.4 GJ per production life.
- Energy efficiency improvement in working conditions
  - Target: estimated energy consumption -30%, 2 MJ per component, 3.6 GJ per production life.
- Multi-process, multi-company distributed control
  - Target: use of the same control along the supply chain, possibility to use the system that would adapt the work sequences, the process routes and machines' behavior to the most efficient working conditions.

# 4    ENEPLAN Business Cases

Besides these technical breakthroughs, additional "non-technical" ones will be triggered that will enable a vertical integration in the value chain and a horizontal integration by the ability to transfer the knowledge to other industrial sectors. ENEPLAN will promote breakthroughs on scientific and technical excellence, moving three at least industrial sectors (automotive, aeronautics and domestic appliances) and their involved partners in the vertical value chain, towards a multi-objective optimized production, by combining excellent research capacities of EU OEMs, SMEs, academic partners and technology providers.

The automotive business case will investigate a seat frame. The current automotive seat frame is manufactured by shaping different steel metal sheets or tubes. The Meta-CAM tool will facilitate the evaluation of different technological scenarios and materials, most suitable for a targeted volume production by taking into account a weight and energy manufacturing process reduction. The results will provide an

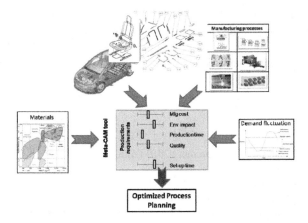

**Fig. 3.** Application of ENEPLAN's approach to the automotive pilot case

optimization of the final production cost and energy and raw material consumption within the target of a specific production rate at the same original product mechanical performance. Alternatives, in terms of forming technologies and the selection of different raw materials, will be evaluated. Optimization of the process by the elimination of steps, due to a reduction in the parts, may be integrated.

The Aeronautics Business case will use as pilot case the Lading Ramp Hinge of a military aircraft. The target with the use of the ENEPLAN's Meta-CAM tool is the energy consumption reduction and the factory's carbon footprint improvement. Moreover, establishing whether other processes are preferable to milling (main processes currently used), for the machining of the produced part and propose alternate process routes.

The household business will use as a pilot case six versions of the front panels of refrigerator doors. These parts contain high quality demands (Visible surfaces without aesthetics faults and all dimensions in tolerances). Currently, the existing process plan requires a lot of transportation between the different stations that increase the energy consumption. The LCA algorithms that will be included in the Meta-CAM tool will aid in finding alternatives and reducing the environmental footprint in the current factory.

## 5    Conclusions

The ENEPLAN project having as its primary objective to help the industry save energy, time and become more flexible, has come up with the development of the ENEPLAN Meta-CAM tool that has already set the specifications of the problem, selected and defined as well as the pilot cases that the Meta-CAM tool will run. The project now is in the phase of modeling and monitoring the business cases processes in order to provide input for the development of the tool. The finalization and validation of the tool is estimated to become true after the April of 2013.

**Acknowledgements.** The work reported in this paper was supported by the collaborative program entitled "Energy Efficient Process planning System – ENEPLAN" which in under the seventh framework program - FoF.NMP.2011-1: "The Eco-Factory: cleaner and more resource-efficient production in manufacturing Program".

# References

1. CECIMO Statistical Toolbox, September 2010 Edition (2010),
   http://www.cecimo.eu
2. EUROSTAT 2012 (Key figures on European business) (2010) ISSN 1830-9720
3. Draft Working Plan of the Ecodesign Directive (2009-2011)
4. Directive of the European Parliament on Energy using Products (2005/32/EC)
5. Dietmair, A., Verl, A.: Energy consumption forecasting and optimization for tool machines. In: Institute for Control Engineering of Machine Tools and Manufacturing Units (ISW), Universität Stuttgart, http://www.mmscience.eu/archives/MM_Science_20090305.pdf
6. Papakostas, N., Efthymiou, K., Georgoulias, K., Chryssolouris, G.: On the configuration and planning of dynamic manufacturing networks. Logistics Research 5(3-4), 105–111 (2012)
7. ENEPLAN site, http://www.eneplan.eu/
8. Jebaraj, S., Iniyan, S.: A review of energy models. Renewable and Sustainable Energy Reviews 10, 281–311 (2006)
9. Bhatt, M.S.: Energy audit case studies I – steam systems. Applied Thermal Engineering 20, 285–296 (2000)
10. Trygg, L.: Swedish Industrial and Energy Supply Measures in a European System Perspective. PhD Thesis, Division of Energy Systems, Linköping University, Sweden (2006)
11. NSF Blue Ribbon Panel: Simulation Based Engineering Science, NSF Report (2006), http://www.nsf.gov/pubs/reports/sbes_final_report.pdf
12. Fu, M.C., Andradóttir, S., Carson, J.S., Glover, F., Harell, C.R., Ho, Y.-C., Kelly, J.P., Robinson, S.M.: Integrating Optimisation and Simulation: Research and Practice. In: Proceedings of the 2000 Winter Simulation Conference, Arlington, VA, December 9-12. IEEE (2000)
13. Tempelmeier, H.: Practical considerations in the optimization of flow production systems. International Journal of Production Research 41(1), 149–170 (2003)
14. Chryssolouris, G., Chan, S., Cobb, W.: Decision Making on the Factory Floor: An Integrated Approach to Process Planning and Scheduling. Robotics and Computer-Integrated Manufacturing 1(3/4), 315–319 (1984)
15. Chryssolouris, G.: Manufacturing Systems: Theory and Practice, 2nd edn. Springer, New York (2006)
16. Chryssolouris, G., Mavrikios, D., Papakostas, N., Mourtzis, D., Michalos, G., Georgoulias, K.: Digital manufacturing: history, perspectives, and outlook. Proceedings of the I MECH E Part B Journal of Engineering Manufacture 222, 451–462 (2008)
17. Chryssolouris, G., Papakostas, N., Mavrikios, D.: A perspective on manufacturing strategy: Produce more with less. CIRP Journal of Manufacturing Science and Technology 1, 45–52 (2008)

# Energy Efficiency Optimisation in Heat Treatment Process Design

Iñigo Mendikoa[1], Mikel Sorli[1], Alberto Armijo[1], Laura Garcia[1], Luis Erausquin[2], Mario Insunza[3], Jon Bilbao[3], Hakan Friden[4], Anders Björk[4], Linus Bergfors[4], Romualdas Skema[5], Robertas Alzbutas[5], and Tomas Iesmantas[5]

[1] Tecnalia Research&Innovation
{inigo.mendikoa,mikel.sorli,alberto.armijo,
laura.garciazambrano}@tecnalia.com
[2] Fundiciones del Estanda
lerausquin@estanda.com
[3] Sisteplant S.L.
{minsunza,jbilbao}@sisteplant.com
[4] IVL Swedish Environmental Institute Ltd.
{hakan.friden,anders.bjork,linus.bergfors}@ivl.se
[5] Lietuvos Energetikos Institutas
{skema,robertas,iesmantas}@mail.lei.lt

**Abstract.** Information and Communication Technology (ICT) tools to support design in terms of energy efficiency optimisation are beginning to come into the market, in particular for energy savings and management in buildings, however little has yet been developed for manufacturing. The work here described is related to the enhancement of existing manufacturing process design methodology and tools with a set of ICT components developed allowing process knowledge based design, simulation and optimisation in terms of energy efficiency. In particular the work described is focused on the heat treatment process of steel casting parts. This process design traditionally consists of a suitable predefined temperature-time curve selection based on personal experience and given customer requirements (material and mechanical properties), yet this curve can actually be optimised in terms of energy consumption and maintenance cost, while keeping required mechanical properties.

**Keywords:** Energy efficiency, Process design optimisation, Heat treatment.

## 1 Introduction

There are several ICT tools to support process design, addressing especially installation customization to the users' needs. Many of them include simulation of processes, which might be used to implicitly analyse energy use within the design processes. Research and technology development attempts to address sustainability issues in process design have been made and several tools are available on the market intending to support users in consideration of sustainability problems. However, a

C. Emmanouilidis, M. Taisch, D. Kiritsis (Eds.): APMS 2012, Part I, IFIP AICT 397, pp. 127–134, 2013.

systematic analysis of energy use within the designed processes and functionality to explicitly support the designer in making decisions relevant for energy efficiency are not provided in most of the currently available design and simulation tools. The current design tools do not explicitly support decisions regarding selection of methods, equipment and materials to use for meeting specifications and for energy efficiency over the whole process life cycle, especially in flexible manufacturing systems asking often for reconfiguration of installations. ICT tools to support design for energy efficiency optimisation are beginning to come into the market, in particular for energy savings and management in buildings, however little has yet been developed for manufacturing.

The work here described is related to the enhancement of existing manufacturing process design methodology and tools with a set of ICT components developed in the framework of DEMI project (FP7-ICT-2009-247831). In particular the work here described is focused on the heat treatment process of steel casting parts and is related to the company *Fundiciones del Estanda* in Spain, allowing this company to address energy efficiency in this process design.

## 2     Manufacturing Process and Energy Consumption Characteristics

Manufacturing process at this company is related to steel casting parts including sub-processes like melting, machining, grinding, cutting and cleaning and heat treatment. This heat treatment process is powered by gas energy, and considering that over 33% of total gas at the company is consumed here, it is reasonable to focus the energy efficient design on this specific sub-process. The main goal is therefore to reduce the energy consumption on the heat treatment process while at least keeping the productivity and resulting mechanical requirements in the steel parts, as well as maintenance costs acceptable.

The specific thermal process design for each piece begins with the selection of the suitable temperature-time curve for the part to be treated, which is defined based on personal experience of experts in charge of process design. The "process design" basically consists of the definition of the Temperature-Time curve for the heat treatment for each type of part, given customer requirements (material and mechanical properties). Predefined Temperature-time curves are normally used, yet these curves can actually be optimised in terms of energy consumption, however this optimisation is currently not done at the company. The DEMI tool being developed is intended to provide the company with the capability of designing optimal heat treatment processes.

Heat treatment process, described by the $T$-$t$ curve, usually consists of some few steps, which can be simplified as an initial heating, temperature holding time t, and a final cooling, but it might be more complex. The considered case study will focus on a particular steel part: brake discs for the high-speed train treated in the Guinea 4 batch furnace. DEMI system will propose the optimal $T$-$t$ curve, consuming minimum gas providing the mechanical requirements, while maintenance costs must remain acceptable so that the new process is profitable. The software can also optimise the process design in terms of minimal maintenance cost, or even use a multicriteria optimisation strategy considering both weighted energy and maintenance cost.

# 3    Process Optimisation with DEMI Tools

DEMI ICT tool consists of several ICT components, three of which are involved in the work being implemented at the manufacturing company, namely, 'Energy Dependency Selector' (EDS) supporting a knowledge based preliminary process design, 'Energy Analyser' (EA) for process optimisation and the supporting 'Energy Simulator' (ES) for energy consumption estimation in specific process configuration. Fig.1 shows the generic process design procedure based on DEMI tools (in grey). All DEMI components communicate each other via web services and sharing information in a Knowledge Repository (KR). In earlier paper the connection between KR-EA-ES for optimisation of configuration of compressed air systems has been described [1].

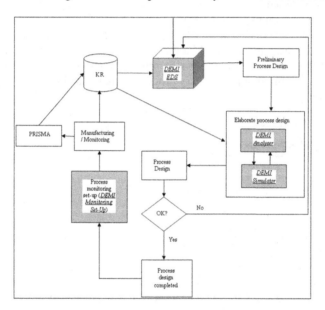

**Fig. 1.** Manufacturing process optimal design with DEMI components

## 3.1    Knowledge Based Preliminary Process Design

Preliminary process design can be quickly defined based on experts' experience, described in terms of rules and successful historic processes. This knowledge based preliminary process design is done with the support of the DEMI component Energy Dependency Selector (EDS), allowing the process designer to quickly figure out the consequences, also in terms of energy consumption, of decisions at process early design stage. EDS component provides a preliminary process design based on two techniques: Case Based Reasoning (CBR) and Rule Based Reasoning (RBR).

**Case Based Reasoning.** This functionality provides historic process designs 'similar' to the target process requirements given by the designer. In this case the requirements are those from the customer, basically material and mechanical properties required.

This functionality requires historic cases database defined and populated including parameters describing the requirements, in addition to those describing the process design. The 'similarity' of historic processes with respect to required parameters values provided by the user is estimated according to the relative weights given for each parameter. The tool finally provides a list of historic processes sorted by similarity. This functionality implementation is based on the *JColibri* tool [2,3] and the process shown in Fig. 2 (left).

**Rule Based Reasoning.** This functionality provides preliminary process design based on experts' experience implemented in terms of 'rules'. The design sequence implemented with the rule based reasoning approach reproduces the way a process designer follows when designing a process: starting from process requirements the tool provides rule based feedback about the basic process design characteristics. This functionality is based on the tool *KnowWE* [4,5], for which several plug-ins have been developed in order to connect it to KR. A basic implementation is shown in Fig. 2 (right), where the user introduces Material and Constraints (mechanical properties required) and the tool provides process parameters intervals based on implemented rules, in this way defining a preliminary process design, matching user requirements, for optimisation.

**Fig. 2.** CBR (left) and RBR (right) implementation for preliminary process design

### 3.2    Process Optimisation

Once a preliminary process design is done with EDS component, Energy Analyser (EA) component provides process optimisation in terms of energy efficiency and/or maintenance cost, keeping required mechanical properties as constraints. EA provides optimal process design, using in turn Energy Simulator (ES) for energy consumption estimation of each potentially optimal design configuration considered.

**Process Optimisation with EA.** DEMI component EA provides the energy optimised process design from the preliminary design provided by EDS, finding minimum energy given ranges on process variables and constraints on requirements variables. Process variables have to be within their given boundaries and constrained by requirements within constraints given by the user. So EA requires information related to the preliminary process definition (provided by EDS) and boundary limits for all the relevant parameters values.

The procedure is basically as follows: EA Client calls EA with the process configuration ID; EA reads configuration ID with info about the nodes from the Knowledge Repository (KR), as well as initial data, boundaries for process variables, and constraints for quality variables from KR; EA starts Matlab, as a server, for process optimisation; For energy process optimisation, EA uses function *fmincon* to find minimum energy given ranges on process variables and constraints on quality variables; EA uses ES as a service to evaluate energy for each iterated process during optimisation, gets energy consumption estimations from ES and is able to predict quality variables (mechanical properties) for each configuration; EA finally sends to KR the process parameters values describing the optimal process design.

**Process Energy Consumption Simulation.** Energy Simulator (ES) estimates the energy consumption of each possible specific process configuration provided by EA component, so that the minimum energy consumption process configuration can be finally selected.

In general, ES is a tool intended for simulation of network system or process, when energy consumption is of interest. ES is constructed as a simulation service able to simulate new/innovative network or system designs and estimate energy use for them. The analytical modelling and simulation is based on "block-based modelling" concept rather than on purely "process-based modelling". It means that whole physical process is decomposed into sub-processes represented by independent blocks (one block for one sub-process). Sub-process is process variable (output of block) related to physical behaviour of other variables (inputs of block) with their weighting coefficients (block parameters). Sub-process may be expressed as a process variable or function dependent on other process variables [6].

ES requires a theoretical model for energy use estimation provided a process configuration. In the case of heat treatment process at *Fundiciones del Estanda* a basic thermodynamic model has been considered. This model expresses fuel (gas) consumption and energy balance (see an example in Fig. 3) of the heat treatment process, taking into consideration the following energy terms: Energy provided by the gas, Energy lost by fumes, Heat stored by parts after treatment, Heat stored by furnace refractory, Heat losses through the furnace walls.

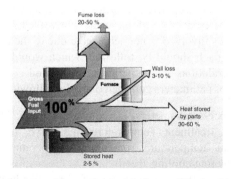

**Fig. 3.** Example of fuel consumption and energy balance of the heat treatment process

This theoretical model is the basis of ES component, also running in Matlab, which receives a given process design from EA. The data needed for this energy consumption estimation are the following, given by the process parameters values describing the process: Material type (specific heat) of the treated parts, Parts load (mass) to be treated, Difference between parts final and initial temperature $(T_{fin}-T_{in})$, Total process time $(t_{fin}-t_{in})=\varSigma t_i$, Configuration of heat treatment process.

Energy balance equation of such a process can be simplified as follows:

$$Q_{gas}P_{CI} = M_F h_F + M_{st}c_{st}\left(T_{fin} - T_{in}\right) + M_{refr}c_{refr}\left(T_{ref-fin} - T_{ref-in}\right) + P_W A_W \left(t_{fin} - t_{in}\right)$$

These terms, considered along the whole process time, have the following meaning:

- Energy provided by the gas, depending on gas consumption (time dependent) and gas calorific power. Total gas consumption is the parameter to be estimated.
- Energy lost by fumes, depending on fumes mass and enthalpy.
- Heat stored by parts after treatment, depending on the parts load, steel specific heat and temperature net increment of the parts.
- Heat stored by furnace refractory, depending on the furnace refractory mass, its specific heat and temperature net increment.
- Heat losses through the furnace walls, depending on energy loss per unit time (time dependent), furnace walls area and process duration.

In order to structure the workflow of power consumption estimation, ES employs four main functionalities: Get configuration (after unique ID from EA is received, ES will connect via web services to the KR and retrieve information about the process configuration), Add blocks (identifies different phases of heat treatment process), Specify connections (creates the heating model from specific phases identified in the previous functionality), Calculate energy use of process configuration (performs estimation of used gas volume together with consumed power).

### 3.3    Mathematical Modeling Approach for Process Optimisation

As described above, in order to optimise the heat treatment process design keeping the resulting steel parts' mechanical properties, some mathematical models have to be ready relating the different sets of parameters involved. If an analytical model considering the physics involved is not achievable due to the problem complexity, an empirical model approach should be followed, which would require a huge historic database allowing correlations among parameters be found.

The different sets of parameters considered are the following:

- Heat treatment process parameters, including: Date/time, Material Load, Type of material and Heat treatment Temperature-time curve, for a simplified process defined by initial temperature, maximum temperature, time at maximum temperature and heating/cooling speed.
- Measured resulting mechanical properties of parts after heat treatment processes, currently stored in quality tests documentation at the company. Mechanical

properties considered are the following: Yield and Ultimate strength, Strain, Resilience and Hardness.

- Maintenance cost parameters of historic processes, currently stored at *Fundiciones del Estanda* by PRISMA software database, provided by the company *Sisteplant* [7]. The main maintenance cost parameters considered are: Mean Time Between Failures (MTBF), Number of breakdowns (per year), Cost of breakdown (average working hours, material, non productive time).

In order to optimise the process design these sets of parameters have to be linked through mathematical models and expressed as objective function. It is important to remark that these models are intended to allow a comparison between different process designs performance, rather than accurate predictions on energy use, maintenance cost or mechanical properties, so that alternative process designs proposed by EA can be simulated by ES, compared by EA and finally an improved process design provided as result part of the optimisation procedure. The relations between sets of parameters and mathematical modelling approach considered are the following:

- Relationship between process design parameters and mechanical properties required. This model is based on experts' considerations about the influence of process parameters over the resulting mechanical properties. In this way a process optimisation can be performed while keeping constraints on mechanical properties. For example, optimal process might have a lower heating speed or maximum temperature, in this way decreasing the energy consumption, while resulting mechanical properties are still kept within specifications.
- Relationship between process design parameters and maintenance cost. According to experts' criteria, the impact of process parameters modifications in maintenance cost can be estimated, and optimisation in terms of maintenance cost performed.
- Relationship between process design parameters and energy consumption. A simplified analytical model has been created, as described in section 3.2, allowing an estimation of energy consumption given a process configuration.

## 4     Conclusions

The set of tools developed and here described allows a manufacturing company dealing with heat treatment to optimise the process in terms of energy efficiency and maintenance costs while keeping the mechanical properties of the treated parts requested by the customer. Tools supporting knowledge based decision making as those described in Energy Dependency Selector component allow the company to keep and reuse the experts' knowledge and experience for a quick preliminary process design, while Energy Analyser and Energy Simulator components support the process design optimisation. All these components can work in a distributed way with a common Knowledge Repository, based on web services.

On the other hand, this set of tools can be adapted to other manufacturing processes where correlations between process parameters and resulting quality parameters can be established, as well as a model for energy consumption estimation, so the approach and tools here presented are portable to other manufacturing processes and therefore to other manufacturing companies.

**Acknowledgements.** The work here described is being developed in the context of project DEMI *"Product and Process Design for AmI Supported Energy Efficient Manufacturing Installations"* (2010-2013), funded by the European Commission under the FP7 (ICT-2009-247831) [8].

# References

1. Friden, H., Bergfors, L., Bjork, A., Mazharsolook, E.: Energy and LCC Optimised Design of Compressed Air Systems: A Mixed Integer Optimisation Approach with General Applicability. In: 2012 UKSim 14th International Conference on Computer Modelling and Simulation, pp. 491–496 (2012)
2. Díaz-Agudo, B., González-Calero, P.A., Recio-García, J.A.: JColibri Tutorial. Facultad de Informatica, Universidad Complutense de Madrid, Spain, http://gaia.fdi.ucm.es/files/people/juanan/jcolibri/downloads/tutorial.pdf
3. Díaz-Agudo, B., González-Calero, P.A., Recio-García, J.A.: Building CBR systems with Jcolibri. Science of Computer Programming 69(1-3), 68–75 (2007)
4. Baumeister, J., Reutelshoefer, J., Puppe, F.: KnowWE – Community based Knowledge Capture with Knowledge Wikis. In: K-CAP 2007: Proceedings of the 4th International Conference on Knowledge Capture, pp. 189–190 (2007)
5. Baumeister, J., Reutelshoefer, J., Puppe, F.: Web–Based Knowledge Engineering with KnowledgeWikis. In: Proc. of AAAI 2008 Spring Symposium on Symbiotic Relationships between Semantic Web and Knowledge Engineering, pp. 1–13. Stanford University, USA (2008)
6. Iešmantas, T., Alzbutas, R.: Designing of energy efficient system considering power consumption and reliability. In: 9th Annual Conference of Young Scientists on Energy Issues CYSENI 2012: International Conference, May 24-25, pp. 179–189. LEI, Kaunas (2012) ISSN 1822-7554
7. http://prisma.sisteplant.com/
8. http://www.demi-online.eu/

# Evaluation and Calculation of Dynamics in Environmental Impact Assessment

Björn Johansson[*], Jon Andersson, Erik Lindskog, Jonatan Berglund, and Anders Skoogh

Production Systems, Chalmers University of Technology, Gothenburg Sweden
{bjorn.johansson,jon.andersson,erik.lindskog, jonatan.berglund,anders.skoogh}@chalmers.se

**Abstract.** In ten years customers will select products not only based on price and quality but also with strong regard to the product value environmental footprint, including for example the energy consumed. Customers expect transparency in the product realization process, where most products are labeled with their environmental footprint. Vigorous companies see this new product value as an opportunity to be more competitive. In order to effectively label the environmental impact of a product, it is pertinent for companies to request the environmental footprint of each component from their suppliers. Hence, companies along the product lifecycle require a tool, not only to facilitate the computing of the environmental footprint, but also help reduce/balance the environmental impact during the lifecycle of the product. This paper proposes to develop a procedure that companies will use to evaluate, improve and externally advertise their product's environmental footprint to customers.

**Keywords:** Discrete event simulation, sustainable production, product lifecycle, environmental analysis, sustainable manufacturing.

## 1 Introduction

Conscious efforts on reducing environmental impact are valuable for companies. Such companies contribute not only to a more sustainable future, but also obtain a competitive advantage towards customers. One example from food and service industry is an award winning restaurant in Sweden called MAX. They reported a reduction of their $CO_2$-emmisions by 44% [1] between 2007 and 2008 by evaluating and improving their product value chain. Moreover, market research shows that 13 times [2] more customers relate their brand to environmental friendly products compared to their main competitor. MAX's sustainability manager states that the latter figure is not the result of an increase in traditional marketing, but derives solely from communication of their products' environmental footprint. This paper describes a current research project called EcoProIT enabling manufacturing industry to evaluate, improve and advertise their environmental footprint through the developed procedure.

---

[*] Corresponding author.

C. Emmanouilidis, M. Taisch, D. Kiritsis (Eds.): APMS 2012, Part I, IFIP AICT 397, pp. 135–141, 2013.

At present, Life Cycle Assessment (LCA) standardized by ISO 14040:2006 and 14044:2006 [3] is by far the most common analysis method for evaluation of environmental footprint. However, there are inherent problems associated with LCA, which reduce its preciseness and limit its value for companies. The main associated problems with traditional LCA analyses are [4]:

- Use lumped parameters and site-independent models.
- Static in nature and disregard the dynamic behavior of industrial and ecological systems.
- Focuses only on environmental considerations, not economic or social aspects.

Hence, it is important to complement LCA with other analysis tools, in order to effectively combine environmental and economic analysis. The EcoProIT project in particular proposes Discrete Event Simulation (DES) as a potent solution, thereby reaping the strengths of DES to perform dynamic and site-specific analyses on product flows along product value chains. Combining the advantages of DES with LCA compensates the above stated weaknesses of traditional LCA. Performing DES and LCA simultaneously in a product value chain offers the advantage to foresee the interaction between resources and helps identify opportunities to reduce waste. In other words, companies will be able to use the EcoProIT tool [5] with combined capabilities of DES and LCA, to label their products and to increase competitiveness. The tool enables continuous improvement of the product realization process with regard to both efficiency and environmental footprint.

## 2    State of the Art

### 2.1    Combined Environmental and Production Systems Analysis

To solve the inherent problems of LCA there are proposals on combining tools for environmental analyses (usually LCA) and tools for evaluation of industrial systems. For example, ecosystem models are combined with basic industrial models such as Activity Based Costing (ABC) [3] and in [6] environmental analyses are combined with the process mapping approach Value Stream Mapping (VSM). Regarding the dynamic aspects, LCA has been combined with Monte Carlo simulations [7] and initial studies have also been performed on integration of LCA and DES [8].

However, the bottom line is that researchers in the area agree on that this is still an immature research area with significant potential [6]. The potential for reducing environmental impact with means of production flow development is actually bigger than the potential of addressing individual manufacturing processes [9]. New research (NIST-Chalmers-Boeing-collaboration) show that more energy is saved by reducing the production lead-time of a product compared to reductions in energy consumption for the value-adding machining processes, which is due to the high energy consumptions during stand-by times of the machines. An additional factor regarded in this project proposal is the potential to benefit from synergy effects from analyzing production and logistic processes throughout the complete product value chain including recycling. This potential is previously evaluated by e.g. [10].

## 2.2    Data Management and Model Credibility

Data management is one of the biggest problems in LCA [3] [4] and this has also traditionally been a problem for production development tools such as DES. An indicator is that 31% of the time for DES is spent on input data management [11]. However, recent research proposes a higher level of automation and integration of data sources in the input data management process [13] [14] and the proposed project will contribute to the incorporation of environmental data in this process. One part in this work is the cooperation with the United States National Institute of Standards and Technology (NIST) on adding environmental parameters to the Core Manufacturing Simulation Data (CMSD) standardization effort [15].

Another important part for model and analysis credibility is to apply a structured and transparent work procedure. This point has recently been addressed in the DES area by efforts from the Fraunhofer Institute in Germany [16] and similar work has also been performed to support combined DES and LCA [5]. The proposed project will contribute to this work by extending these work procedures to regard the entire product value chain and assure correct standardized analyses and trust between involved parties enabling benchmarking between products and companies.

# 3    Project Description

The EcoProIT project brings together researchers on production and environmental system analysis with industrial partners throughout the complete lifecycle of a specific product used in forklift manufacturing. The product is analyzed in three separate settings, raw material extraction/recycling, sub component manufacturing,

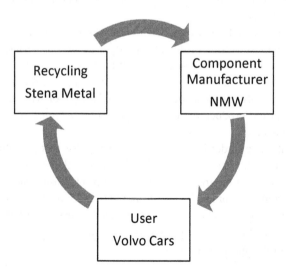

**Fig. 1.** For development and demonstration of the EcoProIT tool, the project will regard companies through the lifecycle of a product

final product manufacturing/use, and then recycled back to the raw material state again. The total cycle will be closed when all three company specific case demonstrators are done, they will then be merged into the complete lifecycle calculation of environmental footprint.

There are three main scientific challenges addressed in the project:

- Efficient management of environmental data.
  How can required data for production performance and environmental impact be jointly collected and processed in an efficient manner?

- Selecting system delimitations.
  How are the system delimitations chosen to ensure objective measurements and, thus, enable comparison?

- Modeling methodology through an entire product lifecycle.
  How are models built and communicated between companies involved in the product lifecycle, in order to assure company integrity as well as correct standardized and credible analyses?

## 4    Level of Innovation

Today, industry can evaluate and declare their products' environmental footprint only for marketing purposes. This is for example applied in several cases in food industry. However, due to limitations in the traditional LCA analysis it is problematic to detailed process analyses and specific results. These drawbacks make it impossible for a specific company to really improve their performance and compete on their environmental footprint.

The proposed tool enables not only declaration of environmental footprint but also continuous work with reduction of this new product value. Furthermore, the tool adds the factors time, location and economy to traditional LCA analyses. The bottom line is that companies in all lines of business can reduce environmental impact and improve economic profit simultaneously. The EcoProIT tool will be associated with competitiveness on the product values *price* and *environmental footprint* in Swedish manufacturing industry.

The significant value in definition of measurements for sustainability performance in manufacturing industry is one contribution. Moreover, the research on dynamic and site specific evaluation of environmental effects in production systems is a requested and not yet researched complement to the popular LCA analysis [3]. Several other actors are identified and collaboration is established with most of the twelve actors described by Herrmann et al. [17] in order to streamline work and reach interoperable and useful results for industrial applications.

## 5     Vision

Product Lifecycle Management (PLM) systems are widely used in large manufacturing companies. They are used to support collaborated work throughout a products life cycle. To conduct the analysis explained in this paper, a structured work method and a helpful tool is needed. However, to support collaborative work between companies and other actors in a life cycle a larger data management system is needed. This project proposes to use PLM likewise software and database structure to enable sharing of results and information. All companies that are involved in a products lifecycle connect to the database structure and share up to date result and analyze. This enables up to date emission declaration for the products analyzed in the system. Figure 2 show how the close linked companies share all information and final result to the public server available for other companies to use in similar studies.

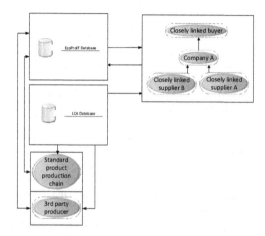

**Fig. 2.** Conceptual data repositories for lifecycle assessment data

## 6     Present Status

The project has reached halfway and two of three parts in figure 1 are completed. The first case study show several advantages with the proposed method compared to LCA concerning the level of details, scalability and dynamical emission values. Results from the study indicated that a large part of the total emission value was related to processes outside the studied company, which directs the need for applying the method to the entire life cycle. The first case study resulted in a proposed method for future work with focus towards the process of gathering environmental input data.

The second case study show how to build a structured output data format that supports validation and verification of the model. Practical experiences show that it is important to early identify the expected input data and information that is possible to retrieve. A DES model built for LCA calculations need other types of information from the real system, i.e. energy consumption and resource consumption for specific processes. Depending on available information the model can be alternately designed.

# 7     Future Research

There are additional efforts ongoing within the field of DES-LCA combination. Examples stated in [18-29] are many different approaches on how to describe instantiated DES-LCA case studies. The majority of these researchers are now working together to find a common solution on how to utilize DES and LCA in a methodological manner to calculate benefits of the combination.

**Acknowledgements.** The authors would like to acknowledge support from ProViking through the EcoProIT project and VINNOVA (Swedish Agency for Innovation Systems). This work has been carried out within the Sustainable Production Initiative and the Production Area of Advance at Chalmers. The support is gratefully acknowledged.

# References

1. MAX Annual Climate Report (2008), http://www.max.se/miljo.aspx (accessed January 16, 2010)
2. Interview with Pär Larshans, HR and Sustainability Manager, MAX Hamburgerrestauranger AB
3. Finnveden, G., Hauschild, M.Z., Ekvall, T., Guinée, J., Heijungs, R., Hellweg, S., Koehler, A., Pennington, D., Suh, S.: Recent Developments in Life Cycle Assessment. Journal of Environmental Management 91, 1–21 (2009)
4. Reap, J., Bras, B., Newcomb, P.J., Carmichael, C.: Improving Life Cycle Assessment by Including Spatial, Dynamic and Place-Based Modeling. In: Proceedings of DETC 2003 ASME (2003)
5. Andersson, J., Johansson, B., Berglund, J., Skoogh, A.: Framework for Ecolabeling using Discrete Event Simulation. In: Proceedings of the 2012 Spring Simulation Multiconference, Orlando, FL, USA (2012)
6. Ball, P.D., Evans, S., Levers, A., Ellison, D.: Zero carbon manufacturing facility – towards integrating material, energy, and waste process flows. Proceedings of the Institution of Mechanical Engineers, Part B: Journal of Engi-neering Manufacture 223(9), 1085–1096 (2009)
7. Maurice, B., Frischknecht, R., Coelho-Schwirtz, V., Hungerbühler, K.: Uncertainty analysis in life cycle inventory. Application to the production of electricity with French coal power plants. Journal of Cleaner Production 8, 95–108 (2000)
8. Heilala, J., Saija, V., Tonteri, H., Montonen, J., Johansson, B., Stahre, J., Lind, S.: Simulation-Based Sustainable Manufacturing System Design. In: Proceedings of the 2008 Winter Simulation Conference, pp. 1922–1930 (2008)
9. Cao, H., Chou, Y.-C.: Mobile Agent Based Integration Framework for Flexible Dynamic Job Shop Scheduling. In: Proceedings of the 2009 ASME Design for Manufacturing and the Life Cycle Conference, San Diego, California, USA, August 30- September 2 (2009)
10. Nagel, C., Meyer, P.: Caught between ecology and economy: end-of-life aspects of environmentally conscious manufacturing. Computers & Industrial Engineering 36, 781–792 (1999)
11. Feifel, S., Walk, W., Wursthorn, S.: LCA, how are you doing today? A snapshot from the 5th German LCA workshop. International Journal of Life Cycle Assessment 15, 139–142 (2010)

12. Skoogh, A., Johansson, B.: Time-consumption analysis of input data activities in discrete event simulation projects. In: Proceedings of the 2007 Swedish Production Symposium (2007)
13. Robertson, N., Perera, T.: Automated data collection for simulation? Simulation Practice and Theory 9, 349–364 (2002)
14. Skoogh, A., Johansson, B., Stahre, J.: Automated Input Data Management: Evaluation of a Concept for Reduced Time-Consumption in Discrete Event Simulation. Simulation: Transactions of the Society for Modeling and Simulation International 88(11), 1279–1293 (2012)
15. SISO – Simulation Interoperability Standards Organization, CMSD Product Development Group. Standard for: Core Manufacturing Simulation Data - UML Model (May 11, 2009)
16. Rabe, M., Spieckermann, S., Wenzel, S.: A New Procedure Model for Verification and Validation in Production and Logistics Simulation. In: Proceedings of the 2008 Winter Simulation Conference, pp. 1717–1726 (2008)
17. Herrmann, C., Thiede, S., Kara, S., Hesselbach, J.: Energy oriented simulation of manufacturing systems - Concept and application. CIRP Annals Manufacturing Technology 60(1), 45–48 (2011)
18. Thiede, S., Herrmann, C., Kara, S.: State of Research and an innovative Approach for simulating Energy Flows of Manufacturing Systems. In: Glocalized Solutions for Sustainability in Manufacturing CIRP Braunschweig (2011)
19. Hesselbach, J., Herrmann, C., Detzer, R., Martin, L., Thiede, S., Lüdemann, B.: Energy Efficiency through optimized coordination of production and technical building services. In: Proceeding of the 15th Conference on Life Cycle Engineering, Sydney (2008)
20. Dietmair, A., Verl, A.: A generic energy consumption model for decision making and energy efficiency optimisation in manufacturing. International Journal of Sustainable Engineering 2(2), 123 (2009)
21. Heilala, J., Vatanen, S., Tonteri, H., Montonen, J., Lind, S., Johansson, B., Stahre, J.: Simulation-based sustainable manufacturing system design. In: Mason, S.J. (Hg.) 2008 Winter Simuation Conference (2008)
22. Hornberger, M.: Total Energy Efficiency Management. Vom Energiemanagementsystem zur Simulation der Energieverbrauchswerte auf Prozessebene. In: Elektronik Ecodesign Congress, München (2009)
23. Johansson, B., Mani, M., Skoogh, A., Leong, S.: Discrete Event Simulation to generate Requirements Specification for Sustainable Manufacturing Systems Design (2009)
24. Junge, M.: Simulationsgestützte Entwicklung und Optimierung einer energieeffizienten Produktionssteuerung. Dissertation, Univ. Kassel (2007)
25. Löfgren, B.: Capturing the life cycle environmental performance of a company's manufacturing system. Göteborg. Chalmers University of Technology (2009)
26. Rahimifard, S., Seow, Y., Childs, T.: Minimising Embodied Product Energy to support energy efficient manufacturing. CIRP Annals - Manufacturing Technology 59, 25–28 (2010)
27. Solding, P., Petku, D., Mardan, N.: Using simulation for more sustainable production systems – methodologies and case studies. Journal of Sustainable Engineering 2(2), 111–122 (2009)
28. Weinert, N., Chiotellis, S., Seliger, G.: Concept for Energy-Aware Production Planning based on Energy Blocks. In: GCSM 2009: Proceedings of the 7th Global Conference on Sustainable Manufacturing, pp. 75–80 (2009)
29. Wohlgemuth, V., Page, B., Kreutzer, W.: Combining discrete event simulation and material flow analysis in a component-based approach to industrial environmental protection. Environmental Modelling & Software 21(11), 1607–1617 (2006)

# Discrete Part Manufacturing Energy Efficiency Improvements with Modelling and Simulation

Juhani Heilala[1], Marja Paju[1], Jari Montonen[1], Reino Ruusu[1], Mikel Sorli[2],
Alberto Armijo[2], Pablo Bermell-Garcia[3], Simon Astwood[3], and Santiago Quintana[3]

[1] VTT Technical Research Centre of Finland, Espoo, Finland
{juhani.heilala,marja.paju,jari.montonen,reino.ruusu}@vtt.fi
[2] Tecnalia, Bilbao, Spain
{mikel.sorli,alberto.armijo}@tecnalia.com
[3] EADS Innovation Works, Filton, Bristol, United Kingdom
{pablo.bermell-garcia,simon.astwood,santiago.quintana}@eads.com

**Abstract.** Energy efficiency has become a key concern in industry due to increased energy cost and associated environmental impacts. It is as well factor on marketing and reputation. Customers require information on the ecological performance of products and the process to build that product. Therefore eco-efficient manufacturing is in our days a matter of competitiveness and economic success. This paper presents industrial driven research and the key findings from production eco and energy efficiency analysis and development projects. Both static and dynamic multi-level modelling and simulation is covered with examples. The use of Value Stream Mapping and Discrete Event Simulation with life cycle inventory data for production eco efficiency analysis is explained. Generic developement steps for process, machine and production system model with environmantal aspects is shown. Development continues in EPES "Eco Process Engineering System for Composition of Services to Optimise Product Life-Cycle"- project.

**Keywords:** Energy efficiency, modeling and simulation, manufacturing.

## 1 Introduction

In order to win future markets, industrial firms are under pressure to achieve sustainability targets related to their products and services. The reduction on materials and energy on products and production systems is acknowledged as a key strategy in this journey [1]. Also the directives and legislation [2] are drivers for environmantal end energy efficincy improvements in manufacturing.

Satisfactory results on manufacturing systems often require detailed studies to understand where and how the energy has been used. This transparency to energy utilization is the basis for optimizing the energy use performance on production systems. Once visibility is achieved, a question remains on the choice on improved decision support methods and tools guiding practitioners on energy efficient investments in manufacturing systems. A current gap is the availability of software

C. Emmanouilidis, M. Taisch, D. Kiritsis (Eds.): APMS 2012, Part I, IFIP AICT 397, pp. 142–150, 2013.
© IFIP International Federation for Information Processing 2013

supporting production engineers in this type of decision making. This is not a simple task since it involves balancing conflicting criteria such as financial costs, energy consumption, equipment reutilization, and manufacturing system availability.

The sustainability assessments of a product, and its corresponding processes, have different emphases. The manufacturing processes, serve to implement a product design, and their constraints are decided by the current product design. To evaluate a manufacturing process, its fulfilment of product design features and requirements need to be considered. For sustainability assessment of a product design, the overall product sustainability performance is the ultimate criteria and the process assessment is only one of the sub-elements. To be specific, the sustainability assessment of a process would not cover the other phases of the manufactured product's life-cycle [3].

An optimized manufacturing process routine does not necessarily mean that the product is optimal concerning its sustainability performance. On the other hand, to achieve optimal overall sustainability performance when designing a product, the corresponding manufacturing processes need to be optimized based on some sustainability criteria and this is one of the aims in the EPES project [16].

Typical tools for eco efficiency analysis of discrete part manufacturing system and processes are Life Cycle Assesment (LCA), Value Stream Map (VSM) and Discrete Event Simulation (DES). This paper reviews those tools for assesstment of energy efficiency in manufacturing, shows challenges and development need as well research results.

## 2    Manufacturing Sustainability with Modelling and Simulation

In addition to the problems for traditional manufacturing modelling and simulation, there are some new challenges for simulation of sustainable manufacturing, such as the lack of [4]:

- Source of the sustainability information, sustainability metrics and indicators
- A reference model to identify appropriate information
- Information models that support simulation for sustainable manufacturing
- Modeling methods for simulation of sustainable manufacturing
- Measures to evaluate sustainability.

### 2.1    Sustainability Indicators

In industry today sustainability measures are common. Ideally measures can be a guide to where you are, where you are heading and how far you are from the ultimate vision. There are parameters (figures you measure), indicators (figures that indicate something) or index (several indicators combined into one). They can be used for benchmarking, decision making, measuring or guiding to improvement on the operational level or enabling companies to identify more innovative solutions to sustainability challenges [5].

Feng & Joung, 2009 [6] describes a multitude of various measurement initiatives for measuring sustainability metrics. It has been recommended to pursue a multi-level approach for metrics, with simple metrics at the highest level. Methodology for sustainable production indicator development has been presented by Velava & Ellenbecker [7]. Examples of indicators have also been presented by Krajnc and Glavic [1]. It should be noted and identifyi the interdependencies between the different indicators. For instance, carbon dioxide emissions are dependent e.g. on the energy consumption and sulfur dioxide air emissions from transportation are dependent e.g. on the sulfur contents of the fuel.

## 2.2    Research on Manufacturing System Modelling and Simulation with Energy Use Parameters

The methods, specifically decicated to production system development are production and material flow simulation, e.g. Discrere Event Simulation and process mapping methods, e.g. Value Stream Mapping.

In Discrete Event Simulation (DES), the operation of a system is represented as a chronological sequence of events. Each event occurs at an instant in time and marks a change of state in the system. DES is well suited for modelling a specific well-defined system, such as a production system. It can provide statistically valid quantitative estimates of performance metrics as-sociated with the system. Integration of sustainability and environmental aspects to simulations is development topic in many research institutes. Currently most of the research efforts have been focused on energy efficiency, examples shown in [8, 9, 10]. Wider scope, sustainability and environmental aspect analysis are shown in [11, 12].

Value Stream Mapping (VSM) relies on Lean principles and identifying and eliminating wasteful activities. It is a process mapping method, and it can be also employed to environmental assessment. The potential of VSM has also been noted by the US Environmental protection agency EPA [13]. EPA has gathered case studies, fact sheets and tools containing techniques for integrating environmental considerations into Lean initiatives and methods [13]. A lot of research has been carried out in various research institutes to use VSM for sustainable production system development.

Typically LCA is conducted for a pre-specified use purpose. It can be decision making, e.g. when comparing two alternative materials, communication purpose, in a form of an environmental product declarations (EPD), or something else. Typically LCA is done for a product system. Use of LCA methods for assessmrent of production system footprint requires specific development in life cycle modeling. In practice light, streamlined or screening LCAs are common since full LCA may be too extensive.

Each analysis method has their limitations and assets which shall be taken into consideration. The essential difference between the three methods is that DES and VSM have generally been used for manufacturing processes and supply chains whereas LCA covers the whole product life cycle including manufacturing, transportation, use, maintenance and end-of-life. LCA method with ISO standardisation (ISO 14040/14044), is solely meant for environmental impact analysis. However DES and VSM have more flexibility in applications and can be used in light environmental analysis. DES is a tool more specifically aimed at production system life-cycle studies. Economic indicators, investment cost and total cost of ownership (TCO) or Activity Based Costing (ABC) analysis can be integrated to DES.

Both LCA and DES require high expertise from the user and computerised tools, while VSM in its simplest form can be done with paper and pencil.

**Use of DES.** In the SIMTER project [11] environmental analysis simulation tool was created (Fig. 1). Data management is in the simulation software interface. The user can control following simulation variables and their relationships: resource – energy; part – material; and system input, system output and layout properties.

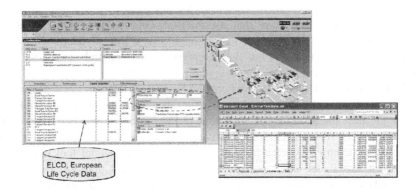

**Fig. 1.** VTT SIMTER Environmental analysis tool interface

Simulation run provides book keeping of events, resource utilisation as well state of the resource (down, idle, busy), material flow statistics, and number of products/parts manufactured (ready, rejected, repair) etc. data. Simulation model and run results can pin point in a detailed way, bottlecks of the system, where and how energy and materials are used, whether material is disposed / recycled, and what emissions and waste are produced. Life cycle inventory (LCI), e.g. energy type and material related data, were either selected from EU-LCA database (http://lca.jrc.ec.europa.eu/lcainfohub/datasetArea.vm) or user editable. Manufacturing process specific data is typically a challenge in the LCI databases.

MS-Excel is used for detailed analytical calculation and summary results can be shown in the simulation software interface. Product, resource or process based and piece count or time frame analysis can be reported using MS-Excel. Similar approach as SIMTER, can be used with other commercial factory simulation tools.

**Use of VSM.** In a recent discrete manufacturing research project Ekoteho [14], methods and tools for environmental assessment were studied. The methods and tools vere divided into those that are used primarily for the assessment of environmental

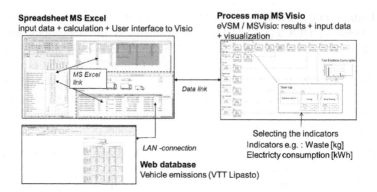

**Fig. 2.** Use of VSM for production system energy efficiency analysis

aspects, such as LCA, and those that use environmental assessment as an add-on element. Add-on tools, such as VSM, require less effort to adapt to existing manufacturing modelling tools, but they compromise on comprehensiveness in the environmental assessment part.

In the project new methodology was created based on VSM (Fig. 2). Choosing the right indicators according to the goal, and setting the system boundaries are essential steps for the new methodology as shown in in Paju et al. (2010) [14]. To test the methodology some simplified and connective process flow chart models were created with eVSM tool (http://www.evsm.com/). eVSM is a commercial tool that creates link between MS Excel and MS Visio. The modelling test platform utilizes pre-selected indicators and limited amount of visible parameters. The test platform had connections to web databases Lipasto (http://www.lipasto.vtt.fi/yksikkopaastot/indexe.htm) to import logistic emission data.

# 3    Genaral Model Development Steps

The general methodology for developing the process-oriented, environmental modules of the sustainability simulation toolkit involves the following steps according to Zhou and Kuhl [15]:

1. Identify sustainability factors and environmental performance measures for systems of interest.
2. Establish simulation state variables to represent the sustainability factors and performance measures.
3. Identify the events in the system that cause changes to the state variables, and translate these system events to simulation events and the associated event triggers.
4. Establish the mathematical, statistical, and logical relationships among the state variables to update and change the values of the state variables as events occur in the system over time.

5. Implement state variables, relationships, and events into a robust, flexible simulation toolkit modules.
6. Perform verification, validation, and testing of the simulation toolkit modules.

The authors have used similar approach in the past and the presented case studies [11, 14] can be implemeted using also other commercial tools. Methodology and tool development for sustainability simulation toolkit continues in the EPES project [16]. The aim of the EPES project is to bring sustainability intelligence to the decision making process for optimisation of the product service system (PSS) life cycle.

In sustainability aspect simulation or any simulation study, one of the first steps is to define the scope of study and select suitable indicators for assesstment. Both VSM and DES, are process oriented and study is focused on manufacturing material flow, process cycle times, resources utilisation, equipment and even human operators activities.

Workstation and manufacturing process level data can be quite similar in LCA, VSM or DES. Here deep understanding of processes and equipment is needed. For sustainability issues we are adding energy flow study, (energy consumption), more detailed consumables study; e.g. materials, (dimensions, type), components, semi products, lubricants, chemicals, waste generation, and also emission study (air emission, aerosol particle, water emission), depending on the scope of the study (see Fig. 3). Equipment simpliest model, include only three states; down (off), idle (stand-by) and busy (working). In more detailed model the busy state energy consumptioncan depend of equipment speed or process load.

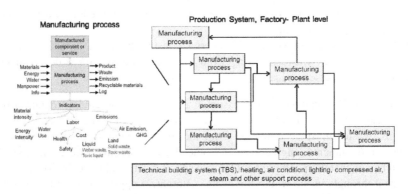

**Fig. 2.** From machine level to plant level analysis of complex process chains

The system level combines the workstations and manufacturing processes together, (Fig. 3, see also case study Fig. 1 and 2). The production system model can aggregate workstation and process level results to the system level. The analysis of material flow can be complex and here DES has advanges over LCA or VSM. DES studies support multi-product environment, detailed bottleneck and production efficiency analysis.

LCI factors, environmental sustainability aspects, do not always have to be incorporated in the simulation itself. Sometimes it is sufficient to combine the results of a simulation with an LCA knowledge base as a post processing phase. For example, a simulation can provide the distributions of different states that a set of production machinery are in during the production process. This can be later combined with the knowledge of the impacts that each state has on the overall LCA indicators.

## 4    Discussion and Conclusion

LCA and its integration with modelling and simulation for the sustainability evaluation of manufacturing systems and processes have been discussed. There is need for comprehensive and structured approach that provides the necessary coherent process design with a strong emphasis on energy- and resource-efficiency. Industrial companies need integrated product-process-production system modelling and simulation approaches for enabling them to select the manufacturing processes and associated manufacturing systems that fulfil production requirements with minimal economic and environmental costs, especially in the field of energy consumption and related emissions. The methods described in chapter 2.2.can be utilised to integrate sustainability assessment. European research project EPES [16] continues the development. In one of the demonstrators the early product concept will be analysed from both productivity and sustainability aspects using simulation as a service by non-simulation expert. The essential questions answered through this assessment step are:

- Productivity KPIs: What production rate can be achieved for a design using a given set of processes and resources?
- Sustainability KPIs: What are the energy consumption, the emissions and the hazardous material waste resulting from the manufacturing for a design using a given set of processes and resources?

Environmental data management is essential in assessing the environmental aspects and the real bottleneck is in getting data for analysis. Site specific data (energy, emissions, waste) must be collected from the existing manufacturing processes or from design documents, engineering and other legacy systems. Life cycle inventory data can be connected to complement the site specific data and to enable sustainability assessment throughout the whole life cycle. Alternative approach could be to transfer the results from life cycle assessment software to the simulation models. The manufacturing system simulation gives opportunity to analyse also multiproduct manufacturing with view to resource, product or time based analysis.

With methdos presented in this paper industry can gain the knowledge to compare different production system alternatives with regards to their life-cycle performance already during the early design phase.

**Acknowledgments.** The research presented in the paper has been carried out within the frames of the EPES, "Eco-Process Engineering System for Composition of Services to Optimize Product Life-Cycle" collaboration project co-funded by the

European Commission under FoF-ICT-2011.7.3-285093 contract. The authors wish to express the acknowledgement to EC for the support and to all project partners for their contributions during the development presented in this paper.

*Disclaimer.* This document does not represent the opinion of the European Community, and the European Community is not responsible for any use that might be made of its content. Mention of commercial products or services in this report does not imply approval or endorsement by authors, nor does it imply that such products or services are necessarily the best available for the purpose.

# References

1. Krajnc, D., Glavic, P.: Indicators of Sustainable Production. Clean Technologies and Environmental Policy 5(3), 279–288 (2003)
2. European Commission. Summaries on Legislation. Environment (2012), http://europa.eu/legislation_summaries/environment/index_en.htm (accessed May 11, 2012)
3. Lu, T., Gupta, A., Jayal, A.D., Badurdeen, F., Feng, S.C., Dillon, O.W., Jawahir, I.S.: A Framework of Product and Process Metrics for Sustainable Manufacturing. In: Proceedings of the Eighth International Conference on Sustainable Manufacturing, Abu Dhabi, November 22-24, 6 p. (2010)
4. Shao, G., Bengtsson, N.E., Johansson, B.J.: Interoperability for Simulation of Sustainable Manufacturing. In: Proceedings of the 2010 Spring Simulation Multi-conference (SpringSim 2010), Orlando, Florida, USA, April 12-16, 10 p. (2010)
5. OECD. Eco-innovation in industry: enabling green growth, pp. 95–155 (2009)
6. Feng, S.C., Joung, C.B.: An Overview of a Proposed Measurement Infrastructure for Sustainable Manufacturing. In: Proceedings of the 7th Global Conference on Sustainable Manufacturing, Chennai, India, December 2-4 (2009)
7. Veleva, C., Ellenbecker, M.: Indicators of sustainable production: framework and methodology. Journal of Cleaner Production 9(6), 519–549 (2001)
8. Cannata, A., Taisch, M., Vallo, E.: Energy Efficiency Optimization through Production Management Decisions in Manufacturing Environment: A Proposal. In: Proceedings of International Conference on Advances in Production Management Systems (APMS 2010), Cernobbio, Como, Italy, October 11-13. IFIP AICT (2010) ISBN: 978-88649-30-077
9. Duflou, J.R., et al.: Towards energy and resource efficient manufacturing: A processes and systems approach. CIRP Annals - Manufacturing Technology (2012) (paper in press), http://dx.doi.org/10.1016/j.cirp.2012.05.002
10. Herrmann, C., Thiede, S., Kara, S., Hesselbach, J.: Energy oriented simulation of manufacturing systems – Concept and application. CIRP Annals - Manufacturing Technology 60, 45–48 (2011)
11. Heilala, J., Vatanen, S., Montonen, J., Tonteri, H., Johansson, B., Stahre, J., Lind, S.: Simulation-Based Sustainable Manufacturing System Design. In: Mason, S.J., Hill, R.R., Mönch, L., Rose, O., Jefferson, T., Fowler, J.W. (eds.) Proceedings of the 2008 Winter Simulation Conference, pp. 1922–1930. IEEE (2008)
12. Lindskog, E., Berglund, J., Lundh, L., Lee, Y.T., Skoogh, A., Johansson, B.: A Method for Determining the Environmental Footprint of Industrial Products Using Simulation. In: Jain, S., Creasey, R.R., Himmelspach, J., White, K.P., Fu, M. (eds.) Proceedings of the 2011 Winter Simulation Conference (2011)

13. EPA. Lean Manufacturing and the Environment. US Environmental Protection Agency (2012), http://www.epa.gov/lean/environment/ (accessed May 11, 2012)
14. Paju, M., Heilala, J., Hentula, M., Heikkila, A., Johansson, B., Leong, S., Lyons, K.: Framework and Indicators for Sustainable Manufacturing Mapping Methodology. In: Proceedings of the 2010 Winter Simulation Conference, Baltimore, MD, USA (2010)
15. Zhou, X., Kuhl, M.E.: Design and Development of a Sustainability Toolkit for Simulation. In: Johansson, B., Jain, S., Montoya-Torres, J., Hugan, J., Yücesan, E. (eds.) Proceedings of the 2010 Winter Simulation Conference (2010)
16. EPES - Eco-process Engineering System for Composition of Services to Optimize Product Life-cycle (2012), http://www.epes-project.eu

# A Parallelizable Heuristic for Solving the Generic Materials and Operations Planning in a Supply Chain Network: A Case Study from the Automotive Industry

Julien Maheut and Jose Pedro Garcia-Sabater

ROGLE – Departamento de Organización de Empresas,
Universitat Politècnica de Valéncia, Camino de Vera S/N, 46022 Valencia, Spain
juma2@upv.es, jpgarcia@omp.upv.es

**Abstract.** A trend in up-to date developments in multi-site operations planning models is to consider in details the different ways to produce, buy or transport products and the distributed decision-making process for operations planning. One of the most generic approaches to support global optimization in those supply chain networks by considering all the different operations alternatives and product structures is the Generic Materials & Operations Planning Problem. This problem can be modelled by a Mixed Integer Linear Programming model capable of considering production, transportation, procurement tasks and their alternatives and other relevant issues such as packaging. The aim of this paper is to introduce the implementation of a parallelizable heuristic method for materials and operations planning and its application to a case of a Supply Chain Network of the automotive industry. The approach uses variants of the GMOP model to overcome traditional MRP systems' limitations.

**Keywords:** Operations Planning, MRP, Generic Materials & Operations Planning, Mixed Integer Linear Programming, Supply Network, Automotive Industry.

## 1 Introduction

Multi-site operations planning in a Supply Chain Network (SCN) is the process that consists in determining a tentative plan about the operations that must be performed on the available capacitated resources geographically distributed in each time period all along a determined horizon time. The planning of these operations not only determines inventory levels of certain products in given locations, labor levels or the use of productive resources but must also determines which located operations, called strokes [1; 2] must be performed to implement the operations plan.

Generally, SCNs are composed by several facilities located in different sites that must serve a set of end products to different customers[3]. Despite belonging to the same SCN or to the same company in some cases, sometimes, the different members themselves do not communicate their exact costs and capacity data[4]. This implies that central planning is impossible and operations planning must be coordinated in a distributed way between the different members of the SCN.

C. Emmanouilidis, M. Taisch, D. Kiritsis (Eds.): APMS 2012, Part I, IFIP AICT 397, pp. 151–157, 2013.
© IFIP International Federation for Information Processing 2013

In the literature, lots of mathematical models that simultaneously solve the materials and operations planning problem in a multi-site context are presented and part of them are reviewed in [2]. The Multi-level Capacitated Lot-Sizing Problem [5; 6] is the most widely covered, but other authors call it the Supply Chain Operations Planning Problem [7] or they include other adjectives when defining it; for example, dynamic [8]. Nevertheless, to the best of our knowledge, GMOP is the only model that simultaneously considers multi-site, multi-level capacitated operations planning problems with lead times, alternative operations (purchasing, transport -replenishment, transshipments and distribution- and production) and returnable packaging. Moreover, the GMOP model that solves in a decentralized way has not yet been studied.

In this paper, a parallelizable heuristic method for operations and materials planning is introduced. Its application in a SN of the automotive industry composed by different facilities geographically distributed is presented. The proposed method is to plan operations in a decentralized manner using agents that take decision based on the results of several MILP model variants to solve the GMOP problem [9; 10].

Section 2 introduces the SCN description and the different operations carried out in it. Section 3 describes the proposed system and the proposed heuristic method briefly and partially. Section 4 proposes a description of the implementation process of the planning approach. Finally, Section 5 introduces a conclusion and future research lines.

# 2    Supply Chain Network Description

The SCN considered in this paper is composed by several plants geographically distributed in Spain. Plants are responsible of processing, treating, assembling and transporting metal parts in different returnable packaging to different customers, mainly car assembly plants of the automotive sector in Europe.

In this case study, global operations planning tasks is a critical process because some of the different SCN members have grown during the last decade and have currently different plants able to perform the same operations or produce the same products in the different locations considering different constraints and costs. Consequently, one of the main concerns of the SCN is to adapt its plans in order to consider all the feasible ways to serve the customers minimizing costs and respecting due dates.

Global operations planning must consider all the operations, tasks that are performed to procure, transform and transport the materials in order to serve a determined end product to the final customer. In the literature, production operations, transport operations and purchasing operations are the most high value added operations considered. Nevertheless, others high value-added operations must be considered like operations considering returnable packaging [11; 12] or alternative operations [13; 14] because they can substantially affect total SCN cost if they are considering. This is, to the best of our knowledge, one of the major concerns for practitioners that the literature has not dealt with extensively.

The emergence of alternative operations in this case study is a direct consequence of the different processes that take place in the different plants. Stamping, cutting, chemical treatment, painting, assembling, dismantling, and finally (un)packaging operations are some of the operations performed in the SCN where alternatives can exist. Besides transport between plants is a very important process since it is necessary to consider the return and transshipments of the returnable packaging. This consideration is necessary since customers demand is not only in quantity of products on each due time, but also customers demand requires a specific packaging.

In addition, each plant has its own work schedule and capacitated resources, and these factors are usually unknown to the others. Moreover, each plant does not want to share information about inventory levels and costs.

# 3    Advanced Planning and Scheduling Module Description

## 3.1    The Designed Procedure for Collaborative Decision Making

The designed system is an Advanced Planning and Scheduling (APS) system. The SCN planning module consists of different types of agents: one warehouse agent, some plant agents and some supplier agents (Figure 1). Agents do not have any artificial intelligence but are able to communicate and make decisions based on specific criteria established preliminarily.

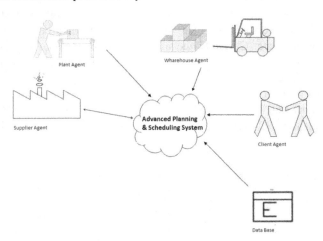

**Fig. 1.** General scheme of the APS System

The warehouse agent knows at all times the inventory levels of products in all the SCN. This agent is the central coordinator and is responsible for transporting finished products between different plants and to the final customers.

The operations planning process starts when a new customers' demand forecast is received (extracted for the MRPs of the different SCN members). First, it is asked to the warehouse agent if the customer-requested product is available in stock in one of the various SCN plants.

If there is sufficient material in at least one of the site, the agent plans how to transport the material to the customer based on specific criteria (cost, due date, run out time in each plant, etc). The decision is made based on the result of a MILP model that considers transport stroke and some constraints about working calendars and truck fleet. Otherwise, the warehouse agent has to act as coordinator and must achieve to get all the material respecting the due date.

To do so, the warehouse agent generates an ordered list of the needed materials. This ordered list is a "bag of material" where there is a quantity of material per request and its due date. For the first product of the list, the warehouse agent asks the different plant agents capable of producing this product. Plant agents can be a plant, a set of resources or even a single specific resource and they are responsible for its assigned internal operations.

Each plant agent then executes its MILP model to determine how much and when can be available the amount of products ordered. Each proposal is offered to the warehouse agent. The latter chooses the option with lower costs.

If the chosen agent plant needed raw material to produce the product, it transmits the information to warehouse agent and this product enters in the tail of the sorted list of material to order.

The agents, before ordering raw material to manufacture an ordered product, will require the product to the warehouse and, if there is not enough, the plant agent of the product will ask the supplier agents the raw material and the possible due dates according to the capacity already assigned.

When the bag is empty, the warehouse agent transfers to different SCN members and the suppliers a personalized plan with the operations to be performed with its corresponding due date. Currently the model does not include a specific transport agent but it is planned for future expansion of the system to take it into account, including more specific constraints.

The operations plan will be used by the different SCN members to create detailed production plans (due dates, delivery dates and lot size), which will be the starting point for sequencing and temporalize. A screen of the tool designed is introduced in Figure 2.

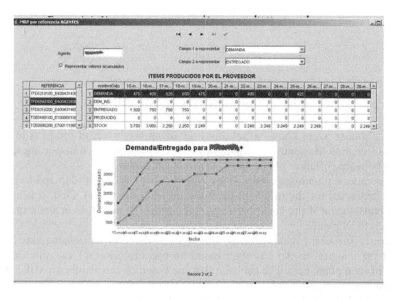

**Fig. 2.** Some results of the planning tool

## 3.2    The MILP Model

The MILP models used for each SCN agent are variants that solve the GMOP problem including backlogs. Each time the warehouse agent requests a product, the associated MILP model is executed to check if it has sufficient capacity for the production of goods (in the requested quantity). Each resource has a limited available capacity, so the agent could not have in certain case the sufficient capacity to serve the order.

In the case the agent do not have enough capacity, the timing or a new amount of product to be serve on time will be determined. The mathematical models are encapsulated in each agent and they are run whenever the agent is solicited.

Procurement strokes are only considered with supplier agent because different alternative procurement operations exist. Because of length constraint, the complete model will not be introduced herein. One generic variant is described in [1; 9; 15].

# 4    Advanced Planning and Scheduling Module Implementation

## 4.1    Implementation Approach

Before tool implementation, the company had its own Enterprise System (ES) which managed an MRP System. In practice, MRPs results were limited to advance the major components production and to merely attempt to maintain one day of demand in stock for each one.

The biggest problem the company faced was that the number of late deliveries had grown in recent years. The reason for this was that the group had grown considerably and had to face and consider an increasing number of end products and production stages. Besides production processes had become more complex with more loading units types, with different facilities to take into account, and with resources, materials and packaging alternatives to be considered.

The existing ES was used to support a certain type of transactions. Plant managers claimed they had sufficient information, and their only complaint was that they did not have sufficient resources (in inventory and machines) to deal with sudden changes in demand.

During implementation, the structure of the existing information system did not change. XML files were created from the existing database (which was supported by conventional BOM files and Routing Files) and were sent to feed the proposed APS system.

During the tool implementation process, the data quality in the ERP systems improved substantially because the facilitator of the new APS (which was in charge of the IT systems) placed pressure on managers to maintain it without our intervention.

After each APS execution, users received the operations plans in Excel spreadsheet files based on an XML format which were designed to suit their requirements.

## 4.2    Implementation Organizational Aspects

Probably one of the major pitfalls in the tool implementation process was that no organizational change occurred. Given the leadership characteristics of the facilitator of IT, we decided to replace the information flow given to users without informing them about the new APS tool.

Thus, tool implementation was transparent to most users who never perceived that they were actually making major changes. The only noted change was that users observed that the data were of a much better quality and that minor changes could be applied to spreadsheet files as they received them. It can be stated that the tool was well-accepted since it was not known to exist as such.

### 4.3    Results in Practice

The implementation process comprised two phases. In the first phase (before Christmas), the head of information systems checked the quality of the results. As he was highly committed to data quality, the data improved substantially. This led to a 33% reduction in delay levels, but also to a 50% increase in stock levels. In the second phase (after Christmas), users began to run operations plans. At that time, delays disappeared completely and only delays due to client requests after deadlines were the source of delays.

Arguably, this reduction was due not only to the use of GMOP models, but also to the MRP system which, until then, had never executed good data quality. However, the use of GMOP models also allows stakeholders to handle packaging flows and alternative operations by generating feasible operations plans and by cutting delays each time without having to consider more machinery resources.

After several years of implementation, the operations planning tool is still executed daily in the company until the present-day. The group's Logistics Manager soon changed after the introduction of the new APS, and the IT facilitator was removed some months afterward. However, the system continues to work, although the company owners now seek a more general (off-the-shelf and state-of-the-art) commercial ERP system. The main problem they now face is to find one that meets their expectations (that considers alternative operations and returnable packaging).

## 5    Conclusions

The proposed system has been successfully implemented in a real SCN. Experiments have been realized to evaluate the different alternatives, taking into account not only the validity of the results in terms of quality but also into account the computation times. The results obtained are practical in the proposed implementation and also revealed to be interesting because it appeared some light features of the system that were not foreseen. The problem has more than 600 end products (considering different types of packaging) and more than 15 agents.

A future research line would be to identify other strategies for ordering products in the bag and evaluate the best strategy in terms of total SCN costs against a centralized MILP model. Another future research line would be to introduce fuzziness in some parameter in case of demand or available capacity data uncertainty.

**Acknowledgements.** The work described in this paper has been partially supported by the Spanish Ministry of Science and Innovation within the Program "Proyectos de Investigación Fundamental No Orientada through the project "CORSARI MAGIC DPI2010-18243" and through the project " Programacion de produccion en cadenas de suministro sincronizada multietapa con ensamblajes/desemsamblajes con renovacion constante de productos en un contexto de inovacion DPI2011-27633". Julien Maheut holds a VALi+d grant funded by the Generalitat Valenciana (Regional Valencian Government, Spain) (Ref. ACIF/2010/222).

## References

1. Maheut, J., Garcia-Sabater, J.P.: La Matriz de Operaciones y Materiales y la Matriz de Operaciones y Recursos, un nuevo enfoque para resolver el problema GMOP basado en el concepto del Stroke. Dirección y Organización 45, 46–57 (2011)
2. Garcia-Sabater, J.P., Maheut, J., Marin-Garcia, J.A.: A new formulation technique to model Materials and Operations Planning: the Generic Materials and Operations Planning (GMOP) Problem. European J. Industrial Engineering 7, 119–147 (2013)
3. Mula, J., Maheut, J., Garcia-Sabater, J.P.: Supply Chain Network Design. Journal of Marketing and Operations Management Research 1, 378–383 (2012)
4. Dudek, G., Stadtler, H.: Negotiation-based collaborative planning between supply chains partners. European Journal of Operational Research 163, 668–687 (2005)
5. Torabi, S.A., Hassini, E.: Multi-site production planning integrating procurement and distribution plans in multi-echelon supply chains: an interactive fuzzy goal programming approach. International Journal of Production Research 47, 5475–5499 (2009)
6. Kanyalkar, A.P., Adil, G.K.: Aggregate and detailed production planning integrating procurement and distribution plans in a multi-site environment. International Journal of Production Research 45, 5329–5353 (2007)
7. de Kok, T.G., Fransoo, J.C.: Planning Supply Chain Operations: Definition and Comparison of Planning Concepts. In: Graves, S.C. (ed.) Handbooks in Operations Research and Management Science Supply Chain Management: Design, Coordination and Operation, vol. 11, pp. 597–675. Elsevier (2003)
8. Buschkühl, L., Sahling, F., Helber, S., Tempelmeier, H.: Dynamic capacitated lot-sizing problems: a classification and review of solution approaches. OR Spectrum (2009)
9. Maheut, J., Garcia-Sabater, J.P., Mula, J.: A supply Chain Operations Lot-Sizing and Scheduling Model with Alternative Operations. In: Sethi, S.P., Bogataj, M., Ros-McDonnell, L. (eds.) Proceedings of the Industrial Engineering: Innovative Networks, 5th International Conference on Industrial Engineering and Industrial Management "CIO 2011", Cartagena, Spain, pp. 309–316. Springer, London (2012)
10. Garcia-Sabater, J.P., Maheut, J., Garcia-Sabater, J.J.: A two-stage sequential planning scheme for integrated operations planning and scheduling system using MILP: the case of an engine assembler. Flexible Services and Manufacturing Journal 24, 171–209 (2012)
11. Pinto, J.M., Chen, P., Papageorgiou, L.G.: A discrete/continuous time MILP model for medium term planning of single stage multiproduct plants, pp. 1–6. Elsevier, B.V. (2007)
12. Scheer, A.W.: Business Process Engineering - Reference Models for Industrial Enterprises. Springer (1994)
13. Lin, J.T., Chen, T.L., Lin, Y.T.: Critical material planning for TFT-LCD production industry. International Journal of Production Economics 122, 639–655 (2009)
14. Escudero, L.F.: CMIT, capacitated multi-level implosion tool. European Journal of Operational Research 76, 511–528 (1994)
15. Maheut, J., Garcia-Sabater, J.P., Valero-Herrero, M.: MILP model for solving the supply chain operations scheduling problem with alternative operations considering delay penalization: a case study of a mass customization company. In: Proceedings of the 41st International Conference on Computers & Industrial Engineering, pp. 289–294 (2011)

# Factory Modelling: Combining Energy Modelling for Buildings and Production Systems

Peter D. Ball[1], Melanie Despeisse[1], Steve Evans[2], Rick M. Greenough[3],
Steve B. Hope[4], Ruth Kerrigan[5], Andrew Levers[6], Peter Lunt[6], Vincent Murray[5],
Mike R. Oates[3], Richard Quincey[5], Li Shao[3], Timothy Waltniel[4],
and Andrew J. Wright[3]

[1] Manufacturing and Materials Department, Cranfield University, UK
[2] Institute for Manufacturing, Cambridge University, UK
[3] Institute of Energy and Sustainable Development, De Montfort University, UK
[4] Toyota Motor Europe, Belgium
[5] Integrated Environmental Solutions Ltd, UK
[6] Airbus Operations Ltd, UK
p.d.ball@cranfield.ac.uk

**Abstract.** Traditionally, manufacturing facilities and building services are analysed separately to manufacturing operations. This is despite manufacturing operations using and discarding energy with the support of facilities. Therefore improvements in energy and other resource use to work towards sustainable manufacturing have been sub-optimal. This paper presents research in which buildings, facilities and manufacturing operations are viewed as inter-related systems. The objectives are to improve overall resource efficiency and to exploit opportunities to use energy and / or waste from one process as potential inputs to other processes. The novelty here is the combined simulation of production and building energy use and waste in order to reduce overall resource consumption. The paper presents a literature review, develops the conceptual modelling approach and introduces the prototype IES Ltd <VE> THERM software. The work has been applied to industrial cases to demonstrate the ability of the prototype to support activities towards sustainable manufacturing.

**Keywords:** Sustainable manufacturing, building energy modelling, resource simulation, factory modelling.

## 1    Introduction

The Bruntland report [1] defines sustainable development as meeting the needs of the present generation without compromising the ability of future generations to meet their own needs. Focusing on sustainable manufacturing there is the need to recognise the triple bottom line of social justice (people), environmental quality (planet) and economic prosperity (profit) [2]. There is significant work underway in both academia and industry to develop tools and techniques for sustainable manufacturing and apply

C. Emmanouilidis, M. Taisch, D. Kiritsis (Eds.): APMS 2012, Part I, IFIP AICT 397, pp. 158–165, 2013.

them for tangible benefit. As a result of rising prices and concerns over energy security and climate change, energy is a major focus. Documented cases and achievements presented on corporate websites show that significant benefits can be obtained. However, it is not until a sustainability mindset is adopted that the opportunities can be identified in the first place.

Sustainable manufacturing [3, 4, 5] (based on environmental conscious manufacturing) is broad in scope, taking a high level view of manufacturing and including the triple bottom line elements. Sustainable manufacturing looks beyond the boundaries of one factory and considers the entire material cycle from material extraction through processing and use to subsequent disposal [6, 7]. Most research in sustainable manufacturing has focused on product design and product end-of-life with relatively little research activity focusing on improving manufacturing systems. Subsequently there is an absence of methodologies for manufacturers to generate improvements within their own facilities [8].

Buildings consume a significant amount of energy to provide heating, cooling, ventilation, lighting and power. Individuals in both buildings and manufacturing systems disciplines use methodologies and tools to guide design and reduce resource use including simulation. Buildings and factory facilities are typically suppliers to manufacturing operations and are managed according to different metrics. There is significant potential for improvement by integrating these areas but there is currently a lack of knowledge, skills and tools.

This paper examines tools for manufacturing buildings and manufacturing systems and the methodologies to support their improvement. In the absence of available tools and methods, the paper presents an approach to combine these areas. Prototype work on integrating them along with sustainable manufacturing tactics is introduced.

## 2    Methodology

The wider aim of this research is to build and apply a modelling tool and assess its applicability. The approach is to use a building and testing cycle by using theories and tools available to create a conceptual model and then simulation modelling tool and to test it in practice.

Literature is drawn from a wide variety of sources in the fields of sustainable manufacturing (SM), sustainable buildings (SB), energy efficiency and modelling. Given that the area is developing both peer reviewed journals as well as commercial sources were used. The literature was used to establish current practice in the SM and SB fields as well as in modelling and simulation.

The modelling approach was developed using literature to capture the Material, Energy and Waste (MEW) flows in a way that they could be represented and modelled both qualitatively and quantitatively. From the conceptual model, a prototype simulation tool developed by extending a commercial building energy software modelling product. Testing used synthetic as well as factory process data.

# 3    Literature

Perhaps as a consequence of the absence of methodologies to transform manufacturing systems, there is a lack of software tools, such as simulation, to support the design and analysis of sustainable industrial systems.  As with the adoption of lean methodologies and 'lean/green' techniques (e.g. [9]), there have been incremental developments in simulation for discrete manufacturing that include energy modelling. As lean methods and manufacturing simulation tools typically capture the visible value-adding processes, the significant energy consuming processes in a factory are ignored.  The facilities that supply steam, air and other services are rarely included. Additionally the building that surrounds the manufacturing operations and part of the manufacturing utilities are ignored and considered separately from manufacturing system design.

Building design and refurbishment is regulated and defined by detailed standards and metrics, particularly building codes and voluntary standards such as BREEAM and LEED.  As with manufacturing systems design, building design is supported by improvement methods and guiding tools that incorporate sophisticated modelling for areas such as comfort and energy performance.

Currently there are no commercially available tools for manufacturers to assess environmental performance, identify improvement areas and help suggest concrete actions across the breadth of the application area described [10]. Additionally, there are few examples of research [9, 11, 12, 13] to bring these domains together. Such work presents conceptual design and specific simulation but does not offer as much benefit as the combination of improvement methodologies and integrated buildings, utilities and production system modelling.

Any sustainable manufacturing modelling tool must be capable of modelling the interaction between the production system and its physical environment – firstly the building itself (including the effect of external factors such as weather data or surrounding buildings) and the locality. For example, sustainable manufacturing tactics include the potential to use local waste to power production processes, or the transfer of waste heat from production to other parts of the factory [14].

# 4    Modelling Considerations

Within most manufacturing operations (especially discrete product flow) material and energy flows vary over time.  For energy the 'quality' will also vary (e.g. production of waste heat at a range of temperatures). To understand the interaction of material and energy changes through time and space dynamic modelling is a possibility [9]. Manufacturing simulation tools are commonly used in modelling materials over time and building simulation tools are well established to model energy use and dissipation over time and space.

Extending Discrete Event Simulation (DES) software to include energy has been achieved [15] and can show what energy is used as a result of production activity. Energy use data can be generated from within the model itself, e.g. by an operating machine, or can be generated after a model run by post-processing the output data. Hence energy consumption data can be driven by a combination of shift hours and machine operation hours. Accounting for energy use is valuable as it can educate users as well as quantitatively inform decision making. However, if the energy (and other resources) are simply accounted for rather than modelled then there is a key drawback; there is no distinction between the input and output of energy.

Modelling the input and output of energy in buildings and production processes is essential to understanding how to make more holistic improvements. The output of energy from production (usually immediately in the form of heat) can impact on the building environment (which can account for up to half a factory's energy consumption). Additionally, understanding what energy is being released (quantity, location, time, quality) is essential for seeking opportunities for reuse. Hence creating building and production models within an energy modelling environment has the potential to model the interaction between those two big energy and other resource consumers. Such modelling could be done in a single modelling software package or from the integration of two specialist packages.

The combination of manufacturing and building simulation techniques is therefore potentially very powerful. For example, they could be used together to understand whether waste heat from air compressors could be used for pre-heating water or whether hot air vented at the end of a process cycle could be used to contribute to space heating in winter. Simulation would be used to understand the potential contribution of waste reuse considering the system complexity and the timing of the heat availability, timing of the heat demand, the heat transfer, spatial aspects, etc.

A software system that combines building simulation with an operational model might use tactics to refer the user to sustainable manufacturing improvements. For example, if the simulation tool was able to model production activity and energy consumption then a comparison of the two could be made and a mismatch could be highlighted. If it was deemed that energy was being used unnecessarily when there was no production (highlighted by a 'tactic') then a link could be made to manufacturing practices to illustrate what solutions other companies implemented.

# 5    Conceptual Model

In order to build a tool to support the pursuit of sustainable manufacturing, a conceptual model must be created that captures the key resource flows and transitions within a factory. The factory will include the production processes and the facility that supports the people and equipment within the building. To use the tool it is necessary to have modelling software, a method by which it is used and a repository of practices (or more specifically tactics) on how to improve the model, see Figure 1.

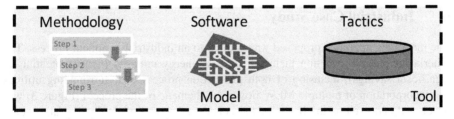

**Fig. 1.** Overview of the modelling tool with method, software and tactics

The software environment will support a model that can contain the utilities and production along with the surrounding building. Some of the utilities will be within the building and some outside. The equipment that consumes and outputs resources are contained within the utilities and production. As the utilities and buildings are potentially affected by the conditions outside the system (or factory) being modelled then the environment is also included. The interrelationships between these modelling components are shown in Figure 2.

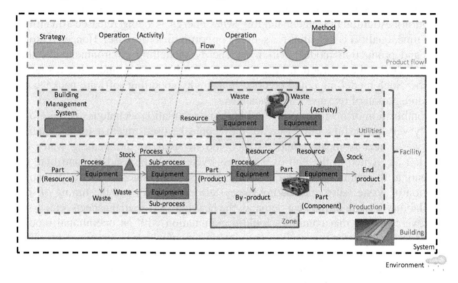

**Fig. 2.** Conceptual model for the software tool

The conceptual model shows the flow of resources through the facility. Parts input and products output are standard elements of production models built in DES software. The building shell and zones within it are standard elements in buildings software. With modelling software that is able to model energy and its transfer then energy and other resources can be modelled for the building (e.g. the heating, ventilation and air conditioning, HVAC) as well as for the production (e.g. the heat and other wastes leaving production equipment).

This generic conceptual model was used to specify the enhancement of existing IES <VE> software to enable the impact of production activity on the wider facility and building to be modelled.

## 6    Industrial Case Study

The modelling approach proposed was applied to an industrial treatment process. The criteria for process selection included: process energy intensity (hence potential for significant savings); inclusion of both production process with surrounding utilities and incorporation of multiple MEW flows. A schematic of the process (Figure 3) was developed and used as the basis for the conceptual model of the facility and then a simulation model (Figure 4) in the prototype <VE> environment.

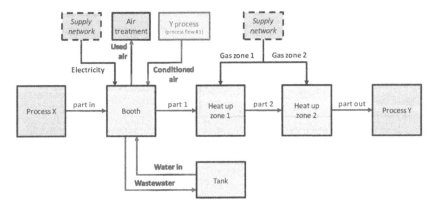

**Fig. 3.** Schematic of the model concept for creation of the software model

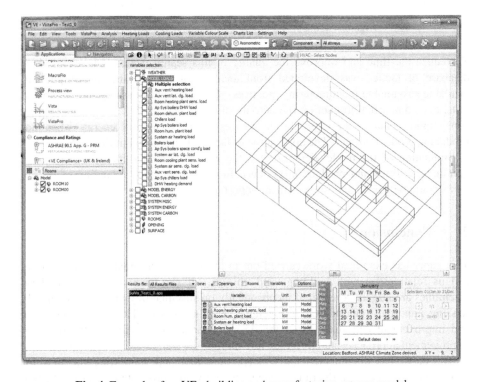

**Fig. 4.** Example of a <VE> building and manufacturing process model

The scale of models containing production and utilities and the complexity of multiple resource flows means that identification of the potential improvements is laborious and skilled. To spot opportunities, users must be able to review each type of flow, their individual timing and their timing relative to other flows based on analysis from first principles as well as experience of other manufacturers' improvements.

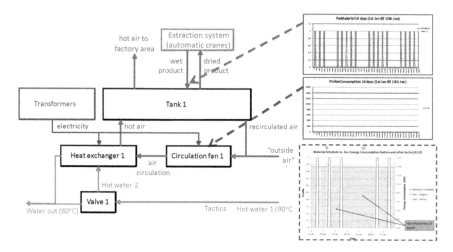

**Fig. 5.** Linking process modelling results to tactics [16]

To reduce the time and improve the quality of this search tactics [14] are used. A database of tactics was developed from analysis of many hundreds of publicly available sustainable manufacturing practices. The tactics have associated automated tests, e.g. comparing production run activity of a production process with the energy consumption data could highlight the process was consuming energy when not producing product output. The application of tactics is illustrated in Figure 5.

Simulation of the model demonstrated the ability to model energy flows across buildings, utilities and production systems. In turn greater understanding of energy flows could be gained and improvement opportunities identified.

## 7     Conclusion

This paper has examined work carried out in the field of sustainable manufacturing and its relationship with buildings and utilities. It has been observed that these disciplines are largely considered independently on sustainability projects, potentially missing important opportunities for better overall solutions. The design, operation and improvement activities across this broad area utilise different skills, different improvement approaches and different software.

The paper has documented the concept of a tool and supporting methods for combined analysis of production systems, ancillary support systems and production buildings. In turn broader and more informed decisions could be made on reducing overall material, energy and resource flows by reducing inputs and reusing wastes.

Future work will encompass software development of further modelling functionality, integration of software workflows to match the activities of the improvement teams and integration of best practices available from manufacturers.

**Acknowledgements.** The authors would like to thank important contributions from the UK's Technology Strategy Board (TSB) and other individuals in Airbus, IES and Toyota contributing to the TSB funded THrough-life Energy and Resource Modelling (THERM) project.

# References

1. World Commission on Environment and Development, Our common future. Oxford University Press, Oxford (1987)
2. Elkington, J.: Cannibals with Forks: The Triple Bottom Line of 21st Century Business. Capstone Publishing, Oxford (1997)
3. Rahimifard, S., Clegg, A.J.: Aspects of sustainable design and manufacture. Int. J. Prod. Res. 45(18-19), 4013–4019 (2007)
4. Seliger, G.: Sustainability in manufacturing: recovery of resources in product and material cycles. Springer, Berlin (2007)
5. Kumazawa, T., Kobayashi, H.: Feasibility study on sustainable manufacturing system. In: 3rd Int. Symposium on Environmentally Conscious Design and Inverse Manufacturing (EcoDesign 2003), Tokyo, Japan, p. 517 (2003)
6. O'Brien, C.: Sustainable production – a new paradigm for the millennium. Int. J. Prod. Econ. 60-61, 1–7 (1999)
7. Allwood, J.M.: What is sustainable manufacturing? Sustainable Manufacturing Seminar Series, pp. 1–32. Cambridge Uni. (February 16, 2005)
8. Despeisse, M., Ball, P.D., Evans, S., Levers, A.: Industrial ecology at factory level – a prototype methodology. Proc. IMechE, Part B: J. Eng. Manuf. 226(10), 1648–1664 (2012)
9. Ball, P.D., Evans, S., Levers, A., Ellison, D.: Zero carbon manufacturing facility – towards integrating material, energy, and waste process flows. Proc. Inst. Mech. Eng. Part B J. Eng. Manuf. 223(9), 1085–1096 (2009)
10. Wright, A.J., Oates, M.R., Greenough, R.: Concepts for the dynamic modelling of energy-related flows in manufacturing. In: Int. Conf. Applied Energy, Suzhou, China, July 6-8 (2012)
11. Oates, M., Wright, A., Greenough, R., Shao, L.: Understanding resource flows in a factory environment. In: Int. Conf. Sustainable Intelligent Manufacturing (SIM), Leiria, Portugal, June 29-July 2 (2011)
12. Hesselbach, J., Herrman, C., Detzer, R., Martin, L., Thiede, S., Lüdemann, B.: Energy efficiency through optimized coordination of production and technical building services. In: 15th CIRP Int. Conf. Life Cycle Engineering, Sydney, Australia, March 17-19 (2008)
13. Michaloski, J.L., Shao, G., Arinez, J., Lyons, K., Leong, S., Riddick, F.: Analysis of Sustainable Manufacturing Using Simulation for Integration of Production and Building Service. In: Symp. Simulation for Architecture & Urban Design (SimAUD), Boston, MA (2011)
14. Despeisse, M., Ball, P.D., Evans, S.: Modelling and tactics for sustainable manufacturing. In: Int. Conf. Sustainable Intelligent Manufacturing (SIM), Leiria, Portugal, June 29-July 2 (2011)
15. Solding, P., Thollander, P.: Increased energy efficiency in a Swedish iron foundry through use of discrete event simulation. In: Winter Simulation Conference, pp. 1971–1976 (2006)
16. Ball, P.D., Despeisse, M., Evans, S., Greenough, R.M., Hope, S.B., Kerrigan, R., Levers, A., Lunt, P., Oates, M.R., Quincey, R., Shao, L., Waltniel, T., Wheatley, C., Wright, A.J.: Modelling energy flows across buildings, facilities and manuf ops. In: Int. Manuf. Conf., Dublin, Ireland (2011)

# Business Modelling for Sustainable Manufacturing

Maria Holgado[1], Donatella Corti[1], Marco Macchi[1], Padmakshi Rana[2],
Samuel Short[2], and Steve Evans[2]

[1] Dept of Management, Economics and Industrial Engineering, Politecnico di Milano
Piazza Leonardo da Vinci, 32, 20133 Milano (Italy)
{maria.holgado,donatella.corti,marco.macchi}@polimi.it
[2] Institute for Manufacturing. University of Cambridge
17 Charles Babbage Road, CB3 0FS Cambridge (UK)
{pr296,sws1001,se321}@cam.ac.uk

**Abstract.** The paper proposes a business modelling process for manufacturing firms to assist them in integrating sustainability into their business model. The process consists of four steps. Expected outputs and questions, driving the analysis and decisions carried along the process, are also included in each step. The proposal is grounded on the state of the art review and a state of practice review done through six exploratory case studies.

**Keywords:** business model, business modelling, sustainable manufacturing, value creation, sustainability.

## 1    Introduction

The changing business landscape, influenced by the increasing awareness of environmental and social impact of industrial activities, is addressing new challenges that stimulates an on-going transformation process leading towards a sustainable industrial system (Evans et al., 2009). Hence, a broader vision for Sustainable Manufacturing has been suggested in the recent years by many authors. A comprehensive definition reflects on Sustainable Manufacturing as '*the ability to smartly use natural resources for manufacturing, by creating products and solutions that, thanks to new technology, regulatory measures and coherent social behaviours, are able to satisfy economic, environmental and social objectives, thus preserving the environment, while continuing to improve the quality of human life*' (Garetti and Taisch, 2012). However, understanding of the term 'sustainability' still varies significantly between manufacturing firms. Some consider mere compliance with environmental legislation to be sustainability; others see waste and cost reduction, or reduction of carbon emissions as sustainability; others view workplace and employee rights or community engagement as sustainability (Bonini et al., 2010). Willard (2005) proposes a 'corporate sustainability continuum', through which firms' progress on the path towards sustainability. Walking along this path will imply changes in the firms that will affect several aspects of their organisation, thus an important innovation process could take place in order to integrate sustainability in

C. Emmanouilidis, M. Taisch, D. Kiritsis (Eds.): APMS 2012, Part I, IFIP AICT 397, pp. 166–174, 2013.

the core purpose of the firm, i.e. in their business model. This integration will need to address two main issues: (i) the value created by the firm should not be only considered in economic terms, hence there is a need for a more holistic view that integrates social and environmental goals (Schaltegger et al., 2011); (ii) from a network perspective, the scope of value needs to include a wider range of stakeholders in a much more explicit manner that involves relationships, exchanges and interactions, besides just economic transactions (Allee, 2011). This paper makes a proposal to this end. After a state of the art review from literature, a state of practice review is presented (section 2): based on their key findings, the methodology for the development of the business modelling process is shortly highlighted (section 3) and the process itself is described (section 4). A discussion is eventually proposed (section 5), to compare our proposal with other processes in literature and to raise the debate on the issues still open in the research agenda.

## 2    Review in Business Modelling

### 2.1    State of the Art Review

The term business model (BM) is widely used in academic and business literature (Richardson, 2008; Zott et al., 2011; Lee et al., 2011). Although there is a general agreement on its basic definition, considered as a simply description of how a firm does business (Richardson, 2008), there is still not theoretical grounding in economic or business studies about this concept (Teece, 2010). BMs have diverse utilities within a firm, such as being a design of the value proposition, creation, delivery and capture mechanisms (Teece, 2010, Osterwalder and Pigneur, 2010) and being a source of innovation (Zott and Amit, 2007, Teece, 2010, Ludeke-Freund, 2010).

Authors such as Chesbrough and Rosenbloom (2002), Braet and Ballon (2007), Richardson (2008), Zott and Amit (2010), Teece (2010), Osterwalder and Pigneur (2010) and Romero and Molina (2011) are key authors in business modelling literature, who have attempted either to describe a business modelling framework or a process. Although without a particular focus on sustainability, their contributions provide a useful overview of the current state of art. Concrete contributions to sustainability-oriented BMs are made by Stubbs and Cocklin (2008), Ludeke-Freund (2010) and Tukker and Tischner (2006), the latter having a focus on Product-Service-System (PSS) as a concrete type of BM. Table 1 summarises their main contributions in terms of what is distinct or novel, that can be (potentially) associated to sustainable business modelling.

As can be deduced from the table, the literature, although comprehensive, is limited in defining and illustrating a business modelling process. The processes primarily guide thinking in generating economic value and do not explicitly embed or consider environmental and social concerns and benefits, nor analyse or include a multi-stakeholder view. Nonetheless, a range of business modelling frameworks is presented that offer a good starting point for developing a business modelling process. The Osterwalder and Pigneur canvas seems the preferable framework for its adaptation to sustainable business modelling: it covers the dominant elements discussed in literature even if, being aligned to what literature is lacking, it is focused on generating economic value and has limited stakeholder inclusion (limited to customer and immediate partners). Governance structure and corporate norms & values are observed – within frameworks – to be important for driving sustainability into BMs.

Key authors in literature have tried to describe a business modelling process, as presented in table 1. However these descriptions are still at a conceptual or exploratory phase, while not much is written about being used in practice. The main drawbacks for sustainable business modelling is the difficulty in embedding sustainability into BM elements and ambiguity in the definition of sustainable BM concept.

**Table 1.** Review of frameworks and processes in business modelling

| Authors | Framework | Process |
|---|---|---|
| Chesbrough and Rosenbloom, 2002 | A framework that embodies strategy and financial modeling and remarks importance of value creation among core company and third parties | --- |
| Tukker and Tischner, 2006 | --- | A process as a methodology for PSS development under a sustainability-based approach |
| Braet and Ballon, 2007 | --- | A process as a cyclic approach; main element of the approach is the categorization of the actors and roles that are active in a given value network |
| Richardson, 2008 | A framework organized around the concept of value; main elements are: value proposition, value creation and delivery and value capture | --- |
| Stubbs and Cocklin, 2008 | A framework for analysis consisting on structural and cultural attributes of sustainable BMs | --- |
| Teece, 2010 | --- | A process with emphasis on value proposition and mechanisms for value capture, focusing primarily on customers and referring exclusively to long-term economic sustainability |
| Zott and Amit, 2010 | A framework with a broader understanding of value creation through interactions along the value network; main elements are: content, structure and governance | --- |
| Lüdeke-Freund, 2010 | A conceptual framework oriented to sustainability strategies driven by eco-innovations and focused on creating an extended customer value | --- |
| Osterwalder and Pigneur 2010 | A framework (named as canvas) proposing a set of elements for the design of BMs: customer segments; value proposition; channels; customer relationships; revenue streams; key resources; key activities; key partnerships; cost structure | A business design process made of 5 phases: Mobilize, Understand, Design, Implement and Manage |
| Romero and Molina, 2011 | A framework providing a multi-value system perspective; multi-stakeholder approach; the role of the customer in the co-creation process | --- |

To sum up, the literature is lacking many sustainability related issues, primarily: (i) the integration of a broader range of stakeholders in business modelling, understanding how value might be perceived for them; (ii) a process for exploring other forms of value, rather than solely economic one, and for analyzing related relationships, exchanges and interactions.

## 2.2    State of Practice Review

This section provides the results of the state of practice reviewed through 6 case studies spread across norm to extreme examples of sustainability, where norm represents an incremental approach to sustainability innovation, and extreme represents a firm seeking to introduce radical change. A semi-structured interview approach was adopted to explore the current practice in the selected cases. Table 2 highlights the results for the norm cases: three cases (case A, C, D) are multinational companies, one is a start-up (case B). Table 3 highlights the results for the extreme cases: one is a start-up (case E), one is a SME (case F). The factors under analysis are: the key drivers for sustainability initiatives (row number 1); the BM innovation processes employed (row number 2); the value network perspective (row number 3).

**Table 2.** Review of business modelling process in practice – norm

|   | A (Food & Agriculture) | B (Laundry equipment) | C (Printing & copying equipment) | D (Food & Agriculture equipment) |
|---|---|---|---|---|
| 1 | Economic motive + climate change + resource limitations | Technology innovation + Customers' increasing awareness of energy and water costs | Economic motive + resource efficiency + customer demand for low cost of ownership | Productivity and sustainability of agricultural land + fuel & time efficiencies |
| 2 | Focus on frugality – efficiency + waste reduction and reuse + formal process for assessing sustainability dimensions of new business initiatives + stakeholder mapping | Technology led firm + little focus on BM, no focus on sustainability per se | Little formal focus on BMs or sustainability per se | PSS as strategic add-on to the core product business + various strategy tools employed to consider customer demands, pricing and distribution channels |
| 3 | Close relationship with growers in supply chain + engagement with local communities around the growers + B2B | Relationships with trial partners for technology development + Partnerships with university for R&D + Focus on developing licensing to major manufacturers | Distributors and resellers + Employees recognized as key resource to the BM | Suppliers of major mechanical systems and software solutions + some wholly-owned distributors and network of other dealers and importers + relationships with customers through employees |

**Table 3.** Review of business modelling process in practice – extreme

|   | E (Personal transportation) | F (Home and Office Furniture) |
|---|---|---|
| 1 | Perceived need for environmental friendly personal mobility solution | Resource efficiency + long-term view of value optimization for the customer and the environment |
| 2 | Systematic innovation process + iterative redesign for optimization + current tools available not considered particularly helpful | Little formal development of business modelling for sustainability + ad-hoc process of business improvement |
| 3 | Network of suppliers for technology, hydrogen infrastructure + local council partners for programme roll-out | Removed intermediaries from distribution network for closeness to customers + Local manufacturing strategy + employees as key resource + Strong ties with customers & suppliers through financing structure + potential for turning firm into employee owned |

Followings are the overall findings of the state of practice review.

- Business modelling often has an organic/ad-hoc approach depending on radical leadership rather than tools and techniques.
- Sustainability is seen more as a detached or isolated concept with difficulty in embedding it in the business purpose and processes.
- Within the stakeholders discussion, their interactions and understanding of value are minimal given the dynamic and complex structure of value networks.
- Governance structure influences whether or not sustainability is successfully incorporated.

### 2.3    Research Gap

The literature and practice review highlights a need for innovation in business modelling process that will assist manufacturing firms in developing and enhancing their BMs to embed sustainability. The existing knowledge in BM development is focused on generating only economic value. To extend the construct of value to include environmental and social benefits through a multi-stakeholder view, a substantial change in the way business are conceived and operated is required. Hence, this paper proposes a business modelling process that assists firms in embedding sustainability into their business, exploring other forms of value (social and environmental) and analysing value exchanges.

## 3    Methodology

The literature and practice reviews on business modelling contributed to the initial development of the proposed business modelling process. Afterwards, the development went through further iterations involving brainstorming sessions, meetings and two exploratory workshops with research and industrial partners. It further involved reviews of EU and international projects and reports and researchers working on other knowledge areas (sustainable manufacturing, value networks) were considered for idea generation and discussion.

## 4    Proposed Business Modelling Process

The business modelling process herein proposed provides a multi-stakeholder view, shared-value creation with different perspectives on value and explicit consideration of environment and society as main elements for developing a sustainable BM. The business modelling process is composed of four steps. Table 4 introduces the description of each step. At the end of the process, it is required to build the governance structure for supporting BM implementation. In particular, the governance structure aims at providing better ways to manage, measure, monitor and control the business activities; hence, it would act as a support for the effective incorporation of sustainability in the BM.

**Table 4.** Business modelling process – description of the steps

|   | STEP | DESCRIPTION |
|---|------|-------------|
| 1 | Purpose of the business | This step attempts to clarify the business concepts in order to go on along next steps, understanding the strategic objectives and firms' position towards sustainability; in particular, it aims at discussing business concepts such as products & service bundles, sustainability values, industry-related needs and opportunities. |
| 2 | Identify potential stakeholders and select sustainability factors | This step aims at identifying (i) the potential stakeholders within the business ecosystem and what they do value and (ii) the sustainability factors leading decisions |
| 3 | Develop the value proposition | This step pursues to envision the value proposition for a firm and its stakeholders |
| 4 | Develop the value creation and delivery system and the value capture mechanism | This step aims at developing the value creation and delivery system and the value capture mechanisms by defining in particular the key activities, key resources, key partners, key channels, key mind-set and the value exchanges for the firm and its stakeholders |

Table 5 presents the four steps of the process identifying the expected outputs as well as several questions that would drive their achievement, as well as the analysis and decisions at each step.

**Table 5.** Business modelling process – steps, expected outputs and questions

|   | STEP | EXPECTED OUTPUTS AND QUESTIONS AT EACH STEP |
|---|------|---------------------------------------------|
| 1 | Purpose of the business | *Concept of industry, products and services bundle, sustainability values (higher level thinking), idea generation/starting point* |
|   |   | • What are the reasons the firm is in business? <br> • Which is the firm's approach towards sustainability? <br> • What are the trends, emerging technologies, opportunities and drivers for the firm's context? (opportunities and drivers for environmental and social sustainability) |
| 2 | Identify potential stakeholders and select sustainability factors | *Stakeholders type, what are they interested in and which sustainability factors are important to them?* |
|   |   | • Who are the possible stakeholders? <br> • What is of value to each stakeholder? <br> • What sustainability factors are important to them? <br> • What are the factors that will drive the firm's decision? |
| 3 | Develop the value proposition | *Value proposition for a firm and its stakeholders* |
|   |   | • What are the value opportunities for the firm? What is(are) the potential value exchange(s)? <br> • What happens if the firm pushes beyond compliance of current accepted standards? <br> • What are the negative potentialities associated to the offering? How can they be eliminated or mitigated? <br> • How can positive social and environmental value be enhanced? <br> • What is the firm's offering – products and services, tangible and intangible benefits – to each stakeholder? |
| 4 | Develop the value creation and delivery system and the value capture mechanism | *Key activities, key resources, key partners, key channels, key mindset. Definition of the value exchanges and value capture for the stakeholders.* |
|   |   | • How is value created and delivered to the identified stakeholders? <br> • What are the activities, resources, suppliers/partners and the relationships with them, network configuration, channels and mind-set? <br> • What are the value exchanges for the firm and the stakeholders? <br> • How is the economic value captured? <br> • How does the firm capture value from public value (environmental and social) creation? <br> • How does other stakeholders capture value? <br> • Is the business model economically, environmentally and socially viable? |

# 5     Discussion

## 5.1     Comparison with Other Business Modelling Processes

This section presents a comparison between our proposed business modelling process and other processes from the literature review[1]. Table 6 shows the steps compounding each process as well as, in the bottom part of the table, their sustainability approaches. It should be noted that our proposal emphasises a comprehensive vision of value (including economic, environmental and social aspects) and a broader multi-stakeholder perspective along all the steps. Another advantage is that it does not address any concrete type of BM, remaining then applicable for a higher variety of firms.

**Table 6.** Comparison among business modelling processes

| | Our proposed business modelling process | Tukker and Tischner, 2006 | Teece, 2010 | Osterwalder and Pigneur, 2010 |
|---|---|---|---|---|
| 1 | Purpose of the business | Analysis on PSS opportunities | | Mobilize |
| 2 | Identify potential stakeholders and select sustainability factors | | Segment the market | Understand |
| 3 | Develop the value proposition | PSS idea generation | Create a value proposition for each segment | |
| 4 | Develop the value creation & delivery system and the value capture mechanism | PSS design | Design and implement mechanism to capture value from each segment | Design |
| | Governance structure – a necessary step but external to our business modelling process | Make the implementation plan | Figure out and implement "isolating mechanisms' to hinder or block imitation by competitors, and disintermediation by customers and suppliers | Implement and manage |
| **Sustainability approach within the business modelling process** | | | | |
| | The three sustainability aspects are considered. It includes a broader vision of stakeholders. Questions in each step provide a guide for sustainability during the whole process. | The three sustainability aspects are considered. It includes a broader vision of stakeholders | Sustainability is only related to economic subsistence and uniqueness of the business model. It is only focused on customer and suppliers. | No specific elements for sustainability are included. It is focused only on economic aspects and considers only customers and business partners. |

## 5.2     Conclusions and Future Research

Firms are attempting to explore BM innovations in order to address the new challenges of sustainable manufacturing and enhance their current BMs by incorporating economic, environmental and social sustainability in a balanced way. A new business modelling process is required that extends consideration to the broader value network, and frames value in terms of economic, social and environmental, rather than just economic aspects. A preliminary business modelling process has then

---

[1] Braet and Ballon, 2007 were not included in the table as they did not develop a process based on steps but a cycle with four phases (Organization, Technology, Service and Financial).

been developed and refined through discussions with industrial partners. Indeed, the business modelling process presented herein has to be understood as a process that may help firms to integrate sustainability fully into the BM and redefine their business logic in order to maximize the value created and delivered through the business ecosystem, while integrating social and environmental value.

Further research is recommended for identifying and enhancing existing tools or developing new tools for business modelling, which will assist in identifying and integrating environmental and social value perspectives in addition to economic value, and in including a multiple-stakeholder approach. The proposed business modelling process is also envisioned as a model for guiding the collection of tools. Further need is testing the business modelling process and its tools in use cases taken from real industrial contexts.

**Acknowledgment.** The paper presents some initial results from "Sustainable value creation in manufacturing networks"(SustainValue) project. The research is funded by the European Community's Seventh Framework Programme (FP7/2007-2013) under grant agreement n°262931.

# References

Allee, V.: Value Networks and the true nature of collaboration, Online edn. Value Networks and Verna Allee Associates (2011)

Braet, O., Ballon, P.: Business Model Scenarios for Remote Management. Journal of Theoretical and Applied Electronic Commerce Research 2(3), 62–79 (2007)

Bonini, S., Gorner, S., Jones, A.: McKinsey Global Survey results: How companies manage sustainability. McKinsey&Company (2010)

Chesbrough, H., Rosenbloom, R.S.: The role of the business model in capturing value from innovation: evidence from Xerox Corporation's technology spin-off companies. Industrial and Corporate Change 11(3), 529–555 (2002)

Evans, S., Bergendahl, M.N., Gregory, M.J., Ryan, C.: Towards a sustainable industrial system. Institute for Manufacturing, University of Cambridge (2009)

Garetti, M., Taisch, M.: Sustainable manufacturing: trends and research challenges. Production Planning and Control 23(2-3), 83–104 (2012)

Lee, J.H., Shin, D.I., Hong, Y.S.: Business Model Design Methodology for Innovative Product-Service Systems: A Strategic and Structured approach. In: Annual SRII Global Conference, pp. 663–673 (2011)

Lüdeke-Freund, F.: Towards a conceptual framework of business models for sustainability. In: Knowledge Collaboration & Learning for Sustainable Innovation ERSCP-EMSU Conference, Delft, The Netherlands (2010)

Osterwalder, A., Pigneur, Y.: Business Model Generation. A Handbook for Visionaries, Game Changers, and Challengers. John Wiley & Sons, Inc., New Jersey (2010)

Richardson, J.: The business model: an integrative framework for strategy execution. Strategic Change 17, 133–144 (2008)

Romero, D., Molina, A.: Collaborative networked organisations and customer communities: value co-creation and co-innovation in the networking era. Production Planning and Control, 1–26 (July 2011)

Schaltegger, S., Lüdeke-Freund, F., Hansen, E.G.: Business Cases for Sustainability and the Role of Business Model Innovation: Developing a Conceptual Framework. Centre for Sustainability Management, Leuphana University, Lueneburg (2011)

Stubbs, W., Cocklin, C.: Conceptualizing a Sustainability Business Model. Organization & Environment 21(2), 103–127 (2008)

Teece, D.: Business models, business strategy and innovation. Long Range Planning 43(2/3), 172–194 (2010)

Tukker, A., Tischner, U. (eds.): New business for old Europe. Product-service development, competitiveness and sustainability. Greenleaf, Sheffield (2006)

Zott, C., Amit, R.: Business Model Design: An Activity System Perspective. Long Range Planning 43(2-3), 216–226 (2010)

Zott, C., Amit, R., Massa, L.: The Business Model: Recent Developments and Future Research. Journal of Management 37(4), 1019–1042 (2011)

Willard, B.: Next Sustainability Wave: Building Boardroom Buy-In. New Society Publishers (2005)

# Embedding Sustainability in Business Modelling through Multi-stakeholder Value Innovation

Samuel W. Short, Padmakshi Rana[*], Nancy M.P. Bocken, and Steve Evans

University of Cambridge, Institute for Manufacturing
17 Charles Babbage Road, Cambridge CB3 0FS, United Kingdom
pr296@cam.ac.uk

**Abstract.** This paper investigates how businesses might create balanced social, environmental and economic value through integrating sustainability more fully into the core of their business. For this purpose a more systematic approach to business model innovation for sustainability is required. A novel value mapping tool is proposed to help firms create value propositions better suited for sustainability. The tool adopts a multiple stakeholder view of value, a network rather than firm centric perspective, and introduces a novel way of conceptualizing value that specifically introduces *value destroyed* and *value missed*, in addition to traditional terms of the core value proposition, and new opportunities for value creation and capture. This will support business modelling for sustainability.

**Keywords:** sustainability, business model, sustainable business model, business model innovation, value creation.

## 1    Background

Current approaches to industrial sustainability such as cleaner production, eco-innovation, and Corporate Social Responsibility (CSR) are enabling industry to reduce un-sustainability. However, these approaches assume that business can continue largely as usual by simply making incremental efficiency and emissions improvements, or giving a little back to society in the form of philanthropic initiatives to offset negative impacts of business. These efforts increasingly appear inadequate to address the growing challenges facing industry and society of climate change, resource scarcity, environmental degradation, and escalating concerns over social sustainability.

A fundamental paradigm shift appears necessary, in which business activities and consumption patterns are aligned with environmental and social objectives. With careful business model redesign it may be possible for mainstream manufacturers to radically improve sustainable performance to deliver greater environmental and social value while at the same time delivering economic sustainability, as suggested by Stubbs and Cocklin (2008), Porter and Kramer (2011), Yunus et al. (2010), and FORA (2010).

---

[*] Corresponding author.

C. Emmanouilidis, M. Taisch, D. Kiritsis (Eds.): APMS 2012, Part I, IFIP AICT 397, pp. 175–183, 2013.

## 1.1    Business Models

A significant number of authors have contributed to the literature on business models and business model innovation. There appears to be reasonably good conceptual understanding, albeit, with several differing perspectives (Teece 2010 and Zott et. al 2011). Richardson (2008), based on a wide range of literature, identifies some common themes, and concisely summarises the elements of business models as: the value proposition (i.e. the offer and the target customer segment), the value creation and delivery system, and the value capture system. Zott and Amit (2010), present the business model from an activity system perspective, and hence view the business model as a network. This exemplifies an emerging view that business models need to be developed with a network rather than firm-centric perspective. Furthermore, Chesbrough and Rosenbloom (2002), Zott and Amit (2010), Teece (2010) and Osterwalder and Pigneur (2010), are key authors who have described a business modelling process.

## 1.2    Sustainable Business Model

A sustainable business model has been defined as 'a business model that creates competitive advantage through superior customer value and contributes to a sustainable development of the company and society' (Lüdeke-Freund 2010). Stubbs and Cocklin (2008) assert that sustainable business models use both a systems and firm-level perspective, build on the triple bottom line approach to define the firm's purpose and measure performance, include a wider range of stakeholders, and consider the environment and society as stakeholders. Sustainable business models as a prerequisite must be economically sustainable. As such, Schaltegger et al. (2011) suggests the objective in business modelling for sustainability is therefore to identify solutions that allow firms to capture economic value from generating public environmental and social value, thereby establishing the business case for sustainability.

## 1.3    Value Innovation and Stakeholders

Business model innovation involves changing 'the way you do business', rather than 'what you do' and must go beyond process and products (Amit and Zott 2012). In other words, business model innovation is about changing the overall value proposition of the firm and reconfiguring the network of stakeholders involved in creating and delivering the value.

At the core of business model innovation is re-thinking the value proposition. Conventionally, business model innovation emphasizes almost exclusively on creating new forms of customer value. To create sustainable business, a more holistic view of the value proposition is required that takes a wider stakeholder perspective (Bowman and Ambrosini 2000), and integrates economic, social and environmental value creation. Hence, the value proposition needs to include benefits to other stakeholders and specifically to society and the environment as well as to customers and the firm. Adapting Donaldson and Preston's (1995) view, six stakeholder types can be observed for sustainable business models and modelling – Customers, investors and shareholders, employees, suppliers and partners, the environment, and society. As Allee (2011) suggests, the scope of value needs to be extended in a much more explicit manner that involves understanding tangible and intangible value flows 1 between stakeholders towards identifying relationships, exchanges and interactions, and opportunities for greater shared-value creation.

### 1.4    Tools for Business Model Innovation for Sustainability

Few tools if any really assist firms in the practical creation of business models for sustainability. The tools and methods currently used are either conceptual or have not been used widely in industry, and typically rely on a well-trained (external) facilitator.

One of the seemingly popular frameworks to support the generic business modelling process is Osterwalder and Pigneur's (2010) business model canvas. While being well-conceived and academically grounded its ability to generate innovative thinking beyond pure economic value creation seems limited due to the narrow view of stakeholder value. Network-centric tools for business model innovation are generally still highly conceptual to date. Tools such as Allee's (2011) Value Network Analysis (VNA) offer an approach to value mapping and understanding shared value creation, which might assist in business modelling. However, VNA maps are complicated and time-consuming to develop, and not specifically intended for business modelling.

## 2    Practice Review

Despite the apparent shortfalls in tools and methods, there are an increasing number of practical examples of firms successfully exploring and innovating for sustainability. A practice review was conducted which consisted of the assessment of case studies in the literature and popular press, augmented with in-depth case studies of five firms that are actively engaging in business model innovation for sustainability. The cases were selected to represent a range of industry sectors, and include start-up, small and medium size enterprises (SMEs) and multinational companies (MNCs). These cases range from an incremental approach to sustainability innovation through to firms seeking to introduce radical change. A semi-structured interview approach was adopted to explore how these firms conceptualise business model innovation for sustainability, and how they are seeking to embed sustainability into the core of their businesses.  Several common themes emerged from the practice review:

---

[1] Examples of tangible value include products, services, money, knowledge, and technology while intangible values include market access, product feedback, and corporate reputation (Allee 2011).

- A common recognition of the need for innovation to embed sustainability in the business by consciously considering environmental and social value.
- Innovations specifically target negative impacts of business, and seek to reduce losses and waste. This appears somewhat distinct from mainstream business where emphasis is on seeking opportunities for new customer-orientated value creation.
- Innovation has been approached generally in an ad-hoc, incremental, and experimental manner, rather than following a prescriptive process or using specific tools.
- Innovations often depend strongly on visionary leadership of a few key individuals.
- The term 'value' was used often (e.g. customer value, economic value) but there seems to be considerable ambiguity about the use and meaning of the term.

Innovation always presents some level of risk and uncertainty for a firm since it requires going beyond what they currently know and do (Chesbrough 2010). Business model innovation for sustainability seems likely to compound this due to the need to consider additional social and environmental dimensions of value. For this reason, and perhaps because of the lack of systematic tools, business model innovation for sustainability to date has relied on somewhat radical leaders, and has to a large extent been avoided by most mainstream manufacturers.

# 3     Research Gap

This paper identifies a need for a tool to assist firms in better understanding sustainable value creation within their business activities, and assist them in developing new business models with sustainability at their core. Specifically, current tools and methods lack a systematic approach for considering value for multiple stakeholders and for innovating the business model for sustainability. In general, a firm-centric approach rather than a network (system) perspective is taken. This paper investigates the following question: *How can sustainability be embedded in the business modelling process through a better understanding of value?*

# 4     Proposed Solution – A Value Mapping Tool

Based on the above review, a value mapping tool is proposed to help companies create value propositions to support business modelling for sustainability. A pilot test of this tool was conducted with a start-up company to develop the approach. The authors conducted further brainstorming against existing industrial examples to further enhance the tool. As a next stage of the research the tool will be comprehensively tested with a wider range of industrial participants. The novel aspects of this tool to address the gap identified in literature and practice are:

- **Systematic assessment of value** based on the observation that business model innovation for sustainability not only needs to seek to create new forms of value, but must also seek to address value that is currently destroyed or missed.

- A **network-centric** perspective for value innovation to ensure optimisation/consideration of value from a total network, or system-wide perspective, rather than narrowly considering a firm-centric view of value.
- A **multiple stakeholder view of value.** Current business modelling processes and tools predominantly focus on customers and partners in the immediate value-chain. This process seeks to expand this range of stakeholders.

## 4.1    Underlying Rationale for the Proposed Value Mapping Tool

The basis of the proposed tool for value mapping is the observation (literature and practice) that product/service industrial networks often create a portfolio of opportunities for value innovation for their various stakeholders as illustrated below in figure 1.

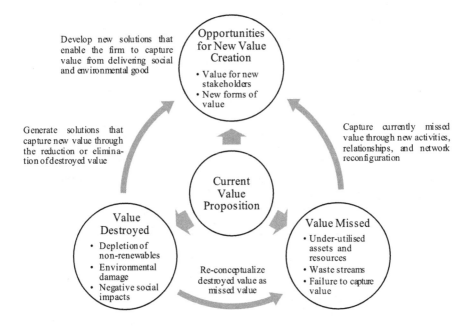

**Fig. 1.** Opportunities for Value Innovation

At the core of this portfolio is the *value proposition* of the network. This represents the benefits derived by each stakeholder in the forms of exchange value involved in creating and delivering a product or service offering, and value in use of that product or service (Lepak et al. 2007). In delivering the value proposition, individual stakeholders and networks collectively may also destroy value through their activities. *Value destroyed* can take various forms, but in the sustainability context is mostly concerning the damaging environmental and social impacts of business activities. The literature often refers to these as negative externalities, but it is felt that this terminology may tend to artificially distance these impacts from the firm.

Furthermore, networks and individual stakeholders also often squander value within their existing business models. This can be conceived as *missed value opportunities*, where individual stakeholders fail to capitalise on existing resources and capabilities, are operating below industry best-practice, or fail to receive the benefits they actually seek from the network. This might be due to poorly designed value creation or capture systems, failure to acknowledge the value, or inability to persuade other stakeholders to pay for the benefit. There are also *new value opportunities*, which tend to be the more usual focus of business model innovation, seeking to expand the business into new markets and introduce new products and services.

## 4.2     Value Mapping Tool

A preliminary tool has been developed to structure the value mapping process as shown in figure 2.

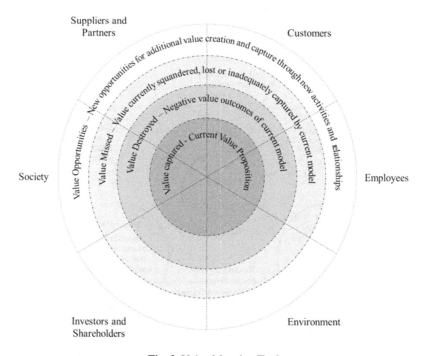

**Fig. 2.** Value Mapping Tool

The design of the tool is based on emphasising:

- **Stakeholder segments.** Each segment represents a relevant stakeholder group in the product/service network. To facilitate a network-centric perspective, the firm is represented as employee and owner stakeholder groups, rather than as a discrete stakeholder.

- **Four representations of value.** The four circles represent the forms of value that are of specific interest to the process of business modelling for sustainability proposed in figure 1. Identifying them separately encourages a more thorough and complete exploration of the current business model, and assists in identifying areas requiring change or improvement.

The circular form of the tool was developed over a series of workshops, to facilitate a holistic system-perspective of value, to encourage equal consideration of all stakeholder interests, and explore the inter-relatedness between stakeholders. Alternative formats such as tabular data capture were tested, but the circular tool better engaged the participants, facilitated discussion of opportunities for value creation, and better stimulated creative lateral thinking.

### 4.3     The Value Mapping Process (Using the Tool)

The process follows several steps:

- The process begins by defining the unit of analysis as the product/service, or portfolio of products/services offered by a business unit, firm, or an industry. The focus is on the offering, rather than the firm, to support a network perspective.
- Stakeholders are identified and placed in each segment of the tool. The starting point is generic stakeholder types, but the tool is populated with specific stakeholders to facilitate the analysis. Specifically society and the environment are included as stakeholders. In a workshop setting it was observed to be beneficial for some segments to initially be left blank to allow later addition during the process.
- A facilitated brainstorming is then used to populate each stakeholder segment in turn with the various forms of value generated for that stakeholder – starting at the centre of the circle and working outwards. This follows a logical progression from the core value proposition by the current business model, outwards to values further removed from the core offering. By following this progression each step builds upon and is informed by each preceding step as illustrated earlier in figure 1.

To maximise the potential of the tool, representatives or suitable proxies for each major stakeholder group should participate in the process to solicit broad perspectives on value. Furthermore, a lifecycle-based approach is introduced to assist participants in identifying all stakeholders and various forms of value throughout each stage in the provision of the product/service from concept through to end-of-life.

## 5     Discussion

Business model innovation seems a key to delivering future sustainability. This paper identifies a gap in current literature and practice for systematic tools to assist firms in business model innovation for sustainability and hence proposes a tool to assist firms and practitioners in mapping value exchanges for sustainability. The tool is intended as a first step in a business modelling process for embedding sustainability into the core purpose of the firm and its network of stakeholders.

To further develop business modelling for sustainability, an approach to assist in transforming the value proposition is needed to help eliminate destroyed value or shift destroyed value into positive opportunities; seek solutions to capture missed value; and integrate new opportunities for value creation. It should be reiterated that the purpose of such innovation is not simply to reduce negatives, but rather to reconceive the business model to deliver sustainability. Amit and Zott (2012) suggest this might be achieved through introducing new activities, new stakeholders, or reconfiguring the existing activities and network in novel ways. A potential practical approach to facilitate this innovation process might be through building upon knowledge of existing and proven business model innovations for sustainability to date. Preliminary work has collated several potential business model innovation archetypes, and these are under analysis to identify defining patterns and attributes that might facilitate grouping and provide mechanisms for achieving value proposition innovation. Further work with industrial partners is planned to develop the business modelling process to refine and demonstrate the approach.

**Acknowledgements.** This paper builds on work undertaken on SustainValue, a European Commission's 7th Framework Programme (FP7/2007-2013). The authors gratefully acknowledge the support of the European Commission, and the contribution of the academic and industrial partners on this project in developing and testing the ideas presented herein.

# References

1. Amit, R., Zott, C.: Creating Value through Business Model Innovation. MIT Sloan Management Review 53(3), 41–49 (2012)
2. Allee, V.: Value Networks and the True Nature of Collaboration, Online edn. Value Net Works and Verna Allee Associates (2011)
3. Bowman, C., Ambrosini, V.: Value Creation versus Value Capture: Towards a Coherent Definition of Value in Strategy. British Journal of Management 11, 1–15 (2000)
4. Chesbrough, H., Rosenbloom, R.S.: The role of the business model in capturing value from innovation: evidence from Xerox Corporation's technology spin-off companies. Industrial and Corporate Change 11(3), 529–555 (2002)
5. Chesbrough, H.: Business Model Innovation: Opportunities and Barriers. Long Range Planning 43(2-3), 354–363 (2010)
6. Donaldson, T., Preston, L.E.: The Stakeholder Theory of the Corporation: Concepts, Evidence, and Implications. The Academy of Management Review 20(1), 65–91 (1995)
7. FORA Nordic project: Green business models in the Nordic Region: A key to promote sustainable growth, Denmark (2010)
8. Lepak, D.P., Smith, K.G., Taylor, M.S.: Value Creation and Value Capture: A Multilevel Perspective. The Academy of Management Review 32(1), 180–194 (2007)
9. Osterwalder, A., Pigneur, Y.: Business Model Generation: A Handbook for Visionaries, Game Changers, and Challengers. John Wiley & Sons (2010)
10. Porter, M.E., Kramer, M.R.: Creating Shared Value. Harvard Business Review (2011)
11. Richardson, J.: The business model: an integrative framework for strategy execution. Strategic Change 17(5-6), 133–144 (2008)

12. Schaltegger, S., Lüdeke-Freund, F., Hansen, E.G.: Business Cases for Sustainability and the Role of Business Model Innovation Developing a Conceptual Framework. Centre for Sustainability Management (CSM), Leuphana University of Lueneburg, Lueneburg (2011)
13. Stubbs, W., Cocklin, C.: Conceptualizing a "Sustainability Business Model". Organization & Environment 21(2), 103–127 (2008)
14. Teece, D.J.: Business Model, Business Strategy and Innovation. Long Range Planning 43, 172–194 (2010)
15. Yunus, M., Moingeon, B., Lehmann-Ortega, L.: Building Social Business Models: Lessons from the Grameen Experience. Long Range Planning 43(2-3), 308–325 (2010)
16. Zott, C., Amit, R., Massa, L.: The Business Model: Recent Developments and Future Research. Journal of Management 37(4), 1019–1042 (2011)
17. Zott, C., Amit, R.: Business Model Design: An Activity System Perspective. Long Range Planning 43(2-3), 216–226 (2010)

# Toward Sustainability Governance in Manufacturing Networks

Teuvo Uusitalo, Markku Reunanen, Katri Valkokari, Pasi Valkokari,
and Katariina Palomäki

VTT Technical Research Centre of Finland
Tekniikankatu 1, P.O. Box 1300, FIN-33101 Tampere, Finland
{teuvo.uusitalo,markku.reunanen,katri.valkokari,
pasi.valkokari,katariina.palomaki}@vtt.fi

**Abstract.** This paper presents a model for addressing sustainability governance in manufacturing networks. The model developed addresses sustainability governance within a manufacturing network as a process to guide the activities of all actors involved toward sustainable development and performance throughout the product life cycle. According to the model, there are three main tasks of sustainability governance: analysing, organising, and developing. These three main tasks are in accordance with company-level approaches but highlight the need for multilevel network governance.

**Keywords:** sustainability, governance, manufacturing networks.

## 1    Introduction

This paper deals with results of an on-going FP7-funded research project entitled 'Sustainable Value Creation in Manufacturing Networks' (SustainValue). The overall goal of the SustainValue project is to develop industrial models, solutions, and performance standards for new sustainable and better-performing production and service networks. One objective of the project is to develop a sustainability governance model for manufacturing networks. This paper presents the first results from the development of this model.

Corporate governance provides the structure through which the objectives of the company are set, and thus it forms the system by which an organisation makes and implements decisions in pursuit of its objectives [1]. The governance model defines 'what to do', 'how to do it', 'who should do it', and 'how it should be measured'. It addresses the rules, processes, metrics, and organisational structures needed for effective planning, decision-making, steering, and control [2]. The main differences between the company and network governance models are related to legal factors, decision-making processes, and control mechanisms. Companies are legal entities with their own goals, and their decision-making is based on internal hierarchical structures (control governance) whereas networks consist of independent actors, who have their own targets and decision-making models.

C. Emmanouilidis, M. Taisch, D. Kiritsis (Eds.): APMS 2012, Part I, IFIP AICT 397, pp. 184–191, 2013.

The European Vision for 2020 report calls for understanding manufacturing as a network of complex and development-oriented relations. The new production paradigm is based on collaborative, value-adding networks, and globalisation has activated a different industrial revolution, leading to a new world distribution of production and markets [3]. Increasing demands for sustainability, however, have created new challenges and emerging opportunities for society and for business. A recent executive study illustrates that companies' perceptions of sustainability are changing. As in the past, company representatives see the potential for supporting corporate reputation. But recently they have also come to expect operational and growth-oriented benefits in cutting costs and pursuing opportunities provided by new markets and products. Additionally, in relation to the social and environmental aspects of sustainability, companies are now integrating sustainability principles into their business by retaining and motivating employees and by saving energy, alongside pursuit of other sustainability goals [4].

Since manufacturing activities at present are organised through networked processes, new models for network governance are needed for ensuring sustainable development and performance of manufacturing operations. These models should enable clear identification of those network actors and stakeholders who influence and can be influenced by the sustainability of the product in the course of its life cycle.

## 2    Value

Sustainability is often perceived from a limited value creation view. The focus has been on an economic, compliance, regulation or legislation perspective, hence raising the need for a more holistic view of sustainable value that integrates economic, social and environmental goals. From a network perspective, the scope of value needs to go beyond customers, immediate partners and shareholders. The scope should consider relationships, exchanges and interactions. Value can be defined as the set of benefits derived by a stakeholder from an exchange. This implies the need for improved understanding of stakeholder value, and the need to seek opportunities for alignment and exchanges between stakeholders. [5]

The development of a common value system in a network context is important in order to support the sustainability of collaborative behaviour [6]. Different value systems of network partners can lead to different perceptions of benefits and non-collaborative behaviours. In order to overcome this, mechanisms to promote transparency and alignment of value systems could be introduced at the level of the governance rules. Research is needed to identify suitable indicators of the collaboration level of each partner. [7]

The key to new sustainable business models is in understanding the value from network perspective. A value network generates value through complex dynamic exchanges between enterprises, customers, suppliers, partners, stakeholders and the community. These networks engage in transactions around goods, services, and revenue. In addition the two other aspects are knowledge value and intangible value or benefits. All three are important in a value network. [8]

# 3    Manufacturing Networks

In traditional manufacturing network operations of suppliers, lead producers (such as OEMs) and customers are seen as independent sequential tasks, which form a value chain. Since the 1990s, however, this pattern has been changing and the theoretical discussion has emphasised the transfer from value chains to value networks [9, 10].

The trend among customers, lead producers (OEMs), and suppliers seems to be to engage in forward transfer in their value chains. This means that customers, lead producers or OEMs outsource manufacturing (give up earlier value chain phases), and their suppliers try to increase services (add later value chain phases and give up some of the earlier phases). Interdependency of operations and co-creation between the actors have been emphasized from several theoretical viewpoints [11, 12, 13].

In the new network economy, the success of a firm depends on its strategic collaboration with other organizations that have an influence on the creation and delivery of its services or products. Manufacturing networks can, therefore, be defined as 'not only a new type of manufacturing system deriving new strategic capabilities and requiring design tools but also posing new theoretical questions about systems and decision processes' [14].

Fjeldstad and Stabell presented a value configuration framework in which value network and value shop are the two alternatives to Michael Porter's traditional concept of value chains [15]. Later on, based on the notion of the value creation framework, Möller et al. have suggested a value continuum framework that includes three generic net types that are current business nets, business renewal nets, and emerging new business nets [16]. Current business nets are value systems with a high level of determination and well-known and well-specified patterns of activities and resources. Emerging new business nets are characterized by radical changes and inherent uncertainty. In between these polar opposites are business renewal nets, which produce incremental local changes in existing value systems. Practical approaches in manufacturing networks can also be characterised by applying three network types. First, the traditional supply networks have the focus on efficiency of processes - the roles and connections between actors are quite well defined. Secondly, in business enhancing networks the focus changes from physical components to competences, while actors try to solve customer's problems together. Thirdly, emergence of radically new business opportunities requires new connections and network members - often over industry sectors. The business models of network actors differ within these network types. Furthermore, each business network evolves over time as network roles, business models, as well as strategies of actors change. Table 1 compares the key characteristics of these value creation frameworks and illustrates their appearance in manufacturing network practises.

**Table 1.** Value creation approaches in manufacturing networks

| Approach | Value network types and their key characteristics | | |
|---|---|---|---|
| Value configuration [13] | Value chain (components as value element) | Value shop (value based on competences) | Value network (connections as value elements) |
| Value continuum [14] | Current business nets (efficiency of operations) | Business renewal nets (incremental changes) | Emerging new business nets (radical changes and uncertainty) |
| Practical approaches in manufacturing networks | Traditional supply networks | Business enhancing networks, like service networks | Innovation networks |

In manufacturing industries value network consist of organizations co-operating with each other to benefit all network members. Lead producer and its suppliers and customers form a typical value network. Value system consists of the suppliers' value networks (who provide input), core company's value network (that produces products), the distributers' and retailer's value networks (who distribute products to customers) and the customers' value networks (who use the products in their own activities) [17].

The focus should be broadened from supplier-lead producer-customer relationships to collaborative relationships [18]. Furthermore, based on system thinking the concept of business ecosystems has been introduced to highlight the importance of a value system, where all stakeholders co-produce value and thereby, value from co-operation is also captured by all stakeholders [19]. In addition to the main actors of a value network (lead producers, their suppliers and customers) also interests of other involved actors (external stakeholders) should be considered. The need to consider sustainability requires tighter collaboration among a wide range of stakeholders. Collaborative networks is one concept that can bring a significant contribution to the better understanding of the stakes and paths towards potential solutions in sustainability. Studies on trust management, value systems, multicultural and multi-legal contexts for collaborative networks can help in the development of better governance methods for sustainable development [20].

## 4    Network Governance Models in Manufacturing

From the standpoint of organisation theory, there are three main governance models: hierarchies (e.g., firms), markets, and networks. Networks are a hybrid model between hierarchies and markets, possessing characteristics from both extremes. Network organisation and management include governance structures that have to do with the degree of central or distributed co-ordination [21].

On the basis of their structure, networks can be divided into hierarchical hub-spoke and multiplex models [22]. In the hub-spoke model, the central actor (i.e., lead producer or OEM) is responsible for the network governance. In contrast, network governance in the multiplex model takes place within and between the network actors. Three distinct types of governance within networks can be identified: i) shared governance, ii) lead-organisation-governed, and iii) network-administrative-organisation-governed [23]. In NAO governance, all activities and decisions are co-ordinated through one organisation specifically created to oversee the network.

Governance structures are what bring actors into working together – the process, rules, and norms by which the network enables participating organisations to influence the network's operations and decision-making. Governance mechanisms can be divided into contractual-based and relational-based governance [24]. Contractual governance emphasises the use of a formalised, legally binding agreement to govern the inter-firm relationship. Relational governance, in contrast, highlights the role of norms of solidarity, flexibility, and information-sharing in the relationship process.

Since networks are mostly composed of autonomous organisations and are not legal entities, the network's participants typically have limited formal accountability for network-level goals, and conformance with rules and procedures is not governed by binding regulations but is voluntary. For goal-directed organisational networks with a distinct identity, governance is still necessary for ensuring that participants engage in collective and mutually supportive action, that conflict is addressed, and that network resources are acquired and utilised efficiently and effectively. Governance involves use of institutions and structures of authority and collaboration to allocate resources and to co-ordinate and control joint action across the network as a whole [25].

## 5    Model for Sustainability Governance in Manufacturing Networks

The present – and especially the future challenge – is to govern sustainability within manufacturing networks and broader business ecosystems. The process towards developing a sustainable manufacturing value network requires reassessing value creation and capturing from the start of a business. Moreover, a more holistic sustainable business model of manufacturing networks should include economic, environmental and social impacts of the business.

The governance model developed illustrates sustainability governance within a manufacturing network as a process for guiding the activities of all actors involved toward sustainable development and performance over a product's life cycle. There are three main tasks of sustainability governance: analysing, organising, and developing as illustrated in the Fig. 1. Through these, the governance model illustrates a process that integrates i) requirements and commitments of stakeholders within the manufacturing network as well as ii) business models and the self-interest of manufacturing-network companies.

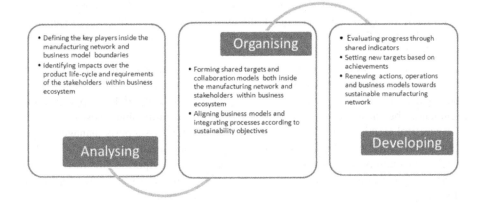

**Fig. 1.** Model for sustainability governance in manufacturing networks

To guide the activities of all actors involved toward the sustainability objectives, companies must first determine the key players in the manufacturing network and the boundaries of the business model. Therefore, the network analysis requires visualisation of the connections (business relationships, ownership, etc.) between the actors. In this phase, an important aspect of the sustainability governance in manufacturing networks is the connection between sustainable development and business models. In order for the network-members to understand the network's value for each member, the objectives, interests, and expectations of each should be covered. Consequently, it is important to assess the requirements and expectations of the stakeholders within the business ecosystem. On the basis of these analyses, companies would be able to identify sustainability impacts over the product life cycle and the requirements imposed for the actors involved.

The analyses of said actors, their requirements, and the total impact direct the organising and management of the sustainability development at network level. Shared targets and collaboration models are formed both inside the manufacturing network and with respect to other stakeholders within the business ecosystem. Alignment of business models and integration of processes in accordance with the sustainability objectives should be carefully considered. Different collaboration models are required for different situations; e.g., the sustainability objectives should be considered when one is deciding with whom to collaborate and how.

In order to ensure continuous improvement as well as renewal, progress should be evaluated via shared indicators and new targets should be set transparently, based on the achievements. Actors will be able to renew actions, operations, and business models together in pursuit of sustainability goals.

# 6    Conclusions

The model developed addresses sustainability governance within a manufacturing network as a process to guide the activities of all actors involved toward sustainable development and performance throughout the product life cycle. According to the model, there are three main tasks of sustainability governance: analysing, organising, and developing. These three main tasks are in accordance with company-level approaches but highlight the need for multilevel network governance.

One of the requirements identified in this study is that sustainability should be integrated into companies' as well as networks' core strategies. The governance model plays an important role for this aim and can be utilised for supporting the alignment of business models and processes with sustainability objectives.

A practical implication of the developed model is that it supports management in analysis and decision-making related to strategic collaboration for sustainability. The model contribution to scientific community is that it supports identification of governance mechanisms related to shared value system in downstream – upstream networking.

The model presented in this paper will be further refined as the SustainValue project progresses. The next version will take into account the advances made in the research carried out in the project. This includes, for example, how governance, corporate norms and values, and ownership structure drive sustainability within the business model and architecture. The model will be further developed and piloted together with companies in order to link it to new methods and tools that will be developed in the SustainValue project as well as to existing methods such as Global Reporting Initiative (GRI).

**Acknowledgements.** The research leading to these results has received funding from the European Community's Seventh Framework Programme (FP7, 2007–2013) under grant agreement 262931. The authors wish to acknowledge the European Commission for their support.

# References

1. ISO 26000:2010: Guidance on social responsibility. International Organization for Standardization (2010)
2. Gewald, H., Helbig, K.: A governance model for managing outsourcing partnership: A view from practice. In: Proceedings of the 39th Hawaii International Conference on System Sciences, HICSS 2006 (2006)
3. European Commission: MANUFUTURE – a vision for 2020: Assuring the future of manufacturing in Europe. Office for Official Publications of the European Communities, Luxembourg (2004)
4. Bonini, S.: The business of sustainability. McKinsey Global Survey results. McKinsey & Company (2011)
5. Evans, S., Rana, P., Short, S.: D2.1 - State-of-practice in business modelling and value-networks, emphasising potential future models that could deliver sustainable value (2012), http://www.sustainvalue.eu/publications/D2_1_Final_Rev1_0_web.pdf (last accessed June 20, 2012)
6. Camarinha-Matos, L.M., Macedo, P.: A conceptual model of value systems in collaborative networks. Journal of Intelligent Manufacturing 21(3), 287–299 (2010)

7. Abreu, A., Camarinha-Matos, L.M.: On the role of value systems to promote the sustainability of collaborative networks. International Journal of Production Research 46(5), 1207–1229 (2008)
8. Allee, V.: Reconfiguring the Value Network. Journal of Business Strategy 21(4), 36–39 (2000)
9. Normann, R., Ramirez, R.: Designing Interactive Strategy: From the Value Chain to the Value Constellation. John Wiley & Sons, Chichester (1994)
10. Peppard, J., Rylander, A.: From Value Chain to Value Network: Insights for Mobile Operators. European Management Journal 24(2-3), 128–141 (2006)
11. von Hippel, E.: Democratizing Innovation. The MIT Press, Cambridge (2005)
12. Dyer, J.H.: Collaborative advantage: winning through extended enterprise supplier networks. Oxford University Press, Oxford (2000)
13. Chesbrough, H.: Open innovation. Harvard Business School Press, Boston (2003)
14. Shi, Y., Gregory, M.: International Manufacturing Networks - to develop global competitive capabilities. Journal of Operation Management 16(2-3), 195–214 (1998)
15. Fjeldstad, Ø.D., Stabell, C.B.: Configuring Value for Competitive Advantage: On Chains, Shops, and Networks. Strategic Management Journal 19(5), 413–437 (1998)
16. Möller, K., Rajala, A., Svahn, S.: Strategic business nets - their type and management. Journal of Business Research 58(9), 1274–1284 (2005)
17. Miltenburg, J.: Manufacturing Strategy – How to Formulate and Implement a Winning Plan. Productivity Press, New York (2005)
18. Vallet-Bellmunt, T., Martínez-Fernández, M.T., Capó-Vicedo, J.: Supply chain management: A multidisciplinary content analysis of vertical relations between companies, 1997–2006. Industrial Marketing Management 40(8), 1347–1367 (2011)
19. Moore, J.F.: The Death of Competition: Leadership & Strategy in the Age of Business Ecosystems. Harper Business, New York (1996)
20. Camarinha-Matos, L.M., Afsarmanesh, H., Boucher, X.: The role of collaborative networks in sustainability. In: Camarinha-Matos, L.M., Boucher, X., Afsarmanesh, H. (eds.) PRO-VE 2010. IFIP AICT, vol. 336, pp. 1–16. Springer, Heidelberg (2010)
21. Valkokari, K., Valkokari, P., Reunanen, M., Palomäki, K., Amirmostofian, A.: D1.2 Towards sustainability governance in manufacturing networks (2012), http://www.sustainvalue.eu/publications/D1_2_final_Rev1_0_web.pdf (last accessed June 20, 2012)
22. Svahn, S., Westerlund, M.: The modes of supply net management: A capability view. Supply Chain Management: An International Journal 12(5), 369–376 (2007)
23. Doz, Y.: Clubs, Clans and Caravans: The Dynamics of Alliance Memberships and Governance. Carnegie Bosch Institute, Berlin (2001)
24. Provan, K.G., Fish, A., Sydow, J.: Interorganizational networks at the network level: A review of the empirical literature on whole networks. Journal of Management 33(3), 479–516 (2007)
25. Poppo, L., Zenger, T.: Do formal contracts and relational governance function as substitutes or complements? Strategic Management Journal 23(8), 707–725 (2002)
26. Provan, K.G., Kenis, P.: Modes of network governance: Structure, management, and effectiveness. Journal of Public Administration Research and Theory 18(2), 229–252 (2008)

# Implementation of Sustainability in Ongoing Supply Chain Operations

Liliyana Makarova Jørsfeldt, Peter Meulengracht Jensen, and Brian Vejrum Waehrens

Center for Industrial Production, Aalborg University, Denmark
{lm,bvw}@business.aau.dk

**Abstract.** The need to take the sustainability agenda beyond its technological outset and include supply chain practices is well-established, but still little has happened and the supply chain has remained largely unaffected. This paper asks why this may be the case and investigates what happens in the translation from ambitious strategic goals to operational practices.

To do this an exploratory case study is presented detailing the efforts of a large Danish manufacturing company to introduce an ambitious sustainability agenda in its ongoing supply chain operations. The study aims to develop a deeper understanding of the inter-functional coordination and operational practices when the sustainability agenda is introduced into supply chain. The study points to a lack of tangible environmental performance measurements and to incoherent functional logics as the main factors preventing effective implementation. We find support for a lack of formalized sustainability integration into operations and clear systemic approach to cross-functional coordination.

**Keywords:** Sustainable Supply Chain Management, Cross-functional Implementation.

## 1 Introduction

The phenomenon of sustainability has in recent years received a great deal of attention by practitioners and academics alike. Simultaneously, in private business sustainability has slowly been accepted as a strategic agenda [1]. The rise of sustainability as a key strategic priority has been due to a number of changes in the manufacturing environment, namely: global competition for resources and escalating deterioration of the environment [2]; rising supply chain cost – regulation in response to environmental protection has changed the cost structure; growing awareness of sustainability issues creates new markets for sustainable products and increases customer pressure for sustainable supply chains [1].

At the same time due to the phenomenon of globalization in the manufacturing environment, a new approach to competitiveness has emerged: the new idea is that it is not single functional area or even firm that competes, but competitive advantages rests in the firms capability to orchestrate the supply chain as a whole [4, 2, 11]. This in turn brings forward issues related to cross-functional and inter-organizational

C. Emmanouilidis, M. Taisch, D. Kiritsis (Eds.): APMS 2012, Part I, IFIP AICT 397, pp. 192–199, 2013.
© IFIP International Federation for Information Processing 2013

coordination and integration of which we know very little when it comes to driving key strategic agendas through. With the intensification of the globalization phenomenon, the supply chain of many companies is increasingly complex and dispersed, which also makes the pursuit of emerging strategic agendas inherently difficult. Furthermore, many companies need to respond to a non-coherent strategic demand, i.e. there is no single strategic demand or performance objective, which means that the company needs to balance diverse demands, which translates into several competing or even diverging performance objectives. There are numerous empirical studies that reveal the existence of managerial problems when sustainability is applied in the supply chain context [1].

The literature on sustainable development in operations documents that tools and techniques for implementation sustainability in the supply chain has been developed over the past 25 years [5, 10]. Among some of the most dominant and applied techniques lifecycle assessment (LCA), reverse logistics, closed loop supply chains, design for disassembly can be mentioned. All confirm the link between sustainability practices in supply chains and competitive advantage in manufacturing companies [6].

# 2     Research Gap

Despite consensus that sustainability is a key competitive parameter and the availability of effective tools, the operational practices in the most companies remain largely unaffected. This is documented in several studies, however, only a few studies empirically investigate this problem on an operational level [12, 13, 14]. Furthermore, these available empirical studies primarily investigate the drivers of environmental behavior and describe the existing practice in order to identify supply chain environmental operational activities, and do not include factors related to the organizational context when implementing sustainability in ongoing supply chain operations and calls have been forwarded to bridge this gap in the literature [2, 7, 13].

Hence the purpose of this study is to go beyond the strategic and corporate realm and, on an operational level, investigate what barriers are preventing companies from adapting sustainability into their supply chains. This purpose leads to the following research question: What are the current organizational barriers preventing companies from implementing and anchoring sustainability in their supply chain practices?

To answer the research question, this study will seek to examine the current organizational set-up and traditional key performance indicators; discuss how sustainable initiatives were approached and motivated in different parts of the supply chain operations; identify challenges of embedding sustainable development in an ongoing supply chain operations; establish the patterns of organizational changes in response to the need of more sustainable manufacturing practice and suggest the solution.

# 3     Research Design

## 3.1     Conceptual Framework for Study

As several different approaches to supply chain management exist, for the purposes of our study we define supply chain management as "the systemic, strategic coordination of the traditional business functions and the tactics across these business functions within a particular company and across businesses within the supply chain, for the purposes of improving the long-term performance of the individual companies and the supply chain as whole" [8].

The study will take a supply chain governance perspective and the framework underlying the study is presented in Figure 1. The framework rests on system view of supply chain management process where the materials and information flows are coordinated from the market to the suppliers through the company, and then detailed organizational elements were drawn additionally in order to understands how new corporate agenda of sustainability affecting cross functional integration and coordination of the ongoing supply chain. The engagement of all partners is considered in the framework. It is done in order to get deep understanding of how partners from support functions and core supply processes are interacting when striving to carry out the strategic agenda.

Strategic agendas that are set by a corporate management strategy are often quite diverse and may draw attention in many different directions. For example cost, quality, responsiveness, and sustainability are each make diverging, but also to some degree mutually reinforcing demands on the organization. Every time a new strategic agenda is set by top management, the need to readdress the supply chain governance form appears: partners from core supply chain processes and support functions have to engage in different ways to carry out tasks set by different strategic agendas and to balance the different strategic agendas.

The discussion will be based on the given framework applying Kahn´s division of integration in cross- functional work, which distinguishes between interaction- based integration and collaboration-based interaction [16]. Finally, the paper will conclude with a discussion of how roles and coordination are affected by the emerging agenda.

## 3.2     Case Selection

As a sample for our study we choose an organization that is well-ahead in its industry in terms of social and environmental performance, while still maintaining economic viability. The company has a global presence with regards to all value chain functions and employs more than 10,000 people in more than 45 countries. It has been working with the sustainability agenda for more than fifteen years. In the past five years sustainability has been established as a key competitive requirement for the future and a very ambitious goal has been publicly announced. In the Danish context the case company represents an extreme case [9] with regards to its focused efforts and ambitious goals to establish sustainable operations, but also with regards to the complexity of implementing the new agenda in the supply chain. The extreme case enables us to study the phenomenon at its edge and is likely to reveal more information [9].

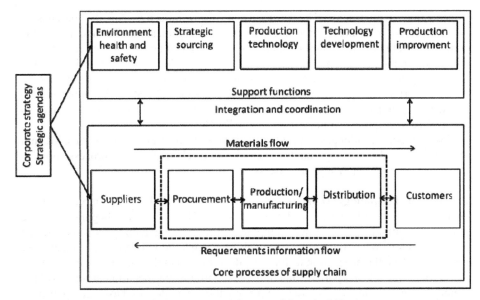

**Fig. 1.** Organizational Context of Sustainability

## 3.3    Data Collection

We used a semi-structured interview protocol to interview actors, who were representing different functions and parts of the supply chain which were engaged in the process of sustainability implementation. In this way we had the necessary flexibility to focus on what was unique at each specific process. It was important to understand how sustainability issues were addressed in the supply chain process and what challenges were experienced during the process of implementation. The case consists of seven subcases – mirroring the different stages of supply chain management and key support functions thereof: the sub-cases differ both in terms of the approach applied to sustainability and in terms of interaction with other parties in the supply chain.

**Environmental Department.** The environmental department was developed with a purpose to ensure and support group strategy towards sustainable development. Being a support function, the department does not pose any power of environmental resources at the company sites. However, the department has a mandate to negotiate the yearly environmental targets for the relevant sites in the organization. The department initiates environmental projects in cooperation with local sites and other departments across the global supply chain, but for the present such projects are only allowed to take place when it does not affect the material flow. The main challenges to implementation identified, were the lack of authority to allocate resources and the need for cross-functional integration around the agenda.

**Purchasing Department.** The primarily business objective for the purchasing department is to ensure appropriate suppliers to organization. To live up to the company's value of sustainability suppliers are estimated and monitored in regard to their CSR practice. While the choice of supplier is mainly driven by cost, informally, CSR assessment is used as indicator for quality. The yearly audit for suppliers is based on performance requirements, which are regularly revised in collaboration with production companies, environmental department, and other functions and in accordance to corporate strategy.

The following challenges were identified: how to measure the value of CSR in a way it can "make a sense" on the operational level of purchase process; how to integrate CSR mindset in support processes.

**Production Technology Department.** The idea to include the requirement from environmental department as well from other stakeholders in the beginning of the process of implementation of new equipment initially was targeting reducing time of implementation. When setting the sustainability agenda into the process of machinery implementation, the production technology department is following the demands from the corporate level. Supportive functions as environmental department and working conditions are mainly the sources of information and do not have real power to change processes of material flow.

The following challenges were identified: lack of technical competencies (knowledge of equipment) from supportive functions; the need to restructure the process to align requirements from all stakeholders in time.

**Production Facilities.** The primary business objectives for production are to manufacture product meeting the delivery time, efficiency and cost. Planning, production technology and quality are the departments that are engaged in decision making regarding processes in production. At present there is no or little formal integration of sustainability in the production process. The governance of sustainability initiatives is perceived as the responsibility of the environmental department and can take place only if it does not interfere with the production process. Because of high priority of cost and other traditional KPIs for the production, the capacity for development remains limited. Few resources can be allocated to sustainability related work and specialized competences have not been developed, and as a consequence the translation from strategic intentions to implementable solutions remains weak.

**Technology Development Department.** In spite of strong strategic intentions towards development of sustainable technology, sustainability is not well integrated in the process. The main reason for this as it was expressed by the environmental engineer is that customers of the technology center (production sites, business development) focus on cost, quality, performance, and environmental criteria are not a key priority. To change the situation, the department has intentions to involve customers and other stakeholders in the early stages of machinery development process. To do so it is planned to formalize procedure of assessment of sustainability on operational level to make it more tangible; to then set-up sustainability targets for new projects while or before specifications are being made an involve customers in this early stage of development; finally when a project is closed to reassess environmental targets for new projects. The main challenges for imbedding sustainability are: how to make sustainability tangible on an operational level, and how to raise awareness of sustainability in the department.

**Logistics Department.** In 2009 the $5^{th}$ Climate Change conference took place in Denmark. It gave a momentum to the initiative of mapping $CO_2$ emissions from transportation on case-company supply chain. A measurement found that one third of overall $CO_2$ emissions of the company were due to transportation. The challenge the department faces is expressed by a transportation manager: Where we go now? How do we operationalize the sustainability strategy and find solutions towards $CO_2$ reduction without compromising traditional performance criteria?

While the existing relationships linkages to transport providers as well as to the productions sites, distribution centers, and warehouse may produce trustworthy information about transportation related $CO_2$ footprint; the logistics function has no influence on flow of components in the operations network. The lack of power to influence the physical flow and the production planning in the operations network remains a key barrier for reaching the ambitious environmental targets stated by corporate strategy. It demands that the logistics department changes its role from simply providing logistics services on demand to them penetrating and influencing the planning system that they respond to.

**The Production Improvement Function.** The primarily business objective of the function is to support and align operations strategy with operations practice in the production sites. With the sustainability agenda as one of the top priorities of corporate strategy, the operations strategy has aimed to incorporate sustainability within its ongoing lean activities. Production improvement is a support function and while it is engaging with group strategy, production sites, environmental department and sales companies to create the focus for production improvements it has limited effect on how the initiatives take effect in the operations flow. Within challenges mentioned is a change in behavior on the shop floor towards practicing a culture and mindset of continuous improvement.

## 4    Discussion and Conclusions

The case company has as one of the Danish frontrunners on sustainability come a long way with its product and process redesign, but it also recognizes that to take the next steps the supply chain needs to be a key contributor of reductions. As can be seen from the case description above the sustainability agenda is met with many challenges once it starts to interfere with the physical flow and its well-established logics and measures of good practice. In the following the framework developed in the section 3.1 will be used as a canvas for discussions as a means of highlighting inter-functional interdependencies related to task performance as well as inter-functional logics and measures of performance.

*Information flow:* sustainability in the case company is driven by two key motives: corporate values regarding responsible behavior and expected growing sustainability demands from customers. Yet, at the present customers do not have direct and concrete demands to sustainability. This means that there is no direct information flow from customers to core operations in the supply chain, but instead this information flow reaches corporate management. As to the information flow between core functions and support functions, it was noted that the sustainability agenda increases the amount of data flowing from operations to the support functions; and to define sustainability targets for different departments' knowledge of specific processes becomes a key priority.

*Material flow:* it is clear from case study that the flow of materials is not as of yet affected by any of sustainability initiatives, due to overriding agendas. Improvements have been made, but mainly with new installations or with technology driven refurbishments where sustainability is a key agenda.

*Cross-functional involvement:* the sustainability agenda brings at least one more new stakeholder in every core supply chain process (the environmental department), but these new stakeholders have only scarcely been involved in these processes. Moreover the nature of involvement of different functions is changing: new technologies are today only certified by the environment department after they have been specified, the environment department does not have the capabilities to be involved in the specification process, and the technology department only has limited knowledge of the environmental impact of new technologies. The analysis of data shows that the sustainability agenda leads to an increase in the number of functional interests involved in the coordination of supply chain processes.

*Interaction vs. collaborative cross-functional integration:* to meet sustainability demands functions are changing the way they work with each other from a sequential interaction based approach to increasing the focus on ongoing collaboration and reciprocal interdependencies. For example, when addressing cost issue, departments communicate with each other using well established and tangible measures. For sustainability few tangible measures exist and the communication is much more directed towards achieving a mutual understanding and forming the basis for collaborating.

Although the case company has come a long way towards implementing sustainability initiatives successfully, this had not had a direct influence on the flow of materials or the planning thereof. To meet the highly ambitious goals of rapid global growth and a related neutral $CO_2$ footprint thereof, the current sustainability initiatives need to be implemented together with material flow oriented initiatives. To cope with the complexity of multifunctional cooperation a systematic approach to sustainability goals should be developed at the operations level: the guidance, the measurement of sustainability that will be tangible for day-to-day work on operational level. One of the solutions can be programme management [17]. The essential purpose of programme management is to direct the numerous and widely dispersed projects so that they not only support the global strategy, but also support a systematic competence and capability build-up in the organization. This is done through balancing between global support and guidelines (e.g. tool-box development, knowledge-sharing platforms, control mechanisms and resource allocation) and local emergent initiatives, incitement and ownership.

# References

1. Lacy, P., Cooper, T., Hayward, R., Neuberger, L.: A New Era of Sustainability. CEO Reflections on Progress to Date, Challenges Ahead and the Impact of the Journey toward a Sustainable Economy. UN Global Compact-Accenture CEO Study (2010)
2. Pagell, M., Wu, Z.: Building a More Complete Theory of Sustainable Supply Chain Management Using Case Studies of 10 Exemplars. J. of Sup. Chain Man. 45(2), 37–56 (2009)
3. Hill, M.R.: Sustainability, Greenhouse Gas Emissions and International Operations Management. International J. of Oper. and Prod. Man. 21(12), 1503–1520 (2001)
4. Goldsby, T.: World Class Logistics Performance and Environmentally Responsible Logistics Practices. J. of Bus. Log. 21(2), 187–208 (2000)
5. Kleindorfer, P.R., Singhal, K., Luk, N., Wassenhove, V.: Sustainable Operations Management. Prod. and Oper. Man. 14(4), 482–492 (2005)
6. Rao, P., Holt, D.: Do Green Supply Chains Lead to Competitiveness and Economic Performance? Int. J. of Oper. & Prod. Man. 25(9), 898–916 (2005)
7. Hald, K.S.: Sustainable Procurement in Denmark 2011- Nogle Foreløbige Resultater. DILF Orientering (5), 6–12 (2011)
8. Mentzer, J.T., DeWitt, W., Keebler, J.S., Min, S., Nix, N.W., Smith, C.D., Zacharia, Z.G.: Defining Supply Chain Management. J. of Bus. Log. 22(2), 1–25 (2001)
9. Yin, R.K.: The Case Study Anthology. Sage Publications, Thousand Oaks (2004)
10. Seuring, S., Muller, M.: From a Literature Review to a Conceptual Framework for Sustainable Supply Chain Management. J. of Clean. Prod. 16(15), 1699–1710 (2008)
11. Dyer, J.H.: Collaborative Advantage: Winning Through Extended Enterprise Supplier Networks. Oxford University Press, Oxford (2000)
12. Holt, D., Ghobadian, A.: An Empirical Study of Green Supply Chain Management Practices amongst UK Manufactures. J. of Man. Tech. Man. 20(7), 933–956 (2009)
13. Porter, M.E., Kramer, M.R.: Strategy & Society. The Link between Competitive Advantage and Corporate Social Responsibility. HBR, 78–92 (December 2006)
14. Bowen, F.E., Cousins, P.D., Lamming, R.C.: Horses for Courses: Explaining the Gap between the Theory and Practice of Green Supply. Green. Man. Int. 35, 41–60 (2001)
15. Lubin, D.A., Esty, D.C.: The Big Idea: The Sustainability Imperative. HBR, 42–50 (May 2010)
16. Kahn, K.B.: Interdepartmental Integration: A Definition with Implications for Product Development Performance. J. of Prod. In. Man. 13, 137–151 (1996)
17. Pellegrinelli, S., Partington, D., Hemmingway, C., Mohdzain, Z., Shah, M.: The Importance of Context in Programme Management: An Empirical Review of Programme Practices. Int. J. Project Man. 25, 41–55 (2007)

# Modular Framework for Reliable LCA-Based Indicators Supporting Supplier Selection within Complex Supply Chains

Carlo Brondi[1], Rosanna Fornasiero[1], Manfredi Vale[2], Ludovico Vidali[1], and Federico Brugnoli[3]

[1] ITIA-CNR, Institute for Industrial Technologies and Automation, Italy
carlobrondi@itia.cnr.it
[2] Aghetera Environment & Development, Italy
[3] Synesis Consortium, Italy

**Abstract.** With increased environmental awareness, a large amount of studies on green supplier selection has been promoted in the past decade. However the application of traditional impact assessments methodologies to fragmented and globalized supply chains is slowed down by provision of reliable data. Therefore, a comprehensive basis for Green Supplier Selection Model (GSSM) is proposed in this paper. In particular this paper proposes an index based on Life-Cycle-Assessment (LCA) to assess environmental burden of the whole company manufacturing activities. The resulting Company Environmental Performance Index (CEPI) can be used for sectoral benchmark to assess Company environmental Eco-Efficiency. The general methodology is presented with two strategic aims: the easy implementation of available data in standardized models and the reliable assessment of best performers within different manufacturing chains. Finally an application of such methodology to industrial cluster is discussed.

**Keywords:** Life Cycle Assessment, Independent information modules, Company Environmental Performance, Green Supply Chain Management, Green Purchasing.

## 1 Scientific Background : Optimizing Sustainability of the Supply Chain

In the current business environment, purchasing process has become critical in adding value to products and a vital determinant to ensure the profitability and survival of a company. Literature reports many different approaches to the topic of purchasing strategies where [1] did a comprehensive review on the past research. Some popular methods include the categorical method, the weighted-point method, the matrix method, the vendor profile analysis, and the Analytical Networking Process (ANP) approach [4]. While literature related to supplier evaluation is plentiful, the works on green supplier evaluation or supplier evaluation that consider environmental factors are rather limited [2-4].

C. Emmanouilidis, M. Taisch, D. Kiritsis (Eds.): APMS 2012, Part I, IFIP AICT 397, pp. 200–207, 2013.

The purchasing process becomes more complicated when environmental issues are considered. This is because green purchasing must consider the supplier's environmental responsibility, depending on product chain assets, in addition to the traditional factors such as the supplier's costs, quality, lead-time and flexibility. The management of suppliers based on strict environmental compliance seems to be not sufficient in view of a more proactive or strategic approach. Noci [4] designed a green vendor rating system for the assessment of a supplier's environmental performance based on four environmental categories, namely, 'green' competencies, current environmental efficiency, suppliers' 'green' image and net life cycle cost, by applying ANP. Main limit in attributing a unique environmental performance index to a company seems to be linked to the management of reliable quantitative scientific set of values which can be considered constant in different comparison.

Life Cycle Assessment (LCA) methodology can represent a good basis to develop a comprehensive index by encouraging companies to look at their technological history placed in other Life Cycle stages as well as their operational efficiency [5]. Appropriate data can be gathered by transcending the boundaries of the company and by offering well-established assessment methodology. Lewandowska et al. [6] accounts like LCA integration within internal environmental management systems may involve barriers both in terms of generation and verification of reproducible results and in terms of final assessment interpretation compliant with rapid business management. The lack of standard approaches for data aggregation from different manufacturers can in fact limit their liability to share data which can result essentials for evaluation in the end-of-pipe phases.

More in detail reliable and comparable results seem to imply pre-definition of system boundaries and allocation criteria [7]. Reference texts suggest that significant portion of the environmental impacts may be neglected due to premature cut-off of impact assessment or by inadequate simplification [8]. Another top concern in many LCA studies seems to be the link of the firm on-site impact with the upstream and downstream processes [9]. Suh et al. [7] proposed the "integrated hybrid LCA", which combine input/output analysis with traditional LCA, as an easy way to assess firm and business sector impact. Such methodology can in fact link the physical flows involved by processes together with economic evaluations and final environmental impacts. As a matter of fact classical LCA modeling requires detailed stages description, reasonably unknown by the same firm, while input-output assessment requires a wider flow assessment which is related to economical and traceable quantities. Gwan et al. [10] and Buxmann et al. [11] proposed calculation methods which are applicable to complex systems having internally recurring unit processes. According to their studies the use of gate-to-gate independent modules and appropriate cut-off criteria can enable a dramatic simplification in Life Cycle Inventory (LCI) and Impact Assessment (LCIA).

# 2    Modular Framework for Company Environmental Performance Assessment

This paper aims to provide a standard methodology to select best "green supplier" within a specific supply chain on the basis of their overall yearly performance. Such criterion is based on a two assessment stages both based on LCA methodology. They are reported in sequence hereafter.

## 2.1    Attribution of an Environmental Profile to Firm Activities

According to literature the assessment of the environmental impact referred to manufacturing activity requires to provide a general tracking of the physical flows involved by companies within a certain time-span. Such assessment provides the basis for a general comparison with other firms. General hypothesis of the proposed modular framework imply a limited adaptation of the integrated hybrid LCA.

System boundaries are fixed coincident with factory physical limits in order to limit data collection within the area of accessible information and to make final data reusable by production managers for internal purposes.

Impact evaluation is provided in terms of cradle-to-gate environmental impact. Complex entering and outgoing flows are partitioned and analyzed as recurrent modules flows (i.e. common auxiliary materials) which are linked to gate-to-gate LCA studies provided by other suppliers or by Life Cycle Analysts. Each environmental impact has been expressed at the endpoint level by using the same common impact categories ($p$) in order to integrate different data. The same environmental firm performance is expressed in terms of resulting cradle-to-gate impact vector ($p_f$) that is parametrically dependent by input and output characteristic flows (figure 1).

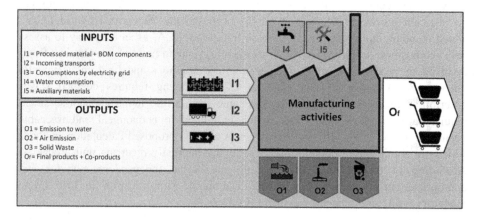

**Fig. 1.** Input-Output flow assessment for Facility Environmental Performance Index calculation

The allocation of environmental impact can imply a subdivision of the whole impact by factory physical production (i.e. mass/number of single item produced yearly by the same facility) or by economic value (i.e. yearly turnover)

Methodology description is summarized in equation 1.

$$P_f = \frac{A\left[\Sigma_{i=1}^T \left(p_{m_i} m_i\right)_{in} + \Sigma_{j=1}^Q \left(p_{m_j} m_j\right)_{out}\right] + B\left[\Sigma_{k=1}^F \left(p_{e_k} e_k\right)_{in} + \Sigma_{h=1}^P \left(p_{e_h} e_h\right)_{out}\right]}{V_f} \tag{1}$$

$$P_C = \Sigma_{f=1}^N P_f \tag{2}$$

In equation 1 Facility Environmental Profile (FEP) is $P_f$, calculated as sum of vector by single contribution of characteristic mass and energy flows (m, e) entering and leaving the production facility boundaries within the same time period (i.e. fiscal year). Each flow quantity is multiplied for the Unitary Impact Profile (UIP) derived from a specific LCA study ($p_m$, $p_e$). Scalar components ($p_1$,...,$p_n$) composing final impact vector (referred to single flows, item, facility or company) are standard endpoint categories in the LCA characterization phase expressed as quantities (kilograms of carbon dioxide equivalents for Global Warming potential, kilograms of $PO_4$ equivalents for Eutrophication Potential,  etc.). Factors A and B are dimensional factors to make congruent the final dimensions with the same impact evaluation format (endpoint categories). Finally variable $V_f$ represent the economic value of the production by the same facility or the number of provided items.

The Company Environmental Profile (CEP) is expressed in equation 2 as vectoral summation $P_C$ of environmental profiles referred to N production facilities $P_f$, composing the analyzed company.

## 2.2    Benchmarking of Environmental Performance at Cluster or Sector Level

Scalar quantities reported in vectoral components of CEP are referred to physical impacts. Interpretation of results can provide useful outcomes to supply manager mainly thorough the comparison of final performance with benchmark values rather than the assessment in absolute terms. Such benchmark values can be referred both to an average performance value and to specific competitor performance value.

In order to get a reliable assessment specific barriers are recognizable. Firstly comparisons confined to few competitors can limit the interpretation of the final values of CEP. In the absence of a reference value the CEP can be insignificant to understand whether a firm is producing a good or bad environmental performance within a supply network. Secondly the vectoral comparison can imply that some scalar components of CEP can be higher or lower than the respective scalar quantity of the competitor CEP (i.e. in a comparison kg of produced $CO_2$ equivalents can be higher while kg of $PO_4$ equivalents can be lower).

In order to overcome such barriers a LCA-based Company Environmental Performance Index (CEPI) is proposed. Initially benchmark values, PS or PCl, for cluster environmental performance are calculated according to two different inventory methods.

— Benchmark values which are referred to statistical input-output approach (NAMEA tables) at sectoral level are calculated in equation 3 (vector $\underline{P_S}$). In equation 3 total impact referred to the cluster level is calculated as sum of vectors related to total flows involved at cluster/sector level. Single quantities of characteristic mass and energy flows (m, e) entering and leaving the sectoral cluster within the same time period (i.e. fiscal year) are multiplied for the corresponding Unitary Impact Profiles (UIP) derived from a specific LCA study ($p_m$, $p_e$). Then each scalar component of the final vector is divided by the number of total companies ($N_S$) owning to the cluster (territorial cluster, national industrial sector etc.) and the total economic production (number of products, total turnover etc.).

— Alternatively the benchmark vector can be assumed coincident with $\underline{P_C}$ in the presence of proper data inventory within a significant company cluster. In equation 4 total environmental impact is calculated as sum of the single company environmental profiles (CEP) and then divided for the number of total companies within the examined cluster ($N_{Cl}$).

$$\underline{P_S} = \frac{A\left[\sum_{y=1}^{L}\left(p_{m_y}m_y\right)_{in} + \sum_{h=1}^{V}\left(p_{m_h}m_h\right)_{out}\right] + B\left[\sum_{z=1}^{D}\left(p_{e_z}e_z\right)_{in} + \sum_{q=1}^{T}\left(p_{e_q}e_q\right)_{out}\right]}{N_S \times E_S} \tag{3}$$

$$\underline{P_{Cl}} = \frac{\sum_{c=1}^{N} P_c}{N_{Cl}} \tag{4}$$

$$I_S = f\left(\frac{P_c - \underline{P_S}}{P_S}\right) \tag{5}$$

$$I_{Cl} = f\left(\frac{P_c - \underline{P_{Cl}}}{P_{Cl}}\right) \tag{6}$$

The resulting benchmark Company Environmental Performance Indexes (CEPI) can be calculated in equation 5 and 6 as vectors $I_S$ or $I_{Cl}$. The scalar components of both index vectors depends on percentage difference between cluster benchmark values, $P_S$ or $P_{Cl}$, and the Company Environmental Profile (CEP).

## 3      Application Case : The Use of Energy in a Territorial Cluster

The methodology has been applied to a territorial district in order to evaluate best performers at environmental level in a manufacturing context. Cradle-to-grave approach has been limited to energy use assessment (Narrow I3 in figure 1).Different companies of different Italian manufacturing sectors owning to the same territorial cluster have been tracked in order to obtain their specific Environmental Profile referred to their energy use.

Firstly the total Environmental Profile have been assesses for 188 companies owning to 12 different manufacturing sectors by evaluating the aggregate Energy consumption in terms of electricity mix , heating gas and district heating in two different years (2005 and 2010). Unitary Impact Profiles assessment included the electricity mix change and combustion technology change at industrial levels for the examined years. Category impact used in the final impact profiles are: Acidification

Potential (kg of $SO_2$ equivalents), Eutrophication potential (kg of Phosphate equivalents), Global Warming potential (kg of $CO_2$ equivalents), Ozone Layer Creation Potential (kg of DCB Equivalents), Photochemical Ozone Creation Potential (kg of Ethene Equivalents).

Secondly a selection of 10 companies has been tracked in terms of economic performance for the same years. Yearly turnover has been used as economic performance indicator in order to make comparable the results among different sectors. Then the respective CEP has been calculated for each company.

Thirdly a benchmark vector $P_S$ has been evaluated within the territorial district by the use of equation 3. More in particular the average environmental profile has been divided for the sectoral turnover at cluster level.

| | Sector | Year 2005 | | | | | Year 2010 | | | | |
|---|---|---|---|---|---|---|---|---|---|---|---|
| | | GWP | ODP | AP | POCP | EP | GWP | ODP | AP | POCP | EP |
| | Manufacturing | kg | kg | kg | kg | kg | kg | kg | kg | kg | kg |
| | Category | CO2 eq | R-11 eq | SO2 eq | C2H4 eq | PO4 eq | CO2 eq | R-11 eq | SO2 eq | C2H4 eq | PO4 eq |
| Cluster 1 | DA | 8,78E-03 | 9,68E-10 | 1,18E-05 | 1,74E-06 | 1,15E-06 | 4,52E-03 | 4,76E-10 | 8,18E-06 | 1,00E-06 | 7,76E-07 |
| Cluster 2 | DE | 7,56E-04 | 6,81E-11 | 1,67E-06 | 1,81E-07 | 1,47E-07 | 6,79E-04 | 6,31E-11 | 1,71E-06 | 1,75E-07 | 1,55E-07 |
| Cluster 3 | DG | 1,98E-02 | 2,00E-09 | 3,49E-05 | 4,32E-06 | 3,20E-06 | 1,23E-02 | 1,25E-09 | 2,48E-05 | 2,86E-06 | 2,31E-06 |
| Cluster 4 | DI | 1,00E-04 | 9,59E-12 | 1,99E-07 | 2,30E-08 | 1,79E-08 | 1,35E-04 | 1,38E-11 | 2,67E-07 | 3,11E-08 | 2,50E-08 |
| Cluster 5 | DJ | 1,11E-04 | 1,19E-11 | 1,62E-07 | 2,26E-08 | 1,55E-08 | 9,21E-05 | 9,91E-12 | 1,55E-07 | 1,99E-08 | 1,49E-08 |
| Cluster 6 | DK | 1,41E-04 | 1,50E-11 | 2,15E-07 | 2,92E-08 | 2,03E-08 | 1,51E-04 | 1,61E-11 | 2,61E-07 | 3,30E-08 | 2,50E-08 |

| | Sector | Year 2005 | | | | | Year 2010 | | | | |
|---|---|---|---|---|---|---|---|---|---|---|---|
| | | GWP | ODP | AP | POCP | EP | GWP | ODP | AP | POCP | EP |
| | Manufacturing | kg | kg | kg | kg | kg | kg | kg | kg | kg | kg |
| | Category | CO2 eq | R-11 eq | SO2 eq | C2H4 eq | PO4 eq | CO2 eq | R-11 eq | SO2 eq | C2H4 eq | PO4 eq |
| Company 1 | DA | C | D | C | C | C | C | C | C | C | C |
| Company 2 | DA | B | B | C | B | B | B | B | C | B | C |
| Company 3 | DE | D | D | D | D | D | D | D | D | D | D |
| Company 4 | DG | B | A | B | B | B | B | B | B | B | B |
| Company 5 | DG | B | B | B | B | B | B | B | B | B | B |
| Company 6 | DI | D | D | E | D | E | C | C | D | C | D |
| Company 7 | DJ | B | B | C | C | C | C | B | D | C | D |
| Company 8 | DJ | D | D | E | E | E | C | C | D | D | D |
| Company 9 | DJ | A | A | A | A | A | E | E | E | E | E |
| Company 10 | DK | D | D | D | D | D | D | D | D | D | D |

**Fig. 2.** Company Environmental Performance Indexes applied to sample companies

Finally Company Environmental Performance Index (CEPI) $I_S$ has been identified by attributing a category label to different percentage difference (see figure 2). Performance categories from A to E have been assigned in correspondence of intervals [x < 0], [0 <x<-0,05*I], [0,05*I<x<0,1*I], [0,1*I<x<0,2*I] and [x>0,2*I], where x is the scalar value of CEP and I is the respective scalar benchmark value.

## 4    Supplier Selection within a Green Supply Chain by Using Performance Index Based on Modular LCA

The application of LCA based indicators can enable supplier selection in complex supply chains through the assessment of environmental impact weighted with the impact of other performance indicators. Environmental sustainability is just one dimension to be considered when evaluating the supply chain configuration. Other dimensions to be considered are cost, time, quality and flexibility as well as collaboration capability of a partner in the SC. The indicators to be considered are linked to the type of business opportunity to be faced by the network. For example in case of customized production it is necessary to focus on indicators of flexibility and service provision more than on cost reduction. The availability of indicators can be based on the following dimensions:

- One-to-one indicators: these indicators allow measuring the performance of a company towards another one and are restricted to the performance of their buyer-seller relationship. This data are available only among the two companies and not accessible by others.
- Many-to-many indicators: in case of collaborative networks where the relationship of buyer-seller is overcome by a cooperative view of the business, it can be advantageous for all companies to share information about each other performance as they are aware of the benefits of making public these information in terms of marketing and return allowing them to give more visibility to their capabilities and stimulate them to perform better.

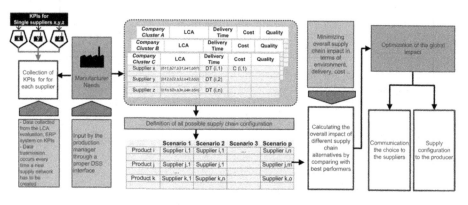

**Fig. 3.** Application of LCA based environmental performance index for supply chain configuration

The calculation of the environmental performance of a company based on the benchmarking proposed in the previous chapter allows to have an evaluation which is not only based on the experience of the company within a specific context but compared with companies in the same sector and other sectors and goes in the direction of sharing information useful to many companies. The approach based on benchmarking at cluster/sector level can overcome the initial problem of a supply chain configuration to retrieve specific data on specific products or components. Aggregating all these different indicators (environmental, time, quality, cost performance, etc.) a company can define different scenarios (SC configurations) where each SC can be characterized by different combination of partners. According to the specific product under development, each manufacturer can give a different level of importance to each indicator category. The decision support system under development is based on a multi-criteria evaluation of the possible performance of the different scenarios.

# 5    Conclusions and Recommendations

A company Environmental Performance Index has been proposed to evaluate the total "green" performance referred to a specific company within a supply cluster. The proposed approach has been applied to SME in a territorial cluster. SMEs can benefit by a suitable application of such methodology. The index assessment allows in facts to emphasize the relative importance of company links with other product chain phases. Consumed and emitted quantities by facilities can be substituted with indexes which are based on their physical environmental impact at global level. Such indexes include the relative contribution of the different suppliers. Secondly CEPI can be applied to a specific company apart from his specific eco-efficiency focus in order to understand their effective environmental burden. Finally CEPI, being based on macro-flows assessments, can be calculated with a standard approach independently from factory technologies and from manufacturing sectors. Finally the assessment reliability can be focused separately on quantity inventory and on unitary impact assessment. Quantity inventory can be monitored yearly by stakeholders who are not necessarily expert in LCA while unitary impact assessment can be based on specific and detailed studies from scientific community. A further step can be represented by the relative weight attribution to the different impact categories during the final selection criteria.

# References

1. Weber, C.A., Current, J.R., Benton, W.C.: Vendor selection criteria and methods. European Journal of Operational Research 50(1), 2–18 (1991)
2. Humphreys, P., McCloskey, A., McIvor, R., Maguire, L., Glackin, C.: Employing dynamic fuzzy membership functions to assess environmental performance in the supplier selection process. International Journal of Production Research 44(12), 2379–2419 (2006)
3. Humphreys, P., McIvor, R., Chan, F.: Using case-based reasoning to evaluate supplier environmental management performance. Expert Systems with Applications 25, 141–153 (2003b)
4. Noci, G.: Designing green vendor rating systems for the assessment of a supplier's environmental performance. European Journal of Purchasing and Supply Management 2, 103–114 (1997)
5. Lozano, S., Iribarren, D., Moreira, T., Feijoo, G.: The link between operational efficiency and environmental impacts - A joint application of Life Cycle Assessment and Data Envelopment Analysis. Science of the Total Environment 407, 1744–1754 (2009)
6. Lewandowska, A., Matuszak-Flejszman, A., Joachimiak, K., Ciroth, A.: Environmental life cycle assessment (LCA) as a tool for identification and assessment of environmental aspects in environmental management systems (EMS). Int. J. Life Cycle Assess. 16, 247–257 (2011)
7. Suh, S.: Functions, commodities and environmental impacts in an ecological-economic model. Ecological Economics 40(4), 451–467 (2004)
8. European Commission, Joint Research Centre, Institute for Environment and Sustainability: ILCD Handbook - General guide for Life Cycle Assessment - Detailed guidance, 1st edn., pp. 99 (2010)
9. Eun, J., Son, J., Moon, J., Chung, J.: Integration of life cycle assessment in the environmental information system. Int. J. Life Cycle Assess. 14, 364–373 (2009)
10. Gwak, J.M., Kim, M., Hur, T.: Analysis of internally recurring unit processes in life cycle Assessment. Journal of Cleaner Production 11, 787–795 (2003)
11. Buxmann, K., Kistler, P., Rebitzer, G.: Independent information modules - a powerful approach for life cycle management. Int. J. Life Cycle Assess. 14(suppl. 1), S92–S100 (2009)

# Sustainable Food Supply Chains: Towards a Framework for Waste Identification

Lukas Chabada[1], Heidi Carin Dreyer[1], Anita Romsdal[2], and Daryl John Powell[1]

[1] Department of Production and Quality Engineering,
Norwegian University of Science and Technology (NTNU), Trondheim, Norway
{lukas.chabada,heidi.c.dreyer,daryl.j.powell}@ntnu.no
[2] SINTEF Technology and Society, Trondheim, Norway
anita.romsdal@sintef.no

**Abstract.** Reduction of waste in food supply chains is an important sustainability issue. More efficient utilisation and management of the resources and values created in food supply chains can contribute to improving competitiveness, and environmental and social responsibility. This study uses the seven wastes approach from lean theory to classify categories of waste in fresh food supply chains and to identify at which stage of the supply chain waste occur. A case is used to illustrate the applicability of the classification. The analysis identifies four categories of waste in the fresh food supply chain; time, distance, energy and mass. The study indicates that the majority of waste is hidden in time, energy and mass categories, related to overproduction, defects and transportation.

**Keywords:** fresh food, waste, lean, food supply chain.

## 1    Introduction

The food sector, represented by farmers, food producers, wholesalers and retailers, creates and manages enormous values and resources. Achieving a sustainable production, distribution and consumption of these values is a significant global responsibility since it affects social development, welfare and health, economic development and competitiveness for actors in the food supply chain, and environmental conditions. The expected population explosion puts direct pressure on global food production (Parfitt et al., 2010, Godfray et al., 2010) and stresses the need for addressing sustainability issues related to the level of waste stemming from resource inefficiencies in food supply chains (Mena et al., 2011).

Cultivating, processing and distributing food which ends up as waste leads to a major loss in value creation (Akkerman et al., 2010). Almost one-third of food produced for human consumption is lost or wasted globally and the level is significantly increasing (Gustavsson et al., 2011). One example of food products being wasted are fresh food products with very short shelf life which need to be processed quickly. A critical question from a logistical point of view is what type of waste are we dealing with and where in the supply chain, and how can new ways to

C. Emmanouilidis, M. Taisch, D. Kiritsis (Eds.): APMS 2012, Part I, IFIP AICT 397, pp. 208–215, 2013.
© IFIP International Federation for Information Processing 2013

control and operate the supply chain contribute to lower the amount of waste. What we know is that a good balance between supply and demand of products in the supply chain will reduce the level of products that will never be sold. We also know that the different stages in the supply chain needs to be integrated, the lead time needs to be kept short, and the inventory level low in order to reduce the risk of creating waste.

There is growing interest in research on waste in food supply chains. Previous studies have concluded that food waste can be found at every stage of the food supply chain (see e.g. Gustavsson et al., 2011). However, lack of studies on systematic and formal definitions and classifications which can assist in defining waste has been identified in research on waste resulting from unnecessary production and distribution activities for high perishable products (Rajurkar and Jain, 2011). This study uses the seven wastes approach from lean which has proved to be very useful for identifying waste in manufacturing processes (Ohno, 1988). The **purpose** of this paper is therefore to use the **seven wastes perspective** from lean in order to develop a **classification for identifying waste in fresh food supply chains**. The classification addresses two research questions (RQ): What **types** of waste can be identified in food supply chains (RQ1)? And **where** in the food supply chain can these wastes be found (RQ2)?

The paper further describes the research methodology and then briefly characterises fresh food supply chains. Next, the seven wastes perspective is used to develop the classification and a case is used to illustrate the applicability of the classification.

## 2      Research Methodology

This research is part of a project focused on sustainable logistics in Nordic fresh food supply chains. The study is carried out by researchers within supply chain management focusing on different aspects of coordination, collaboration, planning and control, and real-time information. The objective of the paper is to develop a classification for waste identification in fresh food supply chains, with focus on producers, wholesalers and retailers. The classification is based on a study of food supply chain and lean theory literature, with particular focus on waste. In order to demonstrate the applicability and relevance of the classification, a Norwegian salad producer is used as an illustrative case. The case was selected due to the fact that the company addresses waste prevention and sustainability as a strategic priority. Data were collected in interviews, discussions and observations during company visits. Interviews and discussions have been conducted in physical meetings and workshops between company representatives and researchers.

## 3      Fresh Food Supply Chain Characteristics

From a supply chain and logistics perspective, there is number of characteristics particular to fresh food supply chains, see Table 1. In general, market and product characteristics tend to push for shorter lead times and higher responsiveness, while the production system with its focus on economies of scale tends to increase lead times (Romsdal et al., 2011). Thus, the way the supply chain and its processes are designed and planned can often result in mismatch of demand and supply, creating high stock levels, increasing the time spent on non-value added operations or contributing to overproduction and increased defects rate.

**Table 1.** Fresh food supply chain characteristics (based on Romsdal et al., 2011)

| Area | Characteristics |
|---|---|
| Product | • High perishability (raw materials, intermediate and finished products) |
| | • Increasing product variety, packaging sizes and receipts |
| Market | • Customers demand frequent deliveries and short response times |
| | • Varying and increasing demand uncertainty |
| | • Limited ability to keep stock |
| | • Cost of lost sales often higher than inventory carrying costs |
| Production system | • Long production lead times, long set-up times, high set-up costs |
| | • Production adapted to high volume, low variety |

Previous studies have identified food waste in all stages of the food supply chain and classified it mostly based on different food product types or production, processing and transportation processes (Parfitt et al., 2010, Gustavsson et al., 2011, Mena et al., 2011). Darlington et al. (2009) pointed out also other wastes in the food supply chain, including bulk waste, water waste, processing waste, packaging waste and overproduction waste. Dudbridge (2011) discusses six out of the seven wastes of lean theory and uses his experience from the food industry to discuss food and other wastes in the food supply chain. His contribution is, however, missing more consistency structure and connection to academic relevance. The discussion above, therefore, shows the lack of attention that has been given to consistent mapping and classifying of different wastes occurring in fresh food supply chains operations.

# 4    Identification of Waste in Fresh Food Supply Chains

The purpose of this paper is to address the gap mentioned above by using the seven wastes from lean as a basis for constructing a classification for waste identification in fresh food supply chains. The study focuses on food producers, wholesalers and retailers in the supply chain. Next, the seven wastes are explained and related to different activities in fresh food supply chains and four wasted categories are identified.

## 4.1    Seven Wastes of Lean and Fresh Food Supply Chains

The systematic identification and elimination of waste is known to be a central element of the Lean Production philosophy (Ohno, 1988, Liker, 2004, Shingo and Dillon, 1989). In order to identify waste in manufacturing processes, Ohno (1988) classifies seven types of waste: Transportation, Inventory, Motion, Waiting, Overproduction, Over-processing, and Defects. Though these seven types of waste have proven to be very useful for identifying waste in the production of discrete automotive components, this type of classification fails to illustrate much of the waste inherent to fresh food supply chains.

Lean theory defines waste as any activity that adds cost or consumes time but does not add value to the customer (Womack and Jones, 2005, Ohno, 1988). Value added activities describe the best combination of processes and operations which are necessary to make the product, delivering the highest quality, for the lowest cost, on time to the customer (Ohno, 1988). In order to find out how much is spent on both value added and non-value added activities, lean theory offers different tools, such as Value Stream Mapping. However, this technique places emphasis on time as a main resource which is wasted. This, however, does not precisely shows all the wastes created in the fresh food supply chain, not including wasted food or energy. Therefore, other categories are added in the proposed waste classification. The categories were chosen on a basis of findings from literature studying operation management considering fresh food characteristics. First category is time which materials, products, equipment, machines and people spend in specific process or operation (Jones and Womack, 2002, Dudbridge, 2011). Second is distance showing how many meters or kilometres were spent on transportation of materials and products (McCarthy and Rich, 2004, Dudbridge, 2011). Third one is energy represented by electricity and fuel spent by tracks, conveyors, fridges, freezers and other equipment and machines (Dudbridge, 2011, Swink et al., 2011). Last suggested category is mass, representing the amount of materials and products which are processed and distributed across the supply chain (Gustavsson et al., 2011, Parfitt et al., 2010).

## 4.2    Towards a Framework for Waste Identification

Below, each of the seven wastes are discussed in terms of the four categories of waste and related to the three actors of the food supply chain; food producers, wholesalers and retailers (based on Ohno, 1988, Jones and Womack, 2002, Dudbridge, 2011).

**Transportation** as itself is a value-added activity bringing the product closer to the customer. Transportation waste is then an unnecessary transportation of materials and products within or outside the company tiding extra **time**, **distance** and **energy**, and by excessive handling of sensitive fresh food products contributing to food waste (Hines and Taylor, 2000). For instance, moving material from and to the distant machine at food producer, transporting materials and products from one place to another just to make a place for new inventory at wholesaler, or moving the products from the store inventory to the shelf and back at retailer stage (Hallihan et al., 1997).

A certain amount of **inventory** is necessary in order to be responsive in fulfilling uncertain customer demand, keeping customer service level high. Inventory waste is therefore characterized as unnecessary inventory in a form of raw materials, work-in-process, or finished goods that exceed what is required to meet customer needs just in time and to meet needs of the process being smoothly performed (Sutherland and Bennett, 2007). This ties extra valuable **time** from shelf life, **energy** of cooling equipment and often leads to food waste. Examples of inventory waste might be all products that are not sold due the deadline determined by safety regulations, or due to product deterioration at every stage of the food supply chain.

**Motion** waste can be defined as **time** spent on unnecessary movements of operator such as unnecessary walking, stretching or reaching for a tool or equipment (Sutherland and Bennett, 2007). Examples are movement of operator to pick the packing tape, reaching for the hammer or walking distance to the pallet while filling the shelf in the store. Motion waste could be reduced by better ergonomics.

**Waiting** waste is an unnecessary waiting of the machines and people spending extra time of labour and energy of idling machines (Sutherland and Bennett, 2007). It might be seen as time operator is waiting to assemble next product or packing machine waiting for products to be delivered or operator waiting for products which should be loaded into a shelf of retail store.

**Overproduction** means making what is unnecessary, when it is unnecessary, and in unnecessary amounts. It occurs when items for which there are no orders are produced. Overproduction in its original sense occurs only at the food producer level when too many products are produced even there is no order for them. On the wholesaler and retailer level, overproduction can be seen as ordering more than is demanded to buffer against uncertainties in demand timing and quantities. Overproduction increases inventory and spends extra **time, distance, energy** and **mass**.

**Over-processing** waste refers to any processes that do not add value to the customer or give more value to the product that is agreed standard. This takes extra **time** and **energy** and increases risk of products being wasted. Examples of this waste are excessive quality check of fresh products at every stage of the supply chain.

**Defects** include wasted materials and products during the production and distribution process, and rejected materials and products which have to be reworked (Dudbridge, 2011, Sutherland and Bennett, 2007, McCarthy and Rich, 2004). Waste from rework includes resources needed to make repairs, while waste from rejects results in waste of **time, energy**, and all other resources put into food products during their production and distribution. The cost of inspecting for defects and responding to customer complaints is also waste related to defects.

Table 2 summarises the discussion above in terms of time, distance, energy and mass, and shows at which stages in the food supply chain they can be identified. The classification shows that time, energy and mass are the most common wastes across the food supply chain and the main contributors are overproduction, defects and transportation followed by inventory waste. On the other hand, the least waste seems to be related to excessive motion.

**Table 2.** Classification of wastes in fresh food supply chains

| Actors in the FSC | Food producers | | | | Wholesalers | | | | Retailers | | | |
|---|---|---|---|---|---|---|---|---|---|---|---|---|
| The 7 wastes / Categories | Time | Dist. | Ener. | Mass | Time | Dist. | Ener. | Mass | Time | Dist. | Ener. | Mass |
| Transportation | X | X | X | X | X | X | X | X | X | X | X | X |
| Inventory | X | | X | X | X | | X | X | X | | X | X |
| Motion | X | | | | X | | | | X | | | |
| Waiting | X | | X | | X | | X | | X | | X | |
| Overproduction | X | X | X | X | X | X | X | X | X | X | X | X |
| Over-processing | X | | X | | X | | X | | X | | X | |
| Defects | X | X | X | X | X | X | X | X | X | X | X | X |

## 5    Case: The Salad Supply Chain

In order to illustrate how the waste classification can be used, a case from the Norwegian food sector is used. The case consists of a supply chain for distribution of processed salads from producer, through a distribution point to a typical grocery store (Yggeseth, 2008, Strandhagen et al., 2011). The shelf life of the salad is around 8-10 days from the production date. The supply chain is illustrated in Fig. 1, showing actors, material and information flow, stock points and physical process.

The factory produces several variants of salads and the production process for most products consists of quality inspections, cutting, washing, and assembly into various product mixes, before packing and storing. Salads are manufactured to stock, but orders from distributors or wholesalers are used for estimating procurement, production, and supply planning. Production planning uses principle of optimal batch-sizing.

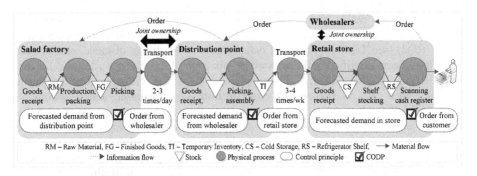

**Fig. 1.** The salad supply chain

Products are kept in stock at the factory until orders arrive. Salads are distributed directly to restaurants and larger institutions and through wholesalers or distribution points to retail stores. From the factory, products are shipped to a distribution point where retailer orders are assembled. The distribution point is merely a cross-docking facility, and within an 8 – 10 hour timeframe the products are transported to retail stores. Accumulated orders are received from a central information system operated by the retail chain's wholesale unit. Throughout the supply chain, products are kept within a strictly regulated temperature zone.

## 6    Discussion and Conclusion

The waste classification from Table 2 can be used as follows. First, on the basis of the seven wastes definitions and proposed wasted categories we try to identify these in the operations of the supply chain. **Transportation** waste could be spotted as unnecessary transport of products between several stock and distribution points. Deeper investigation could show how many man-hours, and how much fuel and electricity is spent unnecessarily. **Inventory** waste can be counted as the amount of products wasted in the multiple stock points and buffers along the supply chain as products waiting for orders to arrive. **Overproduction** waste can be indicated from planning based on forecasting and production planning based on optimal batch-sizes. **Over-processing** waste could be multiple quality checks of salads at four stages in the supply chain (salad factory, distribution point, wholesaler, and retail store). Finally, **defects** waste can be spotted during an excessive handling of temperature sensitive products resulting in waste. Identification of motion and waiting waste in this case would require deeper analysis of the shop floor activities.

From the above, we see that the classification assisted in identifying a number of wastes beyond the simple perspective of volumes of food being wasted or thrown away in the supply chain. We observe that several of the wastes stem from the way the supply chain is designed and managed. For instance, the lack of sharing of real demand data with upstream actors can lead to excessive use of resources put into producing, moving and storing products with no actual order. The multiple stock and handling points along the supply chain also increase lead time, energy and food waste.

This paper has added to the literature on waste in fresh food supply chains by identifying the types of wastes (RQ1) and where these can be found in food supply chains (RQ2) (see Table 2). Different categories of waste (time, distance, energy and mass) have been identified and discussed within each of the seven wastes and for the different supply chain actors. The applicability of the classification has been illustrated in a case. A **theoretical contribution** is an increased understanding of waste in fresh food supply chains. By applying the seven wastes perspective from lean, the paper contributes with new insights into how waste can be identified not only in production but also in the wholesale and retail operations. In **practice**, the classification can assist supply chain actors in analysing their processes and thus provide a basis for identifying the causes of to reduce waste. A **limitation** of the study lies in its limited focus on three supply chain actors and in its limited focus on physical flow only, excluding information flow analysis. The classification suggest the same types of wastes for each actor of the supply chain, However, the priority to reduce these wastes might be different for each of the actors. **Further research** should therefore focus on conducting more empirical cases which would verify and complement the findings of the waste classification Also, the trade-offs between different measures must be evaluated, where for instance less inventory could result in increased transportation waste.

**Acknowledgement.** This study has been made possible by the funding received from Nordic research organization NordForsk via LogiNord project.

# References

1. Akkerman, R., Farahani, P., Grunow, M.: Quality, safety and sustainability in food distribution: a review of quantitative operations management approaches and challenges. OR Spectrum 32, 863–904 (2010)
2. Darlington, R., Staikos, T., Rahimifard, S.: Analytical methods for waste minimisation in the convenience food industry. Waste Management 29, 1274–1281 (2009)

3. Dudbridge, M.: Handbook of Lean Manufacturing in the Food Industry. Wiley Online Library (2011)
4. Godfray, H.C.J., Beddington, J.R., Crute, I.R., Haddad, L., Lawrence, D., Muir, J.F., Pretty, J., Robinson, S., Thomas, S.M., Toulmin, C.: Food security: the challenge of feeding 9 billion people. Science 327, 812–818 (2010)
5. Gustavsson, J., Cederberg, C., Sonesson, U., van Otterdijk, R., Meybeck, A.: Global food losses and food waste. Food and Agriculture Organization of the United Nations, Rome (2011)
6. Hallihan, A., Sackett, P., Williams, G.: JIT manufacturing: the evolution to an implementation model founded in current practice. International Journal of Production Research 35, 901–920 (1997)
7. Hines, P., Taylor, D.: Going lean. Lean Enterprise Research Centre Cardiff Business School, Cardiff (2000)
8. Jones, D., Womack, J.: Seeing the whole. Lean Enterprise Institute, Brookline (2002)
9. Liker, J.K.: The Toyota way: 14 management principles from the world's greatest manufacturer. McGraw-Hill, New York (2004)
10. McCarthy, D., Rich, N.: Lean TPM: a blueprint for change. Butterworth-Heinemann (2004)
11. Mena, C., Adenso-Diaz, B., Yurt, O.: The causes of food waste in the supplier–retailer interface: Evidences from the UK and Spain. Resources, Conservation and Recycling 55, 648–658 (2011)
12. Ohno, T.: Toyota Production System: Beyond large-scale production. Productivity Press, New York (1988)
13. Parfitt, J., Barthel, M., Macnaughton, S.: Food waste within food supply chains: quantification and potential for change to 2050. Philosophical Transactions of the Royal Society of London. Series B, Biological Sciences 365, 3065–3081 (2010)
14. Rajurkar, S.W., Jain, R.: Food supply chain management: review, classification and analysis of literature. International Journal of Integrated Supply Management 6, 33–72 (2011)
15. Romsdal, A., Thomassen, M., Dreyer, H.C., Strandhagen, J.O.: Fresh food supply chains; characteristics and supply chain requirements. In: 18th International Annual EurOMA Conference. Cambridge University, Cambridge (2011)
16. Shingo, S., Dillon, A.P.: A study of the Toyota production system from an industrial engineering viewpoint. Productivity Press, New York (1989)
17. Strandhagen, J.O., Dreyer, H.C., Romsdal, A.: Control Model for Intelligent and Demand-Driven Supply Chain. In: Flynn, B., Morita, M., Machuca, J. (eds.) Managing Global Supply Chain Relationships. Business Science Reference (an imprint of IGI Global), Hersey (2011)
18. Sutherland, J., Bennett, B.: The seven deadly wastes of logistics: applying Toyota Production System principles to create logistics value. White Paper (2007)
19. Swink, M., Melnyk, S., Cooper, M.B., Hartley, J.L.: Managing operations across the supply chain. McGraw-Hill, Irwin (2011)
20. Womack, J.P., Jones, D.T.: Lean solutions: how companies and customers can create value and wealth together. Free Pr. (2005)
21. Yggeseth, F.: Ferskere produkter og mer effektiv logistikk i dagligvarebransjen. Master Thesis, Norwegian University of Science and Technology (2008)

# A Classification of Industrial Symbiosis Networks: A Focus on Materials and Energy Recovery

Vito Albino, Achille Claudio Garavelli, and Vincenzo Alessio Romano

DMMM, Politecnico di Bari,
Viale Japigia 182, 70126 Bari, Italy
{v.albino,c.garavelli,va.romano}@poliba.it

**Abstract.** Industrial symbiosis (IS) has gained more attention in the production economics as the pressure on companies increases for the reduction of waste emissions as well as of primary resources consumption. At present, as the number of IS initiatives increases, many issues about its boundaries, such as the entities involved and the resources shared/exchanged, still continue to remain open. A common classification of IS networks does still not exist.

Input-output matching is the most significant tool to analyze IS. To this aim, we adopt an input-output approach for defining an IS network, and for proposing a classification model at the technical level (i.e. physical flow type, number of production chains involved, and network structure).

The proposed approach is applied to several existing IS networks to describe as it works. This classification framework can be useful for companies to set strategies and for local government to plan policies.

**Keywords:** sustainable production, industrial symbiosis, classification.

## 1  Introduction

Nowadays, problems related to the natural resources consumption, energy usage, Greenhouse Gas (GHG) emissions, and fossil fuel utilization are becoming more and more crucial and relevant. Therefore, there is a need to give further impetus to efficient and eco-innovative production processes, to reduce dependency on raw materials, and to encourage optimal resource use and recycling (UNEP, 2009). Industrial symbiosis (IS) has been considered as one of the most effective solutions to reduce the impact of waste emissions and of primary input consumption moving towards sustainable production models. The Organization for Economic Co-operation and Development has recently identified IS as a tool for systemic innovation vital for future green growth (OECD, 2010). Furthermore, within the Resource Efficiency Flagship Initiative, IS is indicated as a tool that all member states should exploit to help companies work together to make the best use of the waste and by-products they produce (EU, 2011).

Industrial symbiosis has emerged as a sub-field of industrial ecology. "Industrial ecology is the science that provides the conceptual tools to analyze and optimize the flow of energy and materials in production systems" (The Interagency Workgroup on

C. Emmanouilidis, M. Taisch, D. Kiritsis (Eds.): APMS 2012, Part I, IFIP AICT 397, pp. 216–223, 2013.

Industrial Ecology, Material and Energy Flows, 1998). In particular, IS operates at the inter-firm level (Chertow, 2000). However, despite over twenty years of industrial ecology, IS phenomenon is still not clearly defined.

IS has been inspired by the concept of "industrial ecosystem" in which "the consumption of energy and materials is optimized and the effluents of one process ... serve as the raw material for another process" (Frosch and Gallopoulos, 1989). More recently, IS was widely known as "engaging traditionally separate industries in a collective approach to competitive advantage involving physical exchange of materials, energy, water and/or by-products" (Chertow, 2000), whose key success factors are "collaboration and the synergistic possibilities offered by geographic proximity". These keys for the success of IS differ according to the case- and location-specificity of IS, and they have been largely discussed within the recent literature, often achieving not fully agreed results.

Additionally, through the years, the IS network concept has been extended not only to all types of physical and unphysical resources that could be intentionally shared or exchanged (by-products, utilities, and ancillary services) (Chertow, 2007), but also to all the other firm resources such as, for example, knowledge and social processes.

Therefore, IS has been approached from various perspectives (e.g. social, economic, environmental, spatial, organizational, technical). Nevertheless, with the increasing number of IS projects, many issues about IS boundaries, such as the entities involved (firms, organizations, industries, facilities) and the resources shared/exchanged (materials, energy, water, information, expertise), still continue to remain open.

With this regard, focusing on materials and energy physical flows only, and adopting an input-output (I-O) approach, we define an IS network as a set of one or more production chains utilizing their waste materials and residual energy in substitution of primary resources. In particular, we propose a technical classification model of IS networks based on the physical flow type involved, and the production chains sending and receiving it. The study aims at proposing a basic categorization of IS networks, a classification tool, which could be a common ground for successive structural network analyses.

In the next section a specific review of the literature is devoted to the materials and energy flows in IS networks. In the third section the classification model for IS networks is proposed. In the fourth section several case examples are provided. Finally, main conclusions are reported in the last section.

## 2    Materials and Energy in IS Networks

From a technical point of view, a production chain can be considered as an input-output system (Storper and Harrison, 1992) that describes the product flows existing among production processes. Input-output systems may involve many production processes, depending on a specific division and classification of production in processes. In general, the chain may contain the extraction of raw materials, manufacturing, distribution and use of goods. Referring to the environmental sustainability, a sustainable production chain means favouring, for a given output, processes with less use of natural resources (energy and materials) and production of wastes. From the supply perspective, extended supply chains include the reduction and elimination of by-products through cleaner process technologies and lean production techniques, extending chain boundaries as far as to include the source and the destination of all the physical flows used and produced at each chain stage (Albino et al., 2002; 2003). As the opportunity offered by the efficient use of materials (recycling, etc.) and energy stresses the relevance of network of actors, cooperation between actors becomes crucial.

Cooperation can be considered also in terms of industrial ecology. Industrial symbiosis is the main approach introduced by the industrial ecology to explain how industrial ecosystem (Frosch and Gallopoulos, 1989) may work. Two industrial actors operate in IS when they exchange materials and energy to reduce costs, create value, and improve the environment. Although the analysis of the role and level of cooperation between actors of production chains in permitting environmental and economic benefits needs to be explored further, ownership issues are not faced in our study. We aim at describing symbiotic relationships among industrial actors in terms of materials and energy flows only.

Assuming that symbiotic transactions are waste exchanges, the first technical classification of IS networks is proposed by Chertow (2000), identifying ISs i) within a firm, facility or organization, ii) among firms collocated in a defined eco-industrial park, iii) among local firms that are not co-located, and iv) among firms organized "virtually" in a broader region. However, this categorization seems to be in contrast with the Chertow's (2000) IS definition, which indentifies the no well-quantified geographic proximity as the IS key driver. Lombardi and Laybourn (2012) redefine IS as "engaging diverse organizations in a network ... to yield mutually profitable transactions for novel sourcing of required inputs, and value added destinations for non-product outputs". As the decennary National Industrial Symbiosis Programme (NISP) experience in the United Kingdom demonstrates, the localization of the entities exchanging resources, although geographic proximity is often associated with IS, is not essential for the success of IS networks (Lombardi and Laybourn, 2012). Distance between entities can be considered as a business-as-usual factor.

In this scenario, input-output matching is the most significant tool to analyze IS (Chertow, 2000). In input-output matching, firms systematically collect input and output data of companies and try to create links among partners. Recently, Bossilkov et al. (2005) proposed a technical classification of existing IS networks in three dimensions: i) type of resource exchange (water, energy, process or non-process waste, utility sharing); ii) type of processing involved (direct use or reuse, energy recovery or alternative fuels, material recovery, etc.); and iii) type of synergy (bi or multi-lateral, etc.). However, this classification continues to leave ambiguity about IS boundaries. Exchanged/shared resources and involved actors, which should characterize IS networks and distinguish them from other types of resource synergy, are still not clearly defined. As Golev and Corder (2012) affirm, a common classification for IS networks does still not exist.

# 3    A Classification Model for IS Networks

Adopting an input-output (I-O) approach, we define an IS network as a set of one or more production chains utilizing their waste materials and residual energy in substitution of primary resources. Thus, we propose a three-dimensional structural classification model for IS networks by tracking material and energy flows among symbiotic chains. This classification refers to an elementary IS network, i.e. a physical flow type (i.e. one waste-one primary input) shared by one or more actors (i.e. production chains). Starting from this basic categorization, we may represent and classify a more complex IS network as a composition of elementary IS networks.

## 3.1    Physical Flow Type

Let us consider an IS network constituted by one or more production chains.

Let us assume that the waste $l$ output flow is the only waste material flow produced, and the primary input type $k$ the only one required by the IS network. Assuming that the waste $l$ can be used as primary input $k$, we may distinguish the i) material-material, and ii) material-energy flow types. In the first case, the waste $l$ can be directly used in production processes without further transformation as material input, or recycled obtaining the primary input required by the IS network. In the second case, the waste $l$ can be used to produce energy (e.g. alternative fuels).

Now let us suppose that the waste $l$ output is an energy flow, and the primary energy input $k$ the only required by the IS network. Assuming that the waste $l$ can be used as primary input $k$, we may identify the iii) energy-energy flow type, i.e. an energy cascade, such as heat recovery.

## 3.2    Internal and External IS

Let us consider an IS network constituted by one production chain, $\alpha$. Let us assume that the chain $\alpha$ only produces the waste type $l$, and only requires the primary input type $k$. Assuming that the waste type $l$ can be used as primary input $k$, a form of internal IS may occur if the chain $\alpha$ uses the waste $l$ as primary input $k$.

Let us consider now an IS network constituted by two production chains, $\alpha$ and $\beta$, where $\alpha \neq \beta$. Let us assume that the chain $\alpha$ only produces the waste type $l$, and no primary input is required, and the chain $\beta$ only requires the primary input type $k$, and no waste is produced. Assuming that the waste type $l$ can be used as primary input $k$, a form of external IS may occur if the chain $\beta$ uses the waste $l$ as primary input $k$.

## 3.3    IS Network Structure

Let us consider an IS network constituted by two or more production chains. Let us assume that the waste type $l$ is only produced, and the primary input $k$ only required by the IS network. Finally, let us assume that the waste $l$ can be used as primary input $k$. For each physical flow type, depending on the number of production chains sending and receiving it, we may identify the following configurations: i) one-to-one, ii) one-to-$n$, iii) $n$-to-one, and iv) $m$-to-$n$, where $m, n \geq 2$.

In the first case, let us suppose that the IS network is composed by two production chains, $\alpha$ and $\beta$. Moreover, let us assume that the chain $\alpha$ only produces the waste $l$, and no primary input is required, and the chain $\beta$ only requires the primary input type $k$, and no waste is produced. The "one-to-one" configuration occurs if the chain $\beta$ uses the waste $l$ as primary input $k$.

In the second case, let us suppose that the IS network is composed by three production chains, $\alpha$, $\beta$, and $\gamma$. Furthermore, let us assume that the chain $\alpha$ only produces the waste $l$, and no primary input is required, and the chains $\beta$ and $\gamma$ only require the primary input $k$, and no waste is produced. The "one-to-$n$" configuration occurs if the chains $\beta$ and $\gamma$ use the waste $l$ as primary input $k$.

In the third case, let us continue to suppose that the IS network is composed by three production chains, $\alpha$, $\beta$, and $\gamma$. Let us assume that chains $\beta$ and $\gamma$ only produce the waste $l$, and do not require any primary input, and the chain $\alpha$ only requires the primary input type $k$, and no waste is produced. The "$n$-to-one" configuration occurs if the chains $\alpha$ uses the waste $l$ as primary input $k$.

In the fourth case, let us suppose that the IS network is composed by four production chains, $\alpha$, $\beta$, $\gamma$, and $\delta$. Let us assume that chains $\alpha$ and $\beta$ only produce the waste $l$, and do not require any primary input, and chains $\gamma$ and $\delta$ only require the primary input $k$, and do not produce any waste. The "$m$-to-$n$" configuration occurs if chains $\gamma$ and $\delta$ use the waste type $l$ as primary input $k$.

# 4     Case Examples

As we have anticipated at the beginning of the previous section, a complex IS network may be a chain or a network of elementary IS networks. In this section, we describe several case examples of actual IS networks that better fit our classification model, based on a single one waste-one input physical flow type.

Yang and Feng (2008) analyze the Nanning Sugar Co., Ltd. case, which is one of the most successfully examples of a new form of IS emerged in China, inspired by the "circular economy" philosophy. Black liquor generated during the alkaline pulping process passes through a recovery process. On the one hand, alkali recovered is reintroduced into the pulping process; on the other hand, lime sludge is used in substitution of limestone to produce cement. In this case, if we consider each physical flow type as a one waste-one input flow, we have two "one-to-one" configurations, one internal, and one external. However, if we categorize a physical flow type only based on the waste output flow, independently from the obtainable input types, this is an example of a "one-to-$n$" configuration, characterized by a material-material flow, and internal-external IS.

Wolf (2007) investigates the Swedish forest industry in the Östergötland region. Three actors are identified: the pulp mill, the saw mill, and the pellet production plant. Sawdust and wood chip by-products from the saw mill are delivered to the pulp mill to be used as biofuel. Thus, the pulp mill supplies steam and electricity to the saw mill, and to the pellet chain. As shown, this is a "one-to-$n$" IS network, both internal and external, with a material-energy flow, where the pulp mill operates as a conversion process.

Research Triangle Institute (1996) has developed a prototype eco-industrial park for the Brownsville (Texas, U.S.) / Matamoros (Mexico) industrial area, identifying opportunities for symbiotic exchanges among local existing companies. In particular, we focus on scrap plastic re-use. The proposed prototype suggests an IS network composed by a plastic recycler, and three other entities sending their plastic scrap: a textile company, and auto and discrete parts manufacturers. Therefore, plastic may be purchased in the form of plastic pellets by the discrete parts manufacturer, after being processed. This is a "$n$-to-one" configuration, with a material-material flow type, and internal-external symbiosis.

Chertow and Miyata (2011) investigate some IS initiatives of a cluster of companies located in the Campbell Industrial Park in Honolulu, HI, on the island of Oahu. In particular, three organizations bring their used activated carbon to AES Hawaii cogeneration plant as alternative fuels: the Honolulu Board of Water Supply (BWS), Tesoro (i.e. an oil refining company), and the Kalaeloa Cogeneration Plant (i.e. an oil-fired power plant). Both BWS and Tesoro pay AES Hawaii to take and burn the used carbon (McCann, 2005). We may categorize this case as a "$n$-to-one" configuration, with a material-energy flow type, and external IS only.

Mirata and Emtairah (2005) study the case of the industrial town of Landskrona, located in south-western Sweden. Several sectors are included such as chemicals, waste management, metals recycling, and public infrastructures. However, if we consider the local community as a third actor, a heat cascading initiative involves other two entities: steel dust and lead battery recycling companies. Heat from lead acid battery and steel dust recyclers is used for district heating by the local community. A "$n$-to-one"/energy-energy/external IS occurs by tracking the heat flow.

Focusing on utility synergies, Van Beers et al. (2007) investigate the Kwinana Industrial Area, dominated by heavy process industries, and located in Western Australia. In particular, a "$m$-to-$n$"/material-material/internal-external IS occurs by tracking the wastewater flow. In fact, the cogeneration (i.e. Verve Energy) and the chlor-alkali (i.e. Nufarm Coogee) plants send their wastewater to the treatment plant of Tiwest, a company producing titanium dioxide. So, the potable and demineralized water returns to the plants that generate the wastewater flow.

Korhonen (2001) analyzes the regional energy supply system of the Jyvaskyla region in Finland. The Rauhalahti CHP plant, which is a publicly owned body, receives waste wood from a plywood mill, located in the Saynatsalo suburb, and external fuel, such as peat, saw-mill and forestry waste from other actors. Thus, it produces electricity for all households, services and industry in the city, the energy produced by waste is used for district heating, and industrial steam is sent to the Kangas paper mill. This is an example of a "$m$-to-$n$" configuration, with a material-energy flow type, and external symbiosis.

# 5    Conclusions

Industrial symbiosis (IS) is emerging as one of the most effective tools to mitigate environmental impact of industrial activities, by reducing both primary resources consumption and waste emissions. However, no common classification model for IS networks exists (Golev and Corder, 2012). In this paper, adopting an input-output approach, we have defined an elementary IS network based on the single physical flow type (one waste-one primary input) shared among production chains. Furthermore, we have distinguished between internal and external forms of IS. The former occurs when the waste output flow is sent and received by the same chain, the latter when the chain sending and the one receiving it are not the same. These two conditions can co-exist according to the structure of the network. Four possible configurations have been found depending on the number of production chains sending and receiving the physical flow type.

Several case examples of existing IS networks have been also provided. Focusing only on one specific physical flow type (one waste-one primary input), we have classified each case.

The proposed classification model for IS networks does not aim at being an exhaustive categorizing tool, but a basic categorization at the technical level useful for successive network analyses. It can support policy design as network identification provides guidelines for incentives in terms of transportation and environmental legacy issues, as well as of type and size of sectors to be involved in the IS network.

**Acknowledgements.** Financial support provided by the POR Puglia 2000–2006 (CIP_PE007 – "Metodologie innovative per lo sviluppo di mercati organizzati di servizi logistici", CIP_PS092 –"Produzione Distribuita come Sistema Innovativo – DIPIS and CIP_PE109 – "Development of an innovative model for self-evaluation of the degree of corporate social responsibility") is gratefully acknowledged.

# References

Albino, V., Dietzenbacher, E., Kühtz, S.: Analyzing Material and Energy Flows in an Industrial District using an Enterprise Input-Output Model. Economic Systems Research 15, 457–480 (2003)

Albino, V., Izzo, C., Kühtz, S.: Input-output models for the analysis of a local/global supply chain. Int. J. Product. Econ. 78, 119–131 (2002)

Bossilkov, A., van Berkel, R., Corder, G.: Regional Synergies for Sustainable Resource Processing: A Status Report. Centre for Sustainable Resource Processing (CSRP), Perth, Western Australia (2005)

Chertow, M.R.: Industrial symbiosis: literature and taxonomy. Annual Review of Energy and the Environment 25, 313–337 (2000)

Chertow, M.R.: "Uncovering" industrial symbiosis. Journal of Industrial Ecology 11(1), 11–30 (2007)

Chertow, M., Miyata, Y.: Assessing collective firm behavior: comparing Indus-trial Symbiosis with possible alternatives for individual companies in Oahu, HI. Bus. Strat. Env. 20, 266–280 (2011)

European Union (EU), Resource Efficiency Flagship Initiative (2011), http://ec.europa.eu/europe2020/europe-2020-in-a-nutshell/flagship-initiatives/index_en.htm

Frosch, D., Gallopoulos, N.: Strategies for manufacturing. Scientific American 261(3), 94–102 (1989)

Golev, A., Corder, G.D.: Developing a classification system for regional resource synergies. Minerals Engineering 29, 58–64 (2012)

The Interagency Workgroup on Industrial Ecology, Material and Energy Flows 1998. Materials, Washington, DC (1998)

Korhonen, J.: Regional industrial ecology: examples from regional economic systems of forest industry and energy supply in Finland. Journal of Environmental Management 63, 367–375 (2001)

Lombardi, D.R., Laybourn, P.: Redefining Industrial Symbiosis - Crossing Academic–Practitioner Boundaries. Journal of Industrial Ecology 16(1), 28–37 (2012)

McCann, R.: AES Hawaii. Interviews 22 (July 27-October 14, 2005)

Mirata, M., Emtairah, T.: Industrial symbiosis networks and the contribution to environmental innovation: the case of the Landskrona industrial symbiosis programme. Journal of Cleaner Production 13(10-11), 993–1002 (2005)

OECD, Project on Green Growth and Eco-Innovation, OECD (2010)

Research Triangle Institute, Eco-Industrial Parks: A case study and analysis of economic, environmental, technical, and regulatory Issues (1996), http://www.rti.org/pubs/case-study.pdf

Storper, M., Harrison, B.: Flessibilità, gerarchie e sviluppo regionale: la ristrutturazione organizzativa dei sistemi produttivi e le nuove forme di governance. In: Belussi, F. (ed.) Nuovi Modelli D'impresa, Gerarchie Organizzative e Impresa Rete, pp. 209–237. Angeli, Milano (1992)

United Nations Environment Programme (UNEP), Global Green New Deal. Policy Brief (2009), http://www.unep.org/pdf/GGND_Final_Report.pdf

Van Beers, D., Corder, G., Bossilkov, A., Van Berkel, R.: Industrial Symbiosis in the Australian minerals industry - The cases of Kwinana and Gladstone. Journal of Industrial Ecology 11(1), 55–72 (2007)

Wolf, A.: Industrial Symbiosis in the Swedish Forest Industry. Ph.D. thesis, Linköping University, Linköping (2007)

Yang, S., Feng, N.: A case study of industrial symbiosis: Nanning Sugar Co., Ltd. in China. Resources, Conservation and Recycling 52, 813–820 (2008)

# Performance Evaluation in Sustainability Conscious Manufacturing Companies by Using TOPSIS Method

Merve Kılıç and Seren Özmehmet Taşan

Dokuz Eylul University, Department of Industrial Engineering, Izmir, Turkey
mervekilic_35_5@yahoo.com
seren.ozmehmet@deu.edu.tr

**Abstract.** In a manufacturing environment, managing limited resources has always been a main issue for engineers. Recently, the idea of managing limited resources without harming ecological environment adopted by manufacturing sector and sustainable manufacturing has become a key issue. While the concept of sustainability has been recognized, companies need to measure how sustainable they perform. Therefore, sustainability indicators are developed and used in order to assess companies' production activities expediently to sustainable manufacturing. This paper presents a research indicating the application of TOPSIS method on sustainability indicators related to production for two different multi-criteria decision making problems in a sustainability conscious manufacturing company.

**Keywords:** Sustainability, Indicator, Manufacturing, TOPSIS, Performance Evaluation.

## 1 Introduction

In ecology, sustainability is defined as the providing the continuousness of biological systems' variety and productivity. Considering this definition, the term of sustainability is used for managing the resources via long term maintenance of responsibility for environment, economy and society. Sustainability can be evaluated as a problem statement that seeks ways for human and other forms of life will flourish on the planet forever. With the ever increasing interest in sustainability, the companies started to realize the importance and impact of manufacturing their products in a more sustainable way. Sustainable manufacturing refers to that decreasing the negative effects of a product and its production processes on environment, health and welfare of community to minimum level. From raw material to the finished good and even at the recycling phase, the product should cause no or minimum damage to environment and during its production process, environmental resources should be used efficiently. The objectives of sustainable manufacturing are defined by the European Union as creating more value for more (growth) and better jobs, increasing the competition of European industries and the communities in the knowledge century and sustainable development of economies [1]. Since the importance of the sustainable manufacturing has been increased rapidly, companies

C. Emmanouilidis, M. Taisch, D. Kiritsis (Eds.): APMS 2012, Part I, IFIP AICT 397, pp. 224–231, 2013.

show tendency to adopt this concept. Similar to companies' approach which uses financial indicators to determining the business success, there has been needed to measure and evaluate sustainability. However, sustainability can be thought as an abstract concept which is hard to measure. Therefore sustainability indicators are developed and used in order to measure how a company succeeds in the concept of sustainability and sustainable production.

Several researchers have focus on determining indicators for sustainable manufacturing [2-4]. These researchers gave utmost importance to create and define new sustainable manufacturing indicators. However, due to difficulties in determining suitable indicator baseline, there has been a lack of research concerning performance evaluations by using indicators. Practically, various indicators should be considered simultaneously while evaluating the sustainability performance of a manufacturing system. In order to fill this gap, the contribution of this study focuses on the application of TOPSIS method that makes us able to consider various sustainability indicators simultaneously. The remainder of this paper is organized as follows; Section 2 presents the necessary background information regarding to sustainability indicators while focusing on the product indicators. Following, section 3 consists of the brief explanation of the TOPSIS method. Later, section 4 includes the application of TOPSIS method on two different case studies. Finally, conclusions and directions for future researches are given in section 5.

## 2    Sustainability Indicators Related to Manufacturing

The indicator has significance that extends beyond the properties directly associated with the parameter values. Indicators possess a synthetic meaning and are developed for a specific purpose [2]. United Nations (UN) defined indicators for sustainable development considering sociological field of development problems as well as the physical problems [5]. UN grouped indicators according to fields such as poverty, governance, health, education, demographics, natural hazards, atmosphere, land, oceans, seas and coasts, freshwater, biodiversity, economic development, global economic partnership, consumption, and production. In literature, sustainability indicators related to manufacturing are evaluated in three differently named groups such as product, process and management [3]; social, environmental and economic [4] or inputs, operations and products [2]. This paper presents only the indicators related to product. Indicators related with product generally state the impacts of materials used for producing the product, consumption and renewability of the resources used for production and recyclability of a product.

Neto et al. [3] defined nine indicator related to product considering the material usage and renewability, usage of resources such as energy and water and transportation of material and products. Similar to this study, OECD [2] defined product indicators related to materials with the aspects of renewable and non-renewable and also with the content of restricted substance. Energy consumption is also included in to indicators and as an addition; greenhouse gas emission intensity is mentioned. Krajnc and Glavic [4] defined product indicators under the output indicators which is a branch of the main title of the environmental indicators. Additionally, they considered the recyclable materials.

# 3     TOPSIS Method

TOPSIS stands for technique for order preference by similarity to ideal solution developed by Hwang and Yoon [6]. TOPSIS method has several advantages; one of which is the application convenience and simplicity when identifying the suitable alternative quickly. Additionally, it performs similar to various methods that use additive weights and performs better than other methods in most cases.

The TOPSIS method based on the selected alternative should to be found at the shortest distance from the positive ideal solution and farthest from the negative ideal solution. Positive ideal solution represents the best criteria values and conversely the negative ideal solution represents the worst criteria values attainable from all alternatives. TOPSIS can be summarized in six steps (Fig.1). In first step, evaluation matrix is built by listing alternative horizontally and criterions vertically. Second step consists of dividing each center values by the norm of the total outcome vector in order to non-dimensionalize the center values in the evaluation matrix. Third step includes multiplying the matrix's values by normalized weights of each criterion and establishing the relative importance matrix. The fourth step consists of building positive and negative ideal solutions to compare the alternatives with each other. After determining the positive and negative ideal solutions, the separation of each matrix value from the ideals are measured as Euclidean distances in the fifth step. At the sixth step, these distances are transformed into a single metric called relative closeness to the ideal solution. Finally, alternatives ranked according to their closeness to the ideal solution.

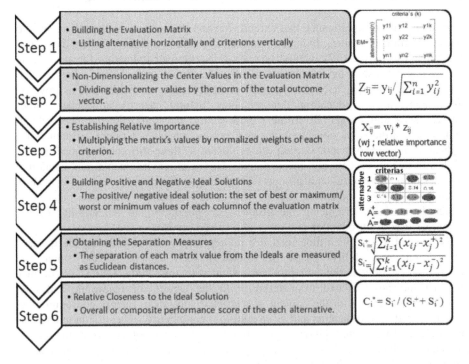

**Fig. 1.** Summary of TOPSIS steps

# 4    Case Studies

In order to present the applications of multi-criteria decision making process for evaluating sustainability indicators in the concept of manufacturing, two different case studies are formed and examined according to company's perception of sustainability. The first case study includes the application of TOPSIS method on the decision making regarding six production period of the company concentrating on three sustainability indicators: product durability, revenues from eco-products and reusable packaging mass. After applying steps mentioned in section 3, the most appropriate period with the strategy that fits to the company's criterions are determined. The second case study includes determining that which product is matched with the firm's philosophy of sustainability. Six eco-products are examined based on the four criterions and the most preferable product with the maximum revenue, shortest production time, involves larger amount of recyclable material and with minimum amount of carbon emission is determined as a result of the study. After applying steps mentioned in section 3, the most appropriate eco-product that fits to the company's perception of sustainability is determined. Finally, results for both case studies are discussed in detail.

## 4.1    Case Study I

This case study concerns with the sustainability performance in Company X over time periods. While producing their ordinary goods the firm decided to enlarge its product range to the new segment: eco-products. During 6 time periods they have been trying to develop a production strategy related to their sustainability perception. Now Company X wants to eliminate the production of ordinary products and focus on the eco-products. The firm concentrates on 3 sustainability indicators: product durability $(I_1)$, revenues from eco-products $(I_2)$ and reusable packaging mass $(I_3)$. They observed the information related these indicators and examined the 6 time periods (see Fig. 2, step 1). There were 6 different strategies in 6 time periods and now the firm wants to evaluate that which strategy is better. According to sustainability policy of Company X, it is better if a product has maximum durability, consists of more reusable package and with the maximum revenue.

Using the information gathered by Company X for 3 sustainability indicators over 6 time periods, TOPSIS method was applied as shown in Fig. 2 and summarized in Fig. 3. The results of TOPSIS showed that the strategy applied on the $6^{th}$ period fits best to the Company X's sustainability perception and the firm decided to continue its production activities with this strategy. Performance criterion of $5^{th}$ period is very close to period 6. From Fig. 3, it is seen that the durability is achieved in $5^{th}$ and $6^{th}$ period to 8 years and revenue obtained from eco-products shows small decrease. It is also seen that the reusable packaging mass is doubled from period 5 to 6. If the firm concentrates on only first 4 periods, it would be difficult to make a choice because the results provided from these periods are very close to each other while data belongs to these periods were varied.

## 4.2    Case Study II

This case study concerns with the sustainability performance in Company X for various products. Company X wants to determine that which product is matched with the firm's policy of sustainability. The relevant data regarding to six products A, B, C,

*Step 1: Building the Evaluation Matrix*

|  | $I_1$ (years) | $I_2$ (million $) | $I_3$ (tones) |
|---|---|---|---|
| **1. Period** | 5 | 100 | 75 |
| **2. Period** | 6 | 230 | 12 |
| **3. Period** | 7 | 170 | 48 |
| **4. Period** | 6 | 170 | 69 |
| **5. Period** | 8 | 400 | 80 |
| **6. Period** | 8 | 300 | 160 |

*Step 2: Non-Dimensionalizing the Center Values in the Evaluation Matrix*

$$Z_{ij} = y_{ij} / \sqrt{\sum_{i=1}^{n} y_{ij}^2}$$

|  | $I_1$ (years) | $I_2$ (million $) | $I_3$ (tones) |
|---|---|---|---|
| **1. Period** | 0.30 | 0.16 | 0.35 |
| **2. Period** | 0.36 | 0.37 | 0.05 |
| **3. Period** | 0.42 | 0.27 | 0.22 |
| **4. Period** | 0.36 | 0.27 | 0.32 |
| **5. Period** | 0.48 | 0.65 | 0.37 |
| **6. Period** | 0.48 | 0.49 | 0.75 |

*Step 3: Establishing Relative Importance*

Establishing relative importance ($w_j$) of the criterion consists of multiplication the matrix values by the normalized weights for each criterion. Normalized weights of the criterions are found with a ten point scale.

|  | Points out of 10 | Norma-lized Values |
|---|---|---|
| $I_1$ | 6 | 0.32 |
| $I_2$ | 8 | 0.42 |
| $I_3$ | 5 | 0.26 |
| Total | 19 | 1 |

|  | $I_1$ | $I_2$ | $I_3$ |
|---|---|---|---|
| **1. Period** | 0.096 | 0.067 | 0.091 |
| **2. Period** | 0.115 | 0.155 | 0.013 |
| **3. Period** | 0.134 | 0.113 | 0.057 |
| **4. Period** | 0.115 | 0.113 | 0.083 |
| **5. Period** | 0.153 | 0.273 | 0.096 |
| **6. Period** | 0.153 | 0.205 | 0.195 |

*Step 4: Building Positive and Negative Ideal Solutions*

The positive ideal solution corresponds to the set of best or maximum values of each column. Conversely, the negative ideal solution constitutes the set of worst or minimum values of each column of the evaluation matrix where A+ and A- are the set of maximum and minimum values of the criteria's.

|  | $I_1$ (years) | $I_2$ (million $) | $I_3$ (tones) |
|---|---|---|---|
| **1. Period** | 0.096 | 0.067 | 0.091 |
| **2. Period** | 0.115 | 0.155 | 0.013 |
| **3. Period** | 0.134 | 0.113 | 0.057 |
| **4. Period** | 0.115 | 0.113 | 0.083 |
| **5. Period** | 0.153 | 0.273 | 0.096 |
| **6. Period** | 0.153 | 0.205 | 0.195 |

$A^+ = \{ 0.153, 0.273, 0.195 \}$    $A^- = \{ 0.096, 0.67, 0.013 \}$

*Step 5: Obtaining the Separation Measures*

The separation of each alternative from the ideal one is given by Euclidean distance.

$$S_i^+ = \sqrt{\sum_{i=1}^{k}(x_{ij} - x_j^+)^2} \quad \text{and} \quad S_i^- = \sqrt{\sum_{i=1}^{k}(x_{ij} - x_j^-)^2}$$

*Step 6: Relative Closeness to the Ideal Solution*

Relative closeness to the ideal solution may call overall or composite performance score of the each alternative.,

$$C_i = S_i^- / (S_i^+ + S_i^-)$$

| | | |
|---|---|---|
| $C_1 = 0.26$ | $C_2 = 0.29$ | $C_3 = 0.25$ |
| $C_4 = 0.29$ | $C_5 = 0.70$ | $C_6 = 0.79$ |

**Fig. 2.** Applying TOPSIS steps to the case-1

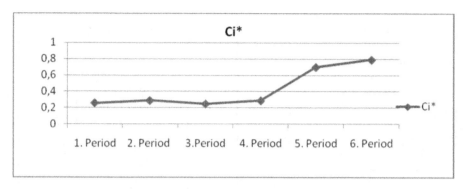

**Fig. 3.** Performance Values for Each Period

**Table 1.** Product Data

|   | Demand (yearly) | Price (per product) | Production Duration (of 1 product) | Recyclability (%) | $CO_2$ Emission (yearly) |
|---|---|---|---|---|---|
| A | 300 | 5000 | 8 hr | 75% | 25 |
| B | 400 | 3000 | 11 hr | 85% | 40 |
| C | 200 | 5000 | 5 hr | 70% | 30 |
| D | 300 | 10000 | 8 hr | 50% | 45 |
| E | 100 | 20000 | 12 hr | 68% | 20 |
| F | 600 | 3000 | 6 hr | 90% | 32 |

D, E and F are shown in Table 1. Data related to production of the six eco-products: annual revenue calculated as multiplication of yearly demand and price per product. For example, from product A: 300*5000 = 1500000. Revenue from eco-product determined as 10500000 and total revenue of the firm recorded as 19500000. The firm produces 12 hour in a day and 5 days in a week. Recycled material costs 600 and normal material costs 1000. According to Company X, the product with the maximum revenue, shortest production time, involves larger amount of recyclable material and with minimum amount of carbon emission is preferable.

Using the information gathered by Company X for 6 products, TOPSIS method was applied as shown in Fig. 4 and summarized in Fig. 5. In the third step, weights are determined according to following calculations; Revenue from eco-products: revenue from eco-products / total revenue = 10.5 /19.5 =0.54; 12 hr production in a day and 5 days in a week, 50 hr production of eco-products : 50 / 60= 0.83; Recycled material costs 600, normal material costs 1000 : 1000/600= 1.66; It means that if the firm spends 1000 on normal material, they produce 1 product; if they spend same value on recycled material they produce 1.66 products; Mass fraction of greenhouse gases: total mass of CO2 equivalents/ total mass of products = 192 / 1900 =0.10. The results of TOPSIS revealed that product F is more suitable for Company X's policy of sustainability. If the data is reviewed, it is seen that the product F shows highest

<table>
<tr><td colspan="2">

*Step 1: Building the Evaluation Matrix*

</td><td colspan="2">

*Step 2: Non-Dimensionalizing the Center Values in the Evaluation Matrix*

</td></tr>
</table>

| | Revenue ($I_1$) | Time ($I_2$) | Recycling ($I_3$) | $CO_2$ Emission ($I_4$) |
|---|---|---|---|---|
| A | 15 | 8 | 75 | 25 |
| B | 12 | 11 | 85 | 40 |
| C | 10 | 5 | 70 | 30 |
| D | 30 | 8 | 50 | 45 |
| E | 20 | 12 | 68 | 20 |
| F | 18 | 6 | 90 | 32 |

$$Z_{ij} = y_{ij} / \sqrt{\sum_{i=1}^{n} y_{ij}^2}$$

| | $I_1$ | $I_2$ | $I_3$ | $I_4$ |
|---|---|---|---|---|
| A | 0.33 | 0.37 | 0.41 | 0.31 |
| B | 0.26 | 0.52 | 0.47 | 0.49 |
| C | 0.22 | 0.23 | 0.38 | 0.37 |
| D | 0.66 | 0.37 | 0.27 | 0.55 |
| E | 0.44 | 0.56 | 0.37 | 0.25 |
| F | 0.39 | 0.28 | 0.49 | 0.39 |

*Step 3: Establishing Relative Importance*

Establishing relative importance ($w_j$) of the criterion consists of multiplication the matrix values by the normalized weights for each criterion.

| | $I_1$ | $I_2$ | $I_3$ | $I_4$ | Total |
|---|---|---|---|---|---|
| Calculated Weights | 0,54 | 0,83 | 1,66 | 0,1 | 3,13 |
| Normalized Values | 0,17 | 0,27 | 0,53 | 0,03 | 1 |

| | $I_1$ | $I_2$ | $I_3$ | $I_4$ |
|---|---|---|---|---|
| A | 0.056 | 0.099 | 0.217 | 0.009 |
| B | 0.044 | 0.140 | 0.249 | 0.014 |
| C | 0.037 | 0.062 | 0.201 | 0.011 |
| D | 0.112 | 0.099 | 0.143 | 0.016 |
| E | 0.074 | 0.151 | 0.196 | 0.007 |
| F | 0.066 | 0.075 | 0.259 | 0.012 |

*Step 4: Building Positive and Negative Ideal Solutions*

The positive ideal solution corresponds to the set of best or maximum values of each column. Conversely, the negative ideal solution constitutes the set of worst or minimum values of each column of the evaluation matrix where A+ and A- are the set of best and worst values of the criteria's.

| | $I_1$ | $I_2$ | $I_3$ | $I_4$ |
|---|---|---|---|---|
| A | 0.056 | 0.099 | 0.217 | 0.009 |
| B | 0.044 | 0.140 | 0.249 | 0.014 |
| C | 0.037 | 0.062 | 0.201 | 0.011 |
| D | 0.112 | 0.099 | 0.143 | 0.016 |
| E | 0.074 | 0.151 | 0.196 | 0.007 |
| F | 0.066 | 0.075 | 0.259 | 0.012 |

$A^+ = \{ 0.112, 0.062, 0.259, 0.007 \}$

$A^- = \{ 0.037, 0.151, 0.143, 0.016 \}$

*Step 5: Obtaining the Separation Measures*

The separation of each alternative from the ideal one is given by Euclidean distance.

$$S_i^+ = \sqrt{\sum_{i=1}^{k}(x_{ij} - x_j^+)^2} \quad \text{and} \quad S_i^- = \sqrt{\sum_{i=1}^{k}(x_{ij} - x_j^-)^2}$$

*Step 6: Relative Closeness to the Ideal Solution*

Relative closeness to the ideal solution may call overall or composite performance score of the each alternative.,

$C_i = S_i^- / (S_i^+ + S_i^-)$

| | | |
|---|---|---|
| $C_A = 0.54$ | $C_B = 0.50$ | $C_C = 0.52$ |
| $C_D = 0.43$ | $C_E = 0.36$ | $C_F = 0.75$ |

**Fig. 4.** Applying TOPSIS steps to the case-2

performance in production time and recyclability out of remaining products. Moreover production time and recyclability have the highest weights out of the other criterions. It is also seen from the graph that products A, B and C shows similar performance according to the firm's philosophy of sustainability.

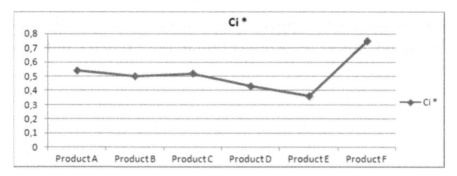

**Fig. 5.** Performance Values of Each Product

# 5     Conclusion

Since importance of sustainability has been increased, companies have shown more tend to manufacture their products in sustainable way. As a result of this tendency to sustainable manufacturing, the creation of sustainability indicators became a hot topic among researchers. Hence the need to measure and evaluate become prominent, the application of indicators in performance evaluation has been ignored. Specifically, this study focused on usage of sustainable manufacturing indicators for performance evaluation and case studies concerning the application of the TOPSIS method which provides advantages of sufficiency and simplicity while identifying the most suitable alternative quickly in case of the conflicting criterion. Future studies will include complex case studies that contain multi-criteria decision making problem of a real company with the real data. Additionally, to reflect the vagueness concept of sustainability, fuzzy TOPSIS will be applied on sustainability indicators and to analyze the outputs of the fuzzy TOPSIS, sensitivity analysis will be used.

# References

1. Westkamper, E.: Manufuture and Sustainable Manufacturing. In: Manufacturing Systems and Technologies for the New Frontier. The 41st CIRP Conference on Manufacturing Systems, pp. 11–14 (2008)
2. OECD, Organization for Economic Co-operation and Development. Sustainable Manufacturing Indicators, http://www.oecd.org/document/48/0,3746,en_21571361_47075996_47855728_1_1_1_1,00.html
3. Raizer Neto, E., Mariotte, M.T., Hinz, R.T.P.: Indicators to Measure Sustainability of an Industrial Manufacturing. In: Innovation in Life Cycle Engineering and Sustainable Development, pp. 111–122 (2006)
4. Krajnc, D., Glavic, P.: Indicators of Sustainable Production. Clean Techn. Environ. Policy 5, 279–288 (2003), doi:10.1007/S10098-003-0221-Z
5. United Nations, Indicators of Sustainable Development: Guidance and Methodologies, 3rd edn. United Nations Publication, Sales No. E.08.II.A.2 (2007) ISBN 978-92-1-104577-2
6. Hwang, C.L., Yoon, K.: Multiple Attribute Decision Making: Methods and Applications. Springer, New York (1981)

# A Decision-Aiding Approach for Residential PhotoVoltaic System Choice: An Application to the French Context

Fredy Huaylla, Lamia Berrah, and Vincent Cliville

Laboratoire d'Informatique, Systèmes, Traitement de l'Information et de la Connaisance,
Annecy le Vieux, France
{huayllfr,lamia.berrah,vincent.cliville}@univ-savoie.fr

**Abstract.** In the last decade the interest for electric production using PhotoVoltaic System (PVS) has strongly increased; namely for the citizen who is able to use roofs or personal surfaces to put in place such systems. For instance, the installed residential PVS capacity has grown to 550 MW (Megawatt) in metropolitan France during the last years. The same trend can be noticed in many developed countries at the same time. However, in light of this investment, people would like to be informed of the different aspects, especially the economic and environmental ones, in order to make their choice. In this sense, this paper deals with the decision-making problem for the residential PVS investment. Different alternatives of module surfaces and PV technology installation are considered and a procedure founded on the ELECTRE approach to aid the citizen in his choice is proposed.

**Keywords:** PhotoVoltaic System, sustainability, energy efficiency, Decision-Aiding, ELECTRE.

## 1 Introduction

Nowadays in different countries, concerns about the environment are taken into account increasingly through energy policies that aim to reduce in the future the effects of the global warming generated by the emission of GreenHouse Gases (GHG). In Europe for example, the European Union (EU) has set as a goal for 2020 the production of 20% of its total consumed energy using Renewable Energy Systems (RES), which would imply a 33% electricity production coming from these kinds of systems [1]. In France, the goals mentioned above would imply a 23% total energy consumed production coming from RES [1]. To achieve this, during the last years French energy policies have promoted the installation of PhotoVoltaic Systems (PVS) mainly through solar plants and residential PVS. As a result, at the end of March 2011, 1146 MW had been installed in metropolitan France, where about half corresponded to residential PVS (integrated into the buildings) [2].

From a general point of view, a PVS is a system composed of PhotoVoltaic (PV) modules and other complementary components called Balance of System (BOS). BOS includes: structures for mounting the modules and the power-conditioning equipment for converting the generated direct current electricity (DC) into alternating

C. Emmanouilidis, M. Taisch, D. Kiritsis (Eds.): APMS 2012, Part I, IFIP AICT 397, pp. 232–239, 2013.

current electricity (AC), with the required form and magnitude for its consumption or insertion in the power grid [3]. PV modules are usually made of mono-crystalline silicon (sc-Si), multi-crystalline silicon (mc-Si) and amorphous silicon (a-Si). The solar energy to electricity conversion yield of each module usually goes in the following order, starting from the bigger: sc-Si, mc-Si and a-Si [4].

Since the installation of a PVS implies an investment, it is logical to compare these kinds of projects with other options. Different criteria are associated to PVS, such as energy, economics, environmental and social criteria, where each criterion has different indicators that can permit an assessment of the performance of the whole system. To cope with such a decision problem, studies have already been made to find the best renewable energy system including PVS. For example, Hauran et al. [1] used a multicriteria-aiding decision method to select the 4 best PVS projects among 16 projects that were presented to the local government of the island of Corsica in France. For that assessment, 7 criteria have been considered, related to energy, environmental, social and economic aspects, such as: total energy produced, ecological degradation, economic and financial benefits to the community, visual impact, etc. In general, the point of view of the evaluation was one that looked for the benefit to the whole community, so economic aspects related to the profitability of the project were not taken explicitly into account [1]. Athanasios et al. [5] assessed 10 power plants considering technological, economic and sustainability aspects through 9 criteria. The ranking of the project is obtained after the application of the AHP - Analytical Hierarchy Process - method. In their study, an emphasis was put on technology and sustainability criteria, giving the conclusion that renewable energy plants were at the top of the evaluation ranking. Again, economic criteria did not consider the profitability of each plant; instead, investment and operational costs were taken into account [5].

If the previous works concern public organisations decisions, they do not have an equivalent for the private investors and particularly for residential investment. In this study, a decision-making problem related to French residential PVS is studied considering energy, economic, environment and esthetic criteria. As a difference from cited works, the profitability of the PVS was taken into account in the economic criteria since, in our case, the considered point of view is the one of an investor (the owner of the dwelling), who, logically, would like to recover his investment. More precisely, for a given location, people of residential sectors willing to produce electric energy by investing in a PVS are faced with the following problem: *Which kind of technology to choose among the three available on the market and what is the total surface to put in place?* Knowing the involved criteria for choosing the PVS, this is a typical multicriteria decision problem of potential alternatives ranking. So using MultiCriteria Decision Aiding (MCDA) methods, namely the outranking ones, can supply interesting information to aid residential people in their choice.

This paper is organised as follows. In Section 2 the French context related to residential PVS systems is summarised. In Section 3 the decision problem is described by the considered alternatives and criteria. Then the ELECTRE III (ELimination and Choice expressing The Reality) outranking method is used to rank the alternatives. Results are discussed before concluding remarks.

## 2     French Policy for Residential PVS

Since 2004, the number of PVS installations in France has grown thanks to the implementation of a tax credit for the material costs of the systems. Since 2006 this increase is higher because of the policy implementation in tariffs that obligates the French electricity company, Électricité de France (EDF), to buy and to pay for the electricity produced by PVS. As a consequence, at the end of March 2011, residential PVS represented more than 550 MW distributed in more than 160 000 installations of less than 10kWp, where 98% had a nominal power of less than 3kWp [2].

Nowadays, French PV policy is maintained although the level of subsidies has been reduced compared to previous years. The policy for residential PVS can be summarised in the following points [6] [7].

- Residential PVS installations of less than 9kWp can enjoy of a tax credit of 11% for the material cost of the system.

- EDF company signs a contract with the owner to buy the electricity produced by the PVS. The tariff is fixed for 20 years at the moment of the contact signing. At the second trimester of 2012, this tariff was 0.3706 €/kWh for installations of a peak power under 9 kWp.

- A Value Added Tax (VAT) of 7% is applied for the material and installation costs for residential PVS of less than 3kWp; although, the TVA rises up to 19.6% for PVS installations of over 3kWp.

- Local governments usually give financial aids for the PVS installation.

Our studied residential PVS are located in the Rhône-Alpes area in France. We assume the valid PV policy in 2012 and the following considerations.

- The PVS accomplishes all the technical constraints required to benefit from the subsidies.

- The solar irradiation over the PV modules, with a slope of 45° and a South orientation, was set to 1408 kWh/m²/year.

- The life time of the installation was set for 20 years.

- The discount rate over the investment was set at 3%.

- The maintenance costs of the PVS were considered 0.

- The dwelling surface was equal to 80 m2 and the final annual energy consumption of a standard French dwelling equal to 137 kWh/m2/year [8].

So a citizen who is interested in installing a PVS on his dwelling roof can describe a given PVS, identified as its module technology and the total modules surface, through the considered criteria (energy, economic, environmental and esthetic) for the assessment study. Thus the possible alternatives can be compared in order to give information for the final choice. But this comparison can be difficult because there is often no Pareto dominance: how to know if a more economic PVS is more attractive than another which is better according to the environmental criteria? So for residential people, a ranking which gives a synthesising view of the potential PVS represents an interesting progress. In this way the MCDA outranking methods supply partial preorder of the potential alternatives [9], *i.e.* a ranking of the considered PVSs according to the preferences of the dwelling owner.

Obviously, aggregation methods like MAUT, AHP, MACBETH or UTA could be used, each of which allows decision-maker to supply total order information [10], [11]. However, such methods need more knowledge to build the utility functions and so remain less understandable for residential investors than the outranking methods that directly use criteria values. The main outranking methods are the ELECTRE family [12] and the PROMETHEE family [13]. Interested readers can find the description of these methods in [14]. The ELECTRE III method which is well adapted to the real life company decision problems as shown by the numerous studies already published, is used in this study [15].

# 3 Decision-Aiding for Residential PVS

## 3.1 Problem Definition

The considered problem is viewed as a ranking problem, *i.e.* the residential investor would like to know what the best alternatives are. In this way it is necessary to define:

- the set of considered alternatives,
- the retained decision criteria,
- the description of each alternative according to the criteria.

Twelve alternative scenarios are considered for our decision problem. For working purposes, each alternative is labelled by the combination of the considered technology ((sc-Si, mc-Si and a-Si) and the total module surfaces (6.25, 12.5, 18.75 and 25 m²). For example: Alternative one = ALT1 = "sc-Si; 6.25 m$^2$".

Six decision criteria are retained, which are:

- *II*, the Initial Investment, *i.e.* the amount of money required at the beginning for installing the PVS.

- $PI = \dfrac{NPV}{II}$, the Profitability of the Investment at the end of the system's life cycle, defined as, with *NPV*: Net Present Value [16].

- $ER = \dfrac{AEP}{AEC}$, the Energy Ratio, with *AEP*: Annual Electricity Production of the PVS, *AEC*: Annual Energy Consumption of the dwelling.

- $EPBT = \dfrac{PE}{AEP}$, the Energy Payback Time with *PE*: Primary Energy used by the PVS during its whole life cycle, *AEP*: Annual Equivalent Primary Energy produced by the PVS [3] [4].

- $GHG = \dfrac{EGE}{TPE}$, the normalised equivalent emissions with *EGE*: Equivalent Grams (of $CO_2$) Emitted during the whole PVS life cycle, *TPE*: Total Produced Electricity during the whole PVS life cycle. [3] [4].

- *Esthetic*, related to the visual impact of the PVS.

The values associated to each criterion for the considered alternatives are given in table 1. They are computed using data from previous works and from current legislation and costs. In this sense for example, values for *EPBT* and *GHG* equivalent emissions are computed from studies made by Fthenakis and Alsema for different PV module technologies [3] [17]. Economic values are computed from current legislation [6] [7] and esthetic values are assigned considering a point of view of a selected potential investor.

**Table 1.** Criteria values

| Alternatives | | | | Criteria | | | |
|---|---|---|---|---|---|---|---|
| Name | Technology, Surface (m²) | II (€) | PI | ER (%) | EBPT (years) | GHG (gCO₂/kWh) | ESTH (1 - 7) |
| ALT1 | sc-Si, 6.25 | 3719 | -0.33 | 9.1 | 3.0 | 75.6 | 7 |
| ALT2 | mc-Si, 6.25 | 3315 | -0.23 | 9.2 | 2.3 | 58.1 | 6 |
| ALT3 | a-Si, 6.25 | 2701 | -0.43 | 7.5 | 1.9 | 50.4 | 5 |
| ALT4 | sc-Si, 12.5 | 7187 | 0.05 | 18.2 | 3.0 | 75.6 | 7 |
| ALT5 | mc-Si, 12.5 | 6380 | 0.2 | 18.3 | 2.3 | 58.1 | 6 |
| ALT6 | a-Si, 12.5 | 5152 | 0.09 | 14.9 | 1.9 | 50.4 | 5 |
| ALT7 | sc-Si, 18.75 | 10656 | 0.18 | 27.3 | 3.0 | 75.6 | 7 |
| ALT8 | mc-Si, 18.75 | 9446 | 0.35 | 27.5 | 2.3 | 58.1 | 6 |
| ALT9 | a-Si, 18.75 | 7603 | 0.27 | 22.4 | 1.9 | 50.4 | 5 |
| ALT10 | sc-Si, 25 | 15759 | 0.11 | 36.3 | 3.0 | 75.6 | 7 |
| ALT11 | mc-Si, 25 | 13955 | 0.27 | 36.7 | 2.3 | 58.1 | 6 |
| ALT12 | a-Si, 25 | 9530 | 0.49 | 29.9 | 1.9 | 50.4 | 5 |

It appears that there is no alternative which is better or less equal to the others according the whole set of criteria (no Pareto dominance). Thus, it is not possible to make a choice from this information. The ELECTRE III method is hence deployed to give more meaningful information.

## 3.2    ELECTRE III Method

From the alternatives description, ELECTRE III ranks the set of alternatives by considering pairwise comparisons according to the Condorcet principle which announces that an alternative outranks another one if it is at least as good according to a majority of criteria without being clearly worst according to the other criteria [18]. The preference relation definition between two alternatives is based on the concordance index which reflects the arguments to favour a given action instead of another one and the discordance index which reflects the argument against this action instead of this other action. The computation of these indexes involves the definition of both criterion preference thresholds and criterion weights representing the criterion's relative importance in the decision-making process. The comparison of the whole pairwise comparisons thanks to mathematical rules allows to give as a final result a partial preorder of the alternatives. Interested readers can find more detailed information in [9] [15]. Note that complementary sensitivity analysis of the description of actions or criteria (thresholds, weight) can be made to reinforce the information for decision-aid.

## 3.3    ELECTRE III Parameters Definition

To proceed with the ELECTRE III software which supports the method, the preference thresholds of indifference and strict preference have to be expressed for each criterion. These values are assigned by the dwelling owner thanks to a dialogue with the ELECTRE method expert who has to explain the meaning of the parameters. The weight definitions of the 6 considered criteria are obtained by the SIMOS method [19]. Both declared thresholds and weights are found in table 2.

In addition, ELECTRE III deployment requires quantitative values for all the criteria, which is not the case for the esthetic criterion. So, linguistic terms must be converted into quantitative values. This transformation leads to integer values that increase with the satisfaction level (a scale from 1 to 7 is retained). Two integers associated to two successive linguistic terms must be different according to the considered strict preference threshold, so the concordance index computation can be consistent.

**Table 2.** Weights and thresholds values

|  | $II$ ($€$) | $PI$ | $ER$ (%) | $EPBT$ (years) | $GHG$ ($gCO_2$/kWh) | $ESTH$ (1-7) |
|---|---|---|---|---|---|---|
| Weight | 2.6 | 1.7 | 2.6 | 0.7 | 0.7 | 1.7 |
| Indifference threshold | 5%*$II$ | 0.05 | 5% | 0.5 | 1 | 1 |
| Strict pref. threshold | 10%*$II$ | 0.2 | 15% | 1 | 5 | 1 |

## 3.4    Results and Discussion

The ranking of the alternatives is given in figure 1. The alternative "ALT12" is considered as better than all the other ones. The alternative "ALT5" is better than the other ones except "ALT12" and is incomparable with "ALT6. So a given alternative can be ranked with possibilities of *ex-aequo* (AlT4, ALT 9) or incomparability (ALT8, ALT 4). Hence, residential people can choose the "ALT12" alternative. To better assess this choice, they can also make a sensitivity analysis regarding:

- the ELECTRE parameters definition (weights and threshold),
- the values describing the alternatives according to the criteria.

The first sensitivity analysis must be carried out when the residential people have hesitated during the questionnaire allowing the ELECTRE deployment. It can also be interesting to simulate different types of people behaviour such as "mainly economic" with the high weight for *PI*, "mainly environmental" with high weights for *EPBT* and *GHG* or for "limited investment capacity" with a high weight for *II*.

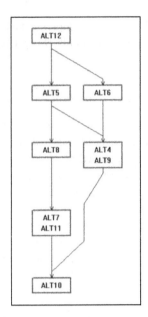

**Fig. 1.** Alternative partial pre-order obtained with ELECTRE

The second analysis is useful to take into account the potential uncertainties concerning the alternative description through the six criteria, namely the technical and economic ones. Indeed, it is well known that energy production depends on environmental factors and that the governmental tax policy can change during the twenty five years of PVS exploitation [20]. Besides the traditional indifference and strict preference thresholds definition, current works are in progress to deal with this point which can modify the initial ranking given in fig. 1. Main contributions of this work were the application of an outranking method to a PVS residential context and the consideration of direct economic benefits, such as the PI.

## 4    Conclusions

This study concerns the residential PVS choice. After a description of the PV module which is the main component of the PVS, the French PVS installation context is presented. From the review of criteria for PVS choice, the study focuses on relevant ones for residential installation. Then the decision-aiding ELECTRE method is briefly described before its application for the PVS residential choice among twelve alternative PVS. The obtained partial preorder is presented and discussed namely through the two complementary sensitivity analyses. Further works for taking into account uncertainties about technical and economic aspects are finally envisaged. Further works for taking into account uncertainties about technical and economic aspects are envisaged as well as the adaptation of the method for the use of PVS installers and resellers.

# References

1. Haurant, P., Oberti, P., Muselli, M.: Multicriteria selection aiding related to photovoltaic plants on farming fields on Corsica island: A real case study using the ELECTRE outranking framework. Energy Policy 39, 676–688 (2011)
2. Leloux, J., Narvarte, L., Trebosc, D.: Review of the performance of residential PV systems in France. Renewable and Sustainable Energy Reviews 16, 1369–1376 (2012)
3. Fthenakis, V.M., Kim, H.C.: Photovoltaics: Life-cycle analyses. Solar Energy 85, 1609–1628 (2011)
4. Sumper, A., Robledo-García, M.: Life-cycle assessment of a photovoltaic system in Catalonia (Spain). Renewable and Sustainable Energy Reviews 15, 3888–3896 (2011)
5. Athanasios, I., Petros, A.: Technological, economic and sustainability evaluation of power plants using the Analytic Hierarchy Process. Energy Policy 37, 778–787 (2009)
6. EDF ENR Énergies Nouvelles Réparties, http://www.edfenr.com/le-photovoltaique/tarif-achat-et-credits-d-impots-photovoltaiques-n799-1.aspx
7. ECOinfos Énergies Renouvelables, http://www.les-energies-renouvelables.eu/energies-renouvelables/9702toutes-les-aides-pour-realiser-son-installation-photovoltaique.html
8. CYTHELIA, http://www.cythelia.fr/maison-zen.html
9. Roy, B.: Paradigms and Challenges. In: Figueira, J., Greco, S., Ehrgott, M. (eds.) Multiple Criteria Decision Analysis. State of the Art Surveys, pp. 3–24. Springer (2005)
10. Guitouni, A., Martel, J.M.: Tentative guidelines to help choosing an appropriate MCDA method. European Journal of Operational Research 109(2), 501–521 (1998)
11. Greco, S., Marques Pereira, R.A., Squillante, M., Yager, R.R.: Preferences and Decisions: Models and Applications, 430 p. Springer, Berlin (2010)
12. Roy, B.: The outranking approach and the foundations of ELECTRE methods. Theory and Decision 31, 49–73 (1991)
13. Brans, J.P., Mareschal, B., Vincke, P.: How to select and how to rank projects: The PROMETHEE method. European Journal of Op. Research 24(2), 228–238 (1986)
14. Martel, J.-M., Matarazzo, B.: Other outranking approaches. In: Figueira, J., Greco, S., Ehrgott, M. (eds.) Multiple Criteria Decision Analysis. State of the Art Surveys, pp. 197–262. Springer (2005)
15. Figueira, J., Mousseau, V., Roy, B.: Electre Methods. In: Figueira, J., Greco, S., Ehrgott, M. (eds.) Multiple Criteria Decision Analysis. State of the Art Surveys, pp. 133–162. Springer (2005b)
16. Chabot, B.: TEC: an analysis economics method (La méthode TEC d'analyse économique). Energy economics cours, Polytech Annecy-Chambéry, France (2012)
17. Alsema, E., de Wild-Scholten, M.: Environmental impact of crystalline silicon photovoltaic module production. In: Material Research Society Fall Meeting, Symposium G: Life Cycle Analysis Tools for "Green" Materials and Process Selection, Boston, MA (2005)
18. Condorcet, J.A.M. Caritat, Marquis De: Essai sur l'application de l'analyse la probabilité des décisions rendues. la pluralité des voix, Imprimerie Royale, Paris (1785)
19. Figueira, J., Roy, B.: Determining the weights of criteria in the ELECTRE type methods with a revised Simos' procedure. Eur. J. of Operational Research 139, 317–326 (2002)
20. Huaylla Roque, F.: Les sytèmes photovoltaïques: caractéristiques et performance, Master Thesis, Université de Savoie, 52 p. (2012) (in French)

# Design of Controlling Supported Sustainability of Manufacturing Enterprises

Eryk Głodziński

Warsaw University of Technology, Faculty of Production Engineering, Warsaw, Poland
e.glodzinski@wip.pw.edu.pl

**Abstract.** In the paper the controlling as a management concept supporting sustainability of enterprises was characterised. Controlling is treated as a very important element of managerial accounting system in manufacturing companies. In the first part of the paper the company sustainability was presented. Next the stages of controlling design were characterised. In the third part of the paper the controlling model was shown. Finally, various controlling supporting instruments enabling the balanced growth of manufacturing enterprises were listed. The relationships between them were presented.

**Keywords:** controlling, design, modelling, management tools.

## 1    Introduction

On global economic market the enterprises should operate basing on the criteria of efficiency, effectiveness and social responsibility. These criteria are the basic assessment factors in decision-taking process of companies applied strategy of balanced growth. In such case, the weight of each criterion is depended on many determinants e.g. economic situation of the company and on the market, competitor's position of company or expectations of society and other stakeholders. The decision-taking process is the major element of management process and should be supported by creating proper information using complementary various management tools. These tools can be divided into three groups: concepts, methods and techniques.

The paper presents the results of research connected with design of controlling as a concept, which supports production management. The research is based on the analysis of selected, existing controlling systems in international companies present on the European market and the application proposal of universal model of controlling design created by S. Marciniak [5] to the manufacturing companies. The main thesis of the paper is the assumption, that controlling will support sustainability of manufacturing enterprises if the design process follows the right methodics. A proposal of the proper methodics will be presented in the paper. The article does not take into consideration the issue of sustainability of products, but analyses sustainability of company by developing the products.

C. Emmanouilidis, M. Taisch, D. Kiritsis (Eds.): APMS 2012, Part I, IFIP AICT 397, pp. 240–249, 2013.
© IFIP International Federation for Information Processing 2013

## 2    Sustainability of the Company with Controlling

Controlling in paper's meaning should deliver proper information for decision-taking process and is associated with the early-warning-system against threats. The controlling connects many planning and control methods/techniques. One of the most important stage of designing the controlling is to choose and integrate these tools in one system targeting on the strategic goals of company.

Sustainability means being able to operate on the market, overcoming the problems which could threaten the normal existence of enterprise, ensuring the company development in long-term period. Regarding the manufacturing enterprise, sustainability in current market conditions can be associated with:

- assembling of goods avoiding the production interruptions (like accidents at work place, equipment failures, delays in material delivery etc.),
- reducing waste (by assembling the goods according to the technological documentation, ensuring the quality of services and the supplied materials, maintenance management etc.),
- recycling the waste when it occurs (re-use the material in other technological processes, store the waste in an environment-friendly way),
- developing all company: units, function and processes, especially manufacturing processes and other supporting processes like R&D, supplying etc.

It will be possible, if the company is able to control its activity, especially in the above mentioned tasks. Control of activity has to be preceded by planning. Both processes should be integrated in the company as one controlling system. In practice, the integration means collaboration of various methods and techniques of management. The issue is to choose the ones which could be used complementary. It is obvious that the system should simultaneously use the results (information) of the above mentioned processes. Aggregation of selected management methods and techniques can proceed by controlling concept. Its main principles are: establishing measurable goals, continuous analysis of target and current data, predicting the future, providing cost account in accountability centres, applying of feedback loops. It is important, that controlling system should not use especially the tools, which can provide contradictory results or cost of providing data is too high in comparison to their decision value.

In the assembled sector of economy planning and control processes are based mainly on the measurable (quantitative) indicators e.g.: degree of the use of production capacity, amount of sales revenue, amount of production costs, number of finished goods in comparing to the waste. However, ensuring the sustainability of company with controlling requires including not only quantitative assessment but qualitative as well. The main issue is applying and aggregating both results in one system. The solution of such a problem could be a design of special assessment system unique for the company or basing on existing tools e.g. created in 1996 by R.Kaplan and D.Norton the Balance Scorecard [3], which divides the goals of company into four perspectives: financial, internal business process, learning and growth, customer. The above mentioned management tool translates a business unit's strategy into tangible objectives and measures. One of the major problem of design process is the measure the factors which are not quantitative. These issues have not been solved satisfactorily by researchers and practicans till today. Nevertheless Balance Scorecard is currently very popular in business and in research works as well. Regarding the works of research, especially Nobel prize winners in economics (J. Stiglitz [7] and P. Krugman [4]) and after the start of worldwide crisis in 2008 the approach to assessment of company activity (object of planning and control) should be partly revised. Now the most important goals of company could be divided into three groups: achieving satisfactory financial result (economic indicators), doing the business regarding the social aspects (connected with employee and society –social indicators) and protecting the natural environment (environment-friendly indicators). Selected groups of criteria are a part of the economics balanced growth theory. The theory is especially important for middle and big enterprises which want to operate and develop on the market in next several years. In such case they have to measure not only financial indicators but non-financial ones as well. Small companies characterise by different range of problems. Vital operating factor for most of them is financial result and sustainability is associated mainly with low-cost operating. Even thought keeping the sustainability in developing economy requires having good social relationship with the society. The relationship is created especially by brand image - key customer care, good supplier network, environmental-friendly behaviours. The last mentioned factor is built minimizing the number of waste and emissions.

## 3    Conditions and Stages of Controlling Design

Before the process of controlling creation starts, the conditions of designing, modelling, implementation, and using the system in specific application area should be researched. Manufacturing enterprises differ from service companies mainly by:

- tangibility of products (the tangibility level is much higher),
- storage possibility,
- level and degree of contact between producers and consumers (the contact between the production force and clients is occasional),
- length of response time between the order and execution (depends on the length of production processes),
- labour intensity and the use of machinery (predominately the high level of automation),
- frequency of replacing the machinery (very often, which influence high level of amortization/depreciation).

In the controlling design process, the efficiency and effectiveness of company operating should have the some priority. It has to be taken into consideration that price and next the quality of products are for customer most often more important than the manufacturing technology or place. The controlling's measurement system should include the formulas, which analyse and asses these indicators. From the perspective of manufacturing enterprise is vital relationship between sales figures, brand image, product launch or product placement. These indicators are hardly measurable (it is necessary to use indirect measures). Regarding the above mentioned issues the controlling design process can be executed in following stages:

1. Analysing business processes regarding the economic, social and environment-friendly goals.
2. Analysing the existing frameworks of enterprise.
3. Choosing the areas supported by controlling and sequence of implementation.
4. Designing new or redesigning business processes regarding the concepts management by processes and targets.
5. Presenting controlling system in the form of model to enable better understanding.
6. Redesigning frameworks.
7. Integration management functions esp. planning and control of production in one system.
8. Designing measurement system of enterprise goals basing on universal model of controlling design [5].
9. Updating the model to the more developed form.
10. Designing motivation system based on responsibility account and results achieved by company staff.
11. Completing the model before test phase.
12. Testing the model.
13. Updating the model after the completed test phase.

The designing process in management generally bases on the principals, which were created for engineering science and economics. They could be adopted in major points in management science. Technical rules of designing the controlling are as follows:

1. Designing should encompass all the structural elements included in the system.
2. Designing should be implemented in two layers:
   a) globally, where all organizational units are the units subject to the design,
   b) structurally, where we design the internal structure of organizational units.
3. Connections should be designed (dependences, coupling) between units of the structure without specifying the mode of implementation of the connection; It is necessary to verify the connections (so-called static verification of relationship between the elements of the system).
4. The time and the sequences of execution of the connections (dependences, coupling) need to be specified.
5. Verification of carefully time identified connections (so-called dynamic verification of te relationship) should be executed.
6. The implementation procedures should be designed in accordance with the system that allows the transformation of the dynamic model of the system into real specificity of the company; It is necessary to complete the implementation procedures with analysis and model management methods.
7. After the procedures have been designed it is necessary to check again the regularity of information flow and decision-taking (simulation); It is necessary to design technical tools supporting the functioning (operating) of the system , mainly of IT nature,
8. The test of practical functioning of the designed system is performed (verification) [6].

Controlling department, situated as a unit supporting top management in access to information, is responsible for protecting and developing the controlling philosophy (methodology consistent and common for each unit of company). Other tasks include:

developing the controlling tools, data aggregation, data benchmarking, reporting, decision recommending. These tasks arise from controlling functions:

- planning and evaluating measured areas,
- planning targets figures,
- monitoring business processes,
- collecting data describing operational activity of company,
- analysing data from data base,
- assessing information,
- creating financial and managerial reports,
- delivering reports to the right people.

Regarding the above mentioned processes and functions, controlling should be focused on following areas (in sequence of applying):

1. Finance (major issues: cost and revenue accounting, analysing incoming and outgoing payments, measuring assets and equity, analysing liabilities etc.).
2. Manufacturing (major issues: providing production capacity, measuring quantity of outputs –especially prime products, checking quality of goods and subcontractor services, checking margins, analysing time schedule etc.).
3. Sale and after sale services (major issues: targeting margins and production capacity, measuring and analysing satisfaction of clients, pointing out key clients etc.).
4. Procurement (major issues: analysing efficiency of deliveries, checking quality of materials, measuring and analysing satisfaction from cooperation with suppliers etc.).
5. Storage (major issues: measuring and analysing quantity of inventories).
6. Maintenance (major issues: checking natural depreciation of machinery, checking productivity of machinery, measuring and analysing satisfaction from cooperation with machinery producers and services etc.).
7. Environment protection (major issues: checking quantity of emissions and non-recycled waste, measuring and analysing impact of company operation on natural environment and economic development etc.).
8. Human resources (major issues: measuring achievement of the person's goals, analysing work performance, targeting gained experience, knowledge and skills etc.).

The above mentioned sequence bases on the criteria: the specifics of the company (due to assembling goods), value of benefits connected with implementation (additional profits or reduction resource consumptions) and opportunity to use other management concept (when it is not necessary to apply controlling in the selected area). Implementation of controlling in selected areas should accompany application of the company controlling. Its main targets are assessing and raising the stakeholder value, protecting the company against threats (in perspectives of economy, society and environment) and planning and controlling activity on the highest level (most aggregated) of the company.

In designing process the vertical integration of planning and control is one of the most difficult issues. In practice it means using the same measures in both processes, which gives opportunity for benchmarking and variance (deviation) analysis. The second form of integration is horizontal approach. It means using measurement system which enables data aggregation. It is possible when all financial and non-financial indicators can be presented in monetary unit. A valuation of non-financial indicators, like environmental-friendly behaviours, is quite a difficult problem to overcome. It is a big challenge for somebody who designs the controlling.

# 4    Model of Controlling System

To ensure both forms of integration and fulfil the established targets all designed elements of controlling should be evaluated before the real application. One of the best methods to achieve it is creating the conceptual model of controlling. It is a theoretical framework that can be used to present in a simple way all elements of controlling and relationship between them.

The controlling model consists at least of:

1. Various structural elements (objects like company and product strategy, data base or using management tools and subjects like key users and end users of controlling system and receivers the information).
2. Relationship between elements constituting this model (in form of mathematical formulas or form presented various data described state of the research subject),
3. Controlling process description (guidelines outlining methodology of planning and controlling).

For better transparency the controlling model should be presented with graph techniques e.g. used in IT the methods of block scheme (fig.1).

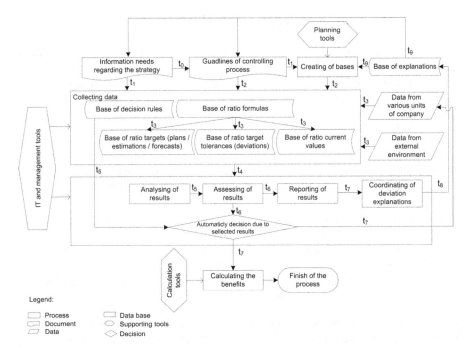

**Fig. 1.** Model of controlling system (Source: own study)

The elements of controlling model are as follows:

- strategy of enterprise based on targets (e.g.: margin, quantity, quality, market position),
- set of sources to obtain external information about resources, technologies, demand, supply etc.,
- set of methods/techniques to obtain external data and information,
- set of sources to obtain internal information about resources, technologies, organisation aspects of the company etc.,
- set of methods/techniques to obtain internal data and information,
- set of methods/techniques for calculation of target data,
- set of methods/techniques for measuring amount of current data,
- set of methods/techniques for analysing, assessing and reporting,
- set of methods/techniques for calculation the benefits in motivation system,
- data bases of: measurements (formulas used for measuring), target indicators (target values for benchmarking), target tolerances (limitations of targets for benchmarking), up-to-date dates (current data presenting actual statement), decision-taking rules in approach to assessing process, explanations (remarks to exceeded limitations).

All the above mentioned elements should be obtained during the designing process of controlling. One of the most important stages by designing process is selecting management tools (methods/techniques) supporting the system.

## 5      Selected Tools Applied in Controlling

The management tools can be described as intangible objects which help to achieve management goals of the company. The literature describes many examples of methods and techniques used by manufacturing companies [2]. Not all of them could be applied in controlling system. It should be focused especially on:

- quantitative presenting of operation activity (core processes) of the enterprise (in approach to: materials, goods in progress, finishing goods, storage goods, goods sold etc.),
- continuous analysis of the company results on operational (especially manufacturing and investment activity) and financial (especially working capital analysis) levels,
- valuating of qualitative aspects of company activity regarding the balance growth theory (especially satisfaction from using goods by the clients),
- the use of variance (deviation) analysis as a leading approach to assessment of the business results,
- providing the feedback loops of information during the manufacturing process,
- connecting various tools of management in one system.

Selection of methods/techniques should take into consideration their cooperation (plan data can be measured and collected next analysed and aggregated, finally evaluated on various level of aggregation, and reported). The tools applied in controlling can be presented regarding the functions of controlling and their usefulness for achieving various goals (fig. 2). These goals, as mentioned previously, results from balance growth development. Such approach requires doing analysis regarding effectiveness and efficiency in economic, social and environmental-friendly areas.

Regarding the controlling philosophy, it is important to use the result from assessment process to improve the sustainability of company. Company staff should be enough motivated to follow the strategy and resulting from it activities. From operational point of view it means, that the above mentioned behaviour is characterised mainly by proper use of management tools, right activity in right time, and continuous improvement of management system. It results in applying the

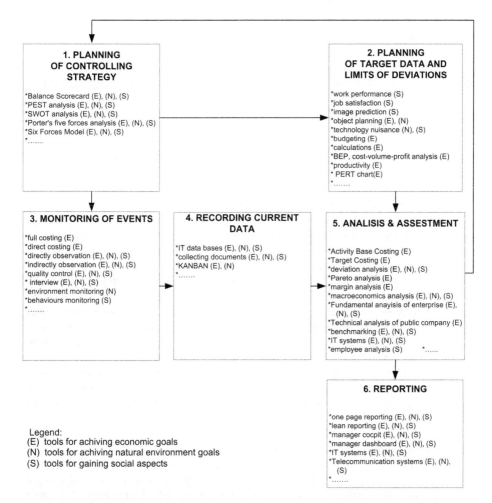

**Fig. 2.** Selected management tools supported controlling in manufacturing enterprise (Source: own study)

motivation system as an element of controlling. The bonuses (benefits for employee calculated from controlling system) have in this case a financial form. If controlling informs about the level of indicators describing company activity (economic, social and environmental aspects), the motivation system will base on measured data. It helps to avoid increasing the additional costs. Bonus system can base on:

- financial result of company,
- financial results of company units,
- financial results of projects/orders etc.,
- change of share value (by public companies),
- level of meeting the budget,
- level of employee absence,
- level of employee innovation,
- share in establishing targets.

In controlling the motivation system should be easy to understand by employees. The formula of bonus calculation should not change during the assessment period of time.

# 6    Conclusions

Sustainability of enterprise can be assessed using the controlling as a "going concern" principle, which is known from financial accounting. This approach means treating controlling as an early warning system, which consists of proper measurements and implemented procedures (decision rules) in action needed situations.

Without controlling concept the management tools generally are used separately. In this case achieving established goals of enterprise is at risk, because each unit of company tries to maximize its own targets. To avoid such situations controlling principles require cooperation and joint use of all enterprise resources. The success of controlling, in meaning of establishing the company sustainability, depends on many factors. Two of them, namely the applied design methodics and supporting management tools have been analysed in the paper. The major assessment areas like: finance, manufacturing, sale, after sale services and procurement have been presented. Summarising, existing and proven (tested) tolls supporting controlling in such system should be used. All elements of the system and the relationship between them have to be expressed in form of conceptual model which helps in its understanding, evaluation and application. For company management is important to link controlling system with motivation system because it results with better efficiency and effectiveness.

**Acknowledgements.** This work partly presents the results of research from a project number N N115 294338, which has been financed by the Polish Ministry of Science and Higher Education in years 2010-2013. The author wants to acknowledge other members of the project from Warsaw University of Technology for their collaboration.

# References

1. Anupindi, R., et al.: Managing Business Process Flows. Principles of Operations Management, p. 276. Pearson Education, New Jersey (2006)
2. Harrison, D.K., Petty, D.J.: Systems for Planning and Control in Manufacturing. Systems and management for competitive manufacture. Newnes Publishing House (2002)
3. Kaplan, R., Norton, D.: Using the Balance Scorecard as a Strategic Management System. Harvard Business Review (January-February 1996)
4. Krugman, P., Wells, R.: Economics. Worth Publishers (2009)
5. Marciniak, S.: Controlling. Filozofia, projektowanie, pp. 101–110. Difin Publishing House, Warsaw (2008)
6. Marciniak, S.: Design and modeling of the controlling in manufacturing enterprise. In: Dilemmas of the Contemporary Economy Facing Global Changes, pp. 219–228. Cracow University of Economics, Cracow (2012)
7. Stiglitz, J.: Globalization and Its Discontents. W.W. Norton & Company, New York (2002)

# Modularization – Enabler for Shop Floor Involvement in Improvement and Development

Bjørnar Henriksen[1], Lars Skjelstad[1], Eva Amdahl Seim[2], and Carl Christian Røstad[1]

[1] SINTEF Technology and Society, 7465 Trondheim, Norway
[2] Norwegian University of Science and Technology, 7491 Trondheim, Norway

**Abstract.** The introduction of modules and product platforms implies a strategy where the scope should encompass not a single product, but a family or an assortment of products. Instead of searching for "an optimal design for an optimal product", the objective should be to create a flexible product design, allowing product variations without requiring changes in the overall product design every time a new variant is introduced. This flexibility in product design and customization has been regarded as a feasible way for leisure boat manufacturers in high-cost countries like Norway to be competitive in the increasingly tougher conditions of the leisure boat market. The incremental development process that we often find in e.g. craft manufacturing, which leisure boat manufacturing can be seen as, is well suited for modularization. A way to introduce a module-based product architecture could be to identify key parts of the products – parts, systems or components that enable the development of modules. This paper describes how modularization makes it easier to address improvement and development in the company. This paper also reports how the focus modularization enabled profound involvements from employees that reduced barriers to change. This, over time, also challenged the traditional "craftsmen culture" into a more change-oriented and proactive culture at shop floor level.

**Keywords:** Modularization, improvement, leisure boat manufacturing.

## 1 Introduction

Craft manufacturing still plays an important role in the economy. Principles and skills related to craft manufacturing have shown to be important for e.g. European economies to compete with new evolving economies (see e.g. Buschfeld et al [1]). However, craft manufacturing also has to adapt to new manufacturing principles in order to be competitive. This paper aims to show how industrial principles could be implemented in an industry characterized by craft manufacturing exemplified by the leisure boat industry.

Building boats is still to a large extent craftwork based on knowledge passed on for generations. Knowledge of boats and the sea is valuable throughout the development process, from the early design stages to the physical assembly of a prototype. During design most of the boat's seaworthiness, durability and performance is determined.

C. Emmanouilidis, M. Taisch, D. Kiritsis (Eds.): APMS 2012, Part I, IFIP AICT 397, pp. 250–261, 2013.

The quality of the craftwork carried out in production determines the final qualities in this regard. Craft manufacturing industries such as the Norwegian leisure boat industry has traditionally been characterized by small-scale production and high levels of customization. The companies are all small and medium sized with limited resources for R&D and investments. Consequently, development processes have been incremental where changes have been carefully introduced over time in new or modified products and solutions.

One of the advantages of craft manufacturing is the involvement of the persons actually making the product. This personal involvement normally results in high quality and a high degree of customization. This also often goes "hand-in-hand" with improvements where the craftsman is continuously looking for improvement-opportunities. However, quality and improvements need to be documented and to some extent standardized for the rest of the company and the next products to be produced.

International business competition is most challenging on cost issues for the Norwegian manufacturers. Neither the qualities nor the seaworthiness of Norwegian boats are threatened in a dramatic way. But, the industry is not prepared for the competition on costs, and quality alone is not enough to win the market.

An increased degree of modularization has been regarded as one important principle that could increase productivity and quality in general for industry (see ex Baldwin and Clark [2]; Ulrich [3]; Pine, [4]). In short, literature suggests that modularity can facilitate increasing the number of products features available while also decreasing costs [5]. The introduction of modules and product platforms implies a strategy where the scope should encompass not a single product, but a family or an assortment of products. Instead of searching for "an optimal design for an optimal product," the objective should be to create a flexible product design, allowing product variations without requiring changes in the overall product design every time a new variant is introduced. This flexibility in product design and customization has been regarded as a feasible way for the leisure boat producers in high-cost countries like Norway to be competitive in the increasingly tougher conditions of the leisure boat market.

However, even though module-based design is an efficient way of reducing product development costs, the steps for the initial module-based product design, the overall product architecture, might be found very resource-demanding for many companies. Modularization could enable more efficient development and improvement processes since this could be done by focusing on separate modules aiming to optimize them, but not necessarily focus on all the modules at the same time. The holistic module-based product architecture reduces the risk of sub-optimization from separate improvement and development initiatives. More of the improvement and development processes could then be addressed to the shop floor level and the unique knowledge from the craftsmen/boat-builders could be activated and better modules/products and processes result. Hence modularization not only enables shop floor involvement in improvement and development, the involvement of employee's e.g. at the shop floor is also a prerequisite for optimized modules and design for manufacturing.

The purpose of this paper is to illustrate how modularization could be the key for more effective production in craft manufacturing by enabling improvement and development processes from shop floor level. This study uses data gathered from group meetings, interviews and observations through a four year long R&D-project in the leisure boat industry in Norway. The project aimed to introduce industrial principles from e.g. lean manufacturing into an industry characterized by craft manufacturing - the leisure boat industry. The methodological approach was case studies where the researchers took an active part in the change processes of two boatbuilding companies and one supplier to boat-builders.

This paper illustrates how the action research approach triggered involvement by the employees in all levels in the companies. In particular we focus on how the shop floor level could be a driving force for improvement and development within modularized product architecture, but also focus on how modularization fits the incremental product development process.

The composition of the paper is as follows: Section 2 presents relevant theoretical perspectives. Section 3 presents the four year long R&D-project and the basic findings from the project. Section 4 focuses on the discussion, and Section 5 concludes.

## 2     Theoretical Perspectives

### 2.1     Manufacturing Paradigms

Even though new management concepts often have been abandoned before they are allowed to fully prove their relevance, we have seen that each new concept has brought new elements to the table. These elements put into a more coherent and holistic context could be regarded as paradigms [6]. Jovane, Koren and Boer [7] have developed a set of criteria to identify and describe different manufacturing paradigms. In Table 1 Henriksen and Rolstadås [8] illustrate how paradigms could be identified based on a set of similar criteria emphasizing knowledge and innovation.

Craft Manufacturing is by Jovane et al. [7] presented as a manufacturing paradigm and is based on making exactly the product that the customer asks for, usually one product at a time in a "pull-type business model": sell (get paid) – design – make – assemble. The processes have a low level of automation, but use skilled and flexible workers.

Hill [9] presents basic principles for the more recent paradigms:

- a discretionary approach to change to ensure that scarce development resources are used in those areas that will yield best returns
- as with process choice, it is necessary to establish and then choose between sets and trade-offs that go hand in hand with each decision
- the infrastructure design must respond to dynamics of reality and much of necessary change can be achieved incrementally
- continuous development is easier to bring about where the responsibility for identifying and implementing improvements is locally based

**Table 1.** Manufacturing paradigms [8]

| Aspects | | Paradigm | | | |
|---|---|---|---|---|---|
| Field | Criteria | Craft manufacturing | Mass manufacturing | Lean manufacturing | Adaptive manufacturing |
| Business model | Started | *1850s* | *1910s* | *1980s* | *2000s* |
| | Customer requirements | *Customized products* | *Low cost products* | *Variety of products* | *Mass customized products* |
| | Market | *Pull. Very small volume per product* | *Push Demand>Supply Steady demand* | *Push-Pull Supply>Demand Smaller volume per product* | *Pull Globalization, segmentation Fluctuating demand* |
| Innovations | Process - enabler | *Electricity Machine tools* | *Moving assembly line and DML* | *FMS Robots Modulized products* | *RMS Information technology* |
| | Innovation process | *Incremental* | *Linear and radical* | *Incremental and linear* | *Incremental and radical* |
| Knowledge | Behavior | *Practical oriented (skills Learning by doing)* | *Centralized decisionmaking. Learning by instructions* | *Decentralized decisionmaking. Continuous improvement Learning by doing* | *Decentralized decisionmaking. Knowledge to be applied instantly* |
| | Knowledge creation | *Tacit knowledge* | *Explicit knowledge* | *Tacit knowledge* | *Tacit and explicit knowledge* |
| | Knowledge base | *Synthetic* | *Analytical* | *Analytical and Synthetic* | *Analytical and synthetic* |
| | Knowledge transfer- challenge | *Externalize knowledge communicating with customers* | *Internalize knowledge, for practical use* | *Externalize knowledge, making it more explicit* | *Continuously externalize and internalize knowledge* |

Lean manufacturing could also be regarded as a manufacturing paradigm [8] and contains many of the above more recent principles. Lean is based on the entirely new approach to manufacturing Japanese companies developed after World War II characterized by an emphasis on reliability, speed, "just-in-time", and flexibility, rather than volume and cost [9]. Foster [10] defines "lean" as "*a productive system whose focus is on optimizing processes through the philosophy of continual improvement*" ([10] p. 87). One crucial insight is that most costs are assigned when a product is designed. As a consequence, product development activities should be carried out concurrently, not sequentially, by cross-functional teams [12]. Modularization is i.e. considered an enabler for flexibility and is also an important element of lean manufacturing.

## 2.2    Involvement in Improvement and Development

Innovations in companies are often a combination of incremental and radical innovations [13]. Importance and innovativeness are often as high for incremental as for radical innovations, but where incremental innovations are going through more PDCA cycle iterations [14] and hence need more time. There is also often interplay between the incremental and radical innovations since the incremental innovations often enlighten the need for more radical innovations.

In manufacturing, innovation is frequently incremental and continuous through for example, quality improvement and various lean approaches, but it can also be radical and disruptive [15]. An important dimension is whether a manufacturing strategy is based on a decentralized process, as in lean. The innovation process is much more decentralized, interactive and incremental within lean manufacturing than in for example mass manufacturing [16]. More people from different backgrounds and skill competencies are involved in the lean improvement process. However from table 1 we also understand that craft manufacturing is even more grounded on experience and tacit knowledge based incremental innovations, than the more fact based lean manufacturing.

## 2.3    Concurrent Engineering

Concurrent engineering is the term that is applied to the engineering design philosophy of cross-functional cooperation in order to create products that are better, cheaper and more quickly brought to market. In concurrent engineering product design and production processes are developed simultaneously by cross-functional teams. The reason for this is the need to capture and integrate different aspects and the voice of the customer throughout the development process [17]. The fundamentals of concurrent engineering could be described by the following four characteristics [18]:

- increased role of manufacturing process design in product design decisions
- formation of cross-functional teams to accomplish the development process
- focus on the customer during the development process
- use of lead time as a source of competitive advantage

Concurrent engineering significantly modifies the sequential development (waterfall method) process and instead opts to use what has been termed an iterative or integrated development method.

A significant part of concurrent engineering is that the individual employee is given much more say in the overall design process due to the collaborative nature of concurrent engineering. Giving the designer ownership plays a large role in the productivity of the employee and quality of the product that is being produced. This stems from the fact that people given a sense of gratification and ownership over their work tend to work harder and design a more robust product, as opposed to an employee that is assigned a task with little say in the general product [19]. There is a motivation for teamwork since the overall success relies on the ability of employees to effectively work together.

## 2.4    Modularization

Modularization is currently in focus as a means for increasing competitiveness in manufacturing. This is achieved by bridging the advantages of: (1) standardization and rationalization, (2) customization and flexibility, and (3) reducing complexity [20]. Module-based design is in the same way as concurrent engineering a way of reducing product development lead time. However modularization also has many other advantages which have made it a key element in manufacturing paradigms such as lean. Modularity allows part of the product to be made in volume as standard modules while product distinctiveness is achieved through combinations or modifications of modules [5].

The cost effects through reduced product development lead time and volume effects from standardization are important, but there are also revenue aspects of modularization: With a modular product platform structure, a set of building blocks (modules) is created with which, through different combinations, a great number of final products can be built. Parts of the product that strategically should vary to satisfy customer needs are well defined and separated from the parts of the product that should be kept as common units. In this way, many variants of final products can be handled without increasing a company's internal complexity.

By breaking a complex product structure into smaller, manageable units, a company can regain control of the product and the product-related activities. Modularity aims at increasing efficiency by reducing complexity. The modular approach implies building an optimal product assortment that takes into consideration development, design, variety, manufacture, quality, purchase, and after-sales service, in other words, the entire product life-cycle. A cornerstone of modularity is the adoption of a common view of the product throughout the entire organization. This opens up a window of opportunities for concurrent engineering and improvement, decentralization and shop floor involvement.

We often find module-based design within incremental product development, where e.g. not all innovations or "novelties" are introduced at the same time. However, the initial module-based product architecture are often described as a systematic approaches with steps such as in Modular Function Deployment (MFD) [20]: (1) design requirements, (2) identification of functions that fulfill the demands and their corresponding technical solutions, (3) technical solutions are analyzed regarding their reasons for being modules, (4) module concepts are then generated and the interface relations of the modules derived are evaluated. In the final step, (5) a specification is established for each module. A systematic approach needs knowledge from people that knows customer demands, service requirements, and from those producing the products. Concurrent engineering could be a key to mobilize and capture this knowledge in development processes.

The tendency towards a more abstract understanding of modularity is further strengthened by the fact that modularization in an industrial context can be seen as reuse of engineering and employee resources for companies that are increasingly aware of knowledge as a competitive advantage [21]. An important part of the knowledge of the company is embedded in the products and reusing modules knowledge saves time and money. It is not necessarily the finished, physical modules that are reused in order to gain the benefits. Also, so-called *intellectual reuse* of earlier stages, like reuse of engineering specifications, testing, process engineering etc, may lead to the desired effects by blurring the boundary between knowledge management and traditional modularization [22].

# 3     The ISB-Project

## 3.1     The Project

The ISB-project (Industrialized Small scale Production of Leisure Boats) was a 4-year R&D-project that started in 2008 at the same time as the global financial crisis hit the leisure boat market. However, the background for the project was not to meet the difficult market situation, but rather the structural challenges from low-cost producers and the larger, more "industrialized" actors in the industry.

The overall objective of the project was to initiate a transformation of the craft-oriented leisure boat production into a more competitive way of production by introducing more state-of-the-art principles from manufacturing. The overall challenge of the project has been to keep or improve the high quality level and customization that is the characteristic of craft manufacturing, and at the same time create more cost-efficiency. This implies becoming more lean and aiming for mass customization. The focus of the project was on modularization and standardization of work processes.

### 3.2    The Partners

The project had three industrial partners, two Norwegian boat-builders and one supplier to boat-builders. There was also two Norwegian R&D partners (SINTEF and the Norwegian University of Science and Technology). The project was co-financed by The Norwegian Research Council.

The boat-builders had different focus and the project was organized in four work-packages with the industrial partners owning three of them, (1) module-based design, (2) standardized work processes and knowledge management, and (3) supply chain integration. The fourth work package was dissemination.

The largest boat-builder (OEM) with models from 25 to 58 feet had a turnover of 16 million € (2011), employed about 80 people (2011), with manufacturing units in two countries in addition to the mother plant, and customers and suppliers from all continents. The other company made 18 to 27 feet boats and had a turnover of about 4 million € (2011).

Even though these two companies have defined product-lines, the level of customization is high. This makes the manufacturing processes difficult to e.g. automate. For instance, the customer's choice of a larger freshwater-tank impacts the boats stability, thus requiring a reconfiguration of installment of other components and adjustments to e.g. brackets and bars. Manufacturing processes are mainly manual and adjustments are made all along the boat manufacturing process. The quality of the boats is perceived by the market as very high, but also with prices in the high end. Boatbuilding also has other typical characteristics of craft manufacturing such as manual experience-based and incremental product development. Tacit knowledge is the basis for improvement and development and a typical statement could be "what happens at the shop floor stays at the shop floor".

The supplier is a key actor in the boatbuilding industry as it is the biggest and most important supplier of their products in the Scandinavian boatbuilding industry. The company has a turnover of about 7 million € (2011) and is within the mechanical engineering industry, but still has many of the same characteristics of craft manufacturing. The case presented in this paper is in particular based on the largest boat-builder, the supplier and the relation between these two companies.

# 4    Involving Shop Floor Level in Improvement and Development

## 4.1    From Skepticism to Driving Force

At an early stage of the ISB-project, the researchers set out to get an overview of the existing design and production processes. The overview of the production was done by setting up work groups basically from the shop floor (production group). Initially these work groups reflected skepticism among the workers for change. They wanted to keep the identity of being a craftsman and they were not very motivated for standardization of work processes. But this changed during the work session where their work processes and challenges where analyzed and documented, and they could see how their work situation could be improved as a result of measures aiming to improve productivity. Waste reduction and other lean methods are example of such methods.

As the production group, under facilitation by researchers, digged deeper into improvement they turned more of their attention from improvement of todays processes and into product design. They identified how their work could be improved and also the products by redesign products or parts. The discussions where also particularly fruitful when the workers/craftsman discussed the particular area of the boat they normally worked on (e.g. engine room). They showed not only good skills in their work/operations, but also an extremely high knowledge, identity and loyalty to the product and boat area as the discussions become concrete to them. During the project the production work groups made several suggestions for modularization, but also involved themselves in the suggestions for other modules such as cockpit, soft-hatch to handle opening/closing a soft-top and cabling/wiring.

An important finding in the project was the need for a structure for capturing the knowledge and initiatives from the shop floor level. This included a more team-oriented organization at shop floor level, and methods like stand-up meetings (10 minutes) as a daily starting point in the mornings as an arena for daily planning and work related issues. The team leader got responsibility for following up issues and suggestions from these meetings e.g. by own decisions or bringing them up to higher level meetings and decision bodies.

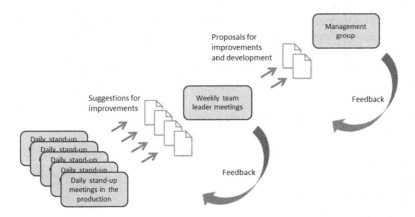

**Fig. 1.** Structure for improvement and involvement from shop floor level

Another important part of the structure for improvement was that discussions and decisions should be more fact-oriented. Thus, tacit knowledge had to be codified through different types of forms, but this also required training of the workers of how to be more explicit. An improvement tool called SMART was developed trough the ISB-project. The methodology resembles the A3 tool in lean, but adjusted to the context of leisure boat manufacturing.

## 4.2    Concurrent Engineering - Internally and with the Supplier

Standardization of work processes is a prerequisite for modularization as this also improves lead times using standardized modules and parts. Further, standardized work processes must be as efficient as possible. Thus, the production/shop floor level needs to be involved concurrently in the design process of products and modules. This was not the case in the companies when the ISB-project started. In fact, boat design had been seen as an "art" where the visual design was the basis and where the design group to a large extent then accomplished the design from the artist with technical and practical solutions and specifications. Even though there were some discussions between the design group and the production, there were no structured concurrent involvements. The same was the case for the involvement of the supplier in the design – they were often just asked to develop and deliver whatever the designer decided, no matter the price (which first became an issue after the supplier had come up with solutions which prolonged the development process).

During the project period several new boat models were launched and the need for å more concurrent development process became clearer. Two years into the project the new 40 feet model was developed as a much more structured project with a proper development team including market and production, and with weekly meetings together with the workers building the prototypes. Also the supplier was more involved in the design process as they got responsibility for developing the "soft-hatch" module. However, the relation between the boat-builder and the supplier was not very structured, and were more based on personal relations and tacit knowledge. This was addressed as a major improvement aspect in the evaluation meeting at the end of the development process of the soft-hatch involving people from the boat-builder (design, production, marketing and sales) and the supplier (including external engineering consultants).

To assure a more concurrent and efficient product development a new lean-oriented project-model was developed based on the following principles:

- understand customer requirements and early focus on gaps
- design to target cost
- make decisions based on facts
- capture and maintain knowledge
- visualize
- "right from me"
- modularization
- early sub-system testing

The project model has several meeting points and learning loops to assure learning and involvement through the project phases: (1) Concept - design brief, (2) Design – solutions and specifications, (3) Prototype – physical design, (4) Validation – testing, evaluation, choice, (5) Production process – suppliers, tools, procedures, and (5) Evaluation – product and processes.

## 4.3    Incremental Modularization Top-down versus Bottom-up

The idea of modularization was not met with enthusiasm, mainly due to the challenge towards business traditions of craftwork explained in 4.1. But a general interest for improving business initiated several initiatives to achieve modularity both in the boat-building companies and the supplier. The main motivation was to increase volumes on some parts. In the biggest boat-building company a work group was set up to focus on modularization.

Even though the ISB-project was aiming for a holistic approach to modularity, a completely modularized new boat is resource demanding and was not the ambitions for the ISB-project. However, the 5 steps of MFD was a reference for our work. This means that the project started with a kind of top-down approach where the work group was going through the basic elements of the new boat model to identify the best possible starting point – the first module to be developed. During work sessions several possible modules where discussed and analyzed but where typically rejected or postponed by the designers under arguments such as, "they could have negative impact on company identity", "on quality" etc. However, the work group agreed on a module or platform that was not visible for the customer, namely the important electric wiring of a boat. Here, new interfaces and new functions based on bus-technology are opening for more standardized marine solutions. The traditional wiring in a medium size boat weights some 250 kg and requires a lot of work and leaves little flexibility for alterations after being installed. Any modification to decrease complexity, volume and weight of this part will reduce installation work and cost.

An example of a more typical top-down module is the introduction of a grid or a stringer inside the bottom of the hull. This is a structure of beams put into the boats inside to give strength to the construction and to provide interfaces towards other major parts, such as pantry, toilets, engines and cockpit. It will in the future be the main module in a boat, opening for a lot of other modules. To introduce this, a lot of engineering has to be done as a total new construction has to be made. First solutions have been introduced, but to fully exploit the potential, several interfaces still have to be worked on. This top-down modularization will in the end represent the biggest potential, and might even change the way boats are built.

The quickest, smallest and most isolated cases are denoted bottom-up initiatives. These are easy to implement because of their minor impact on neighboring parts and designs. They also involve employees in a way that seems to encourage participation. One example is the new so called "soft-hatch", which is a new way of opening the roof of soft-tops. The hatch can be scaled to fit small and large boats, and can be built in series to increase efficiency. The initiative for developing this module was not from a structured top-down process from the design work group. It was rather a result of concrete discussions about a design challenge for the new 40 feet. This discussion involved also the supplier in the ISB-project and resulted in an agreement of outsourcing the design of the new soft-hatch to them.

The process of developing this module is quite typical for how discussions about improvement and development become more fruitful when they are related to a concrete product (or part of a product) and production process. As we have seen from the ISB-project this might end up in modularization. What is important is that these modules are not sub-optimized in a way that reduces the overall performance of the product and processes. They must meet the overall criteria for a holistic product architecture.

# 5    Conclusion

The incremental development process that we often find in e.g. craft manufacturing is well suited for modularization. This means that a company could develop e.g. product modules step by step, and plan how these modules could be replaced or improved incrementally. The ISB-project identified the "wiring" and "inner liner" as examples of modules and platforms from a top-down approach and "hatch-top" as an example of modules developed from concrete discussions at shop floor level and with designers – bottom-up.

The ISB-project has shown how modularization makes it easier to address improvement and development in the company. This is in line with the broader perspectives on modularization where modules also are seen as "knowledge containers". Focus on modules also enabled profound involvements from employees that reduced barriers to change, that over time also challenged the traditional "craftsmen culture" into a more change-oriented and proactive culture at shop floor level. As a result of this cultural change, modules were identified, piloted and implemented in the course of the project.

# References

1. Buschfeld, D., Dilger, B., Heß, L.S., Scmid, K., Woss, E.: Identification of future skills needs in micro and craft(-type) enterprises up to 2020 - Final report. Service Contract No. 30-CE-0319368 European Commission, DG Enterprise and Industry, Unit F.2 – Small Businesses, Cooperatives, Mutuals and CSR; Financed by the European Union, Forschungsinstitut für berufsbildun gim handwerk an der Universität Köln (2011)
2. Baldwin, C., Clark, K.: Modularity in design: An analysis based on the theory of real options. Working paper. Harvard Business School, Boston (1994)
3. Ulrich, K.: The role of product architecture in the manufacturing firm. Working Paper. MIT, Sloan School of Management (1992)
4. Pine, B.J.: Mass Customization. Harvard Business School Press, Boston (1993)
5. Duray, R.: Mass Customizers use of inventory, planning techniques and channel management. Production Planning & Control 15(4), 412–421 (2004)

6. Henriksen, B.: The Knowledge dimension of manufacturing strategy. Doctoral thesis, Norwegian University of Science and Technology (2010)
7. Jovane, F., Koren, Y., Boer, C.R.: A present and future of flexible automation: towards new paradigms. Annals of the CIRP 53(1), 543–560 (2003)
8. Henriksen, B., Rolstadås, A.: Knowledge and manufacturing strategy – How different manufacturing paradigms have different requirements to knowledge. Examples from the automotive industry. International Journal of Production Research 48(8), 2413–2430 (2010)
9. Hill, T.: Operations management: strategic context and managerial analysis. Macmillan, London (2000)
10. Foster, T.S.: Managing quality - Integrating supply chain. Prentice Hall, New Jersey (2006)
11. Womack, J.P., Jones, D.T., Roos, D.: The machine that changed the world: The story of lean Production. Harper Business, New York (1990)
12. Rolstadås, A., Henriksen, B., O'Sullivan, D.: Manufacturing outsourcing – a knowledge perspective. Springer Publishing, London (2012)
13. Deming, W.E.: Out of Crisis Boston. MIT/CAES, Cambridge, MA (1986)
14. Tidd, J., Bessant, J., Pavitt, K.: Managing innovation: Integrating technological, market and organizational change. Wiley, London (2005)
15. Cooper, R.G.: Product leadership: creating and launching superior new products. Perseus, New York (2000)
16. Smith, R.P.: The Historical Roots of Concurrent Engineering Fundamentals. IEEE Transactions on Engineering Management 44(1) (1997)
17. Jo, H.H., Parsaei, H.R., Sullivan, W.G.: Principles of concurrent engineering. In: Concurrent Engineering: Contemporary Issues and Modern Design Tools, pp. 3–23. Chapman and Hall, New York (1993)
18. Rosenblatt, A., Watson, G.: Concurrent Engineering. IEEE Spectrum, 22–37 (July 1991)
19. Ericsson, A., Erixon, G.: Controlling Design Variants: Modular Product Platforms. ASME Press, NY (1999)
20. Miller, T.D., Elgård, P.: Design for Integration in Manufacturing. In: Proceedings of the 13th IPS Research Seminar, Fuglsoe. Aalborg University (1998) ISBN 87-89867-60-2
21. Sanchez, R., Mahoney, J.T.: Modularity, Flexibility, and Knowledge Management in Product and Organization Design. IEEE Engineering Management Review 17 (1996) Reprint from Strategic Management, Special Issue December

# Comparison of Criticality of Configuration Choices for Market Price and Product Cost

Peter Nielsen and Thomas Ditlev Brunoe

Aalborg University, Department of Mechanical and Manufacturing Engineering
{peter,tdp}@m-tech.aau.dk

**Abstract.** The paper presents a quantitative method for determining the criticality of components to costs and sales price in mass customization environments. The method is based information of historically sold configurations and uses backward elimination to arrive at a reduced linear model. The variables included in this model are then the most significant describing variation of (material/salary/total) costs, sales price or profit margin. The method is tested on data from a large manufacturer of mass customized products.

**Keywords:** Mass customization, backward elimination, linear model.

## 1    Introduction

In companies offering customized products, manufacturing costs and sales prices will depend on a particular configuration of a product and those companies often experience that it is not obvious which product properties drive cost and which properties allow for a high sales price. This leads to the fact that it is nontrivial to identify which products are profitable and which are not. In any company it is crucial to continuously evaluate the profitability of the product range, however in companies with a significant product variety such as mass customization or engineer to order companies, this is a challenging task. This evaluation and the resulting development of a product portfolio in mass customizing companies is referred to as solution space development, which is one of three fundamental organizational capabilities which differentiate successful mass customizers from the non successful [11].

In mass customization where it is uncommon to sell and produce more than a few identical products but rather sell high numbers of individually customized products, it makes little sense to evaluate the profitability of a single product. Instead the solution space must be evaluated as a whole. Evaluating the profitability of the solution space can be approached in several different ways. Fundamentally, a qualitative or quantitative approach can be chosen. However, due to the vast complexity of a mass customization solution space in terms of the number of product features and modules, usually leaving a practically infinite solution space, a qualitative approach seems unfeasible indicating that a quantitative approach should be pursued.

C. Emmanouilidis, M. Taisch, D. Kiritsis (Eds.): APMS 2012, Part I, IFIP AICT 397, pp. 262–269, 2013.
© IFIP International Federation for Information Processing 2013

A number of manufacturing processes dependent methods have been developed for cost estimation, implying that the particular method of estimating cost can only be applied to certain processes e.g. casting or welding [4], [5], [12], [13], [13], [17]. Cost estimation methods dependent on the specific product type also exist. In particular much research has been presented within the area of estimating cost during product development for both the finished product and the development process [2], [8], [9], [16], [19]. Kingsman & de Souza [7] introduced a general framework for cost estimation and pricing decisions, but no practical methods for estimating cost are presented. Other studies focus primarily on describing mathematically using synthetic models how customized products can be priced, however primarily compared to similar non-customized products [1], [14].

One of the deficiencies of the approaches found in literature is that most are not specific to mass customization and do thus not take into account a large solution space but focus rather on a single product. Furthermore most are synthetic, meaning that a cost and pricing model must be developed in order to evaluate the product profitability which is complicated by a high variety. Finally a number of the approaches described in literature are product specific rather than generic.

The research objective of this paper is to create an analytic method which can assist companies in evaluating the profitability of a product family based on historical configuration data. By basing the method on historical configuration data, the combinations of modules and features actually sold are evaluated in contrast to a synthetic approach. The research questions of this research presented in this paper are:

1. Which method should be applied to identify which configuration variables are Critical to cost, sales prices and profit margin based on historical configurations?
2. How can the output be analyzed and utilized to identify relations between configuration variables, cost and sales price and profit margin?
3. How may the criticality of configuration variables with respect to cost and sales price be interpreted and utilized to develop the solution space to produce more profitable products?

## 2    Methodology

The aim is in a simple quantitative manner to establish which variables are critical for various costs (typically material and salary costs) and which variables are critical for sales price and high profit margin. The aim is then to identify where there is a gap between these models. I.e. which variables are critical for cost aspects, but not critical for price and profitability in the form of net margin (sales price – variable costs).

The paper utilizes the method for determining the critical of various parameters criticality to cost presented in Brunø and Nielsen [3], developed for Engineer-to-Order cost estimation, and adapts this to a method for comparing the cost aspects and the profit margin per sold product. Due to the complexity of the problem and the number of variables (large number of components and resources involved) considered multiple linear regression must be used [18]. However, since some manner of relations can be expected between the independent variables, all insignificant variables cannot just be removed in one step. To overcome this issue backward elimination is used since in product configuration it seems better to risk dropping variables that explain a given behaviour (in this case of cost or profit margin) than having an overly complex model with several variables explaining the same behaviour [3]. The latter being a potential consequence of using e.g. forward selection.

The principle proposed in this paper of applying backward elimination to the problem is to estimate a (simple) linear model for historical configuration data and corresponding costs or profit margins. This creates a linear model that can explain costs or profit margin for new configurations [10]. The way backward elimination simplifies the linear model is by iteratively removing variables from a large set of data describing a number of historical product configurations and fitting a model to the reduced set of data. The set of variables describing the configurations can contain different types of variables as they are typically related to processes used in the manufacturing/assembly process and Bill of material contents. Since the method reduces the number of variables considerably it is unnecessary to qualitatively select the variables before the method is applied, but merely provide a gross list of variables describing each historical product and a corresponding incurred cost, sales price or profit margin. The result of applying this method (see [3] for further details) is a net list of critical variables fitted to a given dependent variable. In the context of this research the dependent variables will as a minimum be a relevant cost per piece (e.g. registered salary or material cost) sales price and profit margin (preferably a contribution margin excluding the variable costs). An overview of the methodology can be seen in Fig. 1.

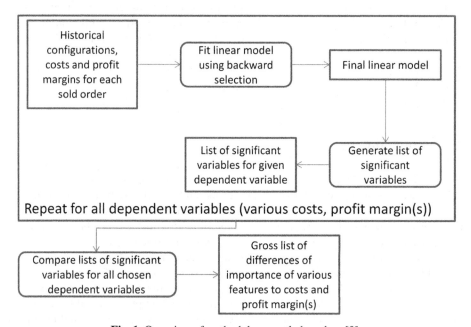

**Fig. 1.** Overview of methodology partly based on [3]

# 3    Case Study Application

The proposed method has been tested on data from a manufacturing company. The case concerns a medium sized company in Denmark producing technical products for domestic water installations which are configured within a predefined solution space. The products share a common structure. The company produces products configured with in a given set of fixed options. The company registers material and salary costs as well as net margin for all sold products. Furthermore a full route and Bill of material is available for all sold configurations.

The initial model contains 194 variables. This is through use of the method presented in Brunø and Nielsen [3] reduced to 22 variables. These results match results achieved by the authors when applying the method to a number of other cases. To simplify the case application of the method the 10 most significant variables for salary, material and profit margin respectively have then subsequently been identified using the method from Brunø and Nielsen (forthcoming). The results are illustrated in Table 1 below.

**Table 1.** Overview of the 10 most significant variables for material cost, salary costs, sales price and profit margin. The variables highlighted with **bold** occur more than once. All dependent variables are calculated per piece.

| Rank of significance | Salary costs | Material costs | Sales Price | Profit margin |
|---|---|---|---|---|
| 1 | **Number of pieces** | **Var6** | Var13 | **Var15** |
| 2 | **Var1** | **Var1** | **Var10** | Var17 |
| 3 | Var2 | **Var10** | **Var7** | **Var12** |
| 4 | **Var3** | **Var5** | **Var5** | **Var1** |
| 5 | **Var4** | **Var4** | **Var4** | **Var8** |
| 6 | **Var5** | **Var3** | Var14 | **Var5** |
| 7 | **Var6** | **Var9** | **Var15** | **Var4** |
| 8 | **Var7** | Var11 | **Var16** | **Var16** |
| 9 | **Var8** | **Var7** | **Number of pieces** | Var18 |
| 10 | **Var9** | **Var12** | **Var9** | Var19 |

From Table 1 it is easy to conclude that there is a relative large overlap between the variables that cause a high material and salary cost (6 out of 10 are the same) although the significance of the variables varies between the two cost structures. It is also easy to conclude that only 5 out of 10 variables that are significant for profit margin are critical for material or salary costs or both. It is interesting also to note that the two most critical variables for profit margin (i.e. the two features most critical to establish the profit margin) are not even on the list of the ten most significant variables for material or salary costs. It is also interesting to note that 6 out of 10 variables that are critical for the sales price (i.e. the price a customer is willing to pay for a piece) are in fact also critical for determining the costs. However, in the same sense it is also very important to note that the variables that are critical for the sales price are only critical for the profit margin 4 out of 10 times. This could indicate that the company is unable to transfer the features that are critical for sales price in to features that are critical for the profit margin.

## 4     Discussion

The following discussion is based on a single case application. This of course somewhat limits the ability to generalize the results. An analysis identifying variables critical to cost and sales price can be utilized for a number of different purposes, however the most obvious opportunities are development of the solution space. Within this area the method could more specifically be applied in cost reduction projects to reduce the cost of expensive features, in adaption of pricing schemes for different features and for identifying non profitable features which should likely be removed from the solution space. However, the method has a main limitation, namely the requirement for a high volume of structured historical data including configuration variables, cost and sales price. As a result, this method cannot be applied for new products which have not yet been sold. Previous research indicates that the model fit increases the less variation is found in the product structure for different configurations. Finally, the method cannot react to changes in cost and pricing structure before a sufficient number of configurations are produced. Fig. 2 illustrates different scenarios for results regarding a specific variable.

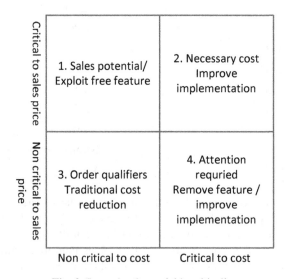

**Fig. 2.** Scenarios for variable criticality

In scenario 1 the variable is critical to the sales price but not the cost, indicating that this particular feature increases the sales price without adding extra cost to the product meaning that this feature can be exploited by e.g. increasing the sales effort for this feature. In scenario 2 the variable is critical to both sales price and cost indicating that the feature is probably necessary since it drives the sales price, however as it is also significant to the cost, efforts for reducing manufacturing costs should be focused here. In scenario 3, the variable is non critical to both sales price and cost, which indicates that these features are not influencing the profitability of the variety in the solution space. However, cost reduction efforts are still relevant in this scenario, but could presumably be addressed as cost reduction of standard product as little variation is found for these variables. In scenario 4, the variable is critical to cost but not to sales price, indicating that attention is required, since this feature basically being priced unacceptably low or the implementation of the feature is too expensive. This suggest that the feature should either be removed, priced higher or be significantly cost reduced to avoid decline in profit margins. The conclusions and suggested actions for the 4 scenarios are to be perceived as indications only. Although for example a variable in scenario 4 may not seem profitable, externalities may imply that it cannot be removed from the solution space or priced differently and thus a qualitative assessment should be performed for each variable. One simple way to apply the information generated and displayed in table 1 is to plot the variables in the matrix illustrated in figure 2. A display of this type comparing salary costs to sales price is presented in figure 3 below.

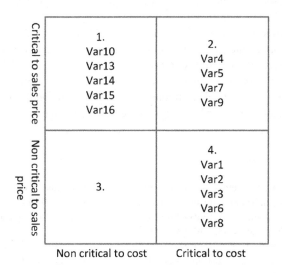

**Fig. 3.** Scenarios for variable criticality comparing salary costs and sales price

As seen from figure 3, there are no variables in the third quadrant. In reality all features not found to be significant by the method and displayed in table 1, are in the quadrant. From the example we can see that we can place 14 variables in the matrix out of a total of 22 variables to begin with. This matches the concept of value engineering seen in e.g. [6], where experiences on value engineering from the automotive industry are presented. The remaining variables then belong to third quadrant. The critical variables from this example then become the five in quadrant 4, i.e. Var1, Var2, Var3, Var6 and Var8. These five variables are insignificant for the sales price, but significant for the salary costs. When redesigning the product (family) it would then be relevant to first focus on these five and try to move them (at first) to quadrant 3 or even 1 or 2 if at all possible. The second step would then be to focus on the variables (features) found in quadrant 2 and investigate if they can somehow be moved to quadrant 1. However, there will always be some variables that are critical for cost variation, so better that they are placed in quadrant 2 than in quadrant 4. It is noteworthy that the variables seem to be equally distributed between the quadrants.

It is important to keep in mind that the approach presented in this paper only addresses the variation in sales price and cost and does thus not address the base cost, i.e. the intercept of the linear model. This cost and sales price is however expected to be defined by a common product platform, i.e. product properties and components which are part of all configured products and can thus be addressed as a non customized product.

## 5    Conclusion

It can be concluded that the method can be used to identify which variables are critical for the costs, sales price and profit margin. It is also noteworthy that in this particular case there is a significant difference between which variables are critical for sales price and costs. It is also possible to conclude that the variables associated with a given feature can be categorized using the developed matrix and that this can serve as a first quantitative step in a redesign process.

Future work will focus on two aspects. First, to further refine the quantitative method for identifying critical components / features. Second, to investigate and implement the method in several redesign processes in practice.

## References

1. Alptekinoglu, A., Corbett, C.J.: Mass Customization Vs. Mass Production: Variety and Price Competition. Manufacturing Service Oper. Management 10, 204–217 (2008)
2. Ben-Arieh, D., Qian, L.: Activity-Based Cost Management for Design and Development Stage. Int. J. Prod. Econ. 83, 169–183 (2003)
3. Brunoe, T.D., Nielsen, P.: A Case of Cost Estimation in an Engineer–to–order Company Moving Towards Mass Customisation. International Journal of Mass Customisation 4, 239–254 (2012)
4. García-Crespo, Á., Ruiz-Mezcua, B., López-Cuadrado, J.L., et al.: A Review of Conventional and Knowledge Based Systems for Machining Price Quotation. J. Intell. Manuf. 1–19
5. H'mida, F., Martin, P., Vernadat, F.: Cost Estimation in Mechanical Production: The Cost Entity Approach Applied to Integrated Product Engineering. Int. J. Prod. Econ. 103, 17–35 (2006)

6. Ibusuki, U., Kaminski, P.C.: Product Development Process with Focus on Value Engineering and Target-Costing: A Case Study in an Automotive Company. Int. J. Prod. Econ. 105, 459–474 (2007)
7. Kingsman, B.G., De Souza, A.A.: A Knowledge-Based Decision Support System for Cost Estimation and Pricing Decisions in Versatile Manufacturing Companies. Int. J. Prod. Econ. 53, 119–139 (1997)
8. Layer, A.: Recent and Future Trends in Cost Estimation. Int. J. Comput. Integr. Manuf. 15, 499–510 (2002)
9. Niazi, A., Dai, J.S., Balabani, S., et al.: Product Cost Estimation: Technique Classification and Methodology Review. Journal of Manufacturing Science and Engineering 128, 563 (2006)
10. Nielsen, P., Petersen, T.D.: Criticality of Components and Specific Configurations in an Engineer-to-Order Environment. In: Proceedings of the 14th International Annual EurOMA Conference (2007)
11. Salvador, F., de Holan, M., Piller, F.: Cracking the Code of Mass Customization. MIT Sloan Management Review 50, 70–79 (2009)
12. Shehab, E., Abdalla, H.: An Intelligent Knowledge-Based System for Product Cost Modelling. The International Journal of Advanced Manufacturing Technology 19, 49–65 (2002)
13. Shtub, A., Versano, R.: Estimating the Cost of Steel Pipe Bending, a Comparison between Neural Networks and Regression Analysis. Int. J. Prod. Econ. 62, 201–207 (1999)
14. Syam, N.B., Kumar, N.: On Customized Goods, Standard Goods, and Competition. Marketing Science, 525–537 (2006)
15. Tornberg, K., Jamsen, M., Paranko, J.: Activity-Based Costing and Process Modeling for Cost-Conscious Product Design: A Case Study in a Manufacturing Company. Int. J. Prod. Econ. 79, 75–82 (2002)
16. Verlinden, B., Duflou, J., Collin, P., et al.: Cost Estimation for Sheet Metal Parts using Multiple Regression and Artificial Neural Networks: A Case Study. Int. J. Prod. Econ. 111, 484–492 (2008)
17. Walpole, R.E., Myers, R.H., Myers, S.L., et al.: Probability and statistics for engineers and scientists. Macmillan, New York (1989)
18. Weustink, I., ten Brinke, E., Streppel, A., et al.: A Generic Framework for Cost Estimation and Cost Control in Product Design. Journal of Materials Processing Tech. 103, 141–148 (2000)

# The Multiple Faces of Mass Customization: Product Design, Process Design and Supply Chain Design

Nico J. Vandaele[1,2] and Catherine J. Decouttere[2]

[1] Katholieke Universiteit Leuven, Faculty of Business and Economics,
Naamsestraat 69, 3000 Leuven
[2] KULAK, E. Sabbelaan 53, 8500 Kortrijk
{Nico.Vandaele,Catherine.Decouttere}@kuleuven.be

**Abstract.** Mass Customization is one of the buzz words of the last decade. However, the purpose of efficiently unfolding multiple variants of a product or service has deep grounded consequences for the business processes and the underlying system. Subsequently, the supply chain structures supporting these processes face many challenges. In this paper we expose an integrated view on mass customization from a design perspective, rooted in a user-oriented design paradigm. First, we want to find an answer to whether mass customization is a feasible business model to guarantee sustainability in the Flemish textile industry. Second, how can the long tail business model be designed in an integrated way, relating product, process and supply chain design. The mass customized product/service design framework is based on field data gathered from a technological innovation supporting programme operational in Flanders' textile industry. Based on these data, some preliminary benchmarking observations can be made which relate to product, process and supply chain design.

**Keywords:** Mass customization, business model innovation, supply chain design.

## 1 Introduction

Mass customization and "the Long Tail" business model, as defined and described by [1], give an answer to the trend of personalization intended at the cost and effort of a standard product or service. "Tailor made" was the traditional way of presenting a perfect fit to a very specific customer need. More specifically for the textile industry, what started off as mainly ergonomic fit (for instance in terms of size), evolved to tailored functionality and individual emotional benefits such as self-expression and uniqueness. The design aspect in the broad sense became an asset creating a willingness to pay. However, companies applying the mass customization business model, need to find a new balance between unique product/service performance and the related cost, while keeping the process and supply chain complexity within feasible limits. Essential elements in this exercise are the co-creation experience, product modularity, and enabling technologies, allowing unique products which are producible in small lot sizes or even in a one-by-one mode.

C. Emmanouilidis, M. Taisch, D. Kiritsis (Eds.): APMS 2012, Part I, IFIP AICT 397, pp. 270–277, 2013.

In the context of the Technological Support Programme for Mass Customization issued by the Flemish Government, we observed and supported the textile and confection industry in Flanders in its transition to mass customization. With an objective of creating sustainable added value and rejuvenating a traditional but struggling Flemish industry in a global context (suffering from delocalisation), the viewpoints from both the customer and the producer are investigated.

# 2 Customization for a Sustainable Textile Industry

**Elements of Sustainability.** Sustainability for the Flemish textile industry is translated in to objectives in terms of social, ecological and economical dimensions. On the social level, it was brought down to "keeping jobs in Flanders". Knowing that large parts of the production in the textile industry has been delocalized from Flanders, we see new activities arising in personalized design, research in technical textiles with new functionalities, automated production of small batches or unique one-of-a-kind products based on efficient technology and experience etc. A lot of these new activities deliver goods and services with a high level of customization.

On the ecological level, the overall carbon footprint of the industry is considered. Key elements driving sustainability in a mass customized textile industry are lower material use due to less scrap, lower transportation and extension of life time of products.

The economic benefits of MC in the textile industry are the result of the transition from a make to stock to a make to order approach. Supply chain related costs such as inventory cost and scrap should be significantly lower. This will depend on the accepted order lead time by the customer of the personalized goods.

The textile industry is known to be highly sensitive to fashion and trends, and each season, this "fashion risk" can lead to significant scrap costs due to unsellable goods.

**Market Environment.** Companies who initially started up with mass customization in a highly customized market, for instance functional sportswear, seem to have a competitive advantage compared to companies who want to make the transition to customization in a market were standard or low customized products and services are the main reference. This is the case with for instance the confection industry or the interior textile industry (curtains and carpets).

However, the theoretical opportunities in the mass production confection industry sector is also high as fashion risk and inventory risks can be minimised by converting away from a mass production business model towards a mass customization business model [8].

**Company Profile.** Reality reveals that the integration of the voice of the customer and the conversion of the sales approach is yet a hard learning curve for traditional companies, as it usually involves a turnaround of both their innovation and processing approach as well as their distribution and supply network. Moreover, the financial benefits of more lean and sustainable operations are not immediately felt as the turnaround to a mass customization network involves the influx of financial resources.

# 3    Business Opportunities from Customization

The literature on Mass Customization is vast and elaborate and traces back to Davis [3]. We refer to [2], [10] for a comprehensive review. The added value of addressing individual needs, whether functional or not, need to be reflected in a positive co-creation experience, which guides the customer in a pleasant way from the understanding of his individual needs through the design process and placing the order of the perfectly matching product. In this way, the negative effect on the purchasing process of an overwhelming range of possibilities can be overcome [9]. The degree to which the product and service should be customized in order to obtain optimal added value, is a key question with implications for the entire business model design. A MC company needs to adopt new skills allowing it to gain and maintain a profound insight in its customer's individual needs and expectations. A highly performing customer knowledge system becomes a necessity.

Already from the conception and development of the products and services, the customization approach will be applied. The product, service and system architecture will be in line with the configuration steps the customer will be invited to take part in. The role of designers and product developers changes towards more openness to the voice of the customer, they will balance between reflecting the company identity and brand essence in the customized products and services and providing guidance and reassurance during the co-creation process where it is expected by the customer.

Accordingly, the processing and the delivery of the product/service has to be performed in an efficient and cost effective manner. In one way or another, multiple technological possibilities are there. The Flemish textile industry has a leading position in technical textiles (used for special purposes like fire protection, healthcare applications, etc.), in implementing three-dimensional body-scanning techniques, in digital printing techniques and many more.

Our double entry research question is as follows:

1. Is mass customization a feasible business model to guarantee sustainability in the Flemish textile industry?
2. How can the long tail business model for a Flemish textile company be designed in an integrated way: product, process and supply chain?

In order to answer these questions, an integrated approach amongst product design, process design and supply chain design is at stake.

# 4    The MC Product, Process and Business Model Design Framework

Against this framework, we give an overview of the dimensions which positively and negatively influence the success of mass customization in the Flemish textile industry, using a multi-dimensional approach based on industry data from 2011. These data were collected based on structured interviews, company audits and group assessments. Important elements from the data collection were grouped into product, process and business model categories. Subsequently we measured some core KPI's from the companies. At this point we only give an overview of some important key value dimensions.

## 4.1    Product/Service Design

Perceived Usefulness (PU) is here measured as a product attribute with a considerable user involvement and is in this context defined as "the value of customization, i.e. the increment of utility a customer gains from a product that fits better to her needs than the best standard product attainable  as perceived by the customer [6]. Examples can be found in sportswear where individual physical characteristics may largely dictate the willingness to deviate from an industrial standard.

Perceived Ease Of Use (PEOU) is the degree to which the co-creation step is pleasant or free of effort for the user. It refers to customer friendly toolkits and configurator applications where the user is led comfortably through his decision process and where positive emotions are elicited during the customizing process.

I Designed It Myself Effect (IDME). Here the feeling of being responsible for the outcome and authoring the design is key. It resembles the 'good' feeling stemming from the actions and the opinions of the customer which turn the product into an element of self-esteem. It is a value-generating effect that arises merely from the fact that the customer is the originator of the product [5].

## 4.2    Process Design

From the process side the degree of Mass Customization (MC) is measured as the degree to which products can be produced, i.e. the ability, to achieve customization, ranging from a solely standard product to a fully customized product.

Process Technology Adaptation (PTA) is the degree to which the company has adapted or employs the adequate process technology to be able to deliver mass customization. Industry known benchmark technologies are used to produce an overall assessment.

## 4.3    Business Model Design

The Point-Of-Sale Effectiveness (POSE) is the degree to which the point of sale is successful in reaching the customer and explaining the benefits of the personalized product offer in an easy way.

Also the organization of the supply chain plays a role and is measured by Supply Chain Network Responsiveness (SCNR). This is measured by the degree to which a company is able to control all the elements leading to responsiveness for mass customization. If many of these supply chain nodes are independent, the harder it is for an independent player herein to deliver a mass customized product.

## 4.4    Key Performance Indicators

In this part we opted to represent all categories of sustainability elements :

Social Gain, defined as the number of jobs kept in Flanders thanks to mass customization.

Ecology Gain, measured by the difference in carbon footprint between mass customization and standard production.

Economic Gain, via the turnover realized by the Mass Customized product families related to the total turnover of all products combined with the growth rate of the company.

The measurement of social gain and ecology gain is not easy but feasible using realistic alternative scenarios and past experiences as benchmarks.

# 5    Preliminary Observations

The measurements on these dimensions have been used to assess the relative position of 17 individual textile companies, who are interested to go along on the road of mass customization. In general, our findings are that there are quite some differences among the MC business models applied and among  the mass customization performance of these companies

## 5.1    Natives and Hybrid Companies

More specific, we noticed that companies who started up applying the mass customization business model, "MC natives" have a higher probability of success than established companies who convert to mass customization ("hybrid" group, Fig 1). The latter evolved to a hybrid business model offering both standard goods and mass customized products. Some of these companies are in a transition phase to a business model fully based on customization, while others consider "customization projects" as a type of innovation next to the core business of mass production of standard products and services. Their intention is not to convert fully to MC but to be present in it. MC natives seem to be slightly better equipped for MC with their process technology and point of sales effectiveness. On average, they have a more profound insight in the user needs and some of these companies were established and are being led by users-innovators. In this group, we find mainly products which are performing functionally better when they fit better, like sportswear. However there is also a group of products which are not perceived as being highly user-centric but which are produced  with  highly performing technology allowing small lot sizes, avoiding large stocks and waste, e.g. in the interior textile business. The hybrid group has not made a final choice for MC yet, and this is observed in many business elements: the culture and employer's mind-set is not equally committed to personalization as it is the case for the MC natives. The business processes, partners and supporting software are not designed for MC, they need to be adapted for it and evolve.

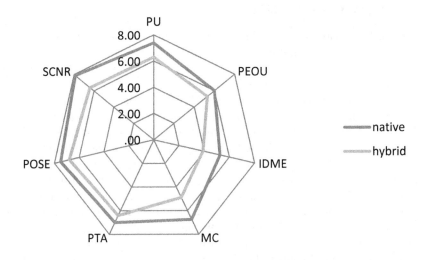

**Fig. 1.** Mass customization natives versus hybrids in terms of key value dimensions

## 5.2    Optimal Degree of Customization Is Key

We also observed that the degree of customization is a crucial decision to be made by the company. It determines the balance between fulfilling user needs and costs. Once it is fixed, it determines nearly all other performance dimensions of the mass customization business model in the company. It also has a certain effect on the PU of competitor's products as it influences the customer expectations towards customization levels of products and services.

In the confection industry, we still observe a certain resistance to maximize personalization. Mainstream customers are not yet massively prepared to share their detailed biometric data from 3D scanning technology in order to obtain better fitting apparel and save time on shopping. On the other hand, e.g. cyclists and other professional athletes do appreciate the additional functionality and are very much willing to go through a personalization process and accept the higher costs involved. The same elevated PU is sensed by mainstream customers in for instance the bedding industry: a highly effective POS, including for instance an "experience module" in the store and additional expert advice, succeeds in creating a much higher willingness to pay for the customized products.

An uncontrollable and quite unpredictable dimension is the IDME. If it is present, it can have a huge impact on willingness to pay. However, it is a factor which seems very hard to initiate or promote. It is likely to be triggered by hypes or trends but we have no evidence hereof yet.

## 5.3     Application of the Model

Additionally to natives and hybrids, some interesting clusters can be delineated where companies can use the information in a peer based setting. A more advanced use of the results is where the assessment leads to a gap analysis with subsequent roadmap construction. The assessment of less controllable pull factors, such as PU and IDME and less controllable cost factors such as PTA (based on state of the art technology) give insight in a theoretical opportunity of a customization. When a certain degree of MC is fixed, it allows to design possible business models with directions for the approach of the customer (PEOU) and the Supply Chain (SCNR, POSE and also PTA) We relate this to the seminal article of Fisher [4], posting that there is a right supply chain for every product. This boils down to the distinction between efficient versus responsive supply chains, serving functional and innovative products respectively. In this way we intend to give additional insight to the textile industry and help them to setup plans to go into the direction of mass customization as a path towards rejuvenation of a suffering industry. We experienced that the representation of the business model building blocks using the business model canvas [7] facilitates company insights in the transition path. We also experienced that introducing sustainability, in the broad sense, and implementing it in decision making, is still a very tough issue.

# 6     Conclusions and Further Research

In short, if we trace back to our research questions posted earlier, we can conclude that:

Mass customization is a viable business model for the Flemish textile industry

The integration of product, process and supply chain design is a way to materialize mass customization.

Future research challenges include the quest for more refined metrics and data collection methods, the inclusion of more companies in to the database and the development of an adequate visualization for better insight and decision making.

**Aknowledgments.** This research is based on a data which was gathered through the technological innovation supporting programme of the Flemish government "Mass customization for the Textile industry" (2012-2014, IWT095011).

# References

1. Anderson, C.: The Long Tail: Why the future of business is selling less of more. Hyperion (2008)
2. Da Silveira, G., Borenstein, D., Fogliatto, F.: Mass customization: Literature review and research directions. International Journal of Production Economics 72, 1–13 (2001)
3. Davis, S.: From future perfect: Mass customizing. Planning Review 17(2), 16–21 (1989)

4. Fisher, M.: What is the Right Supply Chain for your Product. Harvard Business Review, 105–116 (1997)
5. Franke, N., Schreier, M., Kaiser, U.: The "I Designed It Myself" Effect in Mass Customization. Management Science 56, 125–140 (2010)
6. Kaplan, A.M., Schoder, D., Haenlein, M.: Factors influencing the Adoption of Mass Customization: The Impact of Base Category Consumption Frequency and Need Satisfaction. Journal of Product Innovation Management 24, 101–116 (2007)
7. Osterwalder, A., Pigneur, Y.: Business Model Generation. Self Published, Amsterdam (2009), http://www.businesmodelgeneration.com
8. Piller, F.T., Tseng, M.M.: Handbook of Research in Mass Customization and Personalization. World Scientific Publishing Co., Singapore (2010)
9. Schwartz, B.: The paradox of choice: why more is less. HarperCollins (2005)
10. Zipkin, P.H.: The Limits of Mass Customization. MIT Sloan Management Review 42(3), 81–87 (2001)

# Development of a Business Process Matrix
# for Structuring the Implications of Using Configurators
# in an Engineer-To-Order Environment

Olga Willner[*], Manuel Rippel, Matthias Wandfluh, and Paul Schönsleben

ETH Zurich, BWI Center for Industrial Management, Zurich, Switzerland
owillner@ethz.ch

**Abstract.** A methodological application of mass customization principles in engineer-to-order (ETO) processes is expected to lead to shorter lead times, increased quality as well as cost reductions. Product and process configurators, commonly used in mass customization processes, have to be adjusted according to ETO product and process requirements for their successful application in an ETO environment. In this paper the organizational requirements for a successful adaption of configurators to ETO processes are identified and structured. A Business Process Matrix capable of categorizing the implications of using product and process configurators in an ETO environment is developed.

**Keywords:** Engineer-To-Order, Customization, Product Configurator, Business Process, Value Chain.

## 1 Introduction

The publication "From Future Perfect" by Stan Davis in 1987 brought about the advent of mass customization. Mass customization was defined as the capability to produce a wide range of product variants close to mass production prices through flexible and agile processes [1]. Pine [2] operationalized the concept for broad practical application through identifying the core technical enablers for mass customization such as a modular product design or the application of advanced manufacturing and information technologies. At present, in a vast number of industries mass customization production processes can be taken for granted [3]. A technical as well as organizational realization of a broad range of variants is well advanced and solidly based on standardized processes. In particular, a deployment of product and process configurators contributes substantially to ensure efficient and standardized business processes in a mass customization environment [4].

Recent academic research in the field of mass customization almost exclusively focuses on the transition from being a mass producer to becoming a mass customizer. The transition in the opposite direction, the move from being an engineer-to-order (ETO) company to becoming a mass customizer is often neglected [5]. ETO

---

[*] Corresponding author.

C. Emmanouilidis, M. Taisch, D. Kiritsis (Eds.): APMS 2012, Part I, IFIP AICT 397, pp. 278–285, 2013.

companies are defined as companies delivering products which are engineered or optionally reengineered according to the specific requirements of a customer [6]. ETO business processes can be characterized to be highly order specific, knowledge-intensive and of high complexity [7]. A methodological application of mass customization principles in ETO processes is expected to lead to shorter lead times, increased quality as well as cost reductions.

Product and process configurators, commonly used in mass customization processes, have to be adjusted according to ETO product and process requirements for their successful application in an ETO environment. Product structures as well as organizational processes may have to be aligned to novel conditions. A deployment of configurators, originally designed for mass customization purposes, in an ETO environment has a multitude of implications on the business processes along the value chain. The objective of this paper is to develop a Business Process Matrix for categorizing the implications of using configurator solutions in an engineer-to-order environment. This is expected to lead to a structured overview of the most relevant action fields for the implementation of an efficient ETO process along the value chain.

## 2    Research Methodology

The presented results are based on literature analysis and face-to-face interviews. First, literature research was carried out. Academic papers with the words "Engineer-To-Order", "Design-To-Order", or "Mass Customization" used in conjunction with "Product Configurator", "Product Structure" or "Processes" in title, key words or abstract were collected and reviewed. Second, interviews with decision-makers of six Swiss-based production companies from various manufacturing sectors (e.g. production equipment, elevators, pumps) were conducted. To produce robust results, representatives of small and medium enterprises (SMEs) as well as large enterprises were interviewed. The investigated companies varied in maturity levels regarding the deployment of product configurators in ETO processes. The interviews centered on the current state of integrating configurator solutions in ETO processes; both product structure and organizational issues were discussed in detail.

## 3    Results

In the following, a Business Process Matrix for identifying and structuring the organizational implications of using product and process configurators in an engineer-to-order environment is developed. First, the structural setup of the matrix is determined. Then, the core enablers for a successful application of configurators in ETO processes are introduced. Finally, the content of the matrix is derived from literature research and interviews conducted.

## 3.1    Derivation of Business Process Matrix

The solution space of the Business Process Matrix is spanned by a horizontal axis, depicting the business processes, and by a vertical axis, depicting the functional areas of a business organization. Business processes are defined as "a set of logically related tasks or activities performed to achieve a defined business outcome" [8]. In this Business Process Matrix the ETO business processes "Sales", "Design" "Make" and "After Sales" are applied on the horizontal axis [7, 9]. Functional areas are the basis for a functional organizational structure [8]. For this Business Process Matrix the functional areas "Marketing & Sales", "Procurement", "Engineering" and "Production and Logistics" have been identified as being significantly involved in ETO processes. The objective of this matrix is to depict (a) how the tasks along the ETO business process chain are divided between the different functional areas; (b) which information in the form of data is required by whom; (c) which software tools are the enablers for sharing the required information; and (d) which benefits for the business process are achieved through the use of a configurator. To achieve this, the categories "Tasks", "Input data", "Software tools" and "Benefits of configurator" are discussed within the fields of the matrix. The varying impact of the application of configurator solutions on the individual matrix fields is depicted by a color gradation.

## 3.2    Enablers for Configurators in ETO Processes

In this section the core enablers for an application of product and process configurators in ETO processes are introduced and illustrated.

### Product Modeling
An essential prerequisite for an efficient application of configurator solutions in an ETO environment is the description of product structures in product family models. Product structures can be modeled by the application of adaptive or generative methods. In case of an adaptive approach, a suitable parent version is determined from the existing variants to then be adapted to the requirements of the new variant by either developing plus/minus bill of materials (BOM) and operational routings or including dummy positions in product structure templates [9]. A modeling of product structures based on a generative approach takes place through a rule-based configuration of product variants. The definition of new product variants is achieved by the change of parameter values, expressing rules and constraints, that exist in a product configurator [9]. The development of a product family logic, based on modularity and hierarchy principles, contributes to an increased reuse of parts [9, 10]. The definition of a stringent product family logic provides the backbone for leveraging the full benefit of a configurator solution.

### Integrated Information Technologies
Information technologies (IT) are one of the core enablers of mass customization [11], and even more so of engineer-to-order processes. A diverse range of software products is required for an effective management of ETO business processes, e.g. the

sales and after sales phases are often backed up by Customer Relationship Management (CRM) software, the design phase by Computer Aided Design (CAD) systems, the make phase by Enterprise Resource Planning (ERP) systems, Computer Aided Manufacturing (CAM) systems and Manufacturing Execution Systems (MES) [12], and Product Data Management (PDM) and Product Lifecycle Management (PLM) provide support through the complete business process chain [13].

In configurator solutions (here consisting of the modules "sales configurator", "product configurator" and "process configurator") a variety of functionalities are embedded which support different phases of ETO business processes. In the sales phase, the application of a sales configurator supports the generation of valid offer documents. This includes the conversion of customer requirements into commercial specifications (parameterized definition of sales configuration). To be of further use in the design and make phase, commercial specifications have to be converted into technical (dimensioned commercial specifications) and production (including bill of materials and operational routings) specifications, as required by CAD and ERP systems [4]. Whereas the main output of the product configurator is the generation of BOMs based on parameterized product structures, the process configurator provides the appropriate process plans and operational routings.

Applying configurators as stand-alone solutions does not provide a considerable added value. An integration of configurator solutions into the existing IT landscape is crucial to enable an automation of processes, a close collaboration between departments and a proficient exchange of data.

## 3.3    Business Process Matrix

The Business Process Matrix provides a structured approach for decoding the interrelations between business processes and functional areas caused by the deployment of configurators in ETO processes. The matrix is designed with a practical application in mind. In the following, the principal requirements of the different ETO business processes on the configurator solution are described:

### Sales
A potential customer order in the ETO segment is often initiated by an invitation to tender [7]. The generation of a valid offer document, including mapping of customer requirements, definition of commercial characteristics as well as quotation of prices and lead times, is the general objective within the tender stage. Since the success rate for winning a tender is a mere 30% in the ETO sector, fast and cost-efficient processes are required during the tender stage [14]. Therefore, the Marketing & Sales department, usually the interface to the customer during the entire business process chain, has to collaborate closely with various functional areas, e.g. estimated prices and lead times have to be provided by Procurement and Production, the conceptual design has to be developed by Design, the feasibility of the proposed product has to be verified by Production & Logistics.

The integrated application of a configurator solution is disposed to support the collaboration on a technical as well as organizational level. First, a parameterized definition of commercial as well as technical specifications becomes feasible through its deployment. Second, rule-based feasibility and validity checks can be automatized leading to shorter process times and a prevention of manual errors. Third, historical project data systemized and structured by the configurator solution can be consulted for reference.

**Design**

In the ETO segment, products are designed or altered according to order-specific requirements. This tasks reaches from the development of a conceptual design and selection of major components and systems [7] to the concise definition of BOMs and operational routings. On the way, feasibility checks and evaluation of consequences of redesign on functionality and prices might have to be performed.

The application of a configurator solution, backed up by a stringent product family logic can contribute to a systemic reuse of standard and pre-defined components [9, 10]. An increased reuse of parts and components is beneficial for both consistency of business processes and workload of functional areas, e.g. the feasibility of standardized price calculations increases, BOMs and operational routings for subassemblies can be reused, fewer inventories to achieve the same service level required.

**Make**

Production processes in the ETO sector are often highly unpredictable and of low controllability [14, 15]. Bertrand [15] characterizes the ETO market situation as dynamic (strong fluctuations in mix and sales volume in shot and medium term), uncertain (unknown product parts, uncertain lead times, prices and capacities, process uncertainties) and complex (multi-project character of the situation, complex capacity situation). On the other hand, ERP systems are designed to only support production of a limited number of product variants [16, 17] and presume BOMs and operational routings to be static and accurate during production.

A rule-based and consistent preparation of product and process data with the aid of the configurator solutions contributes to a generation of BOMs and operational routings easier processable by ERP systems. Consequently, a preparation of product and process data with the aid of the configurator solutions contributes substantially to process standardization, reduction in errors and decrease in complexity.

**After Sales**

In many markets, after sales is a business process elementary for success [7]. For the provisioning of a proficient after sales service, it is indispensable to know which parts are installed in specific machineries and to have quick access to the right spare parts. Product knowledge aggregated in configurator solutions should therefore be made available to software used in after sales service (e.g. CRM, PDM, PLM systems). Also knowledge relating to operations and maintenance should be fed back from After Sales to Engineering to be used for future improvements [7].

| Functions | Business Processes | | | |
|---|---|---|---|---|
| | **Sales** | **Design** | **Make** | **After Sales** |
| **Marketing & Sales** | *Tasks*: generation of a valid offer document (includes mapping of customer requirements, definition of commercial specifications, quotation of prices and lead times). *Input data*: customer requirements. *Software tools*: sales configurator, CRM software. *Benefits of configurator*: parameterized definition of sales configuration, accessibility of systemized historical project data, partly automated cost calculations. | | | *Tasks*: configuration of services packages, negotiation of service level agreements. *Input data*: customer requirements. *Software tools*: CRM software, PDM system, PLM system. *Benefits of configurator*: accessibility of systemized historical project data. |
| **Procurement** | *Tasks*: estimation of prices and lead times, preliminary selection of subcontractors and suppliers. *Input data*: commercial specifications, supplier data, historical project data. *Software tools*: product configurator, procurement software. *Benefits of configurator*: accessibility of systemized historical project data. | *Tasks*: selection of subcontractors and suppliers, transfer of specifications to suppliers, negotiations on prices and lead times with suppliers. *Input data*: BOMs (preliminary), CAD drawings (preliminary). *Software tools*: product configurator, procurement software. *Benefits of configurator*: automated providing of product and performance specifications to suppliers. | *Tasks*: validation of purchased parts (correct ETO design, correct amount, on time) → supplier evaluation. *Input data*: goods receipt notes, feedback from production. *Software tools*: procurement software, ERP system. *Benefits of configurator*: - | *Tasks*: procurement of spare parts, negotiations on prices and lead times with spare parts suppliers. *Input data*: customer requirements, BOMs. *Software tools*: PDM system, PLM system. *Benefits of configurator*: preparation of historic project data for PDM and PLM systems. |
| **Engineering** | *Tasks*: preliminary development of conceptual design, feasibility check and evaluation of consequences of redesign on functionality and prices, conversion of commercial specifications into technical specifications (preliminary). *Input data*: commercial specifications. *Software tools*: product configurator, CAD system. *Benefits of configurator*: rule-based automation of validity checks, automated generation of BOMs and CAD drawings, parameterized definition of technical specifications, accessibility of systemized historical project data. | *Tasks*: development of conceptual design, feasibility check and evaluation of consequences of redesign on functionality and prices, conversion of commercial specifications into technical specifications. *Input data*: commercial specifications, preliminary technical specifications. *Software tools*: product configurator, CAD system. *Benefits of configurator*: accessibility of systemized historical project data, rule-based automation of validity checks, automated generation of BOMs and CAD drawings, systematic reuse of standard and pre-defined components. | *Tasks*: final design changes. *Input data*: CAD drawings, BOMs. *Software tools*: product configurator, CAD system. *Benefits of configurator*: automated adaption of BOMs and drawings. | *Tasks*: recording of feedback relating to operations and maintenance for future improvements (e.g. Design for Maintainability). *Input Data*: customer feedback. *Software tools*: product configurator, PDM system, PLM system. *Benefits of configurator*: accessibility of systemized historical project data. |
| **Production & Logistics** | *Tasks*: feasibility check (preliminary), capacity check (preliminary), estimation of lead times. *Input data*: technical specifications (preliminary), BOMs (preliminary), CAD drawings (preliminary). *Software tools*: process configurator, ERP system, CAM system, MES. *Benefits of configurator*: support of feasibility and capacity check (based on rules as well as information from previous projects). | *Tasks*: final feasibility check, final capacity check, operational routings (preliminary). *Input data*: technical specifications, BOMs, CAD drawings, operational routings (preliminary). *Software tools*: process configurator, ERP system, CAM system, MES. *Benefits of configurator*: support of feasibility and capacity check (based on rules and consistent preparation of product and process data). | *Tasks*: component manufacturing, assembly, inventory management, operational routings. *Input data*: BOMs, CAD drawings, operational routings. *Software tools*: process configurator, ERP system, CAM system, MES. *Benefits of configurator*: rule-based and consistent preparation of product and process data. | *Tasks*: production of spare parts, spare parts inventory management. *Input data*: BOMs, CAD drawings, operational routings. *Software tools*: ERP system, MES. *Benefits of configurator*: - |

□ low benefits  ▨ average benefits  ▪ high benefits

**Fig. 1.** Business Process Matrix

### 3.4    Implications

The structural deduction of the matrix and its contents illustrate that the Business Process Matrix developed in this chapter is suitable for structuring and contextualizing the organizational adjustments required for the implementation of configurators. Hence, the matrix can be understood as methodological reference in the context of adjusting organizational structures for the successful adaption of configurators to an ETO setting. The matrix depicts that a multitude of fields of action have to be considered when introducing product and process configurators to an ETO environment.

A concise specification of parameterized product structures and, possibly, modular component families is obligatory for the set-up of a fast and efficient product configuration process suitable for ETO products. Furthermore, the selected configuration system has to be fully integrated in the present IT infrastructure and interfaces to existing IT solutions (e.g. CAD, ERP, PLM systems) along the business process chain have to be provided. In this context, a common logic for the conversion and enrichment of data along the dimensions commercial, technical and production characteristics has to be determined. And above all, a close collaboration between all functional areas along the business process chain has to be ensured. Without doubt, an integrated setup of IT systems can contribute considerably to the design of fast and efficient ETO processes. However, due to the immense complexity and low predictability of ETO processes this alone is not sufficient. Only through a company-wide, or even preferable along the whole supply chain, incorporation of skills such as an integrated knowledge management, intercultural competencies and a comprehensive technical-organizational understanding the creation of a competitive ETO process becomes feasible.

## 4    Conclusion

The literature analysis and interviews conducted reveal that a standardized application of configurators in ETO processes still provides a multitude of organizational and technical challenges. This paper contributes to the development and dissemination of a methodology suitable for identifying and structuring the organizational challenges resulting from the deployment of configurators in an ETO environment. A Business Process Matrix for categorizing the implications of using product and process configurators in an engineer-to-order environment is devised. The matrix highlights the most relevant action fields for the implementation of an efficient ETO process along the value chain. Both literature analysis as well as input from practitioners contributed to the design of the Business Process Matrix.

In future research, the authors intend to test and strengthen the Business Process Matrix in practical use cases in various manufacturing companies. This case-based approach is expected to reinforce the practical relevance of the model developed in this paper. The insights gained from the use cases will be applied to refine the Business Process Matrix at hand.

# References

1. Davis, S.M.: Future perfect. Addison-Wesley, Reading (1987)
2. Pine, B.J.: Mass customization the new frontier in business competition. Harvard Business School Press, Boston (1993)
3. Piller, F.T., Moeslein, K., Stotko, C.M.: Does mass customization pay? An economic approach to evaluate customer integration. Prod. Plan. Control 15, 435–444 (2004)
4. Forza, C., Salvador, F.: Managing for variety in the order acquisition and fulfilment process: The contribution of product configuration systems. International Journal of Production Economics 76, 87–98 (2002)
5. Haug, A., Ladeby, K., Edwards, K.: From engineer-to-order to mass customization. Management Research News 32, 633–644 (2009)
6. Caron, F., Fiore, A.: 'Engineer to order' companies: how to integrate manufacturing and innovative processes. International Journal of Project Management 13, 313–319 (1995)
7. Hicks, C., McGovern, T.: Product life cycle management in engineer-to-order industries. Int. J. Technol. Manage. 48, 153–167 (2009)
8. APICS: Dictionary 13th Edition. APICS - The Association for Operations Management, Chicago, IL (2010)
9. Schönsleben, P.: Methods and tools that support a fast and efficient design-to-order process for parameterized product families. CIRP Annals - Manufacturing Technology (2012)
10. Brière-Côté, A., Rivest, L., Desrochers, A.: Adaptive generic product structure modelling for design reuse in engineer-to-order products. Computers in Industry 61, 53–65 (2010)
11. Piller, F.T.: Mass customization and SAP R/3TM - business solutions like SAP R/3 as an enabler of mass customization. Working Paper, University of Wuerzburg, Germany (1997)
12. Flynn, B.B., Sakakibara, S., Schroeder, R.G., Bates, K.A., Flynn, E.J.: Empirical research methods in operations management. Journal of Operations Management 9, 250–284 (1990)
13. Warschat, J.: Enabling IT for mass customization: the IT architecture to support an extended enterprise offering mass-customized products. International J. Mass Customisation 1, 394–401 (2006)
14. Konijnendijk, P.A.: Coordinating marketing and manufacturing in ETO companies. International Journal of Production Economics 37, 19–26 (1994)
15. Bertrand: Production control in engineer-to-order firms. International Journal of Production Economics 3, 3–22 (1993)
16. Aslan, B., Stevenson, M., Hendry, L.C.: Enterprise Resource Planning systems: An assessment of applicability to Make-To-Order companies. Computers in Industry 63, 692–705 (2012)
17. Van Veen, E.A.: New developments in generative BOM processing systems. Prod. Plan. Control 3, 327–335 (1992)

# Designing Rotationally Symmetric Products for Multi-variant Mass Production by Using Production-Technical Solution Space

Guenther Schuh, Till Potente, Christina Thomas, and Stephan Schmitz

Laboratory for Machine Tools and Production Engineering at Aachen University
Steinbachstrasse 19, 52074 Aachen, Germany
{g.schuh,t.potente,c.thomas,st.schmitz}@wzl.rwth-aachen.de

**Abstract.** Highly customized products have led to an irreproducible complexity in product development and order processing process. Today's product design and IT-tools reduce this complexity insufficiently and potentials in administration and manufacturing are not fully lapped. The approach presented in this paper starts the development of a product structure at the manufacturing environment. The aim is to develop a product structure for rotational products that is adapted for manufacturing processes and therefore enabling a cost-effective production. As a result, companies are able to provide their customers with individual product solutions using standardized processes. This enables a technological and production-related flexibility to fulfill growing needs of global markets.

**Keywords:** production-oriented design, product development process, constituent product features, constituent process characteristics, order processing process.

## 1    Introduction

Engineering, process planning and mechanical manufacturing of single and small series manufacturer are facing a high variance of products, labile batch sizes and customer requirements today. Especially companies in the machinery and plant engineering industry producing powertrain and transmission technology are faced with highly individual customer requirements within rotational symmetric products. The companies challenge is to develop competitive products at cost-effective conditions based on existing production processes and products. The aim of this paper is to present an approach, which identifies constituent process features in manufacturing and matches it to the product features. These constituent process features are derived from critical process characteristics. Combined with the constituent product features they are used to establish product development guidelines. The solution is a basis for realizing a cost-effective product design and stable manufacturing.

C. Emmanouilidis, M. Taisch, D. Kiritsis (Eds.): APMS 2012, Part I, IFIP AICT 397, pp. 286–293, 2013.
© IFIP International Federation for Information Processing 2013

# 2 Complexity and Interface Problems in Order Fulfillment and Product Development Process

## 2.1 Technical Challenge Due to Product Complexity

Structural marginally different individual product components - with up to 1000 variations - lead to a high product and process diversity, causing huge fluctuations at the assignment of operation facilities. Figure 1 shows the analysis of process variance regarding the processing time. WZL (Werkzeugmaschinenlabor – Laboratory for Machine Tools and Production Engineering) Industry cases show companies which have more than 90.000 components and over 35.000 products in their portfolio [1]. Even if there are similarities at the product components, cost savings within the product development process and a cost-effective order processing process is not realized. The technical challenge is that due to the complexity and the lack of an evaluation engineers do not have the possibility to systematically chose a more cost-effective and production-oriented constructive solution. The expense and cost influence of the process characteristics in manufacturing because of customized product features is not obvious to the engineer within the design phase.

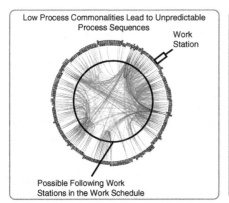
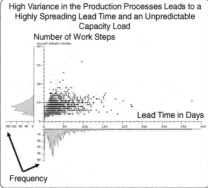

**Fig. 1.** Process Commonalities and Spread of Lead Time of a Production System (Source: WZL RWTH industry cases)

## 2.2 Interfaces and Semantic Problems in Product Development and Order Processing Process as Research Question

In the order processing product engineers, process engineers and manufacturer have different information and views on the product [2]. The high level of division of labor in the industry led to a partition of planning, executing and controlling functions and finally to a very sequential working method, which is mostly based on expert knowledge [1]. The research challenge is about a common understanding of designing product features and their impact on planning and manufacturing. The semantic is actually not able to link engineers knowledge with the needs and requirements of production engineers and manufacturer. Engineers, production engineers and manufacturer all together do not have a common understanding of the product features and the process characteristics because it is insufficiently defined which properties fully describe a rotational symmetric product in their single view.

### 2.3    Not Realized Potential in the Product Development and Order Processing Process

In single and small series manufacturing of machinery and plant engineering, shop fabrication is the dominant manufacturing principle. A various number, often more than 100 different resources, especially the mechanical fabrication such as turning, drilling and milling, is at disposal for the product creation [3]. The increased product-complexity and partly nominal varying product features lead to a high amount of planning and coordinating activities within the order fulfillment process. This results in strewing machining times and total process times within the manufacturing process. Potential analysis and valuations by the industry clarify, that a reduction of product construction by 11%, planning duration by 30% and cutting of the processing time in mechanical manufacturing by 60% [4], are possible saving potentials. This potential demonstrates the industrial relevance of the addressed problem.

## 3      State of the Art in Product Development and Supporting the Order Processing Process

### 3.1    Deficits in Existing Approaches in Product Design

Existing product design methods start at the market needs and do not or not sufficiently consider manufacturing process needs and their influence on the product development.

- Most existing approaches stay on a very functional level in describing product development processes. For designing more cost-effective and innovative products mostly platform and modularity of product architecture approaches are used. Existing approaches disregard the needs of manufacturing and production processes [5-12].
- Market-driven approaches develop methods to design product families and architectures. Concerning market needs and the product communality these approaches aim at profitable product platform regarding manufacturing and redesign costs. Nevertheless these methods do not consider the impact of product features on process features. [13,14]
- The approach of technology push bases the product design on the existing technologies within a company. Generally these approaches are on a more strategic level and do not give detailed solutions to design a product using the production-technical solution space. [15,16]
- Another approach integrates the different company divisions systematically in the platform development process. This method focusses on variance sensitive

manufacturing processes to derive constituent product features for the product design. Nevertheless this method is not specific enough to state definite process features and their influence on product design.[17,18]

## 3.2 Deficits in Supporting Engineering and Development and Industrial Engineering

To support the product development process and the order fulfillment process there are a lot of IT-Tools, such as ERP-, PDM- and CAx-systems [19-21]. It can be stated that there is a certain discharge of routine jobs through the use of current IT-support within the order procedure process. Although single IT-solutions work fairly well, today's IT-support with its interface problems amplify isolated applications and a solid structure of company's divisions [2, 22]. Important information about product design and its impact on the process chain in manufacturing are not sufficient presented by these tools. For example product design is supported by using CAD-systems, which are also used to create drawings for manufacturing. Nevertheless these drawings are not synchronized with the needs of manufacturing. After all important manufacturing information is not included in CAD-systems.

## 3.3 Deficits of Existing Approaches to Control the Complexity within the Product Development Process

Existing methods of product design and IT-systems do not support the product development and order processing processes in that way, that the stated potentials (see chapter 2.3). Critical process characteristics are not systematically detected and linked to product features yet. The reason for that is a very large number of different process parameters and their interaction. It is necessary to identify the main process characteristics e.g. diameter of components, machine tools, which have the greatest impact on administrative expenses and cost-effectiveness in manufacturing. Quantifying the influence of changing product features at the process chain in manufacturing is a perquisite to set product design guidelines for engineers.

# 4 Using Production-Technical Solution Space to Design a Product Structure

As one can see existing tools increase division's product and process knowledge in the product development process insufficiently. Therefore the actual challenge is not to design another supporting tool rather than to develop an approach, which increases a holistic understanding of the process chain. This holistic approach requires cybernetic models with emergent properties. Hence complexity in product design and order processing process is no longer controllable; the problem has to be reduced on a complexity level, where the main challenges still exist. By choosing a focus on the problem's complexity the technical challenge (see chapter 2.1) is addressed.

The approach presented in this paper starts the development of a product structure at the manufacturing environment. Therefore challenges in manufacturing processes first have to be solved so they are working stable and reliable. A product structure is the key to handling product complexity, whereas it can be treated on three levels: the product range level, product level and component level [10]. The understanding of the manufacturing processes and their link to product features helps to avoid complexity within the product design and order processing process. The cost and expense influence in manufacturing of a product feature has to be considered when designing a product. For example a variation of a product feature that causes a high cost impact because of different processes in the production should have a rather small range of variance [5]. This effect is called the variance sensitiveness and is a degree for the cost impact of a process in dependency of the product feature variance. The degree of variance sensitiveness is high if additional features lead to a high increase of process costs [23].

The presented approach will be used for the identification and detection of these process characteristics and their connection on the product features. The approach is divided in the following steps:

1. A target system for the product design has to be defined. Possible target systems can be product flexibility, increasing product economic efficiency or a higher degree of standardization.
2. A product range within an existing product program has to be chosen for the starting phase. This simplification limits the solution space and therefore reduces the necessary complexity.
3. The process chain of the selected products in manufacturing has to be analyzed. As a result main process chains are identified in production.
4. Within the main process chain a stable working process chain has to be selected. This process chain has to be able to manufacture a significant part of a product range and be insusceptible to changing process requirements due to varying products. The selected process chain is the basis for standardized manufacturing processes, which is characterized by short throughput times and leveled process times [24].
5. The selected process chain is used to identify the product components that are produced on this selected process chain by analyzing the corresponding working schedules.
6. A CAD-model based comparison of the selected components and the overall product components of the product program is used to determine further product components that can be produced on this process chain. The CAD-model comparison is supported by a knowledge based classification system for product data [25].
7. The overall received products are used to identify those product features, which make the products producible on the selected process chain. These product features have to be directly linked to the critical process characteristics. This step creates the connection between product and process feature which leads to the constituent product and process features.
8. Deriving design rules for a product structure that can be manufactured on a stable process chain.

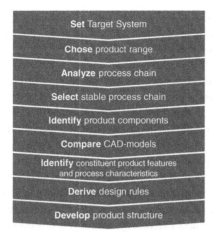

**Fig. 2.** Sequences of the presented approach

9. Consolidation of customer and market needs and design guidelines to develop a product structure which is based on a production-technical solution space.

The common understanding from engineers, production engineers and manufacturer of the dependency of product and process is the prerequisite to solve the research challenge. The aim is to develop a product structure for rotational products that is adapted for manufacturing processes and therefore enabling a cost-effective production. The presented method identifies product features that have a large impact on production costs by quantifying the expenses in manufacturing processes. The developed product structure has the aim to provide a maximum of product individuality by simultaneously standardize the manufacturing processes. After all the product development process is able to provide customized product solutions by using standardized and stabile processes. Elements of mass production such as in-line production are applied to the production of highly customized products. This puts companies into the position to design cost-effective products and production. A technological and production-related flexibility is important to fulfill the growing needs of global markets and to deal with the increased dynamic in the product development process as well as the supply chain within the order process. By applying this concept product and process know-how is constantly available from manufacturing to engineering and development. As a result employees got a persistent view on the product development process as they can now control the complexity of product features and process characteristics.

# 5    Conclusions and Outlook

The stated approach develops a product-structure that is aligned on the company's production. The technical challenge in dealing with product complexity is addressed by focusing on a definite process chain in manufacturing. The research challenge is addressed by the understanding of the link between process characteristics and product features. This is the basis to develop standardized processes in administration and stabile structures in manufacturing. Within the project "Design of innovative modular product platform and value added structures - GiBWert" (see www.gibwert.de), funded by the German Federal  Ministry of Education and Research (BMBF),  a method to systematically link product and process data will be implemented. The aim of this project is a constant product and process tracking system, which realizes complexity restrictions in the product development process. A fundamental part of the research project is to develop a method of detecting and evaluate the variance sensitivity of the production processes.

A validation is still going on at a small business of the machinery and plant engineering that is developing technical solutions for power train and transmission technologies. Process characteristics and product features are now to identify, to classify and to validate. Next exemplary products are used to identify their product features such as Diameter, bore holes, construction materials and surface qualities. After that proper process characteristics such as process times and tool insert have to be analyzed and then linked to the product features. The creation of a constituent product feature model existing of product features and process characteristics will be the next step.

**Acknowledgements.** The research and development project "Design of innovative modular product platforms and value added structures- GiBWert" is funded by the German Federal Ministry of Education and Research (BMBF) within the Framework Concept "Research for Tomorrow's Production" and managed by the Project Management Agency Karlsruhe (PTKA). The main research objective is to develop a product development process for modular product platforms and a holistic method to evaluate possible design scenarios. The author is responsible for the contents of this publication.

# References

1. Brecher, C.: Integrative Production Technology for High-Wage Countries. Springer, Berlin (2011)
2. Wiendahl, H.P.: Betriebsorganisation für Ingenieure, 7th edn. Hanser, München (2010)
3. Hahn, D., Laßmann, G.: Produktionswirtschaft – Controlling industrieller Produktion. Band 1 & 2: Grundlagen, Führung und Organisation, Produkte und Produktprogramm, Material und Dienstleistungen, Prozesse. Physica Verlag, Heidelberg (1999)
4. Schuh, G., Potente, T., Fuchs, S., Schmitz, S.: Wertstromorientierte Produktionssteuerung - Interaktive Visualisierung durch IT-tools zur Bewertung der Logistik- und Produktionsleistung. wt Werkstattstechnik Online Jg. 102, H. 4 (2012)
5. Cai, Y.L., Nee, A.Y.C., Lu, W.F.: Platform Differentiation Plan for Platform Leverage Across Market Niches. Annals of the CIRP 57(1), 141–144 (2008)
6. Farrell, R., Simpson, T.W.: Product platform design to improve commonality in custom products. Journal of Intelligent Manufacturing 14, 541–556 (2003)

7. Gao, F., Xiao, G., Simpson, T.W.: Module-scale-based Product Platform Planning Res. Eng. Des. 20(2), 129–141 (2009)
8. Lindemann, U., Maurer, M., Braun, T.: Structural Complexity Management - An Approach for the Field of Product Design. Springer, Berlin (2009)
9. Pimmler, T., Eppinger, S.: Integration Analysis of product decompositions. Massachusetts Institute of Technology, Cambridge (1994)
10. Ericsson, A., Erixon, G.: Controlling Design Variants: Modular Product Platforms, ASM, New York (1999)
11. Pahl, G., Beitz, W., Feldhusen, J., Grote, K.-H.: Konstruktionslehre, Grundlagen. Springer, Berlin (2007)
12. Kusiak, A., Huang, C.: Development of Modular Products. IEEE Transactions on Components, Packaging and Manufacturing Technology - Part A 19(4) (December 1996)
13. Kumar, D., Chen, W., Simpson, T.W.: A market-driven approach to product family design. International Journal of Production Research 47(1), 71–102 (2009)
14. Martin, M.V., Ishii, K.: Design for variety: developing standardized and modularized product platform architectures. Research in Engineering Design 13(4), 213–235 (2002)
15. Herstatt, C.: Management von technologiegetriebenen Entwicklungsprojekten, Hamburg (2000)
16. Köbler, J.: Modell einer wandlungsfähigen Organisation produzierender Unternehmen, Diss Univ. Stuttgart. Jost-Jetter Verlag, Heimsheim (2006)
17. Schuh, G., Arnoscht, J., Rudolf, S., Korthals, K.: Modular chassis product platform considering variable quantities for an economical electric vehicle production. WGP Konferenz, Berlin (2011)
18. Arnoscht, J.: Beherrschung von Komplexität bei der Gestaltung von Baukastensystemen, Diss. RWTH Aachen, Apprimus Verlag (2011)
19. Thome, R.: Business Software. ERP, SCM, APS, MES - was steckt hinter dem Begriffsdschungel der Business-Software-Lösungen. Lehrstuhl für BWL und Wirtschaftinformatik, Mainfränkisches Electronic Commerce Kompetenzzentrum, Würzburg (2007)
20. Schuh, G., Stich, V., Brosze, T., Fuchs, S., Pulz, C., Quick, J., Schürmeyer, M., Bauhoff, F. High Resolution Supply Chain Management - Optimised Processes based on Self-Optimizing Control Loops and Real Time Data. Production Engineering, Special Issue 1 (2011a)
21. Spur, G., Krause, F.: Das virtuelle Produkt. Management der CAD-Technik. Hanser, München (1997)
22. Beckert, B., Hudetz, W.: Stand und Potenzial produktnaher Datenverarbeitung. PPS Management 7(2), 35–39 (2002)
23. Schuh, G., Arnoscht, J., Bender, D., Bohl, A., Leiters, M., Pokraka, G., Rudolf, S., Schöning, S., Schulz, J., Vogels, T.: Lean Innovation mit Ähnlichkeitsmodellen, Aachen (2011)
24. Schuh, G., Potente, T., Fuchs, S., Thomas, C.: Interactive visualization in production control. In: 2011 17th International Conference on Concurent Enterprising, ICE (2011)
25. Weisskopf, J.: Automatische Produktdatenklassifikation in heterogenen Datenbeständen, Diss. Universität Karlsruhe (TH) (2002)

# Robotics in the Construction Industry: Mass Customization or Digital Crafting?

Ingrid Paoletti and Roberto Stefano Naboni

Politecnico di Milano, Building Environment Science & Technology, Milano, Italy
ingrid.paoletti@polimi.it, roberto.naboni@gmail.com

**Abstract.** The paper discusses the advancement in the mass-customization of building components referring to Robot-Assisted Manufacturing. It is presented how the contemporary employment of Robotics offers a perspective of flexible alternative to traditional serial production system. Different Robot-Assisted fabrication methods are discussed through built experimental case studies at different scales. It is finally argued how Robotic production in architecture is significantly shifting the approach in design towards a model including material and fabrication constraints.

**Keywords:** Mass-Customization, Digital Fabrication, Parametric Design, Robot-Assisted Manufacturing, Additive Production.

## 1 Component Customization in the Construction Industry

Typically construction methods in building industry are based on the principles of mass-production: standardization, modularization and production lines. Compared to other fields, construction industry has not been characterized by the process of evolution which invested most of the manufacturing industry over the last decades with the massive introduction of innovative technologies, such as CNC machines.

While the use of these tools has been introduced in architecture long time ago, they have not determined a productive paradigm shift. Indeed, buildings are in most of the cases assembled from sets of components which are gathered from catalogues provided by the industries.

Starting from the 90s with the introduction of digital tools, the architectural designer's needs increased dramatically in terms of form personalization. Due to the fact that architecture cannot be built in one piece, and requires the prefabrication of components, it is automatically determined the crucial importance of the discretization of complex shapes characterizing the typical design workflow, in which architects conceive buildings just in terms of shape, and later on are facing problems related to construction feasibility.

Within this scenario, robotic fabrication has recently been discovered in the construction industry, after pioneering researches in the early 80s. Architects are especially interested in the robot ability to perform different tasks and in their low price compared to other machines.

C. Emmanouilidis, M. Taisch, D. Kiritsis (Eds.): APMS 2012, Part I, IFIP AICT 397, pp. 294–300, 2013.
© IFIP International Federation for Information Processing 2013

## 2    Robotic Fabrication in Architecture. From Component Customization to Process Customization

Typically the customization of building components is reached through design post-adaptation, in order to fit industrial requirements. As a consequence of studies in the field of emerging technologies and bottom-up design the use of industrial robots has spread dynamically. Robots are multifunctional machines for mass-production, able to accomplish a wide range of works, but mainly used in the automotive industry where they usually do a single routine.

Robotic Fabrication in the construction field has by opposite the implicit advantage to be able of performing a multitude of tasks controlled from a common programming platform. With its employment, the logic of production and mass-customization can change radically for the construction field, shifting from specialized industrial media of production to versatile machine.

This has the potential to revolutionize the current understanding of mass-customization, moving the focus from geometrical post-optimization, to integration of robotic performance within the design process. The use of algorithms to control fabrication tools is natural extension of parametric modeling, helping the understanding of specific fabrication processes and in simulating the kinematics of the machine tool.

In the past few years, architectural faculties such as the ETH Zürich, TU Vienna, University of Stuttgart and the University of Michigan have acquired industrial robots and are actively researching the use of robots in architecture. Nowadays more than twenty architecture faculties in the world are experimenting in the use of industrial robots. However, this research is not limited to academia, with architectural offices like Snøhetta in Norway using robots in-house.

## 3    Parametrically Controlled Robots

The use of industrial robots would normally demand architects to migrate geometries from a CAD software to machines with a linear workflow, essentially converting geometries into working paths. This procedure is essentially transferring construction trajectories, and can be intended as limited in terms of interactions between design and production phases. This lack has recently been overcome by the development of new specific software tools, providing architects with an easier control from design environment to physical production and vice versa. The use of plug-ins such as KUKA PRC and Super KUKA for Grasshopper favors the integration into modeling environments of the dynamic of machines, simulating movements within the CAD space. Architects gained an increased capacity to control robots, and upcoming researches are moving in the direction of strengthening the interaction between design software and machines, in a full integration of the two systems. This paper proposes an overview on the different robotic fabrication procedures nowadays in development, proving how the flexibility of these machines enables architects to experiment a wide range of technical and aesthetic solutions.

# 4    Robotic Additive Fabrication

Additive Fabrication represents the typical construction method employed in architecture and this is the main reason for the recent deep investigation which has been conducted for 3D-Printing at large scale, such as the Italian technology D-Shape and the American-based Contour Crafting. Additive processes can generally offer a wider potential over already established subtractive or formative digital fabrication processes, and in the last years various attempts in this direction have been made using robotic tools.

## 4.1    Bricklaying Robotic Fabrication

A popular example of additive fabrication is the Bricklaying Robot (2006) by Gramazio and Kohler which provides the architects with the possibility to generate brick walls designed parametrically. This system uses Kuka KR150 Robotic Arms to deposit bricks in simple and articulated wall compositions, basically replacing the traditional construction process based on manual work. In this case the robotic fabrication is improving fabrication speed, precision and expanding the formal freedom of the aesthetics of the construction. This technique has been applied for the façade of the Gantenbein Vineyard. In future projection, the authors plan to install the robots directly on building sites, combining the advantages of prefabrication, such as precision and high quality, with the advantages of short transport routes and just-in-time production on the building site. Making use of computer methodologies in the design and fabrication process allows for manufacturing building elements with highly specific forms, which could not be built manually.

# 5    Robotic Transformative Procedures

## 5.1    RoboFold Technology for Metal Sheets

RoboFold is a patented method employed to form metal components with 6-axis industrial robots, especially referring to façade panels. The forming process is achieved by simultaneous work of robots folding sheet metal along curved crease lines, defined by project. The metal sheets are directly transformed by pressure applied on different directions, and no mold-tools are involved in the process. The system was invented by Gregory Epps in 2008, initially conceived for automotive industry and later transferred to construction field. The entire process is simulated in a CAD environment, this means that the design is performed with manufacturing constraints already taken into account since the design process.

Curve Folding is referring almost directly to the art of origami, paper engineering and industrial robot manufacturing. RoboFold uses Rhino3D software with the integration of Grasshopper parametric extension. Currently this system is developed through workshop and education system in various architectural faculties, and through the realization of façade mock-ups and furniture.

## 5.2   Cold Bending of Steel Rods

An alternative transformative technique has been developed by Supermanouvre in collaboration with Matter Design, in order to produce an installation called "Clouds of Venice", exposed in Venice Biennale of Architecture 2012.

This installation is composed by a sequence of bended steel rods, in combination with a custom robotically-assisted CNC bender has been constructed and tested as an alternative to dedicated CNC forming equipment. This combination allowed for the serial creation of accurately defined bends, intervals and rotations. The robot provides the positioning while the bender applies the large forces required.

The operation is based on the proper disposition of three clamps: a collet-gripper mounted on the robot and two die clamps on the bender. One die clamp is used to provide pressure during actual bending, while the other two clamps alternate holding the stock in order to allow the robot to feed and rotate it into the appropriate position. The clamps must be capable of providing enough pressure and friction to counteract the torque resulting from the self-weight of the cantilevering rod.

This fabrication method can be easily implemented for the production of complex steel structures and for more standard applications such as steel reinforced concrete, where the precision and speed of robots can speed up operations which typically require longer time on site.

# 6   Robot Subtractive Fabrication

## 6.1   Hot Wire Cutting Fabrication

A hotwire cutter consists of a thin wire that is heated via an electric current to approximately 200 degrees Celsius and used to cut polystyrene or similar types of thermoplastic foam. The foam vaporizes just ahead of the wire and a minimal energy is required to cut through the stock. The robot-mounted bow-type hotwire has a series of specific constraints that must be embedded within the control software. The primary constraint is speed, while the primary simulation feedback is the positioning of the bow of the tool. The kerf width is directly proportional to the speed, so control over motion is extremely important. The input geometry is most often described by an upper and lower curve, generating a ruled loft between curves, finally generating ruled surfaces. By utilizing 7 axes of the robot simultaneously, large parts can be machined in one step.

A built example of this procedure is The Periscope Tower by Brandon Clifford and Wes Mcgee of Matter Design Studio, a temporary installation designed for the Young Architects Forum Atlanta. For the production a hotwire cutter was mounted onto the robot, creating a multi-axis CNC hotwire-cutter capable of processing 4 meters long EPS blocks.

The designers sought a way to eliminate the excess waste beyond the efficiency of unit nesting, since the methods of fabrication produces no kerf waste and minimal waste which is 100% recyclable material. The fourteen meters height tower was assembled in only six hours.

# 7    Conclusion and Outlook

Despite the potential offered by digital fabrication with CNC machines, construction industry has rarely integrated innovative processes on a large scale, usually due to high costs products, machine low flexibility and time-related concerns. As consequence, complex shapes in architecture are often re-designed after project to fit the construction standard of particular machines. This paper shows an alternative to this typical workflow, focusing on how in the last years the development of robotic fabrication is consistently changing the production perspective towards a new professional paradigm where design software can be integrated with fabrication tools directly in the project.

Robots as universal and programmable machines offer a chance of highflexibility, and the analysis of the reported case studies highlights how the use of industrial robots move the attention from shape-oriented design, to material production system.

The use of robotic fabrication presents different advantages: flexible functionality, changing from a milling machine to a 3D-scanner just by switching its end-effectors; enlarged and geometrically customizable working space; affordable prices if compared with multi-axis Computer Numeric Control (CNC) machines.

This system has yet to compete with mass production and its associated economies of scale in fabricating widely distributed products, but they have already shown the potential to empower customized solutions. These devices can be tailored to local or personal needs in ways that are not practical or economical using mass production lines.

The actual use of robotics under the experiments of several pioneers highlights promising potential and results, but still without a clear vision on how these new tools can be implemented on industrial scale. Within an industrial perspective, the implicit risk of these experiments is to create a new design/fabrication niche, unable to determine an effective impact on the production systems.

In this sense the contemporary use of robotics is limited to the idea of advanced crafting, and the integration on wider scale seems currently hard to be achieved. The analyzed case studies open the idea of "robotic crafting", which could be further adapted to be performed within the context of the building site, more than as a media of industrial prefabrication. Within this scenario it appears fundamental the implementation of more accessible software, in order to be used by less specialized operators.

# References

1. Aigner, A., Brell-Cokcan, S.: Surface Structures and Robot Milling. The Impact of Curvilinear Structured Architectural Scale Models on Architectural Design and Production. In: Ingrid, P. (ed.) Innovative Design and Construction Technologies. Building complex shapes and beyond, pp. 433–445. Maggioli Editore, Milano (2009)
2. Bonwetsch, T., Gramazio, F., Kohler, M.: The informed wall, applying additive digital fabrication techniques on architecture. In: Proceedings of the 25th Annual Conference of the Association for Computer-Aided Design in Architecture, Louisville, pp. 489–495 (2006)
3. Johannes, B., Sigrid, B.-C.: Digital and Physical Computing for Industrial Robots in Architecture. Interfacing Arduino with industrial robots. In: Beyond Codes and Pixels: Proceedings of the 17th International Conference on Computer-Aided Architectural Design Research in Asia, Hong Kong, pp. 317–326 (2012)
4. Sigrid, B.-C., Johannes, B.: Computer Numeric Controlled Manufacturing for Freeform Surfaces in Architecture. In: Kuhlmann, D., Brell-Cokcan, S., Schinegger, K. (eds.) Emotion in Architecture, pp. 20–25. Institut fur Architekturwissenschaften, Wien (2011)
5. Sigrid, B.-C., Johannes, B.: Parametric Robot Control. Intergrated CAD/CAM for architectural design. In: ACADIA 2011: Integration through Computation. Proceedings of the 31st Annual Conference of the Association for Computer Aided Design in Architecture, Banff, pp. 242–251 (2011)
6. Sigrid, B.-C., Johannes, B.: A New Parametric Design Tool for Robot Miling. In: ACADIA 2010: LIFE in:formation, On Responsive Information and Variations in Architecture. Proceedings of the 30th Annual Conference of the Association for Computer Aided Design in Architecture, New York, pp. 357–363 (2010)
7. Sigrid, B.-C., Martin, R., Heinz, S., Johannes, B.: Digital Design to Digital Production. In: 27th eCAADe Conference Proceedings, Session 2009: Modes of Production, Istanbul, pp. 323–329 (2009)
8. Kaczynski Maciej, P., Wes, M., Dave, P.: Robotically Fabricated Thin-shell Vaulting. A method for the integration of multi-axis fabrication processes with algorithmic form-finding techniques. In: ACADIA 2011: Integration through Computation. Proceedings of the 31st Annual Conference of the Association for Computer Aided Design in Architecture, Banff, pp. 114–121 (2011)
9. Knaack, U., Bilow, M., Klein, T.: Rapids. Imagine 04. 010 Publishers, Rotterdam (2010)
10. Kolarevic, B. (ed.): Architecture in the Digital Age. Design and Manufacturing. Taylor & Francis, New York (2005)
11. David, K.O., Karola, D., Steffen, R., Tobias, S., Achim, M.: Performative Architectural Morphology. Robotically manufactured biomimetic finger-joined plate structures. In: 29th eCAADe Conference Proceedings. New Design Concepts and Strategies, Ljubljana, pp. 573–580 (2011)
12. Justin, L., Rachel, V., Yair, K.: Automated Folding of Sheet Metal Components with a Six-axis Industrial Robot. In: ACADIA 2011: Integration through Computation. Proceedings of the 31st Annual Conference of the Association for Computer Aided Design in Architecture, Banff, pp. 144–151 (2011)

13. Parke, M., Diana, T.: Robotic Rod-bending. Digital drawing in physical space. In: ACADIA 2011: Integration through Computation. Proceedings of the 31st Annual Conference of the Association for Computer Aided Design in Architecture, Banff, pp. 132–137 (2011)
14. Andrew, P.: A Five-axis Robotic Motion Controller for the Designers. In: ACADIA 2011: Integration through Computation. Proceedings of the 31st Annual Conference of the Association for Computer Aided Design in Architecture, Banff, pp. 162–169 (2011)
15. Dave, P., Wes, M.: Formation Embedded Design. A methodology for the integration of fabrication constraints into architectural design. In: ACADIA 2011: Integration through Computation. Proceedings of the 31st Annual Conference of the Association for Computer Aided Design in Architecture, Banff, pp. 122–131 (2011)

# Simulation-Based Design of Production Networks for Manufacturing of Personalised Products

Dimitris Mourtzis[*], Michalis Doukas, and Foivos Psarommatis

University of Patras, Lab for Manufacturing Systems and Automation (LMS), Patras, Greece
{mourtzis,mdoukas,psarof}@lms.mech.upatras.gr

**Abstract.** This paper presents a method for the design of manufacturing networks focused on the production of personalised goods. The method, which is implemented to a software tool, comprises of a mechanism for the generation and evaluation of manufacturing network alternative configurations. An exhaustive search and an intelligent search algorithm are used, for the identification of efficient configurations. Multiple conflicting user-defined criteria are used in the evaluation, including cost, time, $CO_2$ emissions, energy consumption and quality. Discrete Event Simulation models of manufacturing networks are simulated for the calculation of performance indicators of flexibility, throughput and work-in-process, and are used for assessing the performance of centralised and decentralised networks. The results obtained through the exhaustive and intelligent search methods are compared. The applicability of the method is tested on a real-life industrial pilot case utilising data from an automotive manufacturer.

**Keywords:** Simulation, Planning, Decentralisation, Personalisation.

## 1 Introduction and State of the Art

The market globalisation trend causes the decentralisation and internationalisation of supply chains and of manufacturing activities [1]. Increased outsourcing is realised by Original Equipment Manufacturers (OEMs) leading to the formation of strong cooperation bonds with their suppliers that have to be coordinated and aligned towards achieving common goals. Innovative production concepts replaced traditional network structures [2]. Moreover, customers demanded personalised products, available at low prices and high quality, at the right time [3]. The demand volatility calls for systems that efficiently deal with uncertainty in inventory planning [4]. Also, globalisation increased $CO_2$ emissions primarily due to production electricity generation methods used [5].

The need for designing and planning efficient manufacturing networks in today's landscape is evident [6]. Current approaches tackle the manufacturing network configuration problem using mathematical programming, bound computation, heuristics, meta-heuristics and sensitivity/stability analysis [7]. Computer simulation,

---

[*] Coressponding author.

C. Emmanouilidis, M. Taisch, D. Kiritsis (Eds.): APMS 2012, Part I, IFIP AICT 397, pp. 301–309, 2013.

nevertheless, has been indispensable for evaluating what-if scenarios for the design and planning problem of manufacturing networks. Discrete Event Simulation (DES) is a necessary tool in order to assess performance indices of dynamic system behaviour [8][9]. Many approaches have been proposed for dynamic manufacturing network management using simulation techniques. A continuous modelling approach for supply chain simulation was applied in the automotive industry and depicted that initial inventory levels and demand fluctuation can create delivery shortages and increased lead times [10]. A DES approach that included a decision-making mechanism was presented in [11]. However, it did not indicate the best configurations of the supply chain but was utilised for identifying potential solutions. A simulation approach that uses meta-heuristics was tested on a newspaper production and distribution problem. The applicability of the method however, was not validated through a real manufacturing problem [12]. The proposed approach in this paper includes a macroscopic investigation of the performance of manufacturing network measured in terms of flexibility, annual throughout and Work-in-Process (WIP) for the identification of efficient configurations for the manufacturing and transportation of personalised products. Concluding, the proven NP-hard problem of identifying efficient manufacturing network configurations [13] requires intelligent methods in combination with simulation [14].

The contribution of the suggested approach can be found in the following. The decision-making mechanism is tightly integrated with the simulation engine because the best alternative schemes that derive from the first comprise the input to the latter. Moreover, the Intelligent Search Algorithm (ISA) that uses three adjustable control parameters is presented and compared to an exhaustive method. ISA is an artificial intelligent search method that is utilised for identifying high quality solutions in a timely manner. ISA can be valuable in cases when exhaustive search is non-feasible due to the required computational effort introduced by the magnitude of the search space [7][15]. Additionally, centralised and decentralised manufacturing networks are compared regarding their performance under highly personalised product demand. Finally, the method is tested on a real-life industrial case utilising data from an automotive manufacturer.

## 2    Manufacturing Network and Product Modelling

The manufacturing network models under investigation consist of traditional centralised manufacturing network (CMN) structures, where assembly tasks can only be performed by the OEM at specific plants and decentralised manufacturing networks (DMN), where, a set of suppliers and dealers (partners) can perform personalisation tasks (e.g. application of the wrap cast carbon) (Fig. 1) [15].

The personalised product under investigation is a hood and a door of a commercial car. The personalisation options are the addition of a custom sticker, a personalised image and a cast carbon wrap. Fig. 2 contains the Bill of Materials (BoM), the Bill of Processes (BoP) and the different Levels of Personalisation (LoP) used in the experiments.

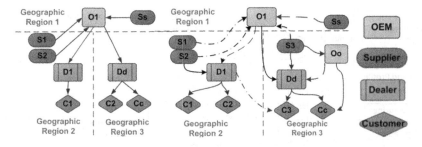

**Fig. 1.** Models of centralised and decentralised manufacturing networks [15]

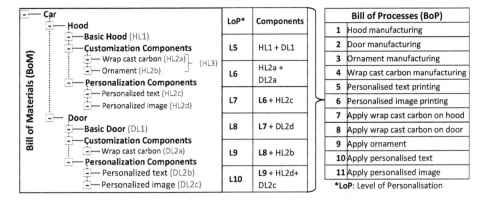

**Fig. 2.** BoM, BoP of the personalised car and LoPs

# 3    Design and Planning Method

The decision-making method includes resource-task assignments. The algorithms used in this procedure are either an Exhaustive Search (EXS) or the ISA. EXS generates the entire search space and identifies the best alternative. Thus, EXS is computationally intensive. ISA is an artificial intelligence search method that utilises three adjustable control parameters [15], namely: SNA (Selected Number of Alternatives) that controls the breadth of the search, DH (Decision Horizon) that controls the depth of the search and SR (Sampling Rate) that guides the search towards high quality paths.

The steps of the decision-making method are: a) form a set of alternatives, b) determine the decision-making criteria, c) calculate the utility value of alternatives, and d) select the best alternative [16][17]. Multiple conflicting criteria are considered simultaneously, based on the design and planning objectives. The best identified schemes are fed into the simulator. Fig. 3 depicts the input-output data and the workflow of the method.

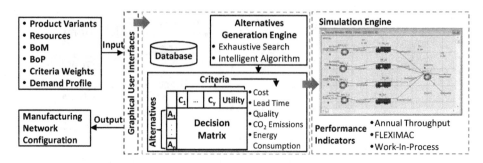

**Fig. 3.** Input-Output and Workflow of the presented approach

## 3.1    Criteria

The quality of the schemes is quantified by the means of the following criteria:

1. *Cost (1)* is the sum of the production and transportation cost (in €) [15][18]:
2. *Lead time (2)* is calculated from the point that an order is placed to the point that it is actually available for satisfying customer demand [15][19]:
3. *Energy Consumption (3)* takes into consideration the Watt specifications and the processing time of each manufacturing resource [18][20]:
4. *$CO_2$ Emissions (4)* are calculated taking into consideration the distance travelled and the emitted grams of $CO_2$ per kilometre [15][18][20][21]:
5. *Quality (5)* is an indicator that takes into account the mean quality of the parts, services that the manufacturing network partner provides and on their respect of due dates and takes values between, calculated based on empirical data [0-100].
6. *Annual Production Rate (6)* is expressed as the mean value of annual production volumes over the complete simulation period [7][19][22].
7. *FLEXIMAC (7)* is a quantification of flexibility, using the processing and flow time of the parts produced and is used to compare two similar networks. It is calculated using the system eigenvalues $\Omega_i$ and computing the amplitude $Q_i$ on those $\Omega$ frequencies. It is then calculated as the average value of the ten largest $Q_i$ [7][15][22].
8. *Work-In-Process (WIP)* is the inventory between the start and end points of the manufacturing system without including raw materials and finished products [23].

Additionally, the following indicators are used to express the resource availability:

*Mean Time Between Failures (MTBF)* is defined for each one of manufacturing network partners. MTBF is based on previous manufacturing knowledge and historical data and takes into account the observed frequency that a supplier fails to deliver the ordered batch, because of resource break-downs or capacity constraints.
*Mean Time To Repair (MTTR)*: The MTTR is calculated for each one of the manufacturing network partners as the time required for them to resume production.

$$C = \sum_{k=1}^{K} Pc_k + \sum_{r=1}^{R} Tr_{Cr} \tag{1}$$

$$L = \sum_{k=1}^{K} Pt_k + \sum_{r=1}^{R} Tt_r + \sum_{k=1}^{K} St_k \tag{2}$$

$$EC = EC_T + EC_P = \sum_{r=1}^{R} D_r * TC + \sum_{k=1}^{K} Pt_k * RW_k \tag{3}$$

$$CE = \sum_{r=1}^{R} \frac{G*D_r}{N} \tag{4}$$

$$QL = \frac{\sum_{k=1}^{K} QL_k}{k} \tag{5}$$

$$AP = \frac{\sum_{i=1}^{n_y} AP_i}{n_y} \tag{6}$$

$$FLEXIMAC = \frac{1}{10}\sum_{i=1}^{10}\frac{1}{2Q_i} \tag{7}$$

where: $Pc_k$: cost of task k (k=1,2,...K), $Tr_{Cr}$: cost of route r (r=1,2...R), Pt: processing time, Tt: transportation time, St: setup time, $EC_T$: the sum of the energy due to transportation (J), D: transportation distance (km), TC: energy consumption per kilometre (J/km) 21, $EC_P$: the sum of the energy for all the processes (J), RW: the Watts of the resource (J/s), grams of $CO_2$ emissions/Km 21, N: number of products in one truck, $QL_k$: the quality of the supplier that performs the task k, $AP_i$: the annual production volume for the i[th] year of simulation and $n_y$: the number of years (simulation period), $Q_i$: the eigenvalues of the system.

## 4     Results and Discussion

As a resource, a selection of machines that are responsible for performing a task (e.g. production of the basic hood) is assumed. The volatile demand profile, as provided by the automotive manufacturer for the simulation experiments, is depicted in Table 1.

Table 1. Demand profile of the car model of the case study

| Month 1 | 2 | 3 | 4 | 5 | 6 | 7 | 8 | 9 | 10 | 11 | 12 | Total |
|---|---|---|---|---|---|---|---|---|---|---|---|---|
| Orders 25.200 | 36.399 | 22.399 | 22.399 | 19.601 | 16.800 | 11.200 | 5.601 | 28.000 | 39.200 | 30.800 | 22.399 | 280x10³ |

The computer simulation experiments were performed on an Intel[TM] i7 3.4GHz computer with 8GB of RAM. Fig. 4 depicts that there is a strong correlation between the Total Number of Alternatives (TNA) and the required Computation Time (CT). The TNA especially in the case of L10 has a difference of 3 orders of magnitude from the L9 case. In the case of L8, the EXS execution was non-feasible due to computational constraints i.e. depletion of the available system memory. It is obvious that the ISA is the preferred method is cases with very large TNA. It is also noted that the CT for L9 and L10 is a projection based on the calculated TNA for these cases.

The values of the criteria the derived from the experiments are included in Fig. 5. Especially for the production of highly personalised products (L8), the Decentralised Manufacturing Network (DMN) depicts significantly reduced criteria values compared to the Centralised Manufacturing Network (CMN). In addition, the ISA yields results that belong to the 10% of the best solutions, in terms of utility value

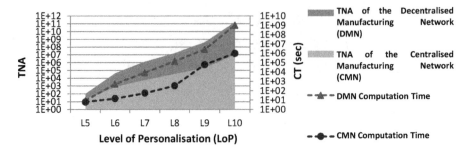

**Fig. 4.** TNA and CT for the CMN and DMN configurations for the different LoPs

(derived from the EXS). Indicatively, the ISA yielded a high quality solution with 23.3% more cost, requiring however, one 1,026 times less CT than the EXS (pie-chart in Fig. 5). In realistic manufacturing cases, EXS is highly ineffective because TNA may be calculated in the order of billions. Thus, a timely and efficient solution can only be then obtained through the utilisation of the ISA. As a result, depending on the design and planning objectives, a trade-off between the time for obtaining the solution and its quality is necessary.

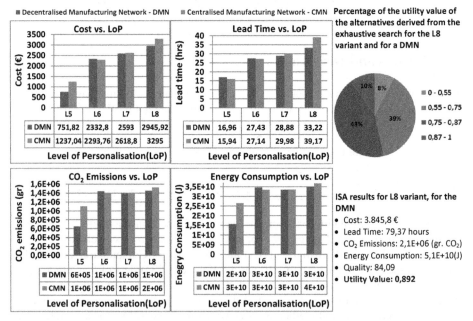

**Fig. 5.** Criteria Values and Utility Value of the EXS and ISA for the CMN and DMN and LoPs

The best configurations identified by the EXS were modelled in a simulator for the calculation of the flexibility, annual throughput and WIP (Fig. 6). The physical "as-is" manufacturing network was first modelled as a digital DES model. This initial model was verified through simulation and any bottlenecks were identified. Afterwards, the truck capacity as well as the buffer sizes were adjusted in all DES models, considering the volume of products and weight constraints. As a result, the transportation and storing activities were optimised in order to minimise idle times and improve machine utilisation. Finally, the initial stock was zero, thus, a ramp-up phase was included in all simulation experiments for the DMN and CMN and for the various LoPs.

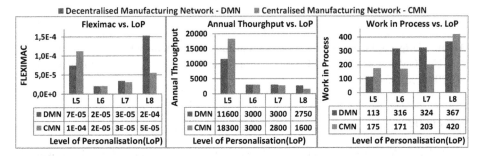

**Fig. 6.** Calculated Indicators for CMN and DMN configurations for the different LoPs

The simulation results depict that the flexibility indices of the CMN configurations are higher for non-customised products, whereas as the LoP increases, DMN displays higher flexibility. The annual throughput follows the same trend. For non-customised products, the CMN is more productive than the DMN ones and as the LoP increases the latter are more productive. The WIP is increasing as the LoP increases for both the CMN and DMN, due to the fact that the number of required processes increases for the production of the final assembly.

# 5    Conclusions and Future Work

The work presented in this paper can support decision-makers during the design of efficient manufacturing network configurations focused on the production of personalised products. The computer simulation experiments depicted the advantages of the decentralised configurations, especially as the LoP increased. The calculated performance indicators of Annual Throughput, Flexibility and Work-in-Process revealed the superiority of the DMN configurations over the CMN under the same personalised product demand. For the case of non-customised products, the CMN configuration yielded better results, as was expected, because traditional CMN configuration were formed to satisfy the needs of mass production, where predictions regarding product demand were reasonably accurate. Moreover, the ISA supported the identification of high quality solutions in cases were an EXS was not feasible to be performed due to the required computation burden. More specifically, the EXS, in the case of the fully personalised product (L8 variant), yielded a result in 2.340 minutes, a non-optimum scenario for real-life manufacturing terms. On the other hand, the ISA yielded high quality results with a deviation of 10,39% in the utility value from the best solution obtained from EXS in 3 minutes, a difference of 3 orders of magnitude. Future work will focus on extending the capabilities of the method. At first the procedure of feeding alternative manufacturing network configurations (DES models) in the simulation engine will be automated. Moreover, additional flexibility indicators will be used for assessing the alternative network configurations. A web-based mechanism for the automatic calculation of the distances between the autonomous manufacturing network entities will be incorporated. Finally, the method will be deployed into a web-based tool.

**Acknowledgments.** This work has been partially supported by the EC funded project "e-CUSTOM - A Web-based Collaboration System for Mass Customisation" (NMP2-SL-2010-260067).

# References

1. Ueda, K., Takenaka, T., Váncza, J., Monostori, L.: Value creation and decision-making in sustainable society. CIRP Annals-Mfg. Tech. 58, 681–700 (2009)
2. The Economist: The Third Industrial Revolution, April 21-27 (2012)
3. Thirumalai, S., Sinha, K.: Customisation of the online purchase process in electronic retailing and customer satisfaction: An online field study. J. of Oper. Mgmt. 29, 477–487 (2011)
4. Radke, A.M., Tseng, M.M.: A risk management-based approach for inventory planning of engineering-to-order production. CIRP Annals-Mfg. Tech. 61, 387–390 (2012)
5. Herrmann, I.T., Hauschild, M.Z.: Effects of globalisation on carbon footprints of products. CIRP Annals-Mfg. Tech. 58, 13–16 (2009)
6. Tolio, T., Urgo, M.: A Rolling Horizon Approach to Plan Outsourcing in Manufacturing-to-Order Environments Affected by Uncertainty. CIRP Annals-Mfg. Tech. 56, 487–490 (2007)
7. Michalos, G., Makris, S., Mourtzis, D.: An intelligent search algorithm-based method to derive assembly line design alternatives. Int. J. of Comp. Int. Mfg. 25, 211–229 (2012)
8. Labarthe, O., Espinasse, B., Ferrarini, A., Montreuil, B.: Toward a methodological framework for agent-based modelling and simulation of supply chains in a mass customisation context. Sim. Mod. Pr. and Th. 15, 113–136 (2007)
9. Persson, F., Araldi, M.: The development of a dynamic supply chain analysis tool: Integration of SCOR and discrete event simulation. Int. J. of Prod. Econ. 121, 574–583 (2009)
10. Pierreval, H., Bruniaux, R., Caux, C.: A continuous simulation approach for supply chains in the automotive industry. Sim. Mod. Pr. and Th. 15, 185–198 (2007)
11. Longo, F., Mirabelli, G.: An advanced supply chain management tool based on modelling and simulation. Comp. & Ind. Eng. 54, 570–588 (2008)
12. Chiang, W.C., Russell, R., Xu, X., Zepeda, D.: A simulation/metaheuristic approach to newspaper production and distribution supply chain problems. Int. J. of Prod. Econ. 121, 752–767 (2009)
13. Garey, M., Johnson, D.: Computers and Intractability – A Guide to the Theory of NP-Completeness, 1st edn. W.H.Freeman & Co Ltd., New York (1990)
14. Yoo, T., Cho, H., Yucesan, E.: Hybrid algorithm for discrete event simulation based supply chain optimisation. Exp. Sys. With Appl. 37, 2354–2361 (2010)

15. Mourtzis, D., Doukas, M., Psarommatis, F.: A multi-criteria evaluation of centralised and decentralised production networks in a highly customer-driven environment. CIRP Annals-Mfg. Tech. 61, 427–430 (2012)
16. Chryssolouris, G.: Manufacturing Systems - Theory and Practice, 2nd edn. Springer (2006)
17. Chryssolouris, G., Dicke, K., Lee, M.: On the Resources Allocation Problem. Int. J. of Prod. Res. 30, 2773–2795 (1992)
18. Mourtzis, D., Doukas, M., Psarommatis, F.: Design and planning of decentralised production networks under high product variety demand. Procedia CIRP (2012), doi: http://dx.doi.org/10.1016/j.procir.2012.07.051
19. Liao, C.J., Shyu, C.H.: An Analytical Determination of Lead Time with Normal Demand. Int. J. of Oper. & Prod. Mgmt. 11, 72–78 (1991)
20. Mourtzis, D., Doukas, M., Psarommatis, F.: Environmental impact of centralised and decentralised production networks in the era of personalisation. Lect. Notes in Prod. Eng, vol. 1, pp. 396–408 (2012), doi:10.1007/978-3-642-30749-2
21. EPA (2010), http://www.epa.gov
22. Alexopoulos, K., Papakostas, N., Mourtzis, D., Gogos, P., Chryssolouris, G.: Quantifying the flexibility of a manufacturing system by applying the transfer function. Int. J. of Comp. Int. Mfg. 20, 538–547 (2006)
23. Hopp, W.J., Spearman, M.L.: Factory Physics: Foundations of Manufacturing Management, 2nd edn. Richard D. Irwin (1995)

# An Empirical Based Proposal for Mass Customization Business Model in Footwear Industry

Golboo Pourabdollahian, Donatella Corti, Chiara Galbusera,
and Julio Cesar Kostycz Silva

Politecnico di Milano, Piazza Leonardo Da Vinci 32, 20133, Milan, Italy
golboo.pourabdollahian@mail.polimi.it, donatella.corti@polimi.it

**Abstract.** This research aims at developing a business model for companies in the footwear industry interested in implementing Mass Customization with the goal of offering to the market products which perfectly match customers' needs. The studies on mass customization are actually mostly focused on product development and production system aspects. This study extends the business modeling including also Supply Chain aspects. The research is based on analyzing Mass Customization application in reality, within some companies operating in footwear industry. Through the real cases of Mass Customization implementation, a business model proposal is developed as an attempt to generalize the empirical findings.

**Keywords:** Mass Customization, Business Model, Footwear industry.

## 1 Introduction

Nowadays globalization has radically changed the industrial environment not only by creating a higher market turbulence and competition but also by increasing number of demanding customers which ask for unique products that perfectly match their needs and preferences. In this regard the adoption of a mass customization (MC) approach has been considered as a proper solution since it provides customers with individualized goods while being efficient at the same time. Considering the increasing interest of a higher number of companies to offer mass customized products, it is crucial to provide companies with a proper business model enabling them to implement MC in a successful manner. Going through literature, we found out that there is no proposal for a MC business model; hence this research aims at developing an empirical based MC business model for footwear industry to support companies since this sector in successful implementation of this strategy. The research is limited to footwear industry due to the fact that business model is highly sector dependent; therefore it is not easy to define a general business model which can be applied in all sectors. Moreover considering the fact that this research is an empirical based study, footwear industry was selected since it is a popular sector for implementation of mass customization with considerable amount of existing and emerging actors in the sector.

C. Emmanouilidis, M. Taisch, D. Kiritsis (Eds.): APMS 2012, Part I, IFIP AICT 397, pp. 310–317, 2013.
© IFIP International Federation for Information Processing 2013

## 2    Business Model: Definition and Reference Structure

From the very early emergence of the term "Business model" by Jones [4] different definitions have been suggested in literature to define the term and its role. These definitions reflect different perspectives which can be targeted by a business model such as value creation, simplification of a complex system, money generation, company behavior representation and etc. In this study we refer to Osterwalder to define business model as "a conceptual tool that contains a set of elements and their relationships and allows expressing a company's logic of earning money."[6] The reference structure for the analysis of a business model in this study is the one proposed by Osterwlader and Pigneur's (called business model canvas) with minor modifications needed to adopt it to the context of interest [7]. The initial business model canvas of Osterwlader and Pigneur includes 9 building blocks that can be logically grouped into 3 areas: Left side relates to efficiency (Key partners, key activities, key resources, and cost structure), the right side relates to value delivery (Customer segment, customer relationship, channels, and revenue streams) and finally the value proposition which is in between. The proposed change is the merging of the costs and revenues blocks into a single one named performance. This is mainly due to the fact that in a mass customization business not only cost and revenue are considered as critical issues but also evaluation of customization and efficiency level of the firm is important. Therefore the final structure of the business model is based on eight blocks illustrated in figure 1.

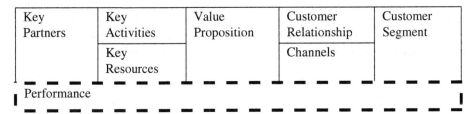

**Fig. 1.** Business model structure

## 3    Research Methodology

In order to come out with the empirical based MC business model for the footwear industry, we selected five companies in different countries operating in footwear industry that propose customized shoes to their customers. The analysis comprehends both cases of small companies and cases of medium/large companies, also already established companies with standard products and start-up mass customized born companies. Data were collected through different primary and secondary sources including: questionnaire, personal interview, papers, releases and publications on scientific magazines, official company website, official financial reports, blogs, forums, communities and online sector magazine release. Table 1 presents a summary of information to introduce the five analyzed cases. For each case study the analysis of the business model in place has been carried out based on the use of the above-mentioned canvas.

**Table 1.** Analyzed case studies

| Company | Country | Foundation year | Size | Mass production beside MC | Type of shoes |
|---------|---------|-----------------|------|---------------------------|---------------|
| A | Germany | 1924 | Large | Yes | Sport |
| B | USA | 1978 | Large | Yes | Sport |
| C | Brazil | 2011 | SME | No | Sneakers |
| D | Germany | 2001 | SME | No | luxury shoes |
| E | Australia | 2009 | SME | No | Women's shoes |

# 4    Cross Analysis

Based on the cases analysis a set of different alternatives for each block of business model were identified and mapped (Table 2). These alternatives are mainly based on best practices of the analyzed companies. Obviously some of them have been applied by only one company while some others are applied by more companies. This is due to the fact that the analyzed cases vary in some factors such as size, customer segment and the level of customization they offer to their customers. In order to better demonstrate the position of each alternative in a MC solution space we defined three pillars for solution space naming product (PR), production system (PS) and supply chain (SC) and we allocated each alternative to the most suitable solution space pillar. This might facilitate for a company the act of focusing on a preferred pillar of solution space without compromising other important aspects of solution space.

**Table 2.** MC alternatives applied in case studies

| BM Block | SS Pillar | Company A | Company B | Company C | Company D | Company E |
|----------|-----------|-----------|-----------|-----------|-----------|-----------|
| Value proposition | PR | Customization (Style, function, fit) | Customization (Style, function) | Customization (Style, packaging), Customer involvement in parts design | Customization (Style, fit), Customers' feedback on raw material quality | Customization (Style), Customized reusable packaging |
| Key activities | PR | Product modularization & components standardization, solution space definition, customers' requirements elicitation | | | | |
| | PS | | | Implement postponement | | |
| | SC | Integrate with logistics partners, Employees training, Information management | Integrate with logistics partners, Employees training | | Integrate with logistics partners, Employees training | Integrate with logistics partners, Employees training |
| Resources | PR | | Designers | | | Designers |

**Table 3.** (*Continued.*)

| | | | | | | |
|---|---|---|---|---|---|---|
| | PS | | | Flexible manufacturing system | | |
| | SC | Online configurator, trained personnel, IT infrastructure | Online configurator | Online configurator | Online configurator, Trained personnel, Point of sale systems | Online configurator, Experts to support customer in co-design |
| Key Partners | SC | Shoe producer, Logistic partner, customers | Shoe producer, Logistic partner, customers | Materials supplier, Logistic partner, customers, web platform provider | Shoe producer, Logistic partner, customers | Shoe producer, Logistic partner, customers |
| Customer Relationship | SC | Online profiles, Social networks, | Online profiles, Social networks, Serious games | Online profiles, Online customized school | Online profiles, Social networks | Online profiles, Social networks, Serious games, Online customized school, Customized relationship, Web-campaign |
| Channels | SC | Online store, physical store, third party retailer | Online store | Online store | Online store, physical store | Online store, physical store, third party retailer |
| Customer Segment | PR | Men & Women, Young web users, International market | Men & Women, Young web users, International market | Men & Women, Young web users, Local market (Brazil) | Women, Young web users, Local market (Germany & UK) | Women, aged between 22-55, International market |
| Performance | PR/PS/SC | Financial indicators | Financial indicators | Financial indicators | Financial indicators | Financial indicators, Limited set of indicators to measure efficacy |

Going through different alternatives applied in each case study three main points should be noticed. In following sections we describe each of these pints.

## 4.1      Implementation of Key Alternatives for MC

Analysis of collected data show that there are some alternatives applied by all five cases involved in this study. This emphasizes the fact that these alternatives should be considered as main attributes of a MC business model in footwear industry and possibly other industries. One of the most notable examples in this regard is "style customization" which is offered as a value proposition by all studied companies. This highlights the point that coming to a mass customization point, aesthetic/style is always a main aspect of customization in footwear industry. The same story is true for product modularization and components standardization which is a critical activity to increase efficiency in mass customization. Other examples in this regard are: Use of online configurator, Customers' requirement elicitation, Web-design and online store.

## 4.2      Lack of Some MC Alternatives Proposed in Literature

One of the notable results of data analysis relates to lack of some MC attributes which are proposed in different studies in literature but have not been implemented in none of the analyzed case studies. A clear example in this regard is knowledge management and knowledge creation. There are numerous studies mention knowledge management and creation as a key issue in mass customization. Franke and Piller point out the importance of acquired knowledge to create a barrier against switching suppliers while Wu et al. emphasize on role of knowledge management in level of service and quality [3],[12]. Surprisingly no company in this study implements knowledge management as a key activity. Another example extracted from analysis is integration of partners in supply chain in order to increase efficiency which has not been followed by analyzed cases. Integration of supplier means the extent to which a supplier could collaborate and manage some inter-organizational activities with manufacturer. In mass customization operations where standardize modularization has been implemented, the role of integrated suppliers are more tangible due to the need of long-term collaboration between manufacturer and supplier.

Implementation of flexible manufacturing systems is another neglected alternative which is considered only by company C. In this case it is not difficult to discover the reason since it is mainly due to the fact that only company C produces shoes in-house and consequently flexible manufacturing systems are considered as a main key resource for them, while the other four companies outsource the whole production which makes them independent to any agile production system. However the story is not so simple when it is related to integrated information system as a key resource. Based on our analysis company A is the only company using integrated information system to facilitate MC implementation. This can be due to many reasons such as high investment, non-readiness of supply chain for information integration, etc. Table 3 illustrates some of the main neglected alternatives by companies.

**Table 3.** Implementation mapping of MC alternatives in literature in analyzed cases

| MC alternative | Company |
|---|---|
| Process modularization [2] | None |
| Implement postponement [13] | C |
| Web-platform and interaction system management [8],[2] | None |
| Flexible manufacturing system [2],[9],[10] | C |
| Integrating partners [8] | A |
| Knowledge management and knowledge creation [3],[11] | None |
| Support customers during co-design [1],[5] | D |

### 4.3    Lack of MC Performance Measurement

As any other company, a mass customization company needs to use metrics in order to keep under control mass customization strategy and in particular to identify commonality and modularity level of products. Although monitoring and performance measurement is considered as a critical issue in MC but only one company uses a few metrics to measure the mass customization level while others never included it as a crucial step in their business model.

## 5    Proposal of MC Business Model

Taking into consideration all the previous considerations, a MC business model for footwear industry is proposed that could support a company in this sector to identify a possible path to implement MC. In order to develop the business model we tried to take into account best practices applied by each company however the proposed business model is not complete since as it has already been mentioned in previous section there are crucial MC alternatives in literature which have not been applied by none of the firms in this study. In this regard a complete business model can be developed through integration of current business model and a literature based MC business model. The following MC business model is a step forward to this aim since it clarifies the most important MC alternatives in a real industrial environment and possible challenges to implement mass customization. This might bring us one step closer to support companies in successful implementation of mass customization. The novelty of the proposed business model is not only based on what mentioned above but also on including supply chain elements in development of business model.

Configuration of the final business model can be an iterative activity by measuring performance of the developed business using indicators mentioned in performance block and revising other blocks to reach the required level of cost, customization and efficiency.

| Key Partners | Key Activities | Value Proposition | Customer Relationship | Customer Segment |
|---|---|---|---|---|
| **Supply chain**: Shoe producer Customers Logistic partner | **Product:** Product modularization Component standardization Solution space definition Customers' needs elicitation **Supply chain:** Integrate with logistic partner Employees training Information management **Production system:** Postponement | **Product:** Co-design Style customization Function customization Fit customization Package customization | **Supply chain:** Co- creation Online profiles Social networks Customized relationship Gamification | **Product:** Young people Web users |
| | **Key Resources** **Supply chain:** Online configurator **Product:** Designers **Production system:** Flexible manufacturing system | | **Channels** **Supply chain:** Online store Physical store Third party retailer | |
| **Performance** **Product/ Production system/ Supply chain:** Financial indicators Customization indicators Efficiency indicators | | | | |

Fig. 2. Proposal of MC business model for footwear industry

## 6    Conclusion

The offer of mass customized shoes is a recent trend in the footwear industry and seems to be a promising business for the coming years that could fulfill evolving customer needs. Some brands have already developed the mass customized line and have entered the business since a few years ago, yet potentialities of mass customization could be further exploited being an opportunity for a higher number of companies. In this paper we propose a framework to support companies operating in shoe sector to develop a MC oriented business model. The proposal is a supporting tool for practitioners during the development of the business model. The decisional process can be more efficient since the framework provides not only a check-list of elements that need to be considered, but also a list of options that have been tested to be successful in the same context. On the other hand, this work adds also insights to the mass customization literature providing a work that take into account at the same time all the elements that need to be configured when a business model has to be developed. Given the high number of variables, the proposed model can be hardly generalized to other sectors, so it is a contribution to the footwear industry. Nonetheless, the applied methodology can be replicated in other industries where mass customization is an opportunity of growth. Next step of this research is the implementation of the proposed framework to support a company not yet mass customized to extend its offer in this direction.

# References

1. Abend, J.: Custom-made for the masses: is it time yet? Journal of Fashion Marketing and Management 2, 48–54 (1996)
2. Blecker, T., Abdelkafi, N.: The Development of a Component Commonality Metric for Mass Customization. Transaction on Engineering Management 54(1), 70–85 (2007)
3. Franke, N., Piller, F.T.: Configuration toolkits for mass customization setting a research agenda. International Journal of Technology Management 6(5/6), 578–599 (2003)
4. Jones, G.M.: Educators, Electrons, and Business Models: A Problem in Synthesis. Accounting Review 35(4), 619–626 (1960)
5. Oleson, J.D.: Path ways to agility: Mass customization in action. John Wiley & Sons, Inc., New York (1998)
6. Osterwalder, A.: The Business Model Ontology - a proposition in a design science approach. Dissertation, University of Lausanne, Switzerland (2004)
7. Osterwalder, A., Pignuer, Y.: Model Generation: A Handbook for Visionaries, Game Changers, and Challengers, 1st edn. John Wiley & Sons, NYC, Hoboken (2010)
8. Piller, F.T.: Mass customization: reflection on the state of the concept. International Journal of Flexible Manufacturing System 16(4), 313–334 (2004)
9. Pollard, D., Chuo, S.: Strategies for Mass Customization. Journal of Business & Economics Research 6(7), 77–85 (2008)
10. Qiao, G., Lu, R., Mclean, C.: Flexible Manufacturing System for Mass Customization Manufacturing. International Journal of Mass Customization 1(2/3), 374–393 (2006)
11. Schreier, M.: The Value Increment of Mass-customized Products: An Empirical Assessment. Journal of Consumer Behaviour 5, 317–327 (2006)
12. Wu, J., Lin, I., Yang, M.H.: The impact of a customer profile and customer participation on customer relationship management performance. International Journal of Electronic Business Management 17(1), 57–69 (2009)
13. Xuan, G.X.: Positioning of customer order decoupling point in mass customization. In: Proceeding of the Sixth International Conference on Machine Learning and Cybernetics, Hong Kong, August 19-22 (2007)

# Mass Customized Large Scale Production System with Learning Curve Consideration

KuoWei Chen and Richard Lee Storch

Industrial & Systems Engineering, University of Washington, Seattle, U.S.A
{kwc206,rlstorch}@uw.edu

**Abstract.** This paper presents the structure for modeling a large scale production system with learning curve considerations. The model will be used to develop a scheduling method that facilitates the production performance for mass customized products. Mass customization is an important manufacturing management strategy but it might lead to unnecessary production losses. Most manufacturing systems' throughput is constrained by one or more bottlenecks and the critical bottleneck may shift from one work station to another. The proposed scheduling method will consider learning curve effects and employ the concept of Shifting Bottleneck Procedure to guide production scheduling decisions. Ultimately, the goal is to improve the throughput of large scale assembly manufacturing systems. A simulation model of a wind turbine assembly line case study is also presented to validate the capability of the proposed method.

**Keywords:** Mass customization, large scale production, learning curves, shifting bottleneck procedure, simulation.

## 1    Introduction

This paper focuses on large scale product industries which are known to produce or assemble large scale products. Examples are commercial airplanes, ships, and wind turbines. A large scale production system often consists of a group of structured organizations to produce a family of complex and customized products in a certain geographic region [1]. There are several crucial characteristics among these industries and the nature of a large scale production system is influenced by its products. The most common characteristics of a large scale production system are long cycle time, low total throughput and limited buffer space. For instance, the total assembly cycle time of a wind turbine nacelle may be up to sixteen hours to be completed and the throughput is limited to five units per week. The buffer space or inventory space may be limited. Long cycle time leads to the limited total production volume in the large scale product manufacturing industry which means total throughput, the average output of a production process per unit time, is limited. In order to improve the total throughput, manufacturing engineers are striving to develop more efficient production process methods.

Mass customization (MC) has been a well known contemporary manufacturing industry management technique, enabling a company to compete with their competitors

C. Emmanouilidis, M. Taisch, D. Kiritsis (Eds.): APMS 2012, Part I, IFIP AICT 397, pp. 318–325, 2013.

in the diverse market. Broadly, the concept of mass customization was first introduced by Davis [2] and he described that manufacturing companies tended to produce goods to serve their relatively large market; meanwhile, satisfying specific needs of individual consumers by customizing products with acceptable cost. However, it is not always free to implement product customization in a production line and the common impact of mass customization on manufacturing trade-offs are important system performances: cost, process time, quality, delivery and volume [3]. Such challenges need to be overcome by those companies who are struggling to achieve mass customization and must consider those performance factors. In spite of a large number of practical approaches and processes for customized product discussed in the literature [4-6], a link between product customization and bottleneck based heuristic with learning curve consideration is still a research area that needs investigation.

This paper proposes the use of learning curve consideration in a bottleneck selection scheduling heuristic to improve the total completion time or system throughput under mass customized large scale product industry. Manufacturers can improve the total throughput by decreasing process time in the bottleneck stage. Those customized products with the similar process on a certain machine are defined as having learning effect when those products are scheduled consecutively. As a result, the customized production system will be closer to the mass production system and then improve the total completion time and throughput. We give a description of bottleneck based heuristic and learning curve effect in Section 2. Section 3 demonstrates the use of learning curve in a bottleneck based scheduling heuristic. Section 4 provides a simulation example which applied the method under a simulated large scale production industry. Section 5 presents the conclusion and future work.

## 2    Background

### 2.1    Bottleneck Based Heuristic

Manufacturing involves many operations on many machines and effective management requires many decisions. There have been many classical scheduling theories for the deterministic problem of scheduling a fixed number of jobs on a given set of machines to improve the production performance such as minimizing makespan, minimizing tardiness, and minimizing lateness. The classical job shop problem can be described as a set of machines that process operations on jobs. Each job has a predefined operation schedule on each machine with the required process time on it [7]. These algorithms can be classified as optimization and approximation algorithms [8, 9]. Among those approximation algorithms, Adams et al. [10] proposed the Shifting Bottleneck (SB) procedure and it is probably the most well known among all heuristics for job shop scheduling problem. A brief statement of the Shifting Bottleneck procedure is as optimizing the sequence on each machine repeatedly, while keeping the sequence of other machines fixed. Each one machine solution is compared with the all others and the machine is identified as the bottleneck machine based on their solution. The SB procedure terminates once all machines have been scheduled. It is generally characterized by following steps to minimize the makespan: bottleneck identification, bottleneck selection, and sequence re-optimization.

## 2.2    Learning Curve Effect

Learning effect has received considerable attention in management science and it can be described as a steady decline in process time when operators perform the same task repeatedly. Dr. Wright [11] first introduced his famous log2 learning curve model in 1936 and this model is still one of the best ways to predict operator's performance. Biskup [12, 13] might be the pioneer to consider the connection between learning effect and scheduling problem and proved that single-machine problem with the consideration of leaning effects remains polynomially solvable for two objectives which are the minimized deviation from a common due date and minimized sum of flow time. Then he introduced a modified formulation to describe the learning effects in scheduling problem with $p_i, i = 1,...,n$ being the normal process time and $p_{ir}$ as the process time of job $i$ if it is scheduled in position $r$ in a sequence (1) as below:

$$p_{ir} = p_i r^a \tag{1}$$

where $a \le 0$ is the learning index, given as the logarithm to the base 2 of the learning rate, and thus for the 80% hypothesis $a = \log_2 0.8 = -0.322$ holds. According to the equation above, the needed process time in position $r$ decreases by the number of repetitions which represents that operators gain experience and skills after repetitive operations.

    Lee et al. [14] discussed the goal of minimizing total completion time for the two machine flow shop problem. They assumed that the same job has different learning effect on different machines and this assumption is common for those multi-machine scheduling problems with learning consideration. A modified equation (2) with learning effect was introduced by Lee and Wu to represent $p_{ijr}$ as the process time of job $i$ if it is scheduled in position $r$ in a sequence on the machine $j$ :

$$p_{ijr} = p_{ij} r^a \tag{2}$$

where $j = 1,...,m$ is the machine index. With respect to the equation above, the needed process time in position $r$ on machine $j$ decreases by the number of repetitions, hence, different processes on each machine might affect the learning situation. According to results in [13-15] scheduling problem with learning curve consideration is considered to have practical impact to manufacturing schedule decision. Besides, it has shown the capability to improve the mass customization production system.

## 3    Methodology

The method we propose is based on the concept of Shifting Bottleneck procedure [10] with learning curve consideration in a large scale customized product production environment. The objective is to improve production performance such as total completion time or throughput by assigning products which have similar process on the bottleneck stage consecutively in order to reduce the process time by utilizing the characteristic of learning curve. Jobs are subject to the constraints that (i) the sequence of machines for each job is prescribed; and (ii) each machine can process only one job at a time. Besides, the processing time of each job might be effected by learning effect when similar processes are scheduled on the same machine consecutively and this causes the processing time of each job on each machine to be changed. Figure 1 presents a flow chart of schedule decision by using bottleneck selection with learning effect consideration.

We start by defining system variables. For instance, $i$ denotes the serial number of job, $j$ denotes the machine or working stage, and $k$ denotes the customization category. Steps 1 and 2 are key steps in this procedure to determine which work station is the real system bottleneck by different criteria. We start to check whether there is any current processing job in the system. If not, the first job is allowed to access into the system according to different dispatching rules and we use first come first served rule here. Otherwise, each work station needs to be measured and analyzed in terms of bottleneck detection criteria. There are basically two well known methods to define the bottleneck in a manufacturing system. The first method is to measure utilization of each work station and the one with highest utilization is considered as a bottleneck. However, it might not be sensitive enough to detect the real bottleneck while there are more than one work stations with same utilization. The second method defines bottleneck by measuring the longest queue line of unprocessed jobs in front of each work station or longest waiting time of each work stage. It is also a simple method to observe the length of queue on each machine in a manufacturing production line. The drawback of this method is lack of accuracy when the maximum of buffer size is limited. The number of unprocessed jobs on more than one busy work stations is restricted by buffer size and this causes difficulty to define a real bottleneck. This is a common situation in the real life especially for large scale production system, for example, an airplane assembly line may just have one buffer space in front each stage. Therefore, we choose the largest waiting time as a bottleneck selection criterion in this paper:

$$\max \left( \frac{\sum_{i=1}^{n} t_{i1} - c_{i0}}{i}, \frac{\sum_{i=1}^{n} t_{i2} - c_{i1}}{i}, ..., \frac{\sum_{i=1}^{n} t_{ij} - c_{ij-1}}{i} \right) \tag{3}$$

for all $j$, where $j = 1...m$ being machine index, $t_{ij}$ denotes the arrival time of job $i$ on machine $j$ and $c_{ij}$ is the completion time of job $i$ on machine $j$.

Once the bottleneck station is determined, we go to the next step to identify relevant job information in order to make schedule decision. Steps 3 and 4 should be performed at anytime to those unprocessed jobs in front of the main system. Under the customization production environment, the information of each job is assumed to be well prescribed according to customer's requirement; however, the assembly

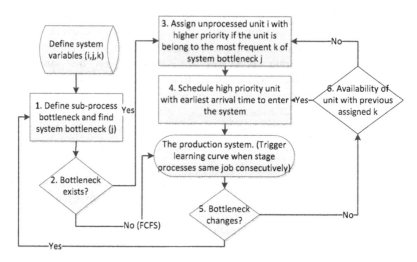

**Fig. 1.** Steps of proposed scheduling procedure with learning effect

sequence can be assigned by the manufacturer to achieve flexible manufacturing. Next, this model accumulates the number for each option in the corresponding work station. Once the bottleneck is determined in Steps 1 and 2, this model assigns those jobs which are in the same job family with most frequent number in the queue of unprocessed jobs corresponding to bottleneck stage with higher priority.  The purpose of this step is to accumulate the same process on the bottleneck stage and then learning effect can be triggered to reduce the process time. This step always schedules those jobs with higher priority first to enter the main system unless the bottleneck changes or there are no more jobs defined as higher priority in the queue of unprocessed jobs in front of the main system. We go back to steps 1 and 2 to re-determine the new bottleneck immediately when the bottleneck changes. Otherwise, this model keeps on steps 3 and 4 to search for the most frequent job family and assign them with higher priority to access into the system if those jobs in the previous majority job family have been all processed to enter the main system.

The final step implements the learning curve on the bottleneck machine to reduce process time when a job is still in the same job family as the previous one. There are numerous descriptions and practical applications of learning curve discussed in the literature [13, 16], however, the proposed heuristic in this paper uses the classic Wright's log2 learning curve model given a learning index $a = \log_2 0.8 = -0.322$ for the 80% hypothesis.

## 4     Simulation and Results

The proposed procedure in section 3 is applied in a simulated example for a wind turbine assembly industry and this model is carried out to analyze the simulation results using the ARENA simulation software. The example assumes a wind turbine company can offer its customers customized nacelles with 3 options ($k = 1...3$) on 15 different categories ( $j = 1,...,15$ ) without supply shortage or other unexpected emergent situation such as labor absence or delay of delivery and the simplified process flow is presented in Figure 2. On the other hand, these jobs all need to process through 15 work stations to be completed with same process sequence in this complex system. There are a total of 700 unprocessed jobs with continuous arrival time and the information of each job is prescribed. This example assumes the buffer space of each work station is restricted to 2 as well as the bottleneck is determined by measuring the largest waiting time.

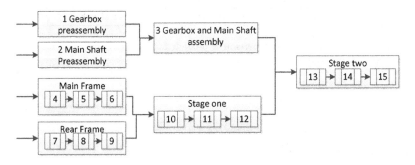

**Fig. 2.** Simplified process flow of nacelles assembly line

According to figure 3, the dash trend presents a schedule decision with traditional first come first serve dispatching rule (FCFS) which means a job is scheduled according to their arrival time. The earlier a job arrives in the queue in front of the main system, the earlier it can be processed into the main system. The solid trend presents a schedule decision using proposed scheduling procedure with learning curve consideration (LC) and it shows that the average completion time has been improved and reduced from around 4016 minutes to 3450 minutes in this wind turbine example.

By following the proposed procedure, every job that arrives in the queue in front of the main system must be checked by the model to determine if it meets the criteria as a higher priority level. It seems that the stage 2 is defined as the primary bottleneck and it consists of sub-processes 13, 14, and 15. Figure 4 (a) (b) (c) depict the process time of individual jobs on each work station respectively. It can be easily seen that learning curve happens on all of three work stations, especially on station (13) and station (14). This also indicates that a work station is determined as a critical bottleneck when there is an exponential decrease period influenced by learning effect. However, a bottleneck might go along with a short learning effect period and this just means the bottleneck changes to another work station quickly in a short time. Besides, learning effect may happen on a non-bottleneck work station according to random combinatorial sequence and this non-bottleneck work station can also benefit by the nature of learning effect.

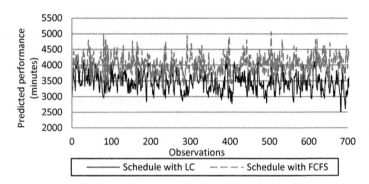

**Fig. 3.** A comparison of predicted completion time

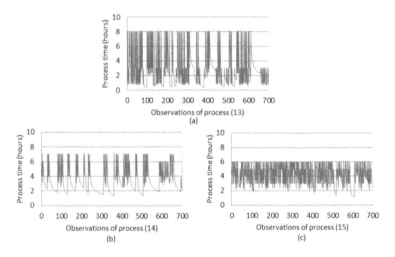

**Fig. 4.** Process time of each job in the bottleneck stage

# 5    Conclusions and Future Work

In the present paper, we propose a structure of modeling with learning effect under mass customization production system. A simulation model also is developed to demonstrate this procedure and analyze the results according to a simulated wind turbine assembly line example. The total completion time has a significant improvement by using the proposed scheduling procedure. This paper concluded that this heuristic has potential capability to improve the performance of a customized production system by assigning job family on bottleneck stage to reduce the process time. In addition, it also can provide manufacturers better scheduling decision support to satisfy customer's demand.

Future development of the method may include (a) using different bottleneck detection method to determine a real bottleneck in a more accurate and sensitive way

(b) comparing the result by different learning curve models, and (c) analyzing the influence of other objectives to the proposed heuristic such as minimizing tardiness or minimizing the variation of completion time. We selected the total completion time as the objective in this paper. Additionally, more complicated and therefore more realistic production systems will be considered.

## References

1. Lu, R.F., Petersen, T.D., Storch, R.L.: Modeling customized product configuration in large assembly manufacturing with supply-chain considerations. International Journal of Flexible Manufacturing Systems 19(4), 685–712 (2008)
2. Davis, S.M.: From "future perfect": Mass customizing. Strategy & Leadership 17(2), 16–21 (1989)
3. Squire, B., et al.: The impact of mass customisation on manufacturing trade-offs. Production and Operations Management 15, 10–21 (2006)
4. Silveira, G.D., Borenstein, D., Fogliatto, F.S.: Mass customization literature review and research directions. International Journal of Production Economics 72, 1–13 (2001)
5. Ulrich, K.T., Eppinger, S.D.: Product Design and Development, 2nd edn. McGraw-Hill (2000)
6. Huang, X., Krista, M.M., Schroeder, R.G.: Linking learning and effective process implementation to mass customization capability. Journal of Operations Management 26(6), 714–729 (2008)
7. Blazewicz, J., Domschke, W., Pesch, E.: The job shop scheduling problem Conventional and new solution techniques. European Journal of Operational Research 93, 1–33 (1996)
8. Jain, A.S., Meeran, S.: Deterministic job-shop scheduling Past, present and future. European Journal of Operational Research 113, 390–434 (1999)
9. Wenqi, H., Alihua, Y.: An improved shifting bottleneck procedure for the job shop scheduling problem. Computers & Operations Research 31(12), 2093–2110 (2004)
10. Adams, J., Balas, E., Zawack, D.: The Shifting Bottleneck Procedure for Job Shop Scheduling. Management Science 34, 391–401 (1988)
11. Wright, T.P.: Factors Affecting the Cost of Airplanes. Journal of Aeronautical Sciences 3, 122–128 (1936)
12. Biskup, D.: Single-machine scheduling with learning considerations. European Journal of Operational Research 115, 173–178 (1999)
13. Biskup, D.: A state-of-the-art review on scheduling with learning effects. European Journal of Operational Research 188(2), 315–329 (2008)
14. Lee, W.-C., Wu, C.-C.: Minimizing total completion time in a two-machine flowshop with a learning effect. International Journal of Production Economics 88(1), 85–93 (2004)
15. Anzanello, M.J., Fogloatto, F.S.: Learning curve models and application: Literaure review and research directions. International Journal of Industrial Ergonomics 41, 573–583 (2011)
16. Roser, C., Nakano, M., Tanaka, M.: Shifting Bottleneck Detection. In: Simulation Conference, vol. 2, pp. 1079–1086 (2002)

# Event-Driven Order Rescheduling Model for Just-In-Sequence Deliveries to a Mixed-Model Assembly Line

Georg Heinecke[1,2], Jonathan Köber[3], Raffaello Lepratti[2], Steffen Lamparter[2], and Andreas Kunz[1]

[1] Institute of Machine Tools and Manufacturing, ETH Zurich, Switzerland
{georghe,kunz}@ethz.ch
[2] Siemens AG, Germany
{georg.heinecke.ext,raffaello.lepratti,
steffen.lamparter}@siemens.com
[3] CLAAS Selbstfahrende Erntemaschinen GmbH, Germany
jonathan.koeber@claas.com

**Abstract.** Today's buyer markets and lean supply chains require build-to-order assembly systems with just-in-sequence (JIS) deliveries. Simultaneously production systems have become prone to supply disturbances (i.e. events) that endanger the synchronized delivery of all JIS components to the assembly line. To uphold production sequence stability, rescheduling is frequently required. Current methods, however, make assumptions that are often insufficiently aligned with real-world problems and focus on production issues while neglecting the implications of today's tight integration of supply chain with production processes. To this end, this contribution derives a general model of a mixed model assembly line. It then proposes and evaluates an event-driven rescheduling model for JIS deliveries. The results indicate that rework due to missing JIS components can be avoided without compromising performance.

**Keywords:** Just-In-Sequence, Mixed-Model Assembly Line, Rescheduling.

## 1 Introduction

Today's buyer markets have forced production systems to shift towards mass customization, where a large product portfolio and many customization options are key success factors for winning customer orders and improving competitiveness [9]. Thus, customer-specific products replaced standardized ones, in the course of which forecasting-based build-to-stock production strategies were abandoned in favour of build-to-order (BTO). It is a demand-driven production approach where a product is scheduled and built in response to a confirmed customer order [6]. Since neither demand volume nor product configurations can be anticipated, however, inventories for highly individualized, costly components were replaced with just-in-sequence (JIS) deliveries. Thus, today a customer order triggers the entire supply chain (SC) where several supply sequences of customer-specific components merge into one 'pearl chain' on an OEM's assembly line, which has two drawbacks. First, the

C. Emmanouilidis, M. Taisch, D. Kiritsis (Eds.): APMS 2012, Part I, IFIP AICT 397, pp. 326–333, 2013.
© IFIP International Federation for Information Processing 2013

production volume of the SC has to align itself with volatile customer demand, requiring flexible and responsive systems [3, 5]. Second, disturbances in JIS processes endanger the synchronized merging of all supply sequences at the OEM and the assembly of a customer-specific product from the respective components [1, 18].

This paper investigates the latter issue because today's global supply networks are prone to disturbances that range from deviations (e.g. transport delays) to disasters (e.g. floods) [2]. Through the seamless connection of lean processes with neither stock nor time buffers, manufacturers are unprotected against disturbances that destabilize the SC system [15]. Risk management can reduce the potential for disasters but it can neither prevent nor efficiently address smaller disruptions and deviations. In these cases companies need a supply chain event management (SCEM) system that identifies disturbances (i.e. events) early through a comprehensive real-time monitoring system (e.g. RFID-based) and suggests counter-measures. These reactions have an operational focus and try to uphold an efficient production despite impending knock-on effects of events. One large group of measures, besides e.g. the reintroduction of time and stock buffers, are adaptions of the production schedule and thus, the pearl chain sequence. However, rescheduling methods make assumptions that are often insufficiently aligned with real-world problems [19, 14, 13] and focus solely on production issues while neglecting the implications of today's tight integration of supply chain with production processes. Despite ample methods [16, 19, 17], planers still find it difficult to react to events and to hold the supply chain stable. Hence, this paper proposes and evaluates a rescheduling approach for a pearl chain sequence of a BTO assembly line that includes implications of event-prone JIS delivery processes.

## 2    Literature Review

The scheduling environment is divided into a static and dynamic environment [19, 16]. In the former, a finite set of orders has to be scheduled without the presence of uncertainty. This paper assumes a *dynamic and stochastic environment* in which an infinite set of orders is subject to uncertainty of some parameters. A scheduling problem of a manufacturer is specified further with the $\alpha \mid \beta \mid \gamma$ notation [13] that refer to the machine environment, processing characteristics and the scheduling objective.

Two of the more complex *machine environments* are job and flow shops that are characterized by the existence or lack of process flow variability, which is due to a multiple stage production process [13]. We model a MMAL and consequently a flow shop where every order has to be processed on the same sequential stages. Assumptions for *processing characteristics* of flow shops differ considerably from job shops and often exclude preemption (i.e. interruption of processing), recirculation, setup times, and machine breakdowns [17]. One important characteristic of flow shops is the availability and size of buffers (i.e. in-process inventories) between stations. A limited buffer implies blocking while a no-wait system like the tact-driven, constantly moving MMAL considered in this paper demands that orders cannot wait between stations and thus production start is delayed until processing is ensured [13]. The problem can be framed as a *proportionate flow shop problem* with equal processing times at each station and without intermittent buffers (MMAL does not halt). The *(re)-scheduling objective* aims either at operational (e.g. asset utilization) or market targets (on-time deliveries) [13]. For instance, makespan is the completion time of the last scheduled order. Its minimization implies a good utilization [13]. Other measures are often a variation of the earliness/tardiness criterion that are sometimes combined with the nervousness criterion to balance permutations [10].

In practice, scheduling is driven by uncertainty [11] while rescheduling is driven by the occurrence of a disturbance. Both concepts can be applied to different degrees in a dynamic and stochastic environment. Approaches with a focus that is entirely offline (i.e. robust scheduling) devise an initial schedule that is not updated while online approaches (i.e. totally reactive scheduling) make all processing decision locally in real-time. A representative for the latter is the choice of the most appropriate dispatching rule [7]. In a dynamic and stochastic environment, predictive-reactive scheduling is the only approach that combines scheduling and rescheduling [19, 16]. It follows a two-step approach where an initial schedule is devised (generation step) and then updated (control step). The interval of an update step is defined as periodic, event-driven, or a combination of both. Since the JIS deliveries to the assembly system are disrupted, a predictive-reactive (re)-scheduling with an event-driven policy is employed. A final aspect is the applied repair strategy that takes effect when a policy triggers a rescheduling. It is characterized by the degree to which it overhauls the initial schedule (partial or complete). This paper presents a partial repair strategy for event-prone JIS deliveries to BTO production systems.

## 3      Problem Formulation

Fig. 1 illustrates a tractor assembly line. From the virtual order bank (VOB), customer orders are sequenced on a weekly basis through a scheduling based on order priority. The scheduled sequence is one week long and fixes the production programme for week 5 – i.e. specific assembly times and the according delivery dates for JIS components. The preceding 4 weeks were scheduled earlier and constitute the frozen zone. It is a pearl chain of over 1200 customer-specific orders that will be assembled over 4 weeks. The length of the frozen zone is determined by the JIS supplier with the longest order to delivery (OTD) time. Around 10 components of the tractor (e.g. drive) are delivered JIS. For each component, a customer can choose between several versions. Thus, each JIS supplier has his own customer-specific sequence that runs in parallel to the order sequence of the manufacturer. They all converge on the assembly line.

From this use case, a model is developed that is generalizable for most BTO assembly systems with JIS deliveries (e.g. automotive industry). Customer orders for a single product arrive randomly in the VOB (see Fig. 1 and Fig. 2), modelled through the Poisson process with exponentially distributed arrival intervals $\lambda$. Customer orders are associated with an order time $o_j$ and a random committed due date $d_j$ that is bound on the lower end by the minimum OTD time of the supply network and its double on the upper end. These limits are largely in accordance with an empirical investigation at the case partner, where they were found to be 4 and 12 weeks respectively [8].

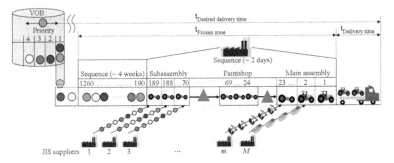

**Fig. 1.** Industrial case study

The SC consists of $M$ suppliers ($1 \leq m \leq M$) that each supplies one station at the MMAL with a component family that comprises $N$ products ($1 \leq n \leq N$) (Fig. 2). When ordering, a customer can select a specific component $n$ of each family to customize his product. The sum of components ordered by a customer constitutes his individual product configuration that is sourced JIS. Each supplier $m$ has a specific OTD time $\zeta_m$ that is subject to random variation due to disturbances. New orders that are not yet sequenced are part of the VOB (see Fig. 2) where orders are sorted by due date $d_j$ from latest to earliest. A one week production schedule is devised weekly with component orders being sent to the suppliers. Within the scheduled sequence of $J$ customer orders ($1 \leq j \leq J$), each order $j$ is associated with a fixed assembly sequence position $s_j$ and thus, a release date $r_j$ when final assembly is scheduled to start.

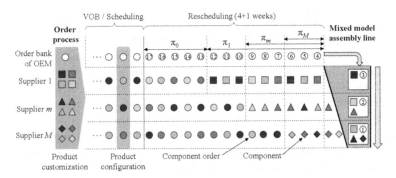

**Fig. 2.** MMAL model with JIS component deliveries

The newly scheduled component orders then successively enter the frozen zones of the $M$ suppliers, depending on $r_j$ and the supplier-specific lead time $\zeta_m$ (see Fig. 2). Once an order enters the frozen zone of supplier $m$, the production of component $n_{mj}$ has begun. Due to this supply chain setup, the mixed model assembly line (MMAL) assembles a total of $n^m$ product variants. Using the $\alpha \mid \beta \mid \gamma$ notation a $Fm \mid p_{mj}=p_j \mid \sum T_j / J$ production system is modelled. It is a *proportional flow shop problem* (PFSP) with $m$ work stations in series; the processing times $p_{mj}$ of order $j$ on station $m$ are identical and equal to $p_j$; the objective function is to minimize the average order-related delivery delay. We assume the MMAL to be a black box where processing times are deterministic and known. A resequencing within the MMAL is excluded (i.e. no mixed-bank buffers [12]). Orders that cannot be assembled due to missing components are moved to the rework area. Completed orders are shipped to the customer and the order-specific tardiness is recorded (if completion time $c_j > d_j$).

# 4    The Multiple Permutable Subsequences Concept

Although providing planning stability, a long frozen zone of e.g. 4 weeks leads to an increase of the probability that disturbances affect supplier sequences. The mismatch between real and planned state of ordered components results in delayed or failed deliveries [4]. Because components are customer-specific, in either case the current sequence position $s_j$ of an order $j$ cannot be hold. Fig. 3 illustrates removal strategies.

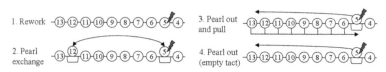

**Fig. 3.** Removal strategies for affected customer orders

The case partner currently moves affected orders to the end of the sequence and advances all others (third strategy in Fig. 3), which has several implications. First, schedule changes have to be communicated to all JIS suppliers, who in turn have to provide the components of advanced orders faster than their frozen zone, which is not always possible and compromises product quality (rush jobs). In urgent cases, emergency transports are devised. Second, the rescheduling policy avoids an empty tact but decreases pearl chain stability since the removal of one order alters the position of the others. This leads to suboptimal due date adherence and confusion on the shop floor. The latter refers to difficulties in aligning the material flow of the right components with the correct machines. Third, high instability with missing or wrong material coupled with a continuously moving assembly line results in rework. While assembly takes a few days, rework can take weeks, further jeopardizing due dates.

To avoid these drawbacks, it is assumed that customer orders are only moved back in the sequence. Thus, strategies two and three in Fig. 3 are invalidated and only 'rework' and 'empty tact' remain. The rework strategy reflects today's supply networks that lack real-time monitoring systems. Components that are delayed or failed are only noticed at the OEM when assembly and component sequences cannot be aligned. The unfinished product then moves to the rework area after assembly. Through a continuously monitored supply chain costly rework is avoided because orders can be removed from the sequence when components are affected by an event. This approach, however, poses the question where the removed order is reinserted into the sequence. To this end, we propose the *multiple permutable subsequences* approach that is based on the insight that the frozen zone is divided into several component sequences that differ in length due to individual OTD times of JIS suppliers (Fig. 4).

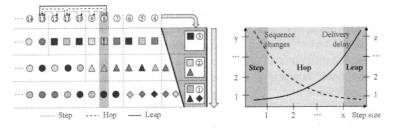

**Fig. 4.** Trade-off between schedule optimality and nervousness during rescheduling

Fig. 2 and Fig. 4 (starting with $s_j = 13$) show that within the *totally permutable subsequence* (TPS) $\pi_0$ orders are easily rescheduled because components are not in production. Hence, the TPS is reduced whenever an order enters the frozen zone of the supplier with the longest OTD, marking the beginning of the *partially permutable subsequences* (PPS) $\pi_m$. Thus, while one component is affected by an event, other components that are already in production would still be delivered on time, which a rescheduling strategy needs to consider. Fig. 4 shows three strategies based on the individual order step size for reinserting an order when it is in the PPS: *step*, *hop* and *leap*. The step strategy moves every order, starting with the delayed order, one sequence position back, resulting in high nervousness but low cumulated delivery delay. In contrast, the hop strategy removes orders based on a criterion (e.g., due date) to balance indicators. Lastly, the leap strategy removes an order from its current position and moves it to the back of the affected component sequence (e.g., from $s_j = 8$ to $s_j = 13$ in Fig. 4). All order sequence positions behind the reinserted order are then increased by one. The resulting empty position (e.g., $s_j = 8$ in Fig. 4) can be filled if another order further down in the sequence is delayed or failed.

# 5    Evaluation

The model with the rework and leap strategies was implemented into Plant Simulation from Siemens PLM Software. The MMAL is supplied by 3 JIS suppliers (drive, engine, and cabin) with a respective lead time of 18, 12, and 6 days and an on-time delivery reliability of 86, 91 and 97% respectively. Each supplier offers 4 different component versions that are randomly chosen by the customer, whose orders arrive according to the Poisson process in mean intervals of 30 minutes. The MMAL assembles 64 different variants and runs at a tact time of 30 minutes. If during assembly customer-specific components are missing, the order is moved to the rework area. The simulation ran for 100 days, including a calibration phase of around 30 days.

Fig. 5 compares the performance of the rework and leap strategies. As outlined earlier, the foremost objective is to have products that do not require rework after assembly. The leap strategy fulfils this requirement by increasing the assembly volume by 23.6% (i.e. products that do not need rework) while virtually eliminating rework that is due to missing components. Through the delay of the product assembly for orders where components are missing, however, the overall production volume is decreased by 3.2% over the simulation time. Furthermore, a total of 765 sequence positions remained empty due to the order removal, which reduces the utilization of the assembly line. The comparison between rework and leap for this indicator is misleading, however, because work stations that lack the correct component are also idle when the rework strategy is applied. Thus, the difference in utilization between the two strategies is less than Fig. 5 suggests. The final indicator is the number of sequence positions that were filled through the application of the leap strategy. These 270 positions became empty through a problem in the supply chain for an order but were filled at a later point in time through the inserting of another order further downstream. As predicted in Fig. 4 and shown in Fig. 5, the leap strategy is associated with a poor performance in regard to the average product delivery delay. It rises from about 4 hours for the rework strategy to more than 20 hours when the leap strategy is applied.

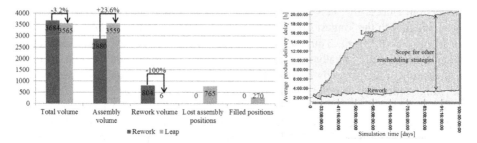

**Fig. 5.** Comparison of the rework and leap strategies

# 6     Summary

Modern BTO production systems are characterized by low inventories for main components that are sourced JIS. The respective component sequences merge seamlessly on the assembly line into a customer-specific product. Trends like global sourcing and lean management, however, have virtually eliminated the scope for variation in the supply processes. Thus, small and large events alike cripple the synchronization of the individual component sequences. A SCEM system identifies these disturbances early through a comprehensive real-time monitoring system and suggests counter-measures. To repair the affected production sequence, this paper presents the multiple permutable subsequences concept that divides the frozen zone into several subsequences of diminishing rescheduling flexibility. The evaluation for one strategy ('leap') showed that through the early removal of affected customer orders from the sequence costly rework due to missing JIS components is avoided. Since the strategy moves an order to the end of the partially permutable subsequence, however, the average product delivery delay is worse when compared to the status quo. Thus, future work focuses on the implementation and evaluation of other strategies that increase performance.

**Acknowledgements.** Part of this work was funded by the Federal Ministry for Economics and Technology (BMWi) under the reference number 01MA10014 'RAN – RFID-based Automotive Network'. Refer to www.autoran.de/en for further details.

# References

1. Christopher, M., Holweg, M.: "Supply Chain 2.0": Managing Supply Chains in the Era of Turbulence. International Journal of Physical Distribution & Logistics Management 41(1), 63–82 (2011)
2. Gaonkar, R., Viswanadham, N.: Analytical Framework for the Management of Risk in Supply Chains. IEEE Transactions on Automation Science and Engineering 4(2), 265–273 (2007)
3. Gunasekaran, A., Ngai, E.: Build-to-Order Supply Chain Management: A Literature Review and Framework for Development. Journal of Operations Management 23(5), 423–451 (2005)
4. Heinecke, G., Köber, J., Kunz, A., Lamparter, S.: Modeling the Basic Cause-Effect Relationship between Supply Chain Events and Performance. In: Kreowski, H.J., Scholz-Reiter, B., Thoben, K.D. (eds.) Proceedings of the Third International Conference on Dynamics in Logistics, LDIC 2012, Bremen, Germany, ch. 13, pp. 163–174. Springer (February/March 2013)
5. Holweg, M., Disney, S.M., Hines, P., Naim, M.M.: Towards Responsive Vehicle Supply: A Simulation-based Investigation into Automotive Scheduling Systems. Journal of Operations Management 23(5), 507–530 (2005)
6. Holweg, M., Pil, F.K.: The Second Century: Reconnecting Customer and Value Chain through Build-to-Order Moving Beyond Mass and Lean in the Auto Industry. The MIT Press, Boston (2004)
7. Jeong, K.C., Kim, Y.D.: A Real-Time Scheduling Mechanism for a Flexible Manufacturing System: Using Simulation and Dispatching Rules. International Journal of Production Research 36(9), 2609–2626 (1998)
8. Köber, J., Heinecke, G.: Hybrid Production Strategy between Make-to-Order and Make-to-Stock – A Case Study at a Manufacturer of Agricultural Machinery with Volatile and Seasonal Demand. Procedia CIRP 3, 453–458 (2012)
9. Kotha, S.: Mass Customization: Implementing the Emerging Paradigm for Competitive Advantage. Strategic Management Journal 16(S1), 21–42 (1995)
10. Lamparter, S., Legat, C., Lepratti, R., Scharnagl, J., Jordan, L.: Event-based Reactive Production Order Scheduling for Manufacturing Execution Systems. In: 18th IFAC World Congress, pp. 2722–2730 (2011)
11. McKay, K.N., Wiers, V.C.: Unifying the Theory and Practice of Production Scheduling. Journal of Manufacturing Systems 18(4), 241–255 (1999)
12. Meissner, S.: Controlling Just-in-Sequence Flow-Production. Logistics Research 2, 45–53 (2010)
13. Pinedo, M.L.: Scheduling: Theory, Algorithms, and Systems. Springer, New York (2008)
14. Portougal, V., Robb, D.J.: Production Scheduling Theory: Just Where is it Applicable? Interfaces 30(6), 64–76 (2000)
15. Radjou, N., Orlov, L.M., Nakashima, T.: Adapting to Supply Network Change. Technical report, Forrester Research (2002)
16. Raheja, A.S., Subramaniam, V.: Reactive Recovery of Job Shop Schedules - A Review. International Journal of Advanced Manufacturing Technology 19, 756–763 (2002)
17. Ruiz, R., Maroto, C.: A Comprehensive Review and Evaluation of Permutation Flowshop Heuristics. European Journal of Operational Research 165(2), 479–494 (2005)
18. Thun, J.H., Hoenig, D.: An Empirical Analysis of Supply Chain Risk Management in the German Automotive Industry. International Journal of Production Economics 131(1), 242–249 (2011)
19. Vieira, G.E., Herrmann, J.W., Lin, E.: Rescheduling Manufacturing Systems: A Framework of Strategies, Policies, and Methods. Journal of Scheduling 6, 39–62 (2003)

# Support to Order Management and Collaborative Production of Customised Garments for Specific Target Groups

Eva Coscia[1], Michele Sesana[1], and Rosanna Fornasiero[2]

[1] TXT e-solutions s.p.a Via Frigia 27 20126 Milano, Italy
{Eva.Coscia,Michele.Sesana}@txtgroup.com
[2] ITIA CNR Via Bassini 15 20133 Milano, Italy
rosanna.fornasiero@itia.cnr.it

**Abstract.** This paper describes a solution for the creation and management of orders and other business documents, necessary for the production and delivery of customised garments. These documents are managed along a supply network that can be quickly set up with the support of a tool for the identification of best partners for the production of the ordered items. The management of the documents leverages on three elements: the adoption of a standard for the interoperability of the business information among different services used in the network; the usage of a tool for quickly and automatically check the documents' contents applying business rules on top of them; a middleware layer that provides a fast way of exchanging the checked documents. The set-up of the supply chain is supported by the Partner Search module which is in charge of managing and improving the manufacturer's knowledge about its potential partners. The solution is validated within an industrial pilot focused on the production of customised knitted items for obese people.

**Keywords:** supply chain management; business document exchange, customized order, partner search.

## 1    Introduction

This paper presents a new approach, developed in the context of the CoReNet[1] project, for the creation of orders and for the production of customized items for specific groups of consumers that have functional and healthy requirements, such as, for example, obese people. The production of a single lot or of small series in a short time and with acceptable prices is a complex task for fashion companies (especially SMEs) that require a support during all the phases of this process, from market analysis and collection design, to item production, delivery and validation by the final consumer.

---

[1] FP7 NMP 260169 *CoreNet* (*Customer-ORiented and Eco-friendly NETworks for healthy fashionable goods*) project website: http://www.corenet-project.eu

C. Emmanouilidis, M. Taisch, D. Kiritsis (Eds.): APMS 2012, Part I, IFIP AICT 397, pp. 334–341, 2013.

The solution presented in this paper supports companies in three business processes: product configuration during the sales process, management of customized orders and other business documents exchanged along the supply chain during production process and the quick set up a of the supply chain for the order fulfilment. These aspects emerged as important steps especially for companies willing to change from standard orders to customized orders where many different parameters have to be verified before production starts.

The usage of standards ensures interoperability of the business documents exchanged between the tools used in the various phases and allows applying checking rules on the information shared by the involved actors along the supply chain. Furthermore, the research of the best partners supporting the manufacturer in the production of the customised items is empowered by a tool for the creation and maintenance of profiles of potential partners providing the partners themselves with the possibility to update their profile with information on their production availability.

## 2    The General Reference Model and a Specific Instantiation: the Knitting Production Business Case

Companies in the Textile, Clothing and Footwear Industry (TCFI), facing the challenge of producing single items or small series of customized items, need support in order to re-design their processes and take advantage of implementing new ICT tools to support them. The CoReNet Reference Model [1] is based on the formalization of the most important business processes requiring collaboration amongst different partners (from product conception and design, to production and delivery), and provides also guidelines along three important dimensions namely organizational changes, ICT and implementation of innovative tools supporting, and knowledge management.

Within this work, the new approach to network management has been validated within an industrial Pilot, called the Knitted Garments Pilot (KGP), where an important fashion company plays the role of the manufacturer. This company, specialized in the production of high-quality fashionable garments, is interested in extending its business to the design and production of garments for obese people, allowing them to order personalized (in sizes and in aesthetical aspects) items. According to the CoRM formalization and the business requirements collected with the company, the new approach proposed for the KGP aims to manage the networks both upstream towards the suppliers and downstream towards the customers and it is based on:

- Organizational revision of the business processes: the sales process is re-engineered to support a new relationship with the customer to ease the formalization of her/his specific needs and to manage the order collection and the product delivery. The relationship with the third parties involved in different working phases need to be based on a more collaborative approach where the third parties can share in a formal way their availability to produce.

- Definition of new ICT tools to support the different phases of sales and order management processes: innovative tools have to be based on integrated provision of advanced services and interoperability with the existing legacies also through the adoption of existing standards for the documents exchanged along the network.

- Change in the knowledge management: the company needs to enlarge the knowledge base on customer requirements and formalize all the different features of the order with specific and dedicated services. This new knowledge base needs to be used during the design phase, in the shop and during production by different actors.

In the specific case of obese people as well as in other target groups like diabetics, elderly etc they have specific requirements for shopping clothes, which are related not only to their sizes, but which require taking a number of measures with the support of dedicated shop assistants or tailors and the production of specific items as well as the need of having fabrics, styles and patterns specific for them. These models and patterns are not always fully available in the shops, therefore the support of an on-line gallery that allows browsing on a number of dedicated items with 3D rendering and possibility of selecting variants would be very useful.

## 3     Background

In literature, there are many different approaches for the order management as well as for the partner search process. These approaches need to be adapated to the needs of customized products. For what concerns order management, while in [10] it is proposed an approach for the qualitative evaluation of the turbulence of the market in [11] it is explained how to increase degree of responsiveness with a new architecture based on Web Services and Ubiquitous Computing technologies for reliable real-time information. The TCFI sector, also analysed in [12,13], is populated by a number of small or micro enterprises, with limited resources for the adoption of innovative IT solutions,  and requires the adoption of order management solutions based on exchange of documents based on SMTP or HTTP rather than on a fully SOA architecture for a step-by-step approach to integration of different modules.

The exchange of business documents along the supply chain for the production of textile and garments need to be formalized in the ModaML/TexSpin standard [5,12,13] that has been included in the results of the eBIZ process [4]; till now the ordering, production and delivery of customized garments, however, is not fully covered by these standards and this work aims to contribute to improve them.

For what concerns the use of different criteria to select partners for supply networks they have been characterized in works developed by [14] and [2] who introduced the utilization of performance measures, usually known as KPIs, to better compare and select the suitable partners for every specific VO (that can be considered a particular type of supply network). These approaches emphasize the importance of selecting partners using a well-defined set of criteria, based on common attributes of each company. Taking into account the improvement of organizations that apply methodologies to measure their performance [16] as well as the improvement of collaborative networks that are establishing inter-organizational Performance Measurement Systems [15], the KPIs can be used as criteria to suggest supply network partners. This strategy has been used also by [7] and [8] who introduced other criteria besides KPIs, like trustworthiness and risk values. [18] also proposed the utilization of KPIs related to collaboration and commitment which are also revised and used in this paper. In literature there are many different KPIs to be used for different scope and applying different perspective to the partners evaluation according to the scope of the network to be created. No shared ontology for modeling KPIs, nor taxonomy of supplies and supply chain roles are available if not restricted to specific sector/application requirements. For the scope of this work, some important KPIs have been selected from literature and from real case studies and have been formalized in the Partner Profile.

# 4    From Customized Order Creation to Collaborative Production

In Figure 1, the processes from the order generation to the delivery of the customised items are depicted and the tools supporting the flow are highlighted with a light dotted grey circle. In particular the following processes are taken into consideration:

- sales process with product configuration
- network configuration process based on partner search
- order management based on standardized document format.

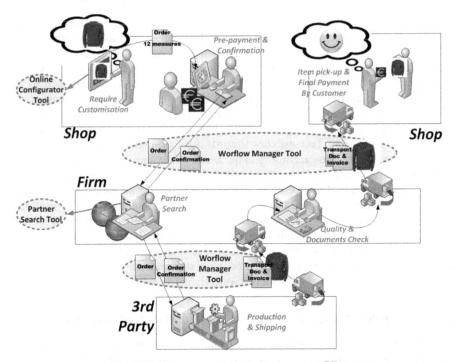

**Fig. 1.** Tool coverage on the knitted garment Pilot

## 4.1    The Sales Process: From Product Configuration to Order Dispatching

The sales process is mainly supported by the introduction of an innovative Configuration user interface to be used by the shop assistant and consists of 3 main parts:

- A configurator used by the company to prepare an on-line collection and to define the customisable parameters made available to the target group of consumers
- A service to quickly get measures of obese people, which allows calculating a set of 12 body measures starting from 3 simple measures.
- An online order preparation and submission tool.

Using a rich graphical user interface, a consumer with the support of the shop assistant can browse a catalogue of items, select and configure them both aesthetically (for example by changing colour, accessories like buttons etc…) and functionally by entering his own measures and specific needs (like larger sizes, functional fabrics and adapted fashion options).

The order is created by a consumer with the support of a shop assistant using the online configurator and is complete of sensible data (related to the consumer and to the prepayment amount); then the order is automatically checked by the system (to avoid errors or incompleteness) and then dispatched to the producer that, with the support of other tools of the pilot, can identify the best suppliers.

## 4.2    The Network Configuration Process: The Partner Search Tool

The network configuration process runs when new $3^{rd}$ parties are needed for knitting or sewing the product requested by the customized order. The process is supported by a Partner Search tool which is based on available capability of each registered potential partner and on KPIs based on their past performance in case they have already collaborate [3]. The selection of partners is based on criteria related to the product features as from the received order but also on criteria to measure the performance of the partner in terms of quality, time, and price. With the Partner Search tool, it is possible to execute multi dimensional searches in order to retrieve partners that provide the best matches towards a set of identified KPIs. These KPIs can be chosen time by time according to the needs of the specific customized order to be produced giving different importance to capabilities, time, cost and quality.

In the specific case of the KGP one of the key criteria for the quick and successful selection of a supplier is the availability of (pre-configured) knitting machines. Therefore the tool can be used at operational level as a collaborative tool since it allows the suppliers to update their profiles with information on availability (in a given time frame) of their machines for the production of specific items. If necessary, the producer exchanges other information with the selected suppliers to plan and execute the production, until the item is physically delivered to consumer at the shop.

## 4.3    The Order Management Process and Use of Data Exchange Standards

The Workflow Manager (WfM) tool seamlessly supports the correct flow of information along a designed process that involves different actors. It applies rules checking the format and the content of the Business Documents and dispatches them to the correct receivers, also providing feedback on errors and anomalies, when necessary. This allows companies to save time when receiving many different orders for customised items, supporting them in dispatching the correct pieces of information to the correct partners.

The WfM architecture is actually based on an Enterprise Service Bus (ESB) that takes care of: managing the exchange of information with external applications/services (on-line configurator, ERP etc.), decoupling the specific way the information is transferred from an external application/service to the ESB and vice versa.

The flow of information generated by the creation of a customized order is usually more complex than the one generated by a standard order, given the amount of data and details to be managed after order collection till the delivery of the item to the final customer. This flow of information needs to be conveyed to the proper actors and tools in a way that is perfectly understandable and manageable by all of them in the shortest possible time. In the case of the TCFI sector, the most natural choice was to evaluate the adoption of the interoperability architecture proposed by eBiz TCF[2] [4] project, that encompasses the Moda-ML[3] standard [5] for Textile and Clothing business documents. The eBIZ processes and documents fitting KGP have been identified and analysed, realizing that eBIZ does not provide a full coverage of the process underlying the creation and management of orders for customized garments. Therefore a set of eBIZ/Moda-ML documents that support the exchange of information for the on-demand production of customized knitted items has been conceived and will end up with the release of a proposal for an extension of the standard, submitted to the ongoing eBIZ CEN workshop[4].

## 5     Conclusions

The KGP scenario presented in this paper describes innovative services to support SMEs in the application of advanced tools for enhanced sales process and collaborative production process. Beyond the benefits deriving by the adoption of a standard for the information exchange, it is important to remark the most innovative aspects emerged by the adoption of the proposed tools in the KGP scenario, are:

- Management of a "customised order" which is presently not supported by the standards in the TCFI sector: This work is a contribution to define a standard format for this kind of order for the Clothing sector, which can be applied to the ordering of different garments, not only knitted items.

- Creation of the order based on collaboration of different actors: the part of the order for "customisation" definition (aesthetical preferences and measures) is done in the on-line configurator and then completed with sensible data in the shop by means of

---

[2] eBiz TCF is a project launched in January 2008 by the European Commission to boost e-business processes in the Textile/Clothing and Footwear (TCF) Industries website: http://ebiz-tcf.eu/

[3] Moda-ML is an initiative that aims to publicly offer tools and format specifications for the data exchange in networks of Textile/Clothing enterprises;website: http://www.moda-ml.org/

[4] eBIZ workshop : http://www.cen.eu/cen/News/PressReleases/Pages/PR-2012-01-23_eBiz.aspx

the ERP company system. The management of the order is fully supported by tools integrated by the WfM.

- Possibility to model through business rules, defined and executed in the WfM properties on the structure and on the content of the documents that are not modelled by the standard.

- Definition and maintenance of information on possible production partners, not only derived from the administrative data but also from their past performances or provided directly, in a collaborative way, by the partners itself.

The integrated solutions that have been designed in order to optimize the automatic exchange of structured information, allow companies to reduces the overall time from the order generation to the production and delivery of a customized product as demonstrated in the KGP. The advantages of the proposed services are that each business partner involved in the process can express rules on the expected contents of the exchanged documents (i.e. presence of a pre-payment description in the order is necessary for its acceptance by the producer) and can specify actions to be triggered (i.e. the order is rejected and a rejection notification is sent to the shop). The advantages of the Partner Search tool are that each partner can collaboratively share its own available capability and the manufacturer can manage in a formal way all partner profiles according to reliable and updated performance measurement. This has demonstrated to increase quality of the partners selected both in terms of reliability and in terms of delivery time.

There are several potential extensions of the solution, among which to provide tool coverage also to support the manufacturer in the selection and publication of garments in the on-line configurator (for example, by providing a virtualisation of the items on obese morphotypes) and check applicability of the solutions to different kind of garments, in particular for those requiring more complex supply chains to be produced. Moreover the proposed solution has been conceived to be applicable to business environments beyond the ordering and production of knitted items and addressing different target groups (not only obese people). For example, the format of the standard documents is general enough to be applied to other kinds of clothes also requiring different sets of personalised measures and the partner profile can be applied as well to other kind of production.

**Acknowledgement.** This work has been partly funded by the European Commission through FP7 NMP *CoreNet* (*Customer-ORiented and Eco-friendly NETworks for healthy fashionable goods*) project (Grant Agreement No. 260169).

# References

1. Zangiacomi, A., Fornasiero, R., Bastos, J., Azevedo, A., Franchini, V., Vinelli, A.: Reference Model Framework for Production of Small Series of Innovative and Fashionable Goods in Manufacturing Networks. In: Azevedo, A. (ed.) Advances in Sustainable and Competitive Manufacturing Systems. 23rd International Conference on Flexible Automation and Intelligent Manufacturing. Lecture Notes in Mechanical Engineering, pp. 1291–1303. Springer (2013)
2. Seifert, M., Eschenbächer, J.: Predictive Performance Measurement in Virtual Organization. In: Camarinha-Matos, L.M. (ed.) Emerging Solutions for Future Manufacturing Systems. IFIP, vol. 159, pp. 299–307. Springer, Boston (2005)

3. Rotondi, D., Piccione, S., Sesana, M., Fornasiero, R.: Semantics and KPIs to improve partners selection for small series production. To be published on 18th International ICE-Conference on Engineering, Technology and Innovation, June 18-20, Munich Proceedings (2012)

4. eBiz TCF Reference Architecture available at http://ebiz-tcf.eu/reference-architecture/

5. ModaML 2011-1 version available at http://www.moda-ml.org/moda-ml/imple/moda-ml-2011-1.asp?lingua=en&pag=0&modo=0

6. Camarinha-Matos, L.M., Oliveira, A.I., Demsar, D., Sesana, M., Molina, A., Baldo, F., Jarimo, T.: VO Creation Assistance Services. In: Methods and Tools for Collaborative Networked Organizations, Springer, New York (2008)

7. Jarimo, T., Salkari, I., Bollhalter, S.: Partner Selection with Network Interdependencies: An Application. In: Camarinlia-Matos, L., Afsarmanesh, H., Ollus, M. (eds.) Network-Centric Collaboration and Supporting Frameworks. IFIP, vol. 224, pp. 389–396. Springer, Boston (2006)

8. Crispim, J.A., Sousa, J.P.: Multiple Criteria Partner Selection in Virtual Enterprises. In: Camarinha-Matos, L.M., Afsarmanesh, H., Novais, P., Analide, C. (eds.) Establishing the Foundation of Collaborative Networks. IFIP AICT, vol. 243, pp. 197–206. Springer, Boston (2007)

9. Wiendahl, H.-H.: Fast and Reliable Order Management Design Using a Qualitative Approach. In: Olhager, J., Persson, F. (eds.) Advances in Production Management Systems. IFIP, vol. 246, pp. 237–244. Springer, Boston (2007)

10. Park, M., Shin, K., Jeong, H., Park, J.: A Framework for Enhancing Responsiveness in Sales Order Processing System Using Web Services and Ubiquitous Computing Technologies. In: Vallespir, B., Alix, T. (eds.) APMS 2009. IFIP AICT, vol. 338, pp. 449–456. Springer, Heidelberg (2010)

11. Gessa, N., Cucchiara, G., De Sabbata, P., Brutti, A.: —A bottom-up approach to build a B2B sectorial standard: the case of Moda-ML/TexSpin. In: Panetto, H. (ed.) — Interoperability of Enterprise Software Applications, Workshops of the INTEROP- ESA International Conference, Geneve, February 22, pp. 249–260. Hermes Science Publishing, Paris (2005) ISBN-1-905209-45-5

12. De Sabbata, P., Gessa, N., Brutti, A., Novelli, C., Frascella, A., D'Agosta, G.: Standard creation and adoption for SME networks. In: Panetto, H. (ed.) Interoperability for Enterprise Software and Applications. Proceedings of the Workshops and the Doctorial Symposium of the I-ESA International Conference 2010 (Workshop: Standards - a Foundation for Interoperability), Coventry, April 13, pp. 41–51. Nacer Boudjlida, ISTE/Wiley (June 2010) ISBN 978-1-84821-270-1

13. Grudzewski, W.M., Sankowska, A., Wantuchowicz, M.: Virtual Scorecard as a Decision-making Tool in Creating Virtual Organisation. In: Camarinha-Matos, L.M., Afsarmanesh, H., Ortiz, A. (eds.) Collaborative Networks and Their Breeding Environments. IFIP, vol. 186, pp. 293–300. Springer, Boston (2005)

14. Gunasekaran, A., Williams, H.J., Mcgaughey, R.E.: Performance measurement and costing system in new enterprise. Technovation 25(5), 523–533 (2005)

15. Lambert, D.M., Pohlen, T.L.: Supply Chain Metrics. International Journal of Logistics Management 12(1), 1–19 (2001)

# Modeling and Simulation Tool for Sustainable MC Supply Chain Design and Assessment

Paolo Pedrazzoli, Marino Alge, Andrea Bettoni, and Luca Canetta

University of Applied Sciences and Arts of Southern Switzerland, ICIMSI, Manno, Switzerland
{paolo.pedrazzoli,marino.alge,andrea.bettoni,
luca.canetta}@supsi.ch

**Abstract.** Supply chain design, management and assessment are key success drivers in nowadays globalised economy. With the advent of new paradigms such as sustainability and mass customization, a new generation of tools is required. This work presents a supply chain simulation tool that allows to take into account the specificity of mass customized markets, efficiently dealing with the adjustable product physical structure and the complexity of handling customized Lot Size One orders. Moreover, this tool is integrated with a sustainable Assessment Engine that allows to configure, since the product design phase, the entire supply chain in a lifecycle perspective. In order to ensure a wide applicability of the tool, this is developed using a client-server architecture and exploiting a Shared Data Model that facilitates the integration of many applications coming from different providers thus giving a powerful decision support tool to companies' decision makers.

**Keywords:** supply chain, simulation tools, mass customization, sustainability.

## 1    Introduction

Mass customization is nowadays an established paradigm that companies, belonging to many different sectors, apply in order to differentiate their proposal and to allow a better fitting of their products with customers' needs. However its implementation is not yet a simple and straightforward process as it deeply depends on the specific characteristics of the reality where it is put into practice. This asks for methodologies to be used as guidelines and specific tools that support the integrated product-process-supply chain design brought forth by mass customization. Unfortunately such comprehensive approaches are, to these days, still lacking [1].

At the same time, the mere evaluation of economic performances is no more suitable in the current global economy. As the concept of sustainability is getting more and more consideration along with customers growing awareness about it, social and environmental issues related to the company business need to be taken into account towards greener and fairer products and supply chains. In the next future, such topics will increasingly set the governments' agenda and drive their decisions – some are already in place – in a shape that could considerably impact on the companies' business. However companies still struggle in finding adequate assessment frameworks for measuring sustainability performance of their supply chains [2].

C. Emmanouilidis, M. Taisch, D. Kiritsis (Eds.): APMS 2012, Part I, IFIP AICT 397, pp. 342–349, 2013.

To this end, within the S-MC-S project, that is co-funded by the European Commission, a collaborative software environment, we will refer to as the S-MC-S System, has been created. This system enables a collaborative and holistic design of a mass customized stable solution space [3] providing a twofold benefit: on the one hand, it allows different design tools covering different compartments of the whole project to share data thus providing support in the handling of the huge and heterogeneous information related to a mass customized solution space; on the other hand, it allows the gathering and formalization of the data needed to carry out a sustainability assessment of the designed solution all along its lifecycle.

This paper will present the conceived environment starting from an overview of the software architecture and Shared Data Model of the proposed system. In the second part, the development of a specific tool for the modeling and simulation of a supply chain for mass customized production will be described. Such tool is meant to overcome the weaknesses of the traditional approaches and to deliver a tool capable to cope with the complex logics of Lot Size One production and delivery driven by mass customization.

## 2    Shared Data Model

As previously said, the first step for laying the foundations of an integrated environment has been the definition of a Shared Data Model [3] where all the involved tools can store and retrieve the relevant information concerning the solution space. This description covers the three main aspects of a product in a lifecycle perspective. First of all the product nature, both in its hierarchical structure and its physical properties. Then the production process which encompasses the whole life of a product from its raw materials extraction down to its end of life treatment. Finally the supply chain, which describes all the involved actors and the carried out transportations of resources which have a role in the product life.

This collaborative description of the product is then used to perform a detailed assessment of its sustainability level. The assessment performed at the design stage of a product enables an iterative feedback between the design choices and the assessment-resulting KPIs based on a sustainable strategy of the company. Detection of problems and investigation of alternatives at this stage is crucial since late recognition and handling of these issues prevents from any effective countermeasures implementation.

In order to enable design of the solution space, a data model has been developed. This data model becomes the common language platform on which all data-providing agents exchange information with the underlining system, thus allowing interaction between them and ensuring consistency of correlated data. Inside the data model five macro areas can be identified as shown in the high-level class diagram of Fig. 1:

- core data entities: contains the project root node and provides elementary building blocks like resources and facilities along with their possible specialized entities as well as descriptive bridges for the other areas;

- product area: models both the resources that compose the product physical structure and how customization choices change the physical structure of the product;
- process area: models the operations which are connected by flows of materials as well as their input and transformed output;
- supply chain area: models the facilities involved in the solution space and the transportations in between them;
- assessment properties area: models assessment properties, representing the characteristics of the data entities used by the Assessment Engine for its calculations.

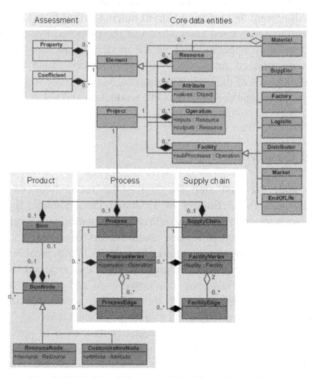

**Fig. 1.** UML Class Diagram of the Shared Data Model

## 3    System Architecture

The second building block of the S-MC-S System is its conceived architecture that is meant to structure the interactions amongst the various design and assessment tools relying on the above described data model. This architecture is based on a client-server model where the server, embodied by the Assessment Engine in Fig. 2, offers specific services and functionalities aimed to implement the full potential of the Shared Data Model platform and of a centralized assessment computation. The server, first of all, handles the persistency of all solution space data, lifting the burden of the developing effort of client specific persistency and providing a centralized repository of shared data on which clients can work collaboratively. The server also exposes locking mechanisms upon shared data to avoid data concurrent modification and to ensure the overall consistency. Moreover the server does not only provide services to handle shared data but it can be also triggered to perform the assessment computation based on the selected assessment model and to return the detailed assessment results back to the calling design tool.

By proposing this architecture the effort to develop a client able to take advantage of the S-MC-S services or even to adapt an existing design tool to it is minimized thus fostering the adoption of the S-MC-S System.

This is the case of the presented supply chain design tool, whose detailed architecture is shown in Fig. 2, where the server part is just sketched for completeness.

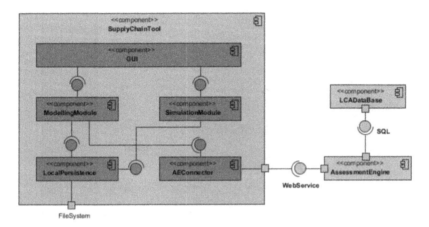

**Fig. 2.** UML Component Diagram of the Supply Chain Tool

## 4    Supply Chain Modeling Tool

Within the context of sustainable production of mass customized goods, as it has been aforementioned, the need for better coordination of the actors involved in the supply chain is recognized as one of the key success factors towards the paradigm adoption. Selection of proper suppliers becomes essential in order to handle the required flexibility needed to sustain the several choices offered to the final customer in an order-driven production. At the same time the ability to predict the system capability to satisfy the incoming orders within the allowed lead time is mandatory if an efficient supply chain is to be set up.

However, the existing supply chain modeling tools don't cope with such a level of detail. Here the customer order is no more an abstract concept representing a product lot to be delivered in time, being aggregated with other customer orders and managed in an undifferentiated way. It has to be represented as a single entity requiring a specific customization of the offered good. To this purpose a tool meant to support modeling and simulation of a mass customization oriented supply chain is here presented.

The definition of the supply chain attains two different levels, logical and geographical supported by related editing panels shown in Fig. 3. The first one allows to model into a graph structure even complex supply chains by defining actors, the macro-processes they carry out and the input/output resources for each one. The second one allows to intuitively geo-position the facilities and to retrieve distances and routes between them for sustainability impact calculation.

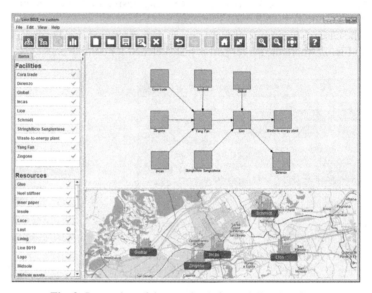

**Fig. 3.** Screenshot of the supply chain modeling interface

# 5     Simulation of the Supply Chain Behavior

The simulation feature of the supply chain tool acts as a decision support platform that enable, at low cost and robust simulation environment, analysis of what-if situations in order to compare alternative supply chains [5]. Furthermore it allows to detect problematic situations like bottlenecks, starving conditions, bullwhip effects under various simulation parameterizations.

This feature exploits a Discrete Event Simulation engine that, upon description of the stochastically variable events occurring in the supply chain, computes its behavior. The tool is provided with an animation feature that allows to graphically verify that the modeled solution is properly working.

One innovative aspect of this supply chain simulation tool is the enhanced description of the product customization aspect. This means that the product samples generated as demand of the various simulated markets are indeed product instances configured from the solution space according to the user-defined product mix. These configurations vary the nature of the different macro-processes applied on each single configured product resulting in different input resources requirements and different output resources productions, as well as different capacity loads and consequent lead times.

For each simulated facility, different strategies and methods can be defined and resulting behaviors simulated. At factory level, production capabilities are triggered by events generated either following a pull or push strategy thus embodying plan of make-to-order, assembly-to-order or make-to-stock productions. At suppliers level, supply agreements which drive the supplier behavior can be postulated for each of the replenished items. Moreover, at markets level, orders generation is driven by its parameterized statistical distribution aimed at representing the expected product mix. The features described above allow to model and simulate typical mass-customization supply chains supporting definition of different decoupling points for the handled resources. This enables proper representation of the different strategies used in order to achieve mass customized goods where standard parts are usually provided make-to-stock whereas highly customized components are produced or supplied only upon reception of customers orders.

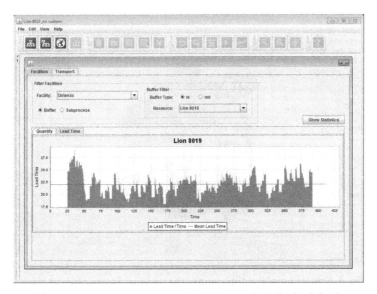

**Fig. 4.** Screenshot of a sample simulation result (order lead time)

As shown in the example of Fig. 4, the simulation results are summarized into an overall supply chain score though they can also be browsed for each facility and for each stock and process linked to it. In this way, it is easier to identify critical processes or facilities and study them deeper into details. Information like order lead time, stock level and stock related costs are available for each resource and the capacity utilization of each production line can also be analyzed.

## 6    Sustainability Assessment of the Supply Chain

Another evaluation layer proposed as support for suppliers selection is the sustainability one. Being connected to the multi-tool S-MC-S System environment, the presented supply chain design tool can exploit the holistic definition of the solution space held in the Shared Data Model in order to calculate its sustainability performances.

Indeed the tool itself completes the information necessary for carrying out the assessment that lie at supply chain level as, for instance, the distances of the covered transportations and the used means or the energy mix used by the facilities based on their geo-position. On the other hand, reuse of detailed definition of the product and production process, defined in other tools, allows to rapidly perform a reliable and complete assessment of the lifecycle sustainability impact of the product solution space.

The outcome [6] consists in the estimation of a total of 40 sustainability indicators (17 environmental, 10 economic and 13 social).

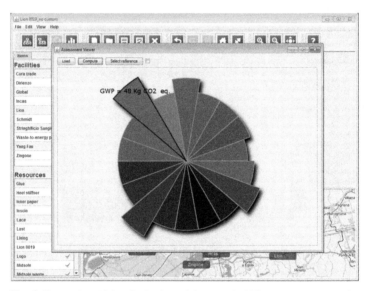

**Fig. 5.** Screenshot of the displaying of the sustainability assessment results

## 7    Conclusions

European Industry is developing methods and enabling technologies towards a customer-oriented and sustainable manufacturing as a key answer to global competitive pressure. This trend has been also understood by policy maker at the European Commission (e.g. as per the "Factory of the Future" multi-annual road-map [7]), and embraced by funding programmes for industrial research (FP7 and Horizon 2020 [8]).

The challenges related with customization lay with the need to efficiently deal with adjustable product physical configuration (whose options must be clearly identified and limited), with the complexity of producing  and handling customized Lot Size One orders, and with the need to cope with sustainability requirements.

The research work here presented focuses on the development of a decision support tool meant to cope with the definition of a proper supply chain for sustainable mass customized products, where current tools fall short. This is done in the framework of the S-MC-S project, that promotes the development of a software environment for the collaborative design of a sustainable mass customized solution space that takes into account product, process and supply chain.

The tool developed uses a client-server architecture and exploits a Shared Data Model that facilitates the integration of many different design tools coming from several providers. The tool empowers a better coordination of the actors involved in the supply chain recognized in the context of sustainable production of mass customized goods, which was one of the limiting factors of mass customization successful implementation. Indeed it supports, through an adherent to reality simulation, the selection of proper suppliers capable to handle the required flexibility in an order-driven production and, at the same time, it fosters the ability to predict the system capability to satisfy the incoming orders within the allowed lead time.

# References

1. Castellano, E., Dolado, J.: Product-processes-supply chain structures alignment for mass customization scenarios. A literature review. In: 4th International Conference on Industrial Engineering and Industrial Management. San Sebastián (2010)
2. Hassini, E., Surti, C., Searcy, C.: A literature review and a case study of sustainable supply chains with a focus on metrics. I. J. of Production Economics 140, 69–82 (2012)
3. Piller, F.T.: Mass Customization: Reflections on the State of the Concept. I. J. of Flexible Manufacturing Systems 16(4), 313–334 (2004)
4. Bettoni, A., Alge, M., Rovere, D., Pedrazzoli, P., Canetta, L.: Towards Sustainability Assessment: Reference Data Model for Integrated Product, Process, Supply Chain Design. In: Proceedings of the 18th International ICE Conference on Engineering, Technology and Innovation. IEEE Press, New York (2012)
5. Chang, Y., Makatsoris, H.: Supply Chain Modeling Using Simulation. I. J. of Simulation 2(1), 24–30 (2000)
6. Canetta, L., Pedrazzoli, P., Sorlini, M., Bettoni, A., Boër, C.R., Corti, D.: Customization and Manufacturing Sustainability: General considerations and footwear investigation. In: Piller, F.T., Chesbrough, H. (eds.) Bridging Mass Customization & Open Innovation. Lulu, Raleigh (2011)
7. European Commission: Factories of the Future PPP Strategic Multi-Annual Roadmap. Publications Office of the European Union, Luxembourg (2012)
8. Community Research and Development Information Service,
   http://cordis.europa.eu

# Agent Based Resources Allocation in Job Shop with Re-entrant Features: A Benchmarking Analysis

Matteo Mario Savino and Antonio Mazza

Department of Engineering, University of Sannio, Benevento, Italy
{matteo.savino,antonio.mazza}@unisannio.it

**Abstract.** Job shop production can be characterized by some unplanned event like re-entrant jobs at a certain stage of the production process. In this case a dynamic allocation management of the resources involved (machines, transporters, etc) can be key factor of success in optimizing some production parameter. The present work studies a multiple objective job shop in which the constraint that a workpiece visits a machine only once is relaxed. The production shop floor has been structured with a Multi Agent System (MAS) able to front dynamically these type of events. A benchmarking analysis is provided to compare the solutions found with other two main dynamic MAS-based systems present in literature.

**Keywords:** Re-entrant Job Shop, Multi-agent system, Resources Allocation Management, Production Scheduling.

## 1 Introduction

Flexibility and re-configurability are crucial issues for modern manufacturing system to meet the demand of continuously changing market and customers' requirements. Reconfigurable manufacturing methodologies were proposed in recent years and considered as an effective approach to achieve flexibility and efficiency of manufacturing systems and related services (Brun et al, 2011). In order to implement re-configurability, intelligent manufacturing philosophies, such as Multi Agent Manufacturing, have been used. In such type of approaches the system is reconfigured through a cooperation and negotiation of distributed and autonomous intelligent entities. Agent-based systems technology has generated lots of excitement in recent years because of its promise as a new paradigm for conceptualizing, designing, and implementing software systems. In the *Technoware* organization to which firms are aiming (Ouzrout et al., 2012) this aspect is particularly attractive to create software operating in distributed and open environments in which problems are essentially of dynamic and stochastic nature. In such context the traditional methods or algorithms like Branch and Bound (BB) and Constrained Based Propagation (CBP) might not be very useful. The aim of the present work is to propose an approach dealing with a dynamic management of a job shop production system featured with re-entrant job possibilities. The cooperation among specific resource agents and a dedicated scheduler agent has made possible the realization of an flexible approach, which effectiveness has

C. Emmanouilidis, M. Taisch, D. Kiritsis (Eds.): APMS 2012, Part I, IFIP AICT 397, pp. 350–358, 2013.

been benchmarked with other recent system present in literature. In the work, we consider a variation of the classical job shop scheduling problem, the reentrant job shop problem, in which it is relaxed the restriction that each job visits a machine only once in the shop floor. In this context the management of this type of event has been made with the aim to obtain a new local reschedule of the required resources.

## 2    Background

Resources allocation management involves several tasks related to the allocation of jobs, or even workers on machines, over a time period to perform a certain management tasks (Groover, 2003; Neubert, Savino, 2009). It is a decision-making process that plays an important role in most manufacturing and service industries (Pinedo, 2005). The most common manufacturing system worldwide is the job shop, which layout is associated with the production of small volumes/large variety products and operates in make-to-order environment. A specific job shop problem is the Re-entrant job shop, originally proposed by Kumar (1993) and considered as the third class of manufacturing system distinguished from job shop and flow shop (Wang and Lin, 2009). The re-entrant job shop scheduling problem extends the classical model by relaxing the restriction that each job visits a machine only once (Zoghby et al., 2004). In this context Fattahi et al. (2011) proposed a bi-objective algorithm which uses the simulated annealing algorithm for the re-entrant manufacturing systems, in order to maximize the production rate of the system and minimize the work in process (NP-Hard class). Wang and Lin, in 2009, proposed to solve the re-entrant job shop system as an ant colony system, developing an agent based simulation platform. Vinod and Sridharan (2009) focused on a simulation-based experimental study of scheduling decision rules, while  Zhou et al. (2008) proposed a model combining Discrete Event System (DES) and Multi-Agent System (MAS) to simulate a real-time job shop working as a test bed to study the performance of control rules and algorithms in dynamic job shop scheduling. MAS are characterized by the presence of two or more agents which interact and work together to perform some set of tasks. An agent may be a piece of software or a hardware that can perceive any changes in its environment and act upon through actuators, as for example in the Microgrids (Logenthiran et al., 2010). MAS have been used to handle both externally and internally driven events disruptive for the planned allocation of manufacturing resources. Tan et al. (2008) developed a MAS based Dynamic Resource Allocation Management (DRAM) System in which each agent is specialized in a sub domain. The system was tested and demonstrated its efficiency in case of unforeseen events like work-pieces delays or machines breakdown, but it was not tested against the problem of re-entrant jobs. According to Deng et al. (2008), re-entrant line is considered as one of the most complex manufacturing processes distinguished from job shop and flow shop. To front the problem they proposed a new model of constructing swarm intelligence on multi-agent system by applying an ant colony scheduling algorithm (ACSA). Wang and Lin (2009) presented a simulation model of a re-entrant line which is based on MAS and HLA (High Level Architecture) in which a new model of constructing an ant algorithm on multi-agent system is proposed to find a satisfactory scheduling scheme.

## 3     Case Study and Architecture

The work considers the shop floor of a firm producing power generators, with a job shop layout in which jobs need to be reworked after some external processing. Fig. 1 gives the layout of a part of the shop floor with a bridge crane as transportation resource.

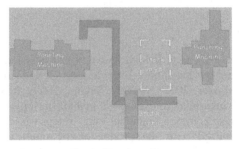

**Fig. 1.** The shop floor

The software agents communicate each other by a Service Oriented Architecture *(SOA)* and though the Contract Net Protocol *(CNP)* in order to perform the allocation of the jobs (Pasatcha and Sunat, 2008). CNP plays an important role in the dynamic characteristics of the agent-based system integration framework, providing a mechanism for agents to interact dynamically (Yun et al., 2009). CNP consists of two types of decision makers: i) managers and ii) contractors. A manager seeks a contractor to complete a task. It sends a request to all eligible contractors for getting bids of the task. After receiving the bids from the contractors, the manager awards the task to the best contractor based on certain criteria (Lau et al., 2006). The present Job allocation system uses the following five types of software agents: Job Agent (JA); Scheduler Agent (SA); Coordinator Agent (CA); Resource Agent (RA); Service Facilitator (SF). Fig. 2 shows the system the relationship between the JA, SA, CA, RA and SF.

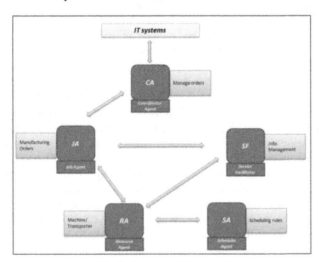

**Fig. 2.** System architecture

CA receives new manufacturing orders and order changes from the ERP system. For orders where the quantity has been reduced, it reports the state of completion and quantities of the WIP that are no longer required by the order. CA performs the following actions: 1. Generating a JA for each manufacturing order; 2. Passing relevant manufacturing order information needed by the JA to manage the completion of the manufacturing order; 2. Cancelling a JA when the manufacturing order is completed. Each JA represents a single manufacturing order receiving the following information: *1. Manufacturing order ID and due date; 2. Product quantity; 3. A listing of the process steps and their corresponding manufacturing lead times.* JA submits a request for the first process in the manufacturing routing of the product to the SF, which publishes the job or service requests. RAs of equipment and transporters that are in operation requests for the job specifications from the SDF. Upon receiving the job specifications, each RA will evaluate if it can handle the job request. In the case of a process job, RAs of process equipment prepare their bids and submit the request to the JA. After the JA has awarded the process job, it will now submit a service request for transportation to move the raw materials or Work in Process (WiP) to the process work centre of the process RA that has just been awarded with the process job, to the SF. RAs of equipment and transporters will request for the job specifications from the SF. Upon receiving the job specifications, each RA will evaluate if it can handle the job request. In this case, as the request is for transportation service, the RAs of process equipment will ascertain and realize that they are not suitable for the job. RAs of transporters will prepare and submit their bids. JA, upon receiving the bids, asks the SF to remove its request, evaluate the bids, and award the job to the RA that has submitted the most favorable bid. When a re-entrant job occurs, the JA is informed by the RA. The JA decides if the current process step should stay with the process equipment until the equipment is serviced and brought back to operation to continue, or to initiate a re-allocation of the current process step to other available equipment. When a process equipment or transporter is switched on to start operation, the RA is created. The RA is destroyed when the process equipment or transporter is switched off. A job that is awarded to the RA of either a process equipment or transporter by a JA, will be communicated to the sub-system controller for execution. The sub-system controller essentially receives job instructions from the RA and periodically sends the job status and the health condition to the RA. Negotiations are summarized in Fig. 3.

The Scheduler Agent (SA) is created to perform a scheduling rule defined according to a specific need of the firm. SA is used to give a precedence to the re-entrant job by associating a flag to each operation to indicate a manufacturing operation previously performed. Each RA sends its waiting queue of tasks to the SA, which arranges the list according to the scheduling rule assigned. Once applied the scheduling algorithm, the SA answers with the updated order of tasks to be executed on the machine. The full list of tasks of each machine is periodically collected and arranged by the SA. The list is dispatched by the machine creating in the meantime a parallel queue of waiting jobs to be ordered. In this way, it is avoided an undefined waiting of tasks characterized by heavy processing time. In the experimental campaign described in the next section, due to the features of the firm, the scheduling

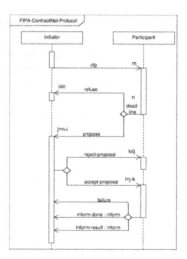

**Fig. 3.** Negotiations

rule which has been applied is the *shortest task first*. The SA is able to collaborate and communicate with the equipments by the use of its two behaviors, named *ReceiveQueue (RQ)* and *ApproveQueue (AQ)*. RQ receives the request made from the machine containing the list of tasks present in queue which must be ordered according to a scheduling rule. *AQ* and *RQ* can be used to establish the priority rule related to the re-entrant jobs, reducing the delay caused by new re-works. Once the list has been ordered, the SA sends the list to the equipment which made the request in order to allow tasks processing.

## 4     The Experimental Campaign

In order to test the system an experimental campaign has been conducted with five main scenarios. In this paper, due to space constraints, we present the most interesting one related to the presence of two re-entrant jobs and a fault on a transporter. The results obtained by the demonstrator are compared applying the DRAM of Luo et al (2009), and the Centralized Scheduling Optimization (CSP) function of Savino and Neubert (2009). The shop floor is composed of five machines typologies ($M_1...M_5$) for the execution of six jobs. Each job task $P_i$ is associated to the corresponding $M_i$ Machine. Tables 1a and 1b shows a comparison between the three systems (SA, DRAM and CSP) for this first case. Process routing, and results concerning Makespan and Average Tardiness are reported for each system.

An additional analysis has been focused on the evaluation of the WiP by considering the average size of each buffer which characterizes a machine. In this case the WiP value represents the number of tasks waiting to be processed in the buffer queue of the machine (Luo et al, 2009).

**Table 1a.** Benchmarking - Routings

| $J_1$ | | | $J_2$ | | | $J_3$ | | | $J_4$ | | | $J_5$ | | | $J_6$ | | |
|---|---|---|---|---|---|---|---|---|---|---|---|---|---|---|---|---|---|
| SA | DRAM | CSP | SA | DRAM | CSP | SA | DRAM | CSP | SA | DRAM | CSP | SA | DRAM | CSP | SA | DRAM | CSP |
| *Product Process Routing (seconds)* | | | | | | | | | | | | | | | | | |
| P1 50 | P1 50 | P3 80 | P1 50 | P5 50 | P1 50 | P1 40 | P2 50 | P5 60 | P1 50 | P1 50 | P1 50 | P1 10 | P5 10 | P2 10 | P1 20 | P5 20 | P4 10 |
| P3 80 | P3 80 | P1 50 | P2 100 | P2 100 | P5 50 | P4 30 | P1 40 | P4 30 | P3 80 | P5 20 | P3 80 | P2 10 | P1 10 | P1 10 | P4 10 | P1 20 | P1 20 |
| P5 60 | P4 60 | P4 60 | P5 50 | P1 50 | P2 100 | P5 60 | P4 30 | P1 40 | P5 20 | P3 80 | P5 20 | P5 10 | P5 10 | P5 10 | P5 20 | P4 10 | P2 10 |
| P4 60 | P2 60 | P5 60 | P2 100 | P4 100 | P4 100 | P2 50 | P3 50 | P3 50 | P4 10 | P2 10 | P4 10 | P1 10 | P4 10 | P4 10 | P2 10 | P3 10 | P5 10 |
| P2 60 | P5 60 | P2 60 | P4 100 | P2 100 | P2 100 | P3 50 | P5 60 | P2 50 | P2 10 | P4 10 | P2 10 | P4 10 | P1 10 | P1 10 | P3 10 | P2 10 | P3 10 |

**Table 1b.** Benchmarking – Delay, Makespan, Tardiness

| $J_1$ | | | $J_2$ | | | $J_3$ | | | $J_4$ | | | $J_5$ | | | $J_6$ | | |
|---|---|---|---|---|---|---|---|---|---|---|---|---|---|---|---|---|---|
| SA | DRAM | CSP | SA | DRAM | CSP | SA | DRAM | CSP | SA | DRAM | CSP | SA | DRAM | CSP | SA | DRAM | CSP |
| **MaxDelay** 30 sec | | | **MaxDelay** 50 sec | | | **MaxDelay** 40 sec | | | **MaxDelay** 60 sec | | | **MaxDelay** 50 sec | | | **MaxDelay** 20 sec | | |
| **Quantity=1** product | | | **Quantity=2** product | | | **Quantity=3** product | | | **Quantity=2** product | | | **Quantity=1** product | | | **Quantity=1** product | | |
| *Makespan (sec)* | | | | | | | | | | | | | | | | | |
| 300 | 315 | 280 | 450 | 490 | 410 | 250 | 270 | 240 | 200 | 220 | 205 | 70 | 75 | 60 | 100 | 110 | 95 |
| *Average Tardiness (sec)* | | | | | | | | | | | | | | | | | |
| 15 | 14 | 12 | 20 | 25 | 17 | 18 | 20 | 16 | 25 | 26 | 22 | 23 | 25 | 20 | 11 | 13 | 10 |

Tab. 2 shows the results obtained with respect to the buffer of Machine 1.

**Table 2.** Average WIP comparison

| Buffer number | Average WIP [# of tasks] | | |
|---|---|---|---|
| | SA | DRAM | CSP |
| *Machine 1* | 2.11 | 2.43 | 2.05 |

The introduction of the SA allows to reduce of a considerable amount the average WIP with respect to DRAM system: the reduction is around 13%. The scheduling rule aims to give execution priority to those tasks characterized by a low completion time, avoiding an increasing of the tasks in queue. We note also that the centralized structure of CSP allows to obtain a better result by reducing WiP of around 3% with respect to the modified version of DRAM. Fig. 4 shows the trend of the WIP with respect to the execution time of all the jobs for Machine 1.

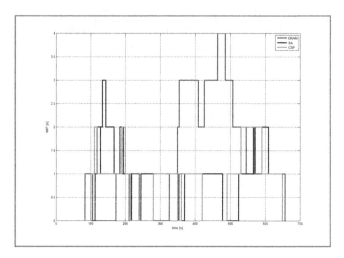

**Fig. 4.** WIP machine 1

SA scheduler provides good results in terms of WIP level by placing in an intermediate situation and reducing the WIP obtained by the application of DRAM scheduler. A further analysis has been conducted in order to evaluate Makespan distribution obtained by the application of the three schedulers. Fifteen simulation runs have been conducted in order to perform this analysis. The average and the standard deviation of the 15 samples are shown in Tab. 3.

**Table 3.** Makespan - Average and standard deviation

|                       | SA  | DRAM | CSP |
|-----------------------|-----|------|-----|
| *Average [sec]*       | 726 | 721  | 727 |
| *Std deviation [sec]* | 20  | 33   | 18  |

In spite of the small difference obtained for the average value, SA and CSP allow to obtain an important result concerning the standard deviation which is now reduced of around 50%. This result indicates that the use of SA and CSP schedulers introduce an uniformity of execution times, i.e. a lower time dispersion. In Fig. 8 we show the trend of execution times by subdividing Makespan range into five classes and associating to each of them the occurrences fitting into the same class. The use of SA and CSP reduce time dispersion and allow to thicken values within some grouping classes. The time necessary to complete the negotiation phase is usually very low (few seconds). The simulations conducted allowed to note that in a negotiation phase, when we have minor products but more jobs, this time takes only the 3% on the total time, instead when we have more products but minor jobs it is slightly higher, with a value maximum equal to 9.5%.

# 5    Conclusions

In this paper a MAS model has been applied for the job shop scheduling in a dynamic manufacturing system with the problem of re-entrant job, in order to give to the system the possibility to react to the events occurring in the real scenario. The model has been created first of all by identifying the agents involved in the system. In the systems developed a scheduler Agent determines the order for the execution of requests requiring the use of a specific resource. An analysis on the results of a case study has been conducted to test the behavior of the model under specified conditions and a combination of events. The results showed a good functionality of the system, highlighted by the improvement the main performance indicator, represented the max tardiness, WiP and Makespan. Good results have been obtained also considering job routing, especially if compared with the other two algorithm present in literature which with the benchmarking has been conducted.

# References

1. Deng, K., Lin, J., Wang, F.: Scheduling of Re-entrant Line Based on Swarm Intelligence. In: International Symposium on Knowledge Acquisition and Modeling, KAM 2008, pp. 323–328 (2008)
2. Fattahi, P., Tavakoli, N., Jalilvand-Nejad, A., Jolai, F.: A hybrid algo-rithm to solve the problem of re-entrant manufacturing system scheduling. CIRP Journal of Manufacturing Science and Technology 57(3), 175–197 (2011)
3. Groover, M.P.: Automation, production systems, and computer integrated manufacturing. Prentice Hall of India Pvt. Ltd., New Delhi (2003)
4. Kutanoglu, E., Sabuncuoglu, I.: An analysis of heuristics in a dynamic job shop with weighted tardiness objectives. International Journal of Production Research 37(1), 165–187 (1999)
5. Logenthiran, T., Srinivasan, D., Khambadkone, A.M., Aung, H.N.: Multi-Agent System (MAS) for Short-Term Generation Scheduling of a Microgrid. In: IEEE ICSET, Kandy, Sri Lanka (2010)
6. Neubert, G., Savino, M.M.: Flow shop operator scheduling through constraint satisfaction and constraint optimisation techniques. International Journal of Productivity and Quality Management 4(5/6), 549–568 (2009)
7. Ouzrout, Y., Savino, M.M., Mazza, A.: PLM maturity model: A multi-criteria assessment in southern Italy companies. International Journal of Operations and Quantitative Management 18(3), 160–17 (2012)
8. Pinedo, M.L.: Planning and scheduling in manufacturing and services. Springer, New York (2005)
9. Savino, M.M., Brun, A., Riccio, C.: Integrated system for mainten-ance and safety management through FMECA principles and fuzzy inference engine. European Journal of Industrial Engineering 5(2), 132–169 (2011)
10. Tan, C.H., Luo, M., Zhao, Y.Z.: Multi-agent approach for dynamic resource allocation. SIMTech technical reports, Singapore (2010)

11. Vinod, Sridharan: Development and analysis of scheduling decision rules for a dynamic flexible job shop production system: a simulation study. International Journal of Business Performance Management 11(1/2), 43–71 (2009)
12. Wong, M.M., Luo, M., Savino, M.M., Meoli, E.: Dynamic batch scheduling in a continuous cycle-constrained production system. International Journal of Services Operations and Informatics 5(4), 313–329 (2010)
13. Wang, F., Lin, J.: A Multi-Agent Architecture for Re-entrant Manufac-turing Line. In: IEEE Global Congress on Intelligent Systems, pp. 3–10 (2009)
14. Zhou, Lee, Nee: Simulating the generic job shop as a multi-agent system. International Journal of Intelligent Systems Technologies and Applications 4(1/2), 5–33 (2008)
15. Zoghby, J., Barnes, J., Hasenbein, J.: Modeling the reentrant job shop scheduling problem with setups for metaheuristic searches. European Journal of Operational Research 167(2, 1), 336–348 (2004)

# Design of a Taxation System to Promote Electric Vehicles in Singapore

Seng Tat Chua and Masaru Nakano

The Graduate School of System Design and Management, Keio University
Kyosei Building, 4-1-1, Hiyoshi, Kohoku-ku, Yokohama, Kanagawa, 223-8526, Japan
c.sengtat@gmail.com, nakano@sdm.keio.ac.jp

**Abstract.** Electric vehicles offer a potential low-carbon alternative to today's gasoline-powered vehicles. In line with global trends, Singapore has expressed interest in promoting electric vehicles on its shores. This paper investigates the effects of taxation, namely tax rebates and carbon taxes, on the penetration of electric vehicles in Singapore. A consumer vehicular preference model was constructed using the logit model, and the effects on the economy determined through an input–output analysis. Multi-objective optimization is then used to find the optimal tax rate. Results indicate that a tax rebate minimizes the negative impact on the economy at a low penetration rate of electric vehicles, whereas a carbon tax minimizes the negative impact on GDP at a high penetration rate of above 60%.

**Keywords:** Electric Vehicles, Sustainable Manufacturing, Socio-Technical Approach, Taxation.

## 1 Introduction

A holistic and socio-technical approach is needed to design a green society with clean energy vehicles (CEVs) in terms of extended social responsibility [1]. Sustainable manufacturing is defined in Nakano [2] as two concepts of 'manufacturing for society, mainly environmental issue' and 'sustainability of manufacturing sector'. Today, automakers are competing globally to develop CEVs. Manufacturing technologies are required that can reduce manufacturing costs and recycle valuable material. Service-oriented architectures, such as the used-battery business, have been developed to encourage consumers to accept EVs. Many national and local governments offer tax incentives to consumers to buy CEVs, and give subsidies to manufacturers to develop technologies such efficient batteries specifically designed for CEVs. This paper focuses on a taxation system to promote electric vehicles.

An integral part of Singapore's electric vehicle test-bedding program is positioning Singapore as a "Living Laboratory." The concept envisions Singapore as a place for companies to leverage its public infrastructure and experience systems-level integration for researching, developing, and testing innovative solutions for electric vehicles in a real environment with human activities.

C. Emmanouilidis, M. Taisch, D. Kiritsis (Eds.): APMS 2012, Part I, IFIP AICT 397, pp. 359–367, 2013.
© IFIP International Federation for Information Processing 2013

This research proposes an optimal taxation rate to increase the adoption rate of electric vehicles while considering the tradeoffs between gains in environmental benefits and reductions in GDP, due to decreased output in the petroleum industry as a result of an increase in the share of electric vehicles.

Two types of taxation will be investigated. The first is a tax rebate levied upon the purchase of an electric vehicle to lower the initial price of an electric vehicle relative to that of a conventional car. By lowering the automobile taxes of electric vehicles through the tax rebate, it is hoped that the price competitiveness of electric vehicles will increase, influencing consumers to make the greener purchase. The second taxation is a carbon tax levied on the fuel used by vehicles during the utilization phase. Taxation during the utilization phase implies that a tax on carbon emissions will be imposed on gasoline in case of a conventional car and electricity in case of an electric vehicle. The carbon tax will vary according to the amount of carbon dioxide emitted, based on the well-to-wheel (WtW) emissions of a vehicle. Because WtW carbon dioxide emissions of conventional cars are higher than that of electric vehicles, consumers will pay a higher carbon tax for conventional cars. The hypothesis is that by further increasing the running cost of conventional gasoline-powered cars through the carbon tax, the price competitiveness of electric vehicles will increase, causing consumers to choose electric vehicles over conventional cars.

## 2    Literature

### 2.1    Singapore and Other Countries

In larger countries such as the United States, Europe and Japan, there has been much interest in past research on the general diffusion process of alternative drive-train technologies [3, 4]. As the intention to promote electric vehicles is a recent development in Singapore, conventional researches based on Singapore as a subject of study have not yet been conducted. There has been largely qualitative research on the success of regulatory and economic instruments in urban environmental policy in Singapore [5]. In quantitative research, areas of focus include modeling of the number of cars in Singapore and comparisons between welfare effects of ownership taxes and usage taxes on cars [6, 7]. However, the effects of the introduction of taxes on the economy and environment have not been reported in conventional studies. In addition, promotion of electric vehicles through taxation has not been studied.

### 2.2    Macro and Micro Modeling

Traditional approaches to model vehicle diffusion can be largely categorized into macro and micro modeling. Macro modeling seeks to explain the aggregate economy whereas micro modeling refers to the representation of the behavior of consumers or smaller entities comprising individuals. While macro models seek to determine the impact on the economy and inter-relations between different sectors of the economy [8], they are founded on the assumption of the price rationality of consumers and do not allow for the construction of a vehicular preference model that includes characteristics beyond cost considerations. In contrast, while micro models are concerned with the vehicular preferences of consumers and the penetration rate of electric vehicles [9], there is insufficient treatment of the effects on the aggregate economy such as industrial structure, GDP, and the interconnections between sectors of the economy. A study on carbon taxation has been studied by using life cycle assessment [10], but GDP is not considered.

This paper thus seeks to harness strengths and compensate for the weaknesses of both macro and micro modeling approaches by combining both macro and micro approaches. The logit model based on past vehicle population data is used to determine vehicular preferences of consumers and predict the share of electric vehicles, while the impact of the proposed taxation on the economy is measured using an input–output analysis.

### 2.3 Tax Rebate and Carbon Tax

Conventional studies [8, 9] have primarily focused on the effects of one particular type of taxation, and merits and demerits of different types of tax policies have not been compared. In addition, while conventional researches have examined the effects of a tax on gasoline, the effects of a carbon tax levied on the "fuel" used by a vehicle, i.e., electricity taxed in case of electric vehicles, have not been studied. This paper, therefore, compares the effects of a tax rebate and a carbon tax based on Well-to-Wheel (WtW) carbon dioxide emission calculations.

## 3    Methodology

The effect of taxation on the share of electric vehicles up to 2020 will first be determined using a consumer vehicular preference model, by considering a projected decrease in the cost of electric vehicles and rising oil prices. The consumer vehicular preference model will be constructed using the logit model, based on past vehicle population data. The consumer utility function described below depends on two variables, i.e., lifecycle cost (LCC) or total ownership cost of a vehicle and previous year's vehicle share (VS). EV and GV denote electric vehicle and gasoline vehicle respectively.

$$f_k = \alpha \, \mathrm{LCC}_k + \beta \, \mathrm{VS}_k \tag{1}$$

$$k \in \{EV, GV\}.$$

Vehicular population data of Singapore, categorized according to type of fuel, released by the Land Transport Authority was used to determine the consumer vehicular preference model. The data from 2006 to 2010 was used for the purpose of this paper. The share of vehicles $S_k$ is then calculated as follows.

$$S_k = exp(f_k) \Big/ \sum_{k=1}^{n} exp(f_k) \tag{2}$$

The impact on the economy is then measured using the input–output analysis by the following equation.

$$X = (I - A)^{-1} F \tag{3}$$

where $X$, $A$, and $F$ refer to domestic product, input coefficient matrix, and final demand, respectively. The 2005 benchmark Input-output tables have been compiled to analyze 136 industrial sectors and commodities [11]. For the purpose of this study, the tables that have been aggregated into 12 industrial sectors and commodities are used. Multi-objective optimization is used to determine the optimal tax that minimizes the adverse effect on the economy and maximizes the reduction in carbon dioxide emissions, based on the following equation:

$$\max_{t} \quad w_1 \Delta ECON(t) + w_2 \Delta CO2(t) \tag{4}$$

$$\text{subject to } 0 \le t \le T_{max}, \tag{5}$$

where $\Delta ECON$ is the increase in gross national output, $\Delta CO2$ is the reduction in carbon dioxide emissions, $t$ is the tax rate, and $T_{max}$ is the maximum tax rate when 99% electric vehicle share is reached. $\Delta ECON$ and $\Delta CO2$ are functions of taxation rate, and their equations are determined by fitting trend lines to the data obtained. The weights on GDP and CO2 are denoted by $w_1$ and $w_2$ respectively. As shown in Table 1, $w_1$ will take on a range of values from $0$ to $1$, and $w_2$ will be calculated using the relation $w_2 = 1-w_1$. The optimal taxation rate for the different combinations of weights will be determined using the SOLVER tool in Microsoft Excel.

**Table 1.** Combination of weights for determination of optimal tax rate

| Weight on GDP ($w_1$) | Weight on CO2 ($w_2$) |
|:---:|:---:|
| 0 | 1 |
| 0.1 | 0.9 |
| 0.2 | 0.8 |
| 0.3 | 0.7 |
| 0.4 | 0.6 |
| 0.5 | 0.5 |
| 0.6 | 0.4 |
| 0.7 | 0.3 |
| 0.8 | 0.2 |
| 0.9 | 0.1 |
| 1 | 0 |

# 4    Results

## 4.1    Effect of Tax Rebate

The cost of vehicles in Singapore is given by the sum of its Open Market Value (OMV), Registration Fee ($140), Additional Registration Fee (100% of OMV) and Excise Duty (20% of OMV). Figure 1 shows that as the amount of the tax rebate for only EVs increases, the share of EVs increases. In the absence of any form of taxation, only a 1.4% share of electric vehicles will be reached in 2020, even after considering the fall in battery costs and rising oil prices. To reach 30% share by 2020, the amount of tax rebate needed is approximately 53% of OMV, which denotes the cost of the vehicle.

In determining the industrial structure, no change in final demand was assumed in the retail trade of vehicles or petrol kiosks/ charging stations. This is because the decrease in demand for petrol-related services will be compensated by the increase in demand for electric vehicle-related services. The trend captured in 2020 is taken to be representative of other years as well. Note that a decrease in demand for gasoline and an increase in demand for electricity cause a corresponding decrease in output in the oil industry and increase in output in the utilities sector. The extent of the decrease in output in the oil industry exceeds the increase in the output in the utilities sector. This can be attributed to the higher price of petroleum and higher efficiency of electric vehicles. In the event that the tax revenue collected by the government increases, it will be returned to the economy via government services in the "Other Services" sector.

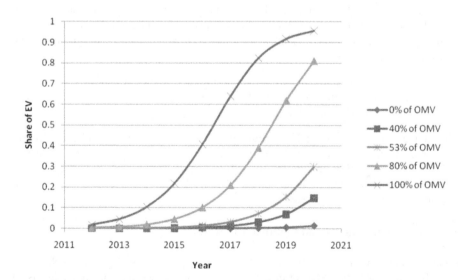

**Fig. 1.** Share of EV against time with different tax rebate rates

## 4.1     Effect of Carbon Tax

Figure 2 shows that as the rate of carbon tax increases, the share of electric vehicles increases. The amount of carbon tax needed to reach an EV share of 30% is SGD 1.66/kg $CO_2$.

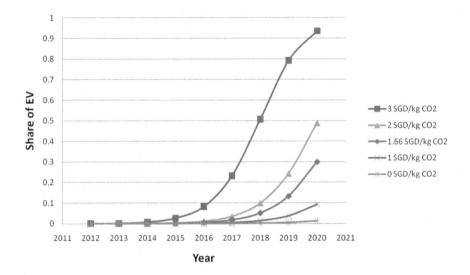

**Fig. 2.** Share of EV against time with different carbon tax rates

For determining the changes to the industrial structure, we assume that a higher overall cost of vehicles as a result of carbon taxation will cause a reduction in the total number of vehicles. This translates into the following changes to the industrial structure:

a) Reduction in final demand in the retail trade of motor vehicles
b) Reduction in final demand in the retail trade of automotive fuels (i.e., petrol kiosks and charging stations)

The changes to the industrial structure after the tax revenue is collected are re-distributed back to the economy. Oil manufacturing and the retail trade industries register the largest dips in output, and other sectors show significant decreases in output not seen in case of a tax rebate. But note that the tax revenue collected increases as the tax rate increases.

## 4.3     Economic Impact and Optimal Tax Rate

It can be seen from Figure 3 that at lower levels of penetration of electric vehicles, a tax rebate mitigates the adverse effect on the economy, whereas at higher levels of penetration, the choice of a carbon tax results in a lower adverse impact on the

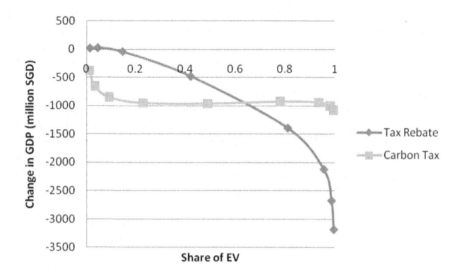

**Fig. 3.** Comparison of economic impact between tax rebate and carbon tax policies

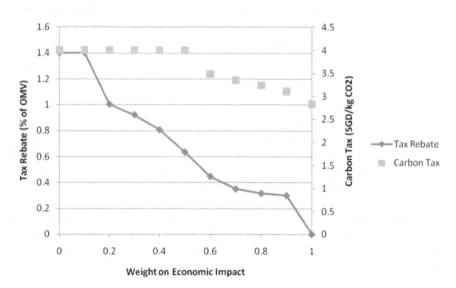

**Fig. 4.** Comparison of optimal tax rates

economy. This is because the carbon tax causes the total number of vehicles to decrease, which in turn results in a decline in the output of the retail trade of automobiles. However, the amount of tax rebate needed to effect a high penetration of electric vehicles causes a significant loss in tax revenues, whereas the increased tax revenue collected with the carbon tax mitigates the decrease in output of the economy as the share of electric vehicles increases.

Figure 4 compares the optimal tax rates determined using multi-objective optimization described earlier. The optimal tax rates for both tax rebate and carbon tax decrease as the weight of their economic impact increases. This is because the higher the taxation, the larger the share of electric vehicles, and consequently, the lower the GDP because of decreased output in the petroleum industry.

Therefore, if the impact on the economy is of more importance, the optimal tax rate should be lower. Note that the optimal tax rates for a carbon tax are skewed toward the region of high values. This is because the gain in environmental benefit outweighs the drop in GDP as a result of an increase in the share of EVs, resulting in less of a need to lower the optimal tax rate even at higher weights of economic impact. In other words, the gain in environmental benefit at all shares of EVs is so significant that lowering the optimal tax rate will not result in substantial benefits from a smaller decline in GDP.

# 5    Conclusion

A tax rebate generally causes both the output of the economy and tax revenue to decrease, whereas a carbon tax causes the output to decrease and the tax revenue collected to increase. In terms of the impact on GDP, with tax revenue assumed to be returned to society, a tax rebate is found to be suitable at a low penetration of electric vehicles, while a carbon tax will minimize the adverse impact on the economy at higher adoption rates of electric vehicles, above 60% share. Therefore, a suggestion for the Singapore government is to first implement a tax rebate to kick-start the promotion of electric vehicles, before switching to a carbon tax when more electric vehicles start plying the roads.

With regard to environmental impact however, a carbon tax will cause a larger reduction in carbon dioxide than a tax rebate at every tax rate owing to a reduction in the total number of vehicles. A recommendation for the Singapore government is to opt for a carbon tax over a vehicle tax rebate if it intends to expedite the penetration of electric vehicles for their environmental benefits.

**Acknowledgments.** This work was supported in part by a Grant in Aid from the Global Center of Excellence Program for "Center for Education and Research of Symbiotic, Safe and Secure System Design" from the Ministry of Education, Culture, Sport, and Technology in Japan.

# References

1. Nakano, M.: Challenges Facing Manufacturing to Move towards a Green Society with Clean Energy Vehicles. In: ElMaraghy, H.A. (ed.) Enabling Manufacturing Competitiveness and Economic Sustainability, pp. 434–438. Springer (2011)
2. Nakano, M.: A Conceptual Framework for Sustainable Manufacturing by Focusing on Risks in Supply Chains. In: Vallespir, B., Alix, T. (eds.) APMS 2009. IFIP AICT, vol. 338, pp. 160–167. Springer, Heidelberg (2010)

3. Struben, J., Sterman, J.D.: Transition challenges for alternative fuel vehicle and transportation systems. Environment and Planning B: Planning and Design 35(6), 1070–1097 (2008)
4. Ueda, T., Muto, S., Morisugi, S.: An economic evaluation of automobile transport control measures that generate negative externalities. Transport Policy Research 1(1), 39–53 (1998)
5. Foo, T.S.: Urban Environmental Policy – The Use of Regulatory and Economic Instruments in Singapore. Habitat Intl. 20(1), 5–22 (1996)
6. Muthukrishnan, S.: Vehicle ownership and usage charges. Transport Policy 17, 398–408 (2010)
7. Olszewski, P., Turner, D.J.: New methods of controlling vehicle ownership and usage in Singapore. Transportation 20, 355–371 (1993)
8. Karplus, V.J., et al.: Prospects for plug-in hybrid electric vehicles in the United States and Japan: A general equilibrium analysis. Transport. Res. Part A (2010), doi:10.1016/j.tra.2010.04.004
9. Tokunaga, S., Muto, S., Huang, Y.H., Sun, L., Okiyama, M.: Modeling analysis of automobile environmental policy. Bunshindo (2008)
10. Nonaka, T., Nakano, M.: The Carbon Taxation by Using LCA including the Manufacturing Phase for Clean Energy Vehicles. In: M4SM Workshop. Euromaintenance 2010 Conference, Verona, Italy (2010)
11. Department of Statistics, Ministry of Trade and Industry, Singapore. Singapore Input-Output Tables 2005 (2010)

# Knowledge Management in Set Based Lean Product Development Process

Robert Furian[1], Frank von Lacroix[1], Dragan Stokic[2], Ana Correia[2], Cristina Grama[2], Stefan Faltus[2], Maksim Maksimovic[3], Karl-Heinrich Grote[4], and Christiane Beyer[5]

[1] Volkswagen AG, Wolfsburg, Germany
{robert.furian,frank.lacroix}@volkswagen.de
[2] Institut für angewandte Systemtechnik Bremen, Germany
{dragan,correia,grama,faltus}@atb-bremen.de
[3] Cranfield University, United Kingdom
m.maksimovic@cranfield.ac.uk
[4] Otto-von-Guericke-Universität Magdeburg, Germany
karl.grote@ovgu.de
[5] California State University, Long Beach, USA
cbeyer@csulb.edu

**Abstract.** The objective of the research is to examine and develop new methods and tools for management of knowledge in Lean Product development. Lean Product development attempts to apply lean philosophy and principles within product development process. Special emphasis is given to the so-called Set Based Lean Design principles. Such product development process requires innovative methodologies and tools for capturing, reuse and provision of knowledge needed for decision making, as well as advanced ICT environment for Knowledge Management (KM).

A Set Based Lean Design toolkit is developed, aiming to support the product developer in making decisions during the development process. This toolkit includes the Lean Knowledge Life Cycle methodology and a set of software tools for KM. The application of the methods and tools is investigated within large automotive industry and its supplier.

**Keywords:** Knowledge management, knowledge based environment, product development process, LeanPPD, Lean development.

## 1    Introduction

In modern manufacturing industry, such as automotive industry, shorter product life cycles and strong competition demand more efficiency in the product development process. Therefore, the product models have to be adapted to the particular market requirements and have to be released fast and cost-efficiently on the markets. However, the product development costs are increasing because of rising diversity of models, fast technology progress and incremental complexity of the automobile [1].

Lean development transforms the philosophy of lean thinking into the product development and the product emerge process. The identification and reduction of

C. Emmanouilidis, M. Taisch, D. Kiritsis (Eds.): APMS 2012, Part I, IFIP AICT 397, pp. 368–375, 2013.

wastes and the boosting of value adding is much more complicated in development because of unique and new project themes with innovative character and development cycles of often about several years. This is contrary to the production, where always similar products in short cycles are produced in exactly defined process chains [2].

In [3] a new paradigm – Lean Product development - is proposed, which takes the lean thinking from waste elimination into value creation. The aim of the research is to develop a comprehensive set of lean methods, methodologies, design techniques and tools to ensure the development of lean product design. Special emphasis is given to the Set Based Design principles. Set Based Lean Design (SBLD) is a methodology similar to DFx and DFMA (Design for Manufacturing and Assembly) [4]. SBLD supports the generation of lean product design and its simultaneous consideration of lean manufacturing required for the physical realization of the product. The following main aspects have to be implemented to the SBLD [3]:

- A method to capture the customer values into a set of designs
- A mechanism to break down these sets to get an optimized final lean design
- The identification of features and tools of the key product

Knowledge reuse is one of the most important factors in increasing efficiency in product development and one of the key factors of the proposed Lean product development. However, due to the inherently unstructured form of knowledge, currently there are obstacles to finding the right knowledge at the right time. In this paper a Knowledge Based Environment (KBE) is proposed, supporting Set Based Lean Product development process, including support for knowledge acquisition and structuring, as well as timely and efficient re-use of previously acquired knowledge. Especially in very large Extended Enterprises, such as the ones typical of the automotive industry, where the knowledge and expertise of a variety of people needs to be used efficiently, such an approach is expected to lead to big improvements in knowledge management. This KBE is the main source of knowledge, from which a set of new designs for a new product is going to be defined [3].

The paper presents a Set Based Lean Design toolkit developed, aiming to support the product developer in making decisions during the development process. This toolkit includes the Lean Knowledge Life Cycle methodology and a set of software tools for KM.

The toolkit is under testing within the Volkswagen Group, which is one of the world's leading automobile manufacturers and the largest car maker in Europe. The toolkit and concepts of Lean Product Development and KBE will the transferred, implemented, tested and evaluated in a development department in the component division of Volkswagen to support the knowledge management in product development and support the product designers in decision making.

# 2    Lean Knowledge Life Cycle

The Lean Knowledge Life Cycle (LeanKLC), developed by [5], was defined as an outcome of the LeanPPD project and provides a methodology for knowledge capture, re-use and creation in product development. The significance of Knowledge is well recognized in the Lean Product Development literature [6, 7, 8, 9, 10, 11]. However, it was observed that current knowledge life cycles methodologies, such as [12, 13, 14, 15], lack supporting tools to be integrated in product development activities in order to provide a Knowledge based environment, which is an important element in LeanPPD [15]. The LeanKLC is addressing both the previous project, as well as the domain knowledge in product development. The LeanKLC follows a sequence of seven stages:

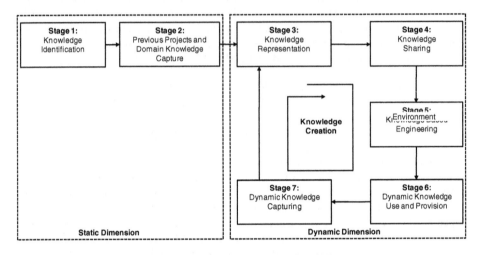

**Fig. 1.** Lean Knowledge Life Cycle [5]

In the first stage, the knowledge relevant in the product development process has to be found and identified. This knowledge is captured and structured in the second phase and categorized into knowledge from previous projects, like lessons learned, or into domain specific knowledge, e.g. design rules. In the next stage, the knowledge has to be represented in a generic way (e.g. OWL) in order to make it usable for ICT tools (e.g. Protégé). The fourth stage is the sharing of knowledge, which requires the storage in a centralized database with a clear structure, before getting implemented in the fifth step in the knowledge based environment (KBE). In the sixth step the knowledge from the KBE is dynamically used and provided to the product development engineers. In the seventh and final stage engineers will dynamically capture new knowledge already while it is created. The previously described stages require different practices, tools and templates, which are currently under development in cooperation with industrial partners within the LeanPPD project and envisioned to be tested in different business cases [5].

# 3    Knowledge Management Software Tool

The analysis of the existing ICT tools indicated that there are no specific SW tools to support Set Based Lean Design. 'Conventional' ICT tools for 'classical' design can (and are) used to support set based design. However, a clear need is identified to develop innovative tools specifically aiming to support KM for SBLD during various phases of the development process.

## 3.1    Requirements

Working as a development engineer in the automotive industry often means working in teams on different parts. Keeping an eye on design changes which have an impact on the design of related parts can lead to a lot of extra work. Especially in set-based design, it is even more complex since the number of possible designs grows significantly with an increasing number of parts sets and parallel designs. The main requirements of the knowledge management software tool, identified by several large industrial companies, are [5]:

- Support knowledge management, i.e. management of product data/ knowledge for SBCE, for different sets of solutions,  provision of design rules, including lean design rules
- Decision making support tools, specifically decisions regarding costs, i.e. tool to explore system sets and evaluate sets for lean production
- Support the re-use of existing designs (sets of solutions), e.g. from previous projects/designs

## 3.2    Implementation of the SW Tool

In order to support the handling of set-based design, based on the above described requirements, a SW tool was implemented to help engineers with the set-based design method. The detailed functions of the tool, for use in product development, were defined by the following:

- Management of parallel design sets: different part sets management with support for set-based lean design
- Part history: documentation of the complete "evolution" of the part, including the management of parallel designs in the different design phases of the part and visualization how the part looked before the change and after the change
- Support in provision of knowledge (rules) including lean design rules
- Support in acquisition of knowledge and report creation including the requests of changes in designs as well as the reasons for accepted and rejected requests
- Re-use of knowledge from previous projects and design-sets
- Support of collaborative work to make department specific knowledge about the requested changes available across all involved departments and automatically inform them about design changes and request their feedback
- Enable search with semantic indexing of keywords to find the knowledge from previous projects

The key concept of the tool is presented in Fig. 2. The tool can be applied at various stages of product development – at system level (whole product) or component level. Its current implementation is focused on a component level, assuming that the SBLD might be applied also at the whole product level. The tool intends to support set based design of components supporting the management of knowledge for sets of design, relations between options etc.

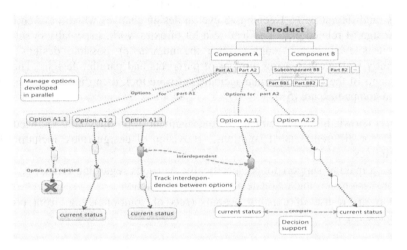

**Fig. 2.** Concept of the SBLD Product Data/Knowledge Management Tool

As mentioned before, the main task of the tool is to help the designer in the management of the sets of design of parts and components. In product development, changes to assemblies and parts have to be done to increase customer value but they also have impact on the shape and function of their nearby assemblies and parts.

The knowledge management tool is easy to integrate in the product development process and can be used during different stages within it:

- In the concept phase where different sets of design have to be evaluated
- In the construction phase of the part, where the 3D-CAD-model and the part list is created
- In the tooling, prototyping and testing phase, where changes from the tool shop and testing have to be implemented in the CAD-drawings

It also provides design knowledge, e.g. design rules of welding plastics or metals, directly to the product developer.

In the module which shows history of the part ("evolution"), the SW tool allows to automatically create reports which contain all changes which have been applied on the part as well as all general information about the part itself. Since design changes result in higher project costs from a certain stage of the project, the SW tool allows to create reports, describing the change, which will be distributed among all involved engineers and departments (planning, tool shop, finances, etc.) to support the decision making if a certain change in the design is necessary or not. Each involved engineer / department can use the SW tool to approve or disapprove the change in the design.

Before the final request to change the design of the part, which has impact on other departments like the planning department or the tool shop, the SW tool supports the designer in providing information about previous or parallel projects which have a similar focus. This provision of knowledge from previous projects and other relevant topics is realized by suggesting other reports, design rules or related projects of possible interest. The SW tool retrieves those documents by querying a search engine whose index is built by an indexing engine (see 3.3). This indexing engine works in the background and automatically indexes all reports and design change requests that are added to the database of the SW tool. No matter if the change in the design of part is applied or not, the new knowledge about this change is annotated and added to the database. In case of rejection, the cause is also annotated and added to prevent other designers from requesting the same change again.

Furthermore a tag cloud showing the most associated keywords to this part allows the designer to directly switch to the related domain knowledge where design and construction knowledge can be obtained.

## 3.3    Knowledge Search Engine and Ontological Structure

The tool provides a special search mechanism to easily find knowledge from previous projects, which includes search by product & part, search by project phase/ date, free text search etc. Furthermore, this can be used to find design rules which are related to the parts and in this way support users in applying lean manufacturing principles.

The approach is to combine the knowledge management tool with an ontological based structuring of data/knowledge for context sensitive enhancement, where product and process knowledge is stored. This ontology is also used to store all extracted context for future reuse. The process is supported by modular services which allow docking onto different systems to monitor and analyze user's interactions and support subsequent services (Context Extraction and Knowledge Search) through monitoring data.

The search is therefore divided into several sub-services. These are:

- Knowledge Monitoring and Indexing
- Context Extraction and Context Model
- Search User Interface

The knowledge monitoring is used to monitor human-computer-interaction in order to extract the actual context to further enhance it with according knowledge. For that, user interaction is being closely monitored, "raw data" collected and enriched with available knowledge. At significantly changed circumstances in the context, configurable defined, all gathered data is forwarded to context extraction services to extract actual context. In a search application, the objective of such monitoring services is to observe user interactions in order to enable context extraction and knowledge enhancing services to provide assistance in refining the search query. In providing e.g. keywords that have been used in similar situations or filter allowing to narrow down search results in an appropriate thematically way, the user is contextually supported in his current situation. Beside the monitored situations, this service also persist meta-information about the knowledge-items which are associated with monitored events. This data is extracted by an appropriate parser and analyser of the Knowledge Monitoring and Indexing services and stored into a Lucene-Index to allow a fast and efficient reuse [17]. Knowledge Items to be index for reuse may reside in any external system, which offers an interface to the outside (e.g. file system, database or WIKI).

To enhance application functionality, monitoring services are monitoring states and conditions in order to trigger other services, for instance "auto-completion services" to give instantaneous feedback to the user during text input. To accomplish that, a monitoring service observes a text box, forwarding text input to a backend service for further processing. This approach enables direct feedback and does not require the user to explicitly trigger the service (e.g. by clicking a button). The overall structure to comprehend the described solution is a Service-oriented Monitoring Architecture (SoMA) within Networked Enterprises [18].

In the product development the use of the search engine and the ontology results in a faster access to information and knowledge that helps the designer in his work. He can faster find structured knowledge from previous projects and search for lean design rules and construction criteria regarding the component he is working on.

# 4    Conclusion

The paper describes a SBLD toolkit developed, aiming to support the product developer in making decisions during the development process. The emphasis is put upon the requirements and the implementation of a knowledge management software tool, which is applied in product development to support SBLD. It is a part of a knowledge based environment and provides set-based lean design rules and domain and specific knowledge to the product designer. This results in a better knowledge management, decision support and communication in product design. Less improvement- and optimization loops are needed because the developer now gets the support of the knowledge management tool. This can save development costs and time in the product development process. The application of the methods and tools is investigated within Volkswagen and its suppliers.

**Acknowledgments.** The work presented is partly carried out in the scope of the current RTD project LeanPPD supported by the Commission of European Community, under NMP - Nanosciences, Nanotechnologies, Materials and new Production Technologies Program under the contract NMP-2008- 214090. This document does not represent the opinion of the European Community, and the European Community is not responsible for any use that might be made of its content.

# References

1. Pahl, G., Beitz, W., Feldhusen, J., Grote, K.-H.: Konstruktionslehre – Grundlagen erfolgreicher Produktentwicklung; Methoden und Anwendung, 7. Auflage. Springer, Berlin (2007)
2. Schuh, G., et al.: Lean Innovation – Ein Widerspruch in sich? In: Hacklin, F., Marxt, C. (eds.) Business Excellence in Technologieorientierten Unternehmen, pp. 13–20. Springer, Berlin (2008)
3. Al-Ashaab, A., Shehab, E., Alam, R., Sopelana, A., Sorli, M., Flores, M., Taisch, M., Stokic, D., James-Moore, M.: The Conceptual LeanPPD Model. In: New World Situation: New Directions in Concurrent Engineering, Part 5, pp. 339–346. Springer, London (2010)
4. Huthwaite, B.: The Lean Design Solution. Institute for Lean Design, Mackinac Island (2004)
5. Maksimovic, M., Al-Ashaab, A., Shehab, E., Sulowski, R.: A Lean Knowledge Life Cycle Methodology in Product Development. In: 8th International Conference on Intellectual Capital, Knowledge Management & Organizational Learning – ICICKM, Bangkok, Thailand (2011)
6. Morgan, J.M., Liker, J.K.: The Toyota Product Development System: Integrating People, Process, and Technology. Productivity Press, New York (2006)
7. Kennedy, M., Harmon, K., Minnock, E.: Ready, Set, Dominate: Implement Toyota's Set-Based Learning for Developing Products. The Oakley Press (2008)
8. Sobek II, D.K., Ward, A.C., Liker, J.K.: Toyota's Principles of Set-Based Concurrent Engineering. Sloan Management Review 40(2), 67–83 (1999)
9. Ward, A.C.: Lean Product and Process Development. Lean Enterprises Inst. Inc. (2007)
10. Mascitelli, R.: The Lean Product Development Guidebook: Everything your design team needs to improve efficiency and slash time-to-market. Technology Perspectives (2006)
11. Oosterwal, D.P.: The Lean Machine: How Harley-Davidson drove top-line growth and profitability with revolutionary lean product development. AMACOM/American Management Association (2010)
12. Bukowitz, W.R., Williams, R.L.: Knowledge Management Fieldbook. Prentice-Hall/FT Management, London (1999)
13. Dalkir, K.: Knowledge management in theory and practice. Butterworth-Heinemann (2005)
14. Firestone, J.M., McElroy, M.W.: Key issues in the new knowledge management. Butterworth-Heinemann (2003)
15. Jashapara, A.: Knowledge Management: An integrated approach. Pearson Education (2004)
16. Al-Ashaab, A., Flores, M., Khan, M., Maksimovic, M., Alam, R., Shehab, E., Doultsinou, A., Sopelana, A.: The Industrial requirements of KBE for the LeanPPD model. In: International Conference on Advances in Production Management Systems (APMS 2010), Cernobbio, Lake Como, October 11-13 (2010)
17. Apache Lucene Search Engine, http://lucene.apache.org
18. Ziplies, S., Scholze, S., Stokic, D., Krone, K.: Service-based Knowledge Monitoring of Collaborative Environments for User-context Sensitive Enhancement. In: Proceedings of the 15th International Conference on Concurrent Enterprising, Leiden, Netherlands (2009)

# Design of Fundamental Ontology for Manufacturing Product Lifecycle Applications

Dimitris Kiritsis[1], Soumaya El Kadiri[1], Apostolos Perdikakis[1], Ana Milicic[1], Dimitris Alexandrou[2], and Kostas Pardalis[2]

[1] LICP laboratory, Ecole Polytechnique Federale de Lausanne, Switzerland
[2] UBITECH, Athens Greece

For APMS 2012 Special Session "Toward the product of the future"

**Abstract.** In today's world of fast manufacturing, high quality demands and highly competitive markets, it has become vital for companies to be able to extract knowledge from their operating data, to manage and to reuse this knowledge in efficient and automated manner. Ontology has proven to be one of the most successful methods in fulfilling this demand and to this day, it has been applied in number of scenarios within companies of all scales. The most appealing features of the ontology are well-defined structure of the knowledge organization; being machine understandable enables automatic reasoning and inference and finally, well defined semantics enables easy interoperability and design of the plug-in modules. Still, one key downfall of ontology is that it usually has to be manually designed from the beginning for each new use-case. This requires highly specialized knowledge experts working closely with the domain experts for, sometimes, significant period of time. In this paper we propose LinkedDesign solution for described issues, as an example of design of fundamental ontology which can be easily adjusted and adopted for different production systems, thus eliminating the need for repetition of entire design process for every individual company. We also discuss and point to a new and challenging fields of research emerging from application of ontology into manufacturing companies, mainly concerning rapidly growing amounts of knowledge which are beginning to exceed human ability to process it.

**Keywords:** Ontology design, Knowledge Management, Design and Manufacturing, Product Lifecycle.

## 1    Introduction

As we enter the knowledge society, ownership of knowledge and information as a source of competitive advantage is becoming increasingly important. In other words, organizations depend more on the development, use and distribution of knowledge based competencies. This is particularly relevant in knowledge intensive processes such as product innovation. Consequently, research and development (R&D) organizations are paying more attention to the concept of managing their knowledge

C. Emmanouilidis, M. Taisch, D. Kiritsis (Eds.): APMS 2012, Part I, IFIP AICT 397, pp. 376–382, 2013.

base in order to increase competitive advantage, through effective decision making and innovation (Nonaka 1991), (Davenport et al. 1996), (Sveiby 1997). Further on, it's becoming increasingly important to enable exchange of knowledge between all stages of product life cycle (PLC), as a prerequisite for optimization of all critical procedures in the design and manufacturing of a product. One of the methods, which has proven to be a very efficient tool for knowledge structuring and exploitation, is ontology. Through the definitions of concepts and relations, it is possible to describe entire domain of interest in a very convenient and details manner. Semantics enrichment opens a possibility for automatic reasoning and inference, which leads to automatic generation of new knowledge. Finally, using different plug-ins, ontology enables interoperability between different systems. All of these benefits are vital in a case of large production companies, which are struggling with ever increasing amounts of data and facing problems of exchanging knowledge between different systems employed for different stages of PLC. This is why it comes as no surprise that ontology has quickly found its place in academic research, as well as industrial research and development.

Popularity and employment of ontology is to some level suppressed by sometimes long and challenging process of ontology design for every specific application. It requires an ontology experts working together with domain experts, often trying to describe highly complex company activities. Although, there are number of standards and methodologies for ontology design, it often comes down to long hours of discussion over hand-sketches. Additional concern is that every domain can be modeled into an ontology in many different ways and it takes experience to be able to judge which is the optimal solution.

LinkedDesign is a FP7 project which, among other things, has a goal of overcoming the above-described problem. It will result in system that allows fast and efficient design and production. LinkedDesign Ontology (LDO) is being designed to utilize knowledge extraction, knowledge structuring, knowledge exchange and knowledge reuse for three use-case companies with highly diverse products and activities. Such challenging task, resolved in a generalized solution which is now applicable for almost every design and manufacturing business, after very light adjustment and installation.

# 2 State of the Art

Ontologies play an important role for many knowledge-intensive applications, since they provide formal models of domain knowledge that can be exploited in different ways. Ontology development has become an engineering discipline, Ontology Engineering, which refers to the set of activities that concern the ontology development process and the ontology life cycle, the methods and methodologies for building ontologies, and the tool suites and languages that support them (Suárez-Figueroa et al. 2011). Foremost methodologies for building ontologies are:

METHONTOLOGY (Gomez-Perez et al. 2004), On-To-Knowledge (Staab et al. 2001), DILIGENT (Pinto et al. 2004) and a new methodology, called the NeOn Methodology (Suárez-Figueroa et al. 2010). The Major ontology languages are: RDF (Klyne & Carroll 2004), RDF Schema (Guha & McBride 2004), OWL (Dean et al. 2004), OWL 2 (Motik et al. 2009) (OWL 2 EL, OWL 2 QL, OWL 2 RL), and SPARQL (Prud'hommeaux & Seaborne 2008). Finally, the leading ontology tools were identified. These are: The NeOn Toolkit (http://neon-toolkit.org/), Protégé (http://protege.stanford.edu/) and TopBraid Composer (http://www.topquadrant.com/products/TB_Composer.html). Ontology design is still one of the relevant research questions and number of methodologies has been developed. As previously mentioned, METHONTOLOGY, On-To-Knowledge, and DILIGENT were up to 2009 the most referred methodologies for building ontologies. These methodologies mainly include guidelines for single ontology construction ranging from ontology specification to ontology implementation and they are mainly targeted to ontology researchers. In contrast to the aforementioned approaches, a new methodology, called the NeOn Methodology, suggests pathways and activities for a variety of scenarios, instead of prescribing a rigid workflow.

The NeOn Methodology for building ontology networks is a scenario-based methodology that supports a knowledge reuse approach, as well as collaborative aspects of ontology development and dynamic evolution of ontology networks in distributed environments. The key assets of the NeOn Methodology are:

- A set of nine scenarios for building ontologies and ontology networks, emphasizing the reuse of ontological and non-ontological resources, the reengineering and merging, and taking into account collaboration and dynamism.
- The NeOn Glossary of Processes and Activities, which identifies and defines the processes and activities carried out when ontology networks are collaboratively built by teams.
- Methodological guidelines for different processes and activities of the ontology network development process, such as the reuse and reengineering of ontological and non-ontological resources, the ontology requirements specification, the ontology localization, the scheduling, etc. All processes and activities are described with (a) a filling card, (b) a workflow, and (c) examples.

All of the named methods are guidelines for creating specific ontology from the beginning. LDO is created as form of template, which can be easily adjusted and adopted by almost any design and manufacturing company, with little or no knowledge about ontology design. The ontology design research is a field in which great amount of work is done within industrial research teams and their results are not always public. Still, to our knowledge. A number of recent works (A. Matsokis & D. Kiritsis 2010), (Kim et al. 2009), (Fiorentini et al. 2008), (Demoly et al. 2012), (Panetto et al. 2012) and (Batres et al. 2007) in various phases of the lifecycle have already provided promising results.

# 3     LinkedDesign Ontology

## 3.1     Methodology for the Design of the Fundamental Ontology

Based on some previous work, a first list of fundamental concepts of all data relevant for the product in all stages of its life cycle has been defined following a bottom-up approach described in (A. Milicic et al. 2012).

In order to design the fundamental ontology, the list of top level concepts has been updated lining up with the NeOn methology (as described in the state of the art), based on the following actions:

a)     Ontology requirements specification: define the purpose, scope, intended end-users, intended uses, ontology requirements analysis (non-functional and functional).
b)     Analysis of existing resources: reusing and reengineering of non-ontological resources (UDEF[1], Standards for product data management); reusing, merging and mapping ontological resources.
c)     Conceptualization and formalization.

## 3.2     The LinkedDesign Fundamental Ontology

The LinkedDesign fundamental ontology can be seen in Figure 1 and some of the top level concepts are given in Table 1.

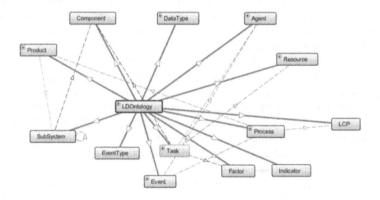

**Fig. 1.** The LinkedDesign Ontology

---

[1] Universal Data Element Framework.

**Table 1.** Top Level Concepts

| No. | Top Level Concepts | Description |
|-----|--------------------|-------------|
| 1 | Task | Groups scheduled actions |
| 2 | Process | Groups all processes |
| 3 | Product | Groups all products |
| 4 | Subsystem | Groups all sub-systems composing a product |
| 5 | Component | Groups all components composing a subsystem |
| 6 | Resource | Groups all the required elements for product manufacturing |
| 7 | Agent | Groups all the agents |
| 8 | LCP | Groups life-cycle phases of the product |
| 9 | Event | Groups the list of event |
| 10 | EventType | Describes the type of the event |
| 11 | Factor | Groups relevant issues related to product which need to be examined |
| 12 | DataType | Describes the obtained data |

## 3.3    Application in the Context of LinkedDesign

LinkedDesign ontology is designed as centralized network of functional unit-ontologies, each dealing with specific task. As sub trees of this core ontology, network contains ontologies which utilize specific needs and requirements of each of three industrial partners. Use-case 1 deals with hot stamping process and aims at analyzing and learning from correlations between production process parameters, geometric and microstructural properties,  and cracks revealed within work pieces, thus enabling a better quality and reducing errors and defects and finally improve and adapt production process. Use-case 2 deals with knowledge based engineering and knowledge capture with KBE systems. The purpose of implementing an ontology for this use-case is the ability to manage KBE solutions (basically KBE Script) and to provide semantics for a business layer which controls the GUI. Use-case 3 deals with lifecycle cost analysis and assessment in order to optimize engineering decisions and facilitate efficient allocation of resources. This use-case aims at exploiting knowledge coming from previous projects and experiences from lifecycle cost analysis perspectives, leading thus to optimize new product's characteristics and costs. Concepts are connected with relations and the rules are defined, describing the functionality of the domain. The graph of the network ontology is shown in figure 2.The idea is that, beside three industrial partners involved in LinkedDesign, practically any company dealing with design and manufacturing will be able to reuse the core, data sources and knowledge subontologies, with a little or no adjustments. They will also have the ability to define and add ontology covering their specific

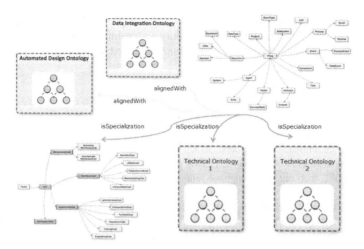

**Fig. 2.** The LinkedDesign Ontology Network

needs if any, as it was done for the three industrial partners. This significantly reduces the resources needed for design of ontology from the beginning and hopefully will lead to even bigger popularization of ontology implementation.

## 4    Open Research Topics

The question which needs to be raised, concerns the increasing amount of knowledge in digital systems. The time when increasing amount of unstructured data was the issue will soon be over, as the research community is progressing in the field of data mining, knowledge extraction and knowledge management. Currently, the most common usage of knowledge bases and ontologies is querying, but this assumes that the user is aware of the topics and amount of available knowledge. The new challenge needs to be in further exploitation of ontology being machine understandable, more precisely, ontology should be very convenient base for the next generation of recommendation systems. Based on a context and data retrieved through ontology, system should be able to assume the profile and the activity of a user, and present him with a knowledge which will be useful to the user, but he wasn't aware of its existence. Such system should come as valuable tool for design & manufacturing community, as this is precisely the field where a number of different-profile users are working on the same product, and it is very difficult to be informed about the details of the product from all stages of product life cycle.

## 5    Conclusion

Implementation of ontology for the industrial needs leads to great partnership where researchers and companies are motivating and inspiring each other for great achievements. LinkedDesign Ontology is a step toward bringing research results closer to their implementation and exploitation. It greatly simplifies the design and usage of ontology for a wide variety of companies as an efficient and productive tool for knowledge management. As the popularity and usage of ontology progresses, there will be more need for further improvements and solutions. There will be new challenges for the research community, such as one proposed in Chapter 4.

# References

Batres, R., et al.: An upper ontology based on ISO 15926. Computers & Chemical Engineering 31(5-6), 519–534 (2007)

Davenport, T.H., Jarvenpaa, S.L., Beers, M.C.: Improving knowledge work processes. Sloan Management Review 37(4), 53–65 (1996)

Dean, M., et al.: OWL web ontology language reference. W3C Recommendation (February 10, 2004)

Demoly, F., Matsokis, A., Kiritsis, D.: A mereotopological product relationship description approach for assembly oriented design. Robotics and Computer-Integrated Manufacturing 28(6), 681–693 (2012)

Fiorentini, X., et al.: Description logic for product information models (2008)

Gomez-Perez, A., Fernández-López, M., Corcho, O.: Ontological Engineering: with examples from the areas of Knowledge Management, e-Commerce and the Semantic Web. Springer (2004)

Guha, R., McBride, B.: RDF Vocabulary Description Language 1.0: RDF Schema (2004)

Kim, K., et al.: Ontology-based modeling and integration of morphological characteristics of assembly joints for network-based collaborative assembly design. Artificial Intelligence for Engineering Design, Analysis and Manufacturing 23(1), 71–88 (2009)

Klyne, G., Carroll, J.J.: Resource description framework (RDF): Concepts and abstract syntax. Changes, 1–20 (February 10, 2004)

Matsokis, A., Kiritsis, D.: An ontology-based approach for Product Life-cycle Management. Computers in Industry 61(8), 787–797 (2010)

Milicic, A., Perdikakis, A., El Kadiri, S., Kiritsis, D., Ivanov, P.: Towards the Definition of Domain Concepts and Knowledge through the Application of the User Story Mapping Method. In: Rivest, L., Bouras, A., Louhichi, B. (eds.) PLM 2012. IFIP AICT, vol. 388, pp. 58–69. Springer, Heidelberg (2012)

Motik, B., et al.: OWL 2 web ontology language: Structural specification and functional-style syntax. W3C Recommendation, 27 (2009)

Nonaka, I.: The knowledge creating company, pp. 96–104 (1991)

Panetto, H., Dassisti, M., Tursi, A.: ONTO-PDM: Product-driven ONTOlogy for Product Data Management interoperability within manufacturing process environment. Advanced Engineering Informatics 26(2), 334–348 (2012)

Pinto, H.S., Staab, S., Tempich, C.: DILIGENT: Towards a fine-grained methodology for Distributed, Loosely-controlled and evolving Engineering of oNTol-ogies. In: ECAI, p. 393 (2004)

Prud'hommeaux, E., Seaborne, A.: SPARQL query language for RDF. W3C Recommendation (January 2008)

Staab, S., et al.: Knowledge processes and ontologies. IEEE Intelligent Systems 16(1), 26–34 (2001)

Suárez-Figueroa, M.C., et al.: Essential In Ontology Engineering: Methodologies, Languages, and Tools (2011)

Suárez-Figueroa, M.C., et al.: gOntt, a Tool for Scheduling and Executing Ontology Development Projects (2010)

Sveiby, K.E.: The new organizational wealth: Managing & measuring knowledge-based assets. Berrett-Koehler Pub. (1997)

# Proposal of an Assessment Model
# for New Product Development

Monica Rossi[1], Sergio Terzi[2], and Marco Garetti[1]

[1] Politecnico di Milano, Milan, Italy
{monica.rossi,marco.garetti}@polimi.it
[2] Università degli studi di Bergamo, Bergamo, Italy
sergio.terzi@unibg.it

**Abstract.** In last decades, New Product Development (NPD) process has become crucial for the company success. Many efforts have been paid in order to identify methods and tools able to improve NPD, but successful models are still missing or not easily followed. Companies find difficult to implement comprehensive models for improving their NPD process, and often they aren't even aware on how they actually are performing it. Which are the main critical areas affecting NPD performances inside the organization? Which are the main opportunities of improvement? Which are the gaps to be fulfilled by a company for acting as a best practice? Both at industrial and academic level, there is the need of a global assessment model able to answer to these – and similar – questions. This paper proposes a tentative model.

**Keywords:** New Product Development (NPD), Assessment Maturity Model, Best Practices, Benchmarking.

# 1    Introduction

During the last ten years, New Product Development not only has been recognized as one of the corporate core functions (Huang et al., 2004), but also as a critical driver for company's survival (Biemans, 2003) and prosperity (Lam et al., 2007). The actual uncertain and turbulent marketplace represents a tough challenge to the NPD process, which is often wasteful and not efficiently performed (Rossi et al., 2011). Companies are trying to come out with new efficient methods and techniques, able to guarantee successful products (Gonzales, 2002) in terms of quality, performance and cost. But a standardized framework, able to lead companies through an efficient and effective NPD process is very hard to introduce, due to the complexity and the variability from company to company of the NPD process itself. The first thing to do in order to improve NPD, is to perfectly understand and correctly address the object of the improvement. The problem is that literature state of the art lacks methodologies and tools capable to assess and evaluate how actually companies manage their whole NPD process. In fact the existing tools are only focused on one single aspect of the NPD process, missing the 360° perspective. This research aims to fill this gap, proposing a reference model able to entirely evaluate the NPD process performance.

C. Emmanouilidis, M. Taisch, D. Kiritsis (Eds.): APMS 2012, Part I, IFIP AICT 397, pp. 383–390, 2013.
© IFIP International Federation for Information Processing 2013

## 2     State of the Art of Assessment Tools

Over the years several assessment tools have been introduced to evaluate specific aspects of the NPD process. Even if they miss the global perspective, they represent a good starting point to be considered in order to develop a comprehensive method. They are listed in the following.

- *Project management maturity assessment methodology:* this method allows comparing the performance gained by similar organizations, evaluating the ratio PM/ROI (project management/ return on investments). Data are collected through a proper questionnaire (Ibbs and Kwak, 2000).
- *RACE (Readiness Assessment for Concurrent Engineering)*: this tool was developed at the beginning of the 1990s at the West Virginia University and it is used in software design and in the mechanical sector to assess the level of application of Concurrent Engineering within NPD. The model assesses two main areas, the organizational part (evaluated in 9 maturity levels) and the information technology part (5 levels are considered) (Wognum 1996). RACE is based on a questionnaire, whose data are represented through a radar chart.
- *CERAM Model (Concurrent Engineering Readiness Assessment Model for Construction)*: this method derives from RACE model; it only differs in some contents, being suited for the construction field. CERAM considers two main perspectives, the process (which is evaluated through eighth levels) and the technology (assessed in four levels) (Khalfan, 2001).
- *BEACON Model (Benchmarking and Readiness Assessment for Concurrent Engineering in Construction)*: this model has been introduced as a complement to the CERAM model. In fact it is able to assess not only process and technology, but also external elements, such as project and people. The efficiency of the organization in project management, the performance of the staff and the efficiency of the technology used in the company are evaluated with a 5 grades scale (Anumba et al., 2007).
- *CMMI (Capability Maturity Model Integration)*: this model was developed in 1987 by SEI (Software Engineering Institute) in order to define the maturity level of the development process. It integrates best practices on improving development process with product maintenance. Five maturity levels are assessed, Ad hoc, Repeatable, Characteristic, Managed and Optimising (Mark et al. 1993).
- *Mis/PyME*: this model is able to assess the processes providing the organization with tools able to facilitate the fulfilment of company's objectives. This assessment model is based on the software indicators of the small and medium enterprises. It focuses on: data, people and performance (Díaz-Ley, 2010).

These assessment tools are considered the most relevant in literature. The visual representation of RACE and BEACON through a radar chart makes them simple and intuitive in representing the AS-IS status. CMMI is valuable for its five maturity levels. The questionnaires used by the models are useful to understand which are the main criticalities and peculiarities of each of the assessed area. But a global model for assessing NPD in its whole is still missing. Basing on the analysed contributions and on empirical experiences, this research aims to fill this gap.

# 3    The Proposed Assessment Model for NPD

The aim of the proposed model is to provide a "picture" of the AS-IS status of the NPD inside a company. To define the NPD maturity is a very tough task, because of the high number of elements concurring in the system, such as people, tools, and methods. For each of these area within NPD, five possible maturity levels, under the acronyms CLIMB, are considered:

- Chaos: the area is usually chaotic and slightly structured.
- Low: the area has a simple formalization and it is barely planned and controlled.
- Intermediate: the area is structured and planned. Standard solutions are normally applied.
- Mature: the area is structured, planned, controlled and measured at its different layers, often through specific quantitative techniques.
- Best practice: the organization reached all the previous stages and the area continuously improves thanks to the analysis of variance of its results. The improvement of NPD performance is reached through incremental and innovative actions.

In order to evaluate the proper maturity level of a company, a questionnaire has been developed for collecting the relevant information within the technical department and a radar chart has been created for the visual representation. They are detailed in the following sections.

## 3.1    The Questionnaire

The questionnaire includes 33 multiple choice questions and tables, used to analyse 3 main perspectives of NPD: Organization, Knowledge Management, Process. These are arranged in 9-areas – respectively 3, 4, and 2. Each area is then evaluated through a variable number of questions. The structure is summarized in Table 1.

Table 1. Structure of the questionnaire

| Macro Area | Area | # Question/ matrix |
|---|---|---|
| Organization | Work Organization | 1-5 |
| | Roles and Coordination | 6-9 |
| | Skills and Competencies | 10-12 |
| Process | Process Management | 13-16 |
| | Activities and Value | 17-20 |
| | Decision Making Factors | 21-24 |
| | Methods | 25 |
| Knowledge Management | Formalization | 26-30 |
| | Computerization | 31-33 |

The chosen areas are suitable to describe the NPD as a whole, overpassing the gap identified in the literature review. A brief description of the selected areas follows:

- *Organization.* This is a huge topic that concerns all the people involved in everyday company's activities. Core elements are division of labour and tasks *(Work Organization)*; coordination of people and activities, roles of engineers and designers *(Roles and Coordination)*; practitioners skills and expertise *(Skills and Competencies)*. When considering NPD, designers assume relevant importance, since the coordination and cooperation between them imply the goodness of the work environment. Moreover, well defined roles and responsibilities result in better organized NPD. Finally, enhancement of individual skills and competences determine a more agile and mature organization and better product performance.

- *Process.* NPD is realized through a – more or less – formalized process, described as a series of steps, activities and tasks to be accomplished in order to define the specifications of a new product, or the upgrade of an existing product. This process can be supported by a huge variety of tools and methods *(Methods)*, such as Design for X techniques, Life Cycle Analysis, etc. The strict control of the NPD process is crucial, such as its continuous monitoring and improvement *(Process Management)*. Moreover the process requires a large number of decisions to be taken every day: a chain of linked choices made considering both internal *(Decision Making Factors)* and external *(Activities and Value)* elements.

- *Knowledge Management.* To maintain and protect the know-how of a company is crucial within any kind of industry. Everyday knowledge is created, shared, retrieved, and displayed; huge amount of data should be handled effectively. The better information are stored, represented, captured, and reused, the more efficient is the NPD. In order to preserve data, these should be formalized and represented in a way understandable by each practitioner inside the company, and easy to be re-used *(Formalization)*. The higher the level of computerization, the faster and more precise the knowledge management process and the communication between people and departments are *(Computerization)*. In order to achieve these results PLM (Product Lifecycle Management) / PDM (Product Data Management) software are suitable to be implemented.

All the 9 areas are numerically evaluated through a proper score given to the related questions, as explained in the next section. Thanks to this score, it is possible to define the maturity level reached by the company in the different areas and it is possible to represent the maturity using a radar chart.

### 3.2     The Radar Chart

The questionnaire is composed by multiple choice questions and tables, associated to a conveniently defined score, used to state the maturity level achieved in NPD by the analysed organization. The Radar Chart (cf. Figure 2) is the way to graphically represent this maturity level. A group of questions determines the score of the area.

Each question is answered with multiple choice descriptive options, which correspond to a numerical value, varying from 0 to 3. The minimum maturity value achievable for the area is obtained when all the answers generate 0 as a reply. Vice versa the best practice level is obtained when all the answers assume value 3. For intermediate answers the value is calculated as normalized score (% value). An example of score calculation is given in following Table (cf. Table 2).

**Table 2.** Example of Scoring of Area

| Skills and Competencies | Answer | Score |
|---|---|---|
| 10. *Product design is heavily based on skills and competence of the actors involved (technicians, designers, managers, etc.). How does the company support training and skill development?* | | |
| a. Any engineer/designer is personally responsible for developing and maintaining his/ her skills. | | 1 |
| b. The company urges the development of strong technical skills, and gives training on the job. | X | 2 |
| c. The company promotes multidisciplinary skills and supports knowledge management activities with formal programs (ex. training plans, rotation between project teams, etc,....). | | 3 |
| d. Other (specify). | | |
| 11. *Is there a responsible trainer that supports training activities inside the organization?* | | |
| a. No, each technician/designer is expected to build his/her skills individually. | | 1 |
| b. Yes, a technician/designer is encouraged to develop his/her own skill from his/her direct supervisor. | X | 2 |
| c. Yes, there is a one-to-one correspondence for tutoring (a junior designer is assigned with a more experienced designer, as a tutor, coach, or mentor). | | 3 |
| d. Other (specify). | | |
| 12. *How effectiveness of training is evaluated in terms of the learning outcomes?* | | |
| a. Using 'visual' evaluation of individual behaviors. | X | 1 |
| b. Using a test before and after the training session. | | 2 |
| c. Using KPIs to assess the impact of training on business performances. | | 3 |
| d. Other (specify). | | |

| *Maximum Achievable Value* | *Achieved value* | *Normalized value for the Area* | |
|---|---|---|---|
| (3+3+3) = 9 | (2+2+1) = 5 | (5/9)*100 = **55.56%** | |

Following this procedure, for each of the 9 areas, is it possible to state the reached maturity level, considering the profiles proposed in Figure 1, and to represent the global results in the radar chart (cf. Figure 2).

| 0-20% | 21-40% | 41-60% | 61-80% | 81-100% |
|---|---|---|---|---|
| Chaos | Low | Intermediate | Mature | Best Practice |

**Fig. 1.** Maturity Levels Profiles

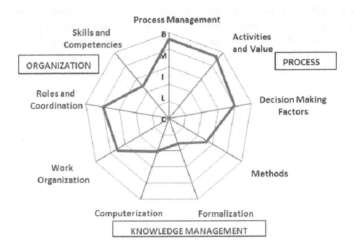

**Fig. 2.** The Radar Chart

# 4     Preliminary Results

Since February 2012 until now a sample of 30 companies has been analyzed. The variety of the sample is quite relevant, has shown in Table 3.

**Table 3.** The Sample

| Number of employees | Small (<50) | Medium (50<= Me <=250) | Large (250< B <= 1000) | Very large (>1000) |
|---|---|---|---|---|
| # companies | 1 | 6 | 11 | 12 |

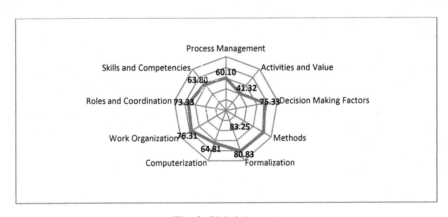

**Fig. 3.** Global Average

Radar chart in Figure 3 displays the average trend of the whole sample. The major criticalities are linked to the definition of the customer value, which is rarely well defined and communicated within the organization. On the contrary the attention paid to knowledge formalization is high. On average, the maturity level of the market is varying between intermediate and mature.

Figure 3 and Figure 4 show the trend of Medium and Very large Enterprises with respect of the global average of the sample. Medium enterprises are close to the global average in terms of *decision making*, *methods* and knowledge *formalization*. Major differences are in *computerization*, *value*, and *organization* macro area perspective, in which they attest under the global trend (cf. Figure 4).

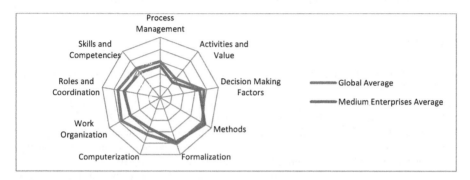

**Fig. 4.** Medium Enterprises vs Global Average

Apart for the *formalization* area, in which they are aligned to the global trend, Very large enterprises are over average for all the considered perspectives (Cf. Figure 5).

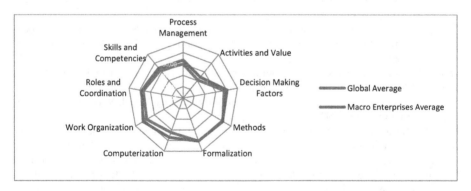

**Fig. 5.** Very large Enterprises vs Global Average

## 5    Conclusions and Future Developments

The aim of the proposed assessment model is to give the possibility to a company to assess its NPD process. Actually companies know the problems they have to face when introducing new products to the market, but they not always consider these criticalities in a whole picture, resulting in a bad focusing of the required improvement efforts. The proposed method gives companies the opportunity to assess themselves, and also to benchmark with competitors.

Further researches will be based on the application of this method in as much companies as possible, in order to test the validity of the model.

**Acknowledgments.** This work was partly funded by the European Commission through the project Lean Product and Process Development – LeanPPD (NMP-2007-214090, www.leanppd.eu). The authors wish to acknowledge their gratitude and appreciation to the rest of the LeanPPD project partners for their contributions during the development of various ideas and concepts presented in this paper.

# References

Anumba, C.J., Ugwu, O., Ren, Z.: Concurrent Engineering in Construction Projects. Taylor and Francis Group (2007)

Biemans, W.G.: A picture paints a thousand numbers: a critical look at b2b product development research. Business & Industrial Marketing 18(6/7), 514–528 (2003)

Díaz-Ley, M., García, F., Piattini, M.: MIS-PyME software measurement capability maturity model – Supporting the definition of software measurement programs and capability determination. Advances in Engineering Software 4, 1223–1237 (2010)

González, F.J.M., Palacios, T.M.B.: The effect of new product develop-ment techniques on new product success in Spanish firms. Industrial Marketing Management 31(3), 261–271 (2002)

Huang, X., Soutar, G.N., Brown, A.: Measuring new product success: an empirical investigation of Australian SMEs. Industrial Marketing Management 33, 117–123 (2004)

Ibbs, W., Kwak, H.Y.: Assessing Project Management Maturity. Project Management Institute 31(1), 32–43 (2000)

Khalfan, M.A., Anumba, C.J., Carrillo, P.M.: Development of a readiness assessment model for concurrent engineering in construction. Benchmarking: An International Journal 8(3), 223–239 (2001)

Lam, P.-K., et al.: Self-assessment of conflict management in client-supplier collaborative new product development. Industrial Management & Data Systems 107(5), 688–714 (2007)

Mark, P., Aulkb, P., Curtis, R., Chrissis, M.: Capability Maturity Model, Version 1.1. Software Engineering Institute (1993)

Rossi, M., Kerga, E., Tasich, M., Terzi. S., : Proposal of a method to systematically identify wastes in New Product Development Process. In: Proceedings of the International Conference on Concurrent Enterprising, ICE 2011, Aachen, Germany, June 20-22 (2011)

Wognum, P.M., Stoeten, B.J.B., Kerkhof, M., De Graaf, R.: PMO-RACE: A Combined Method for Assessing Organisations for CE, Advances in Concurrent Engineering. In: Proceedings of 3rd ISPE International Conference on Concurrent Engineering, Canada, August 26-28, pp. 113–120 (1996)

# Multi-objective Optimization of Product Life-Cycle Costs and Environmental Impacts

Daniele Cerri[1], Marco Taisch[1], and Sergio Terzi[2]

[1] Politecnico di Milano, Department of Management, Economics and Industrial Engineering
Piazza Leonardo da Vinci 32,
20133, Milano, Italy
[2] Università degli Studi di Bergamo, Department of Industrial Engineering
Viale Marconi 5,
24044, Dalmine (Bergamo), Italy
{daniele.cerri,marco.taisch}@polimi.it,
sergio.terzi@unibg.it

**Abstract.** The present paper discusses the development of a model to multi-objective optimization of product life-cycle costs and environmental impacts. In modern world European companies need new competitive factors. Costs along the life-cycle and sustainability could provide two of these. A model to optimize costs and environmental impacts could play a relevant role for engineering the life-cycle of a product. Within this context, the paper conducts a state of the art review of existing solutions. In the end a model is proposed.

**Keywords:** LCA, Life Cycle Assessment, LCC, Life Cycle Costing, Multi Optimization, Genetic Algorithms, Product Life Cycle.

## 1    Introduction

Today, in the modern global world, European companies need to find new competitive factors for facing the low-cost pressure of emerging countries. Sustainability, more and more pushed by international regulations (e.g. Kyoto Protocols, European Directives, etc.), could provide one of these factors: being able to develop eco-friendly, energy-efficient and green products before the others could give a competitive advantage to European industries for the next years. In this research, companies can be supported by methodologies already well-known in literature, like Life Cycle Costing (LCC) and Life Cycle Assessment (LCA), which permit to perform cost and environmental analysis for developing more sustainable products. However, most of the researches available in literature are not able to guarantee the reaching of the optimal solution, but in most of the experiences LCC and LCA are just used for simple evaluations. This paper aims to fill this gap, proposing a model that optimizes product life-cycle costs and environmental impacts at the same time. The paper is organized as follows: Section 2 illustrates the current state of the art of LCC, LCA and optimization methods; Section 3 describes the proposed model, with real application; finally, Section 4 concludes the paper.

C. Emmanouilidis, M. Taisch, D. Kiritsis (Eds.): APMS 2012, Part I, IFIP AICT 397, pp. 391–396, 2013.

# 2     State of the Art

Life Cycle Cost and Life Cycle Assessment are well-known methodologies in the relevant literature. Both have been developed since the '60ies: LCC are "cradle-to-grave" costs summarized as an economic model of evaluating alternatives for equipment and projects [3]; LCA is a technique to assess environmental impacts associated with all the stages of a product's life from-cradle-to-grave [13]. For this paper, it is interesting to analyze the state of the art of optimization applied to LCC and LCA. 39 papers for LCC and 40 papers for LCA, from the last 15 years, have been analyzed. We have classified the contributions in three clusters: (i) simple application of the methodology, (ii) use of a software, (iii) optimization. The first cluster considers papers that barely apply the methodology (LCC or LCA). The second cluster includes contributions that use a software to calculate costs and / or environmental impacts. The third cluster takes into account papers that optimize product life-cycle's costs and / or environmental impacts.

We observe that only few papers consider optimization issues. In percentage, only 20.51% of LCC literature treats about optimization, reduced to 10% in LCA. Evidently, this research area is still emerging and this paper can give a contribution.

Another interesting information is the massive use of software in LCA, while in LCC is practically missing. Use of software in LCA is justified by the increased complexity of the methodology, compared to LCC. The most popular LCA software are: SimaPro, GaBi Software and LCAiT.

Focusing on papers dealing with optimization, the used optimization methods are: Linear Programming, Genetic Algorithm and Particle Swarm Optimization.

In [1] Azapagic and Clift applied 2 algorithms: a single objective linear programming model to optimize LCA and a multi-objective linear programming model to optimize LCA and profit of a chemical plant that produces thermoplastic materials. In [2] the previous authors developed a multi-objective linear programming to optimize LCA (understood as Global Warming Potential), costs and total production of a chemical system that produces 5 boron products. Cattaneo [4] instead use a single objective linear programming model to optimize LCC of a train traction system.

Other 6 papers use genetic algorithm instead of linear programming.

Gitzel and Herbort [8] applied a genetic algorithm to optimize LCC of a DCS (Distributed Control System), using different GA variants. Hinow and Mevissen [9] use genetic algorithm to optimize LCC of a substation, improving the maintenance activities. In Kaveh et al. [10] genetic algorithms, exactly NSGA-2, is used to perform a multi-objective optimization of LCC and initial costs of large steel structures. Here it is possible to see the strong trade-off between initial costs and life cycle costs. Frangopol and Liu [7] and Okasha and Frangopol [12] applied a multi-objective genetic algorithm to optimize three different objectives: LCC, lifetime condition index value and lifetime safety  index value for [7]; LCC, minimum redundancy index and maximum probability of failure for [12]. They are applied on structural maintenance. Dufo-Lopez et al. [6] instead applied the Strength Pareto Evolutionary Algorithm (SPEA) to the multi-objective optimization of a stand-alone PV–wind–diesel system with batteries storage. The objectives to be minimized are the levelized cost of energy (LCOE) and the equivalent $CO_2$ life cycle emissions (LCE). LCE can be viewed as LCA.

Finally, two papers use the particle swarm optimization.

Kornekalis [11] use a multi-objective particle swarm optimization to the optimal design of photovoltaic grid-connected systems (PVGCSs), maximizing Net Present Value (NPV) and the pollutants gas emissions avoided due to use PVGCSs (this can be compared to LCA); Wang et al. [15], instead, applied a Particle Swarm Optimization to minimize LCC of a personal computer.

Genetic Algorithm is a subclass of evolutionary algorithms, where the elements of the search space G are binary strings (G=B*) or arrays of other elementary types [16].

Genetic Algorithms are widely used in LCC and LCA applications for the following reasons:

- They are more efficient than others when number of variables increase;
- They don't have any problem with multi-objective optimization;
- They are suitable for applications dealing with component-based systems (a product could be seen as a chromosome and its components as genes).

# 3    Proposed Model

In this section a model to optimize product life-cycle costs and environmental impacts together is proposed. The model is based on NSGA-2 (Non dominated Sorting Genetic Algorithm). NSGA-2 is one of the most popular and tested Genetic Algorithms. It has three special characteristics: (i) fast non-dominated sorting approach, (ii) fast crowded distance estimation procedure and (iii) simple crowded comparison operator [5]. To perform NSGA-2 it was used GANetXL [14], an add-in for Microsoft Excel.

We have applied NSGA-2 to LCC / LCA optimization. We have defined an experimental scenario composed by a preliminary set of 3 simplified test cases (Table 3), plus the application to a real industrial case, concerning the design of a production line. The performances of NSGA-2 in the introductory test cases have been compared with other two optimization methods, based on linear programming, in order to check the goodness of the proposed model.

**Table 1.** Test parameters

|         | Data Input | Optimal Solutions | Constraint |
|---------|------------|-------------------|------------|
| **Test A** | A | Unique | No |
| **Test B** | B | Pareto Front | No |
| **Test C** | B | Pareto Front | Yes (1) |

In the introductory tests, the life-cycle of a generic product made of 10 subgroups is evaluated. Each subgroup has two alternatives. The data input is composed by 4 types of cost and of 3 kinds of environmental impact. The models must optimize two objectives: minimize the life-cycle-cost and minimize the product life-cycle environmental impact.

Test A was used to see if all the models reach the unique optimal solution, while Test B and Test C were used to see the behaviour of the 3 models with multiple optimal solutions. Test B has no constraints, while Test C has a constraint.

In Test A, all the models reached the optimal solution. In Test B and in Test C, the behaviour of the models were different.

NSGA-2 returns a number of solutions greater than the others two. Also its solutions are not dominated and some of them are surely optimal (compared to WSM, Weighted Sum Model). Then, it is possible to say that NSGA-2 is better than linear programming-based models.

The NSGA-2 model was then applied to a real case, a fraction of an assembly line, designed and manufactured by an Italian company. This line assemblies a small car diesel engine. Five stations were considered: the first is for silicon coating, the second assemblies the base, in the third screws are filled in, the fourth fills screws and rotates the pallets, the last screws the under base. All of these stations can have automatic, semi-automatic or manual alternatives. Each station has 6 alternatives: 3 automatic, 2 semi-automatic and 1 manual. 8 costs and 2 environmental impacts were considered for being optimized. In this case, the algorithm chromosome represents the line and stations represent the genes. The model has two types of constraints: the availability of the fraction of the assembly line must be greater than 0.95; all the stations   must have an alternative. Below we report the model written in analytical form.

$$\min \sum_{i=1}^{30}(Cin * x_i + Ce * x_i + Cric * x_i + Cop * x_i + Ccon * x_i + Cair * x_i + Cmo * x_i + Cmorip * x_i) \tag{1}$$

$$\min \sum_{i=1}^{30}(EIst * x_i + Elel * x_i) \tag{2}$$

Subject to

$$\sum_{i=1}^{6} A_i x_i * \sum_{i=7}^{12} A_i x_i * \sum_{i=13}^{18} A_i x_i * \sum_{i=19}^{24} A_i x_i * \sum_{i=25}^{30} A_i x_i \geq 0.95 \tag{3}$$

$$\sum_{i=1}^{6} x_i = 1 \tag{4}$$

$$\sum_{i=7}^{12} x_i = 1 \tag{5}$$

$$\sum_{i=13}^{18} x_i = 1 \tag{6}$$

$$\sum_{i=19}^{24} x_i = 1 \tag{7}$$

$$\sum_{i=25}^{30} x_i = 1 \tag{8}$$

$$x_i \in \{0,1\} \ i = 1,2,...,30$$

where: *Cin* is initial cost, *Ce* is energy cost, *Cric* is spare parts cost, *Cop* is labor cost, *Ccon* is consumable cost, *Cair* is air cost, *Cmo* is preventive maintenance cost, *Cmorip* is corrective maintenance cost, *EIst* is environmental impact of the station and *Elel* is environmental impact of electric energy. *A* is availability and $x_i$ is binary variable.

So the model must optimize costs and environmental impacts along the product's life cycle, or rather the model must find the best combination of station to optimize the two objective.

Two scenarios were studied: one where the line is installed in Eastern Europe and one where the line is installed in Western Europe. The differences are the labor and maintenance staff costs: in fact in Western Europe they are 3 or 4 times greater than to Eastern Europe.

Fig. 1 and 2 report the results in Eastern Europe and Western Europe scenario.

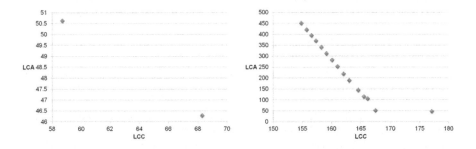

**Fig. 1.** Results (Eastern Europe Scenario)    **Fig. 2.** Results (Western Europe Scenario)

In Eastern Europe Scenario the solution, that minimizes life-cycle cost, is composed of all manual stations, while in Western Europe the solution is composed of all automatic stations. This happens for differences in labor costs: in Eastern Europe, where labor costs are lower, there's convenience to install manual stations, instead in Western Europe it agrees automatic stations. To validate the obtained results, they were subjected to company. It has considered correct the solutions.

# 4    Conclusion

In this paper, a model is proposed to optimize product life-cycle costs and environmental impacts together. It was tested and compared to other two models. Then it was applied to a real case and the results have been validated. This presents some advantages, as (i) relevance for real case and (ii) comparison with other two models, and some criticism, as (i) performances are not evaluated and (ii) LCA not well investigated. The future developments can be (i) the inclusion of effectiveness / performance equations and (ii) the deepening of LCA.

# References

1. Azapagic, A., Clift, R.: Life Cycle Assessment and Linear Programming -Environmental Optimisation of Product System. Computers Chemical Engineering 19, 229–234 (1995)
2. Azapagic, A., Clift, R.: Life cycle assessment and multiobjective optimisation. Journal of Cleaner Production 7, 135–143 (1998)

3. Barringer, H.P.: A Life Cycle Cost Summary. In: ICOMS 2003 (2003)
4. Cattaneo, E.: L'Ottimizzazione della Progettazione tramite il Life-Cycle Cost. Thesis (2009)
5. Deb, K., Pratap, A., Agarwal, S., Meyarivan, T.: A fast and elitist multiobjective genetic algorithm: NSGA-II. Evolutionary Computation. IEEE Transactions 6, 182–197 (2002)
6. Dufo-Lopez, R., Bernal-Agustin, J.L., Yusta-Loyo, J.M., Dominguez-Navarro, J.A., Ramirez-Rosado, I.J., Lujano, J.: Aso: Multi-objective optimization minimizing cost and life cycle emissions of stand-alone PV–wind–diesel systems with batteries storage. Applied Energy 88, 4033–4041 (2011)
7. Frangopol, D.M., Liu, M.: Multiobjective Optimization for Risk-based Maintenance and Life-Cycle Cost of civil infrastructure systems. In: IFIP International Federation for Information Processing, vol. 199, pp. 123–137. Springer, Boston (2006)
8. Gitzel, R., Herbort, M.: Optimizing life cycle cost using genetic algorithms. Journal of Cost Management 22, 34–47 (2008)
9. Hinow, M., Mevissen, M.: Substation Maintenance Strategy Adaptation for Life-Cycle Cost Reduction Using Genetic Algorithm. IEEE Transactions on Power Delivery 26, 197–204 (2011)
10. Kaveh, A., Laknejadi, K., Alinejad, B.: Performance-based multi-objective optimization of large steel structures. Acta Mechanica 223, 355–369 (2011)
11. Kornelakis, A.: Multiobjective Particle Swarm Optimization for the optimal design of photovoltaic grid-connected systems. Solar Energy 84, 2022–2033 (2010)
12. Okasha, N.M., Frangopol, D.M.: Lifetime-oriented multi-objective optimization of structural maintenance considering system reliability, redundancy and life-cycle cost using GA. Structural Safety 31, 460–474 (2009)
13. Scientific Applications International Corporation: Life Cycle Assessment: Principles and Practice. Technical Report, 80 (2006)
14. Savić, D.A., Bicik, J., Morley, M.S.: A DSS Generator for Multiobjective Optimisation of Spreadsheet-Based Models. Environmental Modelling and Software 26, 551–561 (2011)
15. Wang, K., Dai, L., Myklebust, O.: Applying Particle Swarm Optimization (PSO) in Product Life Cycle Cost Optimization. IPROMS, 6 (2009)
16. Weise, T.: Global Optimization Algorithms – Theory and Application. Self Published, 820 (2009)

# A Stochastic Formulation of the Disassembly Line Balancing Problem

Mohand Lounes Bentaha, Olga Battaïa, and Alexandre Dolgui

École Nationale Supérieure des Mines, EMSE-FAYOL,
CNRS UMR6158, LIMOS, F-42023 Saint-Étienne, France
{bentaha,battaia,dolgui}@emse.fr

**Abstract.** The disassembly line balancing problem is studied under uncertainty. Disassembly task times are assumed random variables with known probability distributions. An AND/OR graph is used to model the precedence relations among tasks. The goal is to assign the disassembly tasks to workstations while respecting precedence and cycle time constraints. The objective is to minimize the total line cost including the incompletion cost arising from task incompletion within the cycle time. A stochastic linear mixed integer programming formulation is developed.

**Keywords:** Sustainable Development, Disassembly Line Design, Stochastic Programming, L-shaped Method.

## 1 Introduction

The growing amount of postconsumer products poses challenges for business and society at large [7]. To decrease the amount of waste to be sent to landfills, more and more manufacturers turn to end-of-life processing of products [6]. The selective separation of desired parts and materials, executed by disassembly, is a mandatory step before recycling or remanufacturing [8]. As a consequence, disassembly systems tend to play an important role in industry. Since their design results in complex optimization problems, including disassembly planning, balancing and sequencing, efficient mathematical tools are needed in order to improve their performances and their cost effectiveness. Such tools must take into account the high degree of uncertainty in the structure and the quality of the products to be disassembled because of varying conditions affecting them before they arrive in a disassembly system. This paper deals with the uncertainty related to the disassembly task times and proposes a new mathematical formulation for the stochastic disassembly line balancing problem (DLBP) as well as an exact method to solve it efficiently.

## 2 Problem Formulation

The Disassembly Line Balancing Problem considered here aims to assign a given set of disassembly tasks $I = \{1, 2, ..., N\}$ to an ordered sequence of workstations

C. Emmanouilidis, M. Taisch, D. Kiritsis (Eds.): APMS 2012, Part I, IFIP AICT 397, pp. 397–404, 2013.

$J = \{1,2, \dots, M\}$ under precedence and cycle time constraints. A task cannot be split between two workstations. Disassembly task times $t_i$ are assumed random variables with normal probability distributions having known mean $\mu$ and variance $\sigma^2$, i.e. $t_i = \tilde{\zeta}_i$, $\tilde{\zeta}_i \sim \mathcal{N}(\mu_i, \sigma_i)$, $t_i > 0, i \in I$, [5], [12-13]. The task times of set $I$ are modeled by random vector $\tilde{\xi} = (\tilde{\zeta}_1, \tilde{\zeta}_2, \dots, \tilde{\zeta}_N)$ varying over a set $\Xi \subset \mathfrak{R}_+^N$ in given probability space $(\Xi, \mathcal{F}, P)$. Random variables $\tilde{\zeta}_i, i \in I$ are assumed to be mutually independent. Let $\tilde{\zeta}_i = \alpha_i(\tilde{\xi}), i \in I$.

The precedence relations among tasks are given by an AND/OR Graph (AOG), [2], [10], see Fig. 1. Each subassembly of the product to be disassembled is represented by an auxiliary node $A_k$, $k \in K$ in the AOG. Each disassembly task gives a basic node $B_i, i \in I$ Two types of arcs define the precedence relations between the subassemblies and the disassembly tasks. AND-type arcs (in bold) dictate the normal precedence relation. OR-type arcs (remaining arcs) permit the selection of any of the successors. A dummy task $S$ is introduced into the precedence graph as a sink node, see the figure below.

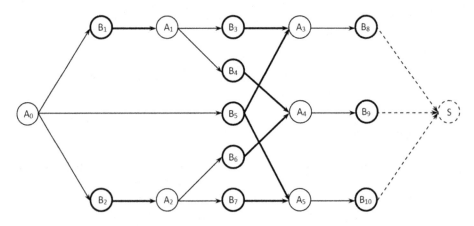

**Fig. 1.** AND/OR precedence graph

The following notations have to be introduced.

**Parameters**

$I = \{1,2, \dots, N\}$, disassembly tasks' index set, $N \in \mathbb{N}^*$;

$J = \{1,2, \dots, M\}$, workstations' index set, $M \in \mathbb{N}^*$;

$K = \{0,1, \dots, G - 1\}$, index set of the AND/OR precedence graph's auxiliary nodes, $G \in \mathbb{N}^*$;

$A_k$ : Auxiliary node of the AND/OR graph, $k \in K$ ;

$B_i$ : Disassembly task, $i \in I$ ;

$S$ : The AND/OR graph's sink node, $t_S = 0$;

$F_c$ : Fixed cost per unit time of operating the workstations;

$q_j$: cost per unit time of exceeding $C_t, j \in J$;

$C_t$ : Cycle time, $C_t > 0$;

$\alpha_i(\tilde{\xi})$ : Random task time of $B_i, i \in I$ ;

$P(k)$ : Predecessors index set of $A_k$, $k \in K$ i.e. $P(k) = \{i|B_i \text{ precedes } A_k\}$;

$S(k)$ : Successors index set of $A_k$, $k \in K$, $S(k) = \{i|A_k \text{ precedes } B_i\}$.

**Decision Variables**

$$x_{ij} = \begin{cases} 1 & \text{if task from } B_i \text{ is assigned to workstation } j, \\ 0 & \text{otherwise.} \end{cases}$$

$$x_{Sj} = \begin{cases} 1 & \text{if sink task } S \text{ is assigned to workstation } j, \\ 0 & \text{otherwise.} \end{cases}$$

$$z_j = \begin{cases} C_t & \text{if } x_{Sj} = 1, \\ 0 & \text{otherwise.} \end{cases}$$

The objective considered in this paper is to minimize the line cost including fixed workstation operating costs and *recourse* costs caused by exceeding $C_t$. A *recourse* variable $y_j(\tilde{\xi}), j \in J$, measures the amount of time exceeding $C_t$ if there is any.

The following model is used for the problem presented.

**Stochastic MIP Formulation (SMIP I)**

$$\min \left\{ F_c \sum_{j \in J} j\, z_j + \mathbb{E}_{\tilde{\xi}} \left[ \sum_{j \in J} q_j\, y_j(\tilde{\xi}) \right] \right\}$$

s.t.

$$z_j = C_t\, x_{Sj}, \forall j \in J \tag{1}$$

$$\sum_{i \in S(0)} \sum_{j \in J} x_{ij} = 1 \tag{2}$$

$$\sum_{j \in J} x_{ij} \leq 1, \forall i \in I \tag{3}$$

$$\sum_{i \in S(k)} \sum_{j \in J} x_{ij} = \sum_{i \in P(k)} \sum_{j \in J} x_{ij}, \forall k \in K \backslash \{0\} \tag{4}$$

$$\sum_{i \in S(k)} x_{iv} \leq \sum_{i \in P(k)} \sum_{j=1}^{v} x_{ij}, \forall k \in K \backslash \{0\}, \forall v \in J \tag{5}$$

$$\sum_{j \in J} x_{Sj} = 1 \tag{6}$$

$$\sum_{j \in J} j\, x_{ij} \leq \sum_{j \in J} j\, x_{Sj}, \forall i \in I \tag{7}$$

$$\sum_{i \in I} \alpha_i(\tilde{\xi})\, x_{ij} - y_j(\tilde{\xi}) \leq C_t, \forall j \in J \tag{8}$$

$$z_j \geq 0, \forall j \in J \tag{9}$$

$$x_{Sj}, x_{ij} \in \{0,1\}, \forall i \in I, \forall j \in J \tag{10}$$

$$y_j(\tilde{\xi}) \geq 0, \forall j \in J \tag{11}$$

The objective function includes fixed and recourse costs, where $\mathbb{E}_{\tilde{\xi}}$ stands for the expected value with the respect to the distribution of the random vector $\tilde{\xi}$:

$$\mathbb{E}_{\tilde{\xi}}\left[\sum_{j\in J} q_j\, y_j(\tilde{\xi})\right] = \int_{\Xi}\left(\sum_{j\in J} q_j\, y_j(\tilde{\xi})\right) dP \tag{12}$$

Note that the integral (12) makes the model nonlinear one.

Constraints (1) ensure the value of $z_j$ to be $C_t$ when dummy task $S$ is assigned to station $j$. Constraint (2) imposes the selection of only one disassembly task (OR-successor) to begin the disassembly process. Constraint set (3) indicates that a task is to be assigned to at most one workstation. Constraints (4) and (5) define OR- and AND-precedence relations, respectively. Constraint (6) imposes the assignment of the dummy task $S$ to one station. Constraints (7) ensure the precedence relations for dummy task $S$. The constraints (8) force the respect of the cycle time limitations. Sets (9)-(11) represent the trivial constraints.

Let $X = \{\, x \mid$ constraints (1)-(7), (9)-(10) are satisfied$\}$ and $L = \{1,2,\dots,L\}, L \in \mathbb{N}^*$. If $\tilde{\xi}$ has a finite discrete distribution $\{(\xi^l, p_l), l \in L\}, p_l > 0, \forall l \in L$ ($p_l$ is the realization probability of $\xi^l$ of $\tilde{\xi}$), then the model presented is an ordinary linear program with a so-called *dual decomposition* structure.

**Deterministic Equivalent (I')**

$$\min\left\{F_c \sum_{j\in J} j\, z_j + \sum_{l=1}^{L} p_l \sum_{j\in J} q_j\, y_j(\xi^l)\right\}$$

s.t.

$$\sum_{i\in I} \alpha_i(\xi^l)\, x_{ij} - y_j(\xi^l) \le C_t, \forall\, j \in J, \forall\, l \in L$$

$$x \in X, y_j(\xi^l) \ge 0, \forall\, j \in J, \forall\, l \in L$$

Depending on the number of realizations of $\tilde{\xi}$, i.e. L, this linear mixed integer program, may become very large in scale, but its particular block structure can be exploited by specially designed algorithms such as the *L-shaped* method, [1], [3-4], [9], [11] which will be developed in the next section.

## 3    Solution Method

**The L-shaped Method**
The main idea of the L-shaped method is to approximate the nonlinear term in the objective function of the two-stage stochastic problems [3]. Assume a finite realizations set $\Xi$ of the stochastic vector $\tilde{\xi}$ such as $|\Xi| = L$. The L-shaped method for the DLBP can be written as follows.

**L-shaped Algorithm**

*Step* 0. Set $\mathfrak{r} = \mathfrak{h} = \upsilon = 0$.

*Step* 1. Set $\upsilon = \upsilon + 1$. Solve the following LP:

$$\min\{c^T x + \varphi\}$$

s.t.

$$A x = b$$

$$\mathcal{D}_v x \geq d_v, v = 1, \dots, \mathfrak{r} \tag{13}$$

$$\mathcal{E}_v x + \varphi \geq e_v, v = 1, \dots, \mathfrak{h} \tag{14}$$

$$x \text{ binary}, \varphi \geq 0$$

Let $(x^\upsilon, \varphi^\upsilon)$ be an optimal solution.

*Step* 2. For $l = 1, \dots, L$ solve the following LP:

$$\min \quad \mathcal{Z} = a^T u^+ + a^T u^-$$

s.t.

$$W y + I u^+ - I u^- = h_l - T_l x^\upsilon$$

$$y \geq 0, u^+ \geq 0, u^- \geq 0$$

$a = (1, \dots, 1)^T$, until for some $l$ the optimal value $\mathcal{Z} > 0$. In this case, let $\sigma^\upsilon$ be the associated simplex multipliers, define

$$\mathcal{D}_{\mathfrak{r}+1} = (\sigma^\upsilon)^T T_l$$

and

$$d_{\mathfrak{r}+1} = (\sigma^\upsilon)^T h_l$$

in order to generate a constraint called a *feasibility cut* of type (13). Set $\mathfrak{r} = \mathfrak{r} + 1$, add constraint type (13) and return to *Step* 1. If for all $l \in L$, $\mathcal{Z} = 0$ , go to *Step* 3.

*Step* 3. For $= 1, \dots, L$ , solve the LP:

$$\min \mathcal{W} = q_l^T y$$

$$W y = h_l - T_l x^\upsilon$$

$$y \geq 0$$

Let $\omega_l^\upsilon$ be the simplex multipliers associated with the optimal solution of problem $l$ above and define

$$\mathcal{E}_{\mathfrak{h}+1} = \sum_{l \in L} p_l (\omega_l^v)^T T_l$$

and

$$e_{\mathfrak{h}+1} = \sum_{l \in L} p_l (\omega_l^v)^T h_l.$$

Let $\theta^v = e_{\mathfrak{h}+1} - \mathcal{E}_{\mathfrak{h}+1} x^v$. If $\varphi^v \geq \theta^v$, stop; $x^v$ is an optimal solution. Else, generate a constraint called *optimality cut* of type (14), set $\mathfrak{h} = \mathfrak{h} + 1$, add constraint type (14) and return to **Step** 1.

This method approximates $\mathbb{E}_{\tilde{\xi}} [\sum_{j \in J} q_j \, y_j(\tilde{\xi})] = \int_{\Xi} (\sum_{j \in J} q_j \, y_j(\tilde{\xi})) \, dP$ using an outer linearization.

Two types of constraints are sequentially added:

- feasibility cuts (13) determining $\{x | \mathbb{E}_{\tilde{\xi}} [\sum_{j \in J} q_j \, y_j(\tilde{\xi})] < +\infty\}$;
- optimality cuts (14), which are linear approximations to $\mathbb{E}_{\tilde{\xi}} [\sum_{j \in J} q_j \, y_j(\tilde{\xi})]$.

## 4    Example

The method presented has been applied to the compass example illustrated in Fig. 2. It is made of seven components: (1) wheel, (2) left leg, (3) right leg, (4) left fixation screw, (5) lead, (6) tip and (7) right fixation screw. The AOG for this example is shown in Fig. 1. The input data for the DLBP is presented in Table 1.

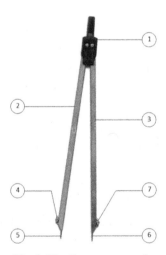

**Fig. 2.** The Compass example

**Table 1.** Input data

| Task | $\mu$ | $\sigma$ | Subassembly | Component | |
|------|------|------|-------------|-----------|--|
| 1 | 0.21 | 0.05 | 1:5 | 6;7 | $|\Xi| = 1024$ |
| 2 | 0.21 | 0.05 | 1:3,6,7 | 4;5 | $J = \{1,2,3\}$ |
| 3 | 0.50 | 0.10 | 2,4,5 | 1;3 | $K = \{0,1,\dots,5\}$ |
| 4 | 0.21 | 0.05 | 1:3 | 4;5 | $F_c = 5$ |
| 5 | 0.50 | 0.10 | 2,4,5/3,6,7 | 1 | $q_j = 7, j \in J$ |
| 6 | 0.21 | 0.05 | 1:3 | 6;7 | $C_t = 0.51$ |
| 7 | 0.50 | 0.10 | 3,6,7 | 1;2 | |
| 8 | 0.21 | 0.05 | -- | 2;4;5 | |
| 9 | 0.50 | 0.10 | -- | 1;2;3 | |
| 10 | 0.21 | 0.05 | -- | 3;6;7 | |

The L-shaped method was implemented in Microsoft Visual C++ 2008. ILOG CPLEX 12.4 was used to solve the model on a PC with Pentium(R) Dual-Core CPU 2.30 GHz and 3Go RAM. The optimal solution contains 2 workstations. Task 5 is assigned to the 1st workstation and tasks {8,10} to the second one. The total line cost is 5.342 when the recourse cost is 0.242. The resolution time was 58 s. The overall idle time of the disassembly line, if mean time of each task selected is considered, is 0.10.

# 5     Conclusion and Perspectives

The disassembly line balancing problem was formulated under uncertainty. A two-stage stochastic linear mixed integer program with fixed recourse was developed to solve it. The formulation presented can be easily adapted for the stochastic assembly line balancing problem as well. Then, the model can be considered for the disassembly task times given by, for example, triangular distribution.

Further research work should be done in order to refine the proposed mathematical model and solution method in order to approach real-world problems where uncertainty does not only concern the disassembly task times but the quantity and the quality of the inputs and outputs of the disassembly line as well.

**Acknowledgement.** This work was partially supported by Research Cluster on Operational Research (GDR RO) of the National Centre for Scientific Research, France.

# References

1. Ahmed, S., Shapiro, A.: The Sample Average Approximation Method for Stochastic Programs with Integer Recourse. Technical Report, School of Industrial & Systems Engineering, Georgia Institute of Technology, 1-24 (2002)
2. Altekin, F.T., Kandiller, L., Ozdemirel, N.E.: Profit-Oriented Disassembly-Line Balancing. International Journal of Production Research 46(10), 2675–2693 (2008)

3. Birge, J.R.: Stochastic Programming Computation and Applications. INFORMS Journal on Computing 9(2), 111–133 (1997)
4. Birge, J.R., Tang, H.: L-shaped Method for Two-stage Problems of Stochastic Convex Programming. Technical Report, College of Engineering, The University of Michigan, 1-10 (1993)
5. Dolgui, A., Proth, J.-M.: Supply Chain Engineering: Useful Methods and Techniques. Springer London Ltd., London (2010)
6. Güngör, A., Gupta, S.M.: A Solution Approach to the Disassembly Line Balancing Problem in the Presence of Task Failures. International Journal of Production Research 39(7), 1427–1467 (2001)
7. Güngör, A., Gupta, S.M.: Issues in Environmentally Conscious Manufacturing and Product Recovery: A Survey. Computers & Industrial Engineering 36, 811–853 (1999)
8. Güngör, A., Gupta, S.M.: Disassembly Line in Product Recovery. International Journal of Production Research 40(11), 2569–2589 (2002)
9. Kall, P., Wallace, S.W.: Stochastic Programming. John Wiley & Sons, Chichester (1994)
10. Koc, A., Sabuncuoglu, I., Erel, E.: Two Exact Formulations for Disassembly Line Balancing Problems with Task Precedence Diagram Construction Using an AND/OR Graph. IIE Transactions 41(10), 866–881 (2009)
11. Ntaimo, L.: Fenchel Decomposition for Stochastic Mixed-Integer Programming. Journal of Global Optimization 55, 141–163 (2013)
12. Sarin, S.C., Erel, E., Dar-el, E.M.: A Methodology for Solving Single-Model, Stochastic Assembly Line Balancing Problem. The International Journal of Management Science 27, 525–535 (1999)
13. Silverman, F.N., Carter, J.C.: A Cost-based Methodology for Stochastic Line Balancing with Intermittent Line Stoppages. Management Science 32(4), 455–463 (1986)

# Incorporating Regularity of Required Workload to the *MMSP-W* with Serial Workstations and Free Interruption of the Operations

Joaquín Bautista, Rocío Alfaro, and Alberto Cano

Universitat Politècnica de Catalunya, Avda. Diagonal 647, 7th floor, 08028 Barcelona, Spain
{joaquin.bautista,rocio.alfaro,alberto.cano-perez}@upc.edu

**Abstract.** We propose a mathematical model to solve an extension to the mixed-model sequencing problem with work overload minimization *(MMSP-W)* for production lines with serial workstations and parallel homogeneous processors and regularizing the required workload. We performed a computational experience with a case study of the Nissan engine plant in Barcelona.

**Keywords:** Manufacturing, Sequencing, Work overload, Linear programming.

## 1 Introduction

Manufacturing lines with mixed products are very common in Just in Time (*JIT*) and Douki Seisan (*DS*) environments. These lines, composed of multiple workstations must be flexible enough to treat different product types.

These lines usually consist of a set ( $K$ ) of workstations laid out in series. Each workstation ( $k = 1, \ldots, |K|$ ) is characterized by the use of the human resources, tools and automated systems necessary to carry out the work assigned to the workstation. The set of tasks assigned to the workstation is called workload, and the average time required to process these tasks at normal activity rates is called workload time or processing time.

An important attribute of these production lines is flexibility. The products (such as engines or car bodies) that circulate through the lines are not completely identical. Although some of the products may be similar or of the same type, they may require different resources and components and therefore may require different processing times.

The desired flexibility of these mixed-product lines requires that the sequence in which the product types are manufactured follow two general principles: (1) to minimize the stock of components and semi-processed products and (2) to maximize the efficiency of the line, manufacturing the products in the least amount of time possible.

A classification of sequencing problems arising in this context was given in [1]:

1. *Mixed-model sequencing.* The aim in this problem is to obtain sequences that complete the maximum work required by the work schedule.

C. Emmanouilidis, M. Taisch, D. Kiritsis (Eds.): APMS 2012, Part I, IFIP AICT 397, pp. 405–412, 2013.
© IFIP International Federation for Information Processing 2013

2. *Car sequencing.* These problems are designed to obtain sequences that meet a set of constraints related to the frequency in which the workstations are required to incorporate special options (e.g., sunroof, special seats or a larger engine) within the products.
3. *Level scheduling.* These problems focus on obtaining level sequences for the production and usage of components.

The *MMSP-W* [2, 3] consists of sequencing $T$ products, grouped into a set of $I$ product types, of which $d_i$ are of type $i$ ($i = 1,...,|I|$). A unit of product type $i$ ($i = 1,...,|I|$), when is at workstation $k$ ($k = 1,...,|K|$), requires a processing time equal to $p_{i,k}$ for each homogeneous processor (e.g., operator, robot or human-machine system) at normal activity, whereas the standard time granted at each station to work on an output unit is the cycle time, $c$.

Sometimes a workstation, $k$, can work on any product a maximum time $l_k$, which is called time window, and is longer than the cycle time ($l_k > c$), which causes that the time available to process the next unit is reduced. When it is not possible to complete all of the work required, it is said that an overload is generated.

The objective of *MMSP-W* is to maximize the total work completed, which is equivalent to minimize the total work overload generated (see Theorem 1 in [4]), sequencing the units on the line, considering the interruption of the operations at any time between the time of completion of one cycle and the time of termination marked by the time window associated with that cycle [5]. In addition, in our proposal we will maintain constant the cumulative time of work required at the workstations in all positions of the product sequence.

# 2    Models for the *MMSP-W*

## 2.1    Reference Models

For the *MMSP-W* with serial workstations, free interruption of the operations and homogeneity of required workload, we begin with several models as reference (see table 1).

**Table 1.** Comparison of the major differences of models $M1$ to $M4$ and $M4\cup3$

|  | M1 | M2 | M3 | M4 | M_4∪3 |
|---|---|---|---|---|---|
| *Objective* | Max V | Min W | Max V | Min W | Min W/ Max V |
| *Start instants* | Absolute $s_{k,t}$ | Relative $\hat{s}_{k,t}$ | Absolute $s_{k,t}$ | Relative $\hat{s}_{k,t}$ | Relative $\hat{s}_{k,t}$ |
| *Variables* | $v_{k,t}$ | $w_{k,t}$ | $v_{k,t}$ | $w_{k,t}$ | $w_{k,t}$, $v_{k,t}$ |
| *Window, t=T* | $l_k \ \forall k$ | $c \ \forall k$ | $l_k \ \forall k$ | $l_k \ \forall k$ | $l_k \ \forall k$ |
| *Rank for $b_k$* | $b_k \geq 1$ | $b_k = 1$ | $b_k \geq 1$ | $b_k = 1$ | $b_k \geq 1$ |
| *Links between stations* | No | No | Yes | Yes | Yes |

The models from the literature, *M*1 [2] and *M*2 [3], do not consider links between workstations. *M*1 is focused on maximize the total work performed, using an absolute time scale at each station and considering more than one homogeneous processor at each workstation. *M*2 is focused on minimize the total work overload with relative time scale at each station corresponding to each processed product unit and only considers one processor at each workstation.

An extension of these models, considering links between consecutive stations, are models *M*3 (*M*1 extended) and *M*4 (*M*2 extended) proposed by [4]. Moreover, considering the equivalence of the objective functions of *M*3 and *M*4, we can combine them and obtain the $M\_4 \cup 3$ [6] model that considers the relative times scales used in *M*4.

## 2.2    Regularity of Required Workload

The overload concentrations at certain times during the workday may be undesirable. One way to avoid this occurrence is to obtain product sequences that regulate the cumulative time of required work at the workstations in all positions of the product sequence.

To do this, first we consider the average time required at the $k^{th}$ workstation to process a product unit, which is the processing time for an ideal unit at workstation $k$. If $\dot{p}_k$ is the average time, then the ideal work rate for station $k$ $\left( k = 1,...,|K| \right)$ is determined as follows:

$$\dot{p}_k = \frac{b_k}{T} \sum_{i=1}^{|I|} p_{i,k} \cdot d_i \qquad k = 1,...,|K| \qquad (1)$$

Consequently, the ideal total work needed to complete $t$ output units at workstation $k$ is:

$$P_{k,t}^* = t \cdot \dot{p}_k \qquad k = 1,...,|K| \ ; \ t = 1,...,T \qquad (2)$$

Moreover, if we consider the actual total work required at the $k^{th}$ workstation to process a total of $t$ product units, of which $X_{i,t} = \sum_{\tau=1}^{t} x_{i,\tau}$ are of type $i$ $\left( i = 1,...,|I| \right)$, then we have:

$$P_{k,t} = b_k \sum_{i=1}^{|I|} p_{i,k} \cdot X_{i,t} = b_k \sum_{i=1}^{|I|} p_{i,k} \left( \sum_{\tau=1}^{t} x_{i,\tau} \right) \qquad k = 1,...,|K| \ ; \ t = 1,...,T \qquad (3)$$

Where $x_{i,t}$ ( $i = 1,...,|I|$ ; $t = 1,...,T$ ) is a binary variable that is equal to 1 if a product unit $i$ is assigned to the position $t^{th}$ of the sequence, and 0 otherwise.

One way to measure the irregularity of the required workload at a set of workstations over the workday is to cumulate the difference between the actual and ideal work required to each output unit at each workstation:

$$\Delta_Q(P) = \sum_{t=1}^{T}\sum_{k=1}^{|K|} \delta_{k,t}^2(P), \quad \text{where } \delta_{k,t}(P) = P_{k,t} - P_{k,t}^* \tag{4}$$

If we consider the properties derived from maintaining a production mix when manufacturing product units over time, we can define the number of units of product type $i$, of a total of $t$ units, which should ideally be manufactured to maintain the production mix as:

$$X_{i,t}^* = \frac{d_i}{T} \cdot t \qquad i = 1,\ldots,|I| \; ; \; t = 1,\ldots,T \tag{5}$$

Therefore, the ideal point $\vec{X}^* = \left(X_{1,1}^*,\ldots,X_{|I|,T}^*\right)$ presents the property of leveling the required workload, because at that point, the non-regularity of the required work is optimal, $P_{k,t} - P_{k,t}^* = \delta_{k,t}(P) = 0$ and then $\Delta_Q(P) = 0$, as shown in (6) (see theorem 1 in [6]):

$$P_{k,t} = b_k \sum_{i=1}^{|I|} p_{i,k} \cdot X_{i,t}^* \Leftrightarrow P_{k,t} = b_k \sum_{i=1}^{|I|} \frac{p_{i,k} \cdot d_i \cdot t}{T} = t \cdot \left( \frac{b_k}{T} \sum_{i=1}^{|I|} p_{i,k} \cdot d_i \right) = t \cdot \dot{p}_k = P_{k,t}^* \tag{6}$$

## 2.3    MMSP-W Model for Workload Regularity

Considering the properties described above and the reference model $M\_4\cup3$ [6], we limit the values of the cumulative production variables, $X_{i,t}$ ( $i = 1,\ldots,|I|$ ; $t = 1,\ldots,T$ ), to the integers closest to the ideal values of production, $X_{i,t}^* = d_i \cdot t/T$ , and then we obtain a new model, the $M\_4\cup3\_pmr$. The parameters and variables are presented below:

Parameters

| | |
|---|---|
| $K$ | Set of workstations ( $k = 1,\ldots,|K|$ ) |
| $b_k$ | Number of homogeneous processors at workstation $k$ |
| $I$ | Set of product types ( $i = 1,\ldots,|I|$ ) |
| $d_i$ | Programmed demand of product type $i$ |
| $p_{i,k}$ | Processing time required by a unit of type $i$ at workstation $k$ for each homogeneous processor (at normal activity) |
| $T$ | Total demand; obviously, $\sum_{i=1}^{|I|} d_i = T$ |
| $t$ | Position index in the sequence ( $t = 1,\ldots,T$ ) |
| $c$ | Cycle time, the standard time assigned to workstations to process any product unit |
| $l_k$ | Time window, the maximum time that each processor at workstation $k$ is allowed to work on any product unit, where $l_k - c > 0$ is the maximum time that the work in progress *(WIP)* is held at workstation $k$ |

## Variables

| | |
|---|---|
| $x_{i,t}$ | Binary variable equal to 1 if a product unit $i$ ($i = 1,\ldots,|I|$) is assigned to the position $t$ ($t = 1,\ldots,T$) of the sequence, and to 0 otherwise |
| $s_{k,t}$ | Start instant for the $t^{th}$ unit of the sequence of products at station $k$ ($k = 1,\ldots,|K|$) |
| $\hat{s}_{k,t}$ | Positive difference between the start instant and the minimum start instant of the $t^{th}$ operation at station $k$. $\hat{s}_{k,t} = \left[ s_{k,t} - (t + k - 2)c \right]^+$ (with $\left[ x \right]^+ = \max\{0, x\}$ ). |
| $v_{k,t}$ | Processing time applied to the $t^{th}$ unit of the product sequence at station $k$ for each homogeneous processor (at normal activity) |
| $w_{k,t}$ | Overload generated for the $t^{th}$ unit of the product sequence at station $k$ for each homogeneous processor (at normal activity); measured in time. |

Model $M\_4 \cup 3\_pmr$:

$$\text{Min} \quad W = \sum_{k=1}^{|K|} \left( b_k \sum_{t=1}^{T} w_{k,t} \right) \Leftrightarrow \text{Max} \quad V = \sum_{k=1}^{|K|} \left( b_k \sum_{t=1}^{T} v_{k,t} \right) \tag{7}$$

Subject to:

$$\sum_{t=1}^{T} x_{i,t} = d_i \qquad\qquad i = 1,\ldots,|I| \tag{8}$$

$$\sum_{i=1}^{|I|} x_{i,t} = 1 \qquad\qquad t = 1,\ldots,T \tag{9}$$

$$v_{k,t} + w_{k,t} = \sum_{i=1}^{|I|} p_{i,k} x_{i,t} \qquad\qquad k = 1,\ldots,|K| \,;\, t = 1,\ldots,T \tag{10}$$

$$\hat{s}_{k,t} \geq \hat{s}_{k,t-1} + v_{k,t-1} - c \qquad\qquad k = 1,\ldots,|K| \,;\, t = 2,\ldots,T \tag{11}$$

$$\hat{s}_{k,t} \geq \hat{s}_{k-1,t} + v_{k-1,t} - c \qquad\qquad k = 2,\ldots,|K| \,;\, t = 1,\ldots,T \tag{12}$$

$$\hat{s}_{k,t} + v_{k,t} \leq l_k \qquad\qquad k = 1,\ldots,|K| \,;\, t = 1,\ldots,T \tag{13}$$

$$\hat{s}_{k,t} \geq 0 \qquad\qquad k = 1,\ldots,|K| \,;\, t = 1,\ldots,T \tag{14}$$

$$v_{k,t} \geq 0 \qquad\qquad k = 1,\ldots,|K| \,;\, t = 1,\ldots,T \tag{15}$$

$$w_{k,t} \geq 0 \qquad\qquad k = 1,\ldots,|K| \,;\, t = 1,\ldots,T \tag{16}$$

$$x_{i,t} \in \{0,1\} \qquad\qquad i = 1,\ldots,|I| \,;\, t = 1,\ldots,T \tag{17}$$

$$\hat{s}_{1,1} = 0 \tag{18}$$

$$\sum_{\tau=1}^{t} x_{i,\tau} \geq \left\lfloor t \cdot \frac{d_i}{T} \right\rfloor \qquad\qquad i = 1,\ldots,|I| \,;\, t = 1,\ldots,T \tag{19}$$

$$\sum_{\tau=1}^{t} x_{i,\tau} \leq \left\lceil t \cdot \frac{d_i}{T} \right\rceil \qquad\qquad i = 1,\ldots,|I| \,;\, t = 1,\ldots,T \tag{20}$$

In the model, the equivalent objective functions (7) are represented by the total work performed ($V$) and the total work overload ($W$). Constraint (8) requires that the programmed demand be satisfied. Constraint (9) indicates that only one product unit can be assigned to each position of the sequence. Constraint (10) establishes the relation between the processing times applied to each unit at each workstation and the overload generated in each unit at each workstation. Constraints (11)-(14) constitute the set of possible solutions for the start instants of the operations at the workstations and the processing times applied to the products in the sequence for each processor. Constraints (15) and (16) indicate that the processing times applied to the products and the generated overloads, respectively, are not negative. Constraint (17) requires the assigned variables to be binary. Constraint (18) establishes the earliest instant in which the assembly line can start its operations. Finally, the constraints (19) and (20) are those that incorporate, indirectly, the regularity of required workload to the *MMSP-W*.

## 3     Computational Experience

To study the behavior of the incorporation of the regularity restrictions of work required into the $M\_4\cup3$, we performed a case study of the Nissan powertrain plant in Barcelona. This plant has an assembly line with twenty-one workstations ($m_1,...,m_{21}$) assembling nine types of engines ($p_1,...,p_9$) that are grouped into three families (4x4, vans and trucks) whose processing times at stations ranging between 89 and 185 *s*.

For the experiment, we considered a set E of 23 ($\varepsilon = 1,...,23$) instances associated to a demand plan of 270 engines, an effective cycle time $c = 175$ *s* and an identical time window for all workstations $l_k = 195$ *s* ($k = 1,...,21$) (see tables 5 and 6 in [4]).

To implement the models, the Gurobi v4.5.0 solver was used on Apple Macintosh iMac computer with an Intel Core i7 2.93 GHz processor and 8 GB of RAM using MAC OS X 10.6.7. The solutions from this solver were obtained by allowing a maximum CPU time of 7200 *s* for each model and for each of the 23 demand plans in the NISSAN-9ENG set.

To estimate the quality of the experimental results, we use the following indicators:

$$RPD(f,\varepsilon) = \frac{f\left(S^*_{4\cup3}(\varepsilon)\right) - f\left(S^*_{4\cup3\_pmr}(\varepsilon)\right)}{f\left(S^*_{4\cup3}(\varepsilon)\right)} \cdot 100 \quad \left(f \in \mathfrak{I} = \{W,\Delta_Q(P)\}; \ \varepsilon \in E\right) \quad (21)$$

$$\overline{RPD}(f) = \frac{\sum_{\varepsilon=1}^{|E|} RPD(f,\varepsilon)}{|E|} \quad \left(f \in \mathfrak{I} = \{W,\Delta_Q(P)\}\right) \quad (22)$$

Table 2 and figure 1 show the results obtained.

**Table 2.** Values of *RPD* for the functions $W$, $\Delta_Q(P)$ and average values ($\overline{RPD}(W)$, $\overline{RPD}(\Delta_Q(P))$) for the 23 instances of the NISSAN-9ENG set.

| $\varepsilon$ | $W$ | $\Delta_Q(P)$ | $\varepsilon$ | $W$ | $\Delta_Q(P)$ | $\varepsilon$ | $W$ | $\Delta_Q(P)$ | $\varepsilon$ | $W$ | $\Delta_Q(P)$ |
|---|---|---|---|---|---|---|---|---|---|---|---|
| 1 | 0.53 | 96.40 | 7 | 1.48 | 91.12 | 13 | -17.48 | 95.59 | 19 | 0.00 | 94.96 |
| 2 | -12.32 | 89.70 | 8 | -15.11 | 94.25 | 14 | -0.71 | 94.35 | 20 | -7.91 | 96.31 |
| 3 | 0.94 | 89.24 | 9 | -2.60 | 94.61 | 15 | -2.08 | 94.58 | 21 | -0.18 | 86.39 |
| 4 | 0.97 | 92.35 | 10 | 0.00 | 87.04 | 16 | -10.57 | 90.42 | 22 | 0.30 | 90.16 |
| 5 | -4.42 | 97.67 | 11 | -56.41 | 95.25 | 17 | -2.09 | 88.91 | 23 | 13.57 | 86.55 |
| 6 | -15.74 | 94.26 | 12 | -1.06 | 96.26 | 18 | -2.31 | 92.08 | $\overline{RPD}$ | -5.79 | 92.54 |

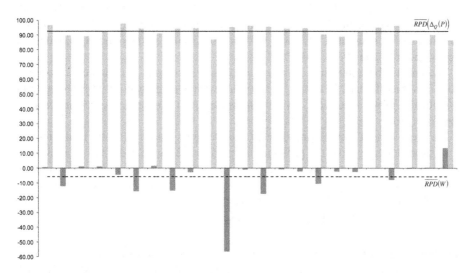

**Fig. 1.** Values of $RPD$ for the functions $W$ (dark grey), $\Delta_Q(P)$ (grey) and average values ($\overline{RPD}(W)$ (dotted line), $\overline{RPD}(\Delta_Q(P))$ (continuous line)) for the 23 instances of the NISSAN-9ENG set.

According to the results (see table 2 and figure 1) we can conclude the following:

- We can only guarantee the optimal solutions for instances 10 and 19, with the limitation of a run time of 7200 $s$,
- The reference model $M\_4\cup3$ achieves a better average overload than $M\_4\cup3\_pmr$ (a difference of 5.79% in $\overline{RPD}(W)$) on the set of 23 instances.
- The incorporation of constraints (8) and (9) into the reference model $M\_4\cup3$ produces a significant improvement in the regularity of the required work ($\overline{RPD}(\Delta_Q(P))$=92,54%).

## 4    Conclusions

We have formulated a model for the *MMSP-W*, $M\_4\cup3\_pmr$, that minimizes the total work overload or maximizes the total work completed, considering serial workstations, parallel processors, free interruption of the operations and with restrictions to regulate the required work.

A case study of the Nissan engine plant in Barcelona has been realized to compare the new model with the reference model $M\_4\cup3$.

The case study includes the overall production of 270 units of 9 different types of engines, for a workday divided into two shifts, and assuming that the particular demands of each type of engine may vary over time. This is reflected in 23 instances, each of them representing a different demand plan.

For the computational experience, the solver Gurobi 4.5.0 was used. The solutions have been found for the 23 instances, allowing a maximum CPU time of 7200 $s$ for each instance. Using this CPU time, we can only guarantee the optimal solutions for the instances 10 and 19.

The results show that the incorporation of the restrictions to regulate the required work into the reference model $M\_4 \cup 3$ produces an average gain of 92,54%, in terms of regularity of required work, while gets worse by an average of 5,79%, in terms of work overload.

We propose as future research lines: (1) to design and to implement heuristics and exact procedures to solve the problem under study; (2) to consider the minimization of the work overload and maximizing the regularity of the work required as simultaneous objectives of the problem; and (3) to incorporate to the proposed models, other desirable productive attributes such as maintenance of the production mix and the regular consumption of products parts, for example.

**Acknowledgements.** The authors greatly appreciate the collaboration of Nissan Spanish Industrial Operations (NSIO). This work was funded by project PROTHIUS-III, DPI2010-16759, including EDRF funding from the Spanish government.

# References

1. Boysen, N., Fliedner, M., Scholl, A.: Sequencing mixed-model assembly lines: Survey, classification and model critique. European Journal of Operational Research 192(2), 349–373 (2009)
2. Yano, C.A., Rachamadugu, R.: Sequencing to minimize work overload in assembly lines with product options. Management Science 37(5), 572–586 (1991)
3. Scholl, A., Klein, R., Domschke, W.: Pattern based vocabulary building for effectively sequencing mixed-model assembly lines. Journal of Heuristics 4(4), 359–381 (1998)
4. Bautista, J., Cano, A.: Solving mixed model sequencing problem in assembly lines with serial workstations with work overload minimisation and interruption rules. European Journal of Operational Research 210(3), 495–513 (2011)
5. Bautista, J., Cano, A., Alfaro, R.: A bounded dynamic programming algorithm for the MMSP-W considering workstation dependencies and unrestricted interruption of the operations. In: Proceedings of the 11th International Conference on Intelligent Systems Design and Applications (ISDA 2011), Córdoba, Spain (2011)
6. Bautista, J., Cano, A., Alfaro, R.: Modeling and solving a variant of the mixed-model sequencing problem with work overload minimisation and regularity constraints. An application in Nissan's Barcelona Plant. Expert Systems with Applications 39(12), 11001–11010 (2012)

# Incorporating Ergonomics Factors into the TSALBP

Joaquín Bautista, Cristina Batalla, and Rocío Alfaro

Universitat Politècnica de Catalunya, Avda. Diagonal 647, 7th floor, 08028 Barcelona, Spain
{joaquin.bautista,cristina.batalla,rocio.alfaro}@upc.edu

**Abstract.** Mixed-product assembly lines have ergonomic risks that can affect the worker productivity and lines. This work proposes to incorporate ergonomic factors to the *TSALBP* (*Time and Space constrained Assembly Line Balancing Problem*). Therefore, we present several elements for new models to assign the tasks to a workstation considering technological, management and ergonomic factors.

**Keywords:** Manufacturing, Assembly Line Balancing, Somatic and Psychic Factors.

## 1    Preliminaries

Circulating units in an assembly line are not identical in manufacturing systems with mixed-product assembly lines, such as in the automotive industry. This difference between product units leads to a change in use of resources (workers, tools, etc.) as well as in consumption of components. Therefore, the assembly line design must deal with balancing. Obviously, technological and management constraints should be considered in the line balancing, according to real situations.

The Assembly Line Balancing Problem (*ALBP*) is a classic problem [1] related to flow-oriented production systems. The problem deals to assign a set of elementary tasks (which may correspond to the assembly or disassembly of a product: motors, batteries, cars...) to a set of workstations or modules. The workstations are usually associated with teams of workers and/or robots, and they apply some of the work that will serve to complete the final product.

Typically, the workstations are arranged in a row, one behind another, and connected by a transport system, which allows movement of the work in progress at constant speed. Each workstation is given a constant time (cycle time, $c$) to complete the work that has been assigned.

Baybars [2] divided the *ALBP* into two classes:

1. The Simple Assembly Line Balancing Problem (*SALBP*).
2. The General Assembly Line Balancing Problem (*GALBP*).

The *SALBP* class contains assembly problems that attempt to minimize the total idle time considering exclusively only two kinds of task assignment constraints:

1. Cumulative constraints, associated with the available time of work in the stations.
2. Precedence constraints, established by the order in which the tasks can be executed.

C. Emmanouilidis, M. Taisch, D. Kiritsis (Eds.): APMS 2012, Part I, IFIP AICT 397, pp. 413–420, 2013.
© IFIP International Federation for Information Processing 2013

Other problems with additional considerations are included in the *GALBP* class [3], like the case in which the assignment of tasks is restricted [4] or when certain tasks must be assigned in block [5].

Some of the limitations in literature [6-7] take into account factors such as: the number of workstations ($m$); the standard time assigned to each workstation ($c$), which is calculated through an average of the processing times of all tasks according to the proportions, of each type of product, that are present in the demand plan, and the available space or area ($A$) to materials and tools to each workstation.

In these conditions we can define a family of problems under the acronym *TSALBP* (Time and Space constrained Assembly Line Balancing Problems) [6-7] that consist on: given a set $J$ of $|J|$ tasks with their temporal $t_j$ and spatial $a_j$ attributes ($j = 1,...,|J|$) and a precedence graph, each task must be assigned to a single station, such that:

- All the precedence constraints are satisfied.
- No station workload time is greater than the cycle time ($c$).
- No area required by the station is greater than the available area per station ($A$).

Then, if we consider the types of limitations defined above, we have eight types of problems, according to the objective of each one of them [6]. For example, the model to the *TSALBP-1* is the following:

$$Min \ z_1 = m \tag{1}$$

Subject to:

$$m - \sum_{k=1}^{m_{max}} k \, x_{j,k} \geq 0 \qquad\qquad \left(j = 1,...,|J|\right) \tag{2}$$

$$\sum_{j=1}^{|J|} t_j x_{j,k} \leq c \qquad\qquad \left(k = 1,...,m_{max}\right) \tag{3}$$

$$\sum_{j=1}^{|J|} a_j x_{j,k} \leq A \qquad\qquad \left(k = 1,...,m_{max}\right) \tag{4}$$

$$\sum_{k=1}^{m_{max}} x_{j,k} = 1 \qquad\qquad \left(j = 1,...,|J|\right) \tag{5}$$

$$\sum_{k=1}^{m_{max}} k \left(x_{j,k} - x_{i,k}\right) \geq 0 \qquad\qquad \left(1 \leq i, \ j \leq |J| : i \in P_j\right) \tag{6}$$

$$x_{j,k} \in \{0,1\} \qquad\qquad \left(j = 1,...,|J|\right) \wedge \left(k = 1,...,m_{max}\right) \tag{7}$$

Where, $x_{j,k}$ is a binary variable that is equal to 1 if a task $j$ ($j = 1,...,|J|$) is assigned to the workstation $k$ ($k = 1,...,m_{max}$), and 0 otherwise; $P_j$ is a parameter that indicates the set of precedent tasks of the task $j$ ($j = 1,...,|J|$) and the objective is to minimize the number of workstations ($m = |K|$).

## 2     The Ergonomic in Assembly Lines

One of the main objectives of the ergonomic is to adapt the operations that the workers must perform to guarantee their safety, welfare and to improve their efficiency.

Although the problems of a poor design of a workstation, in ergonomic terms, affect all areas of employment, manufacturing is one of the most affected. Specifically, the ergonomic risk is present and may affect the performance of workers and the line, in manufacturing assembly lines with mixed-products.

In such environments, ergonomic risk is given basically by the components related to somatic comfort and psychological comfort.

The somatic comfort determinates the set of physical demands to which a worker is exposed throughout the working day. To analyze this type of ergonomic risk, three factors, among others, can be analyzed. These are:

- Postural load: During working hours the workers may adopt repeatedly, inappropriate or awkward postures that can result in fatigue and musculoskeletal disorders in the long run [8].
- Repetitive movements: A workstation may involve a set of repeated upper-limb movements by the worker. This may cause musculoskeletal injuries at long term [9].
- Manual handling: Some tasks involve the lifting, moving, pushing, grasping and transporting objects [10].

By the other hand, the psychological comfort refers to the set of necessary mental conditions that the workers must have to develop their tasks. These conditions are: autonomy, social support, acceptable workloads and a favorable work environment.

## 3     The TSALBP with Ergonomic

Our proposal is to incorporate into the *TSALBP* or in other assembly lines problems the factors that imply these ergonomic problems.

Otto and Scholl [11] employ several techniques to incorporate the ergonomic risks to the problem *SALB-1*.

In a first approximation, given the set $K$ of stations, to each workload $S_k$ assigned at workstation $k$ ( $k = 1,...,|K|$ ), the ergonomic risk $F(S_k)$ is determined. Moreover, a maximum value is established for that ergonomic risk, $Erg$. Consequently, we can add to the original models the following constraints, satisfying: $F(S_k) \leq F(S_k \cup \{j\})$ ( $\forall S_k, \forall j \in J$ ).

$$F(S_k) \leq Erg \qquad \qquad \left( k = 1,...,|K| \right) \qquad (8)$$

Alternatively to the conditions (8), Otto and Scholl propose the *ErgoSALBP-1* with a new objective function composed by two terms [11]; that is:

$$Min \; K'(x) = K(x) + \omega \cdot \xi\big(F(S_k)\big) \tag{9}$$

Where $K(x)$ is the number of workstations; $\omega$ is a weight non-negative and $\xi\big(F(S_k)\big)$ is a function that includes the ergonomic risk factors $F(S_k)$ $\big(k=1,\ldots,|K|\big)$.

Logically, the constraints (8), presented by [11], can be completed if we take into account, in the design of the line, a minimum value to the ergonomic risk. In addition we can consider that this risk depends on the factor (somatic or psychic) that we want. In this situation, we have:

$$F_\phi^{\min} \le F_\phi(S_k) \le F_\phi^{\max} \qquad \big(k=1,\ldots,|K|\big); \; \forall \phi \in \Phi \tag{10}$$

Where $\Phi$ is the set of factors, $F_\phi^{\min}$ and $F_\phi^{\max}$ correspond to the minimum and maximum ergonomic risk to the factor $\phi \in \Phi$, and $F_\phi(S_k)$ is the ergonomic risk at workstation $k \in K$.

Other way to treat the problem is to classify the workstations in several categories (e.g. from 1 to 4) depending on different factors, such as movements, loads, duration, etc. From this point, we can condition the design of the line to the different categories of workstations that are present in a minimum and maximum percentage.

Then, if we define H as the set of ergonomic risk components, in our case, somatics ($\sigma$), psychics ($\varphi$) or both ($\sigma \cup \varphi$), we can find a new classification for the *TSALBP*, that is (see table 1):

**Table 1.** TSALBP_erg typology. The suffixes 1, 2, and 3 refer to the minimization of *m*, *c* and *A*, respectively. The suffix F refers to a feasibility problem. The post-suffix $\eta$ refers to the type of the restriction linked to the human aspects, psychic and somatic, being the element $\eta \in$ H where $\eta = \{\varnothing, \sigma, \varphi, \sigma \cup \varphi\}$. The column "Type" indicates if the problem is one of feasibility (F), mono-objective (OP) or multi-objective (MOP).

| Name | *m* | *c* | *A* | Type |
|---|---|---|---|---|
| TSALBP-F-$\eta$ | Given | Given | Given | F |
| TSALBP-1-$\eta$ | Minimize | Given | Given | OP |
| TSALBP-2-$\eta$ | Given | Minimize | Given | OP |
| TSALBP-3-$\eta$ | Given | Given | Minimize | OP |
| TSALBP-1/2-$\eta$ | Minimize | Minimize | Given | MOP |
| TSALBP-1/3-$\eta$ | Minimize | Given | Minimize | MOP |
| TSALBP-2/3-$\eta$ | Given | Minimize | Minimize | MOP |
| TSALBP-1/2/3-$\eta$ | Minimize | Minimize | Minimize | MOP |

In addition to the above proposals, the assembly line balancing problems with ergonomic conditions can be treated as multi-objective problems.

## 4     An Example

To illustrate the *SALBP-1*, the *TSALBP-1* and the *TSALBP-1-$\sigma$*, we present the following example.

Given a set of eight tasks ($|J| = 8$), whose operation times, $t_j$ ($j = 1,...,|J|$), required space, $a_j$ ($j = 1,...,|J|$), ergonomic risk $F(\{j\})$ ($\forall j \in |J|$) and which precedence graph are shown in figure 1, each task must be assigned to a single stations satisfying the limitations: (1) $c = 20$ *s*; (2) $A = 20$ *m*; and (3) $F^{max} = 60$ *e-s* (ergoseconds).

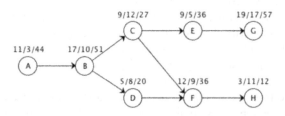

**Fig. 1.** Precedence graph of tasks. At each vertex we can see the tuple $t_j / a_j / F(\{j\})$ corresponding to the task.

Solving the *SALBP-1*, *TSALBP-1*, *TSALBP-1-$\sigma$* we obtain the following results (see Figure 2, Figure 3 and Figure 4, respectively).

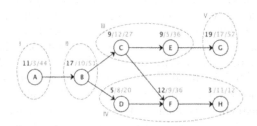

**Fig. 2.** Solution obtained by *SALBP-1* ($m = 5$)

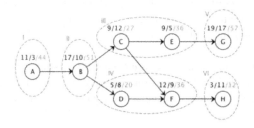

**Fig. 3.** Solution obtained by *TSALBP-1* ($m = 6$)

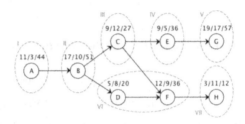

**Fig. 4.** Solution obtained by *TSALBP-1-σ* (*m* = 7)

Considering the *SALBP-1*, the obtained result is (see figure 2) a number of workstations of 5. By other hand, considering the *TSALBP-1* the obtained result is one workstation more that with the *SALBP-1* (figure 3). Finally, if we consider that the ergonomic factor are additive, we can group tasks taking into account, in addition to the cycle time and the area, this factor. Then, we can obtain a result for the *TSALBP-1-σ* (figure 4).

As we can see from the examples, depending on the limiting factors that we consider, the resulting number of stations will be one or other. Obviously, a greater number of conditional factors, means a greater number of workstations.

## 5    Case Study

To evaluate the proposed model and to contrast the influence of constrains relative to the ergonomic factors on the number of workstations of the line, required for *SALBP-1* and *TSALBP-1*, we have chosen a case study that corresponds to an assembly line from Nissan's plant in Barcelona. In fact, the 378 tasks (including the rapid test), that are required in the assembly of a motor (Pathfinder), have been grouped into 36 operations. After to set consistently the potential links, predecessors and successors, between the 36 operations, considering the potential links of the 378 original tasks, and taking into account a cycle time of 180 *s*; an available longitudinal area of 400 *cm*; and a maximum ergonomic risk of 400 *e-s*, we have solved, using the CPLEX solver, the three problems that are the focus of this study (*SALBP-1*, *TSALBP-1* and *TSALBP-1-σ*).

In table 2 we can see the optimal solutions obtained, and the need of more workers when are taken into account more realistic conditions in the assembly line problems. In addition we can see the process time of the operations (*t*), the required area (*a*), the risk factor (*F*) and the workstation where each task has been assigned, for each problem.

In our case, 19 work teams are necessary when only is taken into account the limitation of the cycle time, 21 when the constraints of area are included and 24 when a maximum ergonomic risk must be respected at each workstation.

**Table 2.** Obtained solutions by CPLEX from *SALBP-1*, *TSALBP-1* and *TSALBP-1-σ*

| *j* | *t* | *a* | *F* | *P* | *SALBP-1* | *TSALBP-1* | *TSALBP-1-σ* |
|---|---|---|---|---|---|---|---|
| 1 | 100 | 400 | 200 | - | 1 | 1 | 1 |
| 2 | 105 | 400 | 210 | 1 | 2 | 2 | 2 |
| 3 | 45 | 100 | 90 | 1 | 3 | 3 | 3 |
| 4 | 113 | 300 | 226 | 1, 2 | 3 | 3 | 3 |
| 5 | 168 | 400 | 336 | 1, 2, 4 | 4 | 4 | 4 |
| 6 | 17 | 150 | 34 | 2, 4, 5 | 5 | 5 | 5 |
| 7 | 97 | 250 | 194 | 6 | 5 | 5 | 5 |
| 8 | 50 | 200 | 100 | 2, 3, 7 | 5 | 6 | 6 |
| 9 | 75 | 200 | 150 | 2, 8 | 19 | 6 | 6 |
| 10 | 30 | 100 | 90 | 8 | 6 | 7 | 7 |
| 11 | 65 | 300 | 195 | 8, 10 | 6 | 7 | 7 |
| 12 | 35 | 350 | 105 | 10, 11 | 6 | 8 | 8 |
| 13 | 65 | 50 | 195 | 11, 12 | 7 | 8 | 8 |
| 14 | 115 | 300 | 345 | 12, 13 | 7 | 9 | 9 |
| 15 | 60 | 50 | 180 | 14 | 8 | 9 | 10 |
| 16 | 115 | 100 | 345 | 14, 15 | 8 | 10 | 11 |
| 17 | 60 | 150 | 120 | 13, 14, 16 | 9 | 10 | 12 |
| 18 | 105 | 250 | 210 | 16, 17 | 9 | 11 | 12 |
| 19 | 60 | 150 | 120 | 18 | 10 | 11 | 13 |
| 20 | 100 | 400 | 200 | 18, 19 | 10 | 12 | 14 |
| 21 | 100 | 400 | 200 | 19, 20 | 11 | 13 | 15 |
| 22 | 75 | 200 | 150 | 21, 22 | 11 | 14 | 16 |
| 23 | 75 | 175 | 225 | 21, 22 | 12 | 14 | 16 |
| 24 | 105 | 150 | 315 | 23 | 12 | 15 | 17 |
| 25 | 15 | 100 | 45 | 23, 24 | 17 | 15 | 17 |
| 26 | 35 | 150 | 105 | 24, 25 | 19 | 15 | 20 |
| 27 | 175 | 250 | 350 | 24 | 13 | 16 | 18 |
| 28 | 5 | 0 | 15 | 27 | 14 | 17 | 18 |
| 29 | 165 | 250 | 330 | 27, 28 | 14 | 17 | 19 |
| 30 | 5 | 0 | 15 | 27, 28 | 14 | 17 | 19 |
| 31 | 115 | 150 | 230 | 5, 29 | 15 | 18 | 20 |
| 32 | 60 | 200 | 120 | 29, 30, 31 | 15 | 18 | 21 |
| 33 | 85 | 200 | 170 | 5, 31 | 16 | 19 | 22 |
| 34 | 70 | 200 | 140 | 32 | 16 | 19 | 21 |
| 35 | 160 | 375 | 320 | 31, 33, 34 | 17 | 20 | 23 |
| 36 | 165 | 150 | 330 | 35 | 18 | 21 | 24 |

# 6    Conclusions

From the family of problems *TSALBP*, we propose an extension to these problems attending to the need to improve working conditions of workers in production and assembly lines. The result of this extension is the family of problems *TSALBP_erg*.

Specifically, we formulate the problem *TSALBP-1-σ*, corresponding to the somatic risks, that considers the constraints of cycle time, available area and, in addition, the maximum ergonomic risk to which the workers, assigned to each station, may be subjected.

Through a case study linked to Nissan, we observe that the improvement of the working conditions increases the minimum number of required workers to carry out the same work. By other hand, the reduction of the maximum ergonomic risk admissible, supposes a reduction of the labor cost due to injuries and absenteeism, whose valuation will be object studied in future research.

**Acknowledgment.** The authors appreciate the collaboration of Nissan (NSIO). This work was funded by project PROTHIUS-III, DPI2010-16759, including EDRF funding from the Spanish government.

# References

1. Salveson, M.E.: The assembly line balancing problem. Journal of Industrial Engineering 6(3), 18–25 (1955)
2. Baybars, I.: A survey of exact algorithms for the simple assembly line balancing problem. Management Science 32(8), 909–932 (1986)
3. Becker, C., Scholl, A.: A survey on problems and methods in generalized assembly line balancing. European Journal of Operational Research 168(3), 694–715 (2006)
4. Scholl, A., Fliedner, M., Boysen, N.: Absalom: Balancing assembly lines with assignment restrictions. European Journal of Operational Research 200(3), 688–701 (2010)
5. Battaïa, O., Dolgui, A.: Reduction approaches for a generalized line balancing problem. Computers & Operations Research 39(10), 2337–2345 (2012)
6. Chica, M., Cordón, O., Damas, S., Bautista, J.: Multiobjective constructive heuristics for the 1/3 variant of the time and space assembly line balancing problem: ACO and random greedy search. Information Sciences 180(18), 3465–3487 (2010)
7. Chica, M., Cordón, O., Damas, S., Bautista, J.: Including different kinds of preferences in a multiobjective and algorithm for time and space assembly line balancing on different Nissan scenarios. Expert Systems with Applications 38(1), 709–720 (2011)
8. McAtamney, L., Corlett, E.N.: RULA: a survey method for the investigation of work-related upper limb disorders. Applied Ergonomics 24(2), 91–99 (1993)
9. Colombini, D., Occhipinti, E., Grieco, A. (eds.): Risk Assessment and Management of Repetitive Movements and Exertions of Upper Limbs: Job Analysis, Ocra Risk Indices, Prevention Strategies and Design Principles (2002) ISBN: 978-0-08-044080-4
10. Waters, T.R., Baron, S.L., Kemmlert, K.: Accuracy of measurements for the revised NIOSH lifting equation. Applied Ergonomics 29(6), 433–438 (1997)
11. Otto, A., Scholl, A.: Incorporating ergonomic risks into assembly line balancing. European Journal of Operational Research 212(2), 277–286 (2011)

# Critical Factors for Successful User-Supplier Integration in the Production System Design Process

Jessica Bruch and Monica Bellgran

Mälardalen University, School of Innovation, Design and Engineering, Eskilstuna, Sweden
{Jessica.bruch,monica.bellgran}@mdh.se

**Abstract.** Integration of equipment suppliers in the design of the production system has often been associated with major benefits. However, from a managerial perspective, integration between the user and the suppliers of the production equipment is still challenging. Therefore, the purpose of the research is to explore how manufacturing companies can facilitate and manage equipment supplier integration when designing the production system. Based on an real time case study in the automotive industry 10 critical factors for successful supplier/user integration are identified, which can be classified into three categories: human factors, project management factors and design factors.

**Keywords:** Production system, manufacturing industry, equipment supplier, integration.

## 1 Introduction

For manufacturing companies active on the global market, high-performance production systems that contribute to the growth and competitiveness of the company are essential. Among a wide range of industries it is increasingly acknowledged that superior production system capabilities are crucial for competitive success. However, today's focus is on the operations phase, i.e. the serial production of products, rather than on the previous design of the production system. As a result, production systems are generally designed relatively shortly before their installation [1]. That is also the reason why implementation of lean production in manufacturing industry is largely directed towards improving the operational performance of the production system. This is today true for the global manufacturing industry worldwide. Lean production is the combined set of philosophy, principles and tools for managing their production systems. In the end of the day, however, the real root-cause for many problems and losses in production ends-up with issues that emanate from the design process of either the product or the corresponding production system [2].

The potential of gaining a competitive edge by improving the way the production system is designed is hence ignored, although it is a well-known fact that the production system design process is the foundation for achieving a high-performance production system [3]. Consequently, if the production system is not designed in a proper way, this will eventually end up with disturbances during both start-up and

C. Emmanouilidis, M. Taisch, D. Kiritsis (Eds.): APMS 2012, Part I, IFIP AICT 397, pp. 421–428, 2013.

serial production. The result is evidently low capacity utilization, high production cost and hence low profitability as well as a high environmental impact.

When the process of designing the production system is recognized in industry as a means of achieving the best possible production system, the next step for industry is to actually utilize this design process for innovation and differentiation by the creation of new production processes and technology that supports the need for increased sustainability. Since the technical subsystem of the production system is often designed and built by production equipment suppliers rather than made in-house by the manufacturing company [4], it is critical to successful integrate equipment suppliers when designing the production system. The purpose of this paper is to identify and discuss critical factors facilitating an integrated user-supplier approach when designing production systems working as a means for the creation of better and more sustainable solutions.

## 2    Frame of Reference

### 2.1    User-Supplier Integration Characteristics

The process of designing a production system can be divided into several distinct phases comprising all necessary activities from the analysis to the detailed design of the selected system solution [2]. The ASE model identifies (problem) analysis, (solution) synthesis and (solution) evaluation as the general activities in an engineering design process, which can be transferred to the specification of requirements, generation of concepts and evaluation of concepts when designing the production system [5]. As a result, integration between the user (the manufacturing company) and the supplier (of machines and production equipment) is required in the different activities in each phase of the production system design process, see Figure 1. Although the different phases in the design process are visualized sequentially here, it is important to emphasize that the design process should be considered as an iterative, cyclic process affected in its execution by each project context.

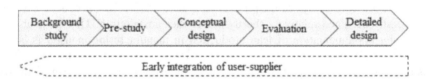

**Fig. 1.** The integration of users and suppliers in the design of the production system [modified from 2]

Despite the potential, from a project management perspective, an integrated user-supplier design approach is still challenging. Integrated design work can be considered as a type of open innovation. Henry Chesbrough defines open innovation as "the use of purposive inflows and outflows of knowledge to accelerate internal innovation and expand the markets for external use of innovation, respectively" [6, p.

1] and the implication of this definition is that companies could and should use both internal and external knowledge, ideas and paths to market, when they seek to maximize returns from the development activities. The study of Enkel et al. [7] shows, that loss of knowledge, higher coordination costs and loss of control and higher complexity are mentioned as frequent risks connected to open innovation activities. Thus, by working together with an equipment supplier, a manufacturing company faces the risk that knowledge about core production processes is transferred to competitors via the equipment suppliers [8]. As such, it is useful to review critical factors for successful user-supplier integration when designing the production system.

## 2.2   Critical Factors

Yin and Ning [9] developed a framework suggesting that  an inter-enterprise information system, a partnering relationship among the participating organizations and an integrated dynamic planning process are critical factors. Focusing on the collaboration between equipment suppliers and users Rönneberg Sjödin et al. [10] argue that more resources should be spent in the early phases as it is important to facilitate intensive collaboration with equipment suppliers. Otherwise, mechanisms important for integration such as meetings, workshops, and teambuilding are limited, which may result in strained relationships, which cannot be recovered at later stages.

Another factor important to consider is an adequate management of information flow between the equipment supplier and the user [11]. In order to realize the benefits of collaboration with an equipment supplier, it is important that the exchanged information is cautiously tailored to the specific needs of the partner. Organizing the collaboration in a formal process and appointing a skilled contact person supports an effective flow of information [11].

Further, even in situations where the equipment supplier has a major role in the design of the production equipment, it seems necessary to maintain certain competencies also within the manufacturing company. Hobday et al. [12] point out that the trend towards outsourcing has made it even more essential to keep in mind the required in-house competences for system integration. Von Haartman and Bengtsson [13] conclude that to be able to benefit from supplier integration, manufacturing companies have to possess corresponding in-house competences.

When integrating the supplier in the design work, an appropriate use and understanding of contracts and governance mechanisms is important. Lager and Frishammer [8] emphasize the need to consider the "nature" dimensions (proprietary/non-proprietary) in order to avoid the unintentional diffusion of important in-house know-how to competitors. Incentives, authority and trust are important tools to govern complex procurement situations involving several actors [14].

# 3   Research Methodology

The research is founded on one real time case study at a Swedish manufacturing company, which gives the possibility of being close to the data, thus enabling a close-up view on patterns, and how they evolve [15]. In line with previous production system design research, our view is that the case study provided a good possibility to capture a more complete and contextual assessment of the process of integrating equipment suppliers in the design work. Clearly, applying a single case study approach suffers from problems of generalization [16]. However, the single case study results created here do not rely on statistical generalization but on analytical generalization, i.e. generalization towards theory, which is a potential provided by the case study methodology.

The study was part of a new product development project, which required the design of a new production system since the new product could not be assembled at the existing production line but required the design and building of new production equipment. The unit of analysis was the production equipment acquisition project at the manufacturing company in which the equipment supplier played a key role in the design and building of the production equipment.

Data was collected between November 2009 and August 2011, where actions and events were observed in real time for 37 days. Overall, being at the company was important for the data collected. For example, on several occasions, project members discussed critical aspects and possible problem solutions at greater length during the lunch break than in project meetings. Data were collected from multiple sources of evidence including passive and active observation, semi-structured interviews and documents aiming at data triangulation. In practice, the same problem or fact was addressed by more than a single source of evidence during the data collection.

The collected data has been analysed according to the guidelines provided by Miles and Huberman [17], i.e. data reduction, data display and conclusion drawing/verification. In order to reduce and display the data in an appropriate way, directly after each time of data collection the findings were summarised and transferred into a worksheet for further analysis. Further, a detailed description of the case was developed. The results from the case study were compared with and related to the existing theory, i.e. enfolding the literature.

## 4    Empirical Findings

The background to the project studied was the need to replace the existing assembly system as a consequence of the design of a new product generation. The idea generation and concept iteration for the production system was carried out under severe time pressure as the time plan for product design was not adhered to and the resources allocated were inadequate at the beginning while the date for start of production was unchangeable. At the manufacturing company, most of the internal work regarding the design of the production equipment was carried out by the production engineering department and the project leader responsible for the industrialization, i.e. the process required when transferring the product design into start of production. The selected equipment supplier was located in Sweden but in another city about 500 km away. The equipment supplier had wide experience as project supplier to the automotive industry and was thus aware of the particular requirements of the automotive industry.

Since there was little room for concept iterations, the case study company commissioned one equipment supplier to design a concept solution between November and December 2009. In parallel, two internal solutions were created based on the earlier ideas of the production engineering manager. The three different concepts were evaluated and synthesized into one final solution, including solutions for production equipment and material supply aspects.

The design of the production equipment followed a formalized process in which the case study company had mapped out different steps or activities that the equipment suppliers had to complete at various points in the process. The activities undertaken in each stage incorporated the transfer of new information from both sides. Since the company normally involves equipment suppliers a considerable amount of standards and rules were used such as the technical requirement specification. However, also new standard documents were created. For example, the manufacturing company put a lot of effort on collecting and documenting more project specific requirements.

To coordinate the work between the user, i.e. the case study company, and the equipment supplier, a time plan was created. The time plan included not only key dates to be kept in the project such as when the factory acceptance test or site acceptance test should be carried out but also several verification occasions, which should take place under the project progress. The verification occasions were summarized in a verification plan, which was used to outline when and how the fulfillment of the specified requirements and the progress of the design and development of the production equipment should be followed up and assessed. In addition, the equipment suppliers and the manufacturing company appointed contact persons. The contact person appointed by the manufacturing company was a production engineering manager who had experience from previous development projects and was also the system designer of the assembly line used for the previous product generation.

Further, during the production equipment acquisition project a number of meetings comprising different participants from the user and supplier company took place. Depending on the purpose of the meetings, employees from different functions with different knowledge were invited. For example, assembly operators attended the discussion about the screen size at each workstation, while employees from the information technology department contributed to the decision about the operating system. The meetings at the manufacturing company offered an opportunity for the equipment supplier to study the manufacturing plant and the assembly of the actual product, to collect information about on-going manufacturing and the production processes connected to the targeted production system part, i.e. the equipment to be built.

# 5    Critical Factors for Successful Integration

The potential of integrating equipment suppliers in the production system design process are compelling. In the studied project, the integration of the equipment supplier resulted into an innovative and new solution based on the access to and application of new technology. Although the potential benefits can be substantial, integrating equipment suppliers in the production system design process is sometimes an uncomfortable way of doing business. In order to achieve successful integration and thus better production systems a total of 10 critical factors were identified, see Table 1. This factors help to identify reduce potential barriers and expand the relationships between the partners.

**Table 1.** Critical factors for improved user-supplier integration in order to accomplish better production system solutions

| Factor | How it contributes to user-supplier integration |
|---|---|
| *Human factors* | |
| Appoint skilled contact person | The contact person enables easily access to missing information and is also used to discuss critical issues. |
| Assign suitable resources | Resources needs to be available to engage in the design process and thus to make integration possible. |
| Build trust | The manufacturing company needs to have confidence in the equipment supplier's capabilities. |
| Core team | A cross-functional team ensures a holistic perspective and speeds up the decision making. Clear and explicit goals should be established. |
| *Project management factors* | |
| Contract | Regulatory issues are clearly defined and help to minimized concerns that either part will take advantage. |
| Formal approaches | Formal methods such as the process applied, documentation and planning facilitates coordination and synchronization of work activities. |
| Frequent face to face meetings | Meetings are used to reduce any equivocality surrounding the process of designing the production system and help to align the culture of the two partners. |
| Information flow | Open communication channels are required to improve decision making and ensure that all partners are updated. |
| *Design factors* | |
| Joined idea generation | Joined idea generation contributes to clear directions and expectations for the project. The creativity of all individuals involved can be utilized in both concept and detailed design. Further, each partner can identify possible benefits. |
| Specified requirements | Specifying as well as understanding requirements of the user contributes to a solution in line with the needs. |

The findings highlighted the importance of the humans involved in the design process from both partners, i.e. the equipment supplier and the manufacturing company. The results of the case study indicate that it is particularly important to have a skilled contact person at the manufacturing company, which is in line with earlier research [12, 13]. This person can be compared to the role of a gatekeeper in new product development projects, i.e. a person which can overcome barriers based on differences such as terminology, norms, and values [18]. The contact person can be considered as a key communicator between both organizations and provide a link between the manufacturing company and the equipment supplier. To have the right competence at the manufacturing company is important to evaluate and judge the appropriateness of the solutions proposed by the equipment supplier.

Further, the empirical findings show that the project management is critical for successful user-supplier integration [1]. The coordination between the equipment supplier and the manufacturing company are likely to benefit from a formal approach [11]. Following this recommendation leads to different initiatives may be established. Effort should be placed on planning activities and establishing a standardized process and documents. The reason for not being able to coordinate the work of the two partners and being late is because the underlying means used are not constructed to support the work at physical dispersed settings. On the other hand by applying for example a structured process gives advices on what work activities needed to be completed at different points in time and what decisions that needed to be accomplished at different points in time. In addition, the findings indicate that in line with prior research [e.g. 10] efforts should also be placed on communicating the expected production system solution internally, i.e. within the own (user) organisation including product designers and the end-user such as operators, and support functions like production engineers or maintenance engineers. Thus, face-to-face meetings could be used to invite also other people outside the core team. By involving end-users as early as possible in the process their input and feedback could be considered when designing the production system thus avoiding late design changes.

Often equipment suppliers are involved when the manufacturing company has already developed its scope of supply including a conceptual solution and the requirement specification. However, the potential benefits that can be achieved by integrating the equipment supplier in the design process are minimised if the equipment supplier is included at this late stage. Thus, there is a need to include equipment suppliers earlier, while at the same time negative effects such as the risk that key competences are distributed to competitors should be minimised. This means that there is a need to look at intellectual factors focusing on achieving a good balance between competition and co-operation. Hence, technical aspects of the buying process need to be addressed [8, 14].

# 6    Conclusions

The purpose of the paper was to identify and discuss critical factors facilitating an integrated user-supplier approach when designing production systems. From the rich database of the real-time case study, a total of 10 critical factors were identified, which in one way or another have an impact on integration between user and supplier. Underlying these factors were three categories: humans, project management and design factors. The three factors are thus related to existing theory. However, what we add is a description of the specific details of user-supplier integration when designing the production system, an issue which has only been addressed to a limited extent.

The research presented in this paper should be seen as a first step to improve the integration between users and suppliers in the design of the production system and clearly more research is needed. For example, our empirical findings revealed somewhat unexpectedly that despite physical distance and organizational boundaries, there were no major coordination problems between the partners. Thus, gaining a better understanding of the barriers for supplier-user integration in the design of the production system is needed to be able to identify ways to overcome them to achieve the creation of better and more sustainable solutions.

# References

1. Bruch, J.: Management of Design Information in the Production System Design Process. PhD thesis, Mälardalen University, Eskilstuna (2012)
2. Bellgran, M., Säfsten, K.: Production Development: Design and Operation of Production Systems. Springer, London (2010)
3. Slack, N., et al.: Operations Management, 2nd edn., Pitman, London, UK (1998)
4. Reichstein, T., Salter, A.: Investigating the sources of process innovation among UK manufacturing firms. Industrial and Corporate Change 15(4), 653–682 (2006)
5. Wiktorsson, M.: Consideration of Legacy Structures enabling a Double Helix Development of Production Systems and Products. Submitted to Springer book on Technology and Manufacturing Process Selection: The Product Life Cycle Perspective (2012)
6. Chesbrough, H.: Open innovation: Researching a New Paradigm for Understanding Industrial Innovation. In: Chesbrough, H., Vanhaverbeke, W., West, J. (eds.) Open innovation: Researching a New Paradigm, pp. 1–12. Oxford University Press, Oxford (2006)
7. Enkel, E., Gassmann, O., Chesbrough, H.: Open R&D and open innovation: exploring the phenomenon. R&D Management 39(4), 311–316 (2009)
8. Lager, T., Frishammar, J.: Equipment supplier/user collaboration in the process industries: In search of enhanced operating performance. Journal of Manufacturing Technology Management 21(6), 698–720 (2010)
9. Yeo, K., Ning, J.: Managing uncertainty in major equipment procurement in engineering projects. European Journal of Operational Research 171(1), 123–134 (2006)
10. Rönnberg Sjödin, D., Eriksson, P.E., Frishammar, J.: Open innovation in process industries: a lifecycle perspective on development of process equipment. International Journal of Technology Management 56(2-4), 225–240 (2011)
11. Bruch, J., Bellgran, M.: Design information for efficient equipment supplier/buyer integration. Journal of Manufacturing Technology Management 23(4) (2012)
12. Hobday, M., Prencipe, A., Davies, A.: Introduction. In: Prencipe, A., Davies, A., Hobday, M. (eds.) The Business of Systems Integration, pp. 1–14. Oxford University Press, New York (2005)
13. Von Haartman, R., Bengtsson, L.: Manufacturing competence: a key to successful supplier integration. International Journal of Manufacturing Technology and Management 16(3), 283–299 (2009)
14. Olsen, B.E., et al.: Governance of complex procurements in the oil and gas industry. Journal of Purchasing and Supply Management 11(1), 1–13 (2005)
15. Leonard-Barton, D.: A Dual Methodology for Case Studies: Synergistic Use of a Longitudinal Single Site with Replicated Multiple Sites. Organization Science 1(3), 248–266 (1990)
16. Yin, R.K.: Case Study Research: Design and Methods, 4th edn. SAGE, Thousand Oaks (2009)
17. Miles, M.B., Huberman, A.M.: Qualitative Data Analysis: An Expanded Sourcebook, 2nd edn. SAGE, London (1994)
18. Tushman, M.L., Katz, R.: External Communication and Project Performance: An Investigation into the Role of Gatekeepers. Management Science 26(11), 1071–1085 (1980)

# Current State and Future Perspective Research on Lean Remanufacturing – Focusing on the Automotive Industry

Elzbieta Pawlik[*], Winifred Ijomah, and Jonathan Corney

Departement of Design, Manufacture and Engineering Management
University of Strathclyde, United Kingdom
elzbieta.pawlik@strath.ac.uk

**Abstract.** Remanufacturing, as one of the most promising product recovery options, is influenced by the uncertainty involved with incoming cores. This poses different organizational and technical challenges to those found in conventional manufacturing. Finding the right strategy is very important to make business more effective and profitable. The combination of remanufacturing and lean manufacturing offers a good opportunity to increase process efficiencies in remanufacturing industry. This paper reviews the current state of practice of lean manufacturing philosophy in the automotive sector, together with an identification of needed further research.

**Keywords:** Remanufacturing Process, Lean Remanufacturing, Uncertainties.

## 1 Introduction

Increased awareness of environmental degradation has precipitated legislative requirements that have drawn attention to product recovery options such as remanufacturing, reconditioning and repair. Of these options, remanufacturing is the only one with which a used product can be brought back to a condition at least equal to that of a new product in terms of quality, performance and warranty (Ijomah 2002).

As such, remanufacturing represents a good opportunity for sustainable development. It retains not only the raw material - as is the case with recycling - but it can also keep a large part of the value added to the raw material during the original manufacturing process. Retaining the shape of raw material avoids the need for further manufacturing processes that are $CO_2$ emitting(Giuntini and Gaudette 2003, Ijomah 2008) and, at the same time, provides significant energy savings by using remanufactured components that require 50-80% less energy to produce than newly manufactured parts (Lund 1984). In addition, remanufacturing creates a new market for employment.

According to Golinska and Kawa (2011) the automotive industry is recognised as one of the most environmentally aware manufacturing sectors. This is illustrated by

---

[*] Corresponding author.

C. Emmanouilidis, M. Taisch, D. Kiritsis (Eds.): APMS 2012, Part I, IFIP AICT 397, pp. 429–436, 2013.

the fact that around 90% of the total worldwide remanufacturing industry belongs to this sector (Kim and Selgier 2006).

This article examines lean remanufacturing practice within the automotive industry by describing the remanufacturing process and its key problems. In addition, the lean manufacturing approach within a remanufacturing context is reviewed. A case study based on an automotive remanufacturing company is presented to illustrate the current state of the research in the application of lean manufacturing within the remanufacturing industry (both positive and negative implications are identified). Finally, the paper ends with conclusions and provides recommendations for future research priorities and directions related to the lean remanufacturing approach.

## 2     Remanufacturing Process

The remanufacturing process usually begins with disassembling used products, known as 'cores', into components, which are then cleaned, inspected, and tested to verify that they meet the required quality standards to be reused without further work. Those that do not meet the requirements can be reprocessed via remanufacturing. If this is not possible due to technological issues or economic reasons, the substandard components are put towards other product recovery options - i.e. recycling - and are replaced with new parts. The remanufactured parts are then reassembled - often together with new parts - into the product (Giuntini and Gaudette 2003). Depending on the product type and volume required, the remanufacturing steps presented above can be undertaken in a different sequence or some may be omitted if the circumstance requires. For example, inspection can be done before the disassembly and cleaning in order to detect damages and select cores that cannot be remanufactured (Sundin 2004). However, some general characteristics remain valid in every remanufacturing process. For example, disassembly always precedes reprocessing and reassembly always succeeds disassembly (Östlin 2008). Figure 2 presents the possible steps (in no specific order) that can be taken during the remanufacturing process.

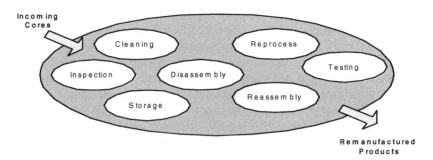

**Fig. 1.** The generic remanufacturing process. (Source: Sundin 2004)

Within the remanufacturing process, managers have to deal with organisational and technical challenges different from those found in conventional manufacturing. The remanufacturing process is inherently influenced by the uncertain condition of the used product e.g. dirt, wear and missing components. Though the arriving cores may be made of the same components, the operations and time required to remanufacture each item will be unique to its condition, while some operations may not be necessary at all. Additionally, the quantity of new components required will depend on the quality of cores - the primary source for supplying remanufactured parts (Giuntini and Gaudette 2003). The significant level of uncertainty in the quality of incoming cores is not the only problem that makes planning and controlling the remanufacturing process more difficult. It is difficult to predict when products will stop fulfilling customer needs, therefore it is often difficult to exactly ascertain the timescale for acquiring necessary cores. This makes the remanufacturing process less predictable than conventional manufacturing (Lundmark at al. 2009). The variability of products is another challenge that occurs in the remanufacturing process in the automotive industry. This is the result of continuous upgrading of the products due to the use of new solutions and technologies or the elimination of design errors (Seitz 2007). In addition, since products are not typically designed for disassembly, the remanufacturing process is more complex. Components that were in good condition can be damaged during the disassembly operation, resulting in higher operational costs (Giuntini and Gaudette 2003). As a result, current remanufacturing processes are more complex and less predictable than conventional manufacturing and require high levels of inspection and testing to achieve high quality products. This can lead to higher remanufacturing costs and longer remanufacturing lead-times. Therefore it is important to find the right strategy to make the remanufacturing process cost effective and thereby contribute to the overall profitability of the remanufacturing business.

# 3    Lean Manufacturing

One way of overcoming the difficulties involved with the remanufacturing process and increase both efficiency and productivity is to apply the principles, tools and methods of lean manufacturing (Seitz 2007, Kucner 2008). Though lean manufacturing philosophy has its roots in the automotive manufacturing industry, Womack and Jones (2003) state that the principles of this approach can be successfully applied to other sectors. They highlight the principles that define lean thinking as (2003):

- *precisely specify **value** by specific product;*
- *identify the **value stream** for each product;*
- *make value **flow** without interruptions;*
- *let the customer **pull** value from the producer;* and
- *pursue **perfection**.*

The entire range of lean manufacturing tools and methods were developed for the practical application of lean thinking. Those tools and methods include: Value Stream Mapping to help generate ideas for process redesign; 5S that allows effective organization of work area; and Kanban, which limits work in process and regulates the flow of goods between the factory, suppliers and customers.

# 4    Lean Remanufacturing

The application of the lean manufacturing approach within a remanufacturing context - Lean Remanufacturing - has only recently gained the attention of researchers and practitioners. Hence, there is little literature on this subject. The combination of remanufacturing and lean manufacturing offers a good opportunity to increase process efficiencies within the remanufacturing industry (Seiz 2007, Kucner 2008).

The first reported study is a case study conducted by Amezquita et al (1998) that focuses on an independent automotive remanufacturer and specifically analyzes the process of remanufacturing clutches. Their analysis shows how the lean manufacturing approach can enhance the effectiveness of the remanufacturing process by developing techniques for lean automation and different methods for the reduction of setup times. Fargher (2003) states that lean manufacturing applied to the remanufacturing operations brings various benefits thanks to the identification and elimination of non-value-added activities through continuous improvement. These benefits include (Seitz 2007):

- Reduction of lead-time;
- Reduced work in process;
- Improved on-time shipments;
- Reduced floor space; and
- Improved quality.

# 5    Research Methodology

The research addresses efforts to improve the remanufacturing process through the application of lean manufacturing practices. As a relatively new topic, there is limited understanding of lean remanufacturing. In order to identify key research challenges and needs within this immature research area we must first understand the current state of the application of lean manufacturing within the automotive remanufacturing industry. A case study is a relevant research strategy that enables a rich understanding of the research context as well as the process being enacted (Saunders et al. 2003). In this instance, the case study took place in an automotive remanufacturing facility in the United Kingdom. During the visit, observation of the shop-floor and semi-structured interviews with Managers were conducted.

## 5.1    Case Study

In order to achieve a better understanding of the lean manufacturing approach within an automotive remanufacturing context, a case study was undertaken. The study is limited to analysis of operational shop-floor activities (focusing on the application of shop floor tools) in automotive remanufacturer, Caterpillar Remanufacturing Ltd (CatReman). Three types of products are remanufactured at CatReman: engines, turbines, and turbochargers. Lean manufacturing methods were first introduced into the company in 2005 and since then the principles and tools have been gradually implemented on a broader scale.

**Case Study Findings**

CatReman started their lean application by introducing a lean manufacturing tool called Visual Control[1] within the facility's most critical areas. Thereafter, the lean approach was implemented within the whole facility, starting with creating current and future state Value Stream Mapping[2], before tools and methods - Pull system[3] (only from customer) and Overall Equipment Effectiveness[4] - were applied. The facility also implemented Total Productive Maintenance[5] for critical machines and is working towards this for all major machinery.

Visual Control is of particular importance for CatReman during the visual inspection process. According to Errington (2009) the inspection step is crucial for remanufacturing. The incorrect assessment of a core or component can cause unnecessary additional operational costs. As remanufacturing is strongly affected by variation in products, those tasked with assessment require precise knowledge of each variation. At CatReman, visual boards are employed that display sample components and give visual and written descriptions of the critical areas for inspecting as well as the acceptable criteria. They are located near to the inspection, machining and the assembly areas, which also have standard worksheets giving the employees the same information. This means that if an operator is unsure of whether the component he or she receives is good enough to remanufacture, he or she can check it at the visual display board. This also serves to remind operators of the importance of quality.

CatReman is also using other forms of visual display boards, such as section (display metrics specific to the section in which they are located) and facility boards (display metrics for the whole facility) to measure, communicate and control the following metrics: people (largely safety and training); quality (warranty to sales, test rejects, etc.); speed (on time delivery, performance to TAKT time etc.) and cost (unplanned overtime, etc.). The top ten most common defects are also presented on the section metrics boards. All of these visual control tools are used to aid the machine operator in the lean process and act as a reminder of the most prevalent quality issues as part of general communications.

Moreover, the plant's layout was significantly changed to be more lean. Employees have a meeting with managers every day, in which they discuss the previous day's production and the coming days production, and disseminate any local or corporate information, such as visits to the factory. There was also the opportunity for employees to voice comments and give feedback to their manager. Each identified problem is

---

[1] Visual Control – *'is any communication device used in the work environment that tells us at a glance how work should be done and whether it is deviating from the standard'(Likker,2004)*

[2] Value Steam Mapping –*'captures processes, material flows, and information flows of a given product family and helps to identify waste in the system.'(Likker, 2004)*

[3] Pull system – *'the preceding process must always do what the subsequent process says'(Likker, 2004).*

[4] Overall Equipment Effectiveness – *'a measure of equipment uptime'(Likker, 2004)*

[5] Total Productive Maintenance - method for improving availability of machines through better utilization of maintenance and production resources

investigated and resolved by using the Ishikawa diagram, 5 why and histograms[6]. These activities have improved the operations within CatReman by:

- Reducing work in process;
- Increasing production control; and
- Providing better service (to increase ability to meet deadlines).

The facility metrics show the benefits of lean manufacturing and are reported corporately each month.

Despite the advantages gained from implementing lean manufacturing tools and methods identified above, it was noticed that not all lean tools and principles were easily and succesfully applied within the remanufacturing context of CatReman.

The pull system within operations is difficult to apply because of the high variability and low repeatability of products. It is also hard to use takt time[7] due to the uncertain condition of cores. Components have to go through different operations to meet the required specification. Some of them will require more time to pass each step and in some cases some operations will be omitted. Additionally, the uncertain condition of components (particularly unique ones) might cause a delay in the reassembly step, because of the need to wait for new components. Because of the high variability of products it is not cost effective to keep stock of all new components that may be needed. However, it was observed that there was a high inventory level of used products. This is a result of the uncertainty in the quantity and timing of incoming cores, i.e. difficulties in predicting the types of cores and when they will arrive at the facility. During the interviews it was found that implementation of 5S is also difficult, since operations on the various components are carried out at the same workplace. As a result, there is a need to keep many different tools at a workstation, not all of which are required regularly. However, reducing the number of tools can cause waste in motion as a result of continuously picking up tools from the store when required. Returned products are usually dirty and this also makes it difficult to keep workplaces clean.

The interviews with Managers identified that Caterpillar has implemented Standard Operating Procedures[8] for all remanufacturing operations - some general (for example for cleaning and inspecting bolts) and some specific to a particular product (for example remanufacturing a cylinder head). They also have Standard Operating Procedures (SOPs) for other processes such as machine maintenance and daily operator checks. This means they can give SOPs to the operator but if additional salvage is required they can not cover it this way. A part might need additional (and not necessarily cost-effective) work because it is not possible to buy new parts (the engine is not in current production) or because the lead-time for the new part is so long. In cases such as this, sometimes other similar used parts are adapted to make the part that is required - breaching SOPs. In this way, SOPs mitigate some of the problems but not entirely effective.

---

[6]Ishikawa chart, 5Why, histogram – are problem solving tools.

[7] Takt time – *'time required to complete one job at the pace of customer demand'*,(*Likker, 2004*)

[8] Standard Operating Procedures – Documented procedures that capture 'best practice'

# 6    Conclusion

The literature review and case study results have confirmed that the lean manufacturing approach brought some important benefits to the automotive remanufacturing sector. On the other hand, the case study also identified that some of the lean manufacturing tools and methods cannot be implemented successfully within automotive remanufacturing operations. Moreover, it was identified that the uncertainty involved in incoming cores (particularly with quality) might be the key problem in the application of the lean manufacturing tools within an automotive remanufacturing shop floor. A similar observation was reported by Östlin and Ekholm (2007)[9] based on their analysis of the toner cartridge remanufacturer company, Scandi-Toner AB. It was observed that the variable processing times and uncertainties in materials recovered limited the implementation of a lean manufacturing approach within that remanufacturing context. As variable processing times are a result of uncertainty in the quality of incoming cores (Lundmark et al. 2009) and the same can be said about the uncertainties in materials recovered, the conclusion might be drawn that uncertainty of incoming cores might be one of the main negative factors for the application of lean manufacturing tools within the remanufacturing context – for every type of product. Despite the fact that difficulties that occur within the remanufacturing process are product type-dependant (Sundin 2004), factors that limit implementation of lean manufacturing arise from its origins. Lean manufacturing has its roots in the Toyota Production System and was developed in the conventional manufacturing sector where uncertainty involved with input is not such an important issue. The lean manufacturing approach was not developed to apply to the variable conditions of remanufacturing. The implementation of some of the principles and tools of lean manufacturing within remanufacturing may require adapting to changeable cores or the elimination of identified constraints. This study provided empirical evidence that identified both positive and negative implications of the role of lean manufacturing within remanufacturing context. However, to make any step to improve lean remanufacturing application, one must acknowledge that one case study is not sufficient and more research is necessary. In particular, there is a need to confirm if uncertainties are indeed the main constraint. Identifying other factors that limit implementation and classifying their relative significance would achieve this.

# References

1. Amezquita, T., Bras, B.: Lean remanufacture of an Automobile clutch. In: Proceedings of First International Working Seminar on Reuse, Eindhoven, The Netherlands, p. 6 (1996)
2. Errington, M.: Business Processes and Strategic Framework for Inspection in Remanufacturing. PhD Dissertation, The University of Exeter, UK (2009)
3. Fargher, J.S.W.: Lean: Dealing with Eight Wastes. ReMaTec News, 24–25 (September 2003)

---

[9] An analysis of the possibility of implementation lean manufacturing methods within toner cartridge remanufacturer.

4. Giuntini, R., Gaudette, K.: Remanufacturing: The Next Great Opportunity for Boosting U.S. Productivity. In: Business Horizons, pp. 41–48 (November-December 2003)
5. Golinska, P., Kawa, A.: Remanufacturing in Automotive industry: Challenges and limitations. Journal of Industrial Engineering and Management 4(3), 453–466 (2011)
6. Ijomah, W.L., McMahon, C.A., Hammond, G.P., Newman, S.T.: Development of design for remanufacturing guidelines to support sustainable manufacturing. Robotics and Computer-Integrated Manufacturing 23, 712–719 (2007)
7. Ijomah, W.L.: A tool to improve training and operational effectiveness In remanufacturing. International Journal of Computer Integrated Manufacturing 21(6), 676–701 (2008)
8. Ijomah, W.L.: A model-based definition of the generic remanufacturing business process. University of Plymouth (2002)
9. Kim, H., Selgier, G.: State of the Art. And Future Perspective Research on the Automotive Remanufacturing – Focusing on Alternator & Start Motor. In: Proceedings Polish-German Workshop on Lean Remanufacturing, Wroclaw, Poland, pp. 113–118 (2006)
10. Koch, T.: Lean Business System. In: Proceedings Polish-German Workshop on Lean Remanufacturing, Wroclaw, Poland, pp. 23–34 (2006)
11. Kucner, R.J.: A socio-technical study of Lean Manufacturing deploymen In the remanufacturing context. PhD Dissertation, The University of Michigan (2008)
12. Liker, J.: The 14 Principles of the Toyota Way: An Executive Summary of the Culture Behind TPS, University of Michigan (2004)
13. Lund, R.T.: Remanufacturing: the experience of the USA and implications for the developing countries, World Bank Technical Paper No.3 (1984)
14. Lundmark, P., Sundin, E., Bjorrkman, M.: Industrial challenges within the remanufacturing system. In: Proceedings of Swedish Production Symposium, pp. 132–139 (2009)
15. Östlin, J., Ekholm, H.: Lean production principles in remanufacturing - a case study at a toner cartridge remanufacturer. In: Proceeding in IEEE International Symposium on Electronics and the Environment, pp. 216–221 (2007)
16. Östlin, J.: On Remanufacturing System: Analysing and Managing Material Flows and Remanufacturing Process. Institute of technology, Linköpings universitet SE-58 183 Linköping, Sweden, THESIS NO. 1192 (2008)
17. Saunders, M., Lewis, P., Thornhill, L.: Research Methods for Business Students, 3rd edn., pp. 169–376. Pearson Education Limited, London (2003)
18. Seitz, M.A.: Automotive Remanufacturing: The challenges European remanufacturers are facing. In: Production and Operations Management Society (POMS) 18th Annual Conference Dallas, Texas, U.S.A (2007)
19. Sundin, E.: Product and Process design for Successful Remanufacturing. Linkoping Studies in Science and Technology. Dissertation No. 906. SE-581 83 Linkoping, Sweden: Department of Mechanical Engineering, Linkoping University (2004)
20. Womack, J.P., Jones, D.T.: Lean thinking: Banish waste and create wealth in your corporation. Free Press, London (2003)

# Understanding Product State Relations within Manufacturing Processes

Benjamin Knoke, Thorsten Wuest, and Klaus-Dieter Thoben

Bremer Institut für Produktion und Logistik GmbH (BIBA),
Hochschulring 20, 28359 Bremen, Germany
{kno,wue,tho}@biba.uni-bremen.de

**Abstract.** Today's manufacturing industry is forced to constantly improve its processes in order to stay competitive in a global market. Already highly optimized in many cases, academics and practitioners must identify furthur optimization potential by taking a closer look at the manufacturing process line. Within this paper, the *product state based view* is briefly introduced as a theoretical basis for the following analysis of relations between product state characteristics along the manufacturing process chain. First, the difference of dependencies and interdependencies are established through a time and process perspective. Possible dependencies are then classified, including theoretical examples. Concluding the paper, the requirements for a mapping of state characteristics are shown and possible opportunities of the presented approach are discussed.

**Keywords:** product state, manufacturing process, (inter-)dependencies, relations.

## Introduction

When it comes to company requirements, manufacturing companies are experiencing more and more challenges from their customers towards product and information quality [1]. At the same time, the manufacturing processes themselves are becoming more complex, as they are no longer being carried out at one single location [2].

Business success of manufacturing companies is directly based on the quality of their processes, so there is a need for constant process improvement [3]. One step towards this goal is to increase the transparency of the processes, which in turn increases understanding of them. The *product state based view* focuses on describing an individual product along an industrial manufacturing process, including the state changes and information involved. It is based around the description of the product through its product state.

The product state within a manufacturing process can be described at any time with holistic knowledge about its relevant characteristics [4]. Despite this deterministic approach, holistic knowledge concerning all state characteristics is neither worthwhile nor feasible. The reasons for not considering a state characteristic can be divided into

C. Emmanouilidis, M. Taisch, D. Kiritsis (Eds.): APMS 2012, Part I, IFIP AICT 397, pp. 437–444, 2013.

three groups [5]. They can either be technical (e.g. not measureable or measurable by destroying the product), financial (e.g. measurement is too costly), or caused by a knowledge gap (e.g. state characteristic is not known). However, some state characteristics can be characterized as relevant regarding their impact on the manufacturing process and the product state.

One way to identify relevant state characteristics is whether they include crucial information needed for each manufacturing process step [5]. Therefore, a product state characteristic that neither impacts the manufacturing process nor influences other product state characteristics may be disregarded. Knowing what the relevant state characteristics do can improves transparency and increases understanding of the manufacturing process itself. The state characteristics are often not independent, but relate to each other and form a complex (manufacturing) system, as well. This paper focuses on the understanding and structure of these relationships between product state characteristics.

# 1     State Characteristics within Manufacturing Processes

First explaining the problem with an initial modeling approach, this chapter then focuses on the relationships between state characteristics in manufacturing processes and in opportunities of application.

## 1.1     Initial Modeling Approach

A generalized model of a manufacturing process is shown in Fig. 1. Product states (S) frame the process steps (P), through which the product is then described by discrete product state characteristics (SC). The term *relation* describes the general connections between SCs. These relations can either be one-directional (dependent, [6]) or bi-directional (interdependent, [7]).

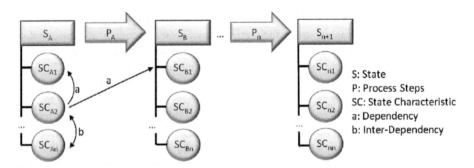

**Fig. 1.** Process model to visualize the relations between state characteristics

The parameters of the manufacturing process also shape SCs. SCs depend partially on process parameters (e.g. cutting speed, damping pressure) of previous process steps. As shown in Fig. 1, these production steps are framed by previous and following states. The extent of the process steps has to be defined according to the modeling degree. It is possible to insert the product states into the process flow after each change of the product (or added value), but it is simpler and more reasonable to merge similar activities according to the modeling focus

The concept becomes significantly more complex through the integration of process parameters into it and will need to be elaborated in further research. An analytical approach towards the modeling of the relations between state characteristics is described in the following section.

## 1.2     Characterization of Possible Relations between State Characteristics

Interdependencies can only occur within a definite product state while dependencies cannot go against the process flow, so any potential shapes of the dependencies and interdependencies can be reduced. This is based on two axioms regarding the temporal restrictions of these connections:

- Dependencies can never go against the process flow, since a state characteristic always has an existing value that only past or present effects can influence.
- Interdependencies can only exist between state characteristics of the same state and time, since a future effect cannot impact the past.

If a decision within the manufacturing process is considered because of an upcoming event, it is in fact not influenced by the future event but by expected requirements and other information existing at the present time of the decision. For example: A car within a manufacturing process is painted red not because a customer is expected to react positively to this specific color at the moment of exchange, but because he had ordered a red car in the past, and this information was already useable during the manufacturing process.

## 1.3     Analytical Approach and Different Types of State Characteristics

As described within the previous section, a SC is also dependent on SCs from previous states. These cross-state relations can add up and become very complex. From an analytical perspective, the relations of SCs can be characterized as mathematical functions. For example, the dependency of a state characteristic SC1 on another state characteristic SC2 is expressed in the term $SC1 = f (SC2)$. If interdependency between these two state characteristics exists, they are described by a common function $f (SC1, SC2)$. These functions can be described either by a mathematical term (e.g. the mass of a cylinder: $m = \rho * l * d^2 * \pi$) or a text (e.g. the overall error ratio is 3% in the dayshift and 5% in the nightshift).

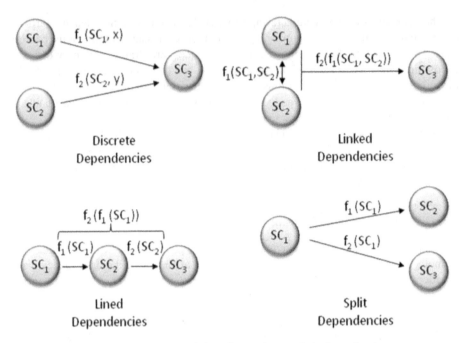

**Fig. 2.** Possible characteristics of state characteristic dependencies

If dependencies between three or more state characteristics exist, four different characteristics can be identified. These types are visualized in Fig. 2. In complex models, these types may appear in combination:

- State characteristics with **discrete dependencies** have independent influence on another state characteristic. This occurs on the condition of additional process parameters $(x,y)$. Since $SC_3$ within the functions $SC_3 = f_1(SC_1)$ and $SC_3 = f_2(SC_2)$ could be eliminated, therefore $f_1(SC_1) = f_2(SC_2)$ would imply a direct connection. This causes the need of additional process parameters, which influence each function $SC_3 = f_1(SC_1, x)$ and $SC_3 = f_2(SC_2, y)$.
- **Linked dependencies** are another form of the connection between state characteristics. In this case, the combination of two or more state characteristics impacts another. If two state characteristics $SC_1$ and $SC_2$ influence $SC_3$ within a linked dependency, they share an interdependency $f_1(SC_1, SC_2)$, and $SC_3$ can be described by the common function $SC_3 = f_1(f_2(SC_1, SC_2))$.
- The sequence of multiple dependencies is defined as **lined dependencies**. If the dependencies $SC_2 = f_1(SC_1)$ and $SC_3 = f_2(SC_2)$ exist, they can be merged into a function $SC_3 = f_2(f_1(SC_1))$.
- Finally a state characteristic can also influence two or more other state characteristics. These **split dependencies** share a common origin and impact different state characteristics. E.g. the functions $SC_2 = f_1(SC_1)$ and $SC_3 = f_2(SC_1)$.

$f(SC_1, SC_2, SC_3, SC_4, SC_5)$

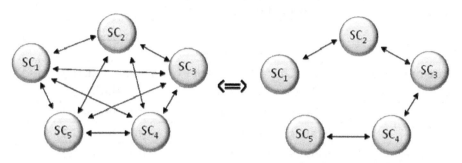

**Fig. 3.** Optional visualization possibilities of multiple interdependencies

If three or more state characteristics share interdependencies, they can be described by a common function. Following this approach, the visualization of all connections is redundant and can be replaced by a chain of interdependencies, as shown in Fig. 3. This can significantly improve the simplicity of a model. Mapping redundant information can be evaded by a structured approach to gather all relevant information. This crucial information is described in the next chapter.

### 1.4  Crucial Information to Map State Characteristic Relations

To benefit from the information of the relations between state characteristics and to share knowledge within a manufacturing process, a map of these relations needs to be modeled. To complete this task, certain information needs to be collected. The necessary data is:

- **Aim and scope:** Needs to be defined in order to create a model that considers relevant elements and neglects irrelevant ones.
- **Modeling degree:** Defines the modeled levels of relations. This includes the number of iterations in describing the relations of elements before and after being connected to state characteristics or process parameters.
- **States and process steps:** Along with their sequence, the states and process steps provide the basic structure of the process. Their sequential arrangement follows the rule of a bipartite graph, for a state is always followed by a process step and vice versa.
- **Process parameters and state characteristics:** The state characteristics and process parameters represent the nodes of the network. Each has to be aligned with the states and process steps.
- **Transfer functions:** The transfer functions describe the relations between state characteristic and process parameters. Collecting the transfer functions, that flow into each node to cover all relations, is sufficient.

A possible modeling form for a structured collection of all relevant data is shown in Table 1. Along with information about the manufacturing process and this data set, the relations of all state characteristics and process parameters are described. A model created on the basis of this data can be applied in multiple applications, which are described within the next section.

**Table 1.** Exemplary structured modeling form to collect all relevant data

| Form of (process-name) | | |
|---|---|---|
| **Aim** | (aim of the model) | |
| **Scope** | (scope and regarded relation levels) | |
| **State or Process Step** | **State Characteristics or Process Parameters** | **Incoming functions of relations** |
| A: (state A) | (state characteristic A.1) | (function A.1.1) |
| | (state characteristic A.2) | (function A.2.1) |
| 1: (process step 1) | (process parameter 1.1) | (function 1.1.1) |
| B: (state B) | (state characteristic B.1) | (function B.1.1) |
| | | (function B.1.2) |
| 2: (process step 2) | (process parameter 2.1) | (function 2.1.1) |
| C: (state C) | (state characteristic C.1) | (function C.1.1) |
| | (state characteristic C.2) | (function C.2.1) |
| 3: (process step 3) | (process parameter 3.1) | (function 3.1) |
| D: (state D) | (state characteristic D.1) | (function D.1.1) |
| | (state characteristic D.2) | (function D.2.1) |

## 1.5    Opportunities for Application of the Concept

The structure of the linked state characteristic concepts provides two different approaches for application. Whenever changes within a manufacturing process occur or have to be implemented, the model of state characteristic relations, when transferred to a PPC, can be applied. If the value of a state characteristic exceeds the acceptable range, the system can be used to create a model with all relevant influences on the state characteristic to identify the problem (Fig. 4, left). Alternatively, if a process parameter has to be changed, the system can be used for the opposite purpose: With a map that provides information about the impact of the change (Fig. 4, right).

A map that contains all information about any relation between state characteristics and process parameters within a manufacturing process tends to become very complex and difficult to handle. To solve this, a model with different hierarchical layers and levels of detail could be applied. One possible approach is to split the model into a meta-model and two sub-models:

- A **meta-model** that provides a general overview on all states and process steps with their aligned process parameters and state characteristics, along with the general process structure.
- A **state-model** that focuses on the relations of a single state or process step, and shows the relations of all process parameters or state characteristics of the focal state or process step.

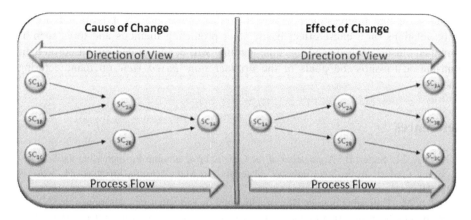

**Fig. 4.** Different opportunities of application

- A **state characteristic-model** that visualizes all relations of a single state characteristic or process parameter, and may include the functions that describe its relations.

With the information described within the previous section, and a defined modeling notation, the automatic generation of such models enters the realm of possibility and may be the outcome of future research.

## 2    Limitation and Outlook

This paper presented an approach to analyze and map relations between state characteristics based on the *product state based view* on collaborative manufacturing processes. After a brief introduction on the importance of transparency and in depth understanding of the own processes, the possible relations, dependencies and interdependencies were presented. The different types of dependencies between state characteristics were then elaborated on, and after a brief presentation on information requirements to apply the approach, the possible opportunities of the concept were discussed.

Overall, the topic of describing relations between state characteristics over a collaborative manufacturing process chain is very complex and, if applied in industry, requires an in-depth understanding and a high transparency of product, process and effects to realize its potential. Theoretically, if an application of the approach is possible, it will help to increase the final product quality and process efficiency by reducing waste and rework through early identification of problems and allocation of information to the right addressee.

The topic itself still needs further research concerning possible ways to identify and describe occurring relations in a practical and efficient way. Early practical insights into the manufacturing processes of an SME (1st tier automotive supplier) have indicated that the complexity of illustrating relations of state characteristics, along a manufacturing process, increases very fast and has to be managed very careful in order to not thwart the goal of increasing transparency for the stakeholders at hand.

Due to these first impressions, parallel to further investigate the possibilities to describe relations on a cause-effect basis, other promising methods and tools such as combined cluster analysis and machine learning will be elaborated on, based on their contribution towards the goals of the *product state based view* on manufacturing processes.

# References

1. Kovacic, M., Sarler, B.: Application of the Genetic Programming for Increasing the Soft Annealing Productivity in Steel industry. Materials and Manufacturing Processes 24, 369–374 (2009)
2. Seifert, M.: Unterstützung der Konsortialbildung in Virtuellen Organisationen durch perspektives Performance Measurement. Dissertation Universität Bremen. Bremen: Mainz Verlag (2007)
3. Linß, G.: Qualitätsmanagement für Ingenieure. München/Wien: Hanser Verlag (2002)
4. Wuest, T., Seifert, M., Klein, D., Thoben, K.-D.: Der Werkstückzustand im Informationsmanagement. Productivity Management 16 (2011)
5. Wuest, T., Klein, D., Thoben, K.-D.: State of steel products in industrial production processes. Procedia Engineering 10, S. 2220–S. 2225 (2011)
6. Farlex, Inc. (2009:2): TheFreeDictionary.com Großwörterbuch Deutsch als Fremdsprache (2009), Online-resource: http://de.thefreedictionary.com/abhängigkeit (last access on August 05, 2012)
7. Miller, G.A., et al.: Dictionary entry overview: What does interdependency mean? (2011), Online-resource: http://www.audioenglish.net/dictionary/interdependency.htm (last access on August 05, 2012)

# Universal Simulation Model in Witness Software for Verification and Following Optimization of the Handling Equipment

Jiří Holík and Lenka Landryová

Department of Control Systems and Instrumentation
VSB – Technical University Ostrava
Ostrava, Czech Republic
jiri.holik@dynamicfuture.cz, lenka.landryova@vsb.cz

**Abstract.** The aim of this work is to verify the working load of forklifts (generally rolling-stock) based on actual transports and following optimization using a universal simulation model in the software Witness. This aim can be characterized in three following phases. In the initial phase, the actual transport data are obtained for a monitored interval and for the distance matrix between the network points of the actual transports. In the second phase, obtained data are implemented into the simulation model and then the simulation is performed to find utilization of all forklifts. In the last phase, the workload is validated and the optimization is performed using Witness Optimizer.

**Keywords:** enterprise, model, monitoring data, optimization.

## 1 Introduction

In companies in which high demands on supply logistics are placed, compliance with the agreed delivery times or deadlines, and work organization itself is emphasized in supplying more end work stations [1]. Solving of deterministic transport systems can be found at specialized literature, [1] or [6] etc. Authors of these publications use mostly mathematical methods for searching results. In this work we apply the already known deterministic access and its characteristic into the simulation tool Witness software [4], [5]. Practical applications of using Witness software are at [4] or [7], [8]. From literature it is also known that the specific requirement occurrence for the deliveries, which can be generally characterized as a demand, usually has a time periodic or random character [1], [6], [7]. Randomness is mainly caused by frequent changes of the produced assortment, also accompanied by limiting the capacity or the number of handling equipment, which in practice can be traced.

This paper analyzes full utilization of the current handling equipment under given conditions for specific requirements for deliveries for a given reference period, and subsequently it validates acquired information about the utilization of handling equipment to allow optimization of their number from the point of view of two optimization criteria. Optimization criteria are chosen on the basis of a universal simulation model created in the Witness environment, suitable for tasks of this nature [4], [5], and their implementation in practice is an alternative engineering solution to managerial methods Just-in-time or Kanban implemented in manufacturing enterprises.

C. Emmanouilidis, M. Taisch, D. Kiritsis (Eds.): APMS 2012, Part I, IFIP AICT 397, pp. 445–451, 2013.
© IFIP International Federation for Information Processing 2013

# 2    Analysis of the Current State of Knowledge

Solving the problems mentioned above is closely related regarding the theory to the tasks of planning cycles of vehicles. Planning cycles of vehicles falls within the scientific theory of transport which was once very successfully developed at the University of Transport and Communications in Žilina, Slovakia. To excellent study materials there can be included [6], in which the problem is well formulated and is followed by a theoretical analysis. There are also approaches to the solution and graphical methods of solution, which can be found in [2], and which are complex for the large number of vehicles and trips.

The subject of an analysis of the current status is the finding of several characteristics that are important input data for subsequent verification of the load of handling equipment. The list of necessary input information is given below in indents. Each area is detailed in the subchapter.

- Information on carried out transports - the deliveries during the reporting period in the past,
- The matrix of distance between transmission points of the network,
- The parameters of handling equipment.

## 2.1    Carried Out Transports

The information about carried out transports is demanded mainly in terms of the format of records that must be followed for the proper functionality of the simulation model. A preview of the data structure for simulation of transport is given below as Table 1. The length of simulation period is not critical, but for the relevance of the results it is useful to have data only for periods with similar volumes of deliveries (of production).

**Table 1.** Records of implemented transport

| Item | Units |
|---|---|
| Date a time of Transport | DD.MM.YYYY HH.MM |
| From - Matrix point | - |
| To - Matrix point | - |
| Number of handling Units | Pallets |
| Material ID | - |
| Group of handling device | - |
| Speed (Loaded) | $m.s^{-1}$ |
| Speed (Unloaded) | $m.s^{-1}$ |
| Loading Time | S |
| Unloading Time | S |

A record containing all information required by the above Table is ideal input data for one or more carried out transports related to FROM WHERE – TO WHERE simulation.

### Date and Time of the Transport

- Date and time of the transport (if this information is not traceable, then any time of the earliest traceable track can be used).

### From - Matrix Point

- Point of matrix representing the starting point of transport network, from where the transport was carried out.

### To - Matrix Point

- Point of matrix representing the destination of transportation networks, from where the transport was carried out.

### Number of Handling Units

- The number of handling units transported within one record made about carried out transport,
- The handling unit can be a pallet, crate, it is necessary to follow for the same handling equipment the same types of handling units - possibly convert to volume units, unless it if needed.

### Material ID

- Identification of transported material, it's optional data item if it is not necessary to statistically follow a transported amount of material types.

### Group of Handling Device

- Identification of specific handling equipment (a forklift), or a group of handling equipment, performing the same activity. Within the group of handling equipment it is necessary to choose the type of handling equipment which will be promptly available for the carried out transport.

### Speed Loaded – Full, Empty

- Indicates the speed in carrying out the handling of the session. There are handlings, which are limited by speed limits for safety reasons, but the speed of handling equipment is usually limited across the transport network (the company).

### Loading Time, Unloading Time

- Specifies the time required for loading (unloading) of a handling unit on (from) handling equipment. Time may vary according to space constraints of locations on the network, depending according to, for example, if it is the floor or a position in a certain height.

## 2.2    Distance Matrix of Points in Transport Network

Since the simulation model works with the real speed of handling equipment, it is also necessary to have real scale of distances between points of transport networks, i.e. points, among which transport is carried out. For the purpose of the simulation model it is sufficient if the carried out transports are completed with information about the distances of all the uniquely determined transport sessions, therefore in any clearly designated routes from - to.

Table 2. Fragment of distance matrix for the simulation model

| FROM / TO | 1 | 2 | 3 | 4 | 5 | 6 | 7 | 8 |
|-----------|-----|------|------|------|------|------|------|------|
| 1 | 0 | 88.2 | 87.3 | 87.7 | 87.7 | 87.4 | 87.5 | 87.7 |
| 2 | 88.2 | 0 | 1.7 | 1 | 0.9 | 1.6 | 1.6 | 1.2 |
| 3 | 87.3 | 1.7 | 0 | 1.3 | 1.1 | 0.5 | 0.6 | 0.8 |
| 4 | 87.7 | 1 | 1.3 | 0 | 0.6 | 1.2 | 1.3 | 0.9 |
| 5 | 87.7 | 0.9 | 1.1 | 0.6 | 0 | 0.7 | 0.7 | 0.3 |
| 6 | 87.4 | 1.6 | 0.5 | 1.2 | 0.7 | 0 | 0.2 | 0.4 |
| 7 | 87.5 | 1.6 | 0.6 | 1.3 | 0.7 | 0.2 | 0 | 0.4 |
| 8 | 87.7 | 1.2 | 0.8 | 0.9 | 0.3 | 0.4 | 0.4 | 0 |

The simulation model reads the requirements from MS Excel workbook, which includes a macro to generate a complete matrix of distances between all points of the network. The generated matrix is read as input to the simulation model. A preview of the distance matrix (network points are indexed) is shown below as Table 2.

## 2.3    Handling Equipment Specifications

Among the main parameters of the handling equipment is speed in a loaded and empty status, and duration of loading and unloading. These parameters must be completed either as a global value, which means that it applies to all transports, or is valid for each transport carried out according to Table 1 in particular. The speed of movement is filled in as the basic unit [ms$^{-1}$] and the duration of loading or unloading in seconds [s].

# 3    Load of Handling Equipment - Current State

After implementing into the MS Excel control workbook simulation experiment can be carried out, reflecting the load of handling equipment in the monitored period, which correspond to the input data.

The output of the simulation model in this phase of work is load charts of all handling equipment, subject to the simulation. The simulation model takes into account parameters such as shifts of handling equipment (their service), or technological operations such as refueling, replacement of battery, etc. Graphical workload is always relative to the useful time shift for the handling equipment. A preview of obtained graphs is shown below as Figure 1.

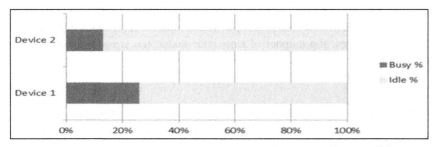

**Fig. 1.** Graphic preview of the handling equipment load for the simulation of the current state

## 4    Optimizing the Number of Handling Equipment Using Witness Optimizer

At the moment, when we are working with more handling equipment within each group, it makes sense to deal with the question of the number of those actually required handling equipment. This question can be approached in a dynamic simulation using the Witness Optimizer tool. This tool allows us to change the input parameters of simulation and subsequently compare observed characteristics, which directly reflect the impacts of these changes.

The optimization module used in this work allows us to change the number of handling equipment within the group of handling devices (device within a group performs the same group of operations) [5]. Optimization can be done with several different algorithms that seek the best solutions according to the defined optimization criteria. These algorithms use heuristic approaches with the possibility to restrict the set of all possible combinations, thus with a finite number of iterations performed. The found solution is therefore not possible to declare with certainty to be the optimal (it would be possible in the simulation case for ALL Combination) [5], but due to the real time given for simulation it is considered the best possible.

The optimization module used in this work is programmed so that you can choose from two contradicting optimization criteria. The first is the cumulative load handling equipment in the group, which can be further understood as a weighted average of all loads of handling equipment belonging to the same group. The second one is the average time required to meet specified requirements for handling. This is the time interval that elapses between the entry requirement for transport until the object is unloaded at the destination point of transport network. Contradicting criteria are chosen to reflect the optimization of the negative impacts. It can be characterized in such way that if we attempt to minimize the average time to meet the need for transport, the negative effect is increasing the number of handling equipment and therefore reducing the value of their cumulative workload. On the other hand, in an effort to maximize the value of the cumulative load, the average time to meet the demand for transport negatively increases.

## 5    Results of the Simulation

After each performed iteration, the initial configuration of the number of handling equipment in each group are recorded in the resulting table as well as values of both optimization criteria. If necessary, it is possible to add other statistics that are needed (amounts transported, the number of trips undertaken, the size of stocks in various parts of the logistics chain, etc.). A preview of the table obtained after optimization is shown below as Table 3.

**Table 3.** Fragment of the resulting comparison of all simulated variants in the optimization

| Watching parameter | Run 1 | Run 2 | Run 3 | Run 4 | Run 5 | Run 6 |
|---|---|---|---|---|---|---|
| AVG waiting for execution of demand | 144 | 148 | 148 | 152 | 154 | 155 |
| No of Group 1 | 8 | 8 | 7 | 8 | 8 | 7 |
| No of Group 2 | 4 | 4 | 4 | 3 | 4 | 3 |
| No of Group 3 | 1 | 1 | 1 | 1 | 1 | 1 |
| No of Group 4 | 7 | 5 | 7 | 7 | 6 | 7 |
| No of Group 5 | 2 | 2 | 2 | 2 | 2 | 2 |
| No of Group 6 | 1 | 2 | 2 | 1 | 1 | 2 |
| Summary | 23 | 22 | 23 | 22 | 22 | 22 |
| Warehouse 1 | 6294 | 6294 | 6294 | 6294 | 6294 | 6294 |
| Warehouse 2 | 8.609 | 8.609 | 8.609 | 8.609 | 8.609 | 8.609 |
| AVG Busy | 31.561 | 33.012 | 31.587 | 32.996 | 32.996 | 33.023 |
| Busy Group 1 | 51.364 | 51.364 | 58.734 | 51.365 | 51.364 | 58.734 |
| Busy Group 2 | 15.098 | 15.098 | 15.098 | 20.131 | 15.098 | 20.131 |
| Busy Group 3 | 51.143 | 51.143 | 51.143 | 51.143 | 51.143 | 51.143 |
| Busy Group 4 | 19.636 | 27.49 | 19.636 | 19.636 | 22.909 | 19.636 |
| Busy Group 5 | 17.304 | 17.304 | 17.304 | 17.304 | 17.304 | 17.304 |
| Busy Group 6 | 31.396 | 15.885 | 15.885 | 31.396 | 31.396 | 15.885 |

A compromise between both contradicting criteria, see Figure 2, can be called the point of balance. The balance point in this case is understood as a generic term. A preview of an intersection of the two criteria is also shown in Figure 2.

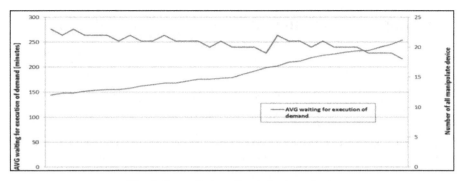

**Fig. 2.** Contradiction of optimization criteria

# 6    Conclusion

This work dealt with an analysis of handling equipment load at specified conditions, using tools from the Witness simulation environment to allow optimization of the number of them from the point of view of two optimization criteria. The chosen optimization criteria are based on a heuristic search for optimal solutions in the final set of defined options. The methodology used in this work is applicable to tasks with a similar focus to find the optimum parameters for the operation of such systems in practice.

**Acknowledgment.** This research is supported by the CP-IP 214657-2 FutureSME, (Future Industrial Model for SMEs), EU project of the 7FP in the NMP area.

# References

1. Daněk, J., Křivda, V.: Fundamentals of Transport (in Czech Základy dopravy), 192 s. VŠB - Technická univerzita Ostrava, Ostrava (2003) ISBN 80-248-0410-7
2. Černý, J., Kluvánek, P.: Fundamentals of Mathematical Theory of Transport (in Slovak Základy matematickej teórie dopravy), 279 s. VEDA, Bratislava (1991) ISBN 80-224-0099-8
3. Plesník, J.: Graph Algorithms (in Slovak Grafové algoritmy), 343 s. VEDA, Bratislava (1983)
4. WITNESS Getting Started Materials. Lanner Group Limited (2010)
5. WITNESS OPTIMIZER - Optimizer Module. Lanner Group Limited (2010)
6. Kluvánek, P., Brandalík, F.: Operational Analysis (in Slovak Operační analýza). ALFA, Bratislava (1982)
7. Holík, J.: Resultes of Selected Systems of Queoing Theory on Simulating program Witness and Theoretic Calculation Comparison (in Czech Komparace výsledků simulace vybraných systémů hromadné obsluhy v simulačním programu WITNESS) VŠB - Technická univerzita Ostrava, Ostrava (2009)
8. Dorda, M., Teichmann, D.: Simulation Using for Modelling of Marshalling Yard Hump Operating (in Czech Využití simulace při modelování provozu na svážném pahrbku seřaďovací stanice). In: 13. Ročník mezinárodní konference Witness 2010, pp. 47–56. Vysoké učení technické v Brně, Brno (2010) ISBN 978-80-214-4107-1

# An Adaptive Kanban and Production Capacity Control Mechanism

Léo Le Pallec Marand, Yo Sakata, Daisuke Hirotani, Katsumi Morikawa
and Katsuhiko Takahashi[*]

Department of System Cybernetics, Graduate School of Engineering, Hiroshima University,
1-4-1, Kagamiyama, Higashi-Hiroshima, 739-8527, Japan
takahashi@hiroshima-u.ac.jp

**Abstract.** This paper proposes an adaptive kanban and production capacity control system as a new production planning and control mechanism for *Just-in-Time* environments to minimize the long term average inventories, Work-In-Process, backorders and operating costs. It is based on the adaptive kanban system proposed by Tardif and Maaseidvaag (2001), but dynamically adjusts both the number of kanbans and the level of production capacity with respect to inventories and backorders. It is expected to be more resistant to changes in the demand than previous *pull* ordering mechanisms. We present how to evaluate its performance for the case of a single-stage, single-product manufacturing process with exponential processing times and demand following a Poisson process. Simulation results under variable demand means are presented.

**Keywords:** Adaptive production capacity, Adaptive kanban system, Markov analysis.

## 1    Introduction

*Just-In-Time* ordering systems, such as the Kanban and Conwip mechanisms, are used for reducing the costs associated with inventories and work-in-process (WIP) while maintaining a high level of service for customers. These systems authorize the release of a production order only when a demand is received from the customer and buffers are allocated to each inventory point to absorb changes in demand or production. However, this is for absorbing stable changes only, if unstable changes appear the allocated buffers cannot absorb them. Therefore *pull* systems are most efficient in environments with stable demand and processing times. The traditional approach is to optimize the number of cards used to control the release of production orders over a period based on demand forecasts. However, using forecasts contradicts the *Just-In-Time* principles and setting the number of cards over a period prevents timely readjustments if environmental conditions change quickly. Therefore, various mechanisms have been proposed to dynamically adjust WIP levels in order to increase the performance of *pull* systems in environments facing demand variability [2].

---

[*] Corresponding author.

C. Emmanouilidis, M. Taisch, D. Kiritsis (Eds.): APMS 2012, Part I, IFIP AICT 397, pp. 452–459, 2013.

The dynamic card controlling mechanism for CONWIP systems [1] adds or subtracts production cards when the manufacturing system's throughput (in make-to-order environments) or service level (in make-to-stock environments) is less or more than a production target. The reactive kanban system [4] dynamically adjusts the number of kanbans, using control charts for monitoring demand inter-arrival times and detecting unstable changes in the demand distribution.

The adaptive kanban system (AKS) was proposed [6] for a single stage manufacturing process. It does not monitor inter-arrival or output times but finished goods and backorders levels. Based on the monitored levels, additional kanban cards are released and captured in addition to initial kanban cards. For setting the AKS, Genetic Algorithm- and Simulated Annealing-based heuristics were compared [3]. Also, the AKS was adapted for a two-stage production line, and the benefits of simultaneously or individually adjusting the number of kanbans at each stage were compared [5].

These systems dynamically adjust the number of production cards, but the amount of WIP is not the only parameter impacting service levels and operating costs. The amount of production capacity also impacts service levels (by conditioning the manufacturing system's throughput) and operating costs (having more capacity than needed is a waste). The mechanism presented here, based on the AKS, dynamically adjusts not only the amount of WIP but also the throughput by changing the amount of active resources. It is expected to minimize inventories, WIP and operating costs while maintaining a high level of service and be more resistant to changes in the demand.

Section 2 presents our Adaptive Kanban and Production Capacity Control system and how to evaluate its performance. We study its performance compared to the Adaptive Kanban system in Section 3 and conclude with brief comments in Section 4.

## 2    Adaptive Kanban and Capacity Control System

For simplicity we restrain our attention to the case of a single-stage, single product manufacturing process MP with $S$ identical parallel servers. We assume demand to follow a Poisson process of rate $\lambda_D$ and an exponential processing time at each server with rate $\mu_P$. These assumptions are quite restrictive but will allow us to use Markovian analysis for estimating the performance of the system and utilized in the literature [1, 3, 5, 6]. We further assume there is no shortage of raw parts, which can be considered true for sufficiently strict service level requirements on the preceding production stage. With the assumption of exponential processing times, parts exit MP with $S$ identical parallel servers according to a state-dependent Markovian process of rate $\mu_P(n)$, where $n$ is the number of orders in MP; $\mu_P(n) = n * \mu_P$ if $n$ smaller than $S$ and $\mu_P(n) = S * \mu_P$ if $n$ greater than $S$.

For the single-stage, single product manufacturing process, we propose an adaptive kanban and production capacity control system (AKCS) based on the AKS. The complete mechanism of AKCS is described in Fig. 1. The decision variables are the number of kanban cards $K$ in original kanban system, the number of additional kanbans $E$, a release threshold $R$ and a capture threshold $C$ in AKS and the number of flexible servers $M$. By setting the decision variables, the total cost $Z$ minimized.

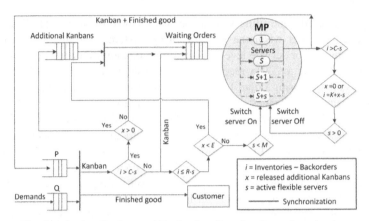

**Fig. 1.** Adaptive Kanban and Production Capacity Control mechanism

The total cost $Z$ consists of the cost for holding inventories and Work-In-Process $I$, the backorders cost $B$, the cost for switching flexible servers $F$, and the cost for operating the manufacturing process $O$, and the unit costs are defined as $h, b, f$, and $d$.

As in the kanban system, all of $K$ kanbans are attached to finished parts stocked in queue P one by one. When a finished part is delivered to the customer, the attached kanban is removed and sent to MP as a production order. If P is empty, new demands are stocked in queue Q as backorders until a part is processed through MP and delivered to the customer.

Furthermore, as in AKS, in addition to $K$ initial kanbans, up to $E$ additional cards can be released into the manufacturing system or captured whenever inventories reach a release threshold $R$ or a capture threshold $C$. When a demand arrives and inventories are equal to $R$ or less, not only an initial kanban but also an additional kanban are released in the manufacturing system as production orders if it is available. If inventories are greater than $C$ when a demand arrives and some additional cards have already been released, the kanban attached to the finished good delivered to the customer is captured.

In our Adaptive Kanban and Capacity Control system (AKCS), not only the number of kanbans but also the production capacity of the manufacturing process is adjusted, by increasing or decreasing the number of active servers in MP. Then, in addition to the initial number of $S$ fixed servers, $M$ flexible servers can be switched on and off to adjust the capacity of M. In the AKCS, finished parts level and on-off of flexible server will be controlled, and costs not only for inventory holding and backorders but also for operating flexible servers will be suppressed.

Increasing capacity is synchronized with demand arrivals while reducing capacity is synchronized with finished parts exits from MP. The flexible servers are switched on when inventories reach $R$ but all additional kanbans have already been released. Flexible servers are switched off when inventories outnumber $C$ but all additional kanbans have already been captured or when the number of busy servers becomes too small (equal to $s$). For the system to be able to return to its initial state $K$ must be greater than $C$, and $C$ equal or greater than $R$. For suppressing costs for inventory holding and backorders, adapting flexible servers is more effective than adapting additional kanbans, however, it leads to an increase in the cost for switching flexible servers. Then, adapting flexible servers only after adapting additional kanbans is considered for suppressing the cost. This system is equivalent to the AKS if $M=0$, and to the traditional kanban system (TKS) if $M=0$ and $E=0$.

Let $i$ be the amount of inventories minus backorders, $s$ the number of active flexible servers and $x$ the number of additional kanbans released at the time. The proposed control rule for adjusting the number of kanbans and flexible servers is shown as follows.

Control rule for additional kanbans:

$$\begin{cases} \text{If } i \leq R\text{--}s \text{ and } x < E \text{ when a demand arrives;} & \text{release a kanban } (x=x+1) \\ \text{If } i > C\text{--}s \text{ and } x > 0 \text{ when a demand arrives;} & \text{capture a kanban } (x=x-1) \end{cases}$$

Control rule for flexible servers:

$$\begin{cases} \text{If } i \leq R-s \text{ and } x=E \text{ and } s < M \text{ when a demand arrives;} & \text{switch on a server } (s=s+1) \\ \text{If } i > C-s \text{ and } x=0 \text{ and } s > 0 \text{ when a part exits MP;} & \text{switch off a server } (s=s-1) \\ \text{If } i=K+x-s \text{ and } s > 0 \text{ when a part exits MP;} & \text{switch off a server } (s=s-1) \end{cases}$$

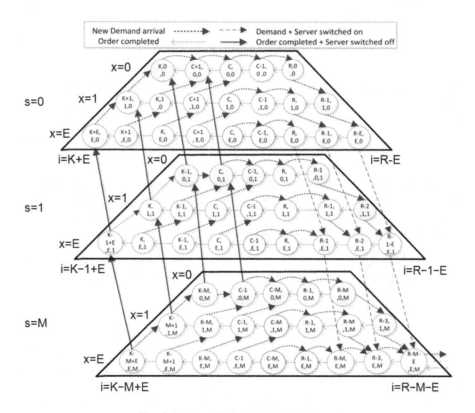

**Fig. 2.** Markov Chain for $E=2, M=2,\ C>R$

Under the assumption of exponential processing times and Poisson demand arrivals, we can model this system as a Markov Chain in terms of states $(i, x, s)$. An example of the Markov Chain of the proposed AKCS is shown in Fig. 2.

If the maximum throughput of MP is greater than the average demand rate then the steady state probability $P(i, x, s)$ of each state exists and can be calculated. Summing the balanced equations of all states $(i, E, M)$ where $i < R-E-M$, we can prove Eq. (1).

$$P(i, E, M) * \mu_P(i, x, s)/\lambda_D = P(i + 1, E, M) \tag{1}$$

Therefore the balanced equations of all states $(i, x, s)$ where $K-s+x < i < R-s-x$ form a finite linear system of $N$ independent equations with $N$ unknown variables $P(i, x, s)$. This system is easy to solve and once the steady probability of each state $(i, x, s)$ has been calculated, and we can estimate the following total cost $Z$ of the system.

$$Z = I + B + F + O \tag{2}$$

Because finished parts and WIP are attached to a kanban, the inventory holding cost $I$ is equal to the average number of cards in the ordering system multiplied by the unit cost $h$ set to 1.

$$I = h * K + h * \sum_{s=0}^{M} \left( \sum_{x=0}^{E} \sum_{i=R-s-x}^{K-s-x} x * P(i, x, s) \right) \tag{3}$$

The backorders cost $B$ is equal to the average amount of backorders multiplied by the unit cost $b$.

$$B = b * \sum_{s=0}^{M} \sum_{x=0}^{E} \sum_{i=0}^{\infty} i * P(-i, x, s) \tag{4}$$

The cost $F$ is equal to the average number of times production capacity is adjusted, multiplied by the unit cost $f$. The first part of the formula is the number of times a server is switched on. The second and last parts are the number of times a server is switched off when $i > C-s$ and $x=0$ or when $i=K+x-s$.

$$F = f * \sum_{s=1}^{M} \left( \sum_{i=R-s-E}^{R-s} \lambda_d * P(i, E, s - 1) + \sum_{i=C-s}^{K-s} \mu_P(i, 0, s) * P(i, 0, s) \right.$$
$$\left. + \sum_{x=1}^{E} \mu_P(K - s + x, x, s) * P(K - s + x, x, s) \right) \tag{5}$$

The cost $O$ is equal to the average number of active servers, multiplied by the unit cost $d$.

$$O = d * S + d * \sum_{s=0}^{M} \left( s * \sum_{x=0}^{E} \sum_{i=R-s-x}^{K-s-x} P(i, x, s) \right) \tag{6}$$

# 3    Performance Study

## 3.1    Expected Performance under Stable Demand

We consider the single stage, single product manufacturing process described in section 3, with $\mu_P = 0.15$, $\lambda_D = 0.2$ and the following cost parameters: $b=1000$, $f=1000$, $d=1$. Table 1 presents the best results obtained with the AKCS for $S+M$ varying from 4 to 6 compared to the best result obtained using the TKS and AKS. Each time, parameters $K$, $E$, $R$, and $C$ were chosen for fixed values of $S$ and $M$ after conducting an exhaustive search over the space of possible values. Here, the optimum number of servers with the AKS and TKS is 4. The AKCS yields better performances only if more than 4 servers are available and the gains are very small. However, cost parameters have a strong impact on performance and this is only a result under the condition of $d=1$ and $f=1000$. Cost parameters could be changed to advantage the AKCS (smaller $f$, bigger $d$). Also Table 1 shows results under stable environment while the AKCS performs much better in unstable environments where there is a great need for adjusting both WIP and capacity (see Section 3.2).

**Table 1.** Performance under stable demand; $d=1$, $f=1000$, $b=1000$

|        | K,E,R,C | S | M | S+M | I+B   | F     | O     | Total  | Gain  |
|--------|---------|---|---|-----|-------|-------|-------|--------|-------|
| TKS    | 7,0,0,0 | 4 |   | 4   | 7.959 |       | 4     | 11.959 |       |
| AKS    | 6,1,5,6 | 4 |   | 4   | 7.926 |       | 4     | 11.926 |       |
| AKCS   | 8,0,0,7 | 3 | 1 | 4   | 9.089 | 0.387 | 3.007 | 12.483 |       |
|        | 7,1,0,5 | 4 | 1 | 5   | 7.687 | 0.170 | 4.002 | 11.859 | 0.57% |
|        | 7,1,0,5 | 4 | 2 | 6   | 7.614 | 0.229 | 4.002 | 11.844 | 0.68% |

For a fixed total number of servers, using more flexible servers leads to bigger inventories, WIP and backorder costs but smaller operating costs. Using Markov analysis we study the impact of the cost ratios $f$ and $d$ on the performance of the AKCS. Demand is considered stable with $\lambda_D=0.2$. Fig. 3 presents the space $(f, d)$ where the local optimum configuration of the AKCS uses $M$ flexible servers, when $b=1000$ and $S+M=5$. As $d$ increases $Op$ increases and using more flexible servers becomes more interesting. As $f$ increases the cost for adjusting capacity increases and performance is reduced. Therefore, if the penalty for switching servers is not prohibitive and $d$ is expensive using more flexible servers may reduce the total cost and improve performance, but if $f$ is too high and $d$ too small, then increasing $M$ reduces performance.

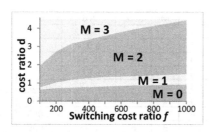

**Fig. 3.** Impact of the cost ratios $f$ and $d$ on the choice of $M$, for $S+M=5$ and $b=1000$

Fig. 4 illustrates the impact of parameter $M$ on the total cost, for $b$=1000 and various values of $f$ and $d$, when the total number of servers is constant. We observe that the expected gain from the AKCS compared to the AKS is very dependent on the cost ratios. For $f$=900 and $d$=0.5, using more flexible servers is counterproductive as the gains from the reduced $O$ are too small to balance $F$ and the increased $I$ and $B$. As $d$ increases so does $O$ but the expected gain from using more flexible servers becomes significant and the effectiveness of increasing $M$ increases. When $d$=3.5, if $f$ varies from 900 to 300 then $F$ decreases and the effectiveness of using more flexible servers increases. We observe that the AKCS outperforms the AKS only if the reduced $O$ outweighs the increase in $I$ and $B$ and if $F$ is not too high, but if these conditions are met, it is able to reduce the total cost.

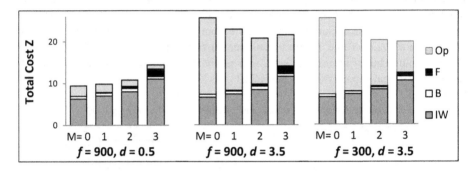

**Fig. 4.** Impact of $M$ on the total cost for $S+M$=5, $b$=1000 and various $f$ and $d$.

## 3.2    Expected Performance under Unstable Demand

The objective of this paper is to propose a Production Planning and Control system more resistant to changes in the demand than existing mechanisms. To assess its performance under unstable demand we conducted a discrete event simulation of a random walk through the Markov Chain. We considered the same manufacturing process and cost parameters as in the preceding study but unstable demand was introduced as follows: the mean of the demand inter-arrival times is set to 3 during the first 25 time units, 5 for the next 25 time units and 7 for the next 25 time units. This pattern repeats itself for the duration of the simulation. We considered a simulation length of

**Table 2.** Simulation under unstable demand mean; $b$=1000, $f$=1000, $d$=1

|      | K,E,R,C | S | M | S+M | I+B | F | O | Total | Gain |
|------|---------|---|---|-----|-----|---|---|-------|------|
| TKS  | 7,0,0,0 | 4 |   | 4   | 55.312 |  | 4 | 59.312 |      |
|      | 9,0,0,0 | 6 |   | 6   | 9.928  |  | 6 | 15.928 |      |
| AKS  | 6,1,5,6 | 4 |   | 4   | 58.766 |  | 4 | 62.766 |      |
|      | 8,1,6,7 | 6 |   | 6   | 9.671  |  | 6 | 15.671 |      |
| AKCS | 8,0,0,7 | 3 | 1 | 4   | 67.589 | 0.067 | 3.195 | 70.851 |      |
|      | 7,1,0,5 | 4 | 1 | 5   | 31.833 | 0.041 | 4.053 | 35.927 |      |
|      | 7,1,0,5 | 4 | 2 | 6   | 25.540 | 0.063 | 4.070 | 29.672 |      |
|      | 10,0,6,8 | 3 | 3 | 6  | 10.437 | 0.699 | 3.462 | 14.597 | 6.9% |
|      | 9,0,4,5 | 4 | 3 | 7   | 9.493  | 0.387 | 4.110 | 13.989 | 10.7% |

1,000,000 time units after a warm up of 100,000 time units. Table 2 presents the results of the best settings from Table 1 and new best settings. Parameters $K$, $E$, $R$, and $C$ were chosen for fixed values of $S$ and $M$ after conducting an exhaustive search over the space of possible values. We observe that our proposed mechanism is much more interesting under unstable demand, as the performance gain compared to the AKS is now 6.9% with the same total number of servers and 10.7% with one more server.

# 4    Conclusion

This paper considered unstable changes in product demand and proposed an Adaptive Kanban and Production Capacity Control system (AKCS) that adjusts both Work-In-Process and production capacity for minimizing the total operating costs while maintaining a high level of service. The AKCS is able to outperform existing ordering systems under certain conditions and is especially interesting in environments facing demand variability where the cost for adjusting production capacity is acceptable and operating costs relatively high. It would be interesting to assess its performance on multi-stage, multi-product environments. The control rule relies only on monitoring inventories and therefore should be easy to implement.

In the present version, production capacity is adjusted only after adjusting the number of kanbans. Instead, releasing a different number of additional kanbans for each capacity level may increase the global performance by better adjusting the amount of WIP to the current manufacturing process capacity and reducing the risk of switching resources on and off in a short succession.

**Acknowledgements.** This work was partially supported by the Grant-in-Aid for scientific research of Japan Society for the Promotion of Science in 2010-2012.

# References

1. Framinan, J.M., González, P.L., Ruiz-Usano, R.: Dynamic Card Controlling in a Conwip System. Int. J. Prod. Econ. 99, 102–116 (2006)
2. Lage, J.M., Godinho, F.M.: Variations of the Kanban System: Literature Review and Classification. Int. J. Prod. Econ. 125, 13–21 (2010)
3. Shahabudeen, P., Sivakumar, G.D.: Algorithm for the Design of Single-stage Adap-tive Kanban System. Comput. Ind. Eng. 54, 800–820 (2008)
4. Takahashi, K., Morikawa, K., Nakamura, N.: Reactive JIT Ordering System for Changes in the Mean and Variance of Demand. Int. J. Prod. Econ. 92, 181–196 (2004)
5. Takahashi, K., Morikawa, K., Hirotani, D., Yorikawa, T.: Adaptive Kanban Control Systems for Two-stage Production Lines. Int. J. Manuf. Tech. Manag. 20, 75–93 (2010)
6. Tardif, V., Maaseidvaag, L.: An Adaptive Approach to Controlling Kanban Systems. Eur. J. Oper. Res. 132, 411–424 (2001)

# Intelligent Manufacturing Systems: Controlling Elastic Springback in Bending

Torgeir Welo

NTNU, Engn. Design and Materials, Rich. Birkelands v. 2B, N-7491, Trondheim, Norway
torgeir.welo.ntnu.no

**Abstract.** A rotary compression bending system with automated closed-loop feedback control has been developed. The overall goal is to improve the dimensional accuracy of formed shapes by transferring in-process data into a steering model for instant springback compensation. An analytical method based on the deformation theory of plasticity was employed to develop a physically-based steering model. Unlike alternative control strategies, the present control strategy is attractive for volume production since the approach does not impact cycle time. More than 150 tests of AA6060 extrusions were conducted to determine the capability of the technology. Prior to forming, the material was exposed to different heat treatments to provoke different stress-strain characteristics. The results show that the springback-angle standard deviations were improved from ±0.41° to ±0.13° by activating the closed-loop feedback system. Since the dimensional process capability is improved by a factor of three, it is concluded that the technology has high industrial potential.

**Keywords:** Forming, machine system, adaptive control, dimensional accuracy.

## 1 Background

European manufacturing companies are currently facing increased competition from low cost countries. One strategy to meet this challenge is developing more automated production technology, providing reduced labor cost while improving product quality. Hence, the future competitiveness of European manufacturing companies is strongly related to their capability in developing and integrating new technology, followed by commercialization of new products that provide superior value to customers.

Despite its long history [1-7], adaptive processing is still a technology that may create competitive advantages in the market place. In bending operations, for example, adaptive control strategies can be used for elastic springback compensation and dimensional control of the final product. One control strategy (A), [8], is to unload the part at an intermediate forming stage and use recorded data to estimate stop position using a predetermined algorithm. A second strategy (B) is to repeat procedure A multiple times until the part geometry meets the desired specifications. Both these strategies are suitable for low-volume production only since the approach increases cycle time. A third strategy (C) is to use a closed-loop feedback scheme and measure parameters such as bending moment, stretch, bend angle and section dimensions, using a steering model for instant prediction of springback. Its main advantage is

C. Emmanouilidis, M. Taisch, D. Kiritsis (Eds.): APMS 2012, Part I, IFIP AICT 397, pp. 460–466, 2013.

producing high-quality parts in one single step without intermediate unloading, making it suitable for volume production. Successful application, however, is strongly dependent on the capabilities of the steering model and the measurement technology used to record instant input data. Automotive product examples where adaptive forming has high value creation potential are shown in Fig. 1. The reader is advised to [9] for more applications and to [10] for research outlook.

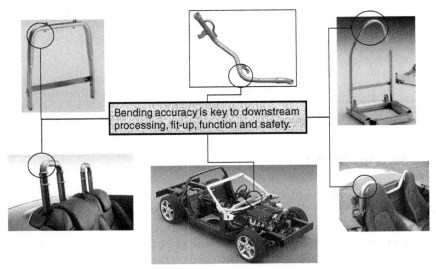

**Fig. 1.** Application examples where springback control in bending is key to product quality

## 2    Technology Brief

The overall goal is to improve the dimensional accuracy of formed shapes using a physically-based steering model for elastic springback compensation. A new rotary draw bending machine system with automated closed-loop feedback control is being developed. In-process measurement data are transferred into an algorithm for instant prediction of springback and bend angle prior to the unloading sequence. The bending system, Fig.2, consists of an electric power unit that is connected to a gearbox. A torque transducer is placed between the gearbox and the entry shaft of the bending arm. The rotation of the bending arm is measured using a rotational transducer connected to the gear. A drawback (sleigh) is mounted underneath the bending arm to eliminate friction as the profile slides against the tool during bending. The drawback is hinged locally at the bending arm to ensure free rotation of the front end of the profile. A pneumatic clamp is used at the rear end of the profile, constraining rotation and translation in the length direction. The lower tool has constant radius and is fixed. The tool's contact surface is made with a protruding ridge to form a local imprint along the inner flange, hence preventing uncontrolled local buckling. During forming, torque and rotation are continuously recorded and fed into a PC-operated control system, which automatically calculates stop position using a steering model. The process is entirely managed by the control system, without any human interference other than specifying the desired bend angle. Due to the control strategy (C) adopted, the cycle time of the bending machine is the same as for conventional draw bending.

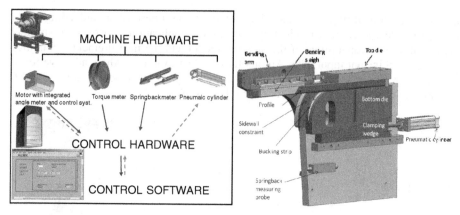

**Fig. 2.** System for automated closed-loop feedback control (left). Mechanical details (right)

# 3    Steering Model

Establishing a continuum-based steering model for springback compensation is a tedious matter, see [11], whose details will be omitted herein. In general, it is essential that the model is capable of capturing the main sources to variability in the bending process, including material parameters such as yield stress and strain hardening as well as dimensional characteristics of the profile. The analytical method used was based on the theory of plasticity using beam theory in combination with a non-linear, closed-form moment-curvature relationship as basis for the predictions. The kinematics and structural scheme of the process are interpreted in Fig. 3. Since elastic springback is essentially a result of the instant moment-to-stiffness ratios, i.e. elastic curvature $\kappa^e(s) = \frac{M(s)}{EI(s)}$, in the entire region A-D prior to unloading, it is important to establish a model that reflects the actual bending moment distribution. Here it is assumed that the bending moment varies linearly from zero at point $A$ to $M_B$ at point $B$, attaining a stationary, maximum value $M_C$ over a transition angle $\Delta\theta_B$ from the profile's first contact point with the die and vanishing over a distance $2 \cdot D$ (depth) inside the clamped region $C$-$D$. The bending moment is a function of instant material properties and the shape of the cross section, while stiffness is only a function of the latter since Young' modulus ($E$) is assumed unaffected by (pre-)deformation.

Fig. 4 shows an overview of the sequential steps included in the calculation strategy to obtain the steering model. In its general form, the solution includes instantaneous input from multiple parameters, including geometrical ones, which would surpass the measurement capabilities of the current system. If the measurements are limited to die rotation and bending moment only, however, the above equation may be converted into a simplified algorithm on the form:

$$\tilde{\varphi} = \frac{\Theta_0 + \hat{c}_0 + \hat{c}_1 \tilde{M}(\tilde{\varphi})}{1 - \hat{c}_3 \tilde{M}(\tilde{\varphi})}$$

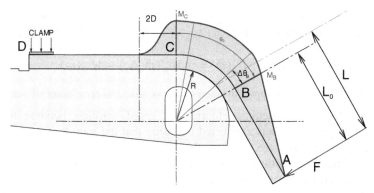

**Fig. 3.** Kinematics and moment distribution used as basis for development of steering model

Here $\tilde{\varphi}$ is the die rotation at end of forming, $\tilde{M}(\tilde{\varphi})$ is the measured moment, $\Theta_0$ is the desired bend angle, and the parameters $\hat{c}_i$ are calibration constants. $\hat{c}_0$ reflects an offset factor due to elastic springback within region $C$-$D$, while $\hat{c}_1$ reflects the elastic springback contribution from regions $A$-$C$, which is the reciprocal of the cross-section's bending stiffness $EI_0$. The constant $\hat{c}_3$ may be interpreted as a correction factor, making springback response non-linear due to inelastic material behavior, shifting contact conditions and cross-sectional distortions.

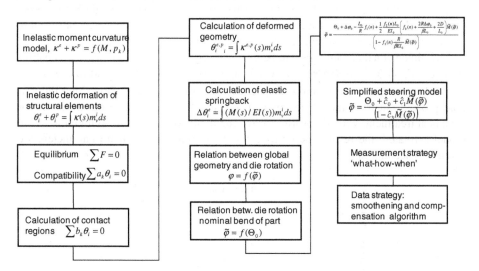

**Fig. 4.** Calculation strategy for development of steering model for springback compensation

## 4     Calibration Procedure

Due to the low inelastic bending resistance of the profile and the use of its variation as input to the steering model, the accuracy of in-process moment readings is key to the success of this technology. Since the torque ($\tilde{M}(\tilde{\varphi})$) and rotation ($\tilde{\varphi}$) are measured directly on the shaft between the gear and the bending arm, the effects of gravity forces ($M_g(\tilde{\varphi})$) and bearing friction ($M_\mu(\tilde{\varphi}, \Delta_i)$) have to be eliminated. Hence

$$\tilde{M}(\tilde{\varphi}) - M_p(\tilde{\varphi}) = \pm M_\mu(\tilde{\varphi}, \Delta_i) - M_g(\tilde{\varphi})$$

where $M_p(\tilde{\varphi})$ is the bending resistance of the profile and $\Delta_i$ is a set of variables that may affect friction (temperature, lubrication, speed, position, bending force, etc). A calibration procedure was conducted to ensure that the transducer would measure the net contribution from the profile in the tests. After zeroing out signals from gravitation and friction, additional tests were run without profile to determine noise. The results showed that the torque standard deviation was 1.2–2.0 Nm within one cycle. The mean value drifted slightly from the first to the last test (1.4–5.0 Nm), reflecting mainly variations from friction.

## 5    Capabilities of Manual and Adaptive Bending

More than 150 bending tests of hollow AA6060 extrusions were conducted to determine the dimensional capability of the technology. In order to provoke different material behaviors, the profiles were aged to different tempers: 'as is'(T1), 60 minutes and 120 minutes at 175 °C, providing initial yield stress range of ± 17%. After bending, the profile was clamped loosely to a fixture and the relative angle between the fixed and the free ends was measured. The repeatability was checked by performing several consecutive measurements of the same profile.

The dimensional capabilities can be evaluated by considering the process capability index, $C_p = B_t/(6 \cdot SD(\Theta))$, in which $B_t$ is the tolerance band and $SD(\Theta)$ is the realized angle standard deviation. Inspecting the results in Fig. 5 shows that the manual process (steering model deactivated) creates three bend angle clusters, one for each heat treatment, with T1-profiles providing the least springback. With the steering model activated, the results merge together, indicating that the main parameters are taken into account in the steering model.

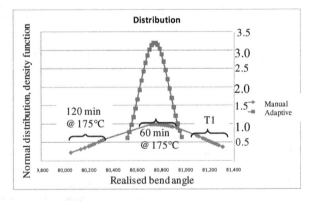

**Fig. 5.** Distributions of bend angle (adjusted to the same mean value) for the two methods

Table 1 shows that the adaptive process is able to reduce the maximum variation from 1.27° to 0.45°. Assuming $B_t = 1.0°$, the adaptive process shows a process capability that is three times better than the manual one. If the bend angle is, say, a standard dimensional feature, $C_p$ >1.33, the manual process would require a tolerance band of 3.26°, whereas the adaptive process would need a tolerance band of ± 0.53° to provide good parts. This result demonstrates that the technology has high industrial potential in terms of improved quality and reduced cost.

**Table 1.** Result summary

|                          | Manual   | Adaptive | Improvement |
|--------------------------|----------|----------|-------------|
| Average bend angle:      | 80.75°   | 79.82°   | NA          |
| Maximum variation:       | 1.27°    | 0.45°    | 282%        |
| Standard deviation:      | 0.41°    | 0.13°    | 315%        |
| $C_p$ ($B_t = 1.0°$):    | 0.41     | 1.25     | 305%        |
| $B_t$ ($C_p$ =1.33) :    | 3.26°    | 1.06°    | 307%        |

## 6    Conclusions and Lessons Learned

Based on this work, the following conclusions can be drawn:

- A new, adaptive bending technology with closed-loop feedback has been developed and validated using full scale experiments;
- The adaptive bending method has proven to dramatically improve the dimensional process capability;
- The technology has great industrial potential in terms of improved dimensional quality and reduced manufacturing costs.

Overall, the main challenge of this work was measuring the bending moment with sufficient accuracy. It turned out that the key was to reduce friction (variations) by replacing sliding bearings with roller bearings for the pivoting bend tool. Doing the machine design all over again, it would be beneficial to use lighter tool and die components to reduce sensitivity to variations since the bending forces are of the same magnitude as the gravity forces for the current concept. It was also a challenge to establish an in-process measurement strategy, relating the datum points of the tool to those of the profile since fit-up is dependent on dimensional accuracy of the incoming part. On the way to commercialization, its robustness and durability in a plant environment must be tested. Finally, since the steering model may utilize additional instant geometry data, future work includes extending measurement capabilities to improve the accuracy of the bending methodology even further.

# References

1. Hardt, D.E., Davis Webb, R., Suh, N.P.: Sheet Metal Die Forming Using Closed-Loop Shape Control. CIRP Annals - Manufacturing Technology 31(1), 165–169 (1982)
2. Hardt, D.E., Roberts, M.A., Stelson, K.A.: Closed-loop shape control of a tool-bending process. Journal of Dynamic Systems, Measurement, and Control 104(4), 317–323 (1982)
3. Jenne, C.J.: Closed loop control of roll bending/twisting: A shape control system for beams. Dep. of Mech. Engineering, Massachusetts Institute of Technology, MSc thesis, 166 pages (1986)
4. Kwok, S.K., Lee, W.B.: "The development of a machine vision system for adaptive bending of sheet metals. Journal of Materials Processing Technology 48(1), 43–49 (1995)
5. Lou, H., Stelson, K.A.: Three-Dimensional tune geometry control for rotary draw tube bending, Part 2: Statistical tube tolerance analysis and adaptive bend correction. J. Manufacturing Sci. Eng. 123(2), 266–271 (2001)
6. Kuzman, K., Geiger, M.: Closed-loop control of the 3D bending process. CIPR Annals - Manufacturing Technology 52(1), 204–208 (2003)
7. Ferreira, J.A., Sun, P., Gracio, J.: Close loop control of a hydraulic press for springback analysis. Journal of Materials Processing Technology 177(1), 377–381 (2006)
8. Chu, H., Stelson, K.A.: Modeling and Closed-Loop Control of Stretch Bending of Aluminum Rect. Tubes. J. Mnf. Sci. and Engn. 125, 113–119 (2003)
9. Kleiner, M., Geiger, M., Klaus, A.: Manufacturing of lightweight components by metal forming. CIRP Anneals – Manufacturing Technology 52(1), 521–542 (2003)
10. Welo, T.: Sheet Metal Forming. In: Chinesta, F., Cueto, E. (eds.) Advances in Material Forming, pp. 175–192. Springer, France (2007)
11. Welo, T., Granly, B.: A New Adaptive Bending Method Using Closed-Loop Feedback Control. Trans. Nonferrous Met. Soc. China (20), 2111–2117 (2010)

# Splitting or Sharing Resources at the Process Level: An Automotive Industry Case Study

Dag E. Gotteberg Haartveit[1], Marco Semini[1], and Erlend Alfnes[2]

[1] SINTEF Technology and Society,
Department of Industrial Management Trondheim, Norway
[2] Department of Production and Quality Engineering,
Norwegian University of Science and Technology, Trondheim, Norway
{dag.haartveit,marco.semini}@sintef.no, erlend.alfnes@ntnu.no

**Abstract.** Original equipment suppliers (OES) supplying the automotive industry are in a business characterized by fierce competition and long contracts. Fulfilling these contracts often implies producing serial parts while an automotive is in serial production and an obligation to provide spare parts after the serial phase. The first period is characterized by large volumes and production based on stable forecasts. The second period implies production for the spare parts marked and this period is characterized by sporadic orders and small volumes. Focused factories theory suggests that production of products with different market and product characteristics should be carried out in separate focus factories. This paper discusses the feasibility of focused factory theory using an OES as an illustrative case, and presents relevant questions to address in order to achieve focus at the process level.

**Keywords:** Focused factories, Operations strategy, Original equipment suppliers, automotive industry.

## 1    Introduction

Original equipment suppliers (OES) supplying the automotive industry are in a business characterized by fierce competition and long contracts. Contracts for supplying original equipment manufacturers (OEM) with serial parts are usually 7 years and when they run out OES's are under obligation to provide spare parts for periods up to 15 years. The first period is characterized by large volumes and production based on stable forecasts. The second period implies production for the spare parts marked and this period is characterized by sporadic orders and small volumes.

Automotive parts are normally mass produced for efficient production in large volumes. The same production system is also utilized for low volume production of spare parts. The spare parts market has the potential of being lucrative for the OES's but serving the market requires flexible production with short lead times [1]. This creates challenges for the OES's. Being able to satisfy the marked requirements of ordinary automotive parts and spare parts demands production systems for, respectively mass production and flexible production. This influences choice of machinery,

C. Emmanouilidis, M. Taisch, D. Kiritsis (Eds.): APMS 2012, Part I, IFIP AICT 397, pp. 467–473, 2013.

operators and production control, and is thereby difficult to combine in one production system. On the other hand, separating the production systems entail duplicating resources and might not be cost efficient.

The purpose of the paper is to present challenges related to focused factories theory and to propose criteria and questions to address in order to achieve focus on the process level based on a comprehensive case study

The case company is a Norwegian subsidiary of a German corporation and is one of the world's largest manufacturers of car bumpers made of aluminum. It supplies bumpers to almost all mayor car manufacturers producing cars in Europe.

Since Skinner [2] introduced the concept of focused factories in 1974, creating this focus by assigning operations resources to satisfy competitive factors has been discussed by scholars. Hill [3] recently described six alternative approaches suggested within theory to find this focus. One of them were the volume approach which Semini et al. [4] applied to propose an organization of the serial and spare part production at the case company in to two different production systems and thereby suggesting two focused factories. This paper will build upon the work of Semini et al. but acknowledge Hill's finding that focus is not necessarily achieved by splitting. In some cases different resources and processes should be shared in order to reach strategic goals [3].

## 2    Literature Review

The literature review chapter will shed light on the pros and cons of applying focused factory theory. The term focused factories is limited to imply *factories within factories* for the remainder of this paper. This limits the scope of the term to i.e. not include decisions related to facility location.

Splitting the factory into two focused factories as was suggested by Semini et al. was thoroughly rooted in literature. Slack and Lewis [5] argues that production systems for products with clearly differing characteristics will not be effective. Porter [6] concurs by arguing that these kinds of production systems makes the company "stuck in the middle" meaning that the production system will have to cater to different, often contradictory goals with the same equipment, organization and processes. Being stuck in the middle leads to issues such as:

- Challenges in regards to choosing right levels of automation, flexibility and integration
- Challenges related to achieving flow oriented layout (product type or process type layout
- Planning and control principles not adapted to production environment or demand patterns
- Challenges related to developing knowledge and know-how for many different product types
- Challenges for the sales and marketing department handling two different markets

While the focused factory theory has been a success for many companies and industries, production of aluminum bumpers where each bumper is a serial part and then a spare part creates extraordinary issues. Production of the same product in its two phases requires the same product knowledge, production equipment and technological know-how etc. Production of a product with these characteristics in two focused factories seems not to be cost efficient and will according to Hyer and Wemmerlov [7] lead to these issues:

- Reduced scale effects and unnecessary duplication of tools and machinery
- Risk of sub-optimizing each factory
- Long lead times and poor utilization of capacity in marked fluctuating situations
- Loss of knowledge and know-how related to each product
- Reduced opportunity for optimized planning due to factory and resource boundaries.

The two previous sections have indicated that there is no clear cut guidance on how to split resources to ensure focus. Hill [3] suggests that the overall focus for an organization should be chosen based on the company's products' order winners and qualifiers. The next chapters will introduce the case company and propose criteria that enable organizations to find its focus by splitting or sharing at the process level.

# 3    Bumper Production

This chapter presents how bumpers are produced at the case company and goes on to explain the alternative operations strategy proposed by Semini et al.[4]

## 3.1    Bumper Production at the Case Company Today

Bumper production essentially consists of three processes. In the casting house, aluminum billets are produced from ingot, scrap metal, and alloying metals. The second process uses these billets to produce profiles of adequate shape and length by means of extrusion and cutting. More than 100 different types of profiles are produced due to unequal shapes and forms of different car models' bumpers. Finally, the third process forms the bumpers. Forming of the bumper is carried out in the bumper plant. Extruded profiles are processed in one of several automated forming lines, carrying out sawing, cutting, tempering, stretch forming, stamping, cutting and washing. Thereafter, all products need to be hardened in furnaces. While some bumpers are finished after hardening, many of them – especially spare parts - need some further processing, such as CNC (computer numerical control) machining, welding, assembly, etc. Serial parts are either sent directly to OEMs or to assembly plants where they are assembled into integrated crash management systems. Spare parts are often sent to OEM-owned central spare parts warehouses. As far as production planning and control is concerned, the forming lines operate with relatively large batches, with batch sizes varying between 2000 and 10000 bumpers.

When a serial part becomes a spare part, it is treated as before. It is often run at the same forming line as before and processed at the same CNC/welding machines. It is also run with the same batch sizes as before, but much more infrequently given their much lower volume. This is again due to relatively complex changeovers, which are particularly challenging for spare parts, since spare parts are produced so infrequently. Often, the tools needed to produce spare parts need considerable maintenance before they are ready for production again. Given that customers often order low quantities of spare parts, has led to considerable stocks of both WIP and finished spare parts, with its associated cost in the form of invested capital, space, maintenance, quality deterioration, administration and handling, and risk of obsolescence.

### 3.2    Two Separated, Dedicated Factories

The corner stone of the new operations strategy proposed by Semini et al. was to separate serial parts production from spare parts production, thereby creating two focused factories [4]. In focused factories, only products with certain characteristics are produced, which allows an increased level of focus. That is, by having separated processes, both physical and planning processes, the two *factories within the factory* can be run with two different focuses, each adapted to the specific needs of each product group. Products can be grouped according to volume, process, product/market, variety geography, or order-winners and qualifiers [3]; the grouping proposed by Semini et. al. [4] was done according to volume (serial parts = high volume; spare parts = low volume). The serial parts factory would produce approximately 15% of the product spectrum, which stand for approx. 80% of the volume. The spare parts factory would produce the remaining 85% of variants, standing for 20% of the volume.

## 4    From Overall Focus to Focusing at the Process Level

The question of achieving focus is not merely an overall question answered by separating production based on product volume as was introduced by Skinner [2] and proposed by Semini et. al. [4] in the previous chapter. The overall focus needs to be brought down on a process level where focus can imply both splitting and sharing individual resources, and various degrees of splitting. The following chapter will present and structure relevant questions to address in order to achieve focus on a process level, and introduce three dimensions of splitting.

### 4.1    Focus at the Process Level

While attempting to organize the production at the case company we realized that achieving focus is a stepwise but also iterative process. One need to decide on an overall focus based on the alternative approaches recapped by Hill [3]. At the same time the processes involved has to be understood and their feasibility to be split or shared for different products examined. If the process is to be split, splitting can be done to different degrees in several dimensions.

The overall focus is chosen based on analysis of the company's product and marked characteristics. Hill argues for achieving focus by focusing production to suit products with the same order winners and qualifiers. If this implies more than one focus the foci needs to be broken down on a process level. Table 1 shows the processes involved in producing aluminum bumpers at the case company. The table was developed based on the mapping guidelines presented in *The extended enterprise model* [8].

**Table 1.** Processes

| Administrative processes | Physical processes | |
|---|---|---|
| Order management | Inbound handling | Assembly |
| Forecasting | Internal transport | Storage |
| Production and inventory control | Production | Packaging and labeling |
| Procurement | - Casting | Outbound handling |
| Quality management | - Extrusion | External transport |
| Tooling | - Forming | |
| Performance measurement | - Machining | |
| Sales and operations planning | - Welding/CNC | |

Each process can be split or shared to achieve the overall strategic goal each foci aims for. In order to make these decisions some questions based on six key criteria needs to be addressed. These criteria and questions are gathered and adapted from theory [3, 7, 9] and structured in Table 2.

**Table 2.** Criterion and guidelines for focusing production systems with differing strategic tasks

| Criterion | Guidelines –questions to address for each process |
|---|---|
| Competitive priority / strategic tasks | How do the product differences affect the particular process? <br> - Are there differing performance objectives? <br> - Are they conflicting? |
| Complexity | Does the process imply that different : <br> - Products need to be handled? <br> - Technologies are used? <br> - Employees work together? <br> - Suppliers/customers are served? <br> Is the existing complexity impeding performance? |
| Utilization | Will splitting result in lower utilization of equipment? <br> Will splitting increase overhead? |
| Investment | Does splitting imply investment requirements? Duplication of equipment? |
| Competence | Is the same competence required for the different products? <br> Will the different foci demand specific product/process knowledge? |
| Flow | What impact does sharing or splitting the process have on the flow between the processes (information, material, etc.)? |

If the answer to the questions implies to split a process, this splitting needs to be decided for three dimensions. Should the two or more focused processes be carried out in different areas with different equipment, but at the same time be organized as one entity with employees servicing both processes? Table 3 illustrates the dimensions and span in degrees of splitting that could be chosen for each process.

**Table 3.** Degrees of splitting

| Dimension | Degree of splitting | |
|---|---|---|
| Spatial/Physical | Co-located – Same equipment | Geographically separated –Different equipment |
| Organizational | Integrated | Disintegrated |
| Job Specialization | Low | High |

## 4.2    Examples from the Case Company

The overall foci for the case company were found by analyzing the company's products order winners and qualifiers as Hill proposed. The result was a *serial part focus* and a *spare part focus*. This differed from Semini et al.'s proposition by not being based on volumes. Some serial products are made in small volumes, but have the same order winners and qualifiers as other serial parts and should be produced with a serial part focus. These two foci should then be evaluated for each process in order to find if the individual process should be shared or split to which degree. The two following examples illustrate briefly these kinds of decisions. They concern two of the 22 processes identified in Table 1.

The first example is a relatively straight forward decision which regards the casting process. The cast house have large scale effects, requires large investments to duplicate and utilization of the equipment is important. The performance objectives for the casting process do not vary between the two foci and the complexity is not influenced. The process at the cast house should therefore be shared and fully integrated along the three dimensions.

The second example is the order management process. Order management at the case company is tightly connected and integrated with customer relations. Each OEM (customer) has its dedicated Key Customer Manager (KCM) which handles contracts and orders from the specific customer. The situation today is that KCM's has the responsibility for both serial and spare parts. KCM's significantly affects operations by influencing order sizes, lead times and end of life production negotiations. The performance objectives in regards to these vary significantly for serial and spare parts. The fundamentals of achieving good spare part production performance are different from serial part production. This knowledge is limited at the case company today and the knowledge that exists is not communicated to KCM's. In regards to utilization of the KCM resources, having more that one KCM per customer is excessive. These KCM's are senior employees with unique relations and knowledge of the customers that is hard and costly to duplicate. Thus, the order management process should be shared, co-located, integrated, but bolstered with employees that can support the KCM's with reaching performance objectives for spare parts. In this regard job specialization should increase in the extended order management process.

# 5    Conclusion

This paper builds on the work by Semini et al.[4], but acknowledge that the authors did not address the question of focused versus shared resources sufficiently. The characteristics of aluminum bumper production imply that some resources and processes should be shared. At the same time it is necessary to split other resources and processes in order to achieve focus. Thus, taking focusing decisions on an overall level is not sufficient. The main contribution of this paper is a presentation of relevant questions to address in order to achieve focus on a process level. The paper introduces three dimensions for which splitting decisions has to be made and briefly explains two focusing suggestions for the case company. A more thorough and complete mapping and evaluation of all processes and resources associated with the production of a bumper at the case company is currently being carried out in order to decide the organization of operations.

Based on the notion that some resources and processes should be shared, opportunities for further research emerge: how should the shared resources be planned and controlled? What kind of principles should be utilized to ensure that the focused parts of the factory get the level of service it should?

**Acknowledgements.** This research was made possible by AUTOPART (AUTOPART - World class, focused spare part production) and SFI NORMAN (SFI - Norwegian Manufacturing Future) supported by the Research Council of Norway.

# References

1. IBM GLOBAL BUSINESS SERVICES, Performance in reserve; protecting and extending automotive spare parts profitability by managing complexity (2008)
2. Skinner, W.: The focused factory. Harvard Business Review 52(3), 113–121 (1974)
3. Hill, A.: How to organise operations: Focusing or splitting? International Journal of Production Economics 112(2), 646–654 (2008)
4. Semini, M., Powell, D., Alfnes, E.: Effective Service Parts Production: A Case Study. In: Proceedings of APMS 2011. Stavanger - University of Stavanger, Norway (2011)
5. Slack, N., Lewis, M.: Operations Strategy, 2nd edn. Pearson Education, Harlow (2008)
6. Porter, M.E.: What is strategy? Published (November 1996)
7. Hyer, N.L., Wemmerlöv, U.: Reorganizing the factory: Competing through cellular manufacturing. Productivity Pr. (2002)
8. Bolseth, S.: The Extent Enterprise Operations Model Toolset. Norwegian University of Science and Technology (2011)
9. Hallgren, M., Olhager, J.: Differentiating manufacturing focus. International Journal of Production Research 44(18-19), 3863–3878 (2006)

# Optimization of Flexible Assembly Systems for Electrical Motors

Mirlind Bruqi[1], Ramë Likaj[1], and Jorgaq Kaqani[2]

[1] Faculty of Mechanical Engineering, Kosovo
{mirlind.bruci,rame.likaj}@uni-pr.edu
[2] Polytechnic University of Tirana, Albania

**Abstract.** The modern assembly systems are fully integrated production systems. They consist of interconnected components of hardware and software. Large flexible assembly systems are being composed of high number of components and managing requires an enormous volume of data. For that reason the controlling and optimization of such systems is too complex. Nowadays that can achieved, using just computers and software tools. In this paper the optimization of product mix for assembly system for electric motors will be described. Also special attention will be given to data security of the information system using cryptography.

**Keywords:** Flexible assembly, optimization, simulation, analysis software, cryptography.

## 1 Introduction

Simulation as a modern concept for system analysis, in particular for production systems is driven by rapid technological development of IT. Various experts have developed numerous algorithms, implementing them in various programming languages. Nowadays an engineer's task is to teach the simulation philosophy in order to be set free from very complex mathematical expressions, creating more space for individual creativity and engineering.

However for simulation of processes, other knowledge is required depending on the field or the level of research.

If we are in a level of a Decision Maker, which requires decisions to be made concerning manufacturing decisions etc, the decision maker should have knowledge of statistics, theory of probability, and a number of other theories linked to buffering and services. Fortunately, modern simulation programs are very advanced, and integrated program packages for statistical preparation of production data and automatic optimization of entire process are included in them. In many cases such simulation process for production system allows very fast and efficient analysis of the stability for the selection of its parameters.

Arena is a simulator, which enables fast and efficient modelling of wide natural and artificial systems. It is a language which is designed for analysis and simulation of a large number of production and logistic systems, warehouses and all service systems. Service systems include: restaurants, post offices, banks, hospitals etc.

C. Emmanouilidis, M. Taisch, D. Kiritsis (Eds.): APMS 2012, Part I, IFIP AICT 397, pp. 474–483, 2013.

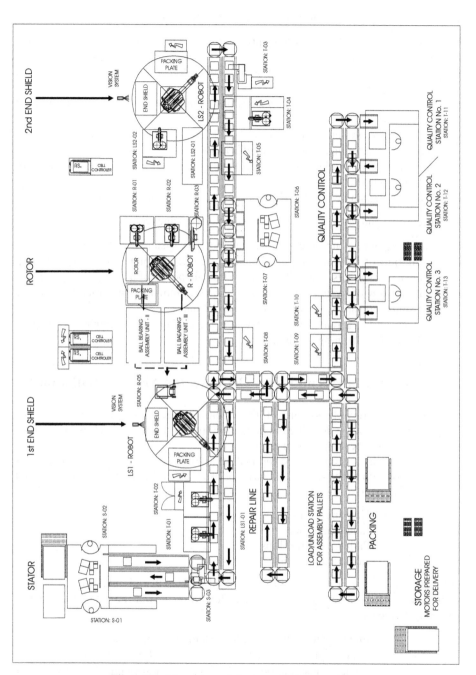

**Fig. 1.** Flexible system of electro-motor's assembling

Systems which can be analysed by Arena are listed below:

- Detailed analysis of each type of production systems, transportation devices and industrial robots,
- Analysis of complex service systems and customer relationship management systems,
- Global analysis of a Supply Chain which include, warehousing, transportation and logistic,
- Prediction of system performance based on key parameters such as; cost, quantity, cycle timing,   and system efficiency,
- Identification of bottlenecks of the Queuing systems and over exploitation of system resources,
- Resource planning of staff, equipments and facilities, materials etc.

By using Arena and its template the following can be achieved:

- **Modelling** of relevant processes within imaginary system boundaries,
- **Simulation** of system in order to understand and interpret complex relationship between its elements,   identification of strategic points of production segments,
- **Visualisation** of system operations by graphic animation in order to facilitate both simulation steps, verification and validation,
- **Analysis** of the current state of the system "as it is" or "how it might be", in order to make better planning for the future.

# 2    System Analysis and Goal Defining, the Aim of Simulation

Activities at the flexible system of the electrical machines assembling are very complex, and need to be described in detail. For the purposes of modelling, only main points of them will be subject of analysis.

The system which is considered for analysis from the entry at the first conveyor as a resource point up to the exit from conveyor as an absorbing point for the parts, and is built by following resources:

- Human resources,
- Industrial robots,
- Pallets with ID chips,
- Rolling conveyors.

In Figure 1 is shown graphically the path of all entities that circulate in the flexible assembling system. The path of material flux through working stations contains following elements:

- Input / Output points of the system given by rectangle,
- Stations given by small circle denoted by R (Resource),
- Logic points or system nodes given as parallelepiped   (N-Node),
- Straight lines represent the conveyors,
- Arrows show the direction of the material flux.

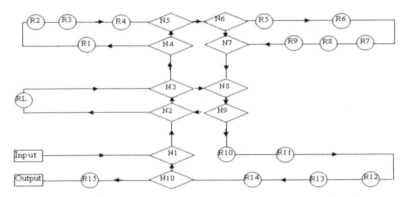

**Fig. 2.** Scheme of material flow through the assembling flexible system

System input represents the source of entities, indicating the input boundary of the system, while output or so-called disappearance point of entities is output boundary of the system. But, the subject of study is analysis of the inner part of the system by considering that all external activities are reduced in two points, input and output. Such approximation brings to the definition the system boundaries.

System allows change the number of resources at working station and also change of material flux depending on overfeed of the system with pallets and to change the frequency of material flux. Therefore, the system input and number of the engaged resources are considered as variables. In the other side, the system is influenced by different demands of the consumers which are made in different timing and in various quantities. These are representing stochastic effects that interfere and put condition to the system itself. The aim of the simulation is to achieve a maximum level of rent ability based on these demands, conditions, schedule and resources.

It is adopted that:

$C_{Ri}$ - are the costs for $i$ resources for the simulation period, $i=1,..,n$,

$C_{Mi}$ - are the material costs of specified product $i$, for $i=1$ to $n$ (Euro)

$C_{Ti}$ - are the costs for waiting time of product-Entity Flow Time $i$ of the system, for $i=1$ to $n$ (Euro)

$\Psi$ - is the objective function.

By the simulation process we are trying to minimise the objective function. This means that if decrease of the costs is achieved the main goal of optimisation is met, meaning that "with minimum utilisation of resources the maximum production volume is obtained, satisfying technical and organization conditions of the system".

Mathematical model is expressed by:

$$min(\Psi) = min\left[\sum_{i=1}^{n} C_{Ri} + \sum_{i=1}^{n} C_{Mi} + \sum_{i=1}^{n} C_{Ti}\right] \tag{1}$$

If $k$- simulations are executed then function (1) has form as given in (2):

$$min(\sum_{j=1}^{k} \Psi_j \ )= min\left\{ \sum_{j=1}^{k} \ l \ [\sum_{i=1}^{n} C_{Rij} + \sum_{i=1}^{n} C_{Mij} + \sum_{i=1}^{n} C_{Tij}] \right\} \qquad (2)$$

So, the simulation that in the best way fulfils the criteria is adopted. This operation is realized with **OptQuest** package which will be described later.

At **OptQuest** is chosen the option:

$$min(\sum_{j=1}^{k} \Psi_j \ ) \approx = \text{minimize}\{\text{Entity.Flow.Time}\} \qquad ...(3)$$

In this case, the only goal was the definition of the objective for our experiments in the assembling flexible system.

A flexible assembly system is an extremely complex production system. This attribute of the system can be described as the reaction of the market, which forces the manufacturer for decreasing a time to bring up the variety products to market. To accomplish this task, the flexible assembly system must quickly respond to the needs of the market. In this case, the system must be able to reconfigure his structure very quickly. These requirements have a large influence on the organization and technology of a production. Effect of these demands is constantly growing complexity and forces the manufactures to strengthen the flexibility of manufacturing and assembling systems.

To achieve these goals, systems must accomplish the following tasks:

- Increase productivity.
- Increase the quality of products and handle integrated quality management with higher efficiency.
- Higher utilization of machines, and stations.
- Quick respond on the external influences and demands.

In order to achieve these tasks and to reduce the complexity of the system itself, the complex global objectives can be transformed into a many simple solutions, which are able to meet local objectives.

These local objectives are based on hierarchical decomposition of time horizon. In this hierarchical framework there are some interconnected decision levels:

- Flexible assembly system for design (long term).
- Flexible assembly system for planning (medium term).
- Flexible assembly system for scheduling and control (short term).

The long term of time horizon means, the period of time on which the decision for design of system is long enough. In that case, in order to reduce the volume of data and the complexity of design process, a lot of activities will be integrated in single assumed activity.

The short term of time horizon means, the period of time by which the decision about system and its components will be made. This short term of time horizon give us an answer about the allocation of system resources in a very short period of time.

In this paper system is presented the simulation model for electrical motors assembly. This model gives the answer about system behavior. Simulation is made in simulation package ARENA. With OptQuest for Arena is carried out the optimization of product mix.

# 3    Description of Flexible Assembly System

The core system consists of industrial robots, assembly stations, transport systems and assembly palettes with ID and memory component. The Assembly stations are thought to be automatic transport systems with few integrated assembly sub-systems. Assembly systems are closed cycle. The assembly pallet is the basic carrier for a product during the assembly cycle. The assembly pallets are moved by conveyer belt system. After each assembly step the quality control check is done. If the state of quality check is positive, then the next assembly operation takes place. If the state of quality check is negative, then palette has to go to the repair station and wait for the shop floor operator. Shop floor operator must try to repair the product. If this is not possible he/she has to remove its content from the system, reset the empty pallet and send it in the direction of loading/unloading station. If repair is done, operator must proceed with palette ID and send it to the assembly cycle. New ID corresponds to the current state of product. Palette with repaired product will be rejected and move to the correct assembly station which is defined by given ID.

After completing the assembly cycle, palette must be in a loading/unloading station. After that, finished product will be unloaded and palette will be given a new status. This system is shown in fig. 3.

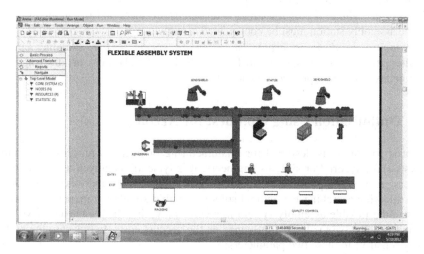

**Fig. 3.** Flexible assembly system

# 4     Entering Samples for Flexible System for Assembling

Another important point of the simulation is to generate data for the working stations known as samples, which is done in a manual and automatic way. Once the system is equipped by a device for identification of pallets and because the system has the possibility of communication with central computer, in this way there is possibility for automatic tracking of data. The data that must be entered in this case are listed in the following:

- Time of arrival of piece at the x station and type,
- Time of piece processing at the station,
- The time between the fall of assembling system and the duration of the fall,
- Schedule of the system, short and long breaks, changes and other organisational restrictions.

# 5     Basic Characteristics of Flexible Assembly Systems

The Simulated flexible complex assembly system deals with following sources of uncertainty and dynamic events:

- *Variable availability, arrival rates and has the incoming parts.*
- *Variable quality of incoming parts* – defective parts have to be removed before, either causing errors in system, or being assembled into finished products.
- *Mixed batch of parts to be assembled* – The assembly station assembling a range of variants of electrical motors types.
- *Variable availability of resources* – resources are tools and machines by which the assembly station must be coordinated directly.
- *Response to dynamic events in assembly system* – For example opening alternative assembly stations to bypass machine breakdowns or allowing more palettes to increase production capacity.

# 6     Optimisation Using Optquest for Arena

OptQuest for Arena is designed for manufacturing or business process consultants, analysts and industrial or systems engineers. It is typically deployed as an enterprise business analysis and productivity tool. OptQuest enhances the analysis capabilities of Arena allowing searching for optimal solutions within simulation models. In order to optimize the flexible assembly system in a case study, first the parameters have to be selected which have the largest influence on the product costs. In this case the system is very sensitive to these two parameters:

1. The number of operators in stations, and
2. The number of products on the batch mixes.

Constrains and profits for each Motor type are resented in Table 1:

**Table 1.** Constrains and profits for each Motor type

|  | Product Type | | | | |
|---|---|---|---|---|---|
|  | A | B | C | D | E |
| Constraints [% in mix] | ≥ 13 | ≥ 10 | ≥ 12 | ≥ 25 | ≥ 30 |
| Costs [Euro / Part] | 17 | 13 | 15 | 28 | 32 |

The numbers of resources in different stations may vary, as shown in Table 2.

**Table 2.** Variable number of resources per station

| Stations | S6 | S10 | S11 | S12 | Repair Line |
|---|---|---|---|---|---|
| Number of Resources | 2 to 3 | 1 to 2 | 2 to 3 | 1 to 2 | 3 to 4 |

These constraints can be added very easily to OptQuest for Arena and the optimization process can begin.

# 7    Optimisation Results

This paper presents simulations model of existing complex FAS.

Simulation model consists of 15 different stations. Additionally, quality control of the system is performed after each assembly station. Purpose of the simulation model is to find the best product mix and optimal numbers of replications on OptQuest for Arena, results are acquired and   presented in the following tables (table 3 and 4).

**Table 3.** The optimal number of resources on stations

| Stations | S6 | S10 | S11 | S12 | Repair Line |
|---|---|---|---|---|---|
| Number of   Resources | 2 | 2 | 3 | 1 | 3 |

**Table 4.** The optimal number of products on batch mixes

| Product Type on batch mix | | | | |
|---|---|---|---|---|
| A | B | C | D | E |
| 15 | 10 | 12 | 33 | 30 |

System security is achieved by using cryptographic methods, by using an algorithm which is designed specifically for FAS. Figure 4 represents an interface for system connection.

**Fig. 4.** Interface FAS connection

The application enables the encryption of various types of files such as "Doc, pdf, doe, dwg etc".

The application features are listed in the following:

- Symmetric encryption 256bit
- Usage of a non-public hash key
- Fast encryption/decryption of large files
- Intel x86 platform based on Windows Operating System
- Non-public algorithm

## 8   Conclusions

Flexible systems for assembling are part of the most sophisticated systems of the time. As such they have the possibility to pass from one assembly program to another in a very short period of time. The flexibility of such systems is its main property. In this way the Passover from one assembly system to another is made in: automatic, semi-automatic way or manually, by replacing the auxiliary devices of robots and machines.

Besides the positive side, these systems also have their negative side. Very often different products are mounted to these systems, and from managerial point of view this is heavy workload because of prior planning and preparations. These preparation tasks include:  choosing an optimal or suboptimal scenario of material, energy and information flow, including human resource organization.

The selection of such scenarios is made through different optimization algorithms such as: finite, limited and random enumeration. Module varies from one system to another, thus this module must be built for each specific system.

The aim of this Paper is to introduce the OptQuest toolbox as new feature of Arena environment for the optimization of complex production systems. The algorithms for the optimization are described in Rockwell Automation handbook OptQuest for Arena.

This paper describes on of the easiest ways for optimization of flexible assembly systems using the OptQuest for Arena. The Results of this study are presented in tables 3 and 4.

# References

1. Bruçi, M., Stopper, M., Bunjaku, A., Stuja, K., Kubat, A.: Optimisation of Flexible Assembly System for Electrical Motors using Opt quest for Arena. In: DAAAM International, Vienna, Austria, pp. 071–072 (2003)
2. Bruçi, M., Bunjaku, A., Stuja, K., Buza, S.: Optimizing of Flexible Palletizing Lines Using Simulation Tools. In: TMT 2005, Antalya, Turkey, pp. 693–696 (2005)
3. Stuja, K., Stopper, M., Bunjaku, A., Bruçi, A.: A concept for scheduling of flexible assembly for electrical motors. In: DAAAM International Scientific Book, Vienna, Austria, pp. 591–598 (2003) ISBN 3-901509-36, ISSN 1726-9687
4. Katalinic, B.: Industrieroboter und flexible Fertigungssysteme für Dehteile. VDI-Verlag, Düsseldorf (1990) ISBN 318-401027-9
5. Rockwell Software, OptQuest for Arena- User's Guide.© 2002 Rockwell Software. Inc., A Rockwell Automatic company, and Optimization Technologies (2002)

# Flexible and Reconfigurable Layouts in Complex Manufacturing Systems

Maria Manuela Azevedo[1,2,*], José António Crispim[2,3], and Jorge Pinho de Sousa[1,2]

[1] Faculty of Engineering, University of Porto, Porto, Portugal
manuela.azevedo@fe.up.pt
[2] INESC TEC, Porto, Portugal
[3] School of Economics and Management, University of Minho, Braga, Portugal

**Abstract.** This paper studies the Facility Layout Problem (FLP) of a first tier supplier in the automotive industry. This complex manufacturing system involves multiple facilities, complex products, and layout reconfiguration constraints. One of the key requirements of this particular system is the need for high levels of flexibility in the reconfiguration of the layouts. This problem is formulated as a mixed-integer programming (MIP), based on a FLP model with multiple objectives and unequal areas. The model allows for two re-configuration types: small and large changes. We explore the application of optimization methodologies to produce efficient and flexible layouts.

**Keywords:** Facility layouts, re-layouts, flexibility, optimization.

## 1    Introduction

The configuration of facility layouts involves the physical organization (of departments, machines, workstations, storage spaces, etc.) inside a plant, facilitating production and material handling, and allowing flexible and efficient operations. The expression "facility layout" is used here in a broad sense since our work is closely related to the literature both on facility location and supply chain design. Due to its practical importance to manufacturing systems competitiveness, this area has attracted a lot of interest from researchers. The reduction of product life cycles and the need to respond rapidly to market changes increase the importance of designing layouts that are more flexible, modular and easily reconfigurable [1]. In the automotive industry, product life cycles are relatively short and technological innovation plays an important role, making it still more important to incorporate the resulting dynamic features into the design process. However the extensive use of databases and benchmark data to test proposed methods often requires the simplification of the characteristics of real production and logistic systems, thus compromising their practical applicability. Moreover this industry produces a large variety of complex products (with many components) and services [2] that significantly increases production and flows complexity.

---

* Corresponding author.

C. Emmanouilidis, M. Taisch, D. Kiritsis (Eds.): APMS 2012, Part I, IFIP AICT 397, pp. 484–493, 2013.

In this work we propose an optimization approach where the facility layout problem is formulated using mixed-integer programming (MIP). Unequal area FLPs are a class of extremely difficult and broad optimization problems arising in many diverse areas [3]. Unfortunately, most of these approaches are based on a single objective while real-world FLPs are naturally multi-objective.

The approach proposed here is meant to tackle FLPs with multiple objectives and unequal areas, as a way to respond to real-world requirements. The model is based on the combination of two sub-models. The first defines the relative position of the departments inside the facilities, and the second defines the relative position of machines inside departments and creates the necessary flows to determine the final layout. The data used to assess and validate the approach was collected from a case study in the automotive industry.

In the next section a brief literature review about facility layouts is presented. Section 3 defines the problem, Section 4 describes our general approach, and Section 5 presents some initial MIP models. Finally in Section 6 we present the preliminary conclusions of this research.

## 2     Literature Review

The Facility Layout Problem (FLP) has been extensively studied and, accordingly, there are numerous related research surveys in the literature ([4], [1] and [5] are some recent examples). There are essentially three types of approaches to solve FLPs (see [4] and[5]): i) optimization: finding optimal layouts; ii) heuristics: finding nearly optimal solutions with hopefully efficient procedures, and iii) simulation: providing a way to assess alternative, potentially interesting solutions. Procedures based on the combination of these different types have also been proposed.

As far as we are aware, there are no studies that focus on layout design involving all the production and storage facilities of a company and only a few studies exhibit detailed and flexible design layouts. For example, Krishnan et al. [6] describe a FLP approach to deal with the uncertainty of product demand in the design of a facility layout, for single-period and multi-period problems. The main drawback of this work is the assumption that all the departments have the same area. González-Cruz and Martínez [7] propose a new multi-criteria entropy-based algorithm for the generation and evaluation of different layout designs of workstations or departments in an industrial plant. However, they do not detail the layout design inside each workstation or department.

Other authors try to further detail the layout design. For example, Kia et al. [8] propose a model for the layout design of a dynamic cellular manufacturing system with product mix and part demands varying during a multi-period planning horizon. They make use of multi-rows layouts to locate machines in the cells configured with flexible shapes. This approach is restricted to cells of production departments. Dong et al. [9] studied the problem of added or removed machines in a plant but with the assumption that the list of machines is known in each period.

The main innovative contribution of our work is that we do not simply focus on machine allocation or department configuration. Instead, we combine in a single approach, the problems in a manufacturing system, associated with machine allocation, department location and flows design. And to design this approach we have taken into account a set of general requirements directly derived from the real problematic situations of the case study.

According to Arabani and Farahani [10] more efforts should be made to incorporate multiple facilities in the analysis of facility location problems in order to effectively handle fluctuating demands originated from miscellaneous customers, industrial sectors and companies. Handling several facilities obviously increases the problem complexity, thus justifying the research presented in this work.

## 3    The Problem

Our problem consists in finding the best physical organization of facilities (departments, machines, workstations, warehouses, etc.) and the best flows of products and raw materials, fostering flexible and efficient operations (see Figure 1). A layout is efficient if the materials flow in a short and rapid way, without waste of time and resources, and it is flexible when it allows fast, cheap and easy to do reconfigurations.

In this work we consider a factory with physically distributed departments (e.g., production, assembly, warehouses, among others). Inside the departments we can have machines, workstations, storage areas and paths that connect them.

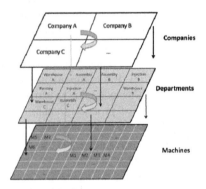

**Fig. 1.** Flows Complexity

In our real-world situation, there is a group of geographically separated facilities (3 factories with 3 warehouses and other production departments) that can produce and store the same type of products and components. Each facility has more or less the same department structure, with the same type of equipment and machines. These facilities are served by a distribution system with trucks to move the raw materials, components and/or products among them. Currently, each facility has warehouses that store the same raw materials, components and products since the production process is common to the factories.

The company works with "projects" that are associated to specific models of a car. A project comprises several parts that are themselves composed by a group of materials or components (see Table 1). These can be produced or assembled by any factory of the group. Each project is assigned to one facility.

**Table 1.** Product Complexty (example)

| Project 1 | | | | | | | | |
|---|---|---|---|---|---|---|---|---|
| Part A | | | Part B | Part C | | | | |
| Comp I | Comp II | Comp III | Comp I | Comp I | Comp II | Comp III | Comp IV | Comp V |

One of the main contributions of this research is the design of a decision-making procedure based on the concepts of "small" and "large" layout changes, making the manufacturing system more dynamic and flexible (see Figure 2).

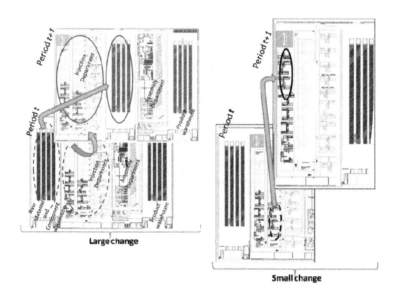

**Fig. 2.** Large and Small changes in a layout (example)

# 4    The Approach

Given its characteristics, this is a rather complex, NP-hard problem [5]. As Arabani and Farahani [10] point out, the main parameters of dynamic problems may significantly change over the planning time horizon, this implying we need to explicitly consider robustness and reliability criteria. Therefore, the models and methods developed to solve these problems should incorporate performance measures or objectives that take risk into account.

The proposed approach (see Figure 3) is a dynamic FLP with multiple objectives and unequal areas, and it is based on the combination of two sub-models: the first defines the relative position of the departments inside various facilities, and the second determines the detailed layout, with the definition of machine positions, inside departments and the associated physical flows.

Our model allows for two re-configuration types: small and large changes. Large changes are required when departments need to be moved from one facility to another or change their position in the same facility, possibly as a result of the arrival of new projects. Small changes are more frequent and consist of reconfigurations inside a department by adding / dropping machines, or by redirecting the flows of materials and products in progress.

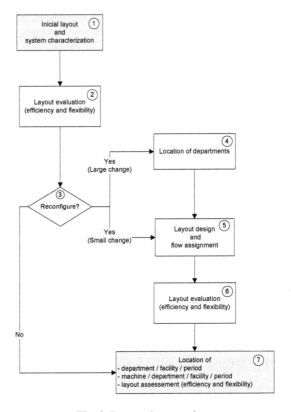

**Fig. 3.** Proposed approach

As presented in Figure 3 this approach consists of 7 steps. In step 1, one makes the system characterization, with parameter values and data. Then in step 2, that information is evaluated, for the multilevel layout of facilities and their departments, in terms of use of equipment and of material flows. These results will be compared to predefined layout efficiency and flexibility targets, in step 3. If the levels of efficiency are satisfactory, the current layout is not changed.

Otherwise, depending on the level of achieved efficiency, the required reconfiguration of the layout can be classified as "large" or "small". For example, if only one department has a low efficiency, only this department needs to be reconfigured, this consisting in a small change (step 5). On the other end, if the whole system has a low efficiency, the reconfiguration is considered to be large (step 4).

In step 4, new locations for the departments are determined, trying to minimize total costs. After changing the positions of the departments, it is necessary to internally reconfigure those departments, and this is done in step 5, by finding the position of machines inside each department and the respective flow assignment, in step 6, the new configuration is evaluated, in terms of efficiency and flexibility. Finally a complete solution is presented (step 7), with the layout configuration of the system, organized in different levels (facilities, departments), as well as the assignment of products to the different machines.

Given the complexity of the problem under analysis and the set of potentially interesting requirements, this approach is intended to be used to analyze different scenarios, namely:

- to centralize the warehouses in one facility;
- to combine departments of the same type in the same facility;
- to produce each product in a specific factory;
- to allow all factories to produce the same products.

The results of this type of analysis will hopefully lead to interesting, valuable guidelines for supporting strategic / tactical decision-making in the company.

# 5    Mathematical Models

Considering the complexity and features of the problem characterized by the case study, we have designed the mathematical models presented in this section. For computational purposes, these models are based on some simplifying assumptions and are formulated as mixed-integer programming, based on a Dynamic Facility Layout Problem with multiple objectives and unequal areas.

## 5.1    General Concepts and Notation

The following general assumptions have been considered:

- the cost of moving machines is known, but it depends on the type of machine and on the type of department;
- the distances between locations are computed between the physical centers of the locations, and measured with a rectilinear distance norm;
- a machine transforms an input into an output (a product), in reality - it can also be a workstation, that assemblies a product or perform other kind of function;
- all departments and machines can be moved to any location inside the facility or to other facility.

*Indices*
$t = 1, 2, \ldots$ - periods of time
$f = 1, 2, \ldots$ - facilities
$i, j = 1, 2, \ldots$ - departments
$l, k = 1, 2, \ldots$ - positions (locations) in a facility or in a department

*General Parameters*
$a_f$ - area of facility f
$a_i$ - area of department i
$r_{lkf}$ - distance between position l and position k, in facility f

## 5.2　Location of Departments ("large changes")

This model makes the allocation of departments to places or positions at facilities, each period of time. This allocation could be maintained the same position from period to the next or change the position in the same facility or even change to other facility.

*Additional parameters*
　　$cr_i$ - fixed cost of shifting department i
　　$q_{ijt}$ - flow (product quantity) between department i and j, in period t
*Decision variables*
$x_{ilft} = \begin{cases} 1 \; if \; department \; i \; is \; placed \; at \; position \; l, \; in \; facility \; f, \; in \; period \; t \\ \quad\quad\quad\quad\quad 0 \; otherwise \end{cases}$

*Model*
$Min \; C1 =$
$$\sum_{t,f,i,j,l,k}[q_{ijt}\,r_{lkf}\left(x_{ilft}\,x_{jkft}\right)] + \sum_{t,i,j,k,l,f1,f2}[\,cr_i\,r_{lf1kf2}\left(x_{ilf1t}\,x_{jkf1t+1}\right)] \quad\quad (1)$$

subject to:

$$\sum_{i,l} a_{if}\,x_{ilft} \leq a_f \quad \forall f,t \quad\quad\quad (2)$$

$$\sum_i x_{ilft} \leq 1 \quad \forall l,f,t \quad\quad\quad (3)$$

$$\sum_l x_{ilft} \leq 1 \quad \forall i,f,t \quad\quad\quad (4)$$

This model aims at minimizing total costs. The first term in the objective function (1) is related to the flows between departments and facilities, representing the material handling costs. The second term represents the reconfiguration cost, incurred when a department changes its position inside a facility or to another facility.

　　Constraints (2) ensure that the total area of a facility is never exceeded. Constraints (3) guarantee that a position in a facility has never more than one department, in each time period. Constraints (4) guarantee that a department is only assigned to one position in a facility, in each time period.

### 5.3    Layout Design and Flow Assignment ("Small Changes")

This model is used to support the design of the detailed layout, determining the positions for the machines inside departments and assigning flows, i.e., allocating the different products to the different machines, in each time period.

*Other indices*
    m,n = 1, 2, ... - machines
    p = 1, 2, ... - type of products

*Additional parameters*
$cr_m$  - fixed cost of shifting machine $m$
$cm_{mp}$ - capacity of machine $m$ when producing product $p$
$q_{mnt}$ - flow (product quantity) between machine $m$ and $n$, in period $t$
$a_m$   - area occupied by machine $m$
$r_{lki}$ - distance between position $l$ and position $k$, in department $i$
$d_{pt}$ - demand of product $p$, in period $t$

*Decision variables*
$$y_{mlit} = \begin{cases} 1 \text{ if machine } m \text{ is placed at position } l, \text{in department } i, \text{in period } t \\ 0 \text{ otherwise} \end{cases}$$
$$u_{mpt} = \begin{cases} 1 \text{ if machine } m \text{ is used to produce product } p, \text{in period } t \\ 0 \text{ otherwise} \end{cases}$$
$b_{pmt}$ - quantity of product $p$, to be produced in machine $m$, in period $t$

*Model*
$$\min C2 =$$
$$\sum_{t,i,n,m,l,k}[q_{mnt}\, r_{lki}(y_{mlit}y_{nkit})] +$$
$$\sum_{t,i1,i2,k,l,m,n}[cr_m\, r_{li1ki2}(y_{nli1t}y_{mki1t+1})] \qquad (5)$$

$$\max E = \sum_{t,m,p,i}(b_{pmt}\, u_{mpit}) \qquad (6)$$

Subject to

$$\sum_{m,l} a_{mi}\, y_{mlit} \leq a_i \quad \forall i,t \qquad (7)$$

$$\sum_m y_{mlit} \leq 1 \quad \forall l,i,t \qquad (8)$$

$$\sum_l y_{mlit} \leq 1 \quad \forall m,i,t \qquad (9)$$

$$b_{pmt} \leq cm_{mp} \quad \forall t,p,m \qquad (10)$$

$$\sum_{f,i,m,p}(cm_p\, u_{mptif}) \geq \sum_p d_{pt} \quad \forall t \qquad (11)$$

This model aims both at minimizing the total cost (5) and at maximizing the layout efficiency (6), in the each period of time. The first objective function (5) is similar to expression (1), with a first part related to the flows between machines, representing the material handling costs inside departments, and the second term representing the reconfiguration costs, incurred when a machine changes its position inside a department. The second objective function (6) maximizes the efficiency of the layout, by increasing the number of machines being used in each period of time.

Constraints (7) ensure that the total area of a department is never exceeded. Constraints (8) guarantee there is no overlap of machines, in each time period. Constraints (9) guarantee that a machine is only assigned to one position in a department, each time period. Constraints (10) verify that the quantity of product assigned to a machine does not exceed the machine capacity. Finally constraints (11) guarantee that the total installed capacity is enough to produce the total demand.

### 5.4     Preliminary Computational Results

These models are now being implemented and tested with IBM ILOG CPLEX Optimizer Studio version 12.2. For the above objective functions, which are not linear, we are using standard reformulation techniques to linearize them.

Preliminary computational results using small, randomly generated instances, seem to be satisfactory, thus validating the approach. It should be noted that, although random, these instances have been designed based on our knowledge of the case study, and seem to reflect the main issues to be solved in practice.

## 6     Conclusions

This work presents some preliminary results of a research project based on a case study involving the reconfiguration of the manufacturing system of a first tier supplier in the automotive industry. This case study considers the entire manufacturing system with multiple facilities. We allow for two types of reconfiguration that differ in the deepness and frequency of the modifications (these alternatives are referred as "large" and "small" changes).

Accordingly the problem was partitioned in two components, and formulated using mixed-integer programming (MIP), based on a FLP model with multiple objectives and unequal areas. This seems to create a useful tool to support the design and re-configuration of flexible layouts, allowing more efficient operations, in rather dynamic environments. A first assessment of the first results of this approach by the decision-makers has shown its potential, thus justifying further developments along this line.

**Acknowledgments.** The authors acknowledge the financial support from FCT, the Portuguese Foundation for Science and Technology (under grant SFRH/BD/33731/ 2009) and from the MIT Portugal Program.

## References

1.  Kulturel-Konak, S.: Approaches to uncertainties in facility layout problems: Perspectives at the beginning of the 21st Century. Journal of Intelligent Manufacturing 18, 273–284 (2007)

2. Marengo, L., Valente, M.: Industry dynamics in complex product spaces: An evolutionary model. Structural Change and Economic Dynamics 21, 5–16 (2010)
3. Ripon, K.S.N., Khan, K.N., Glette, K., Hovin, M., Torresen, J.: Using pareto-optimality for solving multi-objective unequal area facility layout problem. In: Proceedings of the 13th Annual Conference on Genetic and Evolutionary Computation - GECCO 2011, p. 681. ACM Press, New York (2011)
4. Moslemipour, G., Lee, T.S., Rilling, D.: A review of intelligent approaches for designing dynamic and robust layouts in flexible manufacturing systems. The International Journal of Advanced Manufacturing Technology (2011)
5. Drira, A., Pierreval, H., Hajri-Gabouj, S.: Facility layout problems: A survey. Annual Reviews in Control 31, 255–267 (2007)
6. Krishnan, K.K., Jithavech, I., Liao, H.: Mitigation of risk in facility layout design for single and multi-period problems. International Journal of Production Research 47, 5911–5940 (2009)
7. González-Cruz, M.C., Gómez-Senent Martínez, E.: An entropy-based algorithm to solve the facility layout design problem. Robotics and Computer-Integrated Manufacturing 27, 88–100 (2011)
8. Kia, R., Baboli, A., Javadian, N., Tavakkoli-Moghaddam, R., Kazemi, M., Khorrami, J.: Solving a group layout design model of a dynamic cellular manufacturing system with alternative process routings, lot splitting and flexible reconfiguration by simulated annealing. Computers & Operations Research, 1–17 (2012)
9. Dong, M., Wu, C., Hou, F.: Shortest path based simulated annealing algorithm for dynamic facility layout problem under dynamic business environment. Expert Systems with Applications 36, 11221–11232 (2009)
10. Arabani, A.B., Farahani, R.Z.: Facility location dynamics: An overview of classifications and applications. Computers & Industrial Engineering 62, 408–420 (2012)

# Cost Management Practices in Collaborative Product Development Processes

Carlos Barbosa[1], Paulo Afonso[2], and Manuel Nunes[2]

[1] Department of Polymer Engineering, University of Minho, Portugal
cbnuno@dep.uminho.pt
[2] Production and Systems Department, University of Minho, Portugal
{psafonso,lnunes}@dps.uminho.pt

**Abstract.** This study aims at highlighting the current knowledge, practices and effects of collaborative and concurrent new product development processes in the framework of the Portuguese plastic processing industry. By means of a case study approach, the conditioning factors affecting the strategic collaborations among firms are systemized. Mutual dependence, trust, and extensive information sharing were identified as prerequisites factors for a better buyer-supplier interdependence and involvement, as well as for the overall benefit of the supply chain. Moreover, collaborative and concurrent new product development processes ask for the use of cost management practices and advanced technical specifications (standards) which emerge as technical and management tools to achieve higher levels of efficiency and quality at the lower cost. Practices such as target and kaizen costing, value engineering, and design-to-cost, were perceived to play a remarkable positive effect on the internal/external organizational boundaries.

**Keywords:** Cost Management, Inter-organizational Cost Management Practices, Collaborative Strategies, Buyer-Supplier Relationship, New Product Development.

## 1    Introduction

The production systems of the future must be observed in terms of very interlinked production chains. Companies have to take care of costs to meet the descending price rate of the market. Worldwide competition requires continuous productivity improvements and efficient cost control that lead firms assume internally narrow (strategic) competencies and extensive outsourcing. In this way, the interdependence among production partners within a network or supply chain has been increasing.

Such approach pushes to strategic alliances and other types of buyer-supplier cooperation that have led to profitable results [1]. In this context, high levels of inter-firm trust can decrease the transaction costs of the relationship, thus providing competitive advantage for the partners. Furthermore, [2] advocate that the benefits of mutual inter-firm trust can be measurable in financial terms and suggest that managers should pay more attention to the role of inter-firm trust in partner selection

C. Emmanouilidis, M. Taisch, D. Kiritsis (Eds.): APMS 2012, Part I, IFIP AICT 397, pp. 494–501, 2013.

processes. Open-book and other collaborative practices have been mentioned both as a means for improving the cost efficiency of supply chains and as a tool for building trust into customer–supplier relationships. Indeed, they can even support analysts to quantity incommensurable characteristics, such as inter-firm trust.

Many firms form alliances with their suppliers and customers that do not fit into the classical dichotomy of hierarchies and markets. One outcome of these hybrid relational forms is the development of cost management techniques that cross the organizational boundary between buyers and suppliers to reduce costs through collaborative efforts 3]. Thus, high levels of buyer-supplier collaboration not only assumes an exchange of technical knowledge and the synchronization of production flows across supply chain members but, also includes sharing sensitive cost information, which has been usually kept secret by business partners [4].

By means of a case study approach, this study underlines the current knowledge, practice and effects (benefits and detriments) of collaborative and concurrent practices in new product development (NPD) and tests the adherence of a set of conditioning factors within the Portuguese plastic processing industry.

# 2     Literature Review

Inter-Organizational Cost Management (IOCM) practices guide suppliers and buyers to find ways to collaboratively reduce costs during the NPD process and has been shown as a valuable "tool" to manage those systems and increase value to both buyers and suppliers, improving the overall performance of complex and multidisciplinary NPD projects and increasing the overall profits of the value chain.

IOCM can be defined as buyers' and suppliers' coordinated efforts to reduce costs through target costing, value engineering and design-to-cost among other techniques. Past research has primarily argued that such practices depend on component characteristics, relationship characteristics, and characteristics of the transaction. Agndal and Nilsson [5] reported that the deepest collaboration around IOCM issues and the greatest joint use of suppliers' cost information typically occurs in earlier activities in the exchange process, including supplier selection, joint product design and joint manufacturing process development.

In this context, collaborative and concurrent NPD processes ask for the use of a set of practices which emerge as technical and management tools for achieving high standards of efficiency and quality at the lower cost. Firms aiming at implementing this strategy effectively have to pay close attention to several contingency factors on the organizational level and properly manage supplier involvement on the product development process, as well as on the product industrialization and parts supplying at production stage.

Researchers agree on the importance of an alignment between cost management practices in supply chain management and new product development process. However, some view effective cost management practices in supply chain management as critical to successful NPD process while others perceive effective NPD process as critical to successful cost management practices in supply chain management [6-9].

In reality, IOCM practices and new product development process are complementary activities. A new product will be less than totally successful if it is not chain-friendly [10]. On the other hand, international supply chains are reliant on a continuous development of customer-friendly products to distribute efficiently around the globe [10]. Effective cost management practices in supply chain management, particularly in the case of coordinated supply networks, and effective collaborative NPD process should be regarded as cumulative capabilities, that is, they exist simultaneously in a mutually reinforcing fashion [11].

IOCM supply chains and collaborative NPD process share a number of characteristics including an emphasis on customer responsiveness, internal alignment as an elemental starting point, and the coordination of technological developments accomplished through the collective efforts of cross-functional teams representing a mixture of chain members. This movement depends on a combination of innovative organizational practices such as integrated collaborative NPD and coordinated supply networks [12].

The literature emphasizes that the use of IOCM practices results in high level of cost transparency in supply chains and increases overall profits [4, 5]. Several studies demonstrate the relevance of the relationship between effective NPD processes as critical to successful cost management practices in supply chain management [6-9].

# 3     Case Study

## 3.1     Research Method

Different sources of data gathering were used: direct observations and documentation analyses as well as open and semi-structured interviews following a predefined questions guide and research protocol (on average each open interview lasted 60 minutes).

Our approach was firstly to prepare the semi-structured guidelines document and send it to the respondents. Afterwards, we received the semi-structured guidelines replies from the respondents and, consequently, a carefully analyses was performed. The second step of our approach comprehended an open interview by teleconference in order to close the remained gaps from the first step and, additionally, to extend the discussion to practical examples/situations experienced by the companies during the product development process.

## 3.2     Cases

The focus of this study was on a set of three injection-moulding companies (suppliers) with know-how in NPD procedures. The companies, named hereafter as: *PlasNetwork*, *IdeaMaker*, and *NextVision*, are located in the central coast of Portuguese mainland.

These companies were chosen in order to gather important insights from different types of plastic injection moulding companies. While *NextVision*'s activities are centred 100% in automotive industry, the *PlasNetwork* is still not supplying such kind of particular industry. On the other hand, *IdeaMaker*'s activities are balanced between automotive (30% to 40%) and other industries. Therefore, *NextVision* and *IdeaMaker* are 'supported' by the ISO/TS 16949 standards (among others), whereas the *PlasNetwork* holds the ISO 9001:2000 and ISO 14000:2004 registrations.

ISO/TS 16949:2002 uses ISO 9001:2000 as its base specification. It has a focus on customer satisfaction, being important for designing, implementing and maintaining the organization's quality management system. This standard implies greater attention to customer specific requirements and the organization's ability to satisfy them.

*PlasNetwork* is a company with ca. 60 employees that offers a set of transversal services within development, engineering, industrialization and production of plastic products and components. They have the knowledge of gathering and managing the competencies from several organisms: technological centres, mould makers, designers, laboratories, raw materials and equipment suppliers, etc. Working as the consultant centre of an entire network, this firm manages the entire product development process from the concept generation to the delivery of the product. The strongest capability of this company is to manage projects in a very flexible way.

*IdeaMaker* is a second tier supplier of automotive industry. Besides, they also supply package, houseware, and other industries. It is a company with ca. 15 employees divided by several inner activities such as project management, thermoplastics injection (e.g. over-moulding, insert-moulding), assembly lines, ultrasonic welding, quality control, and moulds manufacturing; other competencies, for instance, designing and computer-aided-engineering (CAE) as well as prototyping are outsourced. Interlinking skills throughout the production process provides customers monitoring and technical support until placing the product on the market.

*NextVision* is a much larger company than the previous described. It is a company with ca. 650 employees and its activities have been totally centred in Tier 1 (interior automotive components: centre console, air louvers, radio bezels, armrests, door trims, etc.) customers for about 20 years. Worldwide they are considered one of the major players in terms of air vents production. The company provides complete design, engineering, manufacturing and assembly operations for injection moulded interior subsystems. Other capabilities include painting, multiple interior surface decoration technologies, and an accredited testing laboratory along with a complete computer-aided-design (CAD)/CAE department with in-house rapid prototyping.

# 4    Findings and Discussion

*PlasNetwork* develops the initial ideas/concepts in parallel with customers. This process starts by deeply assessing the customer needs and the product specifications.

This integration (concurrent engineering) takes place earlier in the product development process with the purpose of reducing time-to-market as well as eliminating the probability of errors' propagation along the process.

*"the competitive advantage of our activity is achieved by adding value through collaborative strategies [...] Such approach allows the company to be more agile – that might be tricky to manage [...] it must involve multiple partners as early as possible on the product development process" (PlasNetwork CEO)*

This company aims at holding the ISO/TS 16949 registration in order to supply the automotive industry in a near future. Meanwhile, they have been developing an internal methodology (roadmap) according to that ISO technical specification. Inputs from suppliers/customers are (value-added) perceived as improvements for this methodology. The procedures implemented by the automotive industry are considered, by the interviewed, as the best practices that all companies should follow.

In the non-automotive industry and when the collaboration with the customer is tight the supplier may contributes to redesign the proposed product. This kind of collaboration leads to deeper buyer-supplier relationship that is beyond the functional level, i.e. the collaboration is on an emotional (or co-creation) level meaning a higher confidence and mutual dependence.

*IdeaMaker* develops somehow the abovementioned approach for buyers from the non-automotive sector. Indeed, they look to their customer needs – rethinking – optimizing them with high levels of productivity and innovation. The transfer of skills (collaboration) between partners allows them to offer to the global market better quality final product. As *PlasNetwork*, this company promotes with its non-automotive customers a high level of collaborative strategies at the idea/concept generation phase in order to decrease/optimized costs for both parts. Furthermore, with a transparent cost breakdown approach the company seeks to build customer loyalty.

On the other hand, the product development process for the automotive first tier customers is quite different. Foremost, this industry obliges suppliers to hold the ISO/TS 16949 registration which is a powerful tool that supports top executives, project managers and engineers to develop and control the entire product development process. Secondly, it is impossible to redesign (or alter) the initial concept/part previously idealized by the customer. The collaboration in this kind of environment is much more constricted. In this way, *IdeaMaker* "*intends to open itself to new markets [...] automotive sector requests high processes efficiencies [...] it squeezes the profit margins of its suppliers. [Other sectors] are less stressful... and the objective is to increase profit margins.*" *(IdeaMaker Project & Sales Manager)*

*NextVision* is the paradigm of the second tier suppliers for automotive first tier customers. The customer holds the final authority of the design that is a normal situation in automotive industry at this supply chain level. Moreover, continuous cost reduction during the production process (kaizen costing) is a demand of automotive customers.

This company totally leads its development and production; they have the fully knowledge of all engineering processes. However, if a Tier 2 supplier, such as *NextVision*, does not demonstrate competitiveness on a specific product, the customer has the right to change, due to the nature of the contracts which are protectionist, firstly of OEMs and, secondly of Tier 1. "*It is necessary a robust and competent structure with very specialized staff as well as advanced processes and methodologies [...] The cost of having such structure fits perfectly on the technological environment of the automotive industry [...] which has the capacity to absorb those fixed costs.*" *(NextVision Business Director)*

The company considers customers and suppliers essential parts of its strategy. This collaboration is fundamental for the smooth running of projects within this sector because they can bring important insights to the process of products development.

Thus, results highlight that only crisscrossing effective cost management practices with effective collaborative product development processes lead to successful interdependent buyer-supplier relationships as well as to the overall benefit of the supply chain. Consequently, synergetic alliances are achieved. Figure 1 schematizes a set of in/out organizational conditioning factors that were found to shape the effectiveness of strategic collaboration activities of the three Portuguese plastics injection moulding companies.

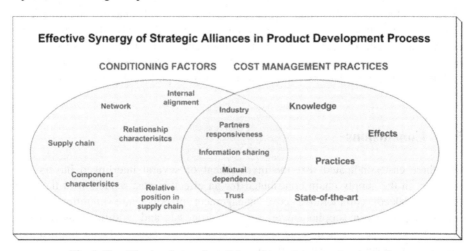

**Fig. 1.** Conditioning factors in collaborative cost management practices

Main conditioning factors that influence the level of collaboration among partners:

- Type of collaboration leadership (traditional: *pull system* / network: *push system*)
- Type of buyer industry (automotive / non-automotive)
- Component characteristics (complex / non-complex)
- Relative position in value chain (essentially OEMs, Tier 1 and Tier 2)
- Partners responsiveness (non-disclosure agreements and contracts)
- Inner personal characteristics (trustful top executive/managers)

The level of information sharing also influences strategic collaborations. This is the result of the mutual dependence levels and trust between customers and supplier. Effectively managing the suppliers' involvement in NPD projects implies the standardization of advanced methods and procedures throughout the value chain.

It is clear that strategic collaborations aim at improving the cost efficiency of the value chains. Accurate knowledge of IOCM state-of-the-art practices contributes to control all important dimensions in product development processes: technical, economic and social. On the literature a set of IOCM practices – which typically occur in early stages – were found: open-book, target costing, value engineering, design to cost, total cost of ownership, among others.

In our study we found that companies under study have been using along the product development process up to – and during – the production stage some of these techniques (e.g. target costing, value engineering, design to cost, and kaizen costing). The use of such practices has remarkable positive effects on internal organizational environment as well as on the entire value chain.

It was perceived from our qualitative approach that the accurate management of these practices leads to several benefits: trust improvement, decrease transaction costs, continuous productivity improvements, efficient cost control, profitable results, increase value to buyers and suppliers, competitive advantages, improve cost efficiency and sustainability of supply chains, high standards of efficiency and quality, and reduce risk. Total cost transparency, or sharing sensitive costs information seems, contrariwise, to be a non-total desirable consequence for the non-automotive suppliers. This is contrary of the intrinsic philosophy behind the IOCM practices.

# 5     Conclusions

The three cases indicated that the involvement of several interlinked buyers and suppliers in the supply chain contributed for an effective cost reduction of the final product. Indeed, collaborative cost management practices are important in the relationship between supplier-buyer, because proposals and modifications made in product design and production processes by a company depend and have implications for operations management in the future.

The studied firms have been applying concurrent and collaborative engineering activities during NPD projects for different industries (e.g. automotive and others), which enable the production of parts and subassemblies (or subsystems) with higher value added. The automotive sector, its meticulousness and vicissitudes, pulls the organizations' skills and performance. Although the higher levels of exigency leading to lower profit margins, this sector is much more predictable and allows increasing the business reflectiveness, management skills, and engineering processes.

It was observed that collaboration levels are a function of companies' inner competencies and the characteristics/complexity of the product. Moreover, the industry type, i.e. the atmosphere of firm's interaction (relative position across the supply chain) and the environment in which the relationship takes place, also plays an important role on the collaboration levels among partners. For instance, the ISO/TS 16949 standard obliges, among many things, a high level of collaboration and cost sharing between buyers and suppliers.

Firms aiming at implementing this strategy effectively have to pay close attention to several contingency factors on the organizational level and properly manage supplier involvement on product development, product industrialization and parts supplying at production stage.

# References

1. Coad, A., Cullen, J.: Inter-Organisational Cost Management: Towards an Evolutionary Perspective. Management Accounting Research 17, 342–369 (2006)
2. Laaksonen, T., Jarimo, T., Kulmala, H.: Cooperative Strategies in Customer–Supplier Relationships: The Role of Interfirm Trust. International Journal of Production Economics 120, 79–87 (2009)
3. Cooper, R., Slagmulder, R.: Interorganizational Cost Management and Relational Context. Accounting, Organizations and Society 29, 1–26 (2004)
4. Kajuter, P., Kulmala, H.: Open-book accounting in networks, Potential Achievements and Reasons for Failures. Management Accounting Research 16, 179–204 (2005)
5. Agndal, H., Nilsson, U.: Interorganizational Cost Management in the Exchange Process. Management Accounting Research 20, 85–101 (2009)
6. Bechtel, C., Jayaram, J.: Supply chain management: a strategic perspective. International Journal of Logistics Management 8, 15–34 (1997)
7. Harmsen, H., Grunert, K., Bove, K.: Company competencies as a network: the role of product development. Journal of Product Innovation Management 17, 194–207 (2000)
8. Randall, T., Morgan, R., Morton, A.: Efficient versus responsive supply chain choice: an empirical examination of influential factors. Journal of Product Innovation Management 20, 430–443 (2003)
9. Narasimhan, R., Swink, M., Viswanathan, S.: On decisions for integration implementation: an examination of complementarities between product-process technology integration and supply chain integration. Decision Sciences 41, 355–372 (2010)
10. Halldorsson, A., Kotzab, H., Mikkola, J., Skjott-Larsen, T.: Complementary theories to supply chain management. Supply Chain Management: International Journal 12, 284–296 (2007)
11. Flynn, B., Flynn, E.: An exploratory study of the nature of cumulative capabilities. Journal of Operations Management 22, 439–457 (2004)
12. Hong, P., Kwon, H., Roh, J.: Implementation of strategic green orientation in supply chain: an empirical study of manufacturing firms. European Journal of Innovation Management 12, 512–532 (2009)

# The Multidisciplinary Virtual Product Development Integrates the Influence of Die Casting Defects in the Mechanical Response

Nicola Gramegna[1,*], Iñigo Loizaga[2], Susana Berrocal[2], Franco Bonollo[3], Giulio Timelli[3], and Stefano Ferraro[3]

[1] ENGINSOFT S.p.A., Padova, Italy
n.gramegna@enginsoft.it
[2] FUNDACION CIE, Bilbao (Vizcaya), Spain
{iloizaga,sberrocal}@cieautomotive.com
[3] University of Padova - DTG, Vicenza, Italy
{bonollo,timelli,ferraro}@gest.unipd.it

**Abstract.** The performance of an Al alloy component when tested under dynamic conditions is defined on the basis of the amount of the absorbed energy during impact and the dampening rate of the striker. These tests can be complex and costly, and sometimes difficult to be realized for some specific components. An useful and "ideal" approach could be the use of numerical simulation tools for virtually testing, but this objective actually remains an ambitious approach, since it requires a deep research of the factors that determine the elasto-plastic material behavior up to fracture. Even more difficult is the characterization of the material in the case of Al alloy diecastings, where the mechanical properties strongly depend on casting defects.

By linking mechanical results with numerical simulation data of filling and solidification, a through-process model is developed to predict the defects' location and amount, thus the structural behavior of die cast components. Furthermore, with particular reference to one demonstrator component, an high pressure die cast steering housing, the innovative correlation between defects (e.g. air inclusion, shrinkage porosity etc.) and mechanical properties has been implemented in MAGMASOFT® simulation tool in order to transfer the realistic local ultimate tensile strength to LS-Dyna FEM code. The multi-objective optimization strategy has been applied to minimize the air entrapment and maximize the local mechanical properties of Al alloy. The final full integrated, and more realistic, approach permits to estimate the single effect of proper Al diecasting design, remaining defects and residual stress on the absorbed energy under impact condition.

**Keywords:** Numerical simulation, HPDC, casting defects, mechanical properties, integrated approach, process optimization.

## 1 Introduction

In the automotive sector, high-pressure die-casting (HPDC) is the preferred foundry process; it is versatile and appropriate for highly engineered components. Unfortunately,

C. Emmanouilidis, M. Taisch, D. Kiritsis (Eds.): APMS 2012, Part I, IFIP AICT 397, pp. 502–509, 2013.
© IFIP International Federation for Information Processing 2013

a limit to large diffusion of HPDC remains the final integrity of castings. The high injection rate of the metal causes turbulences, which form internal and surface defects, such as gas entrapment, and the variable thicknesses of the component itself can lead to a reduced effect of the intensification pressure on the solidification shrinkage [1-3]. Although the classification of diecasting defects is clear, an advanced study is required to understand the correlations between the type, dimension and form of defects and the mechanical properties of diecastings. The first model from this study is described elsewhere [1, 2].

In the present paper, the final quality model is described and applied to a Steering Pinion, i.e. a safety component requiring high quality standards in order to guarantee that it stays oil tight under pressure, and to assure proper fatigue resistance and ductile behavior in case of impact.

# 2   Simulation and Optimization of the Die Casting Process

The design and review of the die cast steering pinion followed the work-flow reported below and acting on a virtual level, before the final physical dynamic testing:

1. process simulation of the existing version of the pinion, and optimization of the HPDC process in order to enhance the quality of the component;
2. identification of the local mechanical properties and residual stresses, and transfer of these information to FEA code for impact analysis;
3. impact simulation using the new model, the pre-stress condition due to residual stresses, and the local mechanical properties at the end of the manufacturing process, in order to determine the most realistic amount of absorbed energy.

## 2.1   Process Simulation of the Original Version of the Casting

The first virtual analysis was performed by using the actual manufacturing parameters and the operating thermal regime of the die. This evidenced the possible causes of filling and solidification defects, with the resulting localized reduction of the mechanical properties. The CAD models, the materials, the lubrication and the movement of the die parts in the production cycle were imported in the software to simulate the thermal behavior of the die. The virtual results were compared with thermal maps acquired by IR camera.

In particular, the analysis showed that the most evident porosity in the casting is due to air/gas entrapped in the center of the area with the greatest thickness. Cross-sections made of the parts and X-ray NDT investigations identify the defect distribution and morphology. The experimental results were in accordance with numerical simulation ones (Fig. 1).

Despite a noticeable variation of thicknesses in the original casting design, the central area of the component, which undergoes the maximum stresses under impact testing, showed some minor interdendritic porosity, mainly located far from the beneficial compacting action resulting from the applied overpressure. An accurate simulation of the cooling rate and the prediction of positions and dimensions of the aforementioned defects represent the basis for working out the local mechanical properties, as further explained.

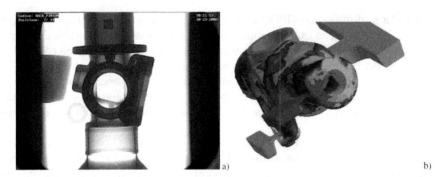

**Fig. 1.** a) X-ray image in comparison with b) defect prediction by numerical simulation

## 2.2    Optimization of the Die Casting

The initial objective of optimizing the mechanical properties of the component can be achieved by modifying the geometry of the component or by varying the diecasting system and the process parameters. Firstly, the thickness of the central cylindrical area was reduced. Furthermore, by using an automatic optimization technique, which allows an advanced research of a multi-objective problem [4, 5], the effect of a single geometric modification to the component was analyzed. The approach adopted is divided into two optimization steps:

- the first step considers the variations of the section of the two gates without any change in the shape of the existing gating and using the original process parameters (solution named ID241 at X=1500 and Y=2750 mbar);
- the second step analyzes a wide range of all possible modifications and variants in order to search out the highest possible quality of the die-casting component (solution named ID882 at X=1500 and Y=1750 mbar) while respecting the constraints imposed by the already existing die, i.e. extractors, orientation, cooling channels, etc..

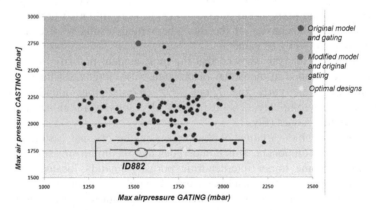

**Fig. 2.** Possible designs for steering pinion plotted as function of the critical overpressure in the casting and the maximum overpressure in the gating system

The design configurations close to the axis of origin minimize even more the aforementioned objectives, but do not respect the minimum temperature of the molten metal at the gate. Fig. 2 evidences the substantial improvement obtained both in comparison with the original version and with the introduction of the new component with a thickness reduction in the central area (Central point at X=1500 and Y=2250 mbar).

**Fig. 3.** Integration of the optimized configurations, ID882 and ID241, in the existing die

The two main objectives of the optimization process are the minimum quantity and pressure of gas entrapped in the casting, and the reduction of the gating system volume, with the simultaneous reduction or absence of turbulence in the same gating. Among the possible designs analyzed by numerical simulation, the design identified as ID882 was chosen, being the best compromise between the dimension and concentration of the residual gas bubbles in the component (measured by the critical volume of the overpressure) and the maximum pressure and dimension of these (the air overpressure) (see Fig. 2). The suggested configurations, namely ID882 and ID241, were integrated in the same die as shown in Fig. 3. The experimental investigations carried out on the castings confirmed the results expected from numerical simulation.

# 3     Determination of the Local Mechanical Properties and Residual Stresses

The effects of process parameters on material properties were experimentally evaluated by using a multicavity die, which enables to cast specimens for mechanical testing. The multicavity die was used to produce castings with different injection parameters and constant geometry model. Microstructural analysis of cross sections shows the presence of several defects, such as cold shut, segregation bands, oxide films, iron-bearing phases and air/gas bubbles entrapped during mold filling. These defects are typical of the high pressure die casting process, and all specimens contain them, but the amount and distribution vary with the process parameters used [2, 6].

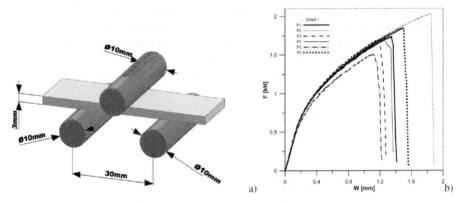

**Fig. 4.** a) Sketch of three point bend test adopted in this work; b) experimental measurements of force (F) versus displacement (W) obtained in bending tests

The bending tests were performed on specimens drawn from a plate produced by the above-described multi-cavity die and the mechanical results were directly correlated with numerical simulations without performing any determination of defect amount. The configuration for the three point bending test is schematized in Fig. 4a., according to ASTM E290-09. As observed in Fig. 4b, the process condition named P5 produced the worst mechanical properties. This is due to the highest metal velocity produced, which causes a turbulent flow and greater gas entrapment. The same variation of process parameters has been applied at virtual level by using the

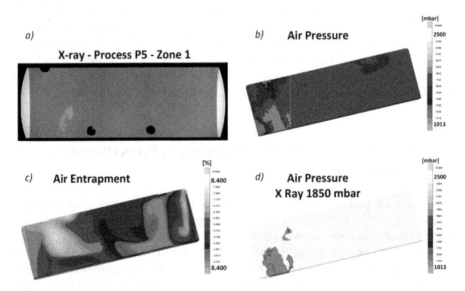

**Fig. 5.** Coherence verification of the numerical simulations of process P5 : a) X-ray images of diecast plate; b) air-pressure criteria; c) air-entrapment criteria; d) air-pressure representation with a value greater than 1850 mbar

MAGMAhpdc module in order to simulate the filling and solidification behavior of multicavity die. Fig. 5 shows air-pressure and air-entrapment images of a region of the plate diecast with P5 process parameters. The X-ray image, acquired from the same location, evidences a good agreement between numerical simulations and experimental data.

For each specimen the simulations results were correlated each other. The aim was to find an empirical relationship between them and the mechanical properties (particularly UTS). The final suggested model, with normalized coefficients, is:

$$\text{UTS} = A - B \times meanairp^b - C \times meanflowlen^c - D \times meanaircontact^d - E \times diffcoolrate^e \quad (1)$$

where UTS is Ultimate Tensile Strength [MPa]; *meanairp* is the mean value of air pressure [mbar] and it identifies the position, severity and dimension of gas entrapment; *meanflowlen* is the path length of the melt [mm] and it shows the possible cooling of the alloy and the impurities due to a less homogeneous fluid-dynamic behavior; *meanaircontact* is the time of metal front in contact with air [sec] and it indicates the degree of risk of oxide formation; *diffcoolrate* is difference between maximum and minimum value of cooling rate in the thickness [°C/s] and it identifies the possible regions of shrinkage porosity.

A "quality mapping" approach [2] was then applied to the steering pinion in order to support advanced design (Fig. 6). By means of a proper tool, this approach can elaborate results from numerical simulation (mold filling, thermal field, defect prediction criteria), with the aim of visualizing the final quality of the casting in terms of defect localization and criticality, local distribution of residual stress and mechanical properties. In comparison to the original cast component which was used as a reference, the last optimization of the shape and process parameters shows that the maximum value of ultimate tensile strength of the material is always in the range of 296-298 MPa.

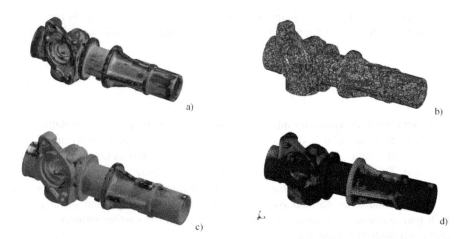

a)

b)

c)

d)

**Fig. 6.** Mechanical properties (UTS) and residual stresses transferred from a CV to a FEM program: a,b) local UTS properties prediction; c,d) residual stress distribution

# 4    The Innovative Integrated Approach

In order to appreciate the effect of the methodology of integration of process simulation and impact simulation, the results of the impact simulation, performed using original geometry and process (curve A) and assuming homogeneous mechanical properties and no residual stress, are compared in Fig. 7a with three different design approaches:

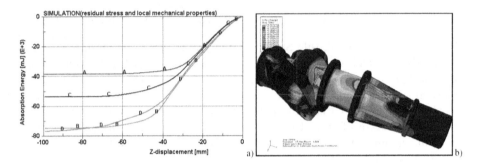

**Fig. 7.** a) Comparison between the results of different impact simulations; b) result of impact test simulation

— curve B) represents the modified model along with the optimized die casting process, without applying the integrated approach;
— curve C) represents the original model and die casting system, but considering the prediction of the localized mechanical properties and the residual stress state;
— curve D) represents the modified model and optimized die casting system, using the integrated approach.

In other terms, the similarity of curves B and D (+3% energy absorbed) is backed up by the local UTS values which are very close to the values normally used in "sound" material.

# 5    Conclusions

The present work describes an integrated approach between process simulation and impact test evaluation of a diecast component, in order to perform a virtual, but realiable, verification of the life of the component from the production stage up to the impact test. The methodology illustrated is specifically directed at the die casting field of light alloys, as it was demonstrated in the practical application on the component studied, and addresses particularly the stages of product design and development which take place in engineering and design offices, in die casting foundries and in end-users industrial companies.

The innovative aspect of the proposed method does not consist in the use of simulation software for the process or the mechanical response, both highly adopted in their fields of application. It consists in the prediction of the mechanical properties as a function of the process, in the prediction of the quality distribution in diecastings and finally in the communication between the different software applications. This makes possible to visualize the realistic mechanical behavior of the cast product and consequently allows the validation and prediction of the mechanical response of the die-cast component at in-service conditions.

**Acknowledgements.** This work was developed with the financial support of the European Project NADIA (New Automotive components Designed for and manufactured by Intelligent processing of light Alloys, NMP-2004-SME 3.4.4.5, contract n.026563-2).

# References

1. Apelian, D., Makhlouf, M.M.: High Integrity Aluminum Die Casting: Alloys, Processes and Melt Preparation. North American Die Casting Association, Des Plaines (2004)
2. Timelli, G., Bonollo, F.: Quality mapping of Aluminium alloy diecastings. Metal. Sci. Tech 26, 2–8 (2008)
3. Gariboldi, E., Bonollo, F., Parona, P.: Handbook of defects in high pressure diecastings. Associazione Italiana di Metallurgia, Milano (2010)
4. Gramegna, N., Baumgartner, P., Kokot, V.: Capabilities of new multi-objective Casting Process Optimisation tool. In: IDEAL International Conference, Lecce (2005)
5. Linares, F., Gramegna, N., Furlan, L., Zamperin, L.: iDP approach to quality assessment and improvement of a diecasting process. In: TCN CAE International Conference, Italy (2003)
6. Timelli, G., Grosselle, F., Voltazza, F., Della Corte, E.: A new reference die for mechanical properties evaluation in die-casting. In: 4rd International Conference High Tech Die Casting, paper no. 35, AIM, Milano (2008)

# Design and Simulation-Based Testing of a Prediction Market System Using SIPS for Demand Forecasting

Hajime Mizuyama

Dept. of Industrial and Systems Engineering, Aoyama Gakuin University,
Sagamihara Kanagawa 252-5258, Japan
mizuyama@ise.aoyama.ac.jp

**Abstract.** Self-adjustable interval prediction securities (SIPS) are newly proposed prediction securities that are suitable for market-based demand forecasting. The whole feasible region of the demand quantity to be estimated is divided into a fixed number of mutually exclusive and collectively exhaustive prediction intervals. Subsequently, a set of winner-take-all-type securities are issued that correspond to these intervals. Each portion of the securities wins a unitary payoff only if the actual sales volume falls in the corresponding interval. The contracts are called SIPS because the borders between the intervals are dynamically and adaptively self-adjusted to maintain the informativeness of the output forecast distribution. This paper first designs a prediction market system using SIPS equipped with a central market maker and then confirms how the system operates through agent-based simulation.

**Keywords:** Agent simulation, collective intelligence, Delphi method, demand forecasting, prediction markets.

## 1    Introduction

In addition to the historical data that are formally owned by a company, fragmentary, dispersed and informal knowledge owned by the company's employees or customers has begun to be treated as a valuable information source for forecasting demand in today's rapidly changing market [1]. Recently, it has been demonstrated that a prediction market can aggregate this dispersed knowledge in a similar, but more efficient manner than the Delphi method [2][3][4]. When a company uses a prediction market to conduct demand forecasting, it usually recruits employees or customers as participants and allows them to trade the fixed-interval prediction securities (FIPS) concerning the demand quantity to be estimated. FIPS are a set of winner-takes-all-type contracts, each of which is tied to a future event that the actual sales volume falls in a specified one among the predetermined set of prediction intervals. Because the intervals are mutually exclusive and collectively comprise the feasible region of the quantity to be estimated, the market prices of the contracts provide a subjective probability distribution of the demand quantity. Some researchers have argued that the scope between the most pessimistic and optimistic prior estimates should be divided into around eight equal-width intervals, and they should be used as the prediction intervals together with the regions lower than and higher than the scope [5].

C. Emmanouilidis, M. Taisch, D. Kiritsis (Eds.): APMS 2012, Part I, IFIP AICT 397, pp. 510–517, 2013.

The approach described above has been shown to be effective when tested in an existing company [6]. Despite its utility, however, this approach has several limitations. Most notably, it does not clearly specify the possible scope of the demand quantity a priori. Ironically, as the potential for capturing information from the prediction market grows, so too does the difficulty associated with properly setting the scope. The output forecast distribution depends on a predefined scope and if it is not appropriately set, the entire market session can be rendered meaningless. To resolve this limitation, Mizuyama and Maeda [1] introduced a new type of prediction securities called the self-adjustable interval prediction securities (SIPS). Like FIPS, SIPS are also a set of winner-take-all-type contracts assigned to prediction intervals. Unlike FIPS, however, in SIPS the borders between the intervals dynamically and adaptively self-adjust over the entire feasible region to maintain the informative quality of the output forecast distribution.

This paper first designs a prediction market system using SIPS suitable for demand forecasting, then verifies how the system operates through agent-based simulation. The remainder of the paper will be organized as follows. First, SIPS and the prediction market system using them will be described. Next, the agent-based simulation model for testing the system will be presented. Following this, simulation experiments and their results will be given. Finally, conclusions drawn from these activities will be offered.

# 2    Prediction Market System Using SIPS

## 2.1    Self-adjustable Interval Prediction Security

Suppose that ten prediction intervals, $I_1 = (-\infty, x_1]$, $I_2 = (x_1, x_2]$, ..., $I_{10} = (x_9, \infty)$, of demand quantity $x$ to be estimated are defined and their corresponding prediction securities are issued. Each unit of these securities is a contract that will pay off a unit amount of money if and only if the realized value of $x$ is actually contained in the corresponding interval. In this situation, the most pessimistic and optimistic prior estimates are $x_1$ and $x_9$ respectively, and the initial possible scope is $(x_1, x_9]$. At the beginning, intervals $I_2, I_3, ..., I_9$ have equal width ($w_0$). If the contracts were FIPS, the borders between intervals $x_1, x_2, ..., x_9$ would not be modified until the entire market session is finished.

In case of SIPS, however, the entire market session is divided into several rounds and the divide-merge operation described below is applied at the end of each round so the borders between the intervals can be appropriately updated.

**Step 1:** Find the interval $I_n$ having the highest value of $D_n$, which is the evaluation measure to be defined later. If the value of $D_n$ is greater than a predetermined threshold, go to **Step 2**. Otherwise, repeat this step after the next round.

**Step 2:** Divide the chosen interval $I_n$:

$$x_{k+1} = x_k \quad (k = 9, 8, ..., n) \tag{1}$$

$$x_n = \begin{cases} x_n - w_0 & (n = 1) \\ (x_{n-1} + x_n)/2 & (n = 2, 3, ..., 9) \\ x_{n-1} + w_0 & (n = 10) \end{cases} \tag{2}$$

**Step 3:** Merge the pair of consecutive intervals $I_m$ and $I_{m+1}$ having the least counter-effect on the evaluation measure:

$$x_k = x_{k+1} \quad (k = m, m+1, ..., 10) \tag{3}$$

Each unit of the prediction security owned by a participant assigned to an interval divided at **Step 2** is automatically exchanged for the pair of the securities corresponding to the sub-intervals that resulted from the split. Similarly, a pair of the securities tied to the intervals merged at **Step 3** is altered into a unit of the new security corresponding to the merged interval. When a participant holds an uneven number of securities to be merged, some redundant units of either one of them will remain. When this occurs, the redundant units are also exchanged for the new merged security so the prices of the other securities and the proportion of the market value of the participant's assets will not change.

The evaluation measure, $D_n$, is defined as follows: The objective of the divide-merge operation is to readjust the definition of prediction intervals so that the hidden collective forecast $f(x)$ can be accurately captured by the price density function $g(x)$, which is defined as:

$$g(x) = g_n = p_n / w_n \quad (x \in I_n) \tag{4}$$

where $p_n$ is the unitary price of the $n$th security and $w_n$ is the width of the $n$th interval (the preset finite value $w_0$ is used for $w_1$ and $w_{10}$, instead of $\infty$, for convenience). Thus, the effect of the operation can be measured by the extent to which distance between $f(x)$ and $g(x)$ is reduced by the operation. When measuring this effect for each interval, since $f(x)$ is an unknown function, a piecewise quadratic approximation constructed from $g(x)$ is used instead, as shown in Fig. 1, where:

$$\int_{x_{n-1}}^{x_n} \tilde{f}(x) \cdot dx = \int_{x_{n-1}}^{x_n} g(x) \cdot dx = w_n \cdot g_n = p_n \tag{5}$$

$$L_n = \begin{cases} 0 & (n = 1) \\ \dfrac{w_n \cdot g_{n-1} + w_{n-1} \cdot g_n}{w_{n-1} + w_n} & (1 < n < 10) \\ 2g_n & (n = 10) \end{cases} \tag{6}$$

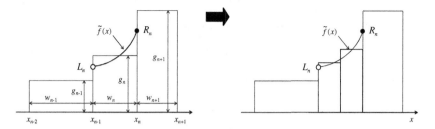

**Fig. 1.** Piecewise quadratic approximation of $f(x)$ before and after division

$$R_n = \begin{cases} 2g_n & (n=1) \\ \dfrac{w_{n+1} \cdot g_n + w_n \cdot g_{n+1}}{w_n + w_{n+1}} & (1 < n < 10) \\ 0 & (n=10) \end{cases} \tag{7}$$

According to this approximation, it is possible to estimate how the division of the $n$th interval will change the shape of $g(x)$ as shown in Fig. 1. Thus, the effect of the division can be evaluated by comparing the distance from $g(x)$ to $\tilde{f}(x)$ between the two graphs in Fig. 1. The reduction in distance resulting from the division can be calculated with a formal distance measure between the distributions, such as a Kullback-Leibler distance, L1-norm, L2-norm, and so on. For the sake of simplicity, this paper uses the L1-distance between $g(x)$ before and after the division as a surrogate measure. Thus, the evaluation measure $D_n$ of dividing the $n$th interval is defined by:

$$D_n = \left| \int_{x_{n-1}}^{\frac{x_{n-1}+x_n}{2}} \tilde{f}(x) \cdot dx - \int_{\frac{x_{n-1}+x_n}{2}}^{x_n} \tilde{f}(x) \cdot dx \right| = \left| \frac{1}{4}(R_n - L_n) \cdot w_n \right| \tag{8}$$

The effect of merging a pair of consecutive intervals can be similarly evaluated.

## 2.2    Central Market Maker for SIPS

Due to the occasional activation of the divide-merge operation, trading SIPS through simple continuous double auction among the participants will be confusing. Thus, this paper provides a computerized market system equipped with a central market maker for trading SIPS. A central market maker in a prediction market accepts any bid/ask requests from a participant as far as she/he agrees with the price offered by the market maker. Accordingly, it resolves the liquidity problem even in a thin market setting.

One of the most well-known and widely-used market-making algorithms for a prediction market is the Logarithmic Market Scoring Rule (LMSR) proposed by Hanson [7][8]. This market maker can handle FIPS. To illustrate, suppose that there are $K$ participants, and participant $k$ has $q_{kn}$ units of the security assigned to the $n$th interval. Given this, the entire security that has been sold thus far is provided by:

$$Q_n = \sum_{k=1}^{K} q_{kn} \qquad (9)$$

The LMSR defines a cost function based on this variable:

$$C(\mathbf{Q}) = b \cdot \log\left[\sum_{n=1}^{10} \exp(Q_n / b)\right] \qquad (10)$$

where $\mathbf{Q} = (Q_1, Q_2, \ldots, Q_{10})$, and determines how much to charge when a participant buys $\Delta\mathbf{q}$ units of the securities using the cost function:

$$\text{Cost} = C(\mathbf{Q} + \Delta\mathbf{q}) - C(\mathbf{Q}) \qquad (11)$$

Thus, the unitary price of the $n$th security is determined by:

$$p_n = \frac{dC(\mathbf{Q})}{dQ_n} = \frac{\exp(Q_n / b)}{\sum_{i=1}^{10} \exp(Q_i / b)} \qquad (12)$$

Unfortunately, simply applying LMSR to SIPS cannot ensure continuity of the securities' unitary prices in addition to the market value of each participant's assets before and after the divide-merge operation. Thus, to resolve this problem, an explicit prior forecast distribution $f_0(x)$ can be introduced and the cost function can be extended accordingly:

$$C(\mathbf{Q}) = b \cdot \log\left[\sum_{n=1}^{10} r_n \cdot \exp(Q_n / b)\right] \qquad (13)$$

where:

$$r_n = \int_{x_{n-1}}^{x_n} f_0(x) \cdot dx \qquad (14)$$

Then, the unitary price of the $n$th security is given by:

$$p_n = \frac{dC(\mathbf{Q})}{dQ_n} = \frac{r_n \cdot \exp(Q_n / b)}{\sum_{i=1}^{10} r_n \cdot \exp(Q_i / b)} \qquad (15)$$

Because of this extension, the division of a certain interval will not affect the respective prices of the securities corresponding to the other intervals and the sum of the prices of the divided securities is equivalent to the price of the original security prior to the division. Gao et al. [9] also extended the LMSR to the real line for interval betting. The fundamental concept of their approach was similar to ours, but our approach is specifically tailored for handling SIPS by introducing an explicit prior forecast distribution.

# 3     Agent-Based Simulation

## 3.1     Simulation Model

To test how the proposed prediction market system using SIPS operates, an agent simulation model was developed. In this model, some computerized trading agents traded SIPS with the central market maker introduced above. Each agent had its own subjective forecast distribution and evaluated its risky assets according to the logarithmic utility function and this subjective forecast distribution. For each agent's trading turn, it chose from three options: (1) buying a unit of security corresponding to a certain prediction interval, (2) selling a unit of security corresponding to a certain prediction interval, and (3) buying and selling nothing. Among these, the option that was chosen maximized the posterior subjective expected utility.

## 3.2     Simulation Experiments

Ten trading agents were modeled in the simulation experiments. They were endowed 100 P\$ at the beginning of a thirty-round market session (P\$ is the unit of the play money used in the simulation, and the unitary payoff of the security is 1 P\$). There were 100 trading turns in each round, and the turns were randomly distributed among the agents. The prior forecast distribution was set as $f_0(x) = N(150, 100)$; the value of the LMSR parameter ($b$) was set at 100; and the threshold value of the divide operation was set as 0.03.

The objective of the simulation experiments was to confirm whether the proposed prediction market system using SIPS can appropriately adjust the scope of forecast according to transaction history. Thus, all the agents were assigned the same Gaussian distribution $f(x) = N(200, 20)$ as the subjective forecast distribution, and initial scope of forecast $(x_1, x_9]$ which was set as (a) being away from the forecast (300, 400], (b) being too wide compared to the forecast (100, 600], or (c) being too narrow compared to the forecast (190, 210].

The output distributions obtained by FIPS and SIPS are illustrated in Fig. 2, 3 and 4. Simulation results confirmed that in all cases, the scope of the forecast is actually modified step-by-step when SIPS is used. After several rounds, it successfully captured the location of the given subjective forecast distribution. How many rounds it took until the scope has been properly readjusted was contingent upon on the difference between the initial scope and the given distribution.

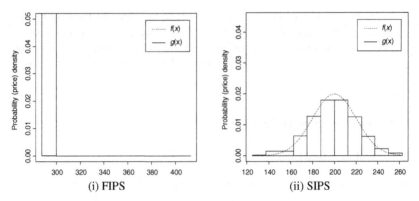

**Fig. 2.** Output distributions in case (a)

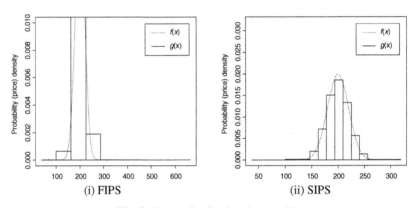

**Fig. 3.** Output distributions in case (b)

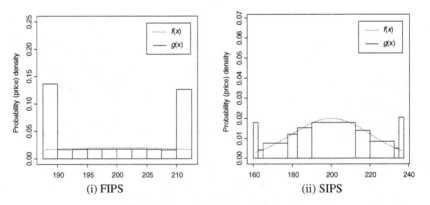

**Fig. 4.** Output distributions in case (c)

# 4    Conclusions

This paper details the design of a prediction market system using SIPS equipped with a central market maker and confirms how the system worked through agent-based simulation. As a result, this chapter has demonstrated that the proposed system can properly adjust the scope of a forecast according to transaction history. This paper assumes that the divide-merge operation splits an interval into two equal-length subintervals, but the point at which the interval should be divided can also be treated as a variable that can affect the performance of SIPS. In addition, the number of intervals need not be ten, and changing the number is relatively straightforward.

The system proposed above is now ready to be tested in a real-world setting. Promising areas in which this system could be applied include the estimation of a new product's demand quantity for a given time period after its launch, the estimation of an existing product's demand quantity during a planned sales promotion, and so on. Further, because the performance of the system also depends on the quality of its users' knowledge, it is not suitable for a product on which knowledgeable users are difficult to find. Finally, the proposed system can currently only handle the demand quantity for a single product in a single time period. To utilize the system in a more traditional setting (i.e., one that includes multiple products and periods), it should be extended to handle multiple related demand quantities in parallel. This presents an interesting challenge that should be undertaken in future research in this area.

**Acknowledgments.** This research was partially supported by the Japan Society for the Promotion of Science, Grant-in-Aid for Scientific Research (B) 20310087.

# References

1. Mizuyama, H., Maeda, Y.: A Prediction Market System Using SIPS and Generalized LMSR for Collective-Knowledge-Based Demand Forecasting. In: Proceedings of the 40th International Conference on Computers and Industrial Engineering (2010)
2. Plott, C.R.: Markets as Information Gathering Tools. Southern Economic Journal 67, 1–15 (2000)
3. Pennock, D.M., Lawrence, S., Giles, C.L., Nielsen, F.A.: The Real Power of Artificial Markets. Science 291, 987–988 (2001)
4. Wolfers, J., Zitzewitz, E.: Prediction Markets. Journal of Economic Perspectives 18, 107–126 (2004)
5. Ho, T.H., Chen, K.Y.: New Product Blockbusters: The Magic and Science of Prediction Markets. California Management Review 50, 144–158 (2007)
6. Chen, K.Y., Plott, C.R.: Information Aggregation Mechanisms: Concept, Design and Implementation for a Sales Forecasting Problem. California Institute of Technology, Social Science Working Paper #1131 (2002)
7. Hanson, R.: Combinatorial Information Market Design. Information Systems Frontiers 5, 107–119 (2003)
8. Hanson, R.: Logarithmic Market Scoring Rules for Modular Combinatorial Information Aggregation. Journal of Prediction Markets 1, 3–15 (2007)
9. Gao, X., Chen, Y., Pennock, D.M.: Betting on the Real Line. In: Leonardi, S. (ed.) WINE 2009. LNCS, vol. 5929, pp. 553–560. Springer, Heidelberg (2009)

# Multi-objective Genetic Algorithm for Real-World Mobile Robot Scheduling Problem

Quang-Vinh Dang, Izabela Nielsen, and Kenn Steger-Jensen

Department of Mechanical and Manufacturing Engineering, Aalborg University,
Fibigerstræde 16, 9220 Aalborg, Denmark
{vinhise,izabela,kenn}@m-tech.aau.dk

**Abstract.** This paper deals with the problem of scheduling feeding tasks of a single mobile robot which has capability of supplying parts to feeders on production lines. The performance criterion is to minimize the total traveling time of the robot and the total tardiness of the feeding tasks being scheduled, simultaneously. In operation, the feeders have to be replenished a number of times so as to maintain the manufacture of products during a planning horizon. A method based on predefined characteristics of the feeders is presented to generate dynamic time windows of the feeding tasks which are dependent on starting times of previous replenishment. A heuristic based on genetic algorithm which could be used to produce schedules in online production mode is proposed to quickly obtain efficient solutions. Several numerical examples are conducted to demonstrate results of the proposed approach.

**Keywords:** Multi-objective, Scheduling, Mobile Robot, Genetic Algorithm.

## 1 Introduction

The automation technology in combination with advances in production management has dramatically changed the equipment used by manufacturing companies as well as the issues in planning and control. With these changes, highly automated and unmanned production systems have become more popular in several industrial areas, e.g., automotive, robot, and pump manufacturing [3]. An automatic production system consists of intelligent and flexible machines and mobile robots grouped into cells in such a way that entire production of each product can be performed within one of the cells. With embedded batteries and manipulation arms, mobile robots are capable of performing various tasks such as transporting and feeding materials, tending machines, pre-assembling, or inspecting quality at different workstations. They have been thus employed in not only small companies which focus on exact applications and a small range of products, but also large companies which can diversify applications in a longer term and larger range. Within the scope of this study, a given problem is particularly considered for a single mobile robot which will automate part-feeding tasks by not only transporting but also collecting containers of parts and emptying them into the feeders needed. However, to utilize mobile robots in an efficient manner requires the ability to properly schedule feeding tasks. Hence, it is

C. Emmanouilidis, M. Taisch, D. Kiritsis (Eds.): APMS 2012, Part I, IFIP AICT 397, pp. 518–525, 2013.

important to plan in which sequence mobile robots process feeding operations so that they could effectively work while satisfying a number of practical constraints.

The problem of scheduling part-feeding tasks of the mobile robot has been modeled in some respects comparable to the Asymmetric Traveling Salesman Problem (ATSP) which belongs to the class of NP-hard combinatorial optimization problems [7]. Among heuristic approaches, Genetic Algorithm (GA) has been widely used in the research areas of TSP, ATSP, or robot task-sequencing problems. Liu and Zheng [10], Moon et al. [12], and Snyder and Daskin [13] discussed about using GAs to solve TSP, while Choi et al. [2] and Xing et al. [14] proposed GAs to deal with ATSP. Zacharia and Aspragathos [15] introduced a method based on GA and an innovative encoding to determine the optimal sequence of manipulator's task points which is considered an extension to the TSP. Beside genetic algorithms, Bocewiz [1] presented the knowledge-based and constraint programming-driven methodology in planning and scheduling of multi-robot in a multi-product job shop taking into account imprecise activity specifications and resource sharing. Hurink and Knust [9] proposed a tabu search algorithm for scheduling a single robot in a job-shop environment considering time windows and additionally generalized precedence constraints. Maimon et al. [11] also presented a neural network approach with successful implementation for the robot task-sequencing problem.

Although there are many related research, the problem of scheduling a single mobile robot with dynamic time windows and restricted capacity where multiple routes have to be carried out has surprisingly received little attention in the literature despite its important applications in practice, e.g. part-feeding task. Such a task must be executed a number of times within time windows which are dependent on starting times of the previous executions of that task, hence, the term, dynamic time windows. The objectives of minimizing the total traveling time of the robot and the total tardiness of the tasks are taken into account to support the global objective of maximizing system throughput. The existing approaches are not well suited and cannot be directly used to solve the problem. Thus, in this paper, a heuristic based on GA, a possibly promising approach to the class of multi-objective optimization, is developed to find efficient solutions for the problem. The advantageous feature of GA is the multiple directional and global search by maintaining a population of potential solutions from generation to generation. Such population-to-population approach is useful to explore all non-dominated solutions of the problem [6].

The remainder of this paper is organized as follows: in the next section, problem statement is described while a genetic algorithm-based heuristic is presented in Section 3. Numerical examples are conducted to demonstrate results of the proposed approach in Section 4. Finally, conclusions are drawn in Section 5.

## 2    Problem Statement

The work is developed for a cell which produces parts or components for the pump manufacturing industry at a factory in Denmark. The essential elements considered in the manufacturing cell consist of an autonomous mobile robot with limitation on carrying capacity, a central warehouse designed to store small load carriers (SLCs), and multiple feeders designed to automatically feed parts to machines of production lines. Besides, every feeder has three main characteristics including maximum level, minimum level, and part-feeding rate to machine. In operation, the robot will retrieve and carry one or several SLCs containing parts from the warehouse, move to feeder locations, empty all parts inside SLCs, then return to the warehouse to unload empty SLCs and load filled ones. To maintain the manufacture of a quantity of products during a given planning horizon, the feeders (tasks) have to be replenished a number of times, the robot consequently has a set of subtasks of tasks to be carried out within time windows. Such a time window of a subtask of a task could be only determined after starting time of the previous subtask of that task. Fig. 1 below shows a layout of the described manufacturing cell.

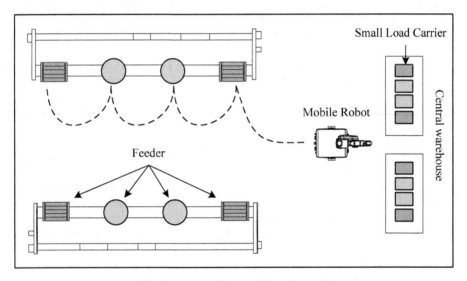

**Fig. 1.** Layout of the manufacturing cell

To enable the construction of a feeding schedule for the mobile robot, assumptions are considered as follows:

- The robot can carry one or several SLC(s) at a time.
- All tasks are periodic, independent, and assigned to the same robot.
- Working time, traveling time between any pairs of locations of the robot, and part-feeding rate to machine of a feeder are known.
- All feeders of machines must be fed up to maximum levels and the robot starts from the ware house at the initial stage.

In order to accomplish all the movements with a smallest consumed mount of battery energy, the total traveling time of the robot is an important objective to be considered. Apart from that, another performance measure is the amount of time a feeder has been waiting to be replenished by the robot. Alternatively, due time of a time window of a feeding task could be considered soft constraint, i.e. schedules that do not meet this constraint are taken into account. In addition, making decisions on which way the robot should provide parts to feeders is a part of real-time operations of production planners. Moreover, concerning the problem belong to NP-hard class, computation time exponentially grows with the size of the problem (e.g. larger number of feeders). It is therefore necessary to develop a computationally effective algorithm, namely GA-based heuristic, which determines in which sequence the feeders should be supplied so as to minimize the total traveling time of the robot and the total tardiness of feeding tasks while satisfying a number of practical constraints.

# 3    Genetic Algorithm-Based Heuristic

In this section, genetic algorithm, a random search method taking over the principle of biological evolution [8], is applied to develop a heuristic which is allowed to convert the aforementioned problem to the way that efficient solutions could be found. The GA-based heuristic shown in Fig. 2 comprises of the following components: genetic representation and initialization; constraint handling and fitness assignment; genetic operators including selection, crossover, and mutation; termination criteria.

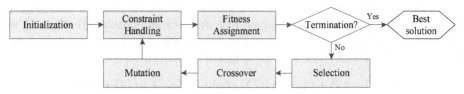

**Fig. 2.** Flow chart of GA-based heuristic

## 3.1    Genetic Representation and Initialization

For the problem under consideration, a solution can be represented by a chromosome of non-negative integers $(0, i, j, ..., i, ..., k)$ which is an ordering of part-feeding tasks of the robot where $i, j, k$: feeder index; $i, j, k = 1 \div n$; $n$: number of feeders. The original length of a chromosome is equal to the total number of subtasks of tasks added the first subtask of task at the central warehouse $(1 + \sum n_i$; $n_i$: number of subtasks of task $i$).

For the initial generation, genes on a chromosome are randomly filled with tasks at feeders. The frequency of such a task is the number of subtasks of that task, in other words, number of times that tasks has to be executed.

## 3.2    Constraint Handling and Fitness Assignment

After initialization or crossover and mutation operations, chromosomes are handled to be valid and then assigned fitness values. A valid chromosome should satisfy two constraints of limitation on carrying capacity $Q_m$ of the robot and time windows of subtasks of part-feeding tasks. For the first type of constraints, to guarantee the robot not to serve more number of feeders than number of SLCs carried in one route, the subtasks of task at the warehouse represented by zeroes are inserted into a chromosome after every $Q_m$ genes starting from the first gene. For instances, if the limitation on carrying capacity of the robot is two SLCs of parts, the chromosome should be restructured to be $(0, i, j, 0, ... , 0, k, l, 0, ... , 0)$.

The second type of constraints requires a subtask of a task to be started after release time and completed by the due time of that subtask, if possible. As mentioned, due time constraints are considered soft constraints. They thus could be modeled as an objective of the total tardiness of part-feeding tasks. The release time and due time could be determined as shown in Equation (1) and (2) below.

$$r_{ik+1} = s_{ik} + (u_i - v_i) \times c_i, i = 1 \div n, k = 1 \div n_i \tag{1}$$

$$d_{ik} = r_{ik} + (v_i \times c_i), i = 1 \div n, k = 1 \div n_i \tag{2}$$

where    $r_{ik}, d_{ik}, s_{ik}$: release time, due time, and starting time of subtask $k$ of task $i$
$u_i, v_i, c_i$: maximum level, minimum level of parts of feeder $i$, and part-feeding rate to machine of feeder $i$

After constraint handling procedure, the objectives of the total traveling time of the robot and the total tardiness of part-feeding tasks are calculated one after another for every chromosome in the population. A weighted-sum fitness function $F$ is then used to assign a fitness value to each chromosome as shown in Equation (3) where $t_{ij}$ is traveling time of the robot from one location to another, $w_i$ is working time of the robot per SLC at feeder $i$, and $\alpha$ is the weighted coefficient.

$$F = \alpha \times \left( \sum_{i,j} t_{ij} \right) + (1 - \alpha) \times \left( \sum_{i,k} (\max \{0, (s_{ik} + w_i/2) - d_{ik}\}) \right) \tag{3}$$

## 3.3    Genetic Operators

Selection, crossover, and mutation are three main genetic operators. For selection, various evolutionary methods could be applied in this problem. $(\mu + \lambda)$ selection is used to choose chromosomes for reproduction. Such selection mechanism guarantees that the best solutions up to now are always in the parent generation [4-5].

Crossover operator generates offspring by combining the information contained the parent chromosomes so that the offspring inherits good features from their parents. The Roulette-wheel selection is used to select the parent chromosomes based on their weighted-sum fitness values. Order crossover (OX) [6] operated with probability $P_c$ will be employed to generate an offspring as follows. Genes having zero values are removed before two cut points are randomly chosen on the parent chromosomes. A string between these cut points in one of the parent chromosomes is first copied to the offspring, the remaining positions are then filled according to the sequence of genes in the other parent starting after the second cut point. When an offspring is produced, it undergoes insertion mutation [6] with probability $P_m$ which selects a gene at random and inserts it in a random position.

## 3.4    Termination Criteria

Termination criteria are employed to determine when the GA-based heuristic should be stopped. Note that making decisions on which sequences the robot should serve feeders is a part of real-time operations of production planners. Therefore, on the one hand if the best solutions over generations do not converge to a value, the maximum generation $G_m$ would be used to stop the run. On the other hand, if the best solution does not improve over $G_c$ consecutive generations, it would not be valuable to continue searching.

## 4    Numerical Examples

The performance of the GA-based heuristic will be tested on several problem instances in this section. Three problems, which are as similar to the real-world case as they can be, are generated with difference number of feeders (namely 3, 5, and 10 feeders), and other system parameters such as limitation on carrying capacity, working time, traveling time of the mobile robot, planning horizon, and characteristics of feeders. The robot is designed to carry up to 3 SLCs at a time to perform part-feeding tasks during a given planning horizon of one hour (corresponding to an eighth of a full production shift). The maximum and minimum levels of parts of feeders are respectively distributed within the ranges of [300, 2000] and [100, 1000] while part-feeding rates in seconds are in-between the interval [1.5, 4.5]. The working times of the robots in seconds at feeders and the warehouse per SLC are respectively distributed within the range of [40, 60] and [25, 40] while the traveling times of the robot in seconds are in-between the interval [20, 60]. Note that the cost matrix of the generated traveling times should satisfy the triangle inequality.

For GA parameters, the population size, $P_c$, $P_m$, $G_m$, and $G_c$ are set to be 100, 0.6, 0.2, 500, and 100, respectively. The weighted-sum fitness function $F$ (Equation 3) will be calculated using one of three different values of the weight coefficient $\alpha$, namely, 0.2, 0.5, and 0.8. The proposed heuristic has been coded in VB.NET, and all the problem instances run on a PC having an Intel® Core i5 2.67 GHz processor and 4 GB RAM. The results for three randomly generated problems in combination with three values of the weighted coefficient $\alpha$ are presented in Table 1 below.

**Table 1.** The best solutions of three generated problems

| Problem | No. of feeder | No. of subtasks of tasks | Weighted coefficient ($\alpha$) | Total traveling time of robot (second) | Total tardiness of tasks (second) | Computation time (second) |
|---|---|---|---|---|---|---|
| 1 | 3 | 11 | 0.2 | 432 | 0 | 0,49 |
| | | | 0.5 | 432 | 0 | 0,63 |
| | | | 0.8 | 428 | 6 | 0,41 |
| 2 | 5 | 24 | 0.2 | 706 | 0 | 1,00 |
| | | | 0.5 | 690 | 4 | 1,12 |
| | | | 0.8 | 682 | 15 | 1,10 |
| 3 | 10 | 42 | 0.2 | 1564 | 0 | 2,52 |
| | | | 0.5 | 1542 | 22 | 2,70 |
| | | | 0.8 | 1528 | 55 | 2,40 |

The total traveling time of the robot, total tardiness of tasks, and computation time shown in Table 1 are the average of 10 runs. It can be observed that as the weighted coefficient $\alpha$ increases, two objectives of each problem instance have opposite trends where the total traveling time of the robot decreases and the total tardiness of tasks increases. In other words, as saving battery energy allowing the robot to be utilized in a longer duration is more important, the robot has a tendency to travel less and vice versa. Similar explanation is also applicable to the total tardiness of part-feeding tasks. Such kinds of solutions in Table 1 are non-dominated solutions for which no improvement in any objective function is possible without sacrificing the other objective function. It also shows that when the size of the problems grows, the computation time of the GA-based heuristic becomes longer, but it is still acceptable (i.e., the largest problem size with 10 feeders and the coefficient $\alpha$ of 0.5 requires 2.7 seconds in average to find the efficient solution). These results provide evidence to prove that the GA-based heuristics could be used to produce efficient schedules within reasonable time in online production mode.

The above solutions are initial schedules for the robot. These schedules serve as input to a Mission Planner and Control (MPC) program which is accessed by using XML-based TCP/IP communication to interact with the robot, Manufacturing Execution System (MES), and the module of GA-based heuristic. In practice, there might be some errors in manufacturing such as machine breakdown, or changes in manufacturing conditions such as characteristics of feeders (e.g. minimum levels of parts), or carrying capacity of the robot. These events will be reported by the MES so that the MPC program can update current states of the shop floor and then call the heuristic module to reschedule part-feeding tasks of the robot. By relaxing the last assumption mentioned in Section 2, the proposed heuristic in turn will use the current states as new input, re-optimize to get alternative schedules, and send these schedules back to the MPC program.

## 5    Conclusions

In this paper, a problem of scheduling a single mobile robot to carry out part-feeding tasks of production lines is studied. To maintain the manufacture of products, it is important for planners to determine feeding sequences which minimize the total traveling time of the robot and the total tardiness of the feeding tasks while taking into account a number of practical constraints. The main novelty of this research lies in the consideration of dynamic time windows and limitation on carrying capacity where multiple routes have to be performed by the single mobile robot. A genetic algorithm-based heuristic was proposed to find efficient solutions for the problem. The results in the numerical examples showed that the proposed heuristic is fast enough to be used to generate efficient schedules compromising the objectives in online production mode. The heuristic may be also used to produce alternative schedules in rescheduling scenarios when there might be some errors or changes in manufacturing conditions. Moreover, the heuristic could be considered to deal with more performance criteria according to requirements of planners, and by investigating different scenarios with various weighted coefficients of those criteria, it can specify which schemes are more beneficial for the manufacturing. For further research, a general model of scheduling multiple mobile robots should be considered together with rescheduling mechanisms to deal with real-time disturbances.

**Acknowledgments.** This work has partly been supported by the European Commission under grant agreement number FP7-260026-TAPAS.

# References

1. Bocewicz, G., Bach, I., Wójcik, R.: Production Flow Prototyping subject to Imprecise Activity Specification. Kybernetes 38, 1298–1316 (2009)
2. Choi, I.C., Kim, S.I., Kim, H.S.: A Genetic Algorithm with a Mixed Region Search for the Asymmetric Traveling Salesman Problem. Comput. Oper. Res. 30, 773–786 (2003)
3. Crama, Y., Kats, V., van de Klundert, J., Levner, E.: Cyclic Scheduling in Robotic Flowshops. Ann. Oper. Res. 96, 97–124 (2000)
4. Dang, Q.-V., Nielsen, I.E., Bocewicz, G.: A Genetic Algorithm-Based Heuristic for Part-Feeding Mobile Robot Scheduling Problem. In: Rodríguez, J.M.C., Pérez, J.B., Golinska, P., Giroux, S., Corchuelo, R. (eds.) Trends in PAAMS. AISC, vol. 157, pp. 85–92. Springer, Heidelberg (2012)
5. Dang, Q.V., Nielsen, I., Steger-Jensen, K., Madsen, O.: Scheduling a Single Mobile Robot for Part-feeding Tasks of Production Lines. In: J. Intell. Manuf. (2012) (accepted)
6. Gen, M., Lin, L.: Network Models and Optimization. Springer, London (2008)
7. Germs, R., Goldengorin, B., Turkensteen, M.: Lower Tolerance-Based Branch and Bound Algorithms for the ATSP. Comput. Oper. Res. 39, 291–298 (2012)
8. Goldberg, D.E.: Genetic Algorithms in Search, Optimization, and Machine Learning. Addison-Wesley, New York (1989)
9. Hurink, J., Knust, S.: A TabuSearch Algorithm for Scheduling a Single Robot in a Job-shop Environment. Discrete Appl. Math. 119, 181–203 (2002)
10. Liu, F., Zeng, G.: Study of Genetic Algorithm with Reinforcement Learning to Solve the TSP. Expert Syst. Appl. 36, 6995–7001 (2009)
11. Maimon, O., Braha, D., Seth, V.: A Neural Network Approach for a Robot Task Sequencing Problem. Artif. Intell. Eng. 14, 175–189 (2000)
12. Moon, C., Kim, J., Choi, G., Seo, Y.: An Efficient Genetic Algorithm for the Traveling Salesman Problem with Precedence Constraints. Eur. J. Oper. Res. 140, 606–617 (2002)
13. Snyder, L.V., Daskin, M.S.: A Random-Key Genetic Algorithm for the Generalized Traveling Salesman Problem. Eur. J. Oper. Res. 174, 38–53 (2006)
14. Xing, L.N., Chen, Y.W., Yang, K.W., Hou, F., et al.: A Hybrid Approach Combining an Improved Genetic Algorithm and Optimization Strategies for the Asymmetric Traveling Salesman Problem. Eng. Appl. Artif. Intell. 21, 1370–1380 (2008)
15. Zacharia, P.T., Aspragathos, N.A.: Optimal Robot Task Scheduling Based on Genetic Algorithms. Robot Comput. Integrated Manuf. 21, 67–79 (2005)

# Multi-camera 3D Object Reconstruction for Industrial Automation

Malamati Bitzidou, Dimitrios Chrysostomou, and Antonios Gasteratos

Laboratory of Robotics and Automation,
Department of Production and Management Engineering,
Democritus University of Thrace,
PME Building, Vasilissis Sophias 12, GR-671 00 Xanthi, Greece
{malabitz,dchrisos,agaster}@pme.duth.gr

**Abstract.** In this paper, a method to automate industrial manufacturing processes using an intelligent multi-camera system to assist a robotic arm on a production line is presented. The examined assembly procedure employs a volumetric method for the initial estimation of object's properties and an octree decomposition process to generate the path plans for the robotic arm. Initially, the object is captured by four cameras and its volumetric representation is produced. Thereafter, a quality check with its respective CAD model is performed and the final details of the 3D model are refined. An octree decomposition technique is utilized afterwards to facilitate the automatic generation of the assembly path plans and translate them to a sequence of movements for the robotic arm. The algorithm is fast, computationally simple and produces an assembly sequence that can be translated to any major robotic programming language. The proposed algorithm is assessed and preliminary experimental results are discussed.

**Keywords:** object assembly, multi-camera system, octree decomposition, 3D reconstruction, industrial automation.

## 1 Introduction

The use of traditional manufacturing machinery such as robotic systems as a way of rapid manufacturing has attracted growing interest in recent years. Intelligent automation is one of the outcomes of this interest and its major impact enables a significant reduction in production time and cost, machining work and product quality. One of the manufacturing processes, in which intelligent automation is applied, is assembly, which constitutes an important stage in product development and accounts for a large proportion of the manufacturing costs. However, assembly still remains one of the least understood manufacturing processes [1]. In this paper an object assembly sequence is planned that incorporates the production of its volumetric model by a multi-camera system, its three-dimensional representation with octrees and its construction implemented by a robot arm of 5 degrees-of-freedom and a gripper. The final goal is to plan a robot arm path consisting of predetermined motions for the assembly of everyday objects.

C. Emmanouilidis, M. Taisch, D. Kiritsis (Eds.): APMS 2012, Part I, IFIP AICT 397, pp. 526–533, 2013.

The rest of this paper is organized as follows. Section 2 provides a review of the related works regarding multi-camera vision systems, automatic assembly planning processes and 3D object representation methods. In section 3 the overview of our system is described and the details about each one of the steps are discussed. Finally, the paper concludes in section 4 where the final remarks about the performance of the algorithm are given along with discussion for future research endeavors.

## 2   Related Work

Technological advances in sensor design, communication, and computing are stimulating the development of new applications that will transform traditional visual systems into pervasive intelligent camera networks. Applications enabled by multi-camera networks are very common in industry. [2]. Systems utilizing multiple visual sensors are required in many manufacturing applications. Over the last few years the state of the art concerning multi-view stereo is improving rapidly. The goal of multi-view stereo is to reconstruct a complete three-dimensional object model from a collection of images taken from known camera viewpoints. A number of high-quality multi-view stereo algorithms have been developed, compared and evaluated [3]. In order to achieve multi-view stereo, systems consists of many visual sensors are usually needed. The uses of multi-camera systems in a variety of tasks premise the determination of optimal sensors configurations. Each system has its own set of requirements, but there is a generic formulation that can be customized to find optimum sensor configurations for all the systems [4].

Sensor planning has been researched quite extensively and several approaches have been developed in the last decades, so there are many different variations depending on the application. A popular set of methods, called next-view planning, attempt to built a model of the scene incrementally by successively sensing the unknown world from effective sensor configurations using the information acquired about the world up to this point [5], [6], [7], [8], [9], [10]. A related set of methods [11] have focused on finding the ideal sensor positions for capturing a static scene from desirable viewpoints assuming that some geometric information about the scene is available. Bordering on the field of graphics, the main contribution of such methods is to develop efficient methods for determining the view of the scene from different viewpoints. Methods that are directly related to ours are those that assume that complete geometric information is available and determine the location of static cameras so as to obtain the best views of an object. This problem was originally posed in the computational geometry literature as the art-gallery problem [12]. The traditional formulation of such problem assumes that two points are called visible if the straight line segment between them lies entirely inside the polygon. Even with such simple definition of visibility, the problem is NP-complete.

The continuous demand for reduced costs but increasing speed and quality in product manufacturing has led to the requirement for the rapid prototyping of solid models prior full-scale production. This is the reason why automatic assembly planning is essential. The series of technical issues addressed in the process of automated assembly planning are the assembly sequence representation at first, the generation and evaluation provided by the assembly assumptions, the calculation of the accuracy and efficiency of the planning process, the integration of the CAD program and finally the motion planning [13]. Numerous algorithms have been exploited for the rapid and effective production of feasible assembly tasks. The vast majority of assembly sequence generators, namely ASG, convert the problem of employing assembly sequences into disassembly ones. During the testing of their feasibility several issues must be considered such as geometrical and mechanical feasibility, manipulability, stability, visibility and used material.

An essential preprocess step of the assembly planning procedure is the three-dimensional representation of the object. The state of the art has changed dramatically over the last years, warranting a new overview in the field. Multiple approaches for assembly, utilize 3D geometry on a regularly sampled three-dimensional grid (volume), either as a discrete occupancy function [14] or as a function encoding distance to the closest surface [15]. The popularity of three-dimensional grids is increasing due to their simplicity and their ability to estimate various kinds of surfaces. A surface can be represented as a set of connected planar facets using polygon meshes, whilst in case of multiple views one can represent the examined scene as a set of depth maps. Among the multitude of existing methods, one can distinguish the use of octree approximation as an approach of compact visualization of computer-aided design models, which was recently reported [16].

## 3    System Overview

The proposed method lies within the category of intelligent assembly path planning methods. The main concept of the algorithm is to produce the volumetric model of the object, represent it using octrees and then create an assembly sequence of predetermined motions. The block diagram of the proposed algorithm is shown in Fig. 1 and the details for every step are given below.

### 3.1    Image Acquisition and Camera Calibration

The system's cameras topology is an application depended task and, therefore, it is based on the desired coverage of the working space taking into account the best combination of number of visual sensors and available bandwidth. In order to provide visual data for accurate 3D object assembly, a four-camera system was assembled inside our lab. The visual sensors are thus, mounted on the four corners of a cube processing $90°$ rotation along their optical axis, $60°$ rotation on the $x$ axis and $150cm$ translation between them. Fig. 2 depicts the system's architecture and shows the position of the cameras inside the cubical structure. The first step of the whole process comprises an initialization phase where the calibration of the multi camera system occurs. The calibration procedure is fast,

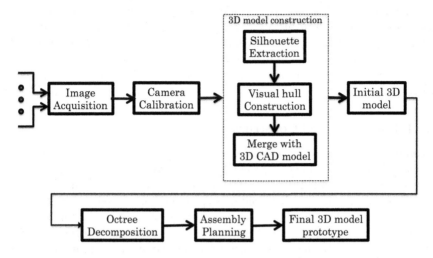

**Fig. 1.** Block diagram of the proposed method

straightforward and results the registration of the cameras to the room coordinate system, employing a classic method [17] realized within the Camera Calibration Toolbox for Matlab [18]. The multi-camera rig acquires static snapshots of the object in a relatively controlled environment. The cameras viewpoints are carefully chosen in a way that will let us acquire the maximum possible shape information from a set of objects images.

**Hardware Configuration.** The proposed vision sensorial framework consists of a four *Flea2* cameras, manufactured by Point Grey Research Inc [19] and are able to capture images of up to $1288 \times 964$ pixels resolution transmitted at a frame rate of 30Hz. They are manufactured using the industrial form factor of similar

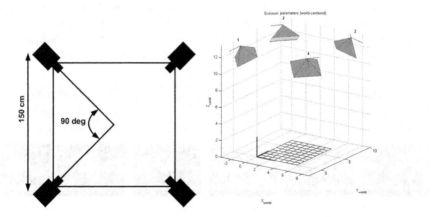

**Fig. 2.** The multi-camera system's architecture

analog cameras and their size is exceptionally small. All cameras are equipped with $6mm$ lenses, which is equivalent to $34.25mm$ in the $35mm$ format, resulting in a working $61.36°$ angular field of view. All four cameras are connected through IEEE 1394b interface to a dedicated master PC, whilst the data transmission is established with the IEEE 1394b transfer protocol using two Point Grey Research PCI Express cards.

## 3.2     Initial 3D Model Construction

Following the camera calibration and image acquisition steps, the obtained image set is then processed in order to produce the first estimation of the 3D model of our examined object. Initially, each image is projected into an array of pixels and an accurate image thresholding approach is employed to result the first black-and-white silhouette of each source photograph as shown in Fig. 3. Having the introductory 2D approximation of the shape of the model consisted of pixels, a background subtraction algorithm isolates the object from its background information. Thereafter, the maximal shape that yields the same silhouettes as the actual object for all views, the so called Visual Hull [20] of the object, is approximated. The Visual Hull is the maximum possible shape that can be retrieved by the object's views and is consistent with its respective silhouettes as seen from any viewpoint in a given region. Once the visual hull of the test object is created it is then merged with its respective 3D CAD model to further refine any discrepancies appeared in the surface of the visual hull. The outcome of this algorithmic step is an initial approximation of the 3D model of the object that will be used as an input for the OcBlox system, analyzed in the next section.

## 3.3     Octree Decomposition

In order to achieve the assembly of the model, a system heavily inspired by the OcBlox one, introduced by [16] is used. It also consists of the octree decomposition technique, the assembly planning and an assembly cell. The proposed system applies octree decomposition to the 3D visual model in order to convert it into approximate octree models. The octree decomposition technique results to hierarchical structure, that subdivides a volume into cubes of varying sizes,

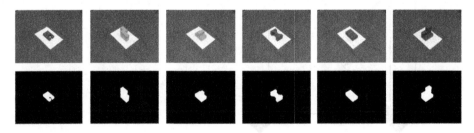

**Fig. 3.** The everyday objects used as an input for the assembly process and their respective black-and-white silhouettes

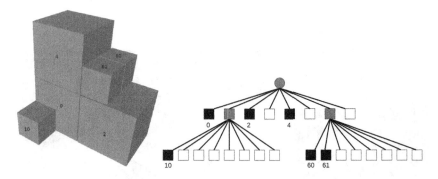

**Fig. 4.** Example of an octree representation

named octants. Among the several cubes a hierarchical tree relationship holds, whereat, each branch is associated to the relative position of the octant in the respective parent node. Octants are distinguished as full, empty or boundary, depending on their relative location in the 3D CAD model: inside, outside or partially inside, respectively. For maximum approximation, full and boundary octants are included in the rough model. The final octree is checked against different criteria, such as the maximum level of decomposition or the minimum size of octant. By concluding the decomposition process, the list of octants form an approximate representation of a 3D CAD model. In this system, octant sizes are limited to particular sizes according to the capability of the manufacturing process. An example of such an octree representation is depicted in Fig. 4.

### 3.4   Assembly Planning

An assembly cell that is used to build cube-based models is developed as shown in Fig. 5 comprising:

1. The SCORBOT-ER 9 Pro (5(a)) industrial robot arm with great accuracy of nominal repeatability of $\pm 0.05 mm$, maximum operation speed: base rotation $140°/sec$, shoulder rotation $123°/sec$, elbow rotation $140°/sec$, wrist pitch $166°/sec$, wrist roll $300°/sec$ and a USB Controller-B with 16 I/O that can be read and generated via an Advanced Control Language (ACL).
2. A workspace where the configuration of the assembly cell is maintained and the cubes that constitute the prototype models are stored. (5(b)).
3. Raw material. Solid cubes of 10, 20 and 40 mm, made of wood with texture additions are used.
4. A camera with frame rate of 25 fps and resolution of 640x480 pixels is also used to recognize each wooden cube's coordinates and project them to the robot arm's coordinate system.

The 3D data extracted from the previous step are the input for the assembly planning system. Thereafter, an estimation of the quantity and dimensions of the wooden cubes needed to assemble the real object is calculated. Their respective

(a) The SCORBOT-ER 9 Pro

(b) A view of the assembly workspace

**Fig. 5.** The robot arm and the workspace used for the assembly cell

coordinates for their correct positioning inside the scene are then computed as well. The outcome of this process is the assembly instructions for the construction of the real prototype from the robotic arm.

## 4    Conclusion

In this paper, a method that performs object assembly using an intelligent vision network is presented. The proposed procedure is based on a volumetric approach for the objects reconstruction resulting to an initial 3D model. After the merging of this 3D model with its 3D CAD design, it can be represented using octree decomposition technique. The final 3D model prototype is constructed by a block of solid cubes positioned inside the assembly cell by the robotic arm. An assembly planning process that generates a sequence of predetermined motions specifies the exact positions of the cubes. The main contribution of the algorithm is the ability to reconstruct an ordinary object using only a system of four cameras. The algorithm is fast, computationally simple and the assembly sequence that is produced can be translated to any robotic programming language. Besides, the computational burden is directly linked to the complexity of objects geometry. The proposed technique is applicable to industrial smart manufacturing systems, to rapid prototyping cells and to standard robotic and machine vision applications.

## References

1. Medellín, H., Corney, J., Ritchie, J., Lim, T.: Automatic generation of robot and manual assembly plans using octrees. Assembly Automation 30(2), 173–183 (2010)
2. Aghajan, H.K., Cavallaro, A.: Multi-camera networks: principles and applications. Academic Press (May 2009)

3. Seitz, S., Curless, B., Diebel, J., Scharstein, D., Szeliski, R.: A comparison and evaluation of multi-view stereo reconstruction algorithms. In: 2006 IEEE Computer Society Conference on Computer Vision and Pattern Recognition, vol. 1, pp. 519–528. IEEE (2006)
4. Mittal, A.: Generalized multi-sensor planning. In: Leonardis, A., Bischof, H., Pinz, A. (eds.) ECCV 2006, Part I. LNCS, vol. 3951, pp. 522–535. Springer, Heidelberg (2006)
5. Hager, G., Mintz, M.: Computational methods for task-directed sensor data fusion and sensor planning. The International Journal of Robotics Research 10(4), 285–313 (1991)
6. Cameron, A., Durrant-Whyte, H.: A bayesian approach to optimal sensor placement. The International Journal of Robotics Research 9(5), 70–88 (1990)
7. Kutulakos, K., Dyer, C.: Recovering shape by purposive viewpoint adjustment. International Journal of Computer Vision 12(2), 113–136 (1994)
8. Maver, J., Bajcsy, R.: Occlusions as a guide for planning the next view. IEEE Transactions on Pattern Analysis and Machine Intelligence 15(5), 417–433 (1993)
9. Ye, Y., Tsotsos, J.: Sensor planning for 3d object search. Computer Vision and Image Understanding 73(2), 145–168 (1999)
10. Miura, J., Ikeuchi, K.: Task-oriented generation of visual sensing strategies. In: Proceedings of the Fifth International Conference on Computer Vision, pp. 1106–1113. IEEE (1995)
11. Sing, B., Seitz, S., Sloan, P.P.: Visual tunnel analysis for visibility prediction and camera planning. In: Proceedings of the IEEE Conference on Computer Vision and Pattern Recognition, vol. 2, pp. 195–202 (2000)
12. O'Rourke, J.: Art gallery theorems and algorithms, vol. 57. Oxford University Press, Oxford (1987)
13. de Mello, L., Lee, S.: Computer-aided mechanical assembly planning, vol. 148. Springer (1991)
14. Slabaugh, G., Culbertson, W., Malzbender, T., Stevens, M., Schafer, R.: Methods for volumetric reconstruction of visual scenes. International Journal of Computer Vision 57(3), 179–199 (2004)
15. Jin, H., Soatto, S., Yezzi, A.: Multi-view stereo reconstruction of dense shape and complex appearance. International Journal of Computer Vision 63(3), 175–189 (2005)
16. Medellín, H., Corney, J., Davies, J., Lim, T., Ritchie, J.: An automated system for the assembly of octree models. Assembly Automation 24(3), 297–312 (2004)
17. Tsai, R.: A versatile camera calibration technique for high-accuracy 3d machine vision metrology using off-the-shelf tv cameras and lenses. IEEE Journal of Robotics and Automation 3(4), 323–344 (1987)
18. Bouguet, J.Y.: Camera calibration toolbox for Matlab (2008)
19. Research, P.G.: Point grey research cameras
20. Laurentini, A.: The visual hull concept for silhouette-based image understanding. IEEE Transactions on Pattern Analysis and Machine Intelligence 16, 150–162 (1994)

# Multimodal Processes Rescheduling

Grzegorz Bocewicz[1], Zbigniew A. Banaszak[2], Peter Nielsen[3],
and Quang-Vinh Dang[3]

[1] Dept. of Electronics and Computer Science, Koszalin University of Technology, Poland
bocewicz@ie.tu.koszalin.pl
[2] Faculty of Management, Dept. of Business Informatics,
Warsaw University of Technology, Poland
Z.Banaszak@wz.pw.edu.pl
[3] Dept. of Mechanical and Manufacturing Engineering, Aalborg University, Denmark
{peter,vinhise}@m-tech.aau.dk

**Abstract.** Cyclic scheduling problems concerning multimodal processes are usually observed in FMSs producing multi-type parts where the Automated Guided Vehicles System (AGVS) plays a role of a material handling system. Schedulability analysis of concurrently flowing cyclic processes (SCCP) executed in these kinds of systems can be considered using a declarative modeling framework. Proposed representation provides a unified way for performance evaluation of local cyclic as well as supported by them multimodal processes. The main question regards of reachability of a SCCP cyclic behavior. In this context, the sufficient conditions guarantee the reachability of both local and multimodal processes cyclic steady state spaces are discussed.

## 1    Introduction

A cyclic schedule [1], [5] is one in which the same sequence of states is repeated over and over again. In everyday practice, cyclic scheduling arises in different application domains such as manufacturing, time-sharing of processors in embedded systems, and in compilers for scheduling loop operations for parallel or pipelined architectures as well as service domains covering such areas as workforce scheduling (e.g., shift scheduling, crew scheduling), timetabling (e.g., train timetabling, aircraft routing and scheduling), and reservations (e.g., reservations with or without slack) [2], [7], [8].

In this paper, such cyclic scheduling problem considered follow from Flexible Manufacturing System (FMS) [3] and employed by them Automated Guided Vehicle (AGV) systems used for material handling. An AGVs provide asynchronous movement pallets of products through a network of guide paths between the workstations. Such flows following production routes are treated as multimodal processes, i.e. sequences of alternating transportation and machining operations. The problems arising concerning material transportation routing and scheduling belong to NP-hard ones. Since the steady state of production flows treated as multimodal processes has periodic character, hence servicing them AGV-served transportation processes (usually executed along loop-like routes) encompass also cyclic behavior.

Many models and methods have been proposed to solve the cyclic scheduling problem [6]. Among them, the mathematical programming approach (usually IP and

C. Emmanouilidis, M. Taisch, D. Kiritsis (Eds.): APMS 2012, Part I, IFIP AICT 397, pp. 534–541, 2013.

MIP), max-plus algebra [8], constraint logic programming [2], [10] evolutionary algorithms and Petri nets [1] frameworks belong to the most frequently used. A majority of them are oriented towards finding a minimal cycle or maximal throughput while assuming deadlock-free processes flow.

In that context, our main contribution is to propose a new declarative modeling based framework enabled to evaluate the cyclic steady state of a given system of concurrent cyclic processes as well as supported by them multimodal cyclic processes. The following questions are of main interest: Does the assumed system behavior can be achieved under the given system's structure constraints? Does the assumed multimodal processes cyclic steady state is reachable from another one?

## 2     Multimodal Processes

Let us consider the above mentioned questions on in the context of Automated Guided Vehicles (AGVs) periodically circulating along cyclic routes (see Fig. 1b) that can be seen as a network of loosely coupled material transportation/handling subsystem modeled in terms of Systems of Cyclic Concurrent Processes (SCCPs) shown in Fig. 1a.

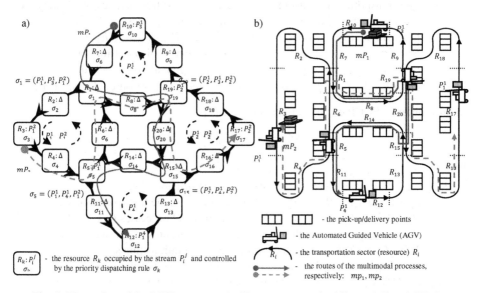

**Fig. 1.** Illustration of the SCCP composed of four processes a) while modeling AGVs b)

Four local *cyclic processes* [2] are considered: $P_1$, $P_2$, $P_3$, $P_4$ and *two multimodal processes* [3] (executed along the parts of local cyclic processes) $mP_1$, $mP_2$, respectively. $P_1$, $P_2$ contain two sub-processes $P_1 = \{P_1^1, P_1^2\}$, $P_2 = \{P_2^1, P_2^2\}$ representing AGVs moving along the same route. The AGVs are used to transport workpieces along transportation routes followed by $mP_1, mP_2$ processes, respectively (Fig 1. b).

## 2.1    Declarative Modeling

The following notations are used [2]:

- $p_i^k = (p_{i,1}^k, p_{i,2}^k, \ldots, p_{i,lr(i)}^k)$ specifies **the route of the local process's stream $P_i^k$** ($k$-th stream of the $i$-th local process $P_i$), and its components define the resources used in course of process operations execution, where: $p_{i,j}^k \in R$ (the set of resources: $R = \{R_1, R_2, \ldots, R_m\}$) – denotes the resource used by the $k$-th stream of $i$-th local process in the $j$-th operation; in the rest of the paper **the $j$-th operation executed on resource $p_{i,j}^k$ in the stream $P_i^k$** will be denoted by $o_{i,j}^k$; $lr(i)$ - denotes a length of cyclic process route. $t_i^k = (t_{i,1}^k, t_{i,2}^k, \ldots, t_{i,lr(i)}^k)$ specifies **the process operation times**, where $t_{i,j}^k$ denotes the time of execution of operation $o_{i,j}^k$.

- $mp_i = \left(mpr_j(a_j, b_j), mpr_l(a_l, b_l), \ldots, mpr_h(a_h, b_h)\right)$ specifies **the route of the multimodal process $mP_i$**, where: $mpr_j(a, b) = \left(crd_a p_j^k, crd_{a+1} p_j^k, \ldots, crd_b p_j^k\right)$, $crd_i D = d_i$, for $D = (d_1, d_2, \ldots, d_i, \ldots, d_w)$, $\forall a \in \{1, 2, \ldots, lr(i)\}$, $\forall j \in \{1, 2, \ldots, n\}$, $crd_a p_j \in R$. The transportation route $mp_i$ is a sequence of sub-sequences of local cyclic process routes. For example, a route of the process $mP_2$ (Fig. 1a) is following: $mp_2 = (R_3, R_4, R_5, R_6, R_1, R_8, R_{19}, R_{20}, R_{15}, R_{16}, R_{17})$.

- $\Theta = \{\sigma_1, \sigma_2, \ldots, \sigma_m\}$ is the set of **the priority dispatching rules**, where $\sigma_i = (s_{i,1}, \ldots, s_{i,lp(i)})$ is the sequence components of which determine an order in which the processes can be executed on the resource $R_i$, $s_{i,j} \in P$.

In that context a SCCP can be defined as a pair [2]:

$$SC = (SC_l, SC_m), \qquad (1)$$

where:

$SC_l = (R, P, \Pi, T, \Theta)$ – characterizes the SCCP structure, i.e.
    $R = \{R_1, R_2, \ldots, R_m\}$ – the set of resources (e.g. the transportation sectors),
    $P = \{P_1^1, \ldots, P_1^a, \ldots, P_n^1, \ldots, P_n^z\}$ – the set of local processes (e.g. AGVs ),
    $\Pi = \{p_1, p_2, \ldots, p_n\}$ – the set of local process routes (e.g. routes of AGVs ),,
    $T = \{T_1, \ldots, T_n\}$ – the set of local process operations times,
    $\Theta = \{\sigma_1, \sigma_2, \ldots, \sigma_m\}$ – the set of dispatching priority rules.
$SC_m = (MP, M\Pi)$ – characterizes the SCCP behavior, i.e.
    $MP = \{mP_1, mP_2, \ldots, mP_u\}$ – the set of multimodal processes, (workpieces),
    $M\Pi = \{mp_1, mp_2, \ldots, mp_u\}$ – the set of multimodal process routes (transportation routes of materials).

The main question concerns SCCP cyclic behavior and a way this behavior depends on direction of local transportation routes $\Pi$, the priority rules $\Theta$, and a set of initial states, i.e., an initial allocation of processes to the system resources.

## 2.2     Cyclic Steady States Space

Consider the following SCCPs state definition describing both the local and multimodal processes allocation:

$$S^k = (Sl^r, MA^k), \qquad (2)$$

where:

- $Sl^r$ – is the state of local processes, corresponding to $S^k$,

$$Sl^r = (A^r, Z^r, Q^r), \qquad (3)$$

where: $A^r = (a_1{}^r, a_2{}^r, \dots, a_m{}^r)$ – the processes allocation in the $r$-th state, $a_i{}^r \in P \cup \{\Delta\}$, $a_i = P_j^k$ – the $i$-th resource $R_i$ is occupied by the local stream $P_j^k$, and $a_i{}^r = \Delta$ – the $i$-th resource $R_i$ is unoccupied.
   $Z^r = (z_1{}^r, z_2{}^r, \dots, z_m{}^r)$ – the sequence of semaphores corresponding to the $r$-th state, $z_i{}^r \in P$ – means the name of the stream (specified in the $i$-th dispatching rule $\sigma_i$, allocated to the $i$-th resource) allowed to occupy the $i$-th resource; for instance $z_i{}^r = P_j^k$ means that at the moment stream $P_j^k$ is allowed to occupy the $i$-th resource.
   $Q^r = (q_1{}^r, q_2{}^r, \dots, q_m{}^r)$ – the sequence of semaphore indices, corresponding to the $r$-th state, $q_i{}^r$ determines the position of the semaphore $z_i{}^r$ in the priority dispatching rule $\sigma_i$, $z_i{}^r = crd_{(q_i{}^r)}\sigma_i$, $q_i{}^r \in \mathbb{N}$. $MA^k$ – the sequence of multimodal processes allocation: $MA^k = (mA_1^k, \dots, mA_u^k)$, $mA_i^k$ – allocation of the process $mP_i$, i.e.:

$$mA_i^k = (ma_{i,1}{}^k, ma_{i,2}{}^k, \dots, ma_{i,m}{}^k), \qquad (4)$$

where:     $m$ – is a number of resources $R$, $ma_{i,j}{}^k \in \{mP_i, \Delta\}$, $ma_{i,j}{}^k = mP_i$ means, the $j$-th resource $R_j$ is occupied by the $i$-th multimodal process $P_i$, and $ma_{i,j}{}^k = \Delta$ – the $i$-th resource $R_j$ is released by the $i$-th multimodal process $P_i$.

The introduced concept of the $k$-th state $S^k$ is enables to create a space $\mathbb{S}$ of feasible states [2]. In this kind of space $\mathbb{S}$ two kinds of behaviors can be considered: **a cyclic steady state** and **a deadlock state** [2].
   The set $mSc^* = \{S^{k_1}, S^{k_2}, S^{k_3}, \dots, S^{k_v}\}$, $mSc^* \subset \mathbb{S}$ is called **a reachability state space of multimodal processes** generated by an initial state $S^{k_1} \in \mathbb{S}$, if the following condition holds:

$$S^{k_1} \xrightarrow{i-1} S^{k_i} \xrightarrow{v-i-1} S^{k_v} \to S^{k_i} \qquad (5)$$

where: $S^a \xrightarrow{i} S^b$ – the next state transition defined in [2], $S^{k_1} \xrightarrow{i} S^{k_{i+1}} \equiv S^{k_1} \to S^{k_2} \to S^{k_3} \to \dots \to S^{k_{i+1}}$ and $S^{k_i} \to S^{k_j}$ means transitions linking two feasible states $S^{k_i}, S^{k_j}$.
   The set $mSc = \{S^{k_i}, S^{k_{i+1}}, \dots, S^{k_v}\}$, $mSc \subseteq mSc^*$ is called **a cyclic steady state of multimodal processes** (i.e., the cyclic steady state of a $SCCP$) with the period $Tm = \|mSc\|$, $Tm > 1$. In other words, **a cyclic steady state** contains such a set of

states in which starting from any distinguished state it is possible to reach the rest of states and finally reach this distinguished state again $S^{k_i} \xrightarrow{Tm} S^{k_i}$.

The cyclic steady state $Sc$ specified by the period $Tc$ of local processes execution is defined in the similar way. Graphically, the cyclic steady states $Sc$ and $mSc$ are described by cyclic and spiral digraphs, respectively. Two cyclic steady states of SCCP from Fig. 1 a) are presented in Fig. 2. Moreover, since an initial state $S^{k_1} \in \$$ leads either to $mSc$ or to a deadlock state $S^*$, i.e. $S^{k_1} \xrightarrow{i-1} S^{k_i} \xrightarrow{v-i-1} S^{k_v} \to S^*$, multimodal processes also may reach a **deadlock state**.

## 2.3  Problem Statement

Consider a SCCP specified (due to (1)) by the given set $R$ of resources, dispatching rules $\Theta$, local $\Pi$, and multimodal processes routes $M\Pi$ as well. Usually the main question concerns SCCP periodicity, i.e. Does the cyclic execution of local processes exist? Response to the above question requires answers to more detailed questions, for instance: What is the admissible initial allocation of processes (i.e. the possible AGVs dockings)? What are dispatching rules $\Theta$ guaranteeing a given SCCP periodicity (in local/multimodal sense)? The problems stated above have been studied in [2-4], [10].

In that context, a new problem regarding possible switching among cyclic steady states can be seen as their obvious consequence. Therefore, the newly arising questions are: Is it possible to reschedule cyclic schedules as to "jump" from one cyclic steady state to another? Is it possible to "jump" directly or indirectly? What are the control rules allowing one to do it? These kind of questions are of crucial importance for manufacturing and transportation systems aimed at short-run production shifts and/or the itinerary planning of passengers (e.g. in a sub-way network).

In terms of introduced notations ($\$, Sc, mSc$) the above questions boil down to the following ones:

*Does there exist a nonempty space MSC of local (Sc) and multimodal (mSc) processes cyclic steady states?*

*Let $mSc_1, mSc_2 \in MSC$. Is the state $mSc_2 \in MSC$ reachable from $mSc_1 \in MSC$?*

## 2.4  Repetitive Processes Scheduling

Searching for response to the first of above stated questions, let us note that a possible cyclic steady state of multimodal processes formulated in terms of CSP can be stated as the following constraints satisfaction problem [2], [3]:

$$CS(SC) = ((\{X, Tc, mX, Tm\}, \{D_X, D_{Tc}, D_{mX}, D_{Tm}\}), C) \tag{6}$$

where: $X, Tc, mX, Tm$ – the decision variables, where $Tc$ and $Tm$ are local and multimodal cycles (periods); $X, mX$ - sequences of operations beginning in local, and multimodal processes, respectively, $D_X, D_{mX}, D_{Tc}, D_{Tm}$ – domains of variables $X, Tc, mX, Tm$, $C$ – constraints determining the relationship among local and multimodal processes, i.e. constraints linking $X, Tc, mX, Tm$. The detailed specification of constraints considered is available in [2], [4].

## 2.5    Cyclic Processes Reachability

Cyclic steady states of multimodal $mSc_i$ and local $Sc_i$ processes are solutions to the problem (6). Considering $mSc_1, mSc_2 \in MSC$ and their $mSc_1^*$, $mSc_2^*$ the following property is hold:

**Property:** *The indirect switching between $mSc_1$ and $mSc_2$ is enabled if two states: $S^a \in mSc_1$ and $S^b \in mSc_2^*$ possessing a common shared allocation $A^x$ there exist.*

The states $S^a$, $S^b$ should not necessarily belong to $mSc_1$ and $mSc_2$. One of them may belong either to a reachability state space $mSc_1^*$ or to $mSc_2^*$. For example, if exist two states $S^a = (Sl^a, MA^a) \in mSc_1$ and $S^b = (Sl^b, MA^b) \in mSc_2^*$ , where $Sl^a = (A^x, Z^a, Q^a)$ and $Sl^b = (A^x, Z^b, Q^b)$ then replacing at the allocation $A^x$ the semaphores $Z^a$ and indices $Q^a$ by $Z^b$, $Q^b$ results in switching from $Sl^a$ to $Sl^b$ ($S^a$ to $S^b$), and consequently in switching from $mSc_1$ to $mSc_2$. That implies the possible indirectly switching between cyclic multimodal processes exist. The cyclic steady states $mSc_1$ and $mSc_2$ are mutually reachable only if they possess the states sharing the same allocations $A^x$. Therefore, the reachability problem (the second of considered questions) of the cyclic steady states space, e.g. regarding of switching between two states $mSc_1 \subseteq mSc_1^*$ and $mSc_2 \subseteq mSc_2^*$, is concluded in the question: Does there exist two states $S^a \in mSc_1$ and $S^b \subseteq mSc_2^*$ ($mSl^a \in mSc_1^*$ and $mSl^b \subseteq mSc_2$) sharing the same allocation $A^x$ of local cyclic processes?

# 3    Illustrative Example

Given the SCCP see Fig. 1. The periods $Tc$ of the cyclic processes steady states $Sc_1$ and $Sc_2$ (local processes behaviors) obtained from the $CS$ (5) the solution while implemented in OzMozart platform (in less than 1 s due to Intel Core Duo 3.00 GHz, 4.00 GB RAM computer) are equal to 18 and 11 t.u., respectively. In turn the periods $Tm$ of the cyclic multimodal processes steady states $mSc_1$ and $mSc_2$ are equal to 55 and 33 respectively.

The obtained cyclic steady states space is shown in Fig 2. The local states are distinguished by "●", while multimodal by "○". In case of multimodal processes $mSc_1$ the completion time for each route is the same and equals to 30 u.t. (see Fig 3). However, in case of $mSc_2$ the completion time for the route $mp_1$ equals to 22 u.t, and 27u.t. for the $mp_2$ (see Fig. 3). That means the longer cycle of the $mSc_1$ implies the longer multimodal processes completion time. So, for a given SCCP the following question can be stated: Does the steady state $mSc_2$ is reachable from $mSc_1$?

Due to the property provided the response is positive, however only if there exist states $S^a \in mSc_1$ and $S^b \in mSc_2^*$ possessing a common shared allocation $A^x$. The $mSc_2$ is reachable from $mSc_1$ in the local state $Sl^{11}$ sharing the common allocation with $Sl^{29}$. The states $S^{29}$ and $S^{30}$ follow the multimodal states $Sl^{11}$, $Sl^{29}$ that can be mutually reachable from each other. Switching from state $Sl^{11}$ to $Sl^{29}$ can be seen as result of change either of semaphores (from $Z^{29}$ to $Z^{30}$) and/or indices (from $Q^{29}$ to $Q^{30}$). The switching assumes the same processes allocation – that means (in terms of AGVS) the same AGVs allocations.

The considered rescheduling from $mSc_1$ to $mSc_2$ employing of switching $S^{29}$ to $S^{30}$ is distinguished by the green line in Fig. 2. Another illustration of such rescheduling provides the Gantt's chart from Fig. 3.

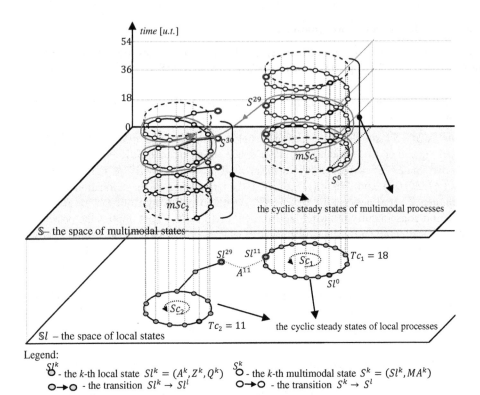

**Fig. 2.** The cyclic steady states spaces of SCCP from Fig. 1

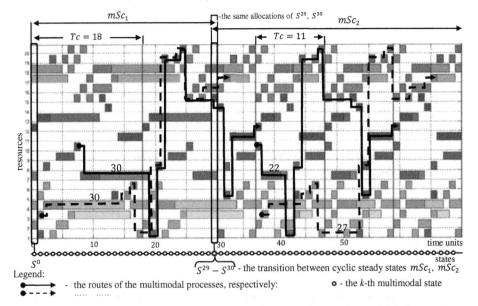

**Fig. 3.** Gantt's chart illustrating the way the cyclic steady state $mSc_2$ can be reachable from $mSc_1$

Note that in the considered case the rescheduling does not disturb execution of multimodal processes.

# 4    Concluding Remarks

Structural constraints limiting AGVS behavior imply two fundamental problems: Does there exist a set of dispatching rules subject to AGVS's structure constraints guaranteeing solution to a CSP representation of the cyclic scheduling problem? What set of dispatching rules subject to assumed cyclic behavior of AGVS guarantees solution to a CSP representation of the cyclic scheduling problem?

In terms of the second question the paper's contribution is the property providing sufficient condition guaranteeing local and multimodal cyclic processes rescheduling. Therefore, the developed conditions can be treated as the new rules enlarging the above mentioned set of dispatching rules. Moreover, the provided conditions complete the rules enabling direct switching between cyclic behaviors [3], [4] for the new rules allowing one to reschedule cyclic behaviors indirectly, i.e. through a set of so called transient states (not belonging to rescheduled cyclic steady states).

# References

1.  Alpan, G., Jafari, M.A.: Dynamic analysis of timed Petri nets: a case of two processes and a shared resource. IEEE Trans. on Robotics and Automation 13(3), 338–346 (1997)
2.  Bocewicz, G., Banaszak, Z.: Declarative approach to cyclic scheduling of multimodal processes. In: Golińska, P. (ed.) EcoProduction and Logistics, vol. 1, pp. 203–235. Springer (2013)
3.  Bocewicz, G., Banaszak, Z.: Declarative approach to cyclic steady states space refinement: periodic processes scheduling. International Journal of Advanced Manufacturing Technology (2012) (in print)
4.  Bocewicz, G., Wójcik, R., Banaszak, Z.A.: Cyclic Steady State Refinement. In: Abraham, A., Corchado, J.M., González, S.R., De Paz Santana, J.F. (eds.) International Symposium on Distributed Computing and Artificial Intelligence. AISC, vol. 91, pp. 191–198. Springer, Heidelberg (2011)
5.  Fournier, O., Lopez, P.: Cyclic scheduling following the social behavior of ant colonies. In: Proceedings of the IEEE International Conference on Systems, Man and Cybernetics, pp. 450–454 (2002)
6.  Levner, E., Kats, V., Alcaide, D., Pablo, L., Cheng, T.C.E.: Complexity of cyclic scheduling problems: A state-of-the-art survey. Computers and Industrial Engineering 59(2), 352–361 (2010)
7.  Liebchen, C., Möhring, R.H.: A case study in periodic timetabling. Electronic Notes in Theoretical Computer Science 66(6), 21–34 (2002)
8.  Polak, M., Majdzik, P., Banaszak, Z., Wójcik, R.: The performance evaluation tool for automated prototyping of concurrent cyclic processes. In: Skowron, A. (ed.) Fundamenta Informaticae, vol. 60(1-4), pp. 269–289. ISO Press (2004)
9.  Smart Nigiel, P.: The Algorithmic Resolution of Diophantine Equations. London Mathematical Society Student Text, vol. 41. Cambridge University Press, Cambridge (1998)
10. Wójcik, R.: Constraint programming approach to designing conflict-free schedules for repetitive manufacturing processes. Digital enterprise technology. In: Cunha, P.F., Maropoulos, P.G. (eds.) Perspectives and Future Challenges, pp. 267–274. Springer (2007)

# Novel Automated Production System
# for the Footwear Industry

Silvio Cocuzza[1], Rosanna Fornasiero[2], and Stefano Debei[1]

[1] CISAS "G. Colombo" – University of Padova, Padova, Italy
{silvio.cocuzza,stefano.debei}@unipd.it
[2] ITIA-CNR, Milan, Italy
rosanna.fornasiero@itia.cnr.it

**Abstract.** The production process of most of the footwear companies working in the market segment of classic, casual, and fashion shoes is still handicraft. Moreover, the actual design and production processes are largely independent, and both of them need the physical prototypes of the semi-finished shoes in order to be accomplished. In this context, the IDEA-FOOT project introduces a new method for the shoe integrated design and production in which most of the production parameters are derived from the shoe 3D CAD model and an innovative automated production plant in which manipulators and automated machines are fully integrated. The aim of this paper is to present the main features of the automated plant, the advantages in using a new integrated design and production process, which is totally new for this market segment, and to analyze the impact of this new production model on the production performance and on the company organization.

**Keywords:** Footwear automation, production systems, robotics, CAD-CAM integration, production performance.

## 1 Introduction

Footwear companies working in the market segment of classic, casual, and fashion shoes, due to the global competition, need to reduce time to market and increase product diversification with small batches production, while keeping a high fashion and quality content of the product. The actual design and production processes are not suitable for this small batches and variegated production.

Indeed, the production process has still a handicraft connotation; most of the production operations are performed manually by workers, and even when automatic machines are used, the operators have to program them manually for each batch of shoes, and the semi-finished shoes and components handling is done by means of conventional conveyors that are manually loaded/unloaded.

Shoe manufacturing of classic, casual, and fashion shoes has a low degree of automation [1], mainly due to the complexity of the product and of the production process. On the other hand, the manufacturing of technical and sportwear shoes is highly automated.

C. Emmanouilidis, M. Taisch, D. Kiritsis (Eds.): APMS 2012, Part I, IFIP AICT 397, pp. 542–549, 2013.

Several works can be found in the literature on the use of automation in different production stations of the shoe manufacturing, such as the automation of the lasting operation [2], of the grinding operation [3], of the roughing and cementing operations [2,4-6], of the bonding of the sole [7], of the finishing operations [2,8], and of the quality control [9]. In the EUROShoE project an automated production plant has been developed for the production of mass-customized shoes [10,11].

The need of the physical prototypes of the semi-finished shoes to have the geometrical information necessary for the design and production phases is the main technological problem of the footwear companies of the considered market segment. Indeed, the actual design and production processes are largely independent, and both of them need the physical prototypes of the semi-finished shoes in order to be accomplished. In the design phase, the semi-finished shoe is necessary for the sequential development of the other shoe components to be assembled, whereas in the production process, the semi-finished product is necessary to program the semi-automatic machines for each batch of shoes.

In this context, the main objectives of the IDEA-FOOT project are:

- the introduction of a new method for the integrated design and production of the shoe, in which the key elements are the 3D CAD design of the shoe components and the transfer of the required geometrical information, tool paths, and production parameters from the design to the production process in a digital standard data format using a CAM S/W;
- the design, construction, test, and validation of the automated production plant in which the aforementioned method is implemented.

The proposed automated production plant is based on a production process that has been redesigned in order to reduce the complexity of the production and to increase flexibility, such as in the lean manufacturing approach [12].

In particular, the automated plant has been designed in order to have a flexible production both in terms of batch size (the minimum batch size is one shoe pair) and in terms of product style diversification.

This is in line with the agile and adaptive manufacturing approaches arisen at the beginning of the last decade as approaches to improve the competitiveness of the companies. Agile production is characterized by the integration of suppliers and customers in the value chain from the design to the production, to the marketing, and to the support services. There are many works applying different dimensions of the adaptive and agile paradigms (such as, for example in [13-16]), both from the point of view of technology improvement (implementation of flexible production systems, information and communication technology (ICT) tools, system integration) and people enhancement (competency management and training at all levels).

The aim of this paper is to present the main features of the automated plant, the advantages in using a new integrated design and production process, which is totally new for this market segment, and to analyze the impact of this new production model on the production performance and on the company organization.

## 2    New Automated Production System

The automated production plant has been realized by means of integrating existing technologies and existing dedicated machines, which have been modified in order to work in an integrated way. All the production operations from the shoe lasting to the shoe bottom processing operations (up to the cementing of the shoe bottom) have been successfully automated.

In the automated plant, manipulators are used both for pick and place and for shoe bottom processing operations. A centralized control S/W, which has been customized for this project (DESMA), is used for the monitoring of the production and for the integration and synchronization of the dedicated production machines, the manipulators, the shoe last identification system (based on radio-frequency identification (RFID) technology), the oven, and the pallet conveyor.

The core of the automated plant is subdivided in two robotic cells: the robotic cell A, in which research and development activities are involved, has been developed by CISAS, and the robotic cell B, in which state of the art technologies are involved, has been subcontracted to DESMA.

In particular, in the robotic cell A the two lasting machines (Brustia) receive the information on the article code for their automatic setup from an RFID chip inserted in the last, and moreover the heel seat and side lasting machine is loaded/unloaded by a manipulator (this was not possible for the toe lasting machine because a skilled operator is needed to assist that operation). On the other hand, in the robotic cell B some technologies already available in the market for the shoe bottom processing of technical and sportwear shoes have been modified for the scopes of this project.

The layout of the automated production plant, which have been defined comparing different solutions in terms of production time, work in progress (WIP), number of human operators, and required space, is presented in Fig. 1.

Before the robotic cell A, a human operator picks the last, the insole, and the upper from the related trolleys, assembles them together and puts the semi-assembled shoe in a trolley (station nr. 7 in Fig. 1).

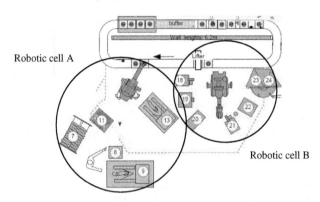

**Fig. 1.** Automated plant layout (Source: S. Cocuzza, Manipulation system for the toe lasting machine, EU FP7 IDEA-FOOT Project, Deliverable D 430.1, p. 5, 2012)

**Fig. 2.** Overall views of robotic cell A (left) and of robotic cell B (right)
(Source: S. Cocuzza, Manipulation system for the other machines of the integrated production cell, EU FP7 IDEA-FOOT Project, Deliverable D 440.1, p. 16-17, 2012)

In the robotic cell A, first some manual operations are performed: a human operator picks the semi-assembled shoe from its trolley and puts it in a conditioning unit (nr. 8); after that operation, the operator places the last in front of an RFID station for the automatic setup of the toe lasting machine (nr. 9), performs the toe lasting operation, and then places the last in the man-robot exchange station (nr. 11), which is also a conditioning unit. Then, a manipulator is used to pick the last from the man-robot exchange station, place the chip of the last in front of a second RFID station for the automatic setup of the heel seat and side lasting machine (nr. 13), load and unload that machine, and finally place the last in the pallet conveyor.

In the robotic cell B, a second manipulator is used to pick the last from the pallet conveyor (after that the last has been processed in the oven and that some optional manual operations have been performed, such as hot air application, cream application, and ironing), perform the shoe bottom processing operations (grinding, hammering, roughing, cleaning with compressed air, and cementing (nr. 18-22)), and then place it in the aspirator (nr. 23-24) to dry the water-based adhesive. The grinding, hammering, roughing, and cementing operations are performed by the robot, which presses the shoe bottom against the related ground-fixed rotating tool.

Two overall views of the robotic cell A and of the robotic cell B of the automated plant, which is installed at the BZ Moda premises, are presented in Fig. 2.

The main features of the new automated production plant are:

- use of manipulators to perform both pick and place and shoe bottom processing operations, thus reducing the processing time and the number of required human operators, and increasing the product quality;
- use of dedicated production machines (for the operations that cannot be performed by robots) that have been modified in order to reduce their setup time and to be loaded/unloaded by means of manipulators;
- implementation of a centralized control S/W for the monitoring of the production and the integration and synchronization of manipulators and automated machines.

The above presented approach represents a solution that can be rapidly adopted by the footwear companies of the considered market segment, in a smooth and gradual change toward automation.

Existing dedicated production machines have been modified in their mechanical and communication interfaces in order to be integrated with the rest of the automated plant and served by manipulators, to receive the setup parameters and tool paths generated automatically by the CAM S/W, and for their automatic setup during the production by using RFID systems.

An RFID tag is used to store in each last the batch information that is called up, when required, to guide the manipulators or the automated machines. The identification code of each shoe model is used in order to recall the production parameters and tool paths from the local databases of the machines and manipulators for their automatic setup in function of the shoe model.

The daily productivity of the automated pilot plant is approximately 320 [pairs/shift] (1 shift = 8 hours), and only 5 human operators are required (considering all the production operations from assembling the last with the insole and the upper up to delasting, excluding the aforementioned optional manual operations).

In the traditional plant with classic conveyor line taken as a reference, 13 human operators are needed, and the daily productivity is 554 [pairs/shift]. In the proposed automated plant, if 2 manipulators are used in the shoe bottom processing robotic cell, the daily productivity can be increased up to 600 [pairs/shift] and the number of human operators can be reduced to 7. Productivity can be additionally increased by adding more manipulators and/or duplicating production stations at the bottlenecks.

Once that the automated plant has been realized, it has been interfaced with the rest of the traditional production plant (including sole application, heel application, finishing, and delasting stations) and small batches of shoes have been produced for validation purposes. The analysis of the produced shoes evidenced that increased quality production operations have been performed, which turned out in high quality finished shoes.

# 3     Impact on Production Performance and on Company Organization

The implementation of the proposed integrated design and production model will contribute to enhance the competitive strength of the footwear companies through leveraging and optimizing the value of knowledge within and across companies by supporting the creation of a sustainable industrial production process. In particular, the solution proposed in this project goes both in the direction of economic sustainability, allowing companies to reduce production costs, and towards environmental and social sustainability, going beyond the lean paradigm.

Time to market will be significantly reduced and footwear companies will have the possibility to be more flexible and responsive in the development of new shoe models. The new production system is extremely flexible both in terms of production of small batches (up to one shoe pair) and in terms of product diversification, with very limited setup time to manage product variants.

Moreover, the relationship between the shoe producer and its suppliers is totally revised: the design of new shoe models will be mainly carried out by the shoe producer with limited intervention of subcontractors, and the production of the shoe components will be made concurrently by the suppliers, saving up to 50% of the design and development time with respect to the actual sequential development of the shoe components based on physical prototypes.

The impact will be on three major dimensions of sustainability: economic, social, and environmental.

Concerning the economic sustainability, an important reduction of the production costs and time to market is envisioned. Moreover, the implementation of these new technologies allows to maintain the production (or, at least, part of it) in the origin country reducing delocalization and assuring workplaces.

Concerning the social sustainability, the introduction of the new integrated design and production method requires the development of new skills and competences both in the area of design, where people have to learn to use new CAD modules, and in the area of production, where workers are asked to do added-value operations in the automated plant. Moreover, the introduction of the new automated production plant improves working conditions: operations that require physical efforts and repetitive manipulations are performed by manipulators, workers are no more involved in risky operations, and the direct contact with harmful substances is eliminated (toxic adhesives have been substituted by water-based adhesives and the operations where leather powder can be breathed causing health problems are carried out in a protected area).

The environmental sustainability of the production processes is nowadays a relevant issue requiring that companies manage the negative externalities caused by their production. In the framework of this project, thanks to the innovative production system, scraps and material waste during the production phase can be significantly reduced (the integration of the design and production phases allows a better organization of the shoe development) and toxic adhesives and solvents are eliminated (water-based adhesives are used).

Based on qualitative information gathered from company managers and technology providers, the analysis of the impact of the implemented technologies on the production performance has been carried out, which can be summarized as follows:

- Impact on flexibility. The production is highly flexible both in terms of batch size (the minimum batch size is one shoe pair) and in terms of product style diversification.
- Impact on productivity. The automated plant productivity is about 320 [pairs/shift]. Nevertheless, productivity can be increased by adding more manipulators and/or duplicating production stations at the bottlenecks.
- Impact on quality. Defects are reduced thanks to the increased accuracy of the automated operations. The product quality is also improved thanks to the upstream improvement in the more precise product design.
- Impact on balancing of production flow. Bottlenecks are eliminated and WIP is minimized thanks to an accurate design of the automated plant and of the centralized control S/W.
- Impact on waiting periods. Waiting periods due to inadequate manufacturing schedules and long production stops for the machines setup are eliminated. The production system is based on an initial plant setup for all the planned production models, which allows to have a seamless flow of production.

- Impact on motion waste. The automated plant design has been optimized so that any operation of workers or machines identified as non-value-adding action is eliminated.
- Impact on capability to find errors. The centralized control S/W generates an alert any time there is a problem in the production so that the worker knows where the problem is located and what caused it.

## 4    Conclusions

The IDEA-FOOT project introduces a new method for the integrated design and production of shoes and an innovative automated production plant in which manipulators and automated machines are fully integrated. Most of the production parameters and tool paths are derived from the shoe 3D CAD model and then transferred to the production using a dedicated CAM S/W. The production data is then recalled in the manipulators and in the production machines by means of RFID systems, thus reducing their setup time. In the automated plant, all the production operations from the shoe lasting to the shoe bottom processing operations (up to the cementing of the shoe bottom) have been successfully automated. A centralized control S/W is used for the monitoring of the production and for the integration and synchronization of manipulators and automated machines. The plant productivity is about 320 [pairs/shift] (1 shift = 8 hours), which can be increased up to 600 [pairs/shift] by adding one manipulator. Productivity can be additionally increased by adding more manipulators and/or duplicating production stations at the bottlenecks. Once that the automated plant has been realized, it has been interfaced with the rest of the traditional production plant and it has been validated by producing small batches of high quality shoes, which demonstrated the accuracy of the production operations. The presented approach, which is totally new for this market segment, allows the reduction of production costs and time to market, with a highly flexible production both in terms of batch size (the minimum batch size is one shoe pair) and in terms of product style diversification. The introduction of automation implies a reduction of the number of human operators required, thus reducing production costs. On the other hand, more qualified workers are needed and their working conditions are improved. Thanks to the new integrated design and production process based on the shoe 3D CAD model, the relationship between the shoe producer and its suppliers is totally revised: the design of new shoe models will be mainly carried out by the shoe producer, and the production of the shoe components will be made concurrently by the suppliers, saving up to 50% of the design and development time. Finally, the improved quality of the production operations implies a significant reduction of scraps and material waste during the production.

**Acknowledgement.** The results presented in this paper have been obtained in the framework of the IDEA-FOOT project (Innovative DEsign and mAnufacturing systems for small series production for European FOOTwear companies) - 7th Framework Programme - Research for the benefit of SMEs - FP7-SME-2008-I - Project n. 232585.

# References

1. Ronthaler, M., de Gea Fernandez, J., Vogele, T.: Automation in the Footwear Industry - Innovative Robotics to Support Complex Artisan Production. Industrie Management 1, 59–61 (2011)
2. Nemec, B., Žlajpah, L.: Automation in shoe assembly. In: Proceedings of the 15th International Workshop on Robotics in Alpe-Adria-Danube Region (RAAD 2006), Balatonfüred, Hungary, pp. 131–136 (2006)
3. Nemec, B., Zlajpah, L.: Shoe grinding cell using virtual mechanism approach. In: Inst. for Syst. and Technol. of Inf. Control and Commun. (ed.), Proceedings of the 5th International Conference on Informatics in Control, Automation and Robotics (ICINCO 2008), Setubal, Portugal, pp. 159–164 (2008)
4. Hu, Z., Marshall, C., Bicker, R., Taylor, P.: Automatic surface roughing with 3D machine vision and cooperative robot control. Robotics and Autonomous Systems 55(7), 552–560 (2007)
5. Rooks, B.W.: Robots bring automation to shoe production. Assembly Automation 16(3), 22–25 (1996)
6. Kochan, A.: Actis and the shoe industry. Assembly Automation 16(3), 30–31 (1996)
7. Tae-Jung, L., Pil-Gyu, P., Jong-Chul, S., Dong-Joo, P., Hee-Tae, A.: A study on development of 3D outsole profile scanner for footwear bonding automation. In: Inst. Control, Autom. & Syst. Eng., Proceedings of the 2001 International Conference on Control, Automation and Systems (ICCAS 2002), Taejon, South Korea, pp. 2857–2860 (2001)
8. Choi, H.-S., Hwang, G.-D., You, S.-S.: Development of a new buffing robot manipulator for shoes. Robotica 26(1), 55–62 (2008)
9. Alcantud, J.A.L., Carbonell, A.A., Asensi, G.D., Balibrea, L.-M.T.: Inspection and quality control based on artificial vision techniques for the automation of manufacturing process in the footwear industry, Proceedings of the Second Asian Conference on Computer Vision (ACCV '95), Ed. In: Li, S., Teoh, E.-K., Mital, D., Wang, H. (eds.) ACCV 1995. LNCS, vol. 1035, pp. 685–689. Springer, Heidelberg (1996)
10. Dulio, S., Boër, C.: Integrated production plant (IPP): an innovative laboratory for research projects in the footwear field. International Journal of Computer Integrated Manufacturing 17(7), 601–611 (2004)
11. Boër, C., Dulio, S.: Mass Customization and Footwear - Myth, Salvation or Reality?. Springer (2007)
12. Womack, J.P., Jones, D.T., Roos, D.: The Machine That Changed the World: The Story of Lean Production. HarperBusiness (2003)
13. Ashall, D., Parkinson, B.: Leaning towards Agile. Manufacturing Engineer 81(1), 27–32 (2002)
14. Gunasekaran, A.: Agile Manufacturing: A Framework for Research and Development. International Journal of Production Economics 62(1), 87–105 (1999)
15. Sharifi, H., Colquhoun, G., Barclay, I., Dann, Z., Agile Manufacturing: A Management and Operational Framework, Proceedings of the Institution of Mechanical Engineers, vol. 215-B, pp. 857-869, 2001.
16. Dashchenko, A.: Manufacturing Technologies for Machines of the Future - 21st Century Technologies. Springer (2003)

# Safety-Guided Design Concerning Standardization's Requirements of Mowing Robots

Spyridon G. Mouroutsos and Eleftheria Mitka

Department of Electrical & Computer Engineering, Xanthi, Greece
{sgmour,em3933}@ee.duth.gr

**Abstract.** Considering the rapidly expanding market for mowing robots to homeowners the noticeable question that arises is what are the safety-guided design requirements that could be applied to production management via safety standards? Standardization attempts to protect human during the interaction with this device. It makes an effort to confine residents by implementing more legible guidelines. There is no correct or incorrect list of hazards, only a list that customers and designers agree that is necessary to be handled. However, the requirements may differ in the design stage. All the design requirements shall be included in the physical system design of the robotic mower. In this paper, the authors believe that it is essential to put forward a comprehensive and systematic list of corrective or preventive measures in order to provide a safety checklist throughout the design stages of robot use. These safety criteria intend to minimize the chance of an accident and offer the adequate protection to users.

**Keywords:** safety-guided design, systemic method, mowing robot, safety requirements, standards.

## 1    Introduction

Recently, everyday people are dreaming about having a device that could be a kind of useful robot. Such robots for residential use, consider capable of taking over chores successfully in the domestic environment. Mowing robot is designed to automatically mow lawn in gardens at any day and time. It is small, compact, silent and easy to transport. The robot can be programmed to mow several areas. During operation, the robot mows the area delimited by the perimeter wire. Its performance depends mostly on the weather conditions (sunlight and temperature), the shape of the garden, the state of blades, the growth of grass and the humidity. It is indented for mowing large areas, preferably at daytime depends on the battery life. Whenever it comes in contact with an obstacle such as branches, small stones, wall or fence, it reverses and follows a different direction. This system uses an irregular movement pattern that is never repeated according to its sensing of growing of lawn.

Since particular safety guidelines for mowing robots do not exist, the authors suggest that their safety-guided design should be based on standards that developed in areas of agriculture and garden equipment. In addition, the methodologies for safety for agricultural equipment [1], safety signs [6], the standard for Robots and Robot Systems [4] providing safety requirements for robot systems, as well as the "Safety

C. Emmanouilidis, M. Taisch, D. Kiritsis (Eds.): APMS 2012, Part I, IFIP AICT 397, pp. 550–557, 2013.

certification requirements for domestic robots", proposed by the authors [7] should be made applicable to robotic lawn-mowers. Every manufacturer should follow the basic instructions summarized in the basic safety standards such as Definitions of Powered Lawn and Garden Equipment [2], Safety Specifications for Commercial Turf Care Equipment [3] and safe features according to Safety Specifications for Turf Care Equipment – Power Lawn Mowers, Lawn and Garden Tractors [5].

With aim to expand and grow the acceptance of robots by the society, the authors propose a new list of safety design constraints. The authors use a systemic method that covers the safety design of the production, managing product (mowing robot) and information (standards) [10].

## 2    Safety-Guided Design

### 2.1    Possible Accidents

The first step in any safety analysis is to define which types of accidents needs to be considered. The definition of an accident derives from the user's experience and from government efforts for systems that are certified by technical committees and corresponding regulations. Accidents are a consequence from ineffective implementation of safety requirements on the design level of the system [9]. In addition, potential accidents of a mowing robot are the following:

**A1.**    Electromagnetic or radio frequency interference may cause person injury.
**A2.**    Severe injury could occur if hair, fingers or clothing of resident are caught in the exposed mechanism of the robot due to indented opening of the cover.
**A3.**    Battery may explode if user does not follow the appropriate procedure and the nearby resident could suffer from electrical shock.
**A4.**    Stones, tools, toys and other loose objects may be thrown by the mower blades leading to harmful injuries.
**A5.**    A resident could be pinned under the robot due to overturning of the robot that is caused by operating in slopes.
**A6.**    A resident could be injured by contact with the blades.
**A7.**    A resident that uses the robot via remote control hits a person or a pet by pulling the mower backward without looking.
**A8.**    The released electrolyte of an intended open of the power pack may cause damages to skin or eyes.
**A9.**    Contact of human with hot parts may cause burns.
**A10.**    The cord/ perimeter wire may lead to tripping hazard.
**A11.**    Electrical component damage due to inadequate cleaning of the device.
**A12.**    A child may fall off and be seriously injured if he rides on an operating robot.
**A13.**    Coexistence everyday problems occur if the robot is moving at high speed.

### 2.2    Adjusting a Level of Severity

A risk management is arranged at early design stages with a risk matrix (counting severity and probability) to agree on which types of hazards shall be mitigated during design stage or to categorize them. Statistically analyzed data estimating the probability of accidents, however, at this specific type of robots, does not exist so far. The safety policy for prioritizing the severity of an accident is that all accidents result in a loss of human life or human injury should be eliminated at the design level.

Level 1:
**A1-1:** Rotating blades catches part of resident's body.
**A1-2:** Coming in contact with any exposed mechanism part of the robot.
**A1-3:** A child rides on an operating robot.
**A1-4:** A resident is pulling the mower backward without paying attention.
**A1-5:** A resident could be pinned under the robot due to overturning.
Level 2:
**A2-1:** Hot parts cause burns.
**A2-2:** A battery could explode.
**A2-3:** The cord/ perimeter wire causes tripping hazard.
**A2-4:** Electromagnetic or radio frequency interference.
Level 3:
**A3-1:** Problems with the coexistence in everyday living.
**A3-2:** Loose objects may be propelled.
**A3-3:** Electrical or electronic component damage.
**A3-4:** Released corrosive electrolyte affects human skin and eyes.

## 2.3     High Level System Hazards

A restricted set of high level system hazards need to be identified combining potentially hazardous conditions with accidents identified at section 2.1. The high-level systems hazards arise from the accidents are the following:

H1. Mechanical hazards (cutting, severing, inadequate velocity) [A4, A6, A13].
H2. Environmental hazards (explosion) [A3].
H3. Tripping and falling hazards [A7, A10, A12].
H4. Thermal hazards (burns) [A9].
H5. Hazards generated by substances [A8].
H6. Electrical hazard [A11].
H7. Hazard generated by radiation [A1].
H8. Hazards generated by neglecting ergonomic principles in machine [A2, A5].

## 2.4     Define Design Constraints

The next step is to define the safety constraints that are considered critical to protect from incidents (Table 1). The greatest challenge is to design such robot that enforces the requirements as much as achievable. Furthermore, we accompanied these protective measures by one real lawnmower in order to prove that implementation of these guidelines are crucial and ought to be applied. The chosen product is Friendly robotics RL850 (Fig. 1).

**Fig. 1.** A commercially available robotic mower (Source: http://www.robomow.com)

**Table 1.** Safety-Guided Design constraints concerning mowing robot's hazards

| HAZARD | SAFETY DESIGN CONSTRAINTS | FRIENDLY ROBOTICS RL 850 |
|---|---|---|
| Electromagnetic or radio frequency interference | • The device shall not be subject to interferences such as high ambient noise, radio transmissions, unshielded computers, infrared remote controllers and magnetic fields.<br>• If the robot is operating in close proximity to another one (by the same or a different manufacturer), then you should make adjustments so that the frequencies of the two robotic devices do not interfere with each other.<br>• Make sure that mower is placed away from light, microwaves, magnetic fields, heat or sound. | • The device shall not be subject to interference cause by nearby metal objects, underground wires, and another wire in a nearby grass, neighbor's lawnmower or another electric device using similar frequency.<br>• The interference shall not lead to calibration failure, ignoring of wire and mowing outside the designated area, changing of direction with no progress. |
| Exposed mechanism | • The mechanism of the robot shall be protected. The respective covers shall be kept in good condition. | • The mowing covering hood shall not collect grass residuals after mowing damp or wet lawn. It shall be inspected and maintained regularly for foreign material using a damp cloth or another similar tool.<br>• The mechanism of Robomow is protected with plastic cover to prevent from bumping or changing it. |
| Explosion of the battery | • Safety features such as battery pack or sealed batteries shall continue to be active in order to protect residents under all emergency circumstances.<br>• User shall be informed by the manufacturer that in case of mowing robot performing on batteries, there exist electrical hazards such as fire, electrical shock or chemical burn hazard in case that battery is mistreated and explosion hazard, if the battery is incorrectly placed [7]. | • The 24V sealed lead acid battery, that is used to drive the three 150W motors on the RL850 and all electronic components ought to be charged at the recommended charging station. Improper charging may causes shock or overheating hazard.<br>• *The charging station ought to be designed according to the following:*<br>• It shall be placed on compact, flat and stable surface with good drainage, on level ground, preferably in a wide span area of the house.<br>• Make sure that water or other liquids is not directed inside the charging station.<br>• The entrance of the charging station shall be positioned so that the robot can enter away from leaves, sticks or twigs.<br>• The charging-station shall be well fastened to the ground.<br>• Deal with any insect with a proper insecticide. |
| Loose objects | • The operational area shall be well defined and operational contingencies detected shall be eliminated by the designer. Such operational contingencies include: inability to determine location in the house; obstacles within its path; not accessible charging station; inability to follow the tasking path.<br>• Guards and shields are designed to protect user. | • Safety features, in case of Robomow [8], such as lift sensor, sensor equipped bumpers, perimeter switch, automatic departure warning alert shall continue to be active in order to protect residents under all emergency circumstances. |

**Table 1.** (*Continued*)

| | | |
|---|---|---|
| Overturning of the robot | • Designer should simulate some test manoeuvres on first use to identify the commands and main functions.<br>• User command execution precisely without putting the resident's life in danger.<br>• The robot shall have easily accessible safety commands and functions, so that the user shall be able to stop the robot in case of overturning.<br>• Emergency stop shall execute the proper stop function in case of overturning. In particular, wiring, communication devices, sensors, electrical and utility connections should meet the performance criteria. | • Robomow is already equipped with an emergency stop switch on the manual controller in order to block its mowing path.<br>• The emergency stop switch shall be applied with a push button switch in series among the battery and the robot. When pushed, the switch shuts-off power to the robot, pausing the turning of motors and blades until the button is released. When power is returned to the robot, the controller will execute the command of the robot. |
| Contact with the sharp rotating blades | • Manual should advice the user to present dramatic description on the hazardous behaviors of mistreating the robot and warn correctly concerning the appropriate safety features.<br>• The replacement of not well-maintained or worn out blades shall not require routine or extraordinary maintenance more than once a year.<br>• User's manual indicates that every maintenance, service, replacement or inspection of worn or damaged parts should be carried out by service experts. | • Blades shall be sharp and offer a safe and effective cut.<br>• Not well-maintained blades will shred the lawn, which can provide an entry point for disease organisms and weaken the grass plant.<br>• It is recommended to replace all three Robomow blades once a year [8]. |
| Pulling the mower backwards without looking | • Online tutorials and help menus shall contain the appropriate instructions, so that users shall have direct access to information on how to operate the robot.<br>• A built-in electronic hardware control system and/or safety operational software shall be selected to force the robot to shut itself down in an emergency.<br>• Mowing robot shall be equipped with an emergency stop switch on the manual controller that ceases the rotation of blades and wheels within seconds. | • The remote emergency stop shall be applied to Robomow with a radio frequency receiver and relay positioned in series among the battery and the robot. When the receiver receives a signal from the remote RF transmitter, the relay ceases the power to the robot blocking any hazardous movement. When power is returned to the robot, the controller will execute the command of the robot. |
| Released electrolyte | • The power pack shall not be able to be opened or spoiled.<br>• The robot ought to be designed so that no additional clothing against hazardous materials and solvents requires to be worn by the user during the charging of the device. | • *Always disconnect Power Pack from Robomow in the following cases:* before clearing blockage/ checking/ cleaning/ working on Robomow or replacing the blades.<br>• Always disconnect Power Pack from Robomow after throw a loose object or in case that Robomow begins trembling irregularly. |
| Contact with hot parts | • *In case that robot containing parts that are likely to overheat, these parts should be constructed so as:*<br>• The temperature of accessible surface does not cause injury to the user.<br>• If gasses and liquids are contained inside the robot, the designer should ensure that any increase of temperature will not cause burn injury. | • Hot parts of Robomow shall not cause burns, the engine and exhaust system shall be kept as cool as possible. |
| The power cord/ perimeter wire causes tripping hazard | • The use of adequate insulation, cable cross-sections, panel covers shall prevent an electrical shock. | • Robomow cables must be embedded inside the body of the robot.<br>• Robomow shall use cable cross-sections and panel covers. |

**Table 1.** (*Continued*)

| A child rides on an operating robot | • Warning signs shall be established to protect residents who may consider that they can ceaselessly be reckless with the operating robot.<br>• Specific responsibilities concerning safety shall be assigned to an adult user.<br>• The robot shall be equipped with a specific audio or visual signal, easily recognizable by everyone, to let people know whether it is on or off. Use a frequency that is not within the range of noise frequencies, in case of an audio signal. | • Safety features of Robomow such as child guard/safety guard, lift sensor, sensor equipped bumpers, warning alert shall continue to be active in order to protect unauthorized persons under all emergency circumstances.<br>• When adjust settings the automatic departure time schedule, do not let Robomow to operate unattended if there are pets, children or people in the vicinity.<br>• Child guard provides a safety feature to offer protect children or unfamiliar bystanders with the safe function of the device to control it easily. |
|---|---|---|
| Electrical of electronic component damage due to inadequate cleaning of the robotic device | • The designer should take into account the fact that objects will be dropped and liquids will be spilled upon the robot, eventually.<br>• Adequate electrical protection shall be provided such as regulators, filters, proper ground circuit. | • The robot electrical equipment should follow the appropriate instructions of the relevant requirements.<br>• An appropriate danger sign for electrical shock shall be generated if needed. |
| Robot is moving at high speed | • Post-manufacture check of the full scale system, about its maximum, minimum, optimal speed and settings, start / end points, path, process.<br>• Speed mode should meet the performance criteria. | • Switch "deadman" shall be applied to Robomow in order to cease the power supply or blocks only the blade or only the rotation of the wheels in case that speed exceeds the manufacturer's specification tolerance.<br>• The emergency stop switch, ought to perform the same function as the switch "deadman" blocking all abnormal high speed movements. |

## 2.5    Assign Responsibility to the User for Implementing Safety Requirements

The responsibility for enforcing each behavioural requirement ought to be assigned to the users of the product as in any production management system. The high-level system requirements for eliminating the hazard was recognized and then enhanced into more distinctive requirements.

However, there is no possibility to develop an ultimate list of requirements that controls every robotic product apart from a restricted list of requirements quite essential with aim to be helpful in a safety analysis. Each production manager has to decide what its specific safety features are possible to certify a particular product. Design takes account of the whole spectrum of the product eliminating human errors by redesigning the equipment.

**HIGH LEVEL SYSTEM HAZARD (1):** Electromagnetic interference.
**Protective measures taken by the user**

- Do not use solvents or benzene for cleaning purpose.
- Do not wash the internal parts of the robot and do not use jets of pressurised water.
- To clean from deposits and residuals from the blade, use an indented brush.
- Use a dry cloth to clean the battery charger and the contact plates.
- Non waterproof robots shall be prevented from washing with liquids and shall be prevented from being turned over in water completely.

**HIGH LEVEL SYSTEM HAZARD (2):** Exposed mechanism.

- To prevent human health, residents shall not open the mower's covering hood with aim to avoid damaging internal electrical components.

**HIGH LEVEL SYSTEM HAZARD (3):** Explosion of the battery.

- Charge the battery in a dry, well-ventilated area where the temperature is moderate.
- Follow the correct procedure for charging.
- Keep all sparks, open flames, and smoking materials away from the battery.
- Keep the battery away from explosive and/or flammable environments.
- Station for battery charging shall not be placed in sites subject to vibration and away from concrete, incline or hard surfaces.

**HIGH LEVEL SYSTEM HAZARD (4):** Loose objects.

- User shall be informed that mowing over objects may cause malfunction to the blade and lead to an injury due to thrown objects from the mower's chute.

**HIGH LEVEL SYSTEM HAZARD (5):** Overturning of the robot.

- Check the slope of the ground and make sure the maximum values allowed.
- User is not supposed to operate the machine on slops or hills. Mow the slope as recommended by the manual.

**HIGH LEVEL SYSTEM HAZARD (6):** Contact with the sharp rotating blades.

- Wear heavy work gloves when working with and around the blades.
- User shall be informed from the manual about maintenance information.

**HIGH LEVEL SYSTEM HAZARD (7):** Pulling the mower backward.

- Look down and behind before and while operating backwards.
- Never try to mow in reverse using the manual controller.

**HIGH LEVEL SYSTEM HAZARD (8):** A child rides on an operating robot.

- The operating area should be clear of people (in particular children, the elderly or disabled people) and domestic animals. Operate the robot at suitable times of the day.
- Do not let a child to ride on a mower or walk along side. Children ought to stay inside the house and supervised so they don't suddenly come into the garden while robot is operating.
- Shut off the product in case of a child coming in the lawn.

**HIGH LEVEL SYSTEM HAZARD (9):** The perimeter wire causes tripping hazard.

- Ensure the robot does not run into obstacles, corners or harmful objects.
- Wear gloves when installing the perimeter wire and driving the wire pegs.
- The power cord shall be fixed firmly to the ground.

**HIGH LEVEL SYSTEM HAZARD (10):** Robot is moving at high speed.

- Never turn on the device in a garage even if the outdoors and openings are opened.

# 3    Conclusion

Safety in a domestic environment is much more complicated, due to the presence of much more untrained people as well as due to many unpredicted situations that might arise. This gave the main thrust to this paper, which attempt to approach the problem of robots safety, from a systemic point of view. This method could be applied as a preventive means at the stages of planning, organizing, directing and controlling the safety design of production in order to reduce the defective procedures that could lead to an incident. Moreover, it could be applied to other types of robot such as biped, toy-robots, personal care, service and automated guided vehicle robots. A robot is considered safe when fulfill the safety standards, which draws from research on the national, and when all requirements that had been pointed out by the authors, are fully satisfied. This Systems-Theoretic framework supports robot's business firm to achieve objectives, increasing firms reputation and facing the competition in the market, while supporting in decision-making related to rapid changes according to specification of the robotic system.

# References

1. ANSI/ASAE S318: Safety for Agricultural Equipment (2009)
2. ANSI/ASAE S323: Definitions of Powered Lawn and Garden Equipment (1983)
3. ANSI B71.4: Safety Specifications for Commercial Turf Care Equipment (2004)
4. ANSI/RIA R15.06: Robots and Robot Systems (1999)
5. ANSI/OPEI B71.1: Safety Specifications for Turf Care Equipment – Power Lawn Mowers, Lawn and Garden Tractors (2003)
6. ASAE S441: Safety Signs (1999)
7. Mitka, E., Gasteratos, A., Kyriakoulis, N., Mouroutsos, G.S.: Safety certification requirements for domestic robots. Safety Science 50, 1888–1897 (2012)
8. Robomow operating and safety manual of Friendly Robotics Acquisition Ltd., http://www.robomow.com/pdf/2010/rl_manual_en.pdf
9. Leveson, N.: Safeware, System Safety and Computers. Addison-Wesley Professional (1995)
10. Mouroutsos, G.S., Mitka, E.: Applying System Safety Engineering to Safety Standards of Domestic Robots. In: 8th HSSS National and International Conference on Systems Approach to Strategic Management, Greece (2012)

# Applying Serious Games
# in Lean Manufacturing Training

M. Messaadia[1], A. Bufardi[2], J. Le Duigou[1], H. Szigeti[3], B. Eynard[1], and D. Kiritsis[2]

[1] Université de Technologie de Compiègne,
Department of Mechanical Systems Engineering, CNRS UMR6253 Roberval
BP 60319, rue du Docteur Schweitzer, 60203 Compiègne Cedex, France
{mourad.messaadia,julien.le-duigou,benoit.eynard}@utc.fr
[2] Ecole plytechnique Fédérale de Lausane (EPFL), Switzerland
{ahmed.bufardi,dimitris.kiritsis}@epfl.ch
[3] DELMIA Dassault Systèmes, 10 Rue Marcel Dassault - 78946 Velizy Villacoublay, France
hadrien.szigeti@3ds.com

**Abstract.** In this paper, we report on the outcomes of one of the most successful training events organized within the framework of ActionPlanT project. This event was planned using the bottom-up approach of the ActionPlanT Industrial Learning model. The "Muscle car" serious game was used to deliver the training content about lean manufacturing to the participants in this event. The feedback received from the participants through the completed questionnaires indicated that serious games are suitable delivery mechanisms for training themes such as Lean Manufacturing.

**Keywords:** ActionPlanT IL model, serious games, Lean manufacturing, ILPE.

## 1    Introduction

Among the challenges of industrial learning (IL) is the inadequacy of learning content and delivery mechanisms to the new learning requirements of the manufacturing workforce.

ActionPlanT project produced a baseline document providing recommendations about instruments, methodologies and activities to deliver effective IL programs for the future e-skills in manufacturing. Among these recommendations is the use of tailored delivery mechanisms for the training of manufacturing workers that take into account their specific needs and constraints.

This paper reports on the outcomes of a training event organized within the framework of ActionPlanT project where a game-based learning mechanism is used to deliver training content to employees from an electronics manufacturing industry.

One of the main activities of ActionPlanT project is the development and validation of a concept for IL, extensively piloted via Industrial Learning Pilot Events (ILPEs) and workshops amongst stakeholders in industry, academia, and the European technology platforms alike.

C. Emmanouilidis, M. Taisch, D. Kiritsis (Eds.): APMS 2012, Part I, IFIP AICT 397, pp. 558–565, 2013.

In ActionPlanT project, an IL model and methodology were developed [1]. Their implementation is executed through the organization of a series of ILPEs where promising delivery mechanisms and manufacturing themes are tested and evaluated for selected target groups. ILPEs are considered as instances of the comprehensive ActionPlanT IL model.

The ActionPlanT IL model is competence-based and is suitable for creating new knowledge assets related to "cutting edge" information and communication technologies (ICTs) for manufacturing, identifying corresponding new professional competencies, and defining relevant learning programs and actions to train workers and engineers to develop these competencies.

The ActionPlanT IL methodology aims at implementing through a number of steps the IL actions defined using the ActionPlanT IL model for a specific learning situation. This includes the identification of the target group and their learning needs, and the choice of adequate delivery mechanisms and appropriate evaluation tools.

The organisation of an ILPE involves 4 main components: the delivery mechanism, the learning theme, the target group, and the training process which encloses the set of activities required to allow delivering the training theme to the target group using the delivery mechanism.

The second section describes the serious game deployment for lean manufacturing training. Third section describes results of applying different types of organization, the evolution from one round to another one and the ILPE evaluation. Finally, the conclusion and future perspectives for ILPE and the evolution of the serious game deployed.

# 2    The ILPE Applying Serious Game in Lean Manufacturing Training

The role of learning for capacity building is seen as paramount for industrial development and enhancing added value. The factors behind the successful industrial learning have not been appropriately conceptualized in the existing academic literature [2]. The ILPE applying serious game in lean manufacturing training will be an evaluation of the industrial learning. The ILPE applying serious game in lean manufacturing training will be an evaluation of the industrial learning, and a way to deepen the theoretical and practical understanding of Industrial learning implementation.

## 2.1    Description of the ILPE and Its Objectives

For the ILPE reported in this paper, we used the bottom-up approach of the ActionPlanT IL model and identified the "application of lean principles" as a professional need for the community (target audience) of employees from an electronics manufacturing industry which guided us to define the appropriate training content that we delivered using a game-based learning mechanism.

One of the main strengths of serious games is their ability to provide job like training environments which is very appreciated by trainees from manufacturing industry.

The main objectives of this ILPE were to test and evaluate the following aspects:

1. the learning process building blocks for competence development in Lean Manufacturing: knowledge, skills, and attitude,
2. the serious game delivery mechanism,
3. team work (collaboration, communication, conflict resolution, group decision making, etc.) of the participants within each team.

This one-day training event was organized for 19 participants from the same company but having different responsibilities.

The serious game exercise was followed by a more formal presentation on Lean principles and the kind of ICT systems that are needed to implement them in modern production organizations. The objectives of the presentation were twofold: (i) to explain to the participants the lean principles they applied in the exercise and (ii) to emphasize the importance of ICT to improve the implementation of Lean principles.

## 2.2    The "Muscle Car" Serious Game

Lean manufacturing can be defined as a business system and a generic process management philosophy with a systematic approach to eliminating waste through continuous improvement [3]. Lean manufacturing and its key principles take their origins from Toyota Production System (TPS) more generally known as lean manufacturing.

The game selected for this ILPE is the "Muscle Car" serious game; it's based on the Lean manufacturing concepts. The purpose of this game is the simulation of car's assembly line. The objective is to assemble as many cars as possible while at the same time keeping the inventory cost as low as possible.

By playing Muscle Car, the participants are expected to face problems and constraints of manufacturing industry that will need to be fixed using different solutions.

The game is based on LEGO® car models where the participants are divided into teams, and compete during 3 rounds of 3 simulated weeks of 5 days. Short breaks simulating the weekends are also considered in the exercise.

Muscle Car is the delivery mechanism used in this ILPE.

## 2.3    Running the Game

The participants in this event were partitioned into two teams. Each participant played a specific role in his team (Autonomous Production Unit (APU) manager, transporter, Final Assembly Line manager, etc.).

In this ILPE, 3 different types of organization were applied and evaluated: traditional, self optimized and lean. The game was run in 3 rounds (a round for each type of organisation) and at the end of each round, the performance of each team was shown to both teams.

Regarding the traditional organization applied in the first round of the game, the participants produced cars according to a specific organization described by the game rules provided by the instructors during the introduction of the ILPE.

Regarding the self optimized organization, the participants of the two teams proposed their own organization in order to fix the different problems and constraints they encountered in the first round of the game where the traditional organization was applied. In each team, the participants collaboratively defined the type of organisation to adopt and collectively agreed on it.

Regarding the lean organization, the participants put some Lean principles provided by the instructors into practice in order to make the production more efficient. It was assumed that the new lean organisation is suggested by a consulting firm specialized in Lean manufacturing. In this new organisation all APUs were reorganized into "Pull Flows": an APU could only produce if there was a demand from its "internal customer", i.e. the APU that consumes its sub-systems.

The game was significantly improved through the introduction of the intermediate round (which does not exist in the original version of the game) where the participants proposed their own organization (self optimized) in order to fix the problems encountered in the first round. The intermediate round allowed the participants to better follow and understand the evolution from a traditional organization to a lean organization and showed that the adoption of lean principles is a normal tendency in a group in the case of organization problems. This was appreciated by both the trainees and the expert trainers.

## 2.4    Muscle Car versus Lean Manufacturing Concepts

There are many tangible benefits associated with lean Manufacturing, such as the automotive industry. Among these benefits we have decreased lead times for customers; reduced inventories for manufacturers; improved knowledge management; more robust processes (as measured by less errors and therefore less rework) [4].

Muscle car is not just a game, but it is the implementation of lean manufacturing concepts through practice and simulation. It's a stimulating and effective teaching tool through participatory and collaborative activities. It strengthens the social dimension and interactions, and ensures the participation and motivates the audience. The serious game is not intended to apply all lean manufacturing concepts, but rather to discuss some concepts in practice.

Among Lean Manufacturing concepts used in this game we find:

- Standardization: concentrates on standardizing best practice in each work area. The game consists to produce two different types of cars with different structure and color. However, we considered standard modules to both types of cars, such as engine, wheels etc. We also establish precise procedures for each APU's work through precise work sequence.
- Kaizen (Continuous improvement): describes an environment where companies and individuals proactively work to improve the manufacturing process. The concept is introduced by the integration of the 2nd round where everybody interacts and exchange, and submit his proposition.
- Kanban: a visual signal to support flow by 'pulling' product through the manufacturing process as required by the customer. In the game Kanban is seen

 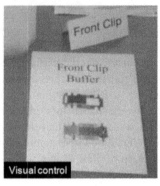

**Fig. 1.** Lean manufacturing concepts illustration

through different APU's of sub-assembly components. APU contains small/large bins for component/module storage (Fig.1). Each bin has a unique label designating the reference, quantity of component, etc.

- Visual control: a method of measuring performance at the 'shop floor' which was visual and owned by the operator team. The concept is introduced progressively, through procedures, the identification of different APU, the transparency of the bins (On each APU it is possible to know the risk of missing components). We introduce in the $3^{rd}$ round Buffers which represent the identification of storage areas (Fig.1).

## 3     Results and Evaluation

The efficiency of each given type of organization was measured using two types of criteria: (i) the number of cars produced (which should be maximized) and (ii) the inventory cost (which should be minimized).

The results of the exercise (number of assembled cars and the inventory cost) are compared in two different ways: (i) for each team according to the different types of organization to see how they are performing with respect to the number of cars produced and the inventory cost, and (ii) between the two teams for each type of organization where the objective is to check whether similar trends are observed within the two teams.

At the end of the serious game we make debrief of the 3 rounds in order to discuss various rounds and especially to show profits of lean manufacturing. Teams will be able to see their mistakes and see for themselves the results.

(Fig. 2) shows inventories obtained during the serious game and presented to players at the end. Three different colors to distinguish different rounds:

- Blue (Traditional factory): first round, where traditional organization was proposed;
- Red (Optimized factory): second round, where teams organize themselves;

- Green (Lean Factory): third round, where the lean manufacturing solution was proposed.

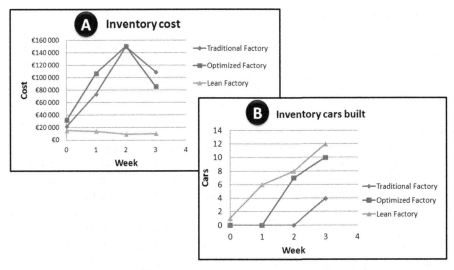

**Fig. 2.** Comparison of "Muscle Car" rounds

(A) Inventory cost: during 3 workweeks each APU will produce parts of car until the final assembly. Every weekend, we made an inventory of parts produced by APU's and don't assembled on the cars. This represents goods in progress and storage costs. For this we assigned a cost to each part.

(B) Inventory cars built: during the game, the goal of participants is to build maximum cars in line with customer's requests. Every weekend, we made an inventory of cars built.

As a result of applying the tree different types of organization, the lean factory organization had the highest number of assembled cars and the lowest inventory cost among the three types of organization for the two teams which means that lean organisation dominates the two other types of organisation since it performs better than them on both criteria.

Another aspect according to these organization and we don't see it through the figure is the working atmosphere. In the first and second rounds participants were working under pressure and moved in all directions. Often they cried out for the part. During the last round, despite the competitive spirit was always present, participants were calmer and focused on their work and did not need to shout.

For the evaluation of the ILPE, a questionnaire was distributed to all the participants during the training session and has been filled-in right after the end of the event. The questionnaire has been structured around the four major building blocks of the learning process (Table 1), which are addressed by the ActionPlanT IL model/methodology, i.e. attitude, knowledge, skills, and competencies [5].

**Table 1.** 4th ActionPlanT ILPE goals regarding attitude, knowledge skills and competencies

|  | Definition | 4th ILPE Goals |
|---|---|---|
| *Attitude* | "Attitude" is a hypothetical construct that represents an individual's degree of like or dislike for an item. Attitudes are generally positive or negative views of a person, place, thing, or event. | Create awareness and attract interest with respect to Lean Manufacturing and the supporting ICTs |
| *Knowledge* | "Knowledge" means the outcome of the assimilation of information through learning. Knowledge is the body of facts, principles, theories and practices that is related to a field of work or study. | Create a basic understanding about the major principles, pillars and limitations of Lean Manufacturing, as well as about the manufacturing ICTs (e.g. MES, ERP, RFID etc.) implementing the underlying principles and enabling lean production |
| *Skills* | "Skills" means the ability to apply knowledge and use know-how to complete well defined tasks. Skills may be cognitive or practical | Apply different schemes for team work organization and information processing in assembly operations, including traditional schemes, self-organization and lean principles |
| *Competencies* | "Competence" means the proven ability to use knowledge, skills and personal, social and/or methodological abilities. Competences may be considered as the interface between the learning and the innovation processes. | Develop the capability of addressing realistic use cases involved in car assembly operations, requiring decision making and optimization of teamwork organization and information processing |

Based on the feedback received from the participants through the completed questionnaires, it was indicated that the "Muscle Car" serious game is a relevant delivery mechanism to learn lean principles and contributes to improve attitude, knowledge, skills and competencies about lean manufacturing.

# 4   Conclusion

Through the discussions between the participants and the instructors after the exercise, it seemed that the participants reached a good understanding of lean manufacturing and showed interest to learn further about it.

The funny side of the game and the competition aspect between the two teams highly influenced the motivation and involvement of the participants in the exercise.

The addition of the intermediate round (self optimized organisation) was very much appreciated by the participants and illustrated the normal transition from traditional organisation to a lean organisation in order to solve organisational problems in a company.

This ILPE showed the great potential of serious games to deliver training content for workers in manufacturing companies. The serious game allows the trainees to learn in a job-like environment.

This kind of training events allows evaluating the compatibility of emerging delivery mechanisms with various training themes in manufacturing industry.

The ActionPlanT IL model and methodology provide efficient tools to organise IL actions for selected target groups.

As perspectives, we envisage the integration of a fourth round, based on ICT integration. This means the establishment of a simplified management information system. Also, ICT allows making information immediately visible to all, through electronic dashboard.

**Acknowledgements.** The research leading to these results has received funding from the European Community's Seventh Framework Programme (FP7/2007-2013) under grant agreement n° 258617.

The work in the ActionPlanT project is a common effort among all its contributing partners: Agoria, EPFL, Fraunhofer IPK, Dassault Systèmes, POLIMI, SAP, Tecnalia, University of Patras, and Platte Consult.

# References

1. Kiritsis, D., Bufardi, A., Mavrikios, D., Knothe, T., Szigeti, H., Majumdar, A.: A competence-based industrial learning approach for factories of the future: A result of the FP7-FoF project ActionPlanT. In: Proceedings of the 4th the International Conference on Computer Supported Education, Porto, Portugal, April 16-18 (2012)
2. Puidokas, M., Jucevicius, G.: The Inter-Organizational Industrial Learning of Lithuanian Furniture Manufacturers in the Value Chains of the Baltic Sea Region. Social Sciences Nr.3(65) (2009) ISSN 1392-0758
3. Womack, J.P., Jones, D.T.: Lean Thinking: Banish Waste and Create Wealth in Your Corporation. Simon & Schuster, New York (1996)
4. Meleton, T.: The Benefits of Lean Manufacturing: What Lean Thinking has to Offer the Process Industries. Trans IChemE, Part A, Chemical Engineering Research and Design 83(A6), 662–673 (2005)
5. Mavrikios, D., Papakostas, N., Mourtzis, D., Chryssolouris, G.: On industrial learning & training for the Factories of the Future: A conceptual, cognitive & technology framework. Journal of Intelligent Manufacturing, Special Issue on Engineering Education (2011), doi:10.1007/s10845-011-0590-9

# Flow and Physical Objects in Experiential Learning for Industrial Engineering Education

David Jentsch, Ralph Riedel, and Egon Mueller

Chemnitz University of Technology, Department of Factory Planning
and Factory Management, Chemnitz, Germany
{david.jentsch,ralph.riedel,egon.mueller}@mb.tu-chemnitz.de

**Abstract.** The paper explores the impact of physical learning objects and learning styles on flow and learning outcomes in industrial engineering education. Learning is conceptualized with the theory of experiential learning. Comparitive case studies yield data involving more than 100 students since 2009. The findings provide a strong argument for utilizing physical objects in education consistent with constructionist theory. It is futhermore found that flow may have negative impact on the learning scope.

**Keywords:** Experiential learning, flow, serious play, case study.

## 1 Introduction

According to Riedel et al. [1] learning is in the curricula of operations management and industrial engineering primarily based on a one-way transfer of concepts and methods. Especially early stages of education in this field are prone to these "transmission" models of learning, where rather fixed ideas are floated into to the learner [2] and personal interaction as well as experimentation is limited.

Research on experiential learning yielded four (respectively nine) learning style types that help to develop curricula allowing for a greater variety of learning processes [2]. The consequent goal is to expose students to a variety of learning opportunities related to different learning styles in order to foster the individual realization of preferred learning processes in different course formats. Adequate learning processes may yield in turn that students immerse themselves into the activity being fully concentrated, absent-minded and even losing all sense of time. These characteristics pertain to what Csikszentmihalyi called flow [3] and seem desirable for effective and positive learning processes in institutions [4, 5].

A second starting point of this article is the notion of the hand-brain-connection rooted in the work of Penfield and Rasmussen [6] and its implication for learning highlighted by Papert's theory of constructionism [7]. This theory may be summarized as learning-by-making and emphasizes that the material used during the learning process is decisive for deep engagement in the task [8], hence for entering the state of flow.

C. Emmanouilidis, M. Taisch, D. Kiritsis (Eds.): APMS 2012, Part I, IFIP AICT 397, pp. 566–573, 2013.

The outlined conceptual building blocks are merged into three subsequent research questions.

1. Do different course formats, implying different learning styles, impact students' experience of flow?
2. How does course material impact flow?
3. How is flow linked to the learning outcome?

Figure 1 summarizes these questions and the given context. The research questions are intended to be explorative.

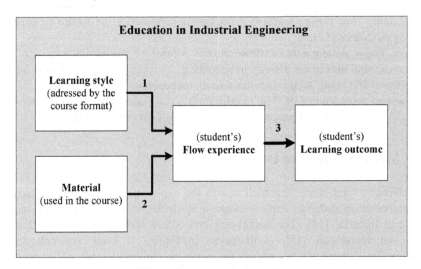

**Fig. 1.** Conceptual framework

The rest of the paper is structured as follows. We will give a brief review on experiential learning and flow theory first. A subsequent section provides an overview on the method and three case studies. Finally, preliminary findings and conclusions are discussed.

## 2    Theoretical Background

### 2.1    Experiential Learning

Experiential learning accentuates the learning process including the total person, e.g. their behavior, emotions and perceptions [2]. Knowledge is therefore created due to two distinct learning processes: The grasping and the transforming of experience [9]. Grasping may be conceptualized as a continuum between concrete experience and abstract conceptualization. Transforming spans from active experimentation to reflective observation.

Combining both process dimensions yields the classical four learning styles (diverging, assimilating, converging, and accommodating) [2] that can be expanded by the work of Abbey et al. [10] into nine styles [2]. We will reconsider these learning styles in order to classify the case studies in section 3.

## 2.2    Flow Theory

The state of flow is strongly linked to positive emotions and can be attained when task requirements and the abilities of the person match, the task is clearly structured, there is immediate feedback, and concentration is undisturbed [3, 11]. Experiencing flow during learning processes is supposed to be linked to improved learning outcomes [12].

Three major dimensions of flow are the control of the activity (control), the absence of mind during the activity indicated e.g. by losing the sense of time (absent-mindedness) and being focused on the activity (concentration) [11].

However, most studies of flow in education seem biased towards computer based games and neglect other types of "material" like physical objects [13].

## 3    Method and Case Description

We selected a case study approach due to the explorative nature of the study and multiple cases in order to explore contrasting differences concerning the learning types and material [14]. The underlying conceptual framework, in accordance to Miles and Huberman [15], is displayed in Figure 1. Data was collected by questionnaires, observations, and interviews with students. Table 1 illustrates the sampling logic and summarizes all three cases.

**Table 1.** Case Overview

|  | Case I: PS | Case 2: LSP | Case 3: PPC |
|---|---|---|---|
| **Material** | 3D (Lego bricks, sensors and actuators, computer) | 3D (Lego bricks) | 2D (paper and pencil, computer) |
| **Experience grasping** | concrete experience (ce) | between ce and ac | abstract conceptualization (ac) |
| **Experience transforming** | active experimentation (ae) | between ae and ro | reflective observation (ro) |

All cases have in common that they represent the exercise module of courses that contain classical "transmission" modules with oral lectures as well.

*Case 1* is part of a course that teaches the fundamentals of facility planning and systems engineering, including requirements engineering and project management. Students are required to build in teams a production system (PS) based on Lego Mindstorms [1, 16, 17]. Figure 2 gives an impression of students building and programming their model. Data is sampled from five runs of the course involving approximately 90 students since 2009.

*Case 2* belongs to an advanced course on leadership skills. Participants work in heterogeneous teams to model a shared understanding of leadership including the various facets of the topics, their personal experience and perceptions. Modeling is realized by means of abstract physical metaphors. The process utilizes a method based on Lego Serious Play (LSP) [8, 17, 18]. Figure 3 gives a workshop-impression. The analysis makes use of data from two courses with 25 students since autumn 2011.

*Case 3* is the exercise of an intermediate course on production planning and control (PPC). Students learn e.g. how to calculate economic lot sizes, use a standard ERP-system and interpret characteristic curves of logistics and production systems. The course is established for almost ten years and mainly held by the second author of this paper. Our in-depth analysis includes 15 participants from the summer term 2012.

**Fig. 2.** Students working on their production system (case I)

**Fig. 3.** Students' shared metaphorical model for leadership as a boat surrounded by high tides (case II)

# 4    Results

Preliminary findings indicate that students experience a high level of flow when experimenting with physical objects especially when combining it with technical problem solving (case 1). However, even more abstract and reflective settings like in case 2 evoke flow-like experiences. The descriptive statistics in Table 2 give evidence for this observation. The measurement is based on questionnaires with four point scales (1 – strong agreement ... 4 – strong disagreement).

**Table 2.** Descriptive Statistics

| Item | Case I: PS | Case 2: LSP (N = 8) | Case 3: PPC (N = 15) |
|---|---|---|---|
| The exercise was fun | M = 1.69* (N = 88) | M = 1.63 | M = 2.20 |
| I knew what to do (control) | M = 1.80 (N = 5) | M = 1.75 | M = 2.33 |
| I forgot time (absent-mindedness) | M = 1.80 (N = 5) | M = 2.50 | M = 2.73 |
| I was completely focused (concentration) | M = 1.80 (N = 5) | M = 2.00 | M = 2.80 |

It is furthermore observable from Table 2 that the utilization of physical material tends to yield positive emotions ("fun") among students. An independent sample t-test showed a significant difference between the means of PS and PPC, $t(101) = 2.775$, $p = .01$ for the item "the exercise was fun". The eta square index ($\eta^2 = .07$) indicated a medium effect size.

Furthermore, most participants agree that physical 3D material helps them to express thoughts and explore complex technical systems. Participants for the LSP case were convinced that 3D models evoke richer communication ($M = 1.63$). One participant stated:

> *"I can use this serious play in creative discussion, where flip charts are too abstract."*

Someone added that the models help when ...

> *"defending your own ideas".*

However, an estimated participants share of 10 to 15% tend to feel unconvertible using physical objects based on Lego bricks. One participant, who was certainly not in the state of flow according to his answers in the questionnaire, stated that he...

> *"[felt] like a child"* and suggested *"to use serious play for school and not for graduate students".*

The learning outcomes are more difficult to grasp. Despite good overall evaluations, some participants indicate that formats with a high degree of concrete experience and active experimentation are fun (case 1 and 2) but the value of the learning remains unclear or too time consuming to be achieved. An example may explain this line of reasoning: A group of students were trying to build a particular production system (case 1). They had spent more than 25 extra hours additional to their class experimenting in a mind-absent flow and were driven by unnecessarily ambitious plans for a fully automated system, but failed to implement their plan with the available material. They decided to quit the exercise and asked for a final consultation with their supervising tutors in early January 2012. Throughout the consultation the students explored their tendency to over-engineer the system and made up their mind for a much simpler solution in order to complete the course. This was apparently a painful experience for the students since they invested long hours into their first concept. However, the most remarkable quotation during the final presentation was the following.

*"The most important learning of this course took place when we failed – to recognize that we were too ambitious and how much it had cost us. That is certainly something useful for the future."*

Further evidence for these unintended learning outcomes can be found in an earlier edition of case 1 in 2011. A participant stated:

*"I did not learn too much from the game itself. What I learned was the importance of good and organized communication – to do intermediate presentations and define a project plan.*
*I found it interesting to see how different roles evolved during the project. There were leaders, thinkers, implementers etc. [...] not everybody is able to lead a project."*

Hence, does this learning prove any value? Fortunately we were able to do a follow up interview in July 2012 with a member of the previously mentioned "over-engineering-group". After participating in the Lego-exercise until February 2012 he had to complete a complex case study concerning facility planning in teamwork from April until July 2012. He suggested the following among several other insights transferred from case 1 to the new task.

*"The tendency of getting obsessed with details was resolved; problems were tackled in a more pragmatic manner. Due to strict milestones and central project controlling (and the related pressure) results were always delivered [...]."*

These insights are certainly some of the basic issues explained in every standard course on project management. However, the self-exposure to a project that is not successful since it lacks these fundamentals seems to provide a suitable alley for students towards really understanding what the course is actually about.

## 5    Discussion and Conclusion

Finally, we may return to the research questions. The first question asked if different course formats impact students' experience of flow. We conclude a tentative yes:

Active experimentation is a supportive condition to enter the state of flow but it is not a sufficient feature. We found flow also in more abstract and reflective situations.

As to the second question, we conclude that material has an impact on entering the state of flow. Especially the modular structure of physical objects allows for an easy entry into the learning process and provides enough complexity to cope with higher levels of skill and abstraction. However, we observed a notable level of cynicism among some participants, which is at least partly due to utilized material. Other researchers [e.g. 19] observed the same issue and argued that cynicism is due to the blurring of the border between private and professional life. We may add that not every course format suits every student due to different learning styles and it is therefore rather simple to derive from the obvious and have objections against using plastic bricks.

Furthermore, our results suggest that flow is linked to the learning outcome (research question 3). The link is established in a rather unexpected manner since high levels of flow yield learning with a scope different to the intended (case 1). From a learning perspective we see a strong need to further enable participants taking responsibility of their own learning when finding themselves in an environment fostering active experimentation and reflecting. We were lucky to find a striking example were high flow and experience based learning was successfully transferred into a new task. However, such success stories need to be further studied in order to give this opportunity to more students.

Despite all limitations of this study, we see a strong argument for physical objects in industrial engineering education and support for the theory of constructionism. Nonetheless, there is a strong need to further elaborate our findings and to study also combinations of physical and digital "cyber" objects in the future.

# References

1. Riedel, R., Jentsch, D., Tröger, S., Müller, E.: Integrating experimental learning into Industrial Engineering curricula – a case study. In: IFAC Conference on Management and Control of Production Logistics MCPL, Coimbra (2010)
2. Kolb, A.Y., Kolb, D.A.: Learning Styles and Learning Spaces: Enhancing Experiential Learning in Higher Education. Academy of Management Learning & Education 4, 193–212 (2005)
3. Csikszentmihalyi, M.: Beyond boredom and anxiety. Jossey-Bass Publishers, San Francisco (1975)
4. Summers, L.H.: On undergraduate education, pp. 63–65. Harvard Magazine (2003)
5. Clinton, G., Rieber, L.P.: The Studio experience at the University of Georgia: an example of constructionist learning for adults. Educational Technology Research and Development 58, 755–780 (2010)
6. Penfield, W., Rasmussen, T.: The cerebral cortex of man; a clinical study of localization of function. Macmillan, Oxford (1950)
7. Papert, S., Harel, I.: Situating Constructionism. Ablex Publishing, Norwood (1991)
8. Gauntlett, D.: Creative explorations: new approaches to identities and audiences. Routledge, Oxon (2007)

9. Kolb, D.A.: Experiential learning: experience as the source of learning and development. Prentice-Hall (1984)
10. Abbey, D.S., Hunt, D.E., Weiser, J.C.: Variations on a Theme by Kolb: A New Perspective for Understanding Counseling and Supervision. The Counseling Psychologist 13, 477–501 (1985)
11. Drenger, J., Gaus, H.-J., Jahn, S.: Does Flow Influence the Brand Image in Event Marketing? Journal of Advertising Research 48, 138 (2008)
12. Shernoff, D.J., Csikszentmihalyi, M., Shneider, B., Shernoff, E.S.: Student engagement in high school classrooms from the perspective of flow theory. School Psychology Quarterly 18, 158–176 (2003)
13. Procci, K., Bowers, C.: An Examination of Flow and Immersion in Games. Proceedings of the Human Factors and Ergonomics Society Annual Meeting 55, 2183–2187 (2011)
14. Voss, C.: Case Research in Operations Management. In: Karlsson, C. (ed.) Researching Operations Management, pp. 162–195. Routledge, New York (2009)
15. Miles, M.B., Huberman, A.M.: Qualitative Data Analysis: An Expanded Sourcebook. Sage Publications, Inc., Beverly Hills (1994)
16. Tröger, S., Jentsch, D., Riedel, R., Müller, E.: The use of LEGO(R) Mindstorms(R) within universitary courses in the field of factory planning and systems engineering. In: Taisch, M., Cassina, J., Smeds, R. (eds.) Experimental Learning on Sustainable Management, Economics and Industrial Engineering. Proceedings of 14th Workshop of the Special Interest Group on Experimental Interactive Learning in Industrial Management of the IFIP Working Group 5.7., pp. 216–225. Politecnico di Milano, Milano (2010)
17. Tröger, S., Jentsch, D., Riedel, R., Müller, E.: Serious Games as a Transfer Method in Industrial Management and Engineering. In: Smeds, R. (ed.) Co-Designing Serious Games, pp. 137–150. Aalto University publication series SCIENCE + TECHNOLOGY, Helsinki (2011)
18. Rasmussen, R.: When You Build in the World, You Build in Your Mind. Design Management Review 17, 56–63 (2010)
19. Fleming, P.: Workers' Playtime?: Boundaries and Cynicism in a "Culture of Fun" Program. The Journal of Applied Behavioral Science 41(3), 285–303 (2005)

# Context Aware E-Support in E-Maintenance

Nikos Papathanassiou[1,2], Christos Emmanouilidis[2],
Petros Pistofidis[1,2], and Dimitris Karampatzakis[2]

[1] Democritus University of Thrace, Greece
{npapatha,pistofid}@ceti.gr
[2] ATHENA Research & Innovation Centre, Greece
{chrisem,dkara}@ceti.gr

**Abstract.** Mobile learning is a powerful addition to the toolset offered by e-Learning solutions. It can extend current e-Learning benefits to provide support and training everywhere, anytime and to anyone registered to have access and with affordable costs. Mobile devices with substantial computational, networking and storage capabilities are ubiquitous today. However, attempts to employ them in training are mostly addressing educational needs of end users with existing competencies in computing, such as students. We propose the development of a specially built mobile learning solution with the aim to provide e-Support to technicians within an e-Maintenance framework. This system will be backed and collaborate with a Learning Management System platform in order to provide on the spot aid and adequate supporting content to maintenance personnel.

**Keywords:** E-support, e-maintenance, mobile learning, e-training, context awareness.

## 1  Introduction

The reported research work aims to combine an integrated e-Maintenance framework with e-Training based on web technologies and supporting mobile devices. The e-Maintenance framework realizes platform-independent Condition-Based Maintenance by integrating an intelligent sensor network deployment, a Computerised Maintenance Management System (CMMS), a knowledge management system and an intelligent maintenance advisor, in the context of the WelCOM project [1]. It can provide an advanced, proactive type of Maintenance support that processes maintenance information throughout the plant, transparently providing it to anyone with authorized access. In this setting, our main aim is to study to what extend the e-Training system can be coupled with the other e-Maintenance components so as to provide context-aware support to shop-floor maintenance personnel and basic training on the system use to stakeholders.

E-Learning can be an effective way to train industrial employees, irrespective of their exact work placement due to some key attributes:

- First, it can offer time and location independent training, which has significant merit in workforce training. Industrial staff is hardly in position to attend formal classes and any probable pressure to become familiar with a new e-maintenance system could easily lead to overkill and negative attitude against the whole system.

C. Emmanouilidis, M. Taisch, D. Kiritsis (Eds.): APMS 2012, Part I, IFIP AICT 397, pp. 574–581, 2013.
© IFIP International Federation for Information Processing 2013

- Second, e-learning can provide a stimulating, intuitive and straight to the point way of delivering technical knowledge that can adapt and readily fit in the everyday schedule of a modern industrial plant.
- Third, e-learning content can be formatted and delivered directly to mobile devices as context-dependent technical support. This has the potential to accelerate the familiarity and facilitate the acceptance of the new training system by maintenance staff.

Modern mobile devices support connectivity, autonomy and offer computing and graphics capabilities that can be exploited to create appealing training environments at affordable cost. In the present work, supporting technical material is provided by a web server running a LMS (learning management system). The aim is to make it easy to locate directly the knowledge part that is requested on the mobile device and to update content regularly to reflect changes in maintenance practice. Our aim is to seek to adhere to e-learning standards, so as to increase the reusability of the content. Lately, our experimentation is focused on methods to seamlessly interconnect a customized mobile interface with the server side e-learning infrastructure. Based on this interconnection and on context-dependent data available from other WelCOM components, we will be able to provide contextualised support to the shop floor staff. Context may refer to different categories, such as user, environment, system, social and service [2]. In an industrial maintenance setting, the context can be quite wide. It may comprise information about specific machine, sensor readings, type of machinery operation, operation and maintenance history, type of maintenance action, possible failures, staff profile and role, as well as relevant services. This information should be communicated between e-Support and the rest of WelCOM e-Maintenance framework tools in a transparent and unobtrusive way, in order to simplify the delivered e-Support interface. Thus, e-Support is adequately offered via web services. Furthermore we seek to employ multiple modalities in human-computer interfaces, including speech interfaces.

## 2    e-Learning and Mobile Learning

In the last decade e-Learning has gained popularity and ubiquity, with relevant research carried out towards a wide spectrum of applications. Interconnectivity offered by ICT pushed the way for the implementation of solutions based on learner-centric Learning Theories, as well as to learning by direct interaction with others, typical in collaborative constructivism and groupware learning. Application of Constructivism and Activity Theory to mobile learning (m-Learning) in relation to acceptance by learners has been studied through questionnaires, highlighting significant advantages, such as learner initiative, improved interactivity and autonomy [3]. Attempts have also been reported to implement known learning theories to develop 3D multimedia courseware [4]. In research focused on engaging learning environments, Augmented Reality (AR) has been employed to deliver new platforms for easy creation of Virtual Scenes without previous programming knowledge [5].

Serious games are shown to bring significant benefits and personalisation options in order to create highly motivating and engaging learning experiences [6]. Employment of social networks in the Learning process has also been studied.

Specifically, Web 2.0 elements, such as participant collaboration and virtual communities were evaluated, noting the connection between social learning networks and the "social constructivism" theory [7]. Work with elementary school pupils has shown how critical it is to deal with e-learning not as simply an extension of printed material but as medium with a multitude of advantages to exploit, like interactivity, multimedia and personalisation [8].

## 2.1 E-Learning Standards

The development costs for quality training material can be brought down by the adoption of Learning Standards that will promote content reusability, interoperability and discoverability. However, these standards still seem inefficient to support modern and engaging learner – system interactions such as multimedia and educational games. An important step to overturn this situation is a project named "Next Generation Learning Environment", carried out by ADL (Advanced Distributed Learning), founders of the SCORM model, one of the most widespread e-learning standards. The primary goal is to provide a standard that will support modern learning experiences, such as games, mobile learning, social networks, learner collaboration and mixed modalities. A straightforward model of integration in Learning Management Systems through improvements in the sequencing procedures has been presented [9].

## 2.2 Industrial Training

Currently demands for improved system productivity, availability, quality, safety and customer satisfaction, highlight the critical role of maintenance as an indispensable activity in industrial production. A significant number of complex factors must be taken into account in modern maintenance and fuel a demand for advanced ICT solutions [10]. The potential impact of an e-Maintenance framework on the implementation of a Condition Based Monitoring strategy is significant [11]. Mobile and collaborative technologies are enabling information and services to become available to the shop floor technical personnel, anywhere and anytime [12]. Furthermore, the concept of a Virtual Factory as an integrated virtual environment that facilitates knowledge and information sharing throughout all industrial production phases is offered as an open alternative to costly proprietary solutions for platform independent monitoring of production assets [13]. A learning engine capable of delivering learning material in the form of 3D knowledge objects to pilots and maintenance technicians in an aviation setting, emphasising access of maintenance technicians to "Learning on Demand (LoD)" instructions and trouble shooting references is an effective training enabler [14].

Industrial Maintenance can benefit from a common accreditation framework that will enhance workers mobility, support enterprise recruitment and enhance staff development. In Europe, such a framework has been set by EFNMS with the definition of competence requirements for maintenance managers and technicians [15], as well as by the PAS55 specification for optimising Asset Management practice, put forward by the Institute of Asset Management in the UK.

## 3    Problem Statement

Developing e-Learning based e-Support for industrial maintenance technicians presents certain challenges:

- Mobile devices pose different restrictions due to monitor sizes, lack of keyboards and mice, limited battery life, unstable network connections and sometimes harsh working conditions. Despite the fact that there are devices with high-end characteristics and industrial design, restrictions have to be addressed to create a usable support application.
- Learners in a typical e-Learning setting would benefit by presenting the learning material gradually, in small sections, with intertwining comprehension questions so as to evaluate their performance and understanding as they proceed through the courses. Technicians on the shop floor would find all these as annoying distractions in their effort to access the exact information they need to perform their job, as they need precise, on the spot information.
- Procedures such as registration, login, course enrolment, searches through a breadth of learning content, are typical in every e-Learning setting. However, they would hinder the work of a technician, even more when he has to interact with other applications, as needed to complete the work orders.

Delivering technical support through mobile devices directly to the technicians on the shop floor, presents some unique benefits that we are planning to exploit:

- Real-time interactions with the supporting material could constitute an invaluable set of information regarding efficiency and appropriateness of the followed procedures and the relevant material. The underlying LMS would record all this information and technicians, engineers or technical managers would have access to it.
- Based on the above, a technician could select to attend a section of the e-learning that is relevant to a difficult part of his task. An engineer, supervisor or technical manager could pinpoint support elements that gather the most inquiries and initiate procedures to update and enrich them. As an example, the e-support system can notify the LMS that there are requests for maintenance actions on a specific machine. Based on this, the LMS can inform supervisors or managers and deliver a short web-based support relevant to the machine, so as to reach a better understanding of the problem at hand and possibly improve performance.
- Context definition in industrial e-support has not received sufficient attention and is usually restricted to localisation and specific user-context. Having a more thorough definition of context in this domain is among our research goals.
- Technically a major challenge we have to face up to is related to the fast and accurate delivery of e-support content to the mobile device. It is clear that under no circumstances this delivery should rely solely on wireless connections, due to number of obstacles, such as metal wall surfaces and roofs that are present in a factory. One solution that was examined initially was to transfer permanently all the supporting material inside the mobile devices. This idea is not satisfactory, first because the volume of this information could easily overload a mobile device and more importantly, it would negate the whole idea of intelligent interaction and collection of feedback by the LMS. Apart from breaking down the content into small

entities, the Learning Objects, a potential solution to this problem is for the technician to be provided only with relevant for his job content. Avoiding redundancies on content delivery, all these objects will undergo custom compression procedures before their transfer to the mobile devices so as to minimize latency. Furthermore, a dynamic caching mechanism can be used to temporarily store large content entities, such as videos, to enhance the user experience.

- Intuitive environment and simplicity are two prerequisite qualities of the proposed solution, in order to minimize the case of rejection from low ICT-skilled users. Although the role of the supervisor is crucial and it is enhanced through the whole e-maintenance system, the e-support platform is expected to be gradually enriched at such level that it will allow for simple tasks to be performed without further human intervention and authorization. Thus, shop floor supervisors can focus on higher level activities.

- Another aspect of simplicity deals with the creation of new content. It is impractical to design a system that will need an ICT expert each time a new element, such as an image, video or technical document has to be added in the supporting database. Therefore, we opt for procedures that will be easily accessible to different staff categories inside an enterprise. The learning support software that will help the creation of new learning objects from raw support data is currently being developed.

A simple sequence diagram, showing the involved processes, invoked by technical staff, is shown in Fig. 1.

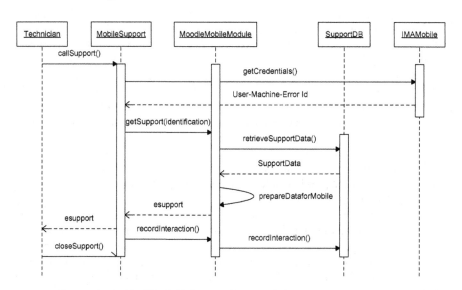

**Fig. 1.** E-Support Sequence Diagram

The above sequence diagram illustrates that the main e-support interaction commences when the technician on the shop floor requests support through the corresponding interface on the mobile device. The native application that is executed on the device proceeds to authorization – context definition procedures by requesting the relevant information from the other e-maintenance components (IMA) through web-services. Consequently, the mobile application contacts the corresponding Moodle module that gathers the requested support material from the learning database by searching based on meta-tags of Learning Objects. This material is processed, i.e. compressed by the module and is been transferred to the mobile device to be presented to the technician.

Essential in the procedure of delivering the appropriate content to each user is the formation of an extended learner profile that will contain constantly updated information about his knowledge, interactions and performance in theoretic learning and industrial work. This profile defines an important part of the context awareness and should be accessible at any time, so that it becomes possible to use the e-Learning system in order to enrich knowledge in the areas that he deems appropriate. It has to be also available to unit or line managers and maintenance supervisors, so they would have the necessary information to suggest improvements on the supporting material and possibly also on the maintenance policy implementation, with the aim to improve the technicians' performance.

Apart from the learner profile, all the learning and supporting content has to be broken down into fine-grained learning objects. These learning objects must be appropriately described and characterized by tags that will enable their search and their instant identification to be delivered to the field worker. The components of this e-Support system, within the WelCOM e-Maintenance architecture are shown in Fig 2.

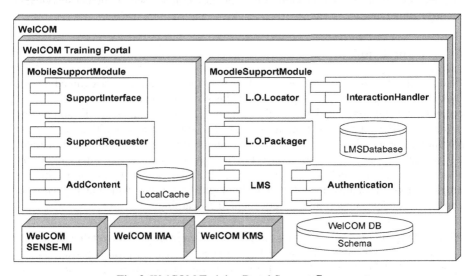

**Fig. 2.** WelCOM Training Portal Support Components

E-support data will be constantly updated and enhanced through the contribution of both managers and technicians. This purely practical knowledge content is expected to formulate a comprehensive library of information about machines and industrial procedures, organised through meta-tags and learning object interrelations in a way that is suitable to the end users, the technicians. As a step further, this library can be redeployed to other parts or subsidiaries of the industry or even to be traded as an asset with industries that use the same machinery.

## 4    Relevant Work

e-Learning has been integrated in m-learning scenarios in various works. The combination of e-learning with m-learning has been tested in a school setting, in order to provide personalised learning [16]. Our work is differentiated in that (a) it addresses industrial training needs (b) knowledge is treated as Learning Objects that are dynamic so as to be updated with user-contributed content, e.g. by the technicians. Furthermore, the nature of the industrial processes themselves makes the provision of all assistive functions, including e-support, fundamentally important. Although a minor latency delay may be tolerated, the delivery of fast and contextually relevant support through mobile devices is one of the requirements in the WelCOM project. The placement of the e-support as a single module inside an integrated e-maintenance framework and the interconnectivity between the autonomous modules though web-services is also considered to be a key contribution.

## 5    Further Work

Currently, our focus is the examination in close collaboration with experts from the industry, of the latest SCORM and IMS standards and composition of a prototype model for our learning objects that will serve the requirements of our project. The development of the Moodle e-Support module has started based on the latest style and security guidelines.

## 6    Conclusion

Placing an e-Learning system as part of a working procedure in a demanding and dynamic setting, such as supporting industrial maintenance technicians, is a considerable challenge and the evaluation of its educational value is among our objectives. E-Support integration should be transparent, intuitive and offer streamlined access to contextually relevant content. It is considered that the integrated e-Training system, comprising both e-Learning and e-Support, would facilitate the adoption of a modern e-Maintenance system. Maintenance staff will be in position to employ more efficiently the offered technological solutions with the provision of context-dependent support and closely coupled e-Learning.

**Acknowledgements.** The author wish to acknowledge the enthusiasm and contribution by the WelCOM  (GSRT grant 09SYN-71-856) project partner's staff, namely KLEEMANN Lifts, National Research Foundation, Prisma Electronics, GDT SA and ATLANTIS Engineering (welcom-project.ceti.gr).

## References

1. Pistofidis, P., Emmanouilidis, C., Koulamas, C., Karampatzakis, D., Papathanassiou, N.: A Layered E-Maintenance Architecture Powered by Smart Wireless Monitoring Components. In: IEEE Conference on Industrial Technologies, ICIT 2012, Athens, Greece, May 19-21, pp. 390–395 (2011)

2. Emmanouilidis, C., Koutsiamanis, R.-A., Tasidou, A.: Mobile Guides: Taxonomy of Architectures, Context Awareness, Technologies and Applications. Journal of Network and Computer Applications 36(1), 103–125 (2013)
3. Liaw, S.-S., Huang, H.-M.: Exploring Learners' Acceptance Toward Mobile Learning. In: Teo, T. (ed.) Technology Acceptance in Education, pp. 145–157. SensePublishers (2011)
4. Noordin, S., Ahmad, W.F.W.: Implementation of design and learning theories in multimedia courseware development: Lines & Planes in 3-Dimensions. In: 2010 Int. Conf. on User Science and Engineering (i-USEr). IEEE (2010)
5. Jee, H.-K., et al.: An augmented reality-based authoring tool for E-learning applications. Multimedia Tools and Applications, 1–11 (2011)
6. Fradinho Oliveira, M., Andersen, B., Pereira, J., Seager, W., Ribeiro, C.: The Use of Integrative Framework to Support the Development of Competences. In: Ma, M., Fradinho Oliveira, M., Madeiras Pereira, J. (eds.) SGDA 2011. LNCS, vol. 6944, pp. 117–128. Springer, Heidelberg (2011)
7. Jones, K., et al.: Social Networks for Learning: Breaking Through the Walled Garden of the VLE. In: Abraham, A., Hassanien, A.-E. (eds.) Computational Social Networks, pp. 417–444. Springer, London (2012)
8. Huang, Y.-M., et al.: Empowering personalized learning with an interactive e-book learning system for elementary school students. Educational Technology Research and Development, 1–20 (2012)
9. Panar, A., Shumaker, T.M. (eds.): Sharable Content Object Reference Model (SCORM®) 2004 4th Edition Testing Requirements (TR) Version 1.1. Advanced Distributed Learning (ADL) Initiative (2009)
10. Arnaiz, A., et al.: Information and Communication Technologies Within E-maintenance. In: Holmberg, K., et al. (eds.), pp. 39–60. Springer, London (2010)
11. Jantunen, E., et al.: e-Maintenance: a means to high overall efficiency. In: Kiritsis, D., et al. (eds.) Engineering Asset Lifecycle Management, pp. 688–696. Springer, London (2010)
12. Emmanouilidis, C., Liyanage, J.P., Jantunen, E.: Mobile solutions for engineering asset and maintenance management. Journal of Quality in Maintenance Engineering 15, 92–105 (2009)
13. Sacco, M., Dal Maso, G., Milella, F., Pedrazzoli, P., Rovere, D., Terkaj, W.: Virtual Factory Manager. In: Shumaker, R. (ed.) Virtual and Mixed Reality, Part II, HCII 2011. LNCS, vol. 6774, pp. 397–406. Springer, Heidelberg (2011)
14. Christian, J., Krieger, H., Holzinger, A., Behringer, R.: Virtual and Mixed Reality Interfaces for e-Training: Examples of Applications in Light Aircraft Maintenance. In: Stephanidis, C. (ed.) HCI 2007. LNCS, vol. 4556, pp. 520–529. Springer, Heidelberg (2007)
15. Franlund, J.: Some European Initiatives in Requirements of Competence in Maintenance. In: Proc. of CM-MFPT 2008, 5th Int. Conf. on Condition Monitoring & Machinery Failure Prevention Technologies, Edinburgh, UK (2008)
16. Nedungadi, P., Raman, R.: A new approach to personalization: integrating e-learning and m-learning. Educational Technology Research and Development, 1–20 (2012)

# Using Behavioral Indicators to Assess Competences in a Sustainable Manufacturing Learning Scenario

Heiko Duin[1], Gregor Cerinsek[2], Manuel Oliveira[3],
Michael Bedek[4], and Slavko Dolinsek[2]

[1] BIBA - Bremer Institut für Produktion und Logistik GmbH, Hochschulring 20,
D-28359 Bremen, Germany
du@biba.uni-bremen.de
[2] Institute for Innovation and Development of University of Ljubljana (IRI UL),
Kongresni trg 12, 1000 Ljubljana, Slovenia
{gregor.cerinsek,slavko.dolinsek}@quest.arnes.si
[3] SINTEF Technology and Society, S.P. Andersens vei 7, 7465 Trondheim, Norway
manuel.oliveira@sintef.no
[4] Graz University of Technology, Brückenkopfgasse 1, 8020 Graz, Austria
michael.bedek@tugraz.at

**Abstract.** This paper introduces a learning scenario created for a serious game to develop competences in the domain of sustainable manufacturing, by applying a Lifecycle Assessment (LCA). A set of behavioral indicators is introduced to assess how particular competences do change while the player is engaged in playing the game scenario. It furthermore presents early evaluation results of the game scenario on a sample of master grade students at the University of Bremen.

**Keywords:** Serious Game, Sustainable Manufacturing, Lifecycle Assessment (LCA), Content Development, Competence-based Learning, Behavioural Indicators.

## 1 Introduction

Manufacturing industries account for a significant part of the world's consumption of resources and generation of waste. Worldwide, the energy consumption of manufacturing industries grew by 61% from 1971 to 2004 and accounts for nearly a third of today's global energy use. Likewise, they are responsible for 36% of global carbon dioxide emissions [1]. Manufacturing industries nevertheless have the potential to become a driving force for the creation of a sustainable society. This requires a shift in the perception and understanding of industrial production and the adoption of a more holistic approach to conducting business [2].

Sustainable manufacturing considers all life-cycle stages, from pre-manufacturing, manufacturing and post-use (holistic view). These stages are spread across the entire supply chain with different partners managing activities at each of these stages. Thus, many players in the manufacturing process must adopt sustainable principles to ensure that higher production standards are met [3].

C. Emmanouilidis, M. Taisch, D. Kiritsis (Eds.): APMS 2012, Part I, IFIP AICT 397, pp. 582–589, 2013.

Therefore, it is quite important to know the environmental impacts of produced products which can be determined by performing a Lifecycle Assessment (LCA). Nevertheless, there are many difficulties associated with the LCA process and traps in its application (conduction and usage), e.g. wrong scoping of the analysis, collecting wrong data, no data available, improper understanding of the production processes, etc. Finally, the success of a LCA analysis depends on the social engineering skills of the analyser to make all responsible managers to support the task.

The training of current and future manufacturing managers needs to achieve two criteria: first, the targeted learning outcomes need to be achieved rapidly, and second, the learners need to be able to apply the learning outcomes into complex, life-like situations and. Competence-based and technology-enhanced learning (TEL) in general and serious games and simulations in particular have recently attracted a great deal of attention as they have the potential to deliver on both accounts [4]. A general introduction to Serious Gaming to support competence development in Sustainable Manufacturing including a requirements analysis has been presented by [5,6]. Serious Gaming has proven to support learners in acquiring new and complex knowledge and is ideally suited to support problem based learning by creating engaging experiences around a contextual problem where users must apply competences to solve these presented challenges [6].

For a comprehensive assessment of the progress of player's competences, behavioral indicators for such a game scenario need to be elaborated. This paper presents the indicators defined for a Sustainable Manufacturing game scenario focusing on carrying out a LCA which includes the competences of 1) information gathering, 2) ability to perform LCA, and 3) decision making.

## 2    Scope of the Sustainable Manufacturing Game scenario

The presented challenges in the education and training for sustainable manufacturing are also addressed by the TARGET project which identified sustainable manufacturing as an emerging field where new competences are required to facilitate the new manufacturing paradigms and technologies [6]. The TARGET (Transformative, Adaptive, Responsive and enGaging EnvironmenT) project aims to develop a novel TEL platform that provides learners with a responsive environment that addresses personalized rapid competence development and sharing of experiences in the domain of project management, innovation and sustainable manufacturing. The TARGET environment consists of a learning process supported by a set of components that constitute the TARGET platform. The core component of the TARGET platform is a serious game combined with virtual world technology, which confronts individuals with complex situations in the form of game scenarios. The serious game facilitates situated learning that results in experiences leading to the development of competences, whilst the interaction within a virtual world enables individuals to externalize their tacit knowledge [7,11].

The sustainable manufacturing game scenario reflects the phases an enterprise has to run through when dealing with sustainability issues. Within the game scenario, the player takes over the role of a Sustainability Manager who was recently hired by the Chief Executive Manager (CEO) of a production company. When starting the game scenario, the player finds himself in a meeting with the CEO and the other managers (i.e. Production Manager, Logistics Manager, Human Resources Manager etc.). The CEO introduces the plan that the LCA) should be conducted concerning the production of a specific product and advises the player to do so. He also urges the other managers to support him. The CEO and the other managers are non-player characters (NPCs) who are driven by the game engine. After the meeting finishes, the player starts to execute the relevant steps of the LCA, i.e. 1) setting the objectives, 2) setting the boundaries, 3) selecting the flow chart, 4) selecting inputs and outputs, 5) deciding on the data for inputs and outputs, 6) setting the impact categories.

In the first phase (scoping of the LCA) the player has to define the objectives and boundaries for the LCA. In order to effectively complete his/her tasks the player needs to gather right and relevant information from different NPCs (i.e. CEO, Production Manager, Shift Manager) and furthermore through accessing the Enterprise Resource Planning (ERP) System or directly visiting the shop floor. For instance, when setting the boundaries, the player can discuss the issue with the CEO, who would advise him/her to focus the LCA on the whole life cycle of the product. On the other hand, player can also discuss the issue with the Production Manager, who would advise him/her to focus the LCA solely on the production of the product. The decision made by the player will have impact on costs, time and the final quality of the LCA. All additional LCA steps required follow the similar logic and the player is virtually free to choose from the data that is available to him/her. The final calculation is done by the virtual LCA tool which also reports whether all necessary data has been entered or not. Finally, the final phase is checking the completeness and consistency of all collected data and evaluating the results in terms of impacts per category. The final result is a report to be created with the virtual LCA tool and delivered to the CEO.

## 3    Measuring Competence Performance in Serious Games

Competence assessment in the field of TEL is usually carried out by on-line questionnaires or test items provided after the learner consumed a set of learning objects. Serious Games offer the opportunity to assess if the player is able to apply a particular competence while he or she is playing the game. In other words, a game scenario may encompass both, learning and test objects at the same time. However, given this potential of serious games, the challenge is to avoid that the player´s flow experience [8] or feeling of presence [9] is impaired. Thus, a non-invasive or implicit assessment procedure is required. Our implicit and non-invasive assessment procedure is based on the interpretation of the player´s actions and interactions within the virtual environment [10]. These actions and interaction, called Behavioral Indicators (BIs) should be valid clues to distinguish between well and poor performing players. The elaboration of BIs starts with the identification and definition of competences to be assessed (see Table 1). The operationalization of BIs leads to formalized functions consisting of parameters that can be measured while the learner is playing the game (game logs). The observation and integration of different BIs constitutes the foundation of an on-line assessment of the level of competence a player has.

**Table 1.** Required Competences for LCA

| ID | Name | Description |
|----|------|-------------|
| C1 | Ability to Perform Life Cycle Assessment (LCA) | It is related to conducting and executing the seven key phases of the LCA concerning a specific product, i.e. 1) setting the objectives, 2) setting the boundaries, 3) flow chart definition, 4) inputs and outputs definition, 5) data gathering, 6) choosing impact categories, 7) interpretation of results with recommendations. |
| C2 | Information Gathering | Concerns getting the "right" information in adequate quality (completeness and correctness) in adequate time. |
| C3 | Decision Making | A very important competence for conducting projects such as the LCA as it requires effective and on-time decisions when 1) setting the objectives; 2) setting the boundaries; 3) flow chart definition; 4) defining inputs / outputs; 5) utilizing gathered data; 6) choosing the impact categories when conducting the LCA. |

The operationalization of the competences and the elaboration of BIs listed in Table 1 was built upon existing theories, frameworks and empirical evidence. Before describing the competences and their BIs in more detail, we will briefly outline the *theory of information foraging* [11] which served as main reference for elaborating BIs for competence C2 (Information Gathering).

### 3.1    Theory of Information Foraging

The theory of information foraging as proposed by [11] aims at describing the strategies that are applied in order to seek for and consume valuable pieces of information (for example, when searching for relevant papers in literature data bases). An ideal information forager gains information from external sources effectively and efficiently. Such external sources encompass a wide range of entities, for example online documents or communication partners. In [11] they are called *patches* and we consider *information sources* as specific subset of them. Information sources in the context of TARGET are e.g. an Enterprise-Resource-Planning (ERP) system or NPCs which are also part of the scenario. An efficient and effective information forager maximizes the rate of gaining pieces of valuable information (in our context called *information objects*) by applying a balanced ratio of explorative and exploitative search activities. These two kinds of activities are mutually exclusive, i.e. the information forager can spend his or her available time on either explorative search behavior (called *between-patch processing*) or exploitative, information consuming behavior (called *within-patch processing*). The information foraging theory provides a profound set of "success indicators". For example *profitability* (the ratio of gain per patch to the cost of within-patch processing) or *rate of information gain* in units of time.

### 3.2    Measuring Performance in Information Gathering

The behavioral indicator used to measure Information Gathering is the number of *information objects* found during the beginning of the game ($t_0$) and a specific point in time $t$. Relating this to the total number of information objects contained in the game scenario provides as a performance indicator the percentage of detected information objects. One could also relate that to the time needed to get a more precise performance indicator for that competence, but for our purpose we just consider the ration of found to the total number of information objects.

**Table 2.** Information Objects hidden in the Game Scenario

| Name | Description and Coding |
| --- | --- |
| Boundary | The boundary is necessary to focus the scope of the LCA. |
| | It is coded as a sentence of the CEO: "I know that the production manager will say "focus on production" but I suggest to focus on the whole life-cycle". |
| Flowchart | A flow chart describes the production and usage processes defining all the (material) inputs and outputs of each step. When the player has selected the boundary he can get the hint from the CEO and the Production Manager which of the provided flow charts in the LCA tool is the right one. |
| Inputs/Outputs | Inputs and outputs describe the flow of energy materials and parts into and out of a production or usage process. |
| | This information object is distributed in sentences of the CEO and the Production Manager. The CEO knows about the sub-parts to be assembled while the Production Manager knows exactly the material and energy inputs and outputs. |
| Data | Data is a collection of correct values for each of the inputs and outputs. Again, this information object is distributed in the game scenario. Many data can be observed when using the ERP system on of the PCs, other, more precise data is told to the player through the Shift Manager. |
| Impact Categories | The impact categories are used as indicators to describe the whole life cycle of the product as green. |
| | The information object is distributed in sentences of dialogs of the CEO and the Production Manager. |

Within the game scenario information objects are coded in either being hidden in a game object or a sentence of a NPC. The two game objects which provide information to the player is a big wall screen showing production processes and a couple of PCs which are accessible by the player showing ERP related data. The NPCs of the scenario are the CEO, the Production Manger, and a shift manager from the production site. All of them are able to answer questions of the player. Table 2 shows which information objects are hidden in the game scenario.

# 4    Evaluation

Evaluation of the Sustainable Manufacturing Scenario has been done 11-13 July 2012 at a laboratory of the University of Bremen. Participants were 24 master students of Management and Industrial Engineering. Evaluation was divided into three steps:

1. All participants filled the first part of a questionnaire with general and scenario related questions to collect demographic data and to assess present understanding of LCA related issues.
2. An instructor introduces the TARGET software and demonstrated how to play it. The participants played the scenario for 20 minutes. After that all participants reflected on their performance related to the three competences mentioned above. The participants have been asked to do a self assessment for the three competences on a scale of 1-9 (where 1 = very poor and 9 = very good) for the phases of beginning, during, and the end of the gaming session. After that, participants were asked how they could improve their performance. All participants played the game for a second time for 20 minutes trying to improve their performance. At the end of the second playing session participants were asked for another self-assessment.
3. Finally, all participants filled the second part of a questionnaire to gather in-game experience, updates on the scenario understanding and general post game evaluation.

The following results are focusing on the question, whether the participants were able to improve their performance in competence Information Gathering.

In the beginning of the first gaming round more than the half of all participants assessed themselves to have only marginal performance in Information Gathering (see Fig. 1). 13 of 24 participants (54%) assessed their own competence on a scale of 1-9 as poor (values between 1 and 3), 8 participants (33%) as medium (values between 4 and 6), and only 3 participants (13%) as good (values between 7 and 9). The highest values participants gave was 7 (3 participants).

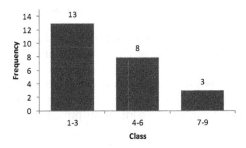

**Fig. 1.** Distribution of participants self-assessment of competence Information Gathering in the beginning of the first round of gaming (n=24)

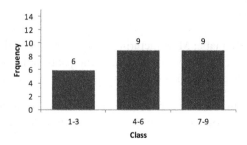

**Fig. 2.** Distribution of participants self-assessment of competence Information Gathering at the end of the second round of gaming (*n*=24)

This situation changed by the end of the second gaming round (see Fig. 2). A total of 75% assessed to have medium to good performance in Information Gathering (37.5% with values between 4 and 6, 37.5% with values greater equal 7). Only 25% assessed themselves still with limited performance. The highest values participants gave was 8 (6 participants).

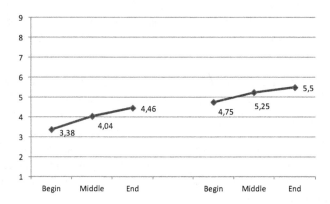

**Fig. 3.** Development of the average of self-assessment of competence Information Gathering (left graph represents first round, right graph represents second round of gaming, *n*=24)

The average value of competence Information Gathering grew from the beginning of the first gaming round to the end of the second gaming round from 3.38 to 5.50 (see Fig. 3).

The results are based on a self-assessment of the players and not on measures taken during game play. Even when the meaning of the performance indicators has been explained there is still the risk that the participants provided incorrect answers.

## 5    Conclusions

This paper introduced a serious game scenario designed to teach the Ability to Perform a Lifecycle Assessment (LCA) and related competences, i.e. Information

Gathering and Decision Making. On the example if Information Gathering it has been shown how a performance indicator can be designed based on behavioral measures. An evaluation with master students at the University of Bremen has been performed showing that during the execution of the game scenario players learned and performed better the longer they played.

**Acknowledgement.** The research reported in this paper has been undertaken within the European Community funded project TARGET under the 7th Framework Programme (IST 231717). The authors of the paper wish to acknowledge the Commission and all participants of the TARGET project consortium for their valuable work and contributions.

# References

1. IEA (International Energy Association): Tracking Industrial Energy Efficiency and CO2 Emissions. Paris, France: OECD/IEA (2007)
2. Maxwell, D., Sheate, W., van der Volst, R.: Functional and systems aspects of the sustainable product and service development approach for industry. Journal of Cleaner Production 14(17), 1466–1479 (2006)
3. WCSD (World Centre for Sustainable Development): E-brochure (2010),
   http://www.pagegangster.com/p/MwNhJ/ (retrieved October 15, 2010)
4. Cerinsek, G., Petersen, S.A., Heikura, T.: Contextually enriched competence model in the field of sustainable manufacturing for simulation style technology enhanced learning environments. Journal of Intelligent Manufacturing 22, 1–15 (2011)
5. Duin, H., Cerinsek, G., Fradinho, M., Taisch, M.: Serious Gaming Supporting Competence Development in Sustainable Manufacturing. In: Cruz-Cunha, M.M. (ed.) Serious Games as Educational, Business, and Research Tools: Development and Design, pp. 47–71. IGI Global, Hershey (2012)
6. Duin, H., Oliveira, M., Thoben, K.D.: A Methodology for Developing Serious Gaming Stories for Sustainable Manufacturing. In: ICE Conference, Munich, Germany, June 21-23 (2012) (accepted conference paper)
7. Andersen, B., Fradinho, M., Lefrere, P., Niitamo, V.-P.: The Coming Revolution in Competence Development: Using Serious Games to Improve Cross-Cultural Skills. In: Ozok, A.A., Zaphiris, P. (eds.) OCSC 2009. LNCS, vol. 5621, pp. 413–422. Springer, Heidelberg (2009)
8. Csikszentmihalyi, M.: Flow: The psychology of optimal experience. Harper & Collins, New York (1990)
9. Slater, M., Wilbur, S.: A framework for immersive virtual environments (FIVE): Speculations on the role of presence in virtual environments. Presence 6, 603–616 (1997)
10. Bedek, M.A., Petersen, S.A., Heikura, T.: From Behavioral Indicators to Contextualized Competence Assessment. In: Proceedings of the 11th IEEE International Conference on Advanced Learning Technologies, pp. 274–276. IEEE (2011)
11. Pirolli, P., Card, S.K.: Information Foraging´. Psychological Review 106(4), 643–675 (1999)

# Lean Product Development: Serious Game and Evaluation of the Learning Outcomes

Endris Kerga[1], Armin Akaberi[1], Marco Taisch[1], Monica Rossi[1], and Sergio Terzi[2]

[1] Politecnico di Milano, Department of Economics, Management and Industrial Engineering,
Piazza Leonardo da Vinci 32, Milano, 20133, Italy
{endris.kerga,armin.akaberi}@mail.polimi.it,
{marco.taisch,monica.rossi}@polimi.it
[2] Università degli Studi di Bergamo, Department of Industrial Engineering Viale Marconi 5,
Dalmine (BG) 24044, Italy
sergio.terzi@unibg.it

**Abstract.** This paper presents a Serious Game (SG) about SBCE (Set-Based Concurrent Engineering), which is one element of Lean thinking in Product Development (PD). The game is structured in two stages that simulate the traditional approach to product concept development called PBCE (Pont-Based Concurrent Engineering) and SBCE approaches. Moreover, this paper presents the learning outcomes gained through running the game in a company. Finally, some practical and theoretical insights gained throughout the game play are introduced.

**Keywords:** Lean Product Development, Set-Based Concurrent Engineering, Serious Game.

## 1    Introduction

Set Based Concurrent Engineering (SBCE) is an element of lean thinking in product development (PD). It is effective at early stages of design when concepts are generated and selected [1], [2]. In a traditional approach which is called Point Based Concurrent Engineering (PBCE), a single concept is selected as early as possible assuming that it will be feasible. However, PD is characterized by uncertainties due to changes in customer requirements, manufacturability issues, sub-system configurations and so on. Thus, often PD project suffers from design reworks due to the so called 'false positive feasibility', where project teams assume a concept is feasible, but will learn later in the development process that it is not [3]. Toyota uses SBCE approach to tackle such a problem by effectively utilizing product knowledge (lesson learned) to generate alternative design concepts. Unless a concept is proven to be infeasible, designers won't eliminate it from a solution set. The unique feature in SBCE process is that design decision is based on proven data. Communication and negotiation within teams are facilitated by a pull event where teams can visualize risk and opportunities using tradeoff and limit-curves. Finally, PD teams converge into an optimal design taking rough objective criteria (such as cost, quality and time), so as the process will continue to detail design stages [1], [2].

C. Emmanouilidis, M. Taisch, D. Kiritsis (Eds.): APMS 2012, Part I, IFIP AICT 397, pp. 590–597, 2013.

In practice, however, the awareness and the adoption levels of SBCE is limited across the industries surveyed [4]. Therefore, the purpose of this paper is to design and validate a learning tool using a serious game approach that enable practitioners to have a hand on experience about SBCE principles and its associated enablers.

In section 2, introduction to the game's features will be introduced. In section 3, a model to evaluate the learning outcomes of the game will be discussed. The results found in the one game play will be presented in section 4, and followed by conclusions in section 5.

## 2 Introduction of SBCE Game

To design the SBCE learning tool a serious game approach is used. In general, the application of games with the aim of education and learning is defined as "Serious games" [5]. In SG, players assume different roles and are involved in simple and complicated decision making processes, which makes it attractive for SBCE process where alternative design exploration and convergence involve multiple-views. Moreover, SG creates a safe and entertaining environment, so that players from the industry freely experiments SBCE process without interfering in an actual PD process.

In the game, players have to design a simplified Airplane structure as shown in Figure1, using different type of LEGO bricks. The Airplane has four sub-systems to be designed (body, wing, cockpit and tail). The game is divided into two stages: Stage one, where players design an Airplane for a given list of customer requirements following a PBCE process; Stage two, where players are provided with the necessary enablers to execute SBCE process. The enablers will help players to explore alternative design concepts, communicate about alternative solutions within a team, and converge into a preferred (a high value) Airplane structure. After each stages, players performances' breakdown in terms of cost and time of development will be provided to facilitate discussion. The game is played in a team of four players and each player represents sub-system departments (body, wing, cockpit and tail).

The main inputs to the Stage one of the game are: Customer requirements and supplier components catalogue. The list of customer requirements to build an airplane structure were made intentionally to be vague, for example, the number of passengers might be from 90 to120 and the wing span could be 7 to 15. Such range of customer requirements (vague) reflect the reality, in which customers often suggest imprecise information, and force designers to explore their concept solutions wide open. In the game, these requirements can be handled in different ways in the Stage one (PBCE process) and in Stage two (SBCE process). Thus, players will understand the advantage of following SBCE than PBCE process to better achieve the customer requirements. In the game, there are five customer requirements: number of passenger (Np), Airplane weight (W) (Airplane structure (Wa) and passengers weights (Wp)), Length of Airplane (L), Wing span (ws) and Tail Span (ts).

The supplier components are LEGO bricks in different sizes and shapes that are used to build body, wing, tail and cockpit. Each brick has circular points on the top, and the number of points on the top of a brick define the characteristics of the component. A single point on a brick has the following character: Cost (10), Lead time or component ordering time (0.5), Capacity (3), Weight (100), Length (1), and Width (1).

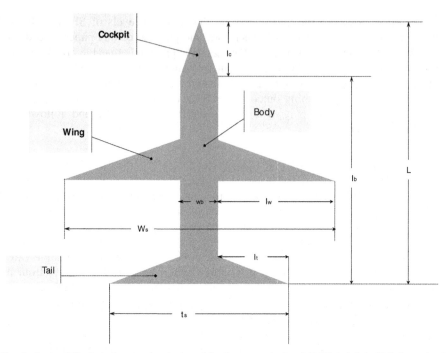

**Fig. 1.** A simplified airplane to be designed in the game (using LEGO bricks). "L": Length of Airplane, "lw": Length of Wing, "lb": Length of Body, "wb": Width of Body, "lc": Length of Cockpit, "Ws": Wing Span, "lt": Length of Tail, "ts": Tail Span.

## 2.1    Stage One and Testing

Taking the customer requirements and the supplier catalogues, players will be asked to build an airplane in this stage. This stage simulates PBCE where players first design an airplane structure, build it and then test it to the constraints. *Design-Build-Test* approach is what many non-lean organizations follow at early stage of design [8]. Once players finish designing and building a prototype design in the first stage, they should submit it to "testing department" to check for stability, flying conditions and dimensional configurations as seen in Table 1.

**Table 1.** Testing constraints

| | |
|---|---|
| Length – Wing span | $\frac{2}{3}L=<ws<L$ |
| Ratio of weight (RW) | $Rw=\frac{Wp}{Wa}<1.25$ |
| *Wa = weights of all airplane components or structure* | |
| *Wp = NP * 60* (Average weight of each passenger) | |
| Airplane stability | $lt<lw$ |
| Alignment between body and cockpit | $lc=wb$ |

The facilitator of the game acts as a testing department. Players will not be given these testing constraints at the start of the game. If the design fails, the prototype should be redesigned. Redesigning has penalty costs and additional time to be penalized. After the first trial the testing constraints will be given to player. If the prototype passes the testing constraints, players will be given the breakdown of their performances in terms of cost and time. The determination of cost and time is executed as follows:

— **Total development cost (C)**

$$C = cost\ of\ components\ (cc) + cost\ of\ iteration\ (ci) + cost\ of\ penalty\ (cp)$$

Where, $cc = Total\ number\ of\ points*single\ point\ cost$, $ci = 30\%\ of\ cost\ of\ components$ (this is an additional cost if players fail to pass testing constraints), and $cp$ (is an additional cost if players fail to meet customer requirements). $cp$ is determined based on unsatisfied customer requirements following the following rules:

| Unsatisfied customer requirement | Np | L | ws | ts | W |
|---|---|---|---|---|---|
| cp | 30%*cc | 40%*cc | 10%*cc | 5%*cc | 20%*cc |

— **Total development time (T)**

$$T = Total\ ordering\ Time\ (tot) + Assembly\ Delivery\ Time\ (ADT) + Iteration\ Time\ (it)$$

Where, $tot = Total\ number\ of\ points*Lead\ time$, $it = 30\%$ of Lead Time, and $ADT = ADTI*tot$. ADTI (Assembly Delivery Time index) is a function of an airplane wing length. ADT variable represents the required time that is needed to assembly the Airplane structure. To determine the ADTI values the following rules are used:

| lw | 3 | 4 | 6 | 7 | 8 | 9 | >10 |
|---|---|---|---|---|---|---|---|
| ADTI | 0.8 | 0.7 | 0.6 | 0.5 | 0.4 | 0.3 | 0.2 |

## 2.2    Stage Two and Supporting Enablers

In Stage two, players will follow a structured SBCE process phases. This stage simulates a different approach than the first. Here, players follow a *Test-Design-Build* approach, and design decisions are made as late as possible until feasibilities are proven. In summary, players will explore, communicate set design solutions, evaluate feasibilities of set of solution and finally converge into a preferred one. The different phases of the Stage two are:

A. *Explore alternative set of designs*: at this phase, players will be supported by QFD (Quality Function Deployment) tool to explore alternative sub-system solutions and able to ingrate customer requirements into an Airplane parameters. QFD is a powerful tool in applying SBCE process, it helps designers to translate rough customer requirements into alternative sub-system solutions [9]. Therefore, each player in a team will explore alternative body, wing, cockpit and tail solutions using its own QFD. This phase is the beginning of a SBCE process in the game.

B. *Communicating set of design solutions*: players at this phase can eliminate Airplane's sub-system solutions that are not compatible. For example, body department might explore alternative feasible body lengths as (11, 12, 14). Meanwhile, cockpit department might generate feasible body of lengths as (12, 13, 14). Therefore, the departments should eliminate incompatible body lengths (11 and 13).

C. *Provision of knowledge from testing department*: from step B, players have complete alternative Airplane solutions which are compatible, but need to filter them using physical constraints. In the game, physical constraints come only from the testing department. Limit-curves are used to generalize knowledge and visually depict solutions which are feasible from testing point of view, see [1, 2, 3] for more details about limit-curves. Therefore, at this phase, players eliminate those Airplane solutions which cannot pass the testing constrains listed in Table 1.

D. *Convergence to a preferred solution*: once alternative feasible Airplanes are identified, estimating the cost and development time of each Airplane solutions help to select the preferred solution. Refer section 2.1 to see the cost and time calculations used.

In summary, the second stage is to lead players through the step-wise phases of SBCE process. The objective is to educate players how to delay decisions early in design phase, and facilitate *test-design-build* approach to avoid unnecessary design reworks and missing customer goals.

# 3    Evaluation Framework for Learning Outcomes

The comparison of performances between the two stages can be taken as a validation mechanism to roughly estimate the advantages of SBCE process (Stage one) over the traditional process (Stage two). However, the main purpose is not to measure the performance leverages of SBCE process using the game. Because, the game is a simplified version of the reality and cannot capture the real complexities of a PD that make a SBCE approach more advantageous (such as product complexity, innovativeness of the product, team size and so on). Therefore, in this paper , it is aimed at measuring the effectiveness of the game to translate the SBCE principles and its associated supporting elements. Given that, it is also aimed at measuring how practitioners have perceived the potential of SBCE process and its elements in improving PD performances.

Garris et.al. identified three level of knowledge aspects in order to measure the effectiveness of a SG[6]:

- *Declarative knowledge*: is the learning of facts or increasing one's knowledge about a subject. In this paper, the understanding of the SBCE principles and its supporting enablers by players are parts of the declarative learning outcomes.
- *Procedural knowledge*: this aspect refers to the learning of procedures, and also to the understanding of patterns of processes and behavior. In the SBCE game, procedural knowledge is related to players ability to associate the specific elements of SBCE process and the benefits of using them to support a better decision making.

- *Strategic knowledge:* Within gaming this aspect has been explained as implementing knowledge from the game in a new (a real-world) situation. Gaming can also contribute to develop reflective competences. Within complex systems, as in PD, it is not only refers to implementing what is taught in the theory but also observing behavior and adapting to new situations. In SBCE game, several complexities have been simplified but adequate challenges are added to enable players to reflect beyond the gaming sessions into real world practices.

Based on the above framework, a structured questionnaire based on the Likert 5 scale has been prepared to measure the learning outcomes of the game. After playing the game with 36 designers (Mechanical, Electrical and Software) and project leaders of the Carel company (www.carel.com), players were asked to evaluate the declarative, procedural and strategic learning aspects of the game. The players have working experience ranging from 4-15 years and age from 25-50 years.

# 4    Results and Analysis

In general, the game has increased the level of awareness of players. Players understand the usage of tradeoff and limit curves to generalize knowledge, and their application in order to explore alternative designs. Communication among teams in SBCE process takes different form than a traditional point based approach, where designers have only once conceptual solution to communicate about. In traditional design approach, it is a norm that a functional team through 'over the wall' of a subsequent function and vice-versa. In SBCE process, different functions pull together their conceptual solutions and check sub-system compatibilities. In the game, players were provided with simple check-list to support communication and negotiation among teams. Though players understand how to use this communication mechanism, some doubts are exhibited on the importance of using such a mechanism. This is due to the simplicity of the Airplane to be designed, but in a real PD problem the complexity grows as more functions have to communicate about the alternative set of solutions.

Figure 2 shows the perceived advantages of following a SBCE process from practitioners perspective. The theoretical advantages of SBCE seems to be confirmed by the practitioners. Most of the designers played the game agreed that the most significant perceived advantages of SBCE are 'facilitate learning about design solutions' and 'avoid design risks'. Using knowledge from past designs and exploration of alternative designs guarantee the PD teams to brainstorm about set of solutions rather than one alternative. Moreover, frontloading the PD process minimize the probability of 'false positive feasibility' to occur. The players perceived also that SBCE reduce the development time and cost. However, such claims cannot be guaranteed if teams are not able to identify when to stop exploring and start converging [7].

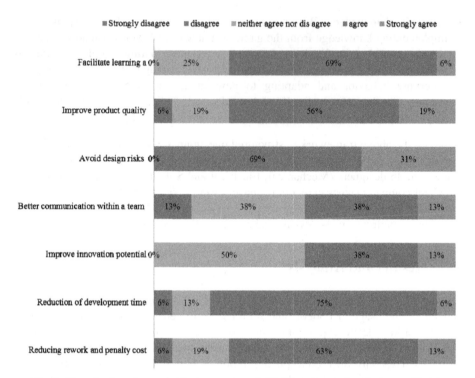

**Fig. 2.** 'Perceived performance' improvements of SBCE process using the game (N=36)

Among the main difficulties that have been mentioned to implement SBCE process is the generation of 'limit-curves'. Limit curves are fundamental to apply SBCE process. They are curves that generalize knowledge of sub-system designs, and designers can see the 'risky' and 'safer' design regions.

However, companies in the current practice don't use such curves to document, represent and share lesson learned or knowledge. Therefore, the main challenge will be to build the necessary competences to capture, represent and share past (static) and current (dynamic) knowledge gained through experimentation.

## 5    Conclusions

Most practical applications of SBCE process are reported from Automotive and Aerospace industries [1, 3, 10, 11]. In other industrial sectors its adoption level is limited. There might be some elements of SBCE process in practice, but its implementation as a structured methodological approach in PD is not prevalent.

In this paper, a Serious Game that can bring a hand on experience is designed and the learning outcomes are measured taking a one company case. The company is in HVAC/R market (www.carel.com), which is different from Automotive and Aerospace industries. However, the players from different background and experience levels acknowledge that SBCE process is a much better approach than PBCE.

Through the assessment, the players identified key advantages and hurdles of applying SBCE process in the company.

In summary, SBCE process is an attractive and sensible approach at early phase of PD compared to PBCE approach. However, companies need to have a structure practices, tools and technologies (enablers) to realize the process. Such enablers are supportive to explore alternative solution, enable set based communication and facilitate convergence to a high value solution.

# References

1. Sobek, D.K., Ward, A.C., Liker, J.K.: Toyota's Principles of Set-Based Concurrent Engineering. Sloan Management Review 40, 67–83 (1999)
2. Ward, A., Liker, J.K., Cristiano, J.J., Sobek II, D.K.: The Second Toyota Paradox: How Delaying Decisions Can Make Better Cars Faster. Sloan Management Review 36, 43–61 (1995)
3. Oosterwal, D.P.: The Lean Machine: How Harley-Davidson Drove Top-Line Growth and Profitability with Revolutionary Lean Product Development. American Management Association, New York (2010)
4. Rossi, M., Kerga, E., Taisch, M., Terzi, S.: Lean Product Development: Fact Finding Research in Italy. In: Proceedings of the International Conference on Industrial Engineering and Systems Management (IESM), Metz, France, May 25-27 (2011)
5. Wouters, P., van der Spek, E.D., Oostendorp, H.: Measuring learning in serious games: a case study with structural assessment. Educational Technology Research and Development 59(6), 741–763 (2011)
6. Garris, R., Ahlers, R., Driskell, J.E.: Games, Motivation, and Learning: A Research and Practice Model. Simulation and Gaming 33(4), 441–467 (2002)
7. Ford, D.N., Sobek, D.K.: Adapting Real Options to New Product Development by Modeling the Second Toyota Paradox. IEEE Transactions on Engineering Management 52(2), 175–185 (2005)
8. Kennedy, M.N.: Product Development for the Lean Enterprise: Why Toyota system is four times more productive and how you can implement it. The Lean Enterprise Institute, Cambridge (2008)
9. Liker, J.K., Sobek, D.K., Ward, A.C., Cristiano, J.: Involving Suppliers in Product Development in the United States and Japan: Evidence for Set-Based Concurrent Engineering. IEEE Transactions on Engineering Management 43, 165 (1996)
10. Bernstein, J.I.: Design Methods in the Aerospace Industry: Looking for Evidence of Set-Based Practices. Master Thesis, Engineering Aeronautics and Astronautics, Massachusetts Institute of Technology (1998)
11. Frye, M.C.: Applying Set Based Methodology in Submarine Design. Master Thesis, System Design and management, Massachusetts Institute of Technology (2010)

# Learning PLM System with a Serious Game

Philippe Pernelle[1], Stephane Talbot[2], Thibault Carron[3],
and Jean-Charles Marty[4]

[1] University of Lyon 1, Laboratory DISP
F-69621 Villeurbanne Cedex, France
philippe.pernelle@univ-lyon1.fr
[2] University of Savoie
F-73000 Chambery, France
stephane.talbot@univ-savoie.fr
[3] Laboratory LIP6
F-75013 Paris , France
thibault.carron@lip6.fr
[4] Laboratory LIRIS
F-69621 Villeurbanne Cedex, France
jean-charles.marty@liris.cnrs.fr

**Abstract.** Despite improvements in educational tools, teaching some elements in the field of production engineering is difficult. In this context, teaching PLM systems remains difficult from a motivation point of view. The purpose of this paper is to propose a highly innovative approach around serious gaming. In the PEGASE project, we have realized an environment for coupling a gaming platform and a content platform in order to enact learning scenarios. This article presents this integration environment which is based on the characterization of business activities within the PLM. Then, we describe the design of scenarios in this platform particularly dedicated to learning PLM systems. We then present the validation of our approach based on different experiments performed with students and with industrial partners.

**Keywords:** Game Base Learning, Serious Game, PLM.

## 1 Introduction

Teaching production engineering is difficult, and particularly for PLM systems. There are many reasons for this. The first reason is that students learn CAD systems without management constraints. When they find out PLM systems, constraints are more visible than the benefits. The second and probably more important, reason is that it is very expensive (in terms of financial cost and human resources) for an educational establishment : Installation, configuration, collaborative projects management...

In this paper, we propose a new approach for learning PLM system: learning a unit with Serious Game. This unit has been produced as part of a research project (PEGASE) that was initially intended to improve the change management. Noting the fact that resistance to change were the same for enterprises

C. Emmanouilidis, M. Taisch, D. Kiritsis (Eds.): APMS 2012, Part I, IFIP AICT 397, pp. 598–605, 2013.

and students, we developed a learning scenario using the playful aspects of the video games. In the first part, we present the concept of this Serious Game, then we present the experiment results that was achieved with students.

## 2  New Learning for PLM Systems

### 2.1  About the Games Learning Bases

Since a few years, Learning Management Systems (LMS) offer functionalities that are recognized as being valuable from different points of view [1]. For instance, students can learn at their own speed. These environments also allow the teacher to evaluate specific activities in a uniform way [2]. LMS allow to structure and to develop distance training. However they have not enough impact on the motivation and the attractiveness. Some students tend to consider LMS as unexciting [3]. So, Game-Based Learning Management System is based on that the way of acquiring knowledge during a learning session is similar to following an adventure in a Role-Playing Game (RPG) [4]. The combination of the two styles is called MMORPG (Massively Multiplayer Online RPG) and offers a good potential for learning reformulated as MMOLE (Massively Multiplayer Online Learning Environment) [5]. Nevertheless, although the students appreciate this approach and that Games-based Learning can significantly enhance learning, there is an obvious need for realistic information about students: skills, actions or behaviors especially for the teacher [6].

The difficulties that teachers face in teaching PLM System to students incited us to find additional motivation thanks to Game-Based Learning (GBL). Although the project below was not initially intended for this, we have conducted experiments to test this.

### 2.2  PEGASE : A Serious Game for PLM

PEGASE project [7] [8] is a Serious Game based on Learning Adventure ("*LA*") [9]. *LA* is a Game-Based Learning Management System representing a 3D environment where the learning session takes place (see Fig. 1). The environment is generic in the sense that it is not dedicated to a particular teaching domain. With the help from a pedagogical engineer, the teacher adapts the environment before the session by setting pre-requisites between sub-activities and by providing different resources (documents, videos, quizzes) linked to the course. Experiments have already been set up for learning Operating Systems as well as Project Management or Object Oriented Concepts in Computer Science. *LA* is thus a platform allowing one to describe, generate and enact different learning environments. The following items define the main characteristics of *LA*:

- A 2D or 3D multiplayer world, split into activity areas;
- Artefacts populating this world: objects, individual or collaborative tools, non-player characters (NPC), players represented by their avatars;

- Possibility to characterize the players / learners through a learner/user model and also through group models;
- Enacting facilities
- Avatar personalisation
- Tracing facilities of players' actions
- Tools for designing scenarios
- Scenario or quest editor, evaluation tools
- Possibility to modify dynamically the environment.

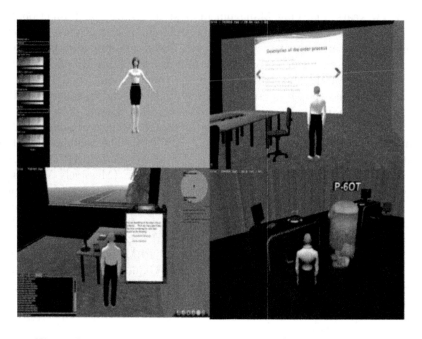

**Fig. 1.** Screenshots of the Learning Adventure (*LA*) environnement

In the PEGASE project, the gaming environment is associated to a content platform (Audros). This content platform is a PLM system very used in SME/SMI. Moreover, a Trace-Based System (TBS) captures the behavioral traces and activity traces. These traces are essential to monitor the progress of the users in the scenario. Thus, after several steps (collection, selection, transformation, aggregation of different traces), we are able to provide specific indicators [10] giving meaningful information to the teacher (see Fig. 2). Moreover, some of these indicators may also be used to update the user model of each student and to present accurate information for the teacher. The interoperability issues have been resolved by relying on a service-oriented architecture [11] (see Fig. 2).

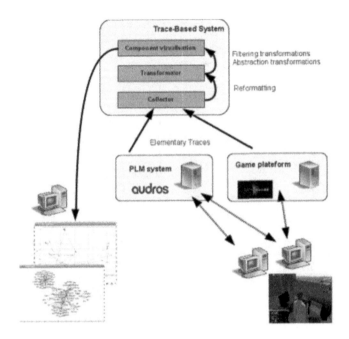

**Fig. 2.** PEGASE architecture

# 3 An Example of a Pedagogical Scenario for PLM

In order to design a pedagogical scenario for PLM, we looked for an industrial process that was sufficiently generic to be used by any student. This process referred to a case study from the plastic industry. The transformation of an industrial process into a pedagogical scenario was achieved thanks to research work concerning gamification [12].

This architecture is generic in sense that it can design any pedagogical scenario. We chose to conceive a first scenario for discovering the main functions of PLM. In the design stage, this classification enables the trainer to build his scenario from a descriptive guide. Initially, the proposed scenario was structured around a simple industrial process (purchase order) described in Figure 3. Without a PLM system, this process is achieved through traditional activities where the risk of error, as well as the tedious tasks involved, should be considered.

In a first part, this process is carried out in the PEGASE Serious Game without any PLM system. The following items and figures describe the corresponding actions:

- Discussion with colleagues and watching a training presentation (see Figure 4);
- Collecting documents in order to complete and visualize the tasks in the process;
- Visualization of the order form, retrieval of information from the archives;

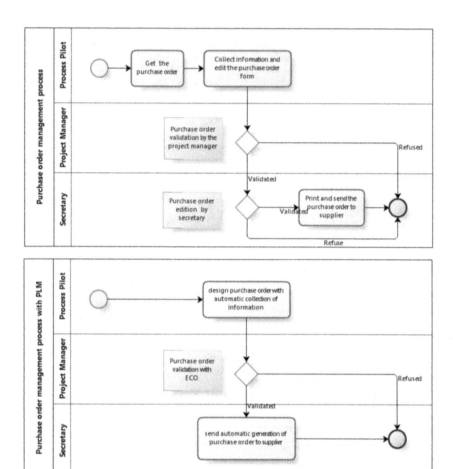

**Fig. 3.** Purchase order management process with and without PLM

- Summary of time-consuming steps (see Figure 5);
- Explanation for creating a purchase order with Audros platform(see Figure 6);

Once the process is carried out without a PLM system, a collective and individual balance of mistakes made by the player is presented. A mini training session on possible solutions to resolve their mistakes with the Audros PLM system is then proposed. The process is therefore performed with a connection to the Audros platform.

*Experiment of this Scenario*

An experiment was carried out from September 2011 to December 2011 in the Technical Institute (Lyon - France) with 224 students. During the experiment, each group of twelve students with their teacher was present in the classroom equipped

**Fig. 4.** PEGASE screenshot: a player interacting with the game environment

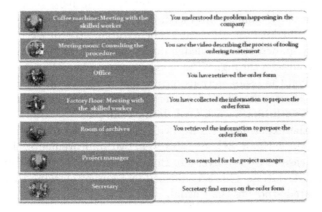

**Fig. 5.** PEGASE screenshot: reminder for the player's tedious tasks

**Fig. 6.** PEGASE screenshot: a player interacting with Audros system

with 12 computers. Each student accessed the virtual environment through his/her workstation, and had a personal (adapted) view on the world. They were explicitly allowed to communicate through the chat tool provided with the system and were warned that they would be observed regarding the use of the system.

As explained before, the course was dedicated to the understanding of the PLM problematic. The learning content dealt with «PLM elementary concepts»: the session was split into two parts: experimenting without (long and tedious) and with a PLM system. The solution (final document) had to be approved by a PLM system expert who was online via the PLM business tool (Audros) and was receiving each document produced. The aim of the session was to assess the knowledge and know-how of the students about the objectives of a PLM system. A story guided the knowledge quest thanks to metaphors. Indeed, the challenge is encouraged through NPC who propose a coherent contest. Immersion is reinforced when the users' actions have a direct impact on the objects of the world. Finally, the teacher was also present in the game via an avatar: it was possible to chat with him, to ask for help for example.

Looking at the experiment results with regard to previous years when this module was done without SG, we observed two improvements. The first is a very slight increase in overall average. However, there is a significant reduction of the standard deviation. This is confirmed by a survey showing that there were fewer unmotivated students than usual.

## 4    Conclusion

In this article, we have illustrated an example of new learning technologies for PLM system. Using a serious game has shown very positive effects. This allows to more easily accept the PLM system constraints. Furthermore, students' motivational level for deepening such systems, is greatly increased.

Naturally, some drawbacks persist: we must recognize that it is very difficult for the teacher to be both present in the game, help the students and regulate the session even with these specific tools. We currently think that we can develop some specific indicators only dedicated to some classical fields of a domain. An interesting perspective could be to develop and propose directly within the indicators some basic regulation actions such as « play specific PLM video » , « propose new activity » or « enable/disable such facility/ies for this student» in order to improve and adapt the learning progression.

The *LA* environment is collaborative, multiplayer and fully observable thanks to traces left by the users during the game. These traces allow us to elaborate collaborative indicators. Moreover, thanks to the feedback collected from these experiments (questionnaires and debriefing sessions directly after the game), we are able to imagine new factual indicators of collaboration exploiting traces left by the users. Future experiments will be done around collaborative activities in the PLM systems. In this brand new scenario (context : futuristic enterprise, multi-role player, handling quality non-conformance process), we want to test some advanced functionalities (ECR, ECO, co-design, ...) around the conception of some complex products.

**Acknowledgement.** We would like to thank the French Ministry for the Economy, Industry and Employment (DGCIS) for the support in the PEGASE project. We would like also to thank G. Dalla Costa, A. Bissay, J. Depoil, L. Kepka, S. El Kadiri, L. Michea and M. Zrouki for their great help in developing this platform.

# References

[1] Dillenbourg, P., Baker, M., Blaye, A., OMalley, C.: The evolution of research on collaborative learning. In: Learning in Humans and Machine: Towards an Interdisciplinary Learning Science, pp. 189–211 (1996)

[2] Hijon, R., Carlos, R.: E-learning platforms analysis and development of students tracking functionality. In: 18th World Conference on Educational Multimedia, Hypermedia and Telecomunications, pp. 2823–2828 (2006)

[3] Prensky, M.: Digital Game-Based Learning. MacGraw Hill (2000)

[4] Squire, K.: Videogames in education. International Journal of Intelligent Games and Simulations 2, 49–62 (2003)

[5] Yu, T.W.: Learning in the virtual world: the pedagogical potentials of massively multiplayer online role playing games. International Education Studies 2(1) (2009)

[6] Galarneau, L., Zibit, M.: Online Game for 21st Century Skills. In: Games and Simulations in Online Learning: Research and Development Frameworks, pp. 59–88. Information Science Publishing, Hersey (2007)

[7] Bissay, A., Zrouki, M., Cheballah, K., Pernelle, P.: Pegase: a platform tool to help change management support during the implementation of a plm system in an industrial company. In: 8th International Conference on Product Lifecycle Management, Eindhoven (2011)

[8] Pernelle, P., Marty, J., Carron, T.: Serious gaming: A new way to introduce product lifecycle management. In: L.U. (ed.) IEEE Workshop on Learning Technology for Education in Cloud 7th International Conference on Knowledge Management in Organizations. Services and Cloud Computing. Services and Cloud Computing, pp. 89–100. Springer (July 2012)

[9] Carron, T., Marty, J.C., Heraud, J.M.: Teaching with game based learning management systems: Exploring and observing a pedagogical dungeon. Simulation and Gaming 39(3), 353–378 (2008)

[10] Gendron, E., Pourroy, F., Carron, T., Marty, J.: Towards a structured approach to the definition of indicators for collaborative activities in engineering design. Journal of Engineering Design 7(3), 195–216 (2012)

[11] Zrouki, M., El Kadiri, S., Pernelle, P., Benmoussa, R.: Caracterisation de services metiers plm: Un exemple d integration dans le cadre du projet pegase. In: 9e Congres International de Genie Industriel (2011)

[12] Mayer, I.S.: he gaming of policy and the politics of gaming: A review. Simulation and Gaming 40, 825–862 (2009)

# Beware of the Robot: A Highly Interactive and Immersive Virtual Reality Training Application in Robotic Manufacturing Systems

Elias Matsas[1], Dimitrios Batras[2], and George-Christopher Vosniakos[1]

[1] National Technical University of Athens, School of Mechanical Engineering, Manufacturing Technology Division, Heroon Polytechniou 9, 15780, Athens, Greece
{imatsas,vosniak}@central.ntua.gr
[2] Presence & Innovation Lab, Arts et Métiers ParisTech, Ingénierium, 4 rue de l' Ermitage, 53000, Laval, France
dbatras@yahoo.gr

**Abstract.** A highly interactive and immersive Virtual Reality Training System (VRTS) is developed, in terms of an educational serious game that simulates the cooperation between industrial robotic manipulators and humans, executing manufacturing tasks. "BeWare of the robot" application ultimately aims at studying the acceptability of human-robot collaboration, when both human and robot share the same workspace. The initial version of the application was evaluated by a group of users. Experimental results on usability and technical aspects are presented and several remarks about users' experience and behavior in the virtual world are discussed.

**Keywords:** Virtual Reality, Safe Human-Robot Cooperation, Manufacturing Training, Interaction, Serious Game.

## 1 Introduction

In not-too-distant future manufacturing systems a need for cooperation and workspace sharing of industrial robots and humans to execute manufacturing tasks will arise. For a long time now, safety of the human interacting with industrial robots is addressed by segregation between humans and robots [1]. Cooperation of human and robot may present an interesting solution that balances productivity, quality, initial capital cost, running cost and flexibility. However, all important physical and "mental" safety issues that arise must be successfully dealt with. Serious games and highly interactive and immersive Virtual or Mixed Reality training applications are preferentially deployed in such cases.

In terms of functionality, VR allows users to be extracted from physical reality in order to virtually change time, space, and (or) interaction type [2]. Virtual Reality-based training systems (VRTSs) are advanced computer-assisted, interactive training systems using VR technology, e.g. allowing proper test and operation of new equipment before it is actually installed [3]. They need to have the necessary physical

C. Emmanouilidis, M. Taisch, D. Kiritsis (Eds.): APMS 2012, Part I, IFIP AICT 397, pp. 606–613, 2013.
© IFIP International Federation for Information Processing 2013

fidelity to mimic the resolution of the physical world in order to be effective for tasks that are characterized by a significant perceptual and/or motor component [4]. Shukla [5] points out the significance of VR in manufacturing training. All VRTSs can be decomposed into three distinct functional parts: (i) output devices, (ii) input devices (mainly for interaction), and, (iii) a VR engine including virtual scene, interaction models, and a graphical representation of the user (avatar) [6].

In the literature, [7] first propose a deictic mode of sensory-motor control with gestures and a HMD for teleassistance, that can be useful for human/robot interaction and control. Morioka [8] developed a new cell production assembly system, in which physical and information supports are provided to the human operators to double productivity. Krüger [9] gives a survey about human-robot cooperation and all available technologies that support the cooperation. Oborski [10] points outs the most important factors of man-machine interaction in advanced manufacturing systems and proposes a method of human attributes modeling for human-machine (robot) interaction. Corrales [11] presents the implementation of real-time proximity queries between humans and robotic manipulators. From another point of view, [12] deal with mental strains of human operators in human-robot cell production systems and propose metrics for a physiologically comfortable collaboration.

In this paper a serious game application named "BeWare of the robot" is presented, simulating tasks of human-robot collaborative tape laying for building aerospace fabric reinforced composite parts. Profiled fabric layers (patches/cloths) are stacked successively inside a die, one on top of the other, until the desired thickness is reached.

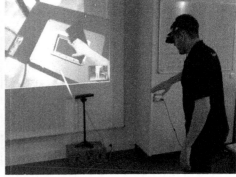

**Fig. 1.** Avatar's hands trying to pick-up the part from the robot (left) and user trying to put the part in the metallic die (right)

Technical aspects of the application development are explained centering on safety issues, such as contacts and collisions that are tackled through "emergencies", i.e. visual stimuli and sound alarms. Preliminary evaluation results by a group of users are presented. Mental safety, i.e. human's awareness of the robot's motion, is the primary objective.

## 2    The Virtual Reality Training System Description and Analysis

Shop-floor environment and its components were developed using Rhinoceros™ and 3ds Max™ for 3D part design and mesh creation. Unity 3d™ game engine was used for assembly, rendering, lighting, physics, simulation, building compilation and programming. "BeWare of the robot" VRTS is a PC standalone build that can run in a typical PC with Windows XP™ and an nVidia™ graphics card supporting 3D stereoscopic vision. An immersive device (HMD) supporting head tracking and a Kinect™ sensor are needed to fully exploit navigation, tracking and immersion capabilities of the system. Communication between Unity 3d and the Kinect™ sensor is implemented with the OpenNI framework. The VRTS incorporates (i) the virtual model of a composites hand layout work-cell, (ii) the model of a Staübli RX90L robotic manipulator, (iii) the skinned model of an avatar created online in evolver.com, with a 3ds Max™ biped attached to it, (iv) interaction scripts in C#, (v) real-time shadows and lighting, and (vi) image, video and audio textures from the real working space. Interaction is mainly based on collision and ray-casting scripts, child/parenting functions, and skeletal tracking of 18 avatar's points.

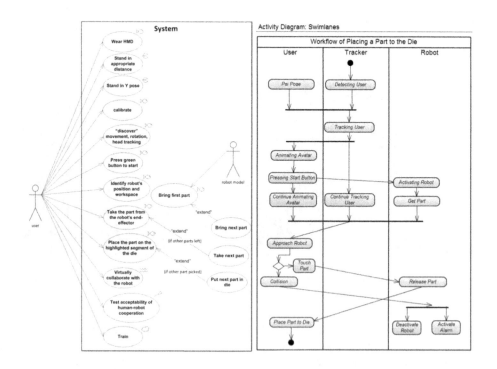

**Fig. 2.** UML Use Case Diagram and Activity Diagram

In order to describe, analyze and decompose the system, Object-Oriented Analysis (OOA) tools and UML 2.0 expressions are used. OOA methods divide the system to its components and make every relation explicit [13]. The Use Case Diagram presented in Fig. 2 defines the required tasks and interactions between the user and the system. The Activity Diagram is a graphical representation of system behavior: flow of actions, activities and transitions. The Structure Diagram provides a detailed analysis of system entities, their attributes, the methods used and the associations between the entities as shown in Fig. 3. OOA tools in VEs can be used as a path for the creation and/or the improvement of the virtual world. In addition, through OOA methods, system knowledge can be captured to build intelligence.

Structure diagram (entities)

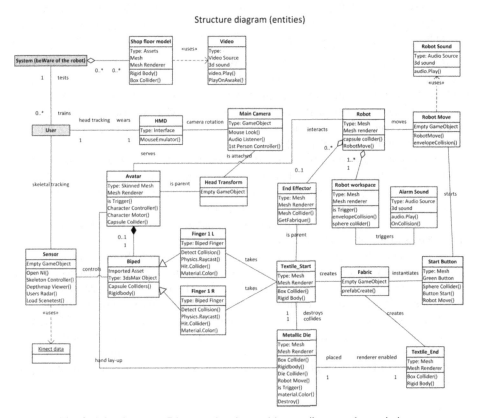

**Fig. 3.** OOA Structure Diagram showing entities, attributes and associations

## 3    Experiment Set-Up and Results

To evaluate both the effectiveness and the usability of the application, as well as to investigate users' experience, a series of experiments were carried out. The participants of the experiment are a group of 30 senior mechanical engineering students (aged between 21 and 31 years), sufficiently familiar with theoretical Robotics and Manufacturing Systems design. None of the students had tested the application before the experiments.

The experimental task required subjects to individually test the "beware of the robot" application; that is to virtually collaborate in sequence with an industrial robot, while sharing the same physical environment. The experimental goal was to test/validate the following hypothesis:

— Highly-interactive and immersive VRTSs may be a successful tool for motor skill training, such as human-robot collaboration testing.
— Immersion and head tracking the user experiences with the use of the HMD boosts the feel of presence and realism. Manufacturing education is therefore enhanced when physical access to equipment is either not possible or potentially hazardous.
— The use of additional audiovisual stimuli (e.g. HD video textures and 3d spatialized sounds from the real environment, real-time shadows and differed lighting) enhances user's experience of presence in the virtual world.

The testing platform consisted of: the "beWare of the robot" application, a PC running Windows XP™ equipped with an nVidia Quadro™ FX1700 graphics card, an eMagin Z800 HMD with stereo ear buds, a Microsoft Kinect™ sensor, keyboard and mouse. Furthermore, in order to be able to reproduce what the users sees through the HMD and to record the experiments with a video camera, we used a projector cloning the displays of the HMD in a wall behind the user.

Experiment's duration was 10 minutes and participants were given detailed instructions orally. After wearing the HMD, subjects were asked to stand in "Y" posture towards the Kinect sensor in order to be detected and calibrated. They, then, had to "discover" system's tracking, moving and rotating capabilities, as well as the objects of the virtual environment. Afterwards, participants had about 6-8 minutes to complete the tasks described in the Use Case Diagram (Fig. 2).

At the end of the experiment, each participant was asked to fill out and submit the online form (questionnaire). This was developed from scratch in order to examine user experience as well as system effectiveness. The questionnaire consisted of 42 questions, grouped into 3 thematic categories (i) participant's personal information, level and experience (14 questions), (ii) immersion, presence and realism (10 questions), (iii) usability, effectiveness, tracking and interaction quality, (18 questions).

Analysis was conducted on three levels: (i) online questionnaires, (ii) task execution video recording and a posteriori observation, and (iii) discussions with each participant.

### 3.1    Results and Discussions

**Presence and Immersion.** Table 1 shows the results of selected questions concerning users' experience in the VRTS. Some interesting findings rise from this table regarding the concepts of presence and immersion. Slater et al. [14] define presence as a subjective phenomenon such as the sensation of being in a VE, while immersion as an objective description of aspects of the system such as field of view and display resolution. In the literature, several theories have been proposed on the nature of presence in immersive VR [15]. Our research focuses more on "presence by involvement"; that is, that both involvement and immersion are thought to be necessary for experiencing presence. Moreover, [16] claim that "presence" and "situation awareness" are overlapping constructs.

In our experiment, a vast majority of participants were feeling as they were really moving in the scene, "involved and present" in the virtual activity. In addition, 93% of the subjects answered that they did not lose their concentration at all during the test. The results also show that a large number of subjects felt like they were really moving an object with their hands, despite the fact that the object did not have physical mass. A posteriori video observation emphasizes the above finding with an intrinsic proprioceptive users' reaction: although subjects were told that they should use one hand, 20% of them used both hands in order to grasp and to carry the workpieces. We also noticed that some users (17%) spontaneously closed their hands and/or fingers in order to grasp the parts (as they would have reacted in the real world), although they were told that our system does not support fingers tracking.

**Table 1.** Users' experience selected results

| Item | SD (1) | D (2) | N (3) | A (4) | SA (5) |
|---|---|---|---|---|---|
| **Presence & Immersion** | | | | | |
| I feel like I was really moving an object with my hand, despite the fact that the object did not have physical mass. | 1 | 7 | 8 | 12 | 2 |
| Wearing the HMD I feel immerged in the virtual environment. | 1 | 0 | 7 | 13 | 9 |
| I feel like I was really moving in the scene. | 0 | 1 | 3 | 5 | 21 |
| Wearing the HMD I feel present and involved in the virtual activity. | 2 | 1 | 5 | 15 | 7 |
| I feel like my behavior in the virtual world didn't change, compared to my behavior in the real world. | 3 | 10 | 9 | 8 | 0 |
| **Usability & Effectiveness** | | | | | |
| I did not encounter any difficulties during the initial calibration process with the Kinect sensor. | 0 | 3 | 3 | 6 | 18 |
| Audiovisual stimuli (alarms) helped me being aware of a potentially hazardous workspace. | 0 | 1 | 1 | 8 | 20 |
| I feel like the avatar followed my movements precisely. | 1 | 2 | 12 | 14 | 1 |
| It was easy to pick-up the workpieces form the robot's end-effector. | 0 | 0 | 9 | 13 | 8 |
| It was easy to navigate/move in the virtual world (ease of movement, restraint). | 0 | 3 | 12 | 12 | 3 |
| I feel that my eyes were tired because of the use of the HMD. | 15 | 10 | 3 | 2 | 0 |
| I feel more like I was participating in an amusing game. | 0 | 2 | 5 | 10 | 13 |
| After the experiment I went through, I believe that human-machine training tasks can be more attractive with the use of "serious games". | 1 | 0 | 2 | 8 | 19 |

**Usability and System Effectiveness.** Although 77% of the subjects had never used the Kinect™ sensor before, only 10% of them encountered some difficulties during the initial detection and calibration process. During the human-robot collaboration procedure, almost all subjects (97%) replied that they easily perceived the red transparent sphere that represented the robot's workspace, and 70% of subjects managed not to enter into the workspace (which was the potentially hazardous area). The survey results show that most of the subjects favorably accepted the use of visual and auditory stimuli (alarms) for the robot's workspace awareness. Note that the red sphere and visual alarms in general may be contradictory with fidelity and realism of VEs, but realism is not always the ultimate goal. In VRTSs learning procedure for example, exaggeration or deformation of real events is "authorized" for complex situations understanding [6].

Concerning the Kinect's™ tracking quality, most of the participants considered that the avatar was following their (tracked) movements precisely, 23% of them, though, pointed out a slight "vibration" in the avatar's movements. On the other hand, observations revealed that 53% of the users sometimes "lost control" of their hands, even instantaneously. That is because experiment tasks required user body rotation towards the sensor, and at the extremes hands tracking is confusing: Kinect™ sensor cannot easily distinguish the left from the right hand. In addition when users turn their body at 180 degrees towards the Kinect sensor, skeletal tracking is lost and although they may continue moving, the avatar remains "frozen" for a while in the last detected posture. Furthermore, 43% of the subjects felt like their movements were altered compared with the real ones; with emphasis in hands "roll" rotation (50%) and body rotation (47%). Nevertheless, 70% of the subjects answered that they easily managed to pick-up the workpieces from the robot's end-effector, while 50% said that it was easy to navigate (walk, rotate, bend etc.) in the virtual world.

Concerning user motivation, 76% of the participants replied that during the experiment they were feeling more as if they were participating in an amusing game, and 90% of the subjects answered that training tasks requiring human-robot collaboration can be more attracting with the use of "serious games".

Eventually, the results suggest a positive prospect for the use of VR for training. In addition, moving around the scene and using real gestures (skeletal tracking) to manipulate objects and to complete the tasks makes learning more active and impressive for learners.

## 4    Conclusion and Future Work

Due to the notions of presence and realism VRTSs and highly-interactive serious games are probably an efficient and safe learning tool to study human-robot collaboration with overlapping workspaces. Through multi-level "invisible" interactions with the Kinect™ sensor skeletal tracking, user experience and behavior in the virtual world can be recorded, studied and analyzed, leading to new knowledge acquisition.

Experiment questionnaire analysis permitted to identify several remarks about user experience in the VE, and helped us pose the question of how virtual world affects user temporal identity in the VE, which will be tackled in an upcoming study.

Moreover, a Mixed Reality version of the application where the user would interact physically with real objects while being tracked and immersed in the virtual world is expected in the near future. Authors are also working on solving the skeletal tracking problems with the use of a second Kinect™ sensor.

**Acknowledgements.** This research has been co-financed by the European Union (European Social Fund–ESF) and Greek national funds through the Operational Program "Education and Lifelong Learning" of the NSRF - Research Funding Program: Heracleitus II, Investing in knowledge society through the European Social Fund.

We wish to thank the participants in the experiments for sharing their experience with us, as well as Dr. Dimitrios Nathanael for his helpful comments concerning the experiment set-up and the questionnaire. We would also like to thank Prof. Simon Richir and Matthieu Lépine for accepting and hosting our application in the exhibition section of Laval Virtual 2012 conference.

# References

1. Helander, M.G.: Ergonomics and Safety considerations in the design of robotics workplaces: A review and some priorities for research. Int. J. of Ind. Ergonomics. 6, 127–149 (1990)
2. Philippe, F., et al.: Le traité de la réalité virtuelle. Les Presses de l'Ecole des Mines de Paris, vol. 2 (2006)
3. Lin, F., Ye, L., Duffy, V.G., Su, C.-J.: Developing virtual environments for industrial training. Information Sciences 140, 153–170 (2002)
4. Nathanael, D., Vosniakos, G.-C., Mosialos, S.: Cognitive task analysis for Virtual Reality Training: the case of CNC tool offsetting. In: Proceedings of ECCE 2010 Conference, Delft, The Netherlands, pp. 241–244 (2010)
5. Shukla, C., Vazquez, M., Chen, F.F.: Virtual Manufacturing: An overview. Computers and Industrial Engineering 31(1/2), 79–82 (1996)
6. Burkhardt, J.-M., Lourdeaux, D., Fuchs, P.: Conception d'un système de RV pour la formation des agents de conduites aux opérations en milieu ferroviaire. In: Grumbach, A., Richards, N. (eds.) Journées Réalité Virtuelle et Cognition, pp. 123–132. ENST, Paris (1999)
7. Pook, P.K., Ballard, D.: Deictic human/robot interaction. Robotics and Autonomous Systems 18, 259–269 (1996)
8. Morioka, M., Sakakibara, S.: A new cell production assembly system with human–robot cooperation. CIRP Annals - Manufacturing Technology 59, 9–12 (2010)
9. Krüger, J., Lien, T.K., Verl, A.: Cooperation of human and machines in assembly lines. CIRP Annals - Manufacturing Technology 58, 628–646 (2009)
10. Oborski, P.: Man-machine interactions in advanced manufacturing systems. Int. J. Adv. Manuf. Technol. 23, 227–232 (2004)
11. Corrales, J.A., Candelas, F.A., Torres, F.: Safe human–robot interaction based on dynamic sphere-swept line bounding volumes. Robotics and CIM 27, 177–185 (2011)
12. Arai, T., Kato, R., Fujita, M.: Assessment of operator stress induced by robot collaboration in assembly. CIRP Annals - Manufacturing Technology 59, 5–8 (2010)
13. Deacon, J.: Object-Oriented Analysis and Design. Pearson Education, Essex (2005)
14. Slater, M., Wilbur, S.: A framework for immersive virtual environments (FIVE): Speculations on the role of presence in virtual environments. Presence 6, 603–616 (1997)
15. Schuemie, M.J., et al.: Research on Presence in Virtual Reality: A Survey. CyberPsychology & Behavior 4(2), 183–201 (2001)
16. Prothero, J.D., Parker, D.E., Furness, T.: Towards a robust, quantitative measure for presence. In: Proceedings of the Conference on Experimental Analysis and Measurement of Situation Awareness, pp. 359–366 (1995)

# Educational Framework of Product Lifecycle Management Issues for Master and PhD Study Programmes

Milan Edl

University of West Bohemia, Faculty of Mechanical Engineering,
Department of Industrial Engineering and Management, Czech Republic
edl@kpv.zcu.cz

**Abstract.** This article focuses on the description and implementation of PLM in the education of students at the University of West Bohemia. The concept is designed to be deployed in both Master's and PhD study programs. It is also used for training research workers in universities and industrial enterprises in the Czech Republic. The entire educational framework is developed in accordance with sustainable management of the product in its entire life cycle.

**Keywords:** PLM, sustainable product, educational framework, factory as product, sustainable production system.

## 1    Introduction

At the outset something should be said about the current state of education in industrial engineering at the University of West Bohemia in Pilsen (UWB). Industrial engineering has an almost 20-year tradition at the University provided by the Department of Industrial Engineering and Management at the Faculty of Mechanical Engineering. The Department has much experience in education and applied research, and also cooperation with industrial partners. In terms of education, it is important to stress that the Department has accreditation for Bachelor, Master and PhD study in the field of industrial engineering and management.

It is precisely this background that has been used to create and improve the educational framework for students at all stages of their education in the field of industrial engineering and Product Lifecycle Management. The three fundamental tenets of the new educational framework are three projects undertaken with assistance from the European Union Structural Fund and the Czech Ministry of Education, Youth and Sports.

It is also important to add that the creation of this educational framework would not have been possible without the experience gained from foreign workplaces.

## 2    Motivation

It is necessary to look at product management from different viewpoints. Not just from a technical perspective, not only from a technical point of view, but we must also add other views. Important factors which are necessary to include are:

C. Emmanouilidis, M. Taisch, D. Kiritsis (Eds.): APMS 2012, Part I, IFIP AICT 397, pp. 614–621, 2013.
© IFIP International Federation for Information Processing 2013

- Reducing the time (maybe timing) of release of product on to the market
- Orientation towards product quality
- Teamwork
- Modularity of product (meta-product)
- Knowledge based approach
- Not undervaluing the second half of the product lifecycle
- Etc...

These conditions should be considered as smart products and intelligent manufacturing systems. What are 'smart products' and 'intelligent manufacturing systems'? It does not mean anything other than the integration of different approaches, tools, ideas, resources, etc., into the final product. Final product can be regarded as the production system, for example, meta-product.

A production system [1] can no longer be seen as the view of F. W. Taylor: Taylorism can be described as: the direction where management methods and means are used that were created and defined in the early 20th century in the USA by F. W. Taylor. Time studies of workers determined that daily tasks were based on the most powerful performances of workers, without taking into account the possibilities and abilities of the average man. Taylorism was based on the idea of homo oeconomicus, who is motivated to work exclusively for material benefits and, as an "isolated individual" willing to submit to a strict, standardized mode of operation.

The production system must be understood as an integral system where it is necessary to apply the elements of intelligence. It is both product development and a combination of all the parts of the product lifecycle.

The following statement [2] was made by Prof. van Brussel from Katholieke Universiteit in Leuven:

**Products and Production Systems Should Be 'Tailor Made' Not 'Taylor Made'!**

The basic idea is clear. It is necessary to satisfy the customer. Modular product is quite advantageous for the efficiency of the product development (if it works).

The production system must be understood as a product, so the modular production system is very important for creating a modular product.

And it is exactly this point of view which is key for industrial engineering education at the University of West Bohemia, and the entire framework of this study programme is based on and gradually modified according to two basic principles. The first is industrial strategy in a Czech and European environment which is based on directives formulated with the support of the Strategic Research Agenda and/or at the Czech governmental level. The second principle is the formulation of the requirements of representatives of Czech industry. These are representatives from companies of various sizes and from varying fields. Feedback from the Czech Technology Engineering Platform (members of Manufuture) was also used.

## 3     Roles of Universities

But it is also essential to look at education in a broader context. What is the role of the University of West Bohemia? The University of West Bohemia in Pilsen has educational, research and application roles. These three pillars are also a source of financing. Education is usually financed by the Ministry of Education. Projects in the field of research, development and innovation are usually financed from the state budget, EU funds and industrial practice. And then there are the financial resources from industrial practice to solve specific industrial problems.

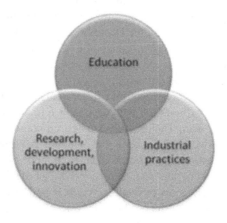

**Fig. 1.** Roles of universities

At the present time, the Department of Industrial Engineering and Management is working on several projects. The first is "Product life cycle in a digital factory environment", the second is "Quality research team focused on the issues of product lifecycle management" and the third is "Creating and enhancing partnerships between universities and practice".

## 4     Proposal and Implementation of an Educational Framework

Based on the identified (or verified) facts, there have been modifications to study programmes both at master's level and also at PhD level. It should be noted that our university students have found employment in industry (industrial plants) and research organizations. There is a need to develop programmes with short to medium term impacts on industry. Therefore, modifications have been made to Master and PhD study programs.

It is also necessary to highlight the cooperation with the following foreign institutions in the creation of an educational framework for PLM at UWB:

- University of Žilina (SK)
- Technical University of Košice (SK)
- University of Zielona Góra (PL)
- University of Bielsko-Biala (PL)
- University of Maribor (SI)
- Fraunhofer-Institut für Fabrikbetrieb und -automatisierung IFF Magdeburg (DE)
- Technical University of Chemnitz (DE)
- Czech Liaison Office for Research and Development (BE)
- SIRRIS (BE)
- Manchester Metropolitan University (GB)

## 4.1    Product Lifecycle in Digital Factory Environment

The project for innovating the Industrial Engineering masters study program is called "Product life cycle in the digital factory environment" [7]. The objective of the project is to innovate the teaching programmes of Bachelor and Master Degree students at the Faculty of Mechanical Engineering at the University of West Bohemia in Pilsen. It will be implemented by the creation of 19 e-learning multimedia modular courses, which will be upgraded to existing programmes. The target group is mainly students with a diverse range of knowledge acquired in the studied subjects (design, technology, production, etc.). Course modules will be used in 38 subjects in six Bachelor's and Master's Degree programmes at three faculties.

Modules developed within the project are as follows:

- Theoretical and System approach for Product Lifecycle Management (PLM) in Digital Factory environment (DF)
  - Digital company
  - System approach to life cycle engineering design in DF environment
  - Legal aspects in connection with the life cycle of the product
  - Virtual reality in DF environments
  - Knowledge management and innovation
  - Performance management processes and increase value-added product in the DF environment
- Technological preparation and support for production in DF environment
  - Design of investment units
  - Design of material handling
  - NC Technology
- Design of production systems (processes) in DF environment
  - Design of production bases
  - Creation and optimization of workplaces
  - Analysis, modelling and optimization
  - Logistics
  - Simulation of manufacturing systems and processes
- Planning and control production and information support in DF environment
  - Methods of Industrial Engineering
  - Production planning

— Integrated management systems and their applications in manufacturing
— Algorithms and their computer support
— Economic analysis and evaluation of production processes and products

These modules are currently implemented in the study programme of Industrial Engineering and Management at the Faculty of Mechanical Engineering, UWB.

## 4.2    Highly Professional Research Team Focused on Product Lifecycle Management and Digital Factory

The project for innovating the Industrial Engineering PhD study programme is called "Highly professional research team focused on the topic of Product Lifecycle Management and Digital Factory" [6]. The basic idea of the project is to improve, streamline and support using specialist knowledge the work of the research centres on the issues of Product Lifecycle Management environment in the Digital Factory at the Faculty of Mechanical Engineering, University of West Bohemia in Pilsen. The project creates specific training modules for acquiring knowledge and skills of researchers and their use in effective research teamwork on the topic. Its character is interdisciplinary and it will be therefore resolved in integrated interdisciplinary research in the fields of design, technology and industrial engineering, which will interconnect into one research team for solving problems using methods and tools of digital business. Furthermore, the cooperation of the team with foreign research teams will be prepared as a necessary condition of quality and sustainability of the research.

In order to fulfil other objectives:

- four industry-oriented research groups at the faculty will be integrated within one multidisciplinary research team,
- the materials for training researchers and doctoral students in this field will be elaborated,
- cooperation of teams with renowned international research centres will be prepared.

Knowledge of individual topics from the field of digital companies based on the use of information technology (CAD, CAM, CAP, ERP, etc.) has a strong tradition at the Faculty of Mechanical Engineering, in the fields of design, technology and industrial engineering (mainly represented by three departments and one research centre). The research of particular topics is currently separated into four research groups that do not cooperate effectively. Therefore, the disconnected research group from the fields of design, technology and industrial engineering will be integrated into an interdisciplinary research team in order to improve and streamline the management team, based on synergies, and to improve performance in solving common problems of digital research companies. These results in the NUTS II Southwest unique research facility focus on training researchers to develop research and practical application of innovations in the issues of the digital enterprise. This method of ensuring the discussed issue is in conformity with the solution originating from foreign research institutions dealing with the concept of digital enterprise.

The research team will consist of academic staff, PhD students and selected students of various disciplines at the Faculty of Mechanical Engineering, along with researchers from industrial companies.

Modules that are being developed within the project are as follows:

- Digital company (DP)
- Product lifecycle management (PLM)
- Enterprise Information Systems and DP
- Knowledge management and DP
- Artificial Intelligence and DP
- Virtual reality and DP
- CAx and DP
- Control via data management and PLM and DP
- Reverse engineering and DP
- Design of production systems and DP
- Assembly, robots and DP
- NC Technology and DP
- Design of production processes and DP
- Logistics and DP
- Production Planning and Control and DP
- Modelling and simulation, and DP
- Evaluation of the performance in the company and DP

The following figure (Fig.2) shows a matrix of relations between individual modules, where value 1 means a weak but existing relationship, 2 means a strong relationship and 3 indicates a very strong relationship.

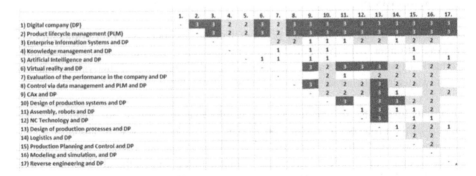

**Fig. 2.** Relationship matrix

The whole concept is conceived as a means for designing modules to create a methodical, logical approach to creating products, from the initial idea through design and production to retail and maintenance and disposal. These modules can be called 'sequential'. However, in order to 'function' these modules need further essential activities which are described in other types of modules. These are called 'profile' modules.

As can be seen from the matrix, all connecting elements are already in the modules, which cover all the other implemented project modules. Other key modules (in terms of connectivity with other thematic units) are Virtual Reality and Planning Manufacturing Processes.

All the modules presented here are included as courses for students of all PhD study areas at the Faculty of Mechanical Engineering, UWB.

### 4.3    Creating and Enhancing Partnerships between Universities and Practice

Improving study programmes is an important step, but it is not the only necessary step that needs to be made. There must be greater interaction with industry and the European Research Area. To this end UWB is also working on the project "Creating and Enhancing Partnerships between Universities and Practice" [8]. This project is aimed at expanding the contacts and cooperation between universities and private and public sectors in order to contribute to the improvement of the design of a competitive workforce. Such cooperation will be mutually beneficial – students will bring into practice the theoretical knowledge of the new organization and a fresh perspective to problem solving, while practitioners will apply their experience in teaching. The development of cooperation and professional skills will also contribute to the conference, interactive workshops and the winter school. The project will be supported by international practice and internships, and participation of foreign experts in interactive workshops, which will not only improve the professional and language skills of the people involved, but also increase international cooperation (joint projects, R & D).

## 5    Conclusion

In conclusion it can be said that positive feedback, especially from companies, is growing stronger over time, and the correctness of moving towards sustainable production systems can be seen. And this is only the beginning of innovation that has not only a technical character, but especially a social dimension.

**Acknowledgements.** In conclusion, we would like to express our thanks for the support of the projects CZ.1.07/2.2.00/15.0397 "Product Lifecycle in Digital Factory Environment", CZ.1.07/2.3.00/09.0163 "Highly professional research team focused on the topic of Product Lifecycle Management and Digital Factory" and CZ.1.07/2.4.00/17.0054 "Creating and Enhancing Partnerships between Universities and Practice" dealt with in the Operational Program Education for Competitiveness.

Special thanks are due to our foreign partners who participated in consultations for the creation of a system for education of PLM at the University of West Bohemia in Pilsen.

# References

1. Edl, M., Kurkin, O.: Innovations Information Management Systems: Product Lifecycle Management. Zielona Góra: Wydawnictwo Instytutu Informatyki i Zarzadzanie Produkcja Uniwesytetu Zielonogórskiego, s. 30–s. 43 (2011) ISBN 978-83-933843-0-3
2. Edl, M.: Řízení životního cyklu produktu (PLM). SmartMotion, Plzeň (2012) ISBN 978-80-87539-04-0
3. Sääksvuori, A., Immonen, A.: Product lifecycle management. 3rd edn., vol. xiii, 253 p. Springer (2008) ISBN 978-354-0781-738
4. Tolio, T.: Design of flexible production systems: Methodologies and tools, vol. xiv, 299 p. Springer, Berlin (2009c) ISBN 35-408-5414-2
5. Stark, J.: Product lifecycle management: 21st century paradigm for product realisation, 2nd edn., vol. xxii, 561 p. Springer, New York (2011) ISBN 08-572-9545-4
6. Product Lifecycle in Digital Factory Environment (2009), http://www.zivdig.zcu.cz (cit. January 05, 2012)
7. Highly professional research team focused on the topic of Product Lifecycle Management and Digital Factory (2009), http://www.vyztymdp.zcu.cz (cit. January 05, 2012)
8. Creating and Enhancing Partnerships between Universities and Practice (2009), http://www.unipranet.zcu.cz (cit. January 05, 2012)

# The Use of Serious Games in the Education of Engineers

Jannicke Madeleine Baalsrud Hauge[1], Borzoo Pourabdollahian[2],
and Johann C.K.H. Riedel[3]

[1] Bremer Institut für Produktion und Logistik, Bremen, Germany
baa@biba.uni-bremen.de
[2] Politecnico di Milano, Milan, Italy
borzoo.pourabdollahian@mail.polimi.it
[3] Nottingham University Business School, Nottingham, UK
johann.riedel@nottingham.ac.uk

**Abstract.** Serious games have been used in the education of engineering students and professionals for decades, but still they have not reached their maximum diffusion. Learning by gaming is often seen as not serious enough within higher education and vocational training. Consequently, gaming as a teaching method is still often excluded from many curricula. Hence, students lack the experience of active knowledge acquisition during lessons and encounter a barrier for successful participation in serious games later. Although a variety of games have been developed and proved successful for the mediation of skills in complex systems (Windhoff, 2001), this paper discusses why we think that serious games should be considered as a suitable learning method for the mediation of skills needed in the education of engineers and secondly to give some examples of current games and experience of their use.

**Keywords:** Serious Games, Engineering Education.

## 1    Introduction

Today manufacturing is often a complex process, involving several partners around the world. The products are more customized and have shorter life-cycle times, which increases the marginal cost per product. As the employee is the person in an organisation that performs and lives collaboration, the organisational success will mainly depend on his/her capabilities to learn and act in a dynamic environment (Windhoff, 2001). Decision makers, like people in general, are prone to the misperceptions of feedback. This means that their performance in complex and dynamic systems is hindered by non-linearity, time delays and feedback structures (Sterman, 1989). Decision making in dynamic systems is hard because it calls for dynamic decision making, which is a stream of decisions closely depending on one another. Thus, the question is: which skills does an employee need in order to perform well in collaborations, and how is it possible to mediate skills in such a way that he/she can act as needed when a new situation arises and how can engineering students be prepared for this during their studies?

Manufacturing and engineering education needs to focus on developing the skills required by new generations of employees; adapting the educational content and its

C. Emmanouilidis, M. Taisch, D. Kiritsis (Eds.): APMS 2012, Part I, IFIP AICT 397, pp. 622–629, 2013.

delivery mechanisms to the new requirements of knowledge-based manufacturing, the provision of integrated engineering competencies, including a variety of soft skills, and the promotion of innovation and entrepreneurship (Taisch, 2011, p.11). In order to achieve this, it is necessary to focus more on multi-disciplinarity and integrated engineering competencies (Taisch, 2011).

## 2    Why Use Serious Games

The term Serious Games mainly refers to games that are primarily designed for non-entertainment purposes. According to Corti (2006) a Serious Game "is all about leveraging the power of computer games to captivate and engage end-users for a specific purpose, such as to develop new knowledge and skills". This unique feature significantly supports new requirements in engineering education; especially those that cannot be taught by traditional means. For example, students can interact in virtual environments, which will confront them with complicated situations in which they need to gather and analyse information to take critical decisions. To reach this goal they are pushed to improve their soft skills, such as communication and negotiation, as well as technical skills. Experience so far with the use of serious games in the education of engineers has shown a positive effect on the students' abilities both, to apply the theoretically gained knowledge and to enhance required business skills for a qualified engineer.

Learning by serious games can be clarified by Kolb's experiential learning cycle, which views learning as a process, which includes four essential phases: Active experimentation and specific experience, Direct experience, Reflexion, and Assesment. Active experimentation and testing lead to direct experience (Straka, 1986). Direct experience allows for reflection on different aspects of the experienced situation both at an individual as well as at a group level. Based upon this reflection, an assessment as well as a definition of the consequences and potential generalization possibilities leads to the awareness of new actions. This experiential learning approach requires a free, self directed and self organized learning process. Effective engineering education needs a learning-by-doing approach characterised by moving from passive perception to active experience. However, there are not enough real life situations that can be used for education or training, since in many real life situations the occurrence of errors or mistakes – which are natural in learning situations – are not acceptable. Simulation games using advanced information and communication technology can be used as a substitute in order to meet this need for active experience (Riis, 1995; Radcliffe & Teakle, 1994).

Creating knowledge by gaming has proved to be particularly effective whenever soft skills are essential and traditional learning methods fail (Windhoff, 2001). Warren and Langley (1999) underscored that decision makers should have access to gaming simulation tools in order for them to cope with the business systems in which they evolve, and to reap strategic management skills. Scholz-Reiter et al. (2002) strongly emphasized the need for the insertion of management games to practitioners and engineering students in organizations and universities, respectively, in order for them to learn specific tasks and aptitudes like communication and co-operation in complex distributed production systems. Up to now, there has not been so much research carried out to understand why specific games work or do not work. This paper presents three case studies of three games to start to understand how they work.

# 3     Case Studies of Serious Games

This section describes three case studies of serious games showing how their pedagogical aims and evaluation results compare. In all three cases we have used a blended learning concept based on Kolb's experiential learning cycle (Kolb, 1984). The experience so far has shown that a well-designed game will not only help the learner to transfer theoretical knowledge to practical skills, but also to transform the gained experience into knowledge so that they can assess previously acquired knowledge and generate new understanding. The games are used by students at masters level and by engineers in industry. The authors have been using serious games for the mediation of skills to engineering students for several years and have collected good feedback both from the students as well as from the analysis of the learning outcomes (Riedel & Baalsrud Hague, 2011). However, with some groups the gaming approach went wrong resulting in a low learning outcome and high stress factors for students. In this paper we analyse why the learning outcome is so dependent on the students' background, and look for mechanisms for improving the learning outcome for the user group with a low learning outcome. A brief description of the games used follows.

## 3.1     COSIGA

Cosiga is a New Product Development (NPD) simulation game. It was designed to tackle the problem of teaching today's engineering and management students the know-how of to design and manufacture new products, to equip them with the experience of design, and to teach them how to deal with the complexities of the new product development process (Riedel, et al. 2001). It is a team player game, played by five people playing in the same room, or in a distributed condition using the internet and telecommunications.   Each person plays a role in the product development process (project manager, designer, marketing manager, purchasing manager and production manager) and works collaboratively together, to specify, design, and manufacture the final product - a type of truck. The product's manufacturability will be put to the test in the simulated factory to produce the final products.

COSIGA enables students to experience the process of new product development from the perspectives of the different disciplines involved in the design process and build their own understanding of the issues of design, manufacture, marketing, project management and purchasing; and the interactions between the disciplines. The game enables students to interact through continuous communication, to share and exchange information, initiate argumentation on problems and concepts, form relationships between pieces of discipline specific information and finally articulate knowledge and make decisions. During their experience with COSIGA students are not really learning about the technical aspects of designing and manufacturing a truck but learning how to increase their awareness of the many complex, often interdependent issues of the design process, through constant information sharing, rationale forming and building their capacity to act, make decisions and create new knowledge.

## 3.2    Beware Game

Beware is a multi-player online game implemented in a workshop setting. The application is used as a training medium for companies involved in supply networks covering the issue of risk management. Currently, Beware is designed with two distinct and independent levels. In the first level, the participant experiences risks within the organization. In this first level, the players have to specify, design and produce a simple product within their company. During the game, the players have to identify upcoming risks and think how to reduce or treat them by developing suitable communication and co-operation strategies as well to define the responsibility of each role. The players can communicate using the inbuilt chat, phones or Skype or also schedule physical meetings to discuss relevant issues.

In the second level, the players are faced with the design, development and manufacturing of an extended product - a cell phone with a range of services. The players use their acquired knowledge and skills in the inter-organisational contract negotiations as well as to carry out the collaborative production in a distributed environment. While the simulated service company takes the consortia's leadership and develops services, the two simulated manufacturing companies develop and produce generic cell phone parts. As the necessary information will be distributed unequally, the students have to cooperate to enable the constant flow of information that will then lead to a constant flow of material. Also there different events and risks included, and the player needs to carry out some risk management tasks.

The game enables students to identify how different types of risks impact differently on the success of the collaboration and also how the impact of risks increases and affects the partners' success over time, if no actions are taken to reduce and control the risks. The students have the possibility to apply risk assessment and risk management methods and thus increase their awareness of risks in production networks as well as the complexity of decision making.

## 3.3    Set-Based Concurrent Engineering Game (SBCE)

Set Based Concurrent Engineering is a concept in new product development based on the lean thinking perspective. It is going to be more diffused in future production systems, due of its advantage in decreasing the time and cost of production. The aim of this serious game is highlighting the benefits of applying the SBCE concept in producing a simplified airplane. It is a teamwork game that includes four members who take the role of each department (body, wing, cockpit and tail). In the first stage players will be asked to design an airplane regarding both customer requirements and supplier components based on a point-based approach and then they will be introduced to the SBCE enablers that they need to execute to design the airplane, with the same data given in the first stage. Finally, after playing the game, players will observe that applying SBCE decreases the time and cost of the design (Kerga, et al. 2011).

# 4    Comparison of the Games' Learning Goals

It is useful to compare the learning goals, or objectives, of the three serious games. The table below shows their learning goals.

**Table 1.** Learning objectives of the three games

| Learning goals | Cosiga | Beware | SBCE |
|---|---|---|---|
| To aid the players to understand the enabling factors which lead to an effectual product development by applying Set-Based Concurrent Engineering. | | | x |
| To help players to understand the new product development process and apply Concurrent Engineering principles and practice. | x | | |
| To impart and improve knowledge of the most common Concurrent Engineering rules and tools. | x | | x |
| To acquire best practice in the Concurrent Engineering domain | x | | |
| To identify, analyse and solve potential problems during Concurrent Engineering | x | | |
| To develop the ability to make decisions in a complex context | x | x | |
| To support the understanding on how to apply methods supporting decision making in a cooperative and competitive environment | | x | |
| To support the understanding of risk assessment and risk management in the supply chain | | x | |
| To learn how to apply risk assessment and risk management methods both in the supply chain as well as within a department. | | x | |
| To identify, analyse and solve potential risks in the supply chain | | x | |
| To demonstrate the challenge to meet both design and customer requirements. | | | x |
| To demonstrate how implementing Set-Based Concurrent Engineering can affect the product development process | | | x |
| To acquire and develop group communication skills | x | x | x |
| To acquire and develop group collaboration skills | x | x | |
| To acquire and improve group problem solving skills | x | x | x |
| To acquire and improve group decision making skills. | x | x | x |
| To acquire and improve group negotiation skills | x | x | |
| To acquire and develop the ability to develop a common understanding with others in a CE Group | x | | |
| To acquire and develop the ability to appreciate, understand and make good use of the contribution of others | x | | |
| To improve risk management skills | | x | |
| To raise awareness, understanding and coping with the typical day-to-day problems in working collaboratively with people from different cultures and languages. | x | | |
| To acquire and develop the ability to collaborate in a European industrial context | x | | |

From the above table we can see that there are a number of similarities between the learning objectives of the games (notwithstanding the fact that two of them are focused on NPD and concurrent engineering). The learning goals address: subject specific domain knowledge, individual skills and group skills: communication, problem solving, decision making, negotiation, etc. All three games were designed to help engineers and students to develop a practical understanding of a specific engineering technique – new product development, risk management and concurrent engineering. However, engineering is not just about the use of specific techniques or methods to solve problems; it is about groups of engineers working cooperatively together. Therefore, all three games place an emphasis upon developing the group skills of the participants.

## 5     Comparison of the Games' Learning Outcomes

The above table summarises the results of several evaluations carried out on the three games. A primary way to tell if a game is simulating the intended process correctly is to examine the communication flow within the game – who is asking who for information and who is supplying information. Various post-game questionnaires were used to determine if the participants had learnt the appropriate concepts. This showed that some concepts were learnt very well, but others less so – eg. the importance of product cost in Cosiga declined after the game, this was due to their being very little emphasis placed on product cost in the game itself (Riedel & Pawar, 2009). Another influence on participants' learning was their prior knowledge and their liking of the gaming method. For the learning from the serious game to be successful the participants need to have the same level of knowledge – if some of the players have inadequate background knowledge, gaming is less successful.

**Table 2.** Learning outcomes of the case study games

| | Social/Soft Skill | Knowledge | | |
| --- | --- | --- | --- | --- |
| | | **Declarative** | **Procedural** | **Strategic** |
| Cosiga | Different types of communication were observed (e.g. ask for information, offer information, request action, etc) and the result demonstrated that the game represented the required communication pattern. Improving multidisciplinary team working and decision making skills. | Understanding the New Product Development concept. Understanding the distribution of knowledge during product development. | Understanding the product development process. Understanding how to collaborate, with downstream and upstream actors. | |

**Table 2.** (*Continued.*)

| | | | | |
|---|---|---|---|---|
| Beware | Different types of communication during the decision making process were observed. | Understanding co-operative production in a distributed environment. Identify the long term impact on decisions made both on own and partners' organization. Supply chain risk management. | Understanding how to redesign the supply chain for reducing risks. Understanding how cost, quality, time, customer service indicators are affected by the production process and the identification and treatment of risks. | Applying several methods supporting risk management. Understanding the long term impact of decisions and long term risks. |
| SBCE | Improving team working and communication skills. Enhancing the decision making skill. | Understanding the difference between two models for NPD: Point-Based and Set-Based CE. Comprehending the enabling drivers in SBCE. Introducing the challenges to develop new products in order to meet dissimilar stakeholders' requirements. | Understanding to consider a set of solutions rather than just one solution. Learning how to employ Set-Based Concurrent Engineering enablers in order to reduce the development time and cost. | |

# 6    Conclusion

The three games discussed in this paper are all used in the education of engineers. The games are used by students at master level and engineers in industry. The authors have been using serious games for the mediation of skills to engineering students for several years and have collected good feedback both from the students as well as from the analysis of learning outcomes. The evaluation of the games showed in general that the players were able to apply the gained theoretical knowledge and also to strengthen their collaboration skills. However, the analysis also showed that the effectiveness of the games was dependent on the group - their level of background knowledge, if it was an inhomogeneous group or a homogenous group, as well as being dependent on their openness for playing games.

**Acknowledgements.** The research reported in this paper has been partially supported by the European Union, particularly through the projects: GaLA: The European Network of Excellence on Serious Games (FP7-ICT-2009.4.2-258169) www.galanoe.eu and ELU: Enhanced Learning Unlimited (FP6-IST-027866).

# References

1. Corti, K.: Games-based Learning; a serious business application. PIXELearningLimited (2006), http://www.pixelearning.com/docs/games_basedlearning_pixelearning.pdf
2. Kerga, E., Rossi, M., Taisch, M., Terzi, S.: Lean Product and Process Development: a Learning Kit. In: 15th IFIP WG 5.7 SIG Workshop, June 5-7, Aalto University, Espoo (2011)
3. Kolb, D.A.: Experiential learning: Experience as the source of learning and development. Prentice Hall, Upper Saddle River (1984)
4. Radcliffe, D.F., Teakle, P.: Contextual Experiences in Concurrent Engineering Learning. In: The National Teaching Workshop, Australia (1994)
5. Riedel, J.C.K.H., Baalsrud Hague, J.: Serious games and the evaluation of the learning outcomes - challenges and problems. In: Cruz-Cunha, M.M., Carvalho, V.H., Tavares, P. (eds.) Computer Games as Educational and Management Tools: Uses and Approaches, pp. 263–279. IGI Global, Hershey (2011)
6. Riedel, J., Pawar, K.: A Report On The Experiences Gained From Evaluating The Cosiga NPD Simulation Game. In: IPDMC 2009, International Product Development Management Conference, June 7-8, Twente University, The Netherlands (2009)
7. Riedel, J.C.K.H., Pawar, K.S., Barson, R.: Academic & Industrial User Needs of a Concurrent Engineering Computer Simulation Game. Journal of Concurrent Engineering: Research & Applications 9(3), 223–237 (2001)
8. Riis, J.O. (ed.): Simulation Games and Learning in Production Management. Chapman & Hall, London (1995)
9. Scholz-Reiter, B., Gavirey, S., Echelmeyer, W., Hamann, T., Doberenz, R.: Developing a virtual tutorial system for online simulation games. In: Proceedings of the 30th SEFI Annual Conference, Firenze, Italy (2002)
10. Sterman, J.D.: Modeling Managerial Behavior: Misperceptions of Feedback in a Dynamic Decision Making Experiment. Management Science 35(3), 321–339 (1989)
11. Swart, J., Wild, J.: A competence based approach for knowledge sharing: building the foundation for Organisational Learning. In: Sixth International Research Conference on Quality, Innovation and Knowledge, Malaysia (2001)
12. Taisch, M., Pourabdollahian, B.: Deliverable 3.1 – SIG Field Report Engineering and Manufacturing. GALA project, Milano (2011)
13. Warren, K., Langley, P.: The effective communication of system dynamics to improve insight and learning in management education. Journal of the Operational Research Society 50, 396–404 (1999)
14. Windhoff, G.: Planspiele für die verteilte Produktion. Entwicklung und Einsatz von Trainingsmodulen für das aktive Erleben charakteristischer Arbeitssituationen in arbeitsteiligen, verteilten Produktionssystemen auf Basis der Planspielmethodik, Aachen (2001)

# Integrating Competence Management into a Coupled Project-System Design Management

Arz Wehbe[1], Christophe Merlo[1,2], and Véronique Pilnière[2,3]

[1] IMS, Université de Bordeaux, 33400 Talence, France
arz.wehbe@u-bordeaux1.fr
[2] ESTIA, Technopole Izarbel, 64210 Bidart, France
{c.merlo,v.pilnière}@estia.fr
[3] CREG-UPPA, Pau, France

**Abstract.** Competence management has recently become an important issue in companies. Closely related to knowledge management, it considers the capacities of an individual to perform by using his/her knowledge. This knowledge management becomes a tool for companies to manage human resources in the long run. The ability to characterize useful competences, to evaluate how they are improved through past experience and successive jobs occupied, and thus to select project team members according to fully or partly existing skills are some of the concerns that business managers have to tackle. This paper focuses on the coordination of design activities in order to propose a tool dedicated to project managers on an operational level to manage skills for better team building. The aim is to improve team performance in the short and long term while preserving a link with the human resources department. Our work is based on the results of the ATLAS project which studies the coupling between systems design and management. We propose an initial tool to manage skills in a design project.

**Keywords:** Collaborative design, skills, design management, project management, forecasting management of employment.

## 1 Introduction and Context

Many studies have examined the human and social dimensions of product design [Lorino, 1996, Perrin, 1999, Boujut and Tiger, 2002]. Indeed, the peculiarity of the design activity is that it is an essentially human activity, not an automated one. [Merlo and Girard, 2003] show that man is both a resource and an actor-engine design process. This is a resource that needs to be controlled, usually by assigning a set of tasks contributing to the overall development objective.

In the context of product development, the logical project [Cleland and Ireland, 2006] and the need for collaboration between several partners [Kvan, 2000] make this an even more important human dimension. Often managers see people as resources having mostly technical knowledge but do consider them mobilized too often in terms of skills. The concern that associating a person and a set of tasks in a logical

C. Emmanouilidis, M. Taisch, D. Kiritsis (Eds.): APMS 2012, Part I, IFIP AICT 397, pp. 630–637, 2013.
© IFIP International Federation for Information Processing 2013

short-term, may present a number of limitations such as: experts required, beginners representatives on low-value activities, a significant turnover between each project, and even during long term projects.

As part of product design, especially for complex systems, our work has led to various proposed models, methodologies and prototypes to integrate the dimensions of the product, as well as process and organization into a common logic of design coordination [Robin et al., 2007]. This integrated approach has helped reconcile the technical and human dimensions of driving design activities through the structuring of projects and performers, planning activities assigned to the actors, the design itself and the performance evaluation of these three dimensions.

One of the areas for improvement proposed here is to study how to include performers in structuring and planning teams based on their competence. Our goal is to integrate management skills as part of an integrated product-process-organization driving the design. In the first section, we describe the ATLAS project, which forms the basis for our thinking. In the next section, we develop our vision of management skills and we make an assessment of what has been implemented in the demonstrator software developed in the ATLAS project. Finally, in the last section, we consider recent developments in management skills for businesses.

## 2    ATLAS Project

The work presented here is based on the ATLAS project, which represents an important step in our work on the conduct of the design. The scientific basis based on the GRAI R & D approach [Girard and Doumeingts, 2004] is formalized by the GRAI Engineering methodology [Merlo and Girard, 2003] to deploy the principles of design steered by the integration of product - process - organization.

The ATLAS project *(Aides et assisTances pour la conception, la conduite et leur coupLage par les connAissanceS – Help and support for design, coordination and their coupling by knowledge)* includes six French academic institutions and two French companies which propose an instrumentation design activity based on the coupling of product design and project design.

Started in 2008, one of the major objectives is the implementation of a demonstrator software to implement mechanisms to ensure the coupling of the object of design (the product or system) and the process of realization (project) in a collaborative environment for concurrent engineering [Prasad, 1996]. The desired result lies behind more consistent and efficient decision-making, as based on information drawn from these two dimensions and consolidated by the aggregation of information from the detailed structuring of the projects and the system.

The different models developed to achieve the objectives of coupling have been presented in [Aldanondo et al., 2008]. The mechanisms that implement them are based on knowledge modeling concepts such as system, reuse, and performance evaluation in the form of variables, constraint programming and feedback.

The demonstrator program targets two categories of users: users involved in system design (designers responsible for these designers) and users responsible for project planning. It has two main modules: The system design module and the project management module.

Each system and each project have associated variables. These variables specify the indicators on which the system will be evaluated (and therefore each subsystem) and the project (and each sub-project). Performance targets to be achieved and constraints can be set by managers (both system and project) and then be checked all along the progress of the design.

A third module focuses on the "management", that is to say on the overall management of this dual system design and project evaluation is used to summarize the performance achieved by going back with the values of variables and offering a synthetic scoreboard, combining variables systems and projects. This module centralizes the exchange between project managers and system by integrating an internal messaging system. It keeps track of the decisions and their justification.

The coupling is provided by various mechanisms built directly in the demonstrator, either independently or integrated in the modules implemented.

The overall architecture of the demo can be described through (Fig. 1), in order to illustrate the interactions between modules. A configuration module completes the architecture of the demonstrator to show the flexibility that can be introduced in relation to the technical assumptions that were retained.

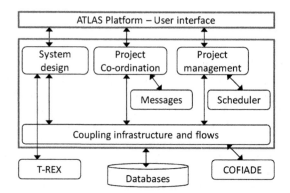

**Fig. 1.** Architecture of ATLAS prototype

In these modules to which are added up additional external tools, in particular: a management tool for feedback *(T-REX, proposed by ENI of Tarbes)* and a constraint propagation engine *(COFIADE, proposed by the Centre Génie Industriel from the Ecole des Mines d'Albi-Carmaux).*

## 2.1    ATLAS Control Design

As part of ATLAS, there are three people in charge of the project: The system and planning managers are at every level, and the project manager that launches the project and appoints the heads of the first level.

This control mode is one of the couplings to manage the coordination of the design. Based on the organizational model of the PPO model (Fig. 2), each level beyond the first is identical and is repeated for each new sub-project.

The coupling is designed to facilitate the impact of decisions made in each of the two-dimensional system and project, and the exchange of relevant information to make a decision comprehensive, relevant and justified, and possibly in a collective context. Different coupling modes have been identified [Aldanando et al., 2008].

For these different coupling modes, the program director (PD), then system manager (SM) defines the design goals for his/here team and deploys them in the form of constraints that apply on the variables he/she selected. The planning manager (PM) does the same with the project-specific objectives such as budget, available resources, and schedules processes and activities. Both must work together to describe the activities that detail the predefined process and validate the allocation of adequate resources. Each of these individuals or stakeholders may rely on a team to assist him in making his decision, not shown in Figure 2.

Everyone then monitors the progress of the design, first overseeing design activities of design and the satisfaction constraints for a system design, and then checking the progress of the schedule, costs and other project constraints. The couplings used (alerts and scoreboard) facilitate the identification of gaps and non-compliance constraints, leading to a collaboration to make new decisions.

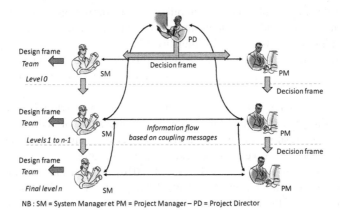

**Fig. 2.** ATLAS organizational Module

The following section discusses the issue of competence management and its implementation in the ATLAS demonstrator.

## 3    Management of Resources by Competences

Questioning the management of resources requires competences to clarify the concept of competences before considering their integration into the control design activities.

For [De Witte, 1994] competences don't have a definition but it is necessary to agree on a common definition to be able to understand. According to Le Boterf, elevator cannot be taken without resorting to a competence [Le Boterf, 2008]. This idea highlights the fact that competence "is never given directly to see: For [De Witte, 1994], competences have never been observed in a microscope.

Even though today there is no clear definition adopted by all, we can see it as a sum of knowledge, know-how and skills. [Le Boterf, 2010] declares that competences are not a state and they are linked to action. For him, competences are a result of three factors: knowing how to act which implies the ability to combine and mobilize relevant resources, the act of willing which refers to the motivation of the individual and a more or less motivating context, and finally the power of acting makes it possible to take responsibility and risk taking of the individual.

[Masson and Parlier, 2004] identify four defining characteristics of competence: it is operative and finalized (it is inseparable from an activity), it is learned (one becomes competent by personal or social building), it is structured (it combines knowing how to act, willing to act and the power of acting), then it is abstract and hypothetical (you cannot directly observe the competence but only its consequences).

[Michel, 1993] considers a competence as an ability to solve problems in an efficient way and in a given context. For our part, we will retain the definition proposed by [Boumane et al., 2006] that involves the definitions of the other authors. "Competence is the ability of a person (actor) to act and react with the required relevance to perform an activity in a work situation". The actor is at the center of the process of selecting, combining and mobilizing their knowledge, skills, abilities and behaviors on the one hand, and environmental resources on the other hand, in order to accomplish a mission defined by the company. "

However, it seems important to add to this definition the notion of "social recognition" developed by [Le Boterf, 1994], provided that the competence is a "knowing how to act".

While it is clear that competence, as we have seen, is an individual behavior, which should be supplemented by the collective dimension of competence. It is inconceivable to separate these two dimensions, as they are interdependent in the design processes that involve, and they call for a many actors.

Based on inputs from Le Boterf [Le Boterf, 2010], we consider that the collective competences are a combination of individual competences. "In the collective design situations, the aim of the process (the intended purpose, the" thing "to do ...) and the process itself (how each one is relevant to the other ...) are built by mutual influence" [Hatchuel, 2008]. In the process of cooperation that arise in the course of work [De Terssac, 2002] during the design activities, other learning rules direct exchanges among the concerned actors: "Learning is therefore necessary at any time and requires exchanges between performers and makers."

## 3.1 Competences Management in Companies

Competences management is an approach that mainly concerns the human resource management, and which tends to replace the traditional management based on position and functions related to this position [Retour, 2002]. In fact in small and middle-sized companies, the establishment of a project team will depend on a single person, the entrepreneur, the technical director or the head of research department, for example. The size of the team will also be reduced, and the choice of assignments does not really arise, because the nature of the tasks will be directly related to the position of the person in the company. Management competences rely on the concept of "versatility" which is reduced to a simple availability management for the actors.

The notion of performance is also very present in this competence approach, as far as decision makers are considered [Defélix and Retour, 2003].

This work shows that competences management is applied here for team building projects and the allocation of some team members on specific tasks, since competences are associated with an activity and a level of competence [Gilbert, 2002]. In a company of a certain size and which has genuine human resources, competences management is divided among people from different backgrounds. Technical managers ask for people around them depending on the qualities or experience they have already established or on which they were advised. Planning or financial project managers are also interested in problems of availability, recruitment based on knowledge or level of competences to be determined. The Human Resources function manages the needs of people as profiles of knowledge / competences, through internal or external recruitment. Beyond the management competences and operational management, the long-term management of these design competences is too often the initiative of the project manager or management when starting a project and does not appear systematically in the primary concerns of the company. Experience accumulated in various projects, but also in various functions throughout the career, can then be taken into account to formalize training schemes in the short term, but also manage the long-term career. Practices are based primarily on mapping competences in 4 distinct levels [Veltz and Zarifian 1994]: Competences required for a specific position; the competences used by the employee in this position; the actual competences gained by the employee; the potential employee's competences, allowing the employee and the company to consider a career development.

Our experience with companies of all sizes in all sectors, we found that competences vary greatly from one company to another.

## 4    Conclusion and Discussion

In the field of project management, and in particular project management product development, the consideration of human resources is recognized as an essential element of project manager activities. Focusing on issues of allocation and availability, these operational concerns are not always in tune with the concerns of long-term human resource departments, for which competences management is an essential tool.

By relying on the results of the ATLAS project, involving the coupling between system design and management of design projects, we have proposed a first pragmatic mechanism for extending the simple assignment management and availability by including the dimension competences. Competences classified by types of competences thus become the milestone between the characterization of an individual by his competences and the ability to select a resource through competences needs. The organizational model of decision making among managers or project leads can oversee the process of decision which transforms this need competences in a planned and validated allocation against indicators performance of the project.

This demonstrator deserves to integrate a concrete management of competences in the design process, but it has some limitations.

First, it would be interesting to incorporate more accurately the situations that mobilize certain competences. For example in Figure 3, the situation in which the person is able to adapt themselves is not specified. As we have seen, a competences that can only be measured in a given situation:

"Adapt to the environment" does not specify the personal and external resources that the person is supposed to mobilize [Le Boterf, 2010]. Furthermore, the notion of competences level is necessary but absent from this first prototype, as we have seen in Section 3, in order to consider a competences planning. In this way it would be possible to evaluate the level required to complete an activity, the level mobilized by an actor in this activity, or the potential level reached by this actor on terms to be defined (eg training). In this way the project manager can master more expected performance by the employees he selects, which directly impacts the performance expected in the project itself.

Thirdly, an inherent difficulty to the complexity of the competence lies in identifying informal competences. They often refer to "embedded knowledge" often implicit, reflected in the speech with "you can see," "you feel good" reflecting for the person the difficulty or the impossibility of accessing such of the type of competence.

Finally and more broadly, if this demonstrator is only a tool, it could be very useful as a source of practical information for planning of jobs and competences.

# References

1. Aldanondo, M., Vareilles, E., Djefel, M., Baron, C., Auriol, G., Geneste, L., Zolghadri, M.: Vers un couplage de la conception d'un produit avec la planification de son développement. In: 7e Conférence Internationale de Modélisation et SIMulation, MOSIM 2008, Paris, France (2008)
2. ATLAS, Aides et assisTances pour la conception, la conduite et leur coupLage par les connAissanceS (2008/2011)
3. Boujut, J.F., Tiger, H.: A socio-technical research method for analyzing and instrumenting the design activity. J. of Design Research, 2 (2002)
4. Boumane, A., Talbi, A., Tahon, C., Bouami, D.: Contribution à la modélisation de la compétence. In: 6e Conférence Internationale de Modélisation et SIMulation, MOSIM 2006, Rabat, Maroc, pp. 3–5 (2006)
5. Cleland, D.I., Ireland, L.R.: Project management: strategic design and implementation. McGraw-Hill Gb, London (2006)
6. De Terssac, G.: Le travail : une aventure collective. Octares Éditions, Toulouse (2002)
7. De Witte, S.: La notion de compétences : problèmes d'approches, dans La compétence, mythe, construction ou réalité ? In: Minet, F., Palier, M., De Witte, S. (eds.), L'Harmattan, Paris, pp. 23–38 (1994)
8. Defélix, C., Retour, D.: La gestion des compétences dans la stratégie de croissance d'une PME innovante: le cas Microtek. Revue Internationale PME 16(3-4) (2003)
9. Gilbert, P.: Jalons pour une histoire de la gestion des compétences. In: Klarsfeld, A., Oiry, É. (eds.) Gérer les Compétences, Des Instruments aux Processus, Cas d'entreprises et Perspectives Théoriques, pp. 11–32. AGRH- Vuibert, Paris (2002)

10. Girard, P., Doumeingts, G.: Modelling of the engineering design system to improve performance. Computers & Industrial Engineering 46(1), 43–67 (2004)
11. Hatchuel, A.: Coopération et conception collective – Variété et crises des rapports de prescription. In: De Terssac, G., Friedberg, E. (eds.) Coopération et Conception, Octares Editions, Toulouse, pp. 101–121 (2008)
12. Kvan, T.: Collaborative design: what is it? Automation in Construction 9, 409–415 (2000)
13. Le Boterf, G.: Construire les compétences individuelles et collectives, 5th edn., Eyrolles, Éditions d'Organisation, Paris (2010)
14. Le Boterf, G.: Pour une nouvelle approche de la compétence: Enjeux, définition, mise en pratique. XVème Journées de Projectique, Bidart, France et Saint Sébastien, Espagne, Octobre 30-31 (2008)
15. Le Boterf, G.: De la Compétence, essai sur un attracteur étrange, Eyrolles, Éditions d'Organisation, Paris (1994)
16. Lorino, P.: Le pilotage de l'entreprise: de la mesure à l'interprétation, Cohérence, Pertinence et Evaluation. In: Cohendet, P., Jacot, J.H., Lorino, P. (eds.) Economica, Paris (1996)
17. Masson, A., Parlier, M.: Les démarches compétence. ANACT, Paris (2004)
18. Merlo, C., Girard, P.: GRAI Engineering: A Knowledge Modelling Method to Co-ordinate Engineering Design. In: 2003 International CIRP Design Seminar, Grenoble, France (2003)
19. Michel, S.: Sens et contresens des bilans de compétences, Editions Liaisons, Paris (1993)
20. Perrin, J.: Pilotage et évaluation des processus de conception, Editions l'Harmattan, Paris, France (1999) ISBN 2-7384-7579-5
21. Prasad, B.: Concurrent engineering fundamentals, vol. 1. Prentice-Hall, Englewood Cliffs (1996)
22. Retour, D.: Le management des compétences, quoi de neuf pour l'entreprise? Management et Conjoncture Sociale, Automne, 7–8 (2002)
23. Robin, V., Merlo, C., Girard, P.: PEGASE: A prototype of software to manage design system in a collaborative design environment. In: Loureiro, S.G., Curran, R. (eds.) 14th ISPE International Conference on Concurrent Engineering, Complex Systems Concurrent Engineering: Collaboration, Technology Innovation and Sustainability, Sao Jose dos Campos, Brazil, pp. 597–604 (2007)
24. Veltz, P., Zarifian, P.: Travail collectif et modèles d'organisation de la production. Le Travail Humain 57(3), 239–249 (1994)

# Model of Skills Development at the Operational Level Applied to the Steel Industry

Ulysses Martins Moreira Filho and Pedro Luiz de Oliveira Costa Neto

Paulista University-UNIP, Graduate Program in Production Engineering
Rua Dr. Bacelar, 1212, 04026-002-São Paulo, Brazil

**Abstract.** The steel sector was one of the pioneers to join the Movement for Quality in Brazil in late 1980, because a significant portion of its revenues came from exports. The steel industry needs massive investment to upgrade its technology, which requires a high level of training of their operators. They must form a human capital capable of producing a laminate to win the preference of its customers. Based on four models of knowledge management: the SECI model, CYNEFIN model, the FIVE DISCIPLINES model and the SEVEN DIMENSIONS model, supported by the Knowledge Management Principles established by Davenport and Prusak, combined with the Criteria for Management Excellence, was developed a Competency Development Model. To validate this model has been carried out a field research in the governance representative of the national steel industry, with the aim to ensure safety in production operations and contribute positively to the manufacture with quality, reliability and competitiveness.

**Keywords:** Excellence in management, quality in operation, knowledge management.

## 1 Introduction

In 1984 Brazil was living a very complicated economic situation due to a strong inflationary process. The model focused on protectionism of domestic industry, allied to an obsolete technological park. This and the effect of globalization forced the Ministry of Industry and Trade to adopt a new attitude to face this reality.

So, the Industrial Technology Department of the Ministry has launched the PADCT – Support Program for Scientific and Technological Development, financed by the Brazilian Government and the World Bank, with the goal of bringing to the Brazilian entrepreneur, clearly and objectively, concepts and methodologies for implementation of "Total Quality" management systems which brought to the various companies in the world, in particular at Japan, gains in productivity, quality and competitiveness.

The Total Quality Management model in the Japanese style gives priority to the PDCA (Plan – Do – Check – Act) cycle management and the use of troubleshooting methods.

C. Emmanouilidis, M. Taisch, D. Kiritsis (Eds.): APMS 2012, Part I, IFIP AICT 397, pp. 638–644, 2013.
© IFIP International Federation for Information Processing 2013

The steel, petrochemical and mining sectors were pioneers in joining this movement, because a significant portion of their revenue comes from export. In the particular case of the steel industry, this model of quality management had a strong echo, due to the influence of the Japanese steel industry, present in a direct or indirect equity participation in this sector in the country.

The advance of scientific and technical knowledge and its dissemination in the productive process significantly changed the way of working, as well as the position of productive agents of the international market. Specificated production of quality with low cost, better capacity and quick innovation as key-factor of success put aside mass production. Holders of technical-scientific knowledge networks assume a privileged position in the world economic scenario [1].

Professional certification is also expanding in the national context, becoming present in a series of forums involving the Ministry of Labour and Employment, the International Labour Organization and the Ministry of Education, while the demand for professional certification of firms grows, as quality assurance strategy and competitiveness in a globalised market. This new reality was being experienced by Brazil.

In this process, the professional qualification in the new contemporary scenario arises as an important element in the composition of the factors influencing the competitiveness of countries, organizations and professionals.

A "new society" of knowledge arises, in which the human being is seen as an asset within organizations, with its own style, individuality and freedom of thought. The human capital is considered one of the main sources of innovation and organizational renewal. It is strengthened the creation of knowledge through activities in the knowledge construction process, generating shared solutions of problems, testing, implementation and integration of new methodologies and tools.

One of the main solutions adopted by Brazilian steel industry to overcome these new challenges posed by the market was the structuring of a standardization system of knowledge, through the certification process. The certification of competence based on the knowledge of the steel industry, established in technical standards or described in guidance manuals, ensures safety in the productive operations and contributes positively to the manufacture of quality products, reliability and competitiveness..

## 2     Objective

The objective of this paper it to present a model for developing skills for operators applied to the steel industry to strengthen its human capital, from the standardization of knowledge, to improve the quality required for excellence in control the production process.

## 3     Methodology

It were performed a multiple case study in steel mills ArcelorMittal, Gerdau, Usiminas, Votorantim and the Brazilian Association of Mining, Metallurgy and Materials, with application of an interview with the representative governance of the

Brazilian steel industry, supported by a questionnaire with fourteen questions divided into three groups: perception of labor offered by the market (questions 1-3), specific knowledge to analyze and solve unforeseen problems (questions 5-11) and ability to achieve professional results (questions 12-14). For this analysis was elaborated a correlation matrix among the indicators of each issue to determine the degree of consistency in relation to the theoretical support.

# 4     Theoretical Background

This study focuses on the development of skills of people who operate equipment for mining and metallurgical industries. To explain the relationship of the problem with the hypothesis, it was drafted a model of competence development, which presents a systemic vision of the three strands that converge to the management of excellence: the information system, the knowledge system and independent data.

The organization information system is the basis for decision-making, structured in the form of management reports, according to the sixth principle of quality "factual approach to decision-making"[2].

The knowledge system is important as far as we nowadays recognize knowledge as one of the more important assets at the organization.

The independent data system is the measurement system of an organization's performance. The structured and systematic measurement enables organizations to monitor their performance and thus quickly make changes on the basis of relevant and reliable information as changes occur in the market [3].

The three systems converge for the management of an organization and excellence permeates the crux of the problem under consideration, which is the competence of persons as the centre of a triangle, whose vertices are the tacit or explicit knowledge [4], the standardization of repetitive tasks [5] and the quality of products offered to consumers [5]; [6]; [7].

In face of a globalized and turbulent scenario, the management model of an organization can be one of the factors for the explanation of the quality of its results and how is done the interrelationship among internal processes.

The construction and strengthening of skills leads to "education and training", because organizations learn through individuals [6]; [7]; [8]; [9].

People need to want actually learn, want growth and be open to innovations. To do so, paradigms should be broken in such a way as to change your mental model of behavior [10]. This leads to standardization of all knowledge acquired throughout life for people who operate the production process, strengthening the human capital and, consequently, its competence.

These skills must be recognized by a third party institution approved by INMETRO – National Institute of Metrology, Standardization and Industrial Quality, the Brazilian responsible institution. By means of a written examination, the operator must demonstrate that dominates the knowledge requirements established in Brazilian technical standards, contributing positively to the production of quality products required by the consumer, within the relevant time limits, i.e., focusing on operational effectiveness, waste control, producing operational safety and its institutional commitment. Every four years, professionals must be reevaluated by the criteria established in the referred qualification standards.

In conclusion, we can say that a management model is the body of knowledge in an organization and to achieve the business autossustainability is essential to stimulate organizational learning, together with the development of specific skills, being able to operate a system that will win the customer's preference.

## 5    Skills Development Model

This model has been structured on the basis of the seven principles of knowledge management established by Davenport and Prusak [11], on the model of knowledge management conceived by Nonaka and Takeuchi [4], the Cynefin model proposed by Snowden and Boone [12], the model of the five disciplines by Senge [10] and the model of the seven dimensions of knowledge management by Terra [13], having as its entrance variable the indicators of refinement of knowledge management from the criteria for Management Excellence by FNQ [3], the Brazilian Quality National Foundation, This model is presented in Figure 1.

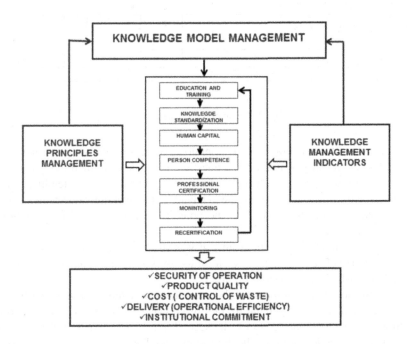

**Fig. 1.** Skills development model [14]

# 6    Discussion and Results

The search results are shown in Figure 2.

| QUESTION | Value Medium | I agree completely (5) | I agree (4) | I partially agree (3) | I partially disagree (2) | I disagree (1) |
|---|---|---|---|---|---|---|
| 1. The recognized problem of lack of skilled labor in the steel industry can be properly resolved in the next 3-5 years? | 2,62 | | | | 2,62 | |
| 2. There are conditions in Brazil to provide adequate training of manpower for the steel industry in the long term? | 3,50 | | | 3,50 | | |
| 3. The low educational qualification of the labor market is offering is one of the obstacles to adequate professional training of operators of the steel industry? | 4,0 | | 4,0 | | | |
| 4. The company clearly recognizes that the way to improved results and it is through a program of education and training? | 4,37 | | 4,37 | | | |
| 5. The company is concerned substantially standardize the knowledge that is at the head of its employees and describe it in operational procedures? | 4,25 | | 4,25 | | | |
| 6. The company recognizes the importance of strengthening its human capital to produce improvements? | 4,25 | | 4,25 | | | |
| 7. Training people is associated with the strategic needs of the company? | 4,62 | | 4,62 | | | |
| 8. The company recognizes that one way of solving functional illiteracy is through training and professional certification? | 4,0 | | 4,0 | | | |
| 9. One of the ways that an organization has to reduce operating costs is the participation of people in solving problems and this is only possible by changing your mindset? | 4,37 | | 4,37 | | | |
| 10. Reducing the number of accidents in a steel plant is directly related to a robust program of education and training? | 4,37 | | 4,37 | | | |
| 11. People no longer only supplier of manpower to be achieved the rank of suppliers of knowledge and skills? | 4,25 | | 4,25 | | | |
| 12. It is through a certification program for people who are adequately assess the level of competence of its employees? | 4,0 | | 4,0 | | | |
| 13. The strengthening of human capital contributes to better decision making in their area of expertise? | 5,0 | 5,0 | | | | |
| 14. The strengthening of human capital contributes to better decision making in their area of expertise? | 4,87 | 4,87 | | | | |
| LEGEND:  ● VALUE MEDIUM        RANGE:  △ LOWER    O SUPERIOR | | | | | | |

**Fig. 2.** The average values profile [14]

In the short term average of the opinions of representative governance of the national steel industry was 2.62 for question 1 and long-term improvement in the perception through actions aimed at reducing the educational gap, tending to a value of 4.0 based on Likert scale. From the behavior of the average value ranging from 4.0 to 5.0 obtained from the point 5 to the point 14, there is a strong correlation with respect to the model.

To provide an analysis of the results, it was structured a correlation matrix among the indicators of each issue, which aims to understand the relationships and interactions, which are set out in Figure 3.

We identified three discrepancies between the respondents, namely: the first is that there is agreement on the standardization of knowledge, but it is not a consensus due to different organizational cultures; the second is that the reduction of accidents in a steel plant is obtained with a solid Education and Training program, emphasized by one group, and another group also adds the responsibility of leadership and governance; third, it is recognized that professional certification is the way to address the functional illiteracy, but in practice what we see is only the assistance to the legal requirements.

| QUESTION | QUESTION / INDICATOR | 1 | 2 | 3 | 4 | 5 | 6 | 7 | 8 | 9 | 10 | 11 | 12 | 13 | 14 |
|---|---|---|---|---|---|---|---|---|---|---|---|---|---|---|---|
| 1 | LABOR | ■ | | | | | ● | | | | | ● | | | |
| 2 | ESPECIFIC KNOWLEDGE | | ■ | | | | | | ● | | ● | | | | |
| 3 | LOW KNOWLEDGE | | | ■ | ● | ● | | | | | | | | | |
| 4 | TRAINING | | | | ■ | | ● | | | | ● | | | | |
| 5 | STANDARDIZATION | | | | | ■ | | | | ● | | | | | ● |
| 6 | HUMAN CAPITAL | | | | | | ■ | | | ● | | | | ● | |
| 7 | STRATEGIES | | | | | | | ■ | ● | | | | | | ● |
| 8 | FUNCTIONALLY ILLITERATE | | | | ● | | | | ■ | | | | ● | | |
| 9 | COST REDUCTION | | | | | | | | | ■ | | ● | | ● | |
| 10 | ACIDENT PREVENTION | | | | | | | | | | ■ | | ● | | ● |
| 11 | SUPPLIER | ● | | | | | | | | | | ■ | | | ● |
| 12 | COMPETENCE | | ● | | | | | | | | | | ■ | | ● |
| 13 | DECISION MAKING | | | | ● | | | ● | | | | | | ■ | |
| 14 | CERTIFICATION | | | | ● | | | | | | | | | ● | ■ |

**Fig. 3.** Correlation between indicators [14]

It was noted that the process approach allows a systemic and a better understanding of the proposed objectives, coupled with the fact that all interviewees were unanimous in asserting that the strengthening of human capital improves the decision-making, and the creation of Corporate Universities by the steel companies is the way to reduce the gap in educational sector.

# 7    Conclusions

The concern of governance is real and imminent in face of the difficulties of acquiring new professionals and the rate of retirement of the current workforce. One cannot fail to mention fierce competition from imported products.

The productive capacity of the Brazilian steel industry for 2015 is estimated at 50 million tons of steel to meet the new planned projects, such as the World Cup 2014, the 2016 Olympic Games and the extraction of oil in deepwater pre-salt.

The model of skills development proposed for the mining-metallurgical sector was ratified by the representative governance of the sector, accounting for 76.2% of steel production in Brazil in 2010, represented by companies ArcelorMittal, Gerdau, Usiminas and Votorantim.

# References

1. Arruda, M.: Qualificação versus Certificação. Boletim Citerfor n° (Maio/Agosto de 2000)
2. ABNT, ABNT NBR 9000:2005-Vocabulário e Princípios. ABNT, Rio de Janeiro (2005)
3. FNQ: Critério de Excelência. Fundação Nacional da Qualidade (2010)
4. Nonaka, I., Takeuchi, H.: Criação do conhecimento na empresa. Campus, São Paulo (1997)
5. Campos, V.F.: Controle da Qualidade Total. Block Editores, São Paulo (1992)
6. Ishikawa, K.: What is Total Quality Contol? The Japanese Way. Prentice-Hall (1985)
7. Feingenbaum, A.V.: Total Quality Control-3° Edição. McGraw Hill Company (1986)
8. Deming, W.E.: Qualidade: A Revolução da Administração. Marques Saraiva, São Paulo (1990)
9. Juran, J.: Planejamento da Qualidade. Livraria Pioneira (1990)
10. Senge, P.M.: A Quinta Disciplina. Best Seller (2009)
11. Davemport, T.H., Prusak, L.: Conhecimento Empresarial. Campus, Rio de Janeiro (1999)
12. Snowden, D.: Complex acts of knowing-paradox and descriptive self-awareness (2002)
13. Terra, J.C.C.: Gestão do Conhecimento: O grande desafio empresarial (2005)
14. Moreira Filho, U.M.: A excelência no controle do processo produtivo com foco no conhecimento e qualidade: Estudo de caso da siderurgia brasileira. UNIP. UNIP, São Paulo (2012)

# Success Factors for PDCA as Continuous Improvement Method in Product Development

Eirin Lodgaard[1,2], Inger Gamme[3], and Knut Einar Aasland[1]

[1] Norwegian University of Science and Technology, Trondheim, Norway
knut.e.aasland@ntnu.no
[2] SINTEF Raufoss Manufacturing, Raufoss, Norway
eirin.lodgaard@sintef.no
[3] Gjøvik University College, Gjøvik, Norway
inger.gamme@hig.no

**Abstract.** In order to maintain sustainability in an ever changing environment, where customer requirements contains a yearly price reduction over the life cycle of a product, decreased time for development of new products and increased product quality, there is an increased need for focus on continuous improvements. A well-known improvement method is the PDCA (Plan-Do-Check-Act), which many companies have succeeded in implementing in the manufacturing department. Not so common, is the use of this method for the development process. The aim of this article is to present success factors which must be in place to succeed in using the specified method, and thereby the desired improvement during continuous improvement initiatives within product development. Management commitment is ranked as most important followed by knowledge about how to use the method, when to apply PDCA, efficient performance and use of internal marketing activities to focusing on the topic.

**Keywords:** Automotive supplier industry, product development, continuous improvement, PDCA.

## 1    Introduction

The long term business sustainability in the automotive supplier industry depends on the ability to face demanding customer requirements. Requirements of a yearly price reduction over the life cycle of a model, decreased time for development of new products and increased requirements and expectations of continuous development of better products and processes for the future are typical for the automotive industry. This requires that companies in the automotive supplier industry continuously improve in all functions of the company, including product development (PD). At least 80 % of the life cycle cost of a product is determined in the early phase of PD. This indicates the importance of how the PD is performed with regards to continuous improvement[1].

Today there are several types of continuous improvement methods in use in the automotive supplier industry, such as LAMDA (Look-Ask-Design-Model)[2], Six

C. Emmanouilidis, M. Taisch, D. Kiritsis (Eds.): APMS 2012, Part I, IFIP AICT 397, pp. 645–652, 2013.
© IFIP International Federation for Information Processing 2013

Sigma[3] and PDCA (Plan-Do-Check-Act)[4, 5]. This research project has chosen to study the PDCA method because it is highly recommended as continuous improvement method in the automotive industry, outlined in the quality standard, ISO/TS 16949[6]. Many companies have successfully implemented the PDCA method in the manufacturing department, but for the future it is important to include the product development as well to be competitive in this demanding industry.

The aim of this paper is to identify success factors when using the established continuous improvement method PDCA, in product development. What success factors must be in place to succeed in using the specific method to achieve the desired improvements during continuous improvement initiative?

## 2     Continuous Improvement in Product Development

Continuous improvement has been in focus in the automotive industry for several decades. It is important to have a never-ending process of performance improvements to gain effective processes in product development [7]. Several companies have succeeded implementing systematic continuous improvement in manufacturing, but few have succeeded in PD. Although many "kaizen" or continuous improvement initiatives are started, the failure rate is high[8]. Lillrank et al reported that two out of three continuous improvement initiatives fail to deliver the desired improvement[9]. This shows the importance of finding out why the failure rate is high and what factors must be in place for successful implementation of continuous improvement in a complex and turbulent environment, such as product development.

## 3     PDCA as a Continuous Improvement Method

In 1950 W. Edwards Deming was invited to Japan by the Union of Japanese Scientist Engineers to teach statistical quality control. He arranged seminars together with manager, focusing on the connection between quality and productivity and the use of statistical process control. He also introduced the Deming wheel which emphasized the importance of constant interaction among research, design, production, and sales to assure better product quality and satisfied customers. The Japanese developed it further to be applied in all problem solving situation and called it PDCA [10]. The PDCA method has been used ever since by the Japanese industry as a systematic continuous problem solving approach. Western industry started to focus on development and implementation of continuous improvement processes in the beginning of the 1980s [11]. Today, this tool is widely outspread in the manufacturing industry and the PDCA is highly recommended in the quality assurance standard ISO/TS 16949 used by the automotive supplier industry.

The PDCA method includes four phases: Plan, Do, Check and Act. The phases are defined in different versions in the literature, but with the same purpose, to continuous improve. We have divided the four phases into seven steps, as shown in figure 1. It starts with identifying the current situation and target for the improvement. Thereafter, to dig deep into the details to discover root causes to avoid jumping to solutions.

After implementation of the actions it is important to study and evaluate the results and if necessary go back to prior phases and modify solutions. The final step is to ensure that the improved level of performance is maintained and to capture what is learned during each of the phases in the PDCA cycle.

Today, the PDCA method is primarily applied in the manufacturing department and less applied in the product development. In manufacturing of a physical product, it is easier to implement the method. In addition, the manufacturing staff is more easily manageable than in the innovative and creative environment of product development. In product development, it is necessary to find a balance between formal processes and creative freedom in order to succeed with continuous improvement.

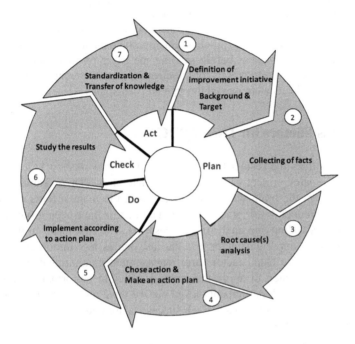

**Fig. 1.** PDCA

# 4    Case Company and Research Method

The following section outlines the case company and the research approach used to conduct this study. The case company is a Norwegian automotive supplier with customers on a worldwide basis. The automotive supplier industry was chosen as a case since they already have a formal requirement, based on ISO/TS 16949, to define a continuous improvement method and to apply the method to assure continuous improvement in the entire company. The chosen case company has a Quality Assurance system, where the PDCA method is chosen to be implemented in the entire organization. They have long experience with continuous improvement methods primarily in the manufacturing department; therefore it is interesting to investigate the product development area and the main critical success factors for successful implementation of the PDCA method.

The research method is based on an extension of the action research approach. The action research is on application of the PDCA method in continuous improvement projects in product development. After finishing several continuous improvement projects in the action research, with the purpose to get experience with PDCA, a brain writing workshop was performed with the aim of defining the success criteria for application of PDCA. The same team participated in both the improvement projects and the brain writing workshop. The participants were professionals from the field of management, simulation, calculations, process and product development, quality assurance and research. Brain writing is a silent, sharing, written creativity method and does not involve group discussion of written ideas during the idea-generation session[12].The brain writing method applied was the 6x3x5 method, which uses the principle: 6 participants writing down 3 ideas in 5 minutes. Each participant starts with writhing down three ideas on a sheet of paper before sending the paper on to person seated on his right-hand side. The next step was to complement ideas on the received sheet. This was continued until the sheets were passed through all participants.

## 5        Success Factors for Use of PDCA

This chapter outlines the results from the brain writing workshop based on the extended action research project with focus on application of PDCA. Table1 summarizes the results from the brain writing workshop with the main success criteria when using PDCA in product development. These main factors have been grouped into five categories, after a coding and analyzing process[13]. The first result in the table was ranked as the most important factor and the last one as less important in the brain writing workshop. The listed factors are: management commitment, knowledge on how to use PDCA, when to apply the method, efficient performance and, internal marketing activities. Each participant picked out the three most important ideas which are shown in the table as subgroups. Each success factor and its subgroup factors will be presented more in-depth.

### 5.1    Management Commitment

Management commitment is ranked as the most important factor in succeeding with your continuous improvement initiatives based on the PDCA method. One possible explanation for this result is that people tend to prioritize the work that the management team wants them to perform. It is not easy to stay motivated working on topics nobody asks for. Imai stated that continuous improvement is the most dominant concept behind good management [10]. Bessant et al. stated that the management is a key variable to maintain the continuous improvement behavior patterns but that  is often poorly understood by themselves [14]. The use of PDCA must be included in the strategy to show that the management really wants to apply the PDCA method. This will help the company to sustain the use of the PDCA method, especially if the management also uses the method.

**Table 1.** Success factors when applying PDCA

| Main Success factor | Subgroup | Number of feasible and relevant ideas |
| --- | --- | --- |
| Management Commitment | • Walk like you talk<br>• Engagement<br>• Sustainability<br>• Included in the strategy | 20 |
| Knowledge on how to use PDCA | • Education<br>• Training of practical use<br>• Knowledge on how to use PDCA in the entire organization<br>• Training included in the budget | 22 |
| When to apply PDCA | • Predefined which type of continuous improvement project | 6 |
| Efficient performance | • A time efficient method<br>• PDCA method applied as simple as possible<br>• Use of PDCA must be a choice in their existing "to do list" | 11 |
| Internal marketing activities | • Use of intranet in general<br>• Publishing of implemented PDCA<br>• Specialist continuous marketing the method<br>• Hang up a notice (A3) in the office area | 13 |

## 5.2    Knowledge on How to Use PDCA

Not surprisingly, the results from the brain writing workshop shows that the entire organization must have performed education in the PDCA method as well as further training in practical use. Educational actions in order to get knowledge about the method are essential to be able to perform continuous improvement initiatives based on PDCA [15]. A firm competitive is not so much production equipment but rather what it knows and how it behaves [8]. Ishikawa stated that continuous improvement starts with education and ends with education [16]. This is supported by Caffyn who found that lack of training is an inhibiting factor for extending continuous improve-ment to the new product development process [17]. Finding from the study done by Yan and Makinde shows that management must prioritize training opportunities to all employees to assure that they really understand what continuous improvement is about [18]. This is substantial to be able to apply the method in a time efficient way as the intention of PDCA is.

### 5.3     When to Apply PDCA

When to apply PDCA is not clearly identified [8]. Not all continuous improvement initiatives require use of PDCA, however purposeful improvement in large or com-plex systems will be appropriate to use PDCA [15]. Common understanding about when to apply the method could be an advantage in order to avoid frustrated employ-ees that do not know what type of continuous improvement initiatives they shall apply the PDCA method on. This will probably be more clarified when the organization has used the PDCA for a while. When you got more experience, then you know when the PDCA can be efficiently applied or not. The dedicated project team in this research study had performed some continuous improvement projects by applying PDCA. In spite of this it was not sufficient to have an overview of when to apply PDCA.

### 5.4     Efficient Performance

Today it is several definitions in the literature of the four phases of PDCA, all with the purpose to assure continuous improvement and problem solving. It is important for organizations to clearly define the concept together with well prepared and user friendly templates. The western companies is known as too fast to conclude on solu-tions therefore it is important to define the first phase clearly and to secure enough time to collect data to achieve fact based solutions [5].

### 5.5     Internal Marketing Activities

The use of intranet, or similar type of mediums, in order to communicate the results from previous improvement projects to the affected part of the organization, is among the participants, defined as an important topic. Use of internal marketing activities to make a clear and credible plan for the organization together with demonstrated results from continuous improvement initiative are essential element in motivating people and to grow culture for continuous improvement [10]. Communication about where the company is heading and how it will get generally make people more enthusiastic about the improvement process. This may indicate that visualization of results from continuous improvements, which must be common for all affected employees, is im-portant to drive successful improvement projects. In a study done by Caffyn and Grantham the results show that all companies studied lacked a strategic approach to the development of continuous improvement, and to capture, share and deploy learn-ing from the improvement [19]. Many people have difficulties sharing knowledge across the team and sometimes even with people in the team. Internal marketing activities can make the knowledge more accessible to others, enable reuse of the knowledge they have, and make it more accessible for others. Capturing and sharing knowledge created is important in delivering high quality products [20].

## 6     Concluding Remarks

Based on action research and a brain writing workshop, involving one of the development teams, we have identified the main success factors and their subgroups to be able to succeed using PDCA in product development. From observations in our study we can propose five aspects which are essential to be aware of if you want to implement the specified improvement method PDCA, in product development. The first, and the most important one, is the commitment by the management. This aspect is of importance to be able to establish the method as a standardized improvement method. As a strategy to solve continuous improvement initiatives, PDCA must be included by the management as method, which they are using in their daily work for the suggested purpose. When to use the defined improvement method, combined with sufficient competence of how to use the method, are the next two success factors. The fourth aspect is to ensure efficient ways to perform the method, such as use well prepared user-friendly templates, with a thought-through common way to perform the improvement issues. The last aspect is to ensure an internal marketing of the application of PDCA method, with specific results from implemented improvement initiatives to show the efficiency of using PDCA. This will contribute on the sustainability of uses of the method if people can see the profit by use of PDCA.

## References

1. Ragatz, G.L., Handfield, R.B., Scannel, T.V.: Success Factors for Integrating Suppliers into New Product Development. Journal of Product Innovation Management 14, 190–202 (1997)
2. Ward, A.C.: Lean Product and Process Development. Lean Enterprise Institute, Cambridge (2007)
3. Bicheno, J., Catherwood, P.: Six Sigma and the Quality Toolbox. Picsie Books, Buckingham (2005)
4. Shook, J.: Managing to Learn. Using the A3 Management Process to Solve Problems, Gain Agreement, Mentor, and Lead. The Lean Enterprise Institute, Cambridge (2008)
5. Sobek, D.K., Smalley, A.: Understanding A3 Thinking, A Critical Component of Toyota's PDCA Management System. Productivity Press, New York (2008)
6. ISO/TS 16949:2009: Quality Management System: Particular Requirements for the Application of ISO 9001:2008 for Automotive Production and Relevant Service Part Organization (2009)
7. Morgan, J.M., Liker, J.K.: The Toyota Product Development System, Integrating People, Processes and Technology. Productivity Press, New York (2006)
8. Bessant, J., Caffyn, S., Gallagher, M.: An Evolutionary Model of Continuous Improvement Behavior. Technovation 21, 67–77 (2001)

9. Lillrank, P., Shani, A.B.R., Lindberg, P.: Continuous Improvement: Exploring Alternative Organizational Designs. Total Quality Management 12, 41–55 (2001)
10. Imai, M.: Kaizen. The Key to Japan's Competitive Success. Random House, New York (1986)
11. Nilsson-Witell, L., Antoni, M., Dahlgaard, J.J.: Continuous Improvement in Product Development. The International Journal of Quality & Reliability Management 22, 753–768 (2005)
12. Heslin, P.A.: Better than Brainstorming? Potential Contextual Boundary Conditions to Brainwriting for Idea Generation in Organizations. Journal of Occupational and Organizational Psychology 82, 129–145 (2009)
13. Miles, H., Hubermann, M.: Quality Data Analysis: A sourcebook. Sage Publications, Beverly Hills (1994)
14. Bessant, J., Caffyn, S., Gallagher, M.: An Evolutionary Model of Continuous Improvement Behaviour. Technovation 21, 67–77 (2001)
15. Langley, G.J.: The improvement Guide. A practical Approach to Enhancing Organizational Performance. Jossey-Bass, San Francisco (2009)
16. Ishikawa, K.: What is Total Quality Control? The Japanese Way. Prentice Hall, Englewood Cliffs (1985)
17. Caffyn, S.: Extending Continuous Improvement to the New Product Development Process. R & D Management 27, 253–253 (1997)
18. Yan, B., Makinde, O.D.: Impact of Continuous Improvement on New Product Development within SMEs in the Western Cape, South Africa. African Journal of Business Management 5, 2200–2229 (2011)
19. Caffyn, S., Grantham, A.: Enabling Continuous Improvement of New Product Development Process. Industry and Higher Education 14, 235–243 (2000)
20. Radeka, K.: Lean Product Development at Playworld System. Target Magazine 27, 10–17 (2011)

# Supporting Production System Development through the Obeya Concept

Siavash Javadi, Sasha Shahbazi, and Mats Jackson

Mälardalen University, School of Innovation, Design and Engineering, Eskilstuna, Sweden
{sji10001,ssi10002}@student.mdh.se,
mats.jackson@mdh.se

**Abstract.** Manufacturing Industry as an important part of European and Swedish economy faces new challenges with the daily growing global competition. An enabler of overcoming these challenges is a rapid transforming to a value-based focus. Investment in innovation tools for production system development is a crucial part of that focus which helps the companies to rapidly adapt their production systems to new changes. Those changes can be categorized to incremental and radical ones. In this research we studied the Obeya concept as a supporting tool for production system development with both of those approaches. It came from Toyota production system and is a big meeting space which facilitates communication and data visualization for a project team. Four lean companies have been studied to find the role of such spaces in production development. Results indicate a great opportunity for improving those spaces and their application to radical changes in production development projects.

**Keywords:** Production system development, Obeya, Kaikaku, Kaizen, Data visualization.

## 1 Introduction

The manufacturing industry is one of the dominant sectors of the European economy providing jobs for around 34 million people, and producing an added value exceeding €1 500 billion from 230 000 enterprises with 20 and more employees. Also, a large part of the growing service sector in Europe is linked to the manufacturing companies. However, the manufacturing industry in Europe faces intense and growing competitive pressure on several fronts.

Although innovative and effective organization of operations has been the basis for industrial success and competition since the days of Ford, current challenges put new and stronger pressure on European manufacturing industry than ever before. Globalization, demographic changes, environmental challenges and new values drives increased demands on resource efficiency, sustainable manufacturing, and innovative and individualized products.

Manufacturing in mature traditional sectors is increasingly migrating to low-wage countries such as China, India, Mexico and Brazil, but these countries are not

C. Emmanouilidis, M. Taisch, D. Kiritsis (Eds.): APMS 2012, Part I, IFIP AICT 397, pp. 653–660, 2013.

standing still in their development. On the contrary, they are rapidly modernizing their production methods and enhancing their technological capabilities - in many cases building new green field sites, which means that they do not only have low labor cost but also the latest technology. In meeting such extensive competition, Swedish manufacturing industry both needs to build on existing strengths and find new ways to compete. One solution is to build on the under-utilized potential of innovative production development instead of mainly emphasizing on the operations phase, i.e. running production. Our industrial historical base and infrastructure give particularly good preconditions for Swedish manufacturing companies to compete with innovative production development as a very effective strategy.

Also, to succeed in developing new efficient products and processes and thereby withstand and handle the global competition, continuous development and improvements as well as radical changes around existing production processes and technology are required. Thus, innovation in relation to production is becoming a crucial area which includes e.g. new business models, new modes of 'production engineering', efficient industrialization of new products and an ability to profit from ground-breaking manufacturing sciences and technologies. Innovation in both new production technology and new ways of working during development and operations is often difficult for competitors to get hold of and copy. Hence, it falls into the competitive advantage category of differentiation as a way to take offensive action in creating a defendable position in industry and generating a superior return on investment, according to Porter (1990)definition.

In summary, the challenges facing the manufacturing sector in Sweden require radical transformations from a cost-based to a value-based focus. An ability to constantly adapt and improve the production operations and working procedures will bring about the required changes. To tackle them appropriately, manufacturing companies need to invest in creativity, entrepreneurship and new innovation models, specifically in the area production system development. Thus, an overall objective and research question is how to support innovation in production system development. One of the tools introduced by lean philosophy is Obeya or war room for development projects which will be explained in details in section 2.2 of this paper. In this research we are trying to illustrate how Obeya or similar meeting places can support innovative production system development.

## 2    Theoretical Framework

### 2.1    Production System Development

Different research traditions have contributed to the current state of knowledge concerning production system development. From an operations strategy perspective, Hayes and Wheelwright (1979) introduced the product-process matrix in order to choose production system layout according to product and process life cycle stage. Miltenburg (2005) defines seven production systems and put them in a matrix in order to analyze similarities and differences between them. However, according to Cochran et al. (2002), Miltenburg (2005) and Hayes and Wheelwright (1979) fail to communicate how lower level design decisions, such as equipment design, operator work content and so on, will affect system performance. These approaches treat production system design as a problem of selecting an appropriate off-the-shelf design from a given set of choices and criteria. Designers are not given the freedom to create a unique production system to satisfy a broad set of requirements in a particular environment.

Examples of research from an industrial engineering perspective in the production system design area are the technology focused book by Bennett (1986), methods based on Integrated Definition for Function Modeling 0 (IDEF0) by for example Wu (2001) and methods based on the function/solution mapping in Axiomatic Design, such as Suh (1990), Kulak et al. (2005), Cochran et al. (2002), and Almström (2005). The system approach is taken on the production system problem by Seliger et al. (1987). Examples of other approaches for systematic design and evaluation of production systems are: Bellgran (1998), Säfsten (2002), Bellgran and Säfsten (2005), Wiktorsson (2000) while methods based on the stage gate method e.g. Ulrich and Eppinger (2003) are developed further by e.g. Blanchard and Fabrycky (1998) and Wu (1994).

Innovation in a production system development perspective is given by Manufuture which describes the need of innovating production by "...important research, innovation and education activities that could transform the competitive basis of producing and delivering products and services that reach a new level in satisfying society's desires and expectations" (Manufuture, 2006).

Innovation in production can also be related to improvements and changes within the production system, innovative production capabilities. In general, two approaches towards production system improvements are commonly recognized: (1) incremental / continuous improvements and (2) infrequent and radical improvements. The first type (called Kaizen in Japanese) is a well-known approach for improving production. Kaizen became widely known after the introduction by Imai (1986) and is widely used within the lean production paradigm. The key characteristics of Kaizen are often described as continuous, incremental improvement in nature, participative, and process-oriented. The concept has been extensively described, and a number of supporting methods and tools have been developed and widely applied in industry.

The radical improvement approach or "Kaikaku" in Japanese has also been conducted by many companies. However, it has been less documented and conceptualized compared to continuous improvement. Radical changes are conducted infrequently, involving some fundamental changes within production and causing dramatic performance gain, and they are often initiated by top or senior management (Yamamoto, 2010).

## 2.2    Obeya

In this paper we studied Obeya as an innovation support tool for production system development with both above mentioned approaches. The Obeya concept is a part of Toyota product development system which has been used as a project management tool in Toyota. The concept was introduced during the development process of Prius in late 90's and since then it has become a standard tool for product development projects in Toyota (Morgan and Liker, 2006) . Obeya in Japanese simply means "big room". However, it has also been called with other names such as "war room", "program room", "control room" and "the pulse room" in different researches and companies. By any name, Obeya is an advanced visual control innovation room where activities and deliverables are outlined and depicted in a visual format to be discussed in frequent meetings. A cross functional team including design and production engineers and other decision makers gathers in a single big room to make real time key decisions on the spot. Andersson and Bellgran (2009) assert that Obeya saves the time since it is not required to move to conference room or others rooms since people are already present in a single room to provide information and answer the questions. In Obeya it is not just the chief engineer who manages the process but all involved people contribute in the decision making process (Liker, 2004), which leads to higher level of cross-functionality in the process (Söderberg and Alfredson, 2009).

Effective data visualization is another benefit of Obeya (Söderberg and Alfredson, 2009). The big room's walls are covered by different types of data to help the project team to make more informed decisions through simple and instant access to all required information in one place simultaneously. Visualized data can be designs and drawings, schedules and plans, technical specifications etc. "Engineers plaster the room's walls and mobile walls with information organized by vehicle part... and this information allows anyone walking the walls to assess program status (quality, timing, function, weight) up to the day" (Morgan and Liker, 2006).

Andersson and Bellgran (2009)describe the benefits of Obeya as following:

- Helping to make plan, do, check and action cycle shorter through gathering all decision makers in a single place
- Facilitating communication between team members through face to face daily contact
- Supporting the product development through combination of effective communication and proper technology
- Providing an infrastructure for idea generation and development for both new products and cost reduction.

Since very few studies have been done about obeya and its application to production development, we studied the current practice of using Obeya or similar meeting places in lean companies directly. We have studied four companies in Sweden who have been working according to the lean principles for several years. The goals of study were to understand

— The uses of meeting places and its contribution to production system development
— The methodology and work process related to those uses
— Data visualization methods and tools used.

# 3    Research Method

To gather required information, semi-structured interview and direct observation techniques were used for the case studies. That type of interview was chosen for this research due to flexibility, allowing discussing and causing to come up with new questions during the interview. At each company along with interviews, production processes observed directly, meeting places were visited and in one of the cases authors participated in the daily morning meeting of the company for daily production issues. All meetings, interviews and visits were documented through voice recording and its transcription as well as taken notes.

All studied companies are a part of international companies or groups which are considered as one of the leading names in their industries. Cases are named company A, B, C and D and they belong respectively to material handling equipment, automotive, construction and automotive parts industries.

Company A has about 1800 employees in 5 assembly lines and 2 production departments. Company b is large size company with almost 1200 employees working in 3 different main departments. Company C is medium size company with almost 100 employees with a single production line. Case D is also a medium size company with almost 150 employees with 5 different product assembly lines.

A cross-case analysis was done in order to compare the gathered information and data from the cases and their uses of meeting places for production system development.

# 4    Results

Gathered data from interviews and visits shows the following results:

A Single meeting place is used in company A to manage daily production problems and Kaizen projects in the whole factory. Every department and line has their own 5 to 10-minute morning meeting in the meeting place. Meetings are held to discuss last day problems of the related line with people related to the problem. Predefined A4 forms are used for registering the problem. Responsible person has 24 hours for finding the root cause and suggesting a temporary or permanent solution for it. Data registration and visualization process are totally manual. Forms and reports are kept on the room walls as a visualization tool for follow ups. A similar space with similar design and tools is also used for problems related to suppliers.

In company B, each department and line has its own meeting places. There is a general design for meeting places in production and assembly departments which includes daily data about quality, production and safety issues. Maintenance department has it is own special room design. There are number of customized visualization tools including different schedules and reports for ongoing maintenance kaizen projects. Generally same process as company A is followed in company B. short meetings about 10 minutes are held every morning with main actors. But no deadline exists for finding the root cause and solution.

Company C has single meeting place which is used for 30-minute morning meetings about production problems, solutions and kaizen projects. Despite other 3 cases, company C's meeting space is in the form of separate room from the production line because of noise disturbance in production line. In addition to conventional visualization tools like white boards, forms and reports, improvements tags are also used to mark source of the problem in the production line. Also digital tools are used for visualizing some information about current situation of production.

Company D has one meeting place for each of its five active production lines. 10-minute morning meetings are held with contribution of line operators and supervisor to mainly follow the production rate and its fluctuations. But some kaizen projects are also followed on those meetings. Few basic visualization tools including white boards and A4 forms for Kaizen projects are used.

In all of the cases Kaizen projects refers to minor production system development mostly initiated by problems in production process, defects in products, deviations from production schedules or safety incidents. Also A3 reports in all cases are more or less similar and come from Toyota data visualization system. They are single piece of A3 paper which simply show and document the whole process of identifying a problem in production system and developing a solution for it (Liker, 2004).

Table 1 shows the summary of the results from gathered data through the interviews and visits.

**Table 1.** Summary of gathered data about production development meeting spaces

| Company | Meeting place type | Purpose | Visualization tools | Meeting time (Minutes) |
|---|---|---|---|---|
| A | Single place for all lines | Kaizen projects | Predefined A4 forms, A3 reports, boards | 5 – 10 |
| B | Multiple customized places for each department | Kaizen projects, General development projects | Predefined A4 reports in the lines, customized reports, schedules and charts for maintenance department, boards | Up to 10 |
| C | Single room for single production line | Kaizen projects | Predefined A4 reports, problem reporting tags, digital screen for production status, boards | Up to 30 |
| D | Multiple places for each assembly line | Production, quality and safety control | Simple quality and production A4 reports, boards | Up to 10 |

## 5    Discussion and Conclusion

As the results indicate, in all cases the meeting spaces are used only for performing incremental changes which are basically minor modifications in production systems. These modifications are mostly initiated by occurrence minor problems in production process, defected products or safety issues and solutions are developed using lean tools like 5whys and 5 Ws which are main tools for preparing A3 reports. Currently there is no indication of using such meeting spaces in radical changes in production system development such as developing and implementing new production system or general   modification in current production systems in those companies. In such cases production system development is mostly considered as a part of product development process according to its dependence to developing new products (Bruch, 2012). But in practice it is a huge complex separate project. Obeya meeting spaces can be used for acquiring and generating production system development information like idea development sessions and designing production system. It can also be a very useful tool for sharing and using information especially during the implementation of radical changes in production systems.

In addition, current meeting spaces are not adequately capable of transferring data and results to involved internal actors like people in other production sites as well as external ones like suppliers. This could be mainly because of total dependence of those spaces to non-digital tools.

As Bruch (2012) explains, design information management as a critical part of production system design and development consist of three main parts: acquiring, sharing and using design information. Obeya or such meeting spaces can be used for these purposes in production system design and development process. Using digital tools can help the two latter parts through facilitating sharing and using acquired data in a faster and more effective manner.

In summary, review of the Obeya concept, its advantages and its current practice in industry shows that it can be applied to other purposes than product development projects. The case studies show that similar meeting places are already used for incremental production system development projects. Radical improvements can even benefit more from this concept because of their nature that needs to implement great changes in a short time which usually demands considerable amount of close teamwork. But to maximize the benefits methods and visualization tools used in a conventional Obeya should be customized to be adapted to this purpose.

## References

1. Almström, P.: Development of Manufacturing Systems - A Methodology Based on Systems Engineering and Design Theory. Chalmers University of Technology, Göteborg (2005)
2. Andersson, J., Bellgran, M.: Spatial design and communication for Improved Production Performance. In: Proceedings of the International 3rd Swedish Production Symposium, Göteborg, Sweden (2009)
3. Bellgran, M.: Systematic design of assembly systems: preconditions and design process planning. PhD Thesis, Linköping University (1998)

4. Bellgran, M., SäFsten, K.: Produktionsutveckling, Utveckling och drift av produktionssystem, Studentlitteratur, Lund (2005) ISBN 91-44-03360-5
5. Bennett, D.: Production Systems Design. Butterworth-Heinemann, London (1986)
6. Blanchard, B.S., Fabrycky, W.J.: Systems Engineering and Analysis (1998)
7. Bruch, J.: Management of Design Information in the Production System Design Process. PhD PhD thesis, Mälardalen University, School of Innovation, Design and Engineering (2012)
8. Cochran, D.S., Arinez, J.F., Duda, J.W., Linck, J.: A decomposition approach for manufacturing system design. Journal of manufacturing systems 20, 371–389 (2002)
9. Hayes, R.H., Wheelwright, S.C.: Link manufacturing process and product life cycles. Harvard Business Review 57, 133–140 (1979)
10. Imai, M.: Kaizen (Ky'zen), the key to Japan's competitive success. McGraw-Hill (1986)
11. Kulak, O., Durmusoglu, M.B., Tufekci, S.: A complete cellular manufacturing system design methodology based on axiomatic design principles. Computers & Industrial Engineering 48, 765–787 (2005)
12. Liker, J.K.: The Toyota Way: 14 Management Principles from the World's Greatest Manufacturer. McGraw-Hill (2004)
13. Manufuture. Assuring the future of manufacturing in Europe (2006), http://www.manufuture.org/
14. Miltenburg, J.: Manufacturing Strategy: How To Formulate and Implement A Winning Plan. Productivity Press (2005)
15. Morgan, J.M., Liker, J.K.: The Toyota Product Development System: Integrating People, Process, and Technology. Productivity Press (2006)
16. Porter, M.E.: The competitive advantage of nations: with a new introduction. Free Press (1990)
17. Seliger, G., Viehweger, B., Wieneke-Toutouai, B., Kommana, S.R.: Knowledge-based Simulation of Flexible Manufacturing Systems. In: The Second European Simulation Multiconference, Vienna, Austria, pp. 65–68 (1987)
18. Suh, N.P.: The Principles of Design. Oxford University Press, USA (1990)
19. Säfsten, K.: Evaluation of Assembly Systems: An Exploratory Study of Evaluation Situations, Linköping, Sweden, Division of Production Systems, Department of Mechanical Engineering (2002)
20. Söderberg, B., Alfredson, L.: Building on Knowledge, An analysis of knowledge transfer in product development. Chalmers University of Technology (2009)
21. Ulrich, K., Eppinger, S.: Product Design and Development. McGraw-Hill, Irwin (2003)
22. Wiktorsson, M.: Performance assessment of assembly systems. KTH, Institutionen för produktionssystem (2000)
23. Wu, B.: Manufacturing Systems Design and Analysis: Context and techniques. Chapman & Hall, London (1994)
24. Wu, B.: A unified framework of manufacturing systems design. Industrial Management & Data Systems 101, 446–469 (2001)
25. Yamamoto, Y.: Kaikaku in production. PhD, Mälardalen Universuty (2010)

# Measurement, Classification and Evaluation of the Innovation Process and the Identification of Indicators in Relation to the Performance Assessment of Company's Innovation Zones

Peter Kubičko[1], Lenka Landryová[2], Roman Mihal'[1], and Iveta Zolotová[1]

[1] Department of Cybernetics and Artificial Intelligence, Technical University Košice,
Letná 9/A, Kosice, Slovak Republic
peter.kubicko@student.tuke.sk,
{roman.mihal,iveta.zolotova}@tuke.sk
[2] Department of Control Systems and Instrumentation, VSB Technical University Ostrava,
17.listopadu 15, Ostrava, Czech Republic
lenka.landryova@vsb.cz

**Abstract.** Continuous renewal of products, services, processes and business collaboration increases the company chances to survival. This article draws attention to the features of innovation zone, which result in innovative products, services, or processes. Our research focuses on the innovation of processes included in innovation zone. In simpler terms, we are engaged in creating a dynamic environment using processes with abilities of permanent improvement of innovation process.

**Keywords:** innovation process, measurement, classification and evaluation of the innovation process, innovation zone, performance indicators.

## 1    Introduction

Measurement and evaluation in the company's (enterprise) innovation zone have an irreplaceable role. In this article we approach the real example of the need for measuring and assessing various levels of innovation zones. As regards the ideas it is often considered too difficult a task as many ideas and suggestions can only be part of an innovation or cannot be directly converted to monetary value. The actual value can be measured by the end customer only, who is the best evaluator of outputs. However, measurement, evaluation and classification were not applied only to the ideas themselves, but our goal is to find the measurable areas of an innovation zone and possible ways of their evaluation.

## 2    Evaluation of Innovation Outputs

The metrics (measurable indicators) that we have identified so far in terms of future production values by estimate only are:  the number of outputs of the innovation

C. Emmanouilidis, M. Taisch, D. Kiritsis (Eds.): APMS 2012, Part I, IFIP AICT 397, pp. 661–668, 2013.
© IFIP International Federation for Information Processing 2013

project, the usefulness in implementation projects (repeatability using one of the outputs), and the number of identified outputs as business opportunities. The number of contracts (signed contracts) transformed from the business opportunities created by innovation outputs is yet the indicator of fair value defined by the customer.

The indicator of a number of outputs of the innovation project indicates only the number regardless of the quality of outputs demonstrating the insufficiency of this indicator. It is therefore advisable to use another indicator that either captures the interest of the future use of some outputs, or measures the actual use thereof. Of course, such a measurement in the first instance requires a questionnaire form of capturing the interest of the individual outputs that provides only an indicative view. If the approach to measure is to capture the used outputs only, so we might get a high accuracy of the indicator, but over time we get information quite late, usually after completion of the project. Therefore, use of another combined indicator (interest survey results, the number of results used) seems to be optimal for the evaluation of ideas. A specific indicator in terms of commercial exploitation of the outputs is the identifier of business opportunities, which, like the previous indicator, has a dual form:

1.  identified business opportunity,
2.  implemented business opportunity.

In addition to measuring the value of innovation ideas it is important to apply the measurement of actual innovation processes and the procedural steps thereof. The process system measurement and process control are natural in the innovation zone because of the dynamically adapting needs of production and the market.

## 3     Measurement and Evaluation of the Innovation Process

We describe the process evaluation by assessing the individual process steps and the possibilities of their improvement. Each step has its own difficulty: its evaluation in terms of automated support, the necessity of investing human effort and possible improvements. It is also necessary to capture weaknesses and existence of defects. To visualize the evaluation process, we chose a sub-process of innovation idea processing. The following assessment is based on the knowledge of the authors of the article, and accordingly we defined the following parameters (KPI-Key Performance Indicators [5]):

**The Level of Automation (LOA)** indicates the level of automated support of the specified step. The aim is to use automated functions for the specified step that focus on usefulness, speed, accuracy and flexibility compared to manual processing.

**The Investment of Human Efforts (IHE)** indicates the level of human efforts in the sense that the smaller the effort, the higher the value of the level. Automation does not always reduce the investment of efforts.

**The Linking with Business Process (LBP)** is a natural indication of the specific step being incorporated into the normal business process.

**The Existence of Deficiency (EOD)** is an indication of redundancy or inefficiency in the operations step or the existence of apparent opportunities for improvement, which have not been applied yet.

**The Added Value (AV)** indicates visible or measurable benefits. Under the added value we understand the benefits that are in line with the company strategy and can either improve the quality of outputs, or bring a reduction of direct costs while the quality remains unchanged, or result in reduced labor.

The indicators can take only three values 0, 1, and 2 representing the minimum, medium, or maximum value of the corresponding indicator.

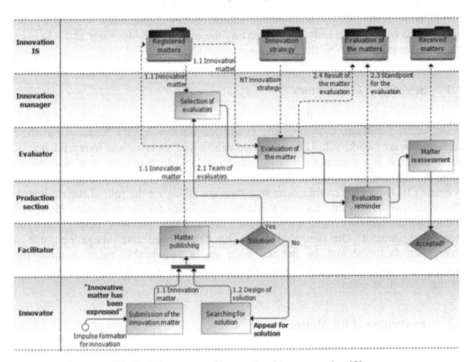

**Fig. 1.** Sub-process of innovation idea processing [2]

### 3.1    Submission of the Innovation Matter

The step of submitting ideas by innovators is easily accessible from the main site of the innovation zone, which is quite comfortable for the promoter of the subject matter when he launches the main site innovation zone. During the normal work day, however, when the user is in one of the many portal sites it is no longer so easy to access. The submission of ideas is available for unregistered users as well as for registered ones. This step could be gradually integrated into the other steps such as the project portal sites.

## 3.2     Matter Publishing

Publishing ideas according to internal rules is trying to capture public comments or getting people interested in sharing the implementation project. Publishing ideas is implemented in an automated way, but the completeness is supervised by the facilitator who before selecting the evaluation team ensures the integrity of the published ideas.

In absence of a description of the solution that may not yet be in possession of the innovator, it also helps the innovator to search for a solution. The communication between the innovator and facilitator is very important and in the current solution this communication is not controlled, but it is left onto the personal activity of the participating actors. Registration of the subject matter is implicitly secured by the portal features and inherently when inserting the idea by the innovator and releasing the same for publication by the facilitator.

## 3.3     Selections of Evaluators

Selection of evaluators of the subject matter is the role of innovation manager. However, the evaluators conduct the evaluation on a voluntary basis within their capabilities and workload. Time synchronization and securing the independence of the evaluation is yet in a position of ethical values. In this step, it is possible to increase the support for the innovation manager in organizing evaluators and acquiring their binding commitment that they are taking on the role of the evaluator. The system also takes into account the motivating factor for the evaluators. However, it does not depend only on the subjective decisions of the innovation manager and the way he applies it. Our knowledge can be summarized into allegations that a motivating factor should be defined with easily enforceable rules, without the unnecessary uncertainty of evaluators about the use or non-use of a motivating factor by the innovation managers.

## 3.4     Evaluation of the Matter

Soon after the first evaluations of ideas it was necessary to improve the evaluation, either compared with a particular goal, or with a specific business issue. Today, the evaluation is in the hands of three randomly selected evaluators that in their perception of reality take into account the potential benefits of the evaluated ideas from different perspectives. For example, the idea that has a society-wide importance need not have business importance for the company. For that reason for the evaluation of ideas a regulation was created that is to guide the evaluators in order to evaluate the prescribed three perspectives:

**Originality:** We are looking for innovative IT solutions (knowledge intensive collaboration solutions: business process repositories, process simulations, large-scale project collaboration systems, scenario-based learning, intelligent helpdesk solutions, etc.). Is your idea unique?

**Feasibility:** We are looking for solutions that can enjoy success in the marketplace or in a company. Is your idea cost-effective, or can it be made so?

**Impact:** If successfully realized, will your idea help turn our current IT challenge into an opportunity?

| | ID | Evaluation Conclusion | Mark 1 | Mark 2 | Mark 3 | Total Score |
|---|---|---|---|---|---|---|
| | 17 | I recommend to test this service with low costs at the beginning. | 4,0 | 3,0 | 3,0 | 10,0 |
| | 19 | Recommend simple and cheap implementation | 4,0 | 3,0 | 3,0 | 10,0 |
| | 40 | I recommend you implement idea with inexpensive solution for processing voice calls driven by process solution. | 4,0 | 3,0 | 4,0 | 11,0 |

**Fig. 2.** Webpart idea evaluation report from idea evaluators [7]

Evaluation forms (templates) are indefinitely available for evaluators. It happens that two evaluators comply with the deadline while the third one delays his or her assessment resulting in a drop in trust from the innovator which is another drawback of this step. All evaluations are automatically recorded and supported by the portal of the innovation zone.

### 3.5    Evaluation Reminder

Reminding the evaluation of the output section allows to create feedback of the production teams and to provide information that is important not only for the implementation phase, but also for the enrichment of information about the production environment and activation of further impulses for new ideas. The output section prepares its viewpoint on the evaluation. This step is purely of an organizational nature and we consider ways to improve this step by the increased collaboration support of the production section that is dedicated to this activity so as to not disturb other planned activities with higher priority.

### 3.6    Matter Reassessment

In conclusion, the final step in the assessment of the previous evaluations and the result is either a rejection or acceptance of the viewpoint, which allows thereafter going into the preparation of the implementation phase of the project.

### 3.7    Searching for Solution

Finding solutions is a step that is necessary if exists an idea which doesn't contain design of technical solution yet. It is used when for the idea there is a need to find appropriate solution and the cooperation with other applicants is welcome. This step has not automated support, which is difficult to establish in this creative activity. It is still necessary to make some effort to find a solution.

# 4    Demonstration of Process Measurement

The following example contains application of defined indicators on the word evaluation of the particular process steps described in the previous chapter. In the table (Table 1) and at the Figure (Fig. 3), there are shown two interpretations of the KPI values for all process steps, matrix and graphical interpretation. Such measurement provides a more realistic vision of the process and options for the optimization and improvement.

**Table 1.** Measurement matrix of the sub-process of innovation idea processing

| | | Process steps (PS) | | | | | | |
|---|---|---|---|---|---|---|---|---|
| | | PS1 | PS2 | PS3 | PS4 | PS5 | PS6 | PS7 |
| | | Submission of the innovation matter | Matter publishing | Selection of evaluators | Evaluation of the matter | Evaluation reminder | Matter reassessment | Searching for solution |
| KPI | LOA | 2 | 1 | 1 | 1 | 2 | 1 | 0 |
| | IHE | 1 | 1 | 0 | 1 | 1 | 0 | 0 |
| | LBP | 1 | 1 | 1 | 1 | 0 | 1 | 1 |
| | EOD | 1 | 0 | 1 | 0 | 1 | 1 | 1 |
| | AV | 2 | 2 | 1 | 2 | 1 | 2 | 2 |

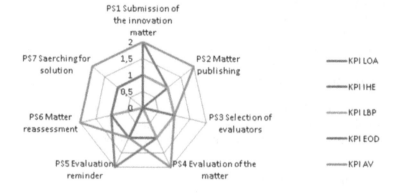

Fig. 3. Chart measurements of process steps

# 5    Conclusion

By the means of the article we demonstrate measurability of general processes of innovation zone, which may be applicable to different types of businesses and organizations dealing with generating innovative ideas in a controllable way and to maximize the added value of its future business. We intend to apply the action of measurement to all of the processes of innovation zone. We consider as important to simulate different business environments in the application verification in order to demonstrate a wide usability of general definition of innovation zone processes (Figure 4) and potential differences related to measurements. We expect that measured values will have different significance (different weight) for different environments, what will be the subject of further research.

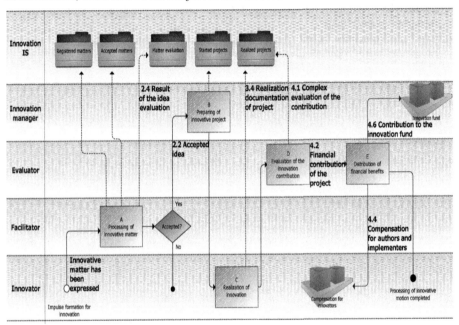

**Fig. 4.** Processes of the innovation zone

**Acknowledgments.** This work was supported by grant KEGA No. 021TUKE-4/2012 (100%). The team also thanks Novitech Company for a willingness, which allowed us to examine conditions for implementation of innovation zones in the real business environment, especially thank the President and Chairman of the Board (Chairman of the Board of Directors), Dr. Attila Toth, for his inspiring advice and transfer of experience to us.

# References

1. Koulopoulos, T.M.: The Innovation Zone, Printed in the united States of America. Davies-Black Publishing (2009) ISBN 978-0-89106-234-9
2. Zolotová, I., Kubičko, P., Landryová, L., Hošák, R.: A design of a reference model of an innovation process and its implementation in business using an innovation zone. In: International Conference on Advances in Production Management Systems, APMS 2011, pp. 1–9 (2011) ISBN 978-82-7644-461-2
3. CREAX Innovation Suite, http://www.creax.com
4. Filipov, S., Mooi, H.: Innovation Project Management. Journal on Innovation and Sustainability 1(1) (2010) ISSN 2179-3565
5. Kaplan, R.S., Norton, D.P.: Balanced Scorecard: Strategický systém měření výkonnosti podniku, p. 261. Management Press, Praha (2002) ISBN 80-7261-063-5 (in Czech)
6. Kaplan, R.S., Norton, D.P.: Using the BSC as a Strategic Management System. Harvard Business Review (1996)
7. Experience from implementation of Innovation zone in Novitech Company, http://izone.novitech.sk/default.aspx

# The Internet of Experiences – Towards an Experience-Centred Innovation Approach

Stefan Wellsandt[1], Thorsten Wuest[1], Christopher Durugbo[2],
and Klaus-Dieter Thoben[1]

[1] BIBA – Bremer Institut für Produktion und Logistik GmbH, Hochschulring 20,
28359 Bremen, Germany
{wel,wue,tho}@biba.uni-bremen.de
[2] University of Bristol, 8 Woodland Road, Clifton BS8 1TN, United Kingdom
Christopher.Durugbo@bristol.ac.uk

**Abstract.** The paper depicts an experience-centred approach for innovation enabled by the Internet of Experiences. Based on findings from innovation research as well as the internet-based approaches of the web 2.0 and the Internet of Things, it is argued that artificial systems, e.g. intelligent products, are capable to make experience on their own out of interactions, similar to user-experience today. After an introduction into the field of "experience" from a knowledge management perspective, a broad definition for experience is suggested. According to this definition, the experience-making possibility of artificial conscious systems is substantiated. Based on these findings, an experience-centred innovation approach, utilizing experience from intelligent objects and human users, is argued. The main outcome of this section is a depiction of the Internet of Experiences.

**Keywords:** Experience, Innovation, Internet of Things, Artificial Consciousness.

## 1 Introduction

Driven by globalization, competition among enterprises and enterprise networks led to the advent of the knowledge worker responsible for constant innovation. Being one step in front of competitors can be a significant core competence resulting in economical, societal and ecological returns. As an effect of shortened product-lifecycles, partially caused by the rapid developments in information and communication technologies, companies had to improve innovation frequency and quality. In order to realize this goal, the innovation process itself was re-thought to take all available sources of innovation into account, be it inside or outside of the enterprise – the idea of *open innovation* was born [1]. One of the richest sources for the new innovation paradigm is the user. The user's experience, created during his daily life and interaction with products and services, is the ideal source for enterprises to learn how to satisfy needs of the people. Importance of the users' experience is also expressed through the development of various tools to capture it, e.g. Living Labs [2]. Changes in the innovation domain were also influenced by

C. Emmanouilidis, M. Taisch, D. Kiritsis (Eds.): APMS 2012, Part I, IFIP AICT 397, pp. 669–676, 2013.

prominent societal shifts, induced by technological paradigms such as the participatory internet.

Over the last years, with the development of web 2.0 after the bursting dot-com bubble [3] and the rise of social networks, the internet itself became more social and a place for communication and social interaction [4]. The social component is steadily becoming more important and builds a basis for new and innovative advances. Within this development, concepts and tools for gathering, sharing and distribution of information and knowledge appeared and became widely popular, Wikipedia being the most famous and most commonly used, LycosIQ [5] or ResearchGate. Another example for knowledge sharing through the internet is Amazon's review function allowing customers to share their experience-based knowledge about products.

User-created content within web 2.0 appears in different forms and qualities ranging from data and information to knowledge and experience. The relation between different qualities of content is illustrated in Fig. 1.

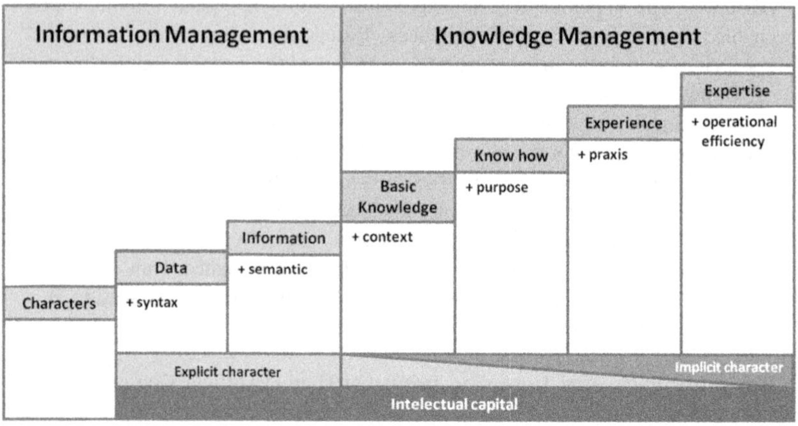

**Fig. 1.** Illustration of information and knowledge management terms (based on [6] & [7])

From a general point of view, most authors support the definition of Probst et. al. that linking of *information* allows its use in a certain field of activity, which can be interpreted as *knowledge* [8]. In Fig. 1, contextualization of data and information towards basic knowledge and know-how is shown. Until *know-how*, it is challenging but possible to save and share, though it becomes hard, if not impossible, for *experience* and expertise due to their individual character.

Referring back to the participative character of web 2.0, another development is interesting called *Internet of Things* (IoT). One of the central ideas of IoT is the extension of the internet into the physical world to embrace everyday objects [9]. The IoT is realized through networked systems of self-organizing objects that interact autonomously, and related processes that lead to an expected convergence of physical things with the virtual world of the internet [10]. One of the central aspects of the IoT is that objects are able to process information, communicate amongst each other and with their environment, and make autonomous decisions, thus becoming "intelligent"

[9], [11], [12]. Closely related to the principles of IoT are intelligent products (IP). A well-accepted definition for intelligent products is the following [13]:

*"[...] a physical and information based representation of an item [...] which possesses a unique identification, is capable of communicating effectively with its environment, can retain or store data about itself, deploys a language to display its features, production requirements, etc., and is capable of participating in or making decisions relevant to its own destiny."*

Up to now, IPs are not intelligent in a human sense [14]. They can be subject of interaction but typically lack complex learning abilities. However, the ability to perceive and communicate experienced situations raises the question how benefits can be taken out of these contents. One idea is to systematically consider their individual experience in order to complement existing open innovation approaches mainly based on user-experience.

This paper intends to identify similarities between two inputs of open innovation processes, i.e. user-experience and potential object-experience, in order to depict a future platform to share experiences – the Internet of Experiences (IoE). In the second section, the approach towards an Internet of Experiences will be introduced. This section covers an overview into experience from a knowledge management perspective and an elaboration on experience in natural and artificial conscious systems. The third section provides a description of the experience-centred approach of the IoE and answers the question of what the IoE could look like. Finally, the paper is concluded and an outlook is given, as well as a short paragraph of the limitations of the approach.

# 2    Approach

The scientific approach that is applied in this paper consists of two aspects: the recent understanding of "experience" from the perspective of knowledge management, and similarities between user-experience and the experience gained by artificial systems such as Intelligent Products.

## 2.1    Experience from a Knowledge Management Perspective

The term "experience" is used and defined differently among research fields. Some of the more prominent fields dealing with experience are cognitive sciences (e.g. enactive framework) and open innovation research (e.g. Living Labs). In *cognitive sciences*, definitions for (human) experience can be found by arguing that experience is closely related to questions about what a situation or an activity feels like [15]. The concept of experience therefore is strongly defined by its subjective character, making it difficult to be addressed in a formal and systematical way in science. This is especially true for scientific disciplines that primarily focus on measurable results like those commonly used in engineering and information technology contexts. While cognitive sciences deal with experience in a broader way, other domains try to focus on certain subjects or categories of experience.

In the area of *open innovation research*, subject of experience are people that interact with products or services – this experience is stated as user-experience. Within innovation research, user-experience is frequently utilized in the context of Living Lab approaches – innovation ecosystems typically utilizing user-experience with ICT technology and related artefacts [16]. User-experience is defined in ISO 9241-210 as *"[...] a person's perceptions and responses that result from the use or anticipated use of a product, system or service"*. It can be expressed through feedback from the users in a codified way (e.g. questionnaire) or interviews. Within innovation ecosystems, formalized user-experience is evaluated and used to create or adapt ICT-services and products respecting user requirements. Other domains specify experience according to different content such as software-experience in computer sciences. According to Conradi and Dybå, software-experience is a composition of experimental data and aggregated models (i.e. knowledge) on these data [17].

The final example for experience raises an important point about the ambiguous relation between knowledge and experience. In order to better distinguish the different terms, especially related to knowledge, the point of origin of different intellectual capital (IC) types is used as illustrated in Fig. 2.

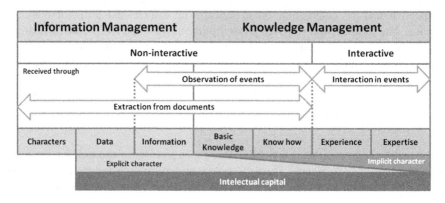

**Fig. 2.** Point of origin for different kinds of intellectual capital (based on [6] & [7])

Points of origin are differentiated into non-interactive (observation and extraction) and interactive ones. Based on this separation, a major difference between knowledge and experience is the fact that the latter is only created during interaction. However, an aspect that makes clear segmentation of IC types difficult is the ambiguous nature of knowledge in literature. As Nonaka proposed in the early 1990s, knowledge consists of explicit and tacit (i.e. implicit) elements [18]. Tacit knowledge can be gained through observation, imitation and practice. In this paper, tacit and explicit character of intellectual capital is seen as a continuum across the four IC types in knowledge management. The main purpose of the continuum is to address difficulties arising from tacit knowledge in relation to the question where it fits best in Fig. 2.

Different scientific perspectives on "experience" result in different understandings and definitions of the term. In order to avoid discussions digressing into the domain of philosophy, or scientific domains where in-depth discussions about "experience" are unavoidable, a broad definition is suggested for the purpose of this work. The definition takes into account findings in cognitive science, open innovation research, points of origin from IC types and is influenced by findings of Davis in [19]:

*"Experience is an individual and in-tangible consequence of an interaction between a conscious system and real or digital entities inside or outside the system. Experience is related to explicit or tacit elements in the form of associated data, information, basic knowledge, or know how."*

### 2.2 Experience in Natural and Artificial Conscious Systems

In the previous sections, it was pointed out that user-experience is a high value source for innovation processes. In this section, it will be examined whether there is evidence for *object-experience* or not. According to the definition proposed in section 2.1, several conditions need to be evaluated in order to assume that experience can be made by artificial systems such as intelligent products:

— The artificial system has to be <u>conscious</u>
— There has to be <u>interaction</u> between artificial system and other entities
— Consequence of the interaction must be <u>individual</u> and <u>in-tangible</u>

The *consciousness* of artificial systems is subject of investigation in the scientific domain of artificial consciousness [20], [21]. Assuming that, for example, an intelligent product is some kind of machine, we likewise assume that there is a general possibility that it can be conscious. The second condition refers to the *interaction* between artificial system and other entities. As described in the introduction, IPs have communication and decision-making abilities enabling interactive behaviour. Therefore, we consider the second condition as fulfilled.

Since the first two conditions are met, artificial systems such as IPs can be seen as generally capable of drawing consequences from interaction. In order to make clear that consequences belong to a specific artificial system, each system needs to have an identifier making it an *individual* element. For IPs, identifiers can be, for example, RFID tags or barcodes. Grounded on the artificial nature of intelligent products, their storage unit (e.g. hard disk) contains digital content. This leads to the conclusion that consequences related to interaction are *in-tangible*. Based on the examination of the three proposed conditions above, it is concluded that artificial conscious systems, like intelligent products, are *capable of making experience*.

## 3 The Internet of Experiences – Experience-Centred Innovation

The general capability of natural (user) and artificial systems (smart product) to make their own experience during interaction, leads to the question how these kinds of experience can be transformed into benefits. Referring back to the introduction of this work, innovation is a key driver of sustaining competitive advantages. While common innovation processes take user-experience into account, it is reasonable to ask if object-experience can be considered likewise. With respect to the developments in the open innovation domain, it is assumed that *the quality of innovations increases with the number of experiencing systems* participating in the innovation process thus creating more valuable outputs. This assumption, but also the important role of experience innovation processes, is supported by findings of Taylor and Greve [22].

Artificial conscious systems, such as intelligent products, are connected through the Internet of Things. Through this network, data and information are shared to allow new product-based services and enable new product functionalities. With the experience-making ability of IPs, "things" in the IoT can go beyond simple sensing (collection of data and information). From a knowledge perspective, they can become actors, sharing through the internet what they learned or explored. Since the participative internet is already a place where experience is discussed, new actors providing additional input from a new perspective seem to be promising. The networked character of the internet can also help to handle interrelated user- and object-experience in order to derive further conclusions. The joint consideration of *user-experience and object-experience* could be beneficial, for example, to identify requirements for new products and services.

User behaviour or specific requirements that aren't articulated by users (e.g. through questionnaire or interview) might be revealed by considering the perspective that intelligent products, as interaction counter-parts, can take. IPs could reason interaction behaviour of formerly experienced situations and consolidate with similar or complementary products through the internet. The *consolidation process* is meant to identify whether an experience is related to a single or multiple spatial-temporal contexts. Based on the consolidation, the artificial system proposes aspects with hidden innovation potential. Examples for these aspects can be complementary functions of an existing product (incremental innovation) or novel products (radical innovation). These suggestions can be further elaborated and consolidated based on user-experience in the internet, potentially leading to better and/or faster innovation. This depiction of the Internet of Experiences is summarized in Fig. 3.

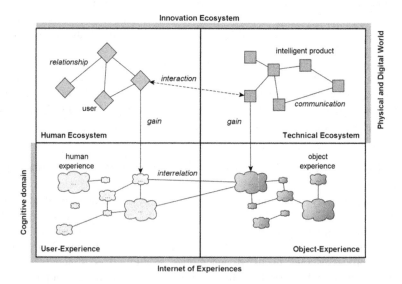

**Fig. 3.** Depiction of the Internet of Experiences

# 4    Conclusion and Outlook

The paper depicted an innovation approach that is centred on experience utilizing an Internet of Experiences. Based on developments in the areas of web 2.0, IoT, knowledge management and open innovation, an experience-centred approach – the Internet of Experiences – seems promising to complement human-centred innovation with experiences from artificial systems. Different understanding of "experience" in scientific domains was presented in order to suggest a wider definition for the term. Grounded on this definition, the general experience-making ability of artificial systems was argued. Concluded from these findings, an experience-centred innovation approach and the Internet of Experiences are depicted.

Since the experience-centred approach of this work is still under development, further effort needs to be done to provide sufficient foundation for the assumptions of this work (e.g. experience-making ability) and derived theoretical concepts. Some of the unaddressed challenges related to this work are closely based on the current state of research about intelligent artificial systems, e.g. machine learning, artificial consciousness or Internet of Things. For example, artificial systems, such as intelligent products, often-times lack cognitive abilities compared to artificial systems inside of laboratory environments. Other issues are the ontological relationships between experiences as well as the importance of experience and other intellectual capital types for the innovation process. Furthermore, it needs to be elaborated how user-experience and object-experience can be combined on operational level in order to facilitate innovation.

# 5    Limitations

The intention of the introduced approach in this work is not to deeply elaborate what "experience" is, especially in relation to the domains of neurosciences and the human brain. Furthermore, the large field of cognitive sciences is only covered briefly to give a basic understanding of aspects that should be considered when dealing with experience as such.

# References

1. Chesbrough, H.: Open Innovation. Harvard Business School Press, Boston (2003)
2. Eriksson, M., Niitamo, V., Oyj, N., Kulkki, S.: State-of-the-art in utilizing Living Labs approach to user-centric ICT innovation - a European approach (2005)
3. O'Reilly, T.: What is Web 2.0: Design Patterns and Business Models for the Next Generation of Software. Communications & Strategies (65), 17–37 (2007)
4. Gosling, S.D., Augustine, A.A., Vazire, S., Holtzman, N., Gaddis, S.: Manifestations of Personality in Online Social Networks: Self-Reported Facebook-Related Behaviors and Observable Profile Information. CyberPsychology, Behavior & Social Networking 14(9), 483–488 (2011)

5. Alby, T.: Web 2.0 – Konzepte, Anwendungen, Technologien. Hanser Verlag, Munich (2006)
6. North, K., Güldenberg, S.: Produktive Wissensarbeit(er) – Antworten auf die Managementherausforderungen des 21. Jahrhunderts. Gabler Verlag, Wiesbaden (2008)
7. Auer, T.: ABC des Wissensmanagements, http://pwm.at/wp-content/uploads/2010/11/688_tmpphpKCYP1E.pdf (accessed: May 2012)
8. Probst, G., Raub, S., Romhardt, K.: Wissen managen – Wie Unternehmen ihre wertvollste Ressource optimal nutzen. Gabler Verlag, Wiesbaden (2006)
9. Mattern, F., Floerkemeier, C.: From the Internet of Computers to the Internet of Things. In: Sachs, K., Petrov, I., Guerrero, P. (eds.) Buchmann Festschrift. LNCS, vol. 6462, pp. 242–259. Springer, Heidelberg (2010)
10. Brand, L., Hülser, T., Grimm, V., Zweck, A.: Internet der Dinge – Perspektiven für die Logisitk. Zukünftige Technologien Consulting 80 (2009)
11. Isenberg, M.A., Werthmann, D., Morales-Kluge, E., Scholz-Reiter, B.: The Role of the Internet of Things for Increased Autonomy and Agility in Collaborative Production Environments. In: Uckelmann, D., Harrison, M., Michahelles, F. (eds.) Architecting the Internet of Things, pp. 195–228. Springer, Heidelberg (2011)
12. Hribernik, K.A., Hans, C., Kramer, C., Thoben, K.-D.: Service-oriented, Semantic Approach to Data Integration for an Internet of Things Supporting Autonomous Cooperating Logistics Processes. In: Uckelmann, D., Harrison, M., Michahelles, F. (eds.) Architecting the Internet of Things, pp. 131–158. Springer, Heidelberg (2011)
13. McFarlane, D., Sarma, S., Chirn, J.L., Wong, C.Y., Ashton, K.: Auto ID systems and intelligent manufacturing control. Eng. Appl. of Artificial Intelligence (16), 365–376 (2003)
14. Erickson, T.: Social systems: designing digital systems that support social intelligence. AI & Soc. 23, 147–166 (2009)
15. Rhode, M.: Enaction, Embodiment, Evolutionary Robotics: Simulation Models for a Post-Cognitivist Science of Mind. In: Kühnberger, K.-U. (ed.) Atlantis Thinking Machines. Atlantis Press, Paris (2009)
16. Folstad, A.: Living Labs for Innovation and Development of Information and Communication Technology: A Literature Review. The Electronic Journal for Virtual Organizations and Networks 10, 99–131 (2008)
17. Conradi, R., Dybå, T.: An empirical study on the utility of formal routines to transfer knowledge and experience. In: Proceedings 8th European Software Engineering Conference, pp. 268–276 (2001)
18. Nonaka, I.: The Knowledge-Creating Company. Managing for the long term: Best of HBR (November-December 1991); Harvard Business Review, 162–171 (July-August 2007)
19. Davis, M.: Theoretical Foundations for Experiential Systems Design. In: Proceedings of the 2003 ACM SIGMM Workshop on Experiential Telepresence, Berkeley, CA, USA, pp. 45–52 (2003)
20. Haikonen, P.: The Cognitive Approach To Conscious Machines. Imprint Academic, Exeter (2003)
21. Koch, C., Tononi, G.: Can Machines Be Conscious? IEEE Spectrum, 55–59 (June 2008)
22. Taylor, A., Greve, H.R.: Superman or the Fantastic Four? Knowledge Combination and Experience in Innovative Teams. The Academy of Management Journal 49(4), 723–740 (2006)

# Innovating a Business Model for Services
# with Storytelling

Morten Lund

Center for Industrial Production, Aalborg University
ml@business.aau.dk

**Abstract.** In recent years, the notion of business models has been able to innovate the way companies create new business opportunities. However, because business models most often rest on a complex interplay of several actors, there is a need to be able to explore the nature of a business model.

This paper will propose to describe a business model by means of storytelling. Also, the paper will introduce the notion of archetypes of business models with the aim to seek a pattern in the light of the numerous business models available. Two cases will illustrate and discuss storytelling and archetypes, giving rise to conclude that they represent a valuable approach to understanding and innovating business models.

**Keywords:** Business models, Free-business models, narratives, storytelling, business model innovation, archetypes.

## 1    Introduction

The growing interest in understanding and innovating business models in recent years is most likely a result of an increased recognition that a successful business model can be a game changing factor in competition or in entering a new market. However, as a novel concept, many questions arise of both theoretical and practical nature. To explore some of these issues, a Danish research program "ICI" was initiated aimed to inspire and assist participants in a development process of innovating new global business models in a network of smaller, traditional industrial companies and new e-business companies. The research program has shown that a novel approach is needed to illustrate how a new business model may look, especially to provide a picture of an emerging business model that can persuade interested parties what they may gain and which role they would be supposed to play. We have experienced that storytelling represents a fruitful approach which we intend to discuss in this paper.

Furthermore, both practice and theory include quite a large number of different business models. This has led us to explore if patterns may be identified by way of the notion of business model archetypes. From the research program we have selected two related cases that will illustrate elements of storytelling. In addition, they will form a basis for discussing the notion of archetypes that will also be illustrated by existing business models. In this paper, we shall first introduce the notion of business models, storytelling and archetypes. Then the two cases will be presented, followed by a discussion. Finally, the paper will be concluded.

C. Emmanouilidis, M. Taisch, D. Kiritsis (Eds.): APMS 2012, Part I, IFIP AICT 397, pp. 677–684, 2013.
© IFIP International Federation for Information Processing 2013

## 1.1    Business Models

Business model theory as a separate research area is relatively young. Until 2000, the notion of business models was largely related to the preserve of internet-based businesses [Mason 2011]. But since then, research on business models has intensified accompanied by an escalating quantity of literature from both practitioners and academia. The area of business models is thus still young and also quite dispersed. The field as a stand-alone is just starting to make inroads into top management journals, but the conceptual base is still thin [Zott, Amit & Massa 2011].

The definition of the term business model has been discussed substantially over the last decade. From a simple definition, e.g. "Business model is a statement of how a firm will make money and sustain its profit stream over time" [Zhao 2010] to definitions including partners or stakeholders, e.g. "A conceptual tool that contains a set of elements and their relationships and allows expressing the business logic of a specific firm. It is a description of the value that a company offers to one or several segments of customers and the architecture of the firm and its network of partners for creating, marketing and delivering this value and relationship capital, to generate profitable and sustainable revenue stream" [Osterwalder et al., 2004]

We have come to the conclusion that a business model is too multifaceted to be defined in any simplistic way. Overall, a business model consists of two elements; what the business does, and the way in which the business gains profit.

There have been attempts to describe business models as systems consisting of a variation of building blocks, e.g. the Business Model Canvas [Osterwalder XXXX], which describes a business model by means of nine interrelated building blocks. Osterwalder's work has provided a popular framework for describing, understanding and innovating business models for a company. The framework has been used successfully in our research program but has also shown limitations. We have found that several companies and individuals can be considered actors forming a network in a new business model. There is a need to develop a framework for each partner [stakeholder] and for the network as a whole. Another limitation is the static nature of the business model canvas, in view of the desire to generate new ideas.

## 1.2    Storytelling

Storytelling exists throughout all cultures and is an inevitable part of human communication and interaction. Stories can pass on accumulated knowledge, ideas, and values, as for example used in anthropology. Through stories we are creating a narrative image of constructions enabling us to explain complex things, for example proposed as part of corporate strategy development, Kotter [1990], Riis & Johansen [2003]. In this paper narratives and stories are treated as synonyms, ignoring the semantic discussion on the distinction between narrative and storytelling.

Magretta [2002] gained considerable attention by identifying business models as "stories that explain how enterprises work". According to Magretta, business models did not only show how the firm made money but also answered fundamental questions such as: "who is the customer? and "what does the customer value?"

In comparison to a traditional strategy statement, a story is told focusing on what actors do and through such a process description it is explained how money, information and goods and services flow between actors, including customers. In this way, it becomes clear to actors what their role will be, as well as their expected benefits and obligations.

In our research program we have learned that a story evolves through interaction with actors, as they contribute with ideas and own experience and express their preferences. Furthermore, a story can be told in many different ways. On the one hand, it is important to be open for new and innovative ways of expressing a story; on the other hand, we should seek generic elements or questions expected to be addressed in a story.

We found that storytelling may be an important approach for developing a business model in a network of companies and individuals with different backgrounds and qualifications. The process of developing a story serves as a platform for a constructive dialogue for combining different opinions into a coherent business model.

## 1.3    Archetypes

The notion of archetypes represents an attempt to identify generic patterns or classes that may be used as inspiration for developing a specific business model.

Although it is desirable to develop archetypes for successful business models, there is no single, well-defined classification of business model archetypes in the literature. Osterwalder applies the term pattern as an expression that comes from the world of architecture. I his use of the term it stands for the idea of capturing architectural design ideas as archetypal and reusable descriptions.

One may argue that patterns can be formed at a macro and a micro level in an industry or a business. The macro level of business models archetype may express roles in an industry, e.g. wholesaler, consultants, distributor, production, banks, etc. They show how corporations interact with stakeholders of their business model in distinct patterns. For example, Miles & Snow [1978] showed how companies could exists side by side in an industry [books for the educational market] with generic different business models. The macro level business models may consist of variations in patterns. For example, differences between a supermarket and a food wholesale basically lie in the costumer segment. Although the basic business model of "primarily selling products manufactured by others" and the revenue models seem to be alike, only differentiated by quantity and assortment, the two business models are very different. The relationship with suppliers [stakeholders in the business model] is different. In the wholesale business model, suppliers often have relations directly with the customers, discussing price, exclusivity etc. The cost structure is different based on the average turnover per customer. These are examples of small variations in business models at the micro level.

Focusing on micro level business models enables development of specific archetypes of business models describing typical patterns in one or more interrelated building blocks of a business model. As an example, Anderson [2009] presents four revenue model archetypes. He explores how things can be "Free" implying how a product may be provided for free, yet still supporting a viable business model. Sometimes "free" is not really free. "Buy one, get one for free" is just another way of saving 50 per cent off when you buy two. "Free gift inside" really means that the cost of the gift has been included in the overall product. "Free shipping" typically means that the price of shipping has been built into the product's markup. He defines the Free business model as cross-subsidies essentially based on the phrase "there's no such thing as a free lunch." This means that one way or another the food must be paid for, if not by you directly then by someone else whose interest it is to give you free food. Andersen demonstrates that there are different "Free business models archetypes".

Within the broad world of cross-subsidies, Andersen describes four main categories or archtypes. One of the archetypes is "Freemium", a common revenue model on the Internet. It can be described as a revenue model where 5% of the customers pays for 95%, e.g. Skype. The reason for this model to function is that the cost of a Skype customer is close to nothing, and the revenue on the 5% is enough to cover the operation cost. In this example the revenue model archetype provides universally understood pattern enabling us to ask the question "could your business adopt this cost structure?"

This classification focuses on the value paid by customers. Based on our research, this represents an important dimension for identifying archetypes of business models. Other dimensions may be added, e.g. from the Business Model Canvas.

## 2     Two Case Companies

### 2.1     Methodology

Two comparative case studies will be presented aimed to illustrate the notion of storytelling and archetypes. The first case study is based on a longitudinal in-depth qualitative case study over a period of two and a half years of a Danish start-up in the media industry, C-Spot. The network of companies and individuals behind C-Spot developed a clever business model for outdoor advertising through a new IT platform. The second case study is based on interviews and a workshop in the global industrial enterprise, Otis Elevator Company.The longitudinal study of Cspot was an interventionist research project [Lukka 2005]. Our research group followed CSpot from before the company was founded until now, involving the founders, the CEO and senior staff from the company, as well as four business partners, consultants and researchers. The project had a defined goal to invent a new global business model for the company. During the research project, there have been numerous meetings, workshops, reports and semi-structured interviews, which are recorded and/or documented with minutes, pictures or video. The terminology of the business model was introduced to all participants, and especially the use of the Business Model Canvas [Osterwalder 200x], and narratives exemplifying existing, successful business models. The second case study, Otis, is based on semi-structured interviews and a workshop. The semi-structured interviews were conducted with a senior sales manager from the Danish division of Otis. Background information on the Danish elevator industry is based on semi-structured interviews with three industry professionals, statistics and data from official public databases. CSpot is a Danish start-up company, founded in 2009. The business idea was to establish a new advertising channel consisting of a network of physical advertising screens in shop windows set up in areas with a high frequency of pedestrian traffic and showing a constant flow of live messages. The idea of CSpot originated from an idea of using all the empty shop windows that increased in numbers as a result of the financial crisis, but it quickly became apparent that existing shops were just as interested. The screens are connected by a genius virtual platform offering inexpensive advertising opportunities at affordable prices targeting small and local businesses as well as large campaigns. The business model success is based on a radically different cost structure and at the same time a new value proposition to advertisers. Compared to existing advertising channels, the CSpot's channel is different in many ways; e.g. their key value proposition is instant advertising. Usually, e.g. at AFA JCDecaux and Clear Channel, marketing has to plan ahead, produce posters, distribute and put them up. With the Cspot system, advertisers simply go to their website. Here, advertisers choose where and when to show their campaign. Either the advertiser uploads existing material or uses the free online spot builder. This enables customers to advertise instantly and relevant. For example, a local restaurant could put out an offer, if it is a slow night, or if the weather turns to rain. The local department store can attract customers with an attractive offer. The cost structure is also different. In addition to the obvious savings from production and distribution cost of a static media, CSpot came up with a clever model, reducing infrastructure cost drastically. The competitors like AFA JCDecaux and Clear Channel have great costs placing their billboards on house ends or by paying for public exterior. CSpot managed to attract more than 100 sites based on the model: your window space and power in exchange for a quantity of free advertising on the system in your local area. In fact the only cost for Cspot is setting up the screen, maintenance and the GSM Internet connection. Despite the immediate success in creating a good business model, it was difficult to attract large advertisers that often are managed by advertising agencies. The main reason for this is lack of documentation of the effect and the number of people who view the screens. A solution was discussed to install surveillance in every CSpot, providing automatic counting. But the investment was simply too high. The Otis Elevator Company is the worlds largest manufacturer of elevators and escalators. The Danish branch's business model is a typical "service business" where the key activities are to install, modernize and perform services on elevators, escalators and moving walkways. The key resources are knowhow, skilled employees and access to spare parts and tools from the main company. The Danish elevator industry seems to be segmented into two types of businesses. The global actors that are present nationally and local/regional actors. The global actors such as Otis, Thyssen-Krupps, Schindler and Kone all seem to follow the same "services business model" as described. The local actors primarily focus on service and renovation of existing installed elevators, a few on new elevators. From interviews with industry professionals including the case company Otis, they all seemed to agree that the business is all about the services contracts. It is well known in the industry that the global actors often sell new elevators near cost prices, making money on the service.

## 3     Empirical Discussion

The two cases represent different situations with respect to innovating a business model. The first case, CSpot, developed a new idea from scratch by a few core members of a network that was gradually expanded as the business model emerged. The second case, OTIS, took the existing business model as point of departure and sought to expand it by augmenting new activities, new actors, and new revenue models.

In this section we shall discuss how storytelling and the notion of archetypes were used in the process of developing an innovative business case, and in particular discuss some of the challenges experienced. It is interesting to note that the second case was originated as an offspring of the first case. The cases serve multiple purposes; primarily to introduce various principles of applying a storytelling approach that may give rise to conclude that they represent a valuable approach to understanding and innovating business models. Second, to show how two business models can be merged in a complimenting business model.

### 3.1     Using Storytelling to Tackle Business Model Challenges

The CSpot case emerged as a trial-and-error, explorative process with many themes being addressed simultaneously. It was difficult to find a common revenue model that could demonstrate the benefit to investors and customers. Two approaches were tried. Inspired by the Osterwalder Business Model Canvas, the notion of storytelling was introduced as a means of combining different ideas into a story telling what would take place when a service is offered, and how actors would interact.

The second approach was to be inspired by existing, successful business models. In the CSpot case, the story of Google's business model served to understand new facets of a business model, in particular to use knowledge about users as an asset. For example, Google uses the location of users when a search is made, providing a more relevant link between customers and advertisers. This generates additional income, because search becomes more effective.

This story inspired the development of a business model in the CSpot case. For example, how could CSpot location data create additional value for advertisers and also generate more revenue for CSpot, and how could CSpot provide value to users so they would interact with spots. This led to the idea of getting users to take a picture with their smartphone, and to provide spots with 2D barcodes opening for virtual connection to customers. As a result, a new revenue model emerged where advertisers would pay a provision if they get a customer. At the same time, it created a potential relationship to customers with new business opportunities.

The story of Google generated many questions that served as a vehicle for a structured process of understanding the challenges and potentials of the CSpot business model, and of developing a story of an innovative business model. This also proved useful when new spot partners were introduced during the process.

At the end of the development of the CSpot business model, an idea came up that elevators were a perfect place for a CSpot because of the attention you have from people using an elevator and the knowledge it is possible to generate about their background and interests. As a result, it was decided to contact the OTIS company for an explorative discussion.

### 3.2     Why Should Otis Implement CSpots in Elevators?

The Danish branch of Otis has a clear business model that may be defined at a macro level as a "services business model". The revenue of the company is among the best in the industry, and the company has a substantial market share and track record. All in all, the business model seems to be working, and Otis profits from this. Why should Otis implement CSpots in elevators? Or could the question be rephrased: why should Otis add a new business model or change an existing that is working.

At a workshop, an Osterwalder Business Model Canvas was created identifying the existing business model. It revealed that customers were unlikely to pay more for the service of Otis. How could this be addressed? Based on the archetypes introduced by Anderson [2009], the facilitator introduced several existing business models of offering services or products for free. This generated a constructive dialogue on how installation of CSpots in elevators could create revenue for both the owner of an elevator and Otis. Otis showed great interest in different cross-subsidies models, e.g. CSpot paying for the service in exchange for advertising space, enabling Otis to offer Free service to their customers. During the workshop the facilitator introduced the "business model questions" used in the CSpot Case. This enabled validation on the integration between two business models. E.g. the technology present in Otis elevators offers different value proportions to the CSpot business model. Otis elevators can count passengers based on a weight average and count the numbers of trips. This providing advertisers with more accurate data, increasing profit for CSpot. Although not yet implemented, the workshop showed that innovation of an existing business model may be facilitated by use of existing, successful business models organized in a spectrum of archetypes ensuring a broad explorative process.

## 4     Conclusion

In view of the complex interplay of several actors forming a business model, this paper has discussed the idea of describing a business model by means of storytelling, explaining how the interplay of enterprises works to generate value for customers as well as partners. Two case studies illustrated how storytelling could serve as a means of combining different ideas and perspectives into a unified presentation of a business model. Also the story of existing, successful business models may serve as a vehicle for an innovative, collaborative process with many actors.

The notion of archetypes was introduced to inspire a broad innovative process. We chose to focus on revenue models and presented and used a special category under the heading "Free service". In the Otis case, this provided a new way of looking at the existing business model. However, there is a need to further explore the notion of archetypes, for example to identify other revenue models and to introduce other dimensions of a classification. A pragmatic approach would be to use existing successful business models as a basis for identifying patterns and classes.

The emerging area of business models has been able to innovate the way companies create new business opportunities. However, many challenges arise in connection with working in practice with business models. This paper has pointed to new directions of carrying out a collaborative process involving several actors by introducing the notion of storytelling and archetypes and by showing how they may serve as vehicles for creating an overall image combining different ideas and viewpoints.

# References

Anderson, C.: Free, the future of radical price. Random House (2009)

Osterwalder, A., Pigneur, Y.: Towards Business and Information Systems Fit through a BMO. Working paper, Ecole des HEC. University of Lausanne (2003)

Osterwalder, et al.: Business Model Generation: A Handbook for Visionaries, Game Changers, and Challengers. John Wiley (2010)

Osterwalder, A.: An e-Business Model Ontology for the Creation of New Management Software Tools and IS Requirement Engineering. Working paper, Ecole des HEC, University of Lausanne

Lukka, K.: Approaches to case research in management accounting: the nature of empirical interventio and theory lunkage. In: Jönsson, S., Mouritsen, J. (eds.) Accounting in Scandinavia - The Northern Lights. Stockholm, pp. 375–399. Copenhagen Business School Press, Copenhagen (2005)

Mason, K., Spring, M.: The sites and practices of business models. Industrial Marketing Management 40, 1032–1041 (2011)

Magretta, J.: Why Business Models Matter. In: HBR, pp. 3–8 (May 2002)

Miles, R.E., Snow, C.C.: Organizational Strategy, Structure and Process. McGraw-Hill, New York (1978)

Morris, M., Schmindehutte, M., Allen, J.: The entrepreneur's business model: Toward a unified perspective. JBR 58(6), 726–735 (2003)

Kotter, J.P.: A force for change: How leadership differs from management. The Free Press (1990)

Riis, J.O., Johansen, J.: Developing a manufacturing vision. Production Planning and Control 14(4), 327–337 (2003)

Stewart, D.W., Zhao, Q.: Internet marketing, business models, and public policy. Journal of Public Policy 19, 287–296 (Fall 2000)

Zott, Amit, Massa: The Business Model: Recent Developments and Future Research. Journal of Management 37 (2011); 1019 originally published online (May 2, 2011)

# Business Strategy and Innovativeness: Results from an Empirical Study

Gündüz Ulusoy[1], Gürhan Günday[1], Kemal Kılıç[1], and Lütfihak Alpkan[2]

[1] Faculty of Engineering and Natural Sciences, Sabanci University,
Istanbul, Turkey
{gunduz,ggunday,kilic}@sabanciuniv.edu
[2] Faculty of Management, Gebze Institute of Technology, Kocaeli, Turkey
alpkan@gyte.edu.tr

**Abstract.** This study reports on the testing of the hypothesis that there is a positive relationship between business strategy and innovativeness. Business strategy is defined here to include market focus strategy, technology development strategy, and operations priorities - including cost, quality, delivery / dependability, and flexibility. An empirical study is conducted based on data collected using a questionnaire developed. 184 manufacturing firms from different industries in the Northern Marmara region in Turkey participated in the study. Multivariate statistics techniques and structural equation modeling are employed. The results have been affirmative supporting the hypothesis. Market focus and technology development factors are found to mediate the effects of operations priorities on innovativeness. That market focus, technology development and cost efficiency have direct effects on innovativeness is another finding of managerial importance.

**Keywords:** Business strategy, innovativeness, empirical study, structural equation modeling.

## 1 Introduction

This study aims to test the hypothesis that there is a positive relationship between business strategy and innovativeness. Business strategy is defined here to include market focus strategy, technology development strategy, and operations priorities - also called manufacturing capabilities in the literature- including cost, quality, delivery/dependability, and flexibility (see e.g., Hayes and Wheelwright, 1984; Leong et al., 1990). The foremost aim of firms is to survive in the market while generating profit. In the highly dynamic market conditions of today, firms are under the pressure of strong competition in order to gain competitive advantage and to upgrade the efficiency of work and innovation provides them with an effective tool for that purpose, since innovations are among the essential resources through which firms contribute to increased employment, economic growth, and competitive strength. The purpose of innovation is to launch newness into the economic area. As stated by Metcalfe (1998), when the flow of newness and innovations desiccate, the firm's economic structure settles down in an inactive state with little growth.

C. Emmanouilidis, M. Taisch, D. Kiritsis (Eds.): APMS 2012, Part I, IFIP AICT 397, pp. 685–692, 2013.

Four different innovation types are employed in this research: product, process, marketing and organizational innovations (OECD, 2005). We define here innovativeness to embody some kind of measurement contingent on an organization's proclivity towards innovation (Salavou, 2004).

## 2    Data Collection and Measurement of Variables

### 2.1    Data Collection

A questionnaire consisting of 311 individual questions was developed to be filled in by the upper managers of manufacturing companies. The questionnaire was updated based on the experience gained through a pilot test phase covering 10 firms. Afterwards data was collected over a 7-month period in 2006-2007 in textile, chemical, metal products, machinery, domestic appliances and automotive industries in the Northern Marmara region of Turkey. These industries were selected to represent the major manufacturing sectors in Turkey. A manufacturing business unit was selected as the unit of analysis. A total of 184 usable questionnaires were obtained resulting in a response rate of 11%. All the respondents completing the questionnaire were from the top (52%) or middle management (48%). For each sector, number of firms in the sample turned out to be representative, since no significant difference has been detected between the population and the sample percentages.

The profile of the resulting sample presented in Figure 1 illustrates its diversity in terms of firm characteristics. Firm size is determined by the number of full-time employees (up to 50: small, $50 \leq$ medium $<250$, $\geq 250$: large). In addition to the number of full-time employees, for a firm to be classified as large it is required to have an annual revenue $\geq 50$ M€. For small and medium firms, four annual revenue brackets are defined so as to have a balance between small and medium firms. Firm age is determined by the year production had started (up to 1975: old; $1975 \leq$ moderate$<1992$; $\geq 1992$: young). Joint stock companies constitute 73% of the sample with the remaining being limited companies. 19% of the firms in the sample have some level of foreign direct investment.

### 2.2    Measurement of Variables

As we will see in the following, the questions for measurement purpose are asked using a 5-point Likert scale. Such subjective measures possibly bring in manager bias, but are widespread practice in empirical researches (Khazanchi et al., 2007).

First we will deal with the questions concerning the business strategy constructs. The variables of market focus are given in Table 1. A 5-point Likert scale is employed to assess how important each one has been for the firm in the last three years with a scale ranging from 1=extremely unimportant to 5= extremely important.

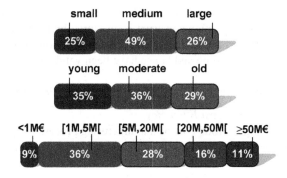

**Fig. 1.** Sample profile

**Table 1.** Variables Associated with Market Focus Strategy

| | |
|---|---|
| 1 | Making incremental changes in current products for current markets. |
| 2 | Developing new products for current products. |
| 3 | Entering new markets with current products. |
| 4 | Entering new markets with new products. |

**Table 2.** Variables Associated with Technology Development Strategy

| | |
|---|---|
| 1 | Developing new technology. |
| 2 | Improving its own technology. |
| 3 | Improving technology developed by others. |
| 4 | Using technology developed by others. |

For technology development strategy, on the other hand, for responding to the question on "the level of resource allocated to execute technology development strategy over the last three years" the 5-point Likert scale employed ranges from 1= no resource allocated to 5= all available resources are allocated. The variables are listed in Table 2. For both market focus and technology development the variables are adapted from Akova et al. (1998).

The questions about operations priorities are provided in Table 3. They are asked using a 5-point Likert scale and inquiring how important each operations priority is for the firm with the scale ranging from 1=extremely unimportant to 5= extremely important. Here we adopt cost, quality, flexibility and delivery/dependability as operations priorities, which have become widely used as statements of the competitive dimensions of manufacturing firms. The variables of the four different operations priorities' measures are adapted from existing OM literature. The base of items asked regarding these operations priorities are adapted mainly from Boyer and Lewis (2002), Alpkan et al. (2003), Noble (1997), Ward et al. (1998), Vickery et al. (1993), Kathuria (2000) and Olson et al. (2005).

Innovation constructs are associated with those four different innovation types mentioned earlier. Each innovation construct is measured by its original measurement items, which are developed accordingly. Therefore, innovation measures used in this research are new for the literature and hence have been validated.

**Table 3.** Variables Associated with Operations Priorities

| | |
|---|---|
| *Variables Associated with Cost Efficiency* | |
| 1 | Decreasing the total cost of manufacturing processes. |
| 2 | Decreasing the total cost of internal and external logistics processes. |
| 3 | Decreasing the operating costs. |
| 4 | Increasing the personnel productivity. |
| 5 | Decreasing the input costs. |
| 6 | Decreasing the personnel costs. |
| *Variables Associated with Flexibility* | |
| 1 | Increasing the capability of flexible use of current personnel and hardware for non-standard products. |
| 2 | Increasing the capability of producing non-standard products. |
| 3 | Decreasing the rejection rate of product orders with non-standard specifications. |
| 4 | Increasing the capability to change the current machine schedule depending on changing the order priorities. |
| 5 | Increasing the capability of flexibility in product processes. |
| 6 | Increasing the capability of flexibility to change the order priorities depending on the status of the orders. |
| 7 | Increasing the capability of manufacturing personnel to work in varying operations and processes. |
| *Variables Associated with Dependability/Delivery* | |
| 1 | Increasing the delivery speed of end products. |
| 2 | Decreasing the duration from start of manufacturing process to the end of delivery. |
| 3 | Increasing the ability to meet the delivery commitments. |
| 4 | Decreasing the duration from taking an order to the end of delivery. |
| 5 | Increasing the ability for just in time delivery. |
| 6 | Decreasing the difficulties associated with delivery to a minimum. |
| *Variables Associated with Quality* | |
| 1 | Increasing the customers' perception for product and service quality. |
| 2 | Increasing the product and service quality compared to competitors. |
| 3 | Decreasing the customer complaints. |
| 4 | Decreasing the quantity of waste, scrap and rework. |
| 5 | Decreasing the quantity of defective intermediate and end products. |
| 6 | Decreasing the number of returns from customers. |

For the measurement of different types of innovative capabilities the respondents are asked to indicate "to what extent the innovations implemented in their organization in the last three years related to the following kinds of activities" on a 5-point Likert scale ranging from 1=not implemented, 2=imitated from national markets, 3=imitated from international markets, 4=currently practiced endogenous innovations are improved, 5=original indigenous innovations are implemented. Due to space limitation we will refer the reader to Günday et al. (2011) for a complete list of variables used for the measurement of product, process, market and organizational innovations.

# 3    Analysis and Results

The multivariate data analysis is performed in three stages using statistical software packages SPSS v17 and AMOS v16.

In the first stage, principal component analysis (PCA) with varimax rotation is conducted to find out the underlying dimensions of business strategy items and innovativeness. PCA on business strategy items produced 6 factors with latent root criterion and the average of communalities was 0.551. All the variables given in Tables 1-3 are included in the factors. The six factors obtained are assigned the following titles: quality, flexibility, delivery and dependability, cost efficiency, market focus, and technology development strategies. The total variance explained is 55.1%. The Cronbach $\alpha$ values are $\geq 0.62$ suggesting construct reliability.

The PCA on innovativeness extracted 5 factors with eigenvalues $> 1$, which are labeled based on the variables involved:  Organizational, marketing, process, incremental product, and radical product innovations. The total variance explained is 63.7%. The Cronbach $\alpha$ values are $\geq 0.7$ suggesting construct reliability. Then we construct an aggregate innovativeness factor as the average of five innovation factors obtained with a Cronbach $\alpha=0.812$, indicating acceptable reliability.

**Table 4.** Correlation Analysis of Business Strategies

| | Mean | Std Dev | Inn | Qual | CEff | Flex | Dep | MFoc | Tech |
|---|---|---|---|---|---|---|---|---|---|
| Innovativeness | 2.81 | 0.84 | 1 | 0.193 (*) | 0.228 (**) | 0.206 (**) | 0.178 (*) | 0.373 (**) | 0.323 (**) |
| Quality | 4.68 | 0.43 | (*) | 1 | 0.551 (*) | 0.240 (**) | 0.415 (**) | 0.130 | 0.222 (**) |
| Cost Efficiency | 4.40 | 0.51 | (**) | (**) | 1 | 0.346 (**) | 0.457 (**) | 0.154 (*) | 0.191 (*) |
| Flexibility | 3.72 | 0.73 | (**) | (**) | (**) | 1 | 0.517 (**) | 0.195 (*) | 0.091 |
| Depend /Delivery | 4.36 | 0.57 | (*) | (**) | (**) | (**) | 1 | 0.203 (**) | 0.120 |
| Market Focus | 3.67 | 0.82 | (**) | | (*) | (*) | (**) | 1 | 0.235 (**) |
| Tech. Dev. | 2.80 | 0.82 | (**) | (**) | (*) | | | (**) | 1 |
| (**) $p<0.01$;   (*) $p<0.05$ | | | | | | | | | |

The second stage involves correlation and regression analysis. The correlation analysis indicates a strong positive association between innovativeness and business strategy factors (Table 4). Significant one-to-one positive relationships of the aggregated factors are extracted from the correlation analysis. All business strategy factors correlate very significantly to innovativeness with $p<0.01$ except quality and dependability/delivery ($p<0.05$). Therefore, we can generally deduce that the higher importance given to operations priorities, market focus and technology development are associated with increased innovative capabilities.

**Table 5.** Effects of Business Strategies on Innovativeness

| Independent Variables | Standard | $p$-Value |
|---|---|---|
| Cost Efficiency | 0.115 | 0.190 |
| Quality | 0.051 | 0.547 |
| Depend/Delivery | -0.058 | 0.511 |
| Flexibility | 0.108 | 0.189 |
| Market Focus | 0.315 | 0.000 |
| Technology | 0.209 | 0.004 |

This regression model is statistically very significant ($p<0.01$) and the independent variables express 24.6% ($R^2=0.246$) of innovativeness. However, when business strategies have entered together to the multiple regression, only market focus ($\beta=0.315$; $p<0.01$) and technology development ($\beta=0.209$; $p<0.01$) have significant positive effects on innovativeness (Table 5). Thus, despite the fact that the model is significant, multiple regression analysis reveals only some business strategies have statistically significant effects over innovativeness. Moreover, correlation analysis already indicated all business strategy factors had significant one-to-one correlation to innovativeness. Hence, post hoc analysis reveals that market focus and technology development factors mediated the effects of cost efficiency, dependability/delivery, quality and flexibility factors on innovativeness.

In the third stage, based on the arguments above, a single-step Structural Equation Modeling (SEM) is performed to depict the relationship between business strategies and innovativeness with the simultaneous estimation of both measurement and structural models by AMOS v16 and analyzed according to goodness-of-fit indices. The resulting proposed paths of relations matching business strategies to innovativeness are presented in Figure 2. It summarizes the main findings of SEM analysis. The estimates on the arrows are regression weights and the estimates on the box corners are the squared multiple correlations. Each regression weight estimate in the model is statistically significant ($p<0.05$). 23% of the innovativeness can be explained by that model. Market focus and cost efficiency have direct effects on innovativeness.

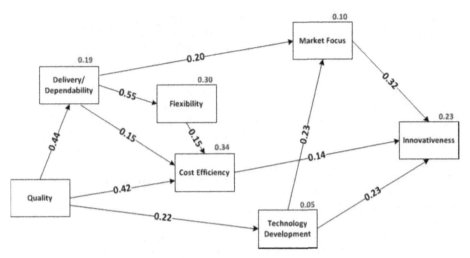

**Fig. 2.** Path analysis of business strategy components and innovativeness

# 4    Conclusions

In this paper, the hypothesis that there is a positive relationship between business strategy and innovativeness has been tested. The analysis is based on an empirical study conducted covering 184 manufacturing companies from the Northern Marmara region of Turkey. The findings summarized above expose the positive relationship between business strategy and innovativeness despite mediating effects between variables. Hence, the hypothesis put forward is supported.

The finding that market focus and technology development factors mediate the effects of operations priorities on innovativeness reveals the supporting role of operations priorities on these factors. That market focus, technology development and cost efficiency have direct effects on innovativeness is a further verification of this web of interactions of great managerial importance. But cost efficiency also depends on the manufacturing capabilities -quality, delivery/dependability, and flexibility. In order to be cost efficient, the firm has to manage all these capabilities in a complementary way rather than trading one against the other.

**Acknowledgement.** This research was supported by a grant from the Scientific and Technological Research Council of Turkey (TUBITAK) (SOBAG-105K105).

# References

1. Akova, B., Ulusoy, G., Payzın, E., Kaylan, A.R.: New Product Development Capabilities of the Turkish Electronics Industry. In: 5th International Product Development Management Conference, Como, pp. 863–876 (1998)
2. Alpkan, L., Ceylan, A., Aytekin, M.: Performance impacts of operations strategies: a study on Turkish manufacturing firms. International Journal of Agile Manufacturing 6, 57–65 (2003)

3. Boyer, K.K., Lewis, M.W.: Competitive priorities: Investigating the need for trade-offs in operations strategy. Production and Operations Management 11, 9–20 (2002)
4. Günday, G., Ulusoy, G., Kılıç, K., Alpkan, L.: Effects of innovation types on firm performance. International Journal of Production Economics 133, 662–676 (2011)
5. Hayes, R.H., Wheelwright, S.G.: Link manufacturing process and product life cycles. Harvard Business Review, 133–140 (January-February 1979)
6. Kathuria, R.: Competitive priorities and managerial performance: A taxonomy of small manufacturers. Journal of Operations Management 18, 627–641 (2000)
7. Khazanchi, S., Lewis, M.W., Boyer, K.K.: Innovation-supportive culture: The impact of organizational values on process innovation. Journal of Operations Management 25, 871–884 (2007)
8. Leong, G., Snyder, D., Ward, P.T.: Research in process and content of manufacturing strategy. Omega 18, 109–122 (1990)
9. Metcalfe, J.S.: Evolutionary Economics and Creative Destruction. Routledge, London (1998)
10. Noble, M.A.: Manufacturing competitive priorities and productivity: An empirical study. International Journal of Operations & Production Management 17, 85–99 (1997)
11. OECD: Oslo Manual: Proposed Guidelines for Collecting and Interpreting Technological Innovation Data. 3rd edn., Paris (2005)
12. Olson, E.M., Slater, S.F., Hult, G.T.M.: The performance implications of fit among business strategy, marketing organization structure, and strategic behavior. Journal of Marketing 69, 49–65 (2005)
13. Salavou, H.: The concept of innovativeness: Should we need to focus? European Journal of Innovation Management 7, 33–44 (2004)
14. Vickery, S.K., Droge, C., Markland, R.E.: Production competence and business strategy: Do they affect business performance? Decision Sciences 24, 435–455 (1993)
15. Ward, P.T., Mccreery, J.K., Ritzman, L.P., Sharma, D.: Competitive priorities in operations management. Decision Sciences 29, 1035–1046 (1998)

# International R&D and Manufacturing Networks: Dynamism, Structure and Absorptive Capacity

Patricia Deflorin[1], Maike Scherrer-Rathje[2], and Helmut Dietl[1]

[1]Department of Business Administration, University of Zurich, Switzerland
(patricia.deflorin,helmut.dietl)@business.uzh.ch
[2]Institute of Technology Management, University of St. Gallen, Switzerland
maike.scherrer@unisg.ch

**Abstract.** We analyze the absorptive capacity (AC) process of a manufacturing company with central R&D and an internationally distributed manufacturing network. Prior research shows that an implementation of the lead factory (LF) is especially supportive if the international manufacturing network struggles with implementing new products and processes. We analyze determinants of AC and show that, in addition to prior related knowledge of the receiving plant, structure can have an even stronger influence. We show that in the case of a low level of prior related knowledge and a low level of AC within the receiving plants as well as high technological heterogeneity between plants and LF, the implementation of an LF may not lead to the expected result. In addition, we conclude that the analysis of the AC process has to move from a single unit to a network. This helps to understand the AC concept in the context of multinational companies.

**Keywords:** Absorptive capacity, Lead factory, New product introduction.

## 1 Introduction

Developing and maintaining absorptive capacity (AC) is critical to the long-term survival and success of a company. We apply the sequential process framework of AC as proposed by Lane et al. (2006): recognizing and understanding potentially valuable new external knowledge through exploratory learning, assimilating new knowledge through transformative learning, and using the assimilated knowledge to create new knowledge through exploitative learning.

It is our purpose to show, based on the analysis of a new product introduction (NPI) within a manufacturing company with internationally distributed plants, how organizational antecedents, specifically structural drivers and related prior knowledge influence the efficiency and effectiveness of the AC process. To understand the AC output, we must consider its activities, starting with R&D and ending with the production of the product. An analysis of the AC process must supersede an isolated focus on R&D activities. The AC process must instead span over the R&D and production network. We analyze the assumption that the Lead Factory (LF) concept helps to overcome a low level of prior related knowledge in the receiving plants and a low AC

C. Emmanouilidis, M. Taisch, D. Kiritsis (Eds.): APMS 2012, Part I, IFIP AICT 397, pp. 693–700, 2013.
© IFIP International Federation for Information Processing 2013

level. The implementation of an LF concept aims to support the knowledge of receiving plants. Therefore, if the level of prior related knowledge of the plants differs within the international production network, the implementation of an LF concept could be a solution that would improve the efficiency and effectiveness of the AC process and its outcome. We highlight the usefulness of the lead factory concept. Further, we show that, despite a low level of prior related knowledge within the receiving plants, the implementation of the lead factory concept may still not be sufficient and may result in a lower level of AC efficiency and effectiveness than expected.

## 2     Review: Organizational Antecedents, AC and Outcome

Many researchers have analyzed the different factors influencing the AC process and its outcomes. Based on a literature analysis, Volberda et al. (2010) have developed an integrative framework of AC. The framework consists of managerial antecedents, intra-organizational antecedents, inter-organizational antecedents, and prior related knowledge. These factors are assumed to influence the efficiency and effectiveness of the AC process. Further, environmental conditions moderate the AC process and its outcome. We focus our analysis on intra-organizational antecedents, more specifically, the influence of the organizational form on the AC process as well as the relationship to prior related knowledge (see Fig. 1).

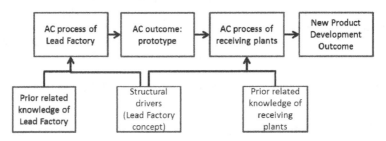

**Fig. 1.** The lead factory concept and its influence on AC outcome

### 2.1     AC Process

We apply the multidimensional view of AC as proposed by Cohen and Levinthal (1990) and Lane et al. (2006). The first step in the process entails the exploratory learning needed to recognize and understand new external knowledge. The second dimension focuses on the assimilation of knowledge through transformative learning. Finally, the third dimension focuses on exploitative learning and how it is used to assimilate new knowledge. The separation between the three different dimensions of AC helps to recognize the different nature of the processes in achieving an understanding of the relationship between the factors influencing the efficiency and effectiveness of the AC process and the AC process itself.

## 2.2     Structural Drivers of the Lead Factory Concept

We focus our analysis on the internal drivers of AC, specifically the organizational structure of a firm. A firm's knowledge base cannot be separated from its organizational structure (Grant, 1996). Lane et al. (2006) highlight the need to focus attention on the structure, policies, and processes within the organization that affect knowledge transfer, sharing, integration, and creation. They highlight the importance of understanding the influence of these factors, as they seem to drive the efficiency and the effectiveness of the firm's AC (Lane et al., 2006). We focus our analysis on the structure of the lead factory concept and how such a structure influences the efficiency and effectiveness of the AC process.

The link between R&D and manufacturing with respect to the success of new product introductions (NPI) has been analyzed and proven important in many studies (Kessler and Chakrabarti, 1999, Swink, 1999). Many problems in NPI can be traced to a lack of R&D–manufacturing coordination (Swink, 2003). To overcome these coordination issues, companies have started to implement a lead factory (Ferdows, 1997). A lead factory is the strategic heart of the manufacturing network, as it links R&D and the manufacturing department and acts as a knowledge incubator. It translates R&D knowledge into manufacturing knowledge (Deflorin et al., 2012). It also develops the production processes and documents and produces the prototype. In addition, the employees of the lead factory support the production ramp-up within the receiving plants. The role of the lead factory, also called the center of excellence, has been the focus of several studies (Leonard-Barton, 1995, Ferdows, 1997, Frost et al., 2002). We assume that the lead factory concept influences the efficiency and effectiveness of the AC process and its outcome. We therefore analyze how the structural drivers of the lead factory concept influence the AC process of the lead factory and the receiving plant.

## 2.3     Prior Related Knowledge

Prior related knowledge is often seen as a most important antecedent to AC (Cohen and Levinthal, 1990). Existing knowledge helps in the recognition of new knowledge and its assimilation. In addition, plants with a low level of prior related knowledge are often in need of external support (e.g., a lead factory). The importance of prior related knowledge, however, has been challenged. We analyze how the factors "prior related knowledge" and "structural drivers" jointly influence the AC process and its outcome.

## 2.4     AC Outcome

Research on AC is often focused on R&D, and output is measured with innovation-related performance measures or is directly linked to overall firm performance (Volberda et al., 2010). As we expand the research focus on the process of new product introduction (from R&D to serial production), we measure the efficiency and effectiveness of the NPI output.

# 3    Methodology

We applied a qualitative case study approach in order to gain new insights into the relationship between structure, prior related knowledge, the AC process, and NPI output. Thus, we collected data from each of the AC process steps by employees responsible for implementing new products through structured interviews. In addition, we attended meetings of NPI project leaders and analyzed archival sources. This exploratory research method embodies the theory-building approach of Yin (1994) and Eisenhardt (1989). The unit of analysis is the NPI process of a Swiss manufacturing company called Machinery, Inc. The analyzed NPI was started within the central R&D department. The following process steps were investigated: development (R&D), prototyping (lead factory), and serial production (receiving plant).

# 4    Case Analysis: Transferring Knowledge between R&D, LF and CN Plant

Machinery Inc. has a central R&D department, a lead factory (LF) and decentralized plants. The following analysis focuses on the link between R&D, LF and a receiving plant in China (CN). Machinery Inc. is a traditional machinery producer with strong and experienced R&D and production departments in Switzerland. Due to the increasing price pressure and the growing market in China, Machinery Inc. decided to build a new plant in the country. To help the Chinese plant develop the required capabilities and knowledge stock, the company decided to implement the lead factory concept. The Swiss plant acts as a lead factory. It is highly interlinked to the R&D department, translates the developed product into production requirements, and develops the first prototype/product and the respective processes. The knowledge required to produce the machine is then transferred to the Chinese plant (CN), the receiving plant. The CN plant translates the new knowledge into its own operating environment, adapts procurement and starts producing the serial production.

## 4.1    LF Concept, Prior Related Knowledge and AC Process Outcome of the LF

To translate external knowledge into new products, R&D recognizes, assimilates and applies knowledge (Lane et al., 2006). This knowledge is then transferred to the LF. The LF recognizes and assimilates knowledge and translates the R&D material (e.g., drawings) into production knowledge. Concretely, the department develops processes required to develop the first prototype. The assimilated knowledge is then translated into applied knowledge – the production of the prototype.

The implementation of the LF concept has led to the following structural drivers which influence the AC process of the LF. First, R&D and LF are part of the same cultural background and speak the same linguistic language. The plants are physically close, and there is intensive formal and informal information sharing. The relationship between R&D and LF is strong, as the employees have known each other for many years. These structural drivers positively influence the AC process of the LF.

Both departments are experts in their respective fields. Due to the many NPIs during the last 50 years, both departments have a high level of related knowledge. This knowledge helps the LF employees to recognize knew knowledge and assimilate it. The prior related knowledge has a strong influence on the efficiency and effectiveness of the AC process. The employees of the LF are familiar with NPI and the recognition and translation of R&D information into the production environment. Therefore, the prior related knowledge of the LF positively influences the AC process and leads to a fast and dependable AC output; i.e., the prototype.

The LF employees state that the assimilation, transformation and application of the transferred knowledge do not lead to difficulties because of the structural drivers and the prior related knowledge stated above. The number of loops needed to adapt the R&D output to the LF's production requirements is low and because of the structural drivers of the concept and the related prior knowledge, effective and efficient. The output of the LF's AC process, i.e., the prototype of the new product, is dependable, fast and achieves a high quality level. The left side of Fig. 2 summarizes the findings.

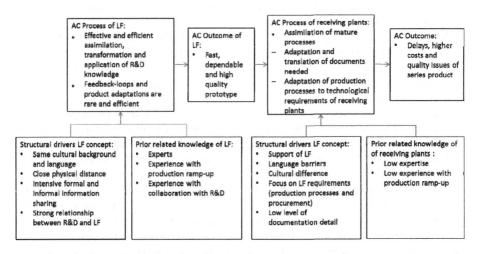

**Fig. 2.** The LF concept, prior related knowledge, AC process and outcome

## 4.2    LF Concept, Prior Related Knowledge and AC Process Outcome of the Receiving Plant

The CN plant receives the knowledge transferred from the LF. The receiving plant must recognize the new knowledge, transform it into its own production requirements and apply it with the goal of reaching serial production of the new product.

The transferred process and product documentation are of high quality. The R&D documents have already been improved based on the input gained while producing the prototype. Therefore, the AC outcome of the LF positively influences the AC process of the receiving plant.

Considering the structural drivers, a mixed influence on the AC process of the receiving plant is visible. Due to the intermediary responsibilities of the LF, employees support the transfer and help the CN employees to recognize and assimilate the new knowledge. The recognition and assimilation, however, is negatively influenced through language barriers and cultural distance. Documents have to be adapted and translated, leading to a negative influence on the efficiency and effectiveness of the AC process. The central R&D is focused on the requirements of the LF. R&D employees are well informed about the equipment and capabilities of the Swiss plant and develop the product accordingly. Further, the production process and its documentation are developed according to the specifications of the Swiss plant. In addition, the procurement is also focused on the Swiss requirements. Therefore, the assimilation and application of the knowledge within the LF only partly supports the AC process within the CN plant. In addition, due to the close and long-term relationship between R&D and LF, the documentation is not as detailed as it should be in order to allow an easy and fast adaptation of the documents and processes. The transformation needed within the CN plant is time consuming and often results in a lower quality level of the final product than the prototype constructed from the lead factory. Despite the positive effect of the LF concept, depending on the intensity of the aforementioned factors, the negative effects may have a stronger influence on the efficiency and effectiveness of the AC process.

After the assimilation of the transferred knowledge, full serial production begins (application). The low labor and material cost advantage should lead to a better cost performance. However, as the machines were constructed according to Swiss standards and only partially adapted, some of the anticipated cost savings were not achieved. For example, the engine of the machine was still delivered from the Swiss standard supplier because the CN plant did not have enough time and experience to define a comparable supplier. In addition, the production employees did not have the capabilities to improve the processes designed to achieve additional cost savings.

The analysis of the influence of the prior related knowledge available at the CN plant revealed the following issues. Due to the relatively young age of the plant, employees do not have the same experience and expertise as their Swiss counterparts. Despite being in the position to receive an already-tested product and documentations from the LF, the structural drivers of the LF concepts necessitate that the knowledge received be transformed into its own production requirements. This transformation is difficult and time consuming, as CN plant employees are not used to assimilating knowledge or adapting and improving production processes; the respective prior knowledge is missing, and the AC level is low.

Based on the output of the central units (R&D and LF) and the AC process of the CN plant, the NPI leads to the following results. The prototype was produced quickly and was proven dependable with a high level of quality. The recognition, assimilation and application process within the CN plants, however, was time consuming and the delivery of the series was delayed. In addition, there was a quality difference between the prototype and the CN-produced machines; for example, the machines were produced with different types of steels, and the CN steel was not rust free. The expected costs were only partially achieved. The strong focus on the Swiss production requirements prevented a successful transfer and full cost-saving potential.

# 5    Discussion

Machinery Inc. has invested in new plants in order to become internationally competitive and to be able to serve new and expanding markets. The new plants, however, have difficulties in recognizing, assimilating and applying knowledge. The supporting activities from the LF were implemented to strengthen the AC process within the receiving plant. The analysis of the structural drivers from the lead factory concept reveals that the concept has its weaknesses, which became visible while analyzing the efficiency and effectiveness of the AC process. The main structural issue of the LF concept stems from the focus of the LF requirements, leading to new assimilation needs within the receiving plants. The need to assimilate knowledge within the receiving plant is still present if the receiving plant has built up its knowledge stock. These negative effects out of the structural drivers of the lead factory, however, would not apply if the LF and the receiving plant applied identical technologies and process steps. Therefore, the higher the technological heterogeneity between the plants, the lower the positive effects of the structural drivers of the LF concept.

The analysis of the AC processes of the LF and receiving plants leads to a different structural possibility for Machinery Inc. To overcome the issues related to the strong focus on the LF's requirements, central R&D could transfer the knowledge to a local team of developers (application development). The application developers would know the requirements of the CN plant and would therefore be able to adapt the documents to the local needs. In addition, this structural solution should strengthen the efficiency and effectiveness of the AC process of the CN plant as there are no language barriers between the application developers and the plant. In addition, there would be only a short distance and no cultural differences. This solution would ensure the assimilation of the transferred knowledge and allow an efficient and effective application without neglecting local advantages and without the additional costs of a lead factory.

# 6    Conclusion

We strengthen the construct of AC in exploring its important determinants. We argue that, in addition to prior related knowledge as a determinant of AC, structure can have an even stronger influence. Further, we show that the activities described in the AC process framework span different network units (R&D, LF and plants). The consequences of the chosen structural solution reveal that an analysis of the AC process and outcome should span the whole network and move away from the single analysis of the R&D activities. Therefore, the unit of analysis moves from a single unit to a network. This helps in the understanding of the AC concept in the context of multinational companies.

Our framework shows the relationship between organizational structure and AC. More specifically, we analyze the effect of the lead factory concept. The analysis of Machinery Inc. shows that in the presented circumstances, the negative effect from the chosen structural solution seems stronger than the positive effects from the supporting activities of the LF. We therefore come to the preliminary conclusion that it is important to understand under which circumstances the lead factory concept is more or less suitable. Technological heterogeneity between the plants may reduce the positive effect of the LF concept and lead to a lower efficiency and effectiveness of the AC process than expected. The lead factory concept seems to be most suitable if there is high technological homogeneity between the plants and if the LF and the AC levels of the receiving plants are sufficiently high. Otherwise, the support of the lead factory may still be insufficient to assimilate and apply the transferred knowledge.

From a managerial perspective, different structural solutions must be implemented to strengthen the AC output. Based on the results of this single case study, we propose that in the case of high technological homogeneity, the implementation of an LF may be suitable. In the case of high technological heterogeneity, however, the strengthening of the AC output may be supported with the implementation of a local application development to overcome the negative influence of the LF's structural drivers on the efficiency and effectiveness of the AC process.

# References

Cohen, W.M., Levinthal, D.A.: Absorptive Capacity: A New Perspective on Learning and Innovation. Administrative Science Quarterly 35, 128–152 (1990)

Deflorin, P., Dietl, H., Lang, M., Scherrer-Rathje, M.: The Lead Factory Concept: Benefiting from an Efficient Knowledge Transfer. Journal of Manufacturing Technology Management 23, 517–534 (2012)

Ferdows, K.: Making the Most of Foreign Factories. Harvard Business Review 75, 73–88 (1997)

Frost, T.S., Birkinshaw, J.M., Ensign, P.C.: Centers of Excellence in multinational corporations. Strategic Management Journal 23, 997–1018 (2002)

Grant, R.M.: Prospering in Dynamically-Competitive Environments: Organizational Capability as Knowledge Integration. Organization Science 7, 375–387 (1996)

Kessler, E.H., Chakrabarti, A.K.: Speeding Up the Pace of New Product Development. Journal of Product Innovation Management 16, 231–247 (1999)

Lane, P.J., Koka, B.R., Pathak, S.: The reification of absorptive capacity: A critical review and rejuvenation of the construct. Academy of Management Review 31, 833–863 (2006)

Leonard-Barton, D.: Wellsprings of Knowledge. Harvard Business School Press, Boston (1995)

Swink, M.: Completing projects on-time: how project acceleration affects new product development. Journal of Engineering and Technology Management 20, 319–344 (2003)

Swink, M.: Threats to new product manufacturability and the effects of development team integration processes. Journal of Operations Management 17, 691 (1999)

Volberda, H.W., Foss, N.J., Lyles, M.A.: Perspective - Absorbing the Concept of Absorptive Capacity: How to Realize Its Potential in the Organization Field. Organization Science 21, 931–951 (2010)

# Building a Conceptual Model for Analyzing Sustainability Projects Aiming at Technology Transfer: A Terminological Approach

Deise Rocha Martins dos Santos Oliveira[1,2], Irenilza de Alencar Nääs[1],
Ivo Pierozzi Júnior[2], and Oduvaldo Vendrametto[1]

[1] Paulista University-UNIP, Graduate Program in Production Engineering,
Dr. Bacelar St. 1212, São Paulo, Brazil
`irenilza@gmail.com, oduvaldov@uol.com.br`
[2] Embrapa Agricultural Informatics, Dr. André Tosello Avenue, 209,
Barão Geraldo, P.O. Box 6041, 13083-886, Campinas, SP, Brazil
`deise.oliveira@gmail.com, ivo@cnptia.embrapa.br`

**Abstract.** R&DI institutions have adopted solutions based on Portfolio Management Project (PMP) to select the best projects in terms of both cost and strategic results. The candidate projects must meet sustainability requirements, since investments in sustainability have emerged as the most important global issue for business, industry, government, and academia. The objective of this research was to develop a conceptual model for analyzing a portfolio of sustainability projects. Such a portfolio provides descriptors widely recognized to support technology transfer, notably in the agricultural domain. This conceptual model was developed from a case study of Embrapa (Brazilian Agricultural Research Corporation). Although the proposed model has become a simple tool, the results revealed it is interesting for reclassification of the Embrapa's projects, pointing to solutions on sustainability with a potential for technology transfer.

**Keywords:** Portfolio Management Project, Embrapa's project portfolio, Standardized categoriation system, Agrovoc, Thesaurus.

## 1 Introduction

Every institution is subject to limited resources, either material, financial or personal. To reduce inefficient allocation of resources is essential to implement a selection process for identifying what are the projects of highest priority and value.

Institutions without clear criteria for selecting projects face high-risk investment in wrong projects. Clearly, such institution requires a rational and concrete process capable of justifying the decisions on project selection. The focus should not be just in terms of cost, but also concerning the return that such projects can offer. In doing so, some projects must be eliminated or even delayed according to the value they contribute to an institution mission [1].

C. Emmanouilidis, M. Taisch, D. Kiritsis (Eds.): APMS 2012, Part I, IFIP AICT 397, pp. 701–707, 2013.

In searching for choices that add value and justify their investments, many institutions have adopted solutions based on Portfolio Management Project (PMP). These solutions provide a repository of projects that allow for monitoring results and facilitating the capture of lessons learned from the strategic decisions taken in the past [2], besides other advantages.

In particular, R&DI institutions have adopted solutions based on PMP not only to reduce direct and indirect costs, but also to eliminate redundant and inefficient projects [3]. The selected projects aim at providing solutions capable of encompassing technologies, products and services (TPS) designed to meet the needs of the market. The challenge, however, goes further: it is not enough to have technologies, products and services that satisfy human needs, such solutions must be sustainable across time and space, and in environmental, social and economic dimensions.

Sustainability has emerged as the most important global issue for business, industry, government, and academia. According to WCED [4], sustainable development is a process in which there is harmony between resource exploitation, the direction of investments, the orientation of technological development and institutional changes that enrich both present and future, as a potential for meet the needs and aspirations of human beings. It is inserted in all productive sectors, particularly in agriculture, which is a sector that requires attention due to the interfaces that its activities establish with environment, economy and society in general. Moreover, agriculture is the sector responsible for the production of raw materials for food, fiber and, more recently, for alternative energy.

Issues of sustainable agriculture are related to human survival. The use of land, soil and water, global climate change, food safety, vegetal and animal sanity are some of the Government concerns, but also became part of our day-to-day lives. The environmental, social and economic aspects make it clear that technologies, products and services are priorities for any program on sustainable agriculture and livestock.

The objective of this research was to develop a conceptual model that facilitates the analysis of a portfolio for sustainability projects. Such portfolio provides descriptors widely recognized to support technology transfer, notably information related to the sustainability of agricultural activities. This conceptual model was developed from a case study of Brazilian Agricultural Research Corporation (Embrapa).

## 2    Methodology

The terminological conceptual model is proposed to investigate a project's database developed by Embrapa. It is important to learn with past experiences to plan future projects, always considering the companies' mission and strategies. In this research, the aim is to reach projects focused on sustainability and technology transfer.

The proposed model is based on a theoretical referential explored in processes of documentary analysis, organization and knowledge representation. Such a model borrows some elements from the Concept Theory, the Faceted Classification Theory; the General Terminology Theory; and the Communicative Terminology Theory [5-7].

The proposed model assumes that all the knowledge is based in concepts which human mind organizes everything that can be understood in the real world. The concepts can be represented by words that are part of a special vocabulary, called terminologies. This model can facilitate the information recover and organization process.

To initiate this process, a user can enter terms describing the research (sustainability and technology transfer) into AGROVOC thesaurus. AGROVOC thesaurus is a terminological resource that contains over 40,000 concepts about food, nutrition, agriculture, fishery, forestry, environment and other related areas. It was developed in English and it is held by the Food and Agriculture Organization (FAO), an organization linked to the United Nations (UN) and headquartered in Rome, Italy [8]. AGROVOC is part of Agriculture Information Management Standarts (AIMS) that is a web portal managed by FAO and that disseminates standards and good practices in information management for the support of the right to food, sustainable agriculture and rural development.

A thesaurus is a system (or model) for knowledge organization and representation that evolves progressively in terms of structure and function of specialized vocabularies, and where synonyms, polysemies or associative and hierarchical relationships between terms are established according to a pattern internationally recognized [9].

Based on the keywords "sustainability" and "technology transfer", submitted to AGROVOC, we built up a list of generic terms for the agricultural domain. From those generic terms, we recovered the related terms and, subsequently, it was performed a mapping of the terms extracted. Based on these terms, a standardized categorization system is then organized to represent the best descriptors for technologies, processes or services regarding the agricultural sector. The projects are organized into a hierarchical tree [10] and the keywords retrieved from the Embrapa's project portfolio can be either submitted again for new analysis, or used to select projects whose results are related to sustainability and have potential for technology transfer. The same methodology can be used for any or different group of words. Actually, when the words are submitted to AGROVOC, it is not compulsory that they really have related words. In this case, we found some related words, and this helped us in the research.

It is important to note that, originally, the projects and the database were written in Portuguese. Portuguese is one of the 21 languages presented by AGROVOC. So, this work was done in that language. Only for this paper, we translated into English, using the terms shown by AGROVOC.

We adopted a methodology of exploratory research that, according to Gil [11], it is designed to provide an overview on a particular fact, not formulating accurate hypotheses. So, our theoretical referential was based on a literature survey comprising the domains of sustainability and technology transfer.

We performed the case study at Embrapa. In Brazil, Embrapa is an institution focused on RD & I with a mission to provide solutions for the sustainable development of agriculture [12]. Its bibliographical asset and its project portfolio are vast, covering many different subjects. But only from late 90's, the subject on sustainability has received a special attention. The main questions for this research were: What projects are those? What were their results? Do they still feasible nowadays?

The case study was conducted by extracting keywords announced by the authors from Embrapa's project portfolio, which is composed of 14,736 projects, comprising the period from 1994 to 2009.

# 3    Results and Discussion

In institutions of RD & I, the TPS are developed from research projects. In general, these institutions work with a project portfolio often designed with different logics of organization and planning. However, these portfolios rarely establish strategies a priori for transferring of the generated knowledge. If this issue is thought afterwards, it can create conflicts of interest or even technical and administrative barriers, such as those related to intellectual and industrial property, or copyright, in addition to rework to its evaluation from this point of view.

According to Cribb [13] technology transfer is understood as the displacement of technological knowledge from one place to another. According to Tigre [14], an innovation only produces comprehensive impact when it is spread widely across companies, sectors and regions, unleashing new ventures and creating new markets. Tigre also says that the dynamics of diffusion can be understood as the adoption path of a technology in the market, with focus on the characteristics of technology and other elements that influence its pace and direction.

As we mentioned previously, we performed a case study taking into account the Embrapa's project portfolio with the purpose of validating the conceptual model for analyzing sustainability projects aiming at technology transfer. The purpose is to understand what was done in the past and plan future projects for the Organization.

In this model, we assume that all knowledge is based on concepts under which the human intellect categorizes all the things that we understand in the real world. The concepts can be represented by words that make special vocabularies, called terminologies. Thus, by means of terminological resources, the proposed model aims at facilitating the recovery and reorganization of the desired information. A sketch of the proposed model is depicted in Figure 1.

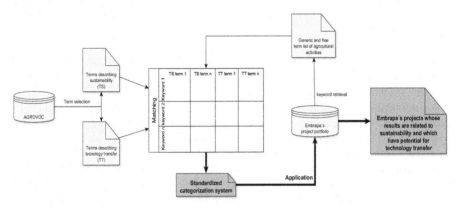

**Fig. 1.** A general view of the proposed model for analyzing sustainability projects

First, we entered the word "sustainability" into AGROVOC and recovered 17 related terms, as can be seen in Table 1.

**Table 1.** Related terms available at AGROVOC related to sustainability

| Relationship Type* | Term |
|---|---|
| RT | Ecology |
| RT | natural resources |
| RT | agroecosystems |
| RT | biological production |
| RT | sustainable land management |
| RT | integrated land management |
| RT | sustainable development |
| RT | balance of nature |
| RT | low input agriculture |
| RT | sustainable agriculture |
| RT | conservation tillage |
| RT | sustainable forestry |
| RT | socioeconomic development |
| RT | alternative agriculture |
| RT | farm inputs |
| RT | draught animal cultivation |
| RT | resource management |

**\*Legend:** Standardized relationships of a thesaurus: "used for" (UF); "broader term" (BT); "narrowed terms" (NT);"related terms"(RT).

In the next step, we then entered the term "technology transfer" into AGROVOC and found 17 related as presented in Table 2.

**Table 2.** Related terms available at AGROVOC related to technology transfer

| Relationship Type* | Term |
|---|---|
| UF | application of technology |
| BT | Activities |
| NT | diffusion of research |
| NT | innovation adoption |
| RT | Research |
| RT | pilot farms |
| RT | Patents |
| RT | appropriate technology |
| RT | Modernization |
| RT | diffusion of information |
| RT | digital divide |
| RT | research networks |
| RT | communication technology |
| RT | extension activities |
| RT | Innovation |
| RT | Exhibitions |
| RT | technological changes |

**\*Legend:** Standardized relationships of a thesaurus: "used for" (UF); "broader term" (BT); "narrowed terms" (NT); "related terms" (RT).

Subsequently, it was performed a mapping of the terms extracted from texts of the projects with those consulted on AGROVOC, building up a specific system for categorization to represent the best descriptors related to sustainability and technology transfer.

As a result, we found 581 projects having the term sustainability and 611 projects containing the term technology transfer. In the next step, we searched for the terms sustainability and technology transfer together into the Embrapa's project portfolio and found 44 projects, which represents only 0.3% of the total (14,736).

Through the model application, it was possible to explore a certain term. For instance, from the term sustainability, 17 keywords were generated, and other 17 words were generate for the term technology transfer, enhanced the input of a search system to retrieve information.

## 4     Conclusions

In this work we proposed a conceptual model for analyzing sustainability projects aiming at technology transfer for institutions of R&DI. We performed a case study by using the Embrapa's project portfolio to validate the model.

We summarize the main results of the case study at Embrapa, as follows:

- Major of the projects were developed without criteria that are relevant at the present time. So we need to find different ways to extract knowledge from the Embrapa's project portfolio;
- This conceptual model can be used with any group of words, and not only with sustainability or technology transfer;
- The historical context at Embrapa has not prioritized issues of sustainability and technology transfer. Such issues have received special attention since the 90's.
- The model is simple, flexible, and can be easily adapted to other R&DI institutions.

We believe that this model can be easily adapted to meet the requirements of solutions based on Portfolio Management Project (PMP) in institutions of R&DI. As a continuation of this work, we are now analyzing the proposed model, considering both efficiency (use of resources) and effectiveness (achieving positive results for the organization) issues, and also analyzing their risks.

## References

1. Cooper, R.G., Edgett, S.J., Kleinschmidt, E.J.: Portfolio management for new products. Perseus Books (1998)
2. Levine, H.A.: Project Portfolio Management: A Practical Guide to Selecting Projects, Managing Portfolios, and Maximizing Benefits (Jossey-Bass Business & Management). John Wiley & Sons (2005)
3. Martino, J.P.: R&D project selection. John Wiley & Sons (1995)

4. WCED. Our Common Future. The World Commission on Environment and Development, p. 400. Oxford Univ. Press, Oxford (1987)
5. Bufrem, L.S., Gabriel Jr., R.F.: The appropriation of concept as an object in the scientific periodical literature in information science. Inf. 16(esp), 52–91 (2011)
6. de Campos, M.L.: Documentary language: theories underlying their preparation. EDUFF, Niterói (2001) (in Portuguese)
7. Carlan, E., Medeiros, M.B.B.B.: Systems of Knowledge Organization in view of Information Science. RICI: R.Ibero-amer. Ci. Inf. 4(2), 53–73 (2011) (in Portuguese)
8. Agrovoc (2012), http://aims.fao.org/website/AGROVOC-Thesaurus/sub
9. Zeng, M.L.: Knowledge organization systems (KOS). Knowledge Organization 35(2-3), 160–182 (2008)
10. Lévy, P., Authier, M.: The knowledge trees. Editora Escuta, São Paulo (1995) (in Portuguese)
11. Gil, A.C.: Methods and techniques of social research. Atlas, São Paulo (1999) (in Portuguese)
12. Embrapa, http://www.embrapa.br
13. Cribb, A.Y.: Determinants of technology transfer in the Brazilian agribusiness food: identification and characterization. Journal of Technology Management & Innovation 4(3) (2009) (in Portuguese)
14. Tigre, P.B.: Innovation management: the economics of technology in Brazil. Elsevier, Rio de Janeiro (2006)

# Finding Optimal Resources for IT Services

Sumit Raut[1,*] and Muralidharan Somasundaram[2]

[1] TCSL, Kolkata, India
sumit.raut@tcs.com
[2] TCSL, Chennai, India
muralidharan.somasundaram@tcs.com

**Abstract.** This paper studies the resource management problem in IT services, where service request arrives to resource management group (RMG) and RMG needs to allocate resources to a request for a service based on availability of resources and service requirement start date. We propose an approach to find optimal number of resources in the context of Poisson arrivals, and service times & lead-times are exponentially distributed. We provide an exact mathematical queuing model for optimal number of skilled resources needed based on waiting time cost, idle time cost and revenue from a customer service for a guaranteed service level agreement. We tested the model with real life data for various types of requirements and analytical results show the benefits of the proposed approach.

**Keywords:** IT services, Queuing, resource allocation, delay, waiting time.

## 1    Introduction

IT services business is a knowledge intensive industry where highly skilled resources are needed to meet demand for day-to-day services. Typically customers arrive with their requests to resource management group (RMG) for their service for a particular booking date and RMG needs to provide the skilled resources for the given booking date. The customer request needs to go through two stages of a process: (i) keep the request in RMG server till booking date and (ii) RMG allocates skilled resources to complete the request. Early allocation of skilled resources (i.e., before booking date) to request may lose opportunity to allocate resources of other possible future requests, i.e., paying wages while there is no realization of revenue and deterioration in service level. Delay in allocation of skilled resources indicates loss of demand resulting in revenue loss of service provider. Hence, it is important to estimate the right number of resources and active bench (safety stock) in dynamic IT services environment. The problem complexity increases when there is also possibility of substitution and multiskilling. This paper studies the resource allocation (or optimal bench) problem and applied queuing theory approach to determine the optimal number of resources which would also help to decide the active bench and number resources need to be

---

*  Room: 4B-14, TCSL, BIPL, Sector-V, Salt lake, Kolkata – 700093.

C. Emmanouilidis, M. Taisch, D. Kiritsis (Eds.): APMS 2012, Part I, IFIP AICT 397, pp. 708–715, 2013.

trained for a particular skill. In past, several authors discussed the aspects of determining of optimal number of servers in a different stream of research. Some of the relevant literatures are described below:

Grassmann [6] states that: "In respect to real life, all models are approximations." He argues that it may not be practical to apply exact mathematical queuing models to real problems, and offers a number of practical methods for finding the number of servers in waiting line systems. Bassamboo et al. [4] offer a dynamic model for determining the number of agents and the assignment of arrivals to agents in large call centers using an asymptotic approximation approach, and Borst et al. [5] consider an M/M/s system with a large number of servers (s), and propose an asymptotic approximation for finding the optimum staffing levels. Radmilovic et al. [10] provide a method to determine optimum number of servers and optimum server capacity with considerations of bulk arrival rate and estimate the impact in cost with changes of number of servers, group size and bulk arrival rate. Fazel et al. [7] presents an alternative approximate method for analyzing large M/M/s systems, which is highly accurate, and considers both the cost of customer waiting and the staffing cost to develop a model that determines the optimum number of servers that would minimize the total cost. Yang et al. [12] studies the optimal resource allocation in time-reservation systems where customers arrive at a service facility and receive service in two steps; in the first step information is gathered from the customer, which is then sent to a pool of computing resources, and in the second step the information is processed after which the customer leaves the system. They used dynamic programming approach to determine near-optimal number of processors follows a step function with as extreme policy the bang-bang control. They also provide new fundamental insights in the dependence of the near-optimal policy on the distribution of the information gathering times.

All the above works consider the system where jobs are serviced in First-Come-First-Serve (FCFS) order, and how the optimal number of servers varies across workloads. In addition, these queuing models does not consider real-life constraints (except Yang et al. [12]) and impractical to use them for large service centers or industry.

There are few researchers who have been used queuing models successfully for a variety of real-life problems. Some of the real-life solutions examples are for a variety of organizations including police patrol scheduling (Kolesar el al. [8]), staffing of supermarkets (Ittig [9]), tele-retailing (Andrew et al. [2]), and call centers (Artalejo et al. [3]). These models are commonly used by service organizations to determine the number of servers through trial and error. The available queuing models, however, become exceedingly complex and cumbersome for analyzing large service centers, and the trial and error approach becomes impractical. Therefore, finding the optimum number of resources in a large service industry to provide optimal level of service for different customers at different point of time needs special attention in research.

The main difference between the existing literature and our work is that we aim to (1) optimize the resource allocation cost, idling cost and revenue from servicing customers through effectively releasing resources and estimating right number of resources and (2) satisfy SLA (Service Level Agreement) constraint on the delay of a job, where delay is not same as waiting time. This is in contrast to the aforementioned works which have not focused on resource release time while obtaining number of skilled resources needed for a guaranteed SLA guarantee.

We organized the papers as follows: In Section 2, we describe the model formulation. Section 3 describes the simulation study and results. Conclusions and future directions of research are provided in Section 4.

## 2     Model Formulation

The resource allocation of a service request in IT industry has done through two stages (refer Fig. 1): (i) In the first stage, RMG receives requests and allocates the resource to service as per starting date of service; (ii) In the second stage, resources perform the service as per request/competency.

**Fig. 1.** Resource Allocation Process

*Parameters Definition and Assumptions:*

- Request arrival (X) follows Poisson distribution with mean $\lambda$ (per day)
- Service time (T) of a request (X) follows Exp. distribution with mean $1/\mu$ (in day)
- Request arrival date and request start date to process are $A_x$ and $B_x$, respectively
- Lead time represents as $L = B_x - A_x$, and follows Exp. distribution with mean $1/\mu_l$
- Number of server is S.

The first stage of resource allocation process of RMG is represented by the queuing system where request is arriving with Poisson process (X) in infinite number of servers (since, RMG only need to store the information in this stage) with infinite capacity systems and request leaves the system once it reaches at start-date of service. The time between requests follows exponential distribution (Y) with mean $1/\lambda$. The service time / stay time of a request in first stage is followed exponential distribution with mean as average lead time $(1/\mu_1)$. The requests' depart from the first stage would be allocated to second stage of RMG process, i.e., the arrival process of request to second stage is same as departure process of first stage. Therefore, the departure process is $D = Y + L$ and the distribution is as follows:

$$f(D = d) = \int_0^d f(L = d - y) * f(Y = y)dy = \int_0^d \mu_1 * e^{-\mu_1(d-y)} * \lambda * e^{-\lambda y}dy =$$
$$\frac{\lambda * \mu_1}{(\lambda - \mu_1)}\left[e^{-\mu_1 d} - e^{-\lambda d}\right] \qquad (1)$$

The expected value of departure process:

$$E(D) = \frac{1}{\mu_2} = \frac{\lambda + \mu_1}{\lambda \mu_1} \tag{2}$$

The second stage of resource allocation process of RMG is represented by the queuing system where request arrival process as request departure process from first stage, i.e., follows hypo-exponential distribution and service time follows exponential distribution with mean $1/\mu$. Based on the queuing model, we approximate the system in G/M/1 queuing model (this can be expanded for G/M/S queuing model and for different customer priority (Adan et al. [1])). The delay time distribution of this model is given below (Adan et al. [1], White et al. [11]):

$$P(W \le t) = 1 - \sigma * e^{-\mu(1-\sigma)t} \tag{3}$$

Where $\sigma = \tilde{D}(\mu - \sigma\mu)$, $\tilde{D}$ is a moment of request arrival process in second stage.

Moment of request arrival process in second stage of RMG process is as follows:

$$\tilde{D}(s) = \left(\frac{\mu_1}{\mu_1 + s}\right) * \left(\frac{\lambda}{\lambda + s}\right) \tag{4}$$

Now, the equation (4) is represented as

$$\sigma = \left(\frac{\mu_1}{\mu_1 + \mu - \sigma\mu}\right) * \left(\frac{\lambda}{\lambda + \mu - \sigma\mu}\right) \tag{5}$$

The expected delay time of the system is given below:

$$E(W) = \int_0^\infty t * \mu \sigma(1 - \sigma) * e^{-\mu(1-\sigma)t} = \frac{\sigma}{\mu(1-\sigma)} \tag{6}$$

The distribution of conditional delay time W|W>0 is as follows:

$$P(W > t | W > 0) = \frac{P(W > t)}{P(W > 0)} = \frac{\sigma * e^{-\mu(1-\sigma)t}}{\sigma} = e^{-\mu(1-\sigma)t} \tag{7}$$

The expected value of conditional delay time W|W>0 can be obtained as:

$$E(W|W > 0) = \int_0^\infty t * \mu (1 - \sigma) * e^{-\mu(1-\sigma)t} = \frac{1}{\mu(1-\sigma)} \tag{8}$$

From the equation (5) and (8), the unique root $\sigma$ is calculated as follows:

$$\sigma = \left(\frac{\mu_1}{\mu_1 + \left(\frac{1}{E(W|W>0)}\right)}\right) * \left(\frac{\lambda}{\lambda + \left(\frac{1}{E(W|W>0)}\right)}\right) \tag{9}$$

*Functional relationship of service rate ($\mu$) with unique root ($\sigma$):*
From the equation (5), we can write the equation as follows:

$$\sigma = \left\{\frac{1}{1 + (1-\sigma)*\frac{\mu}{\mu_1}}\right\} * \left\{\frac{1}{1 + (1-\sigma)*\frac{\mu}{\lambda}}\right\} \tag{10}$$

Suppose, $\sigma = 1 - k$, $A = \frac{\mu}{\mu_1}$ and $B = \frac{\mu}{\lambda}$

Then, the equation (10) can be written as:

$$(1 - k)(1 + kA)(1 + kB) = 1$$

$$k = \frac{-(A+B-AB) \pm \sqrt{(A+B+AB)^2 - 4AB}}{2AB} \tag{11}$$

Since at weekly level service rate ($\mu$) $\leq 1$, average lead-time ($1/\mu_1$) $\geq 1$ and the actual arrival rate ($\lambda$) $\geq 1$ for IT service industry (in most project cases), then, $B \leq 1$ and the value of ($A + B$) is always greater than or equal to $AB$. Therefore, $k$ can be written as

$$k = \frac{-(A+B-AB) + \sqrt{(A+B+AB)^2 - 4AB}}{2AB} \tag{12}$$

Now, the relation between service rate $\mu$ and unique root $\sigma$ is as follow:

$$(1 - \sigma)\mu = \frac{-\left(\frac{\lambda}{\mu_1} + \frac{\mu_1}{\lambda} - \mu\right) + \sqrt{\left(\frac{\lambda}{\mu_1} + \frac{\mu_1}{\lambda} + \mu\right)^2 - 4\mu_1\lambda}}{2} \tag{13}$$

## 2.1 Determination of Optimal Number of Server or Service Rate

Allocating too many resources results in decrease waiting time but comes at high allocation costs and allocating too few skilled resources leads to long waiting times. Therefore, the problem is formulated as follows:

Minimize the expected number of customer's delays and idle resources

$$W_{cost} * E(D) * \frac{\sigma}{\mu(1-\sigma)} + R_{cost} * \left(1 - \frac{E(D)}{\mu}\right) \tag{14}$$

Maximize revenue by service (Revenue per unit * Avg. customer depart from system)

$$Rev * E(D) * \frac{1}{E(S)} = Rev * E(D) * \mu * (1 - \sigma) \tag{15}$$

Where, $W_{cost}$ is average delaying cost, $R_{cost}$ is average resource idle cost per day (i.e., fixed cost per day (pay bill) incurs for each resource and this pay bill need to incur after finishing their work) and Rev is the average revenue for service per day.

For priority customers, IT service providers are bounded by obligation to provide the service must. Therefore, we consider delaying time should not exceed t time-length with confidence level 95% as constraint as follows:

$$P(W \leq t) = 1 - \sigma * e^{-\mu(1-\sigma)t} > 0.95 \tag{16}$$

The above optimization problem is solved using Gradient search method and produces local optimal solution or optimal number of resources.

## 3 Simulation Study

We consider the resource allocation problem for different competencies in IT service industry for simulation study. We capture six months data on different competency requests arrival (request date, start date) and allocation/service (fulfilled date) details for our analysis. From the above data set, we derive lead time (start date – request date), delay (min (fulfilled date – start date, 0), and waiting time (min (fulfilled date – request date, 0). We derive the service rate from the equation (8 & 9) using arrival rate, delay and lead-time information.

We observed that there are more than 200 competency levels in the dataset. We also observed that the variability is too high in each competency level and most of the cases data is intermittent. Hence, we group the competency as per their similarities, where one competency/skill can be substituted to other. In this way, the total number of competency groups is turned out fifteen. Some of the competency groups are: SAP-ERP, ORACLE-ERP, Programming, etc. The arrival patterns of some of the competency groups are given in Fig. 2.

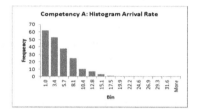 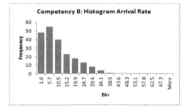

**Fig. 2.** Arrival patterns of different competency

The mapping of queuing model to resource management problem in IT-service is measured by error in the estimated delay with actual delay observed. $W_{real}$ denotes the mean delay of serving of each competency group in IT-service process and $W_{model}$ denotes the mean delay (refer equation 8) which derived from two-stage queuing model. The mapping error % ($MAPE_{comp}$) for each competency is represented as shown below:

$$MAPE_{comp} = \frac{|D_{real,comp} - D_{model,comp}|}{D_{real,comp}} * 100 \qquad (17)$$

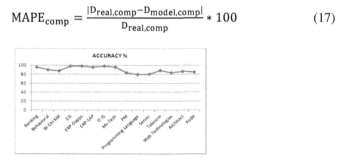

**Fig. 3.** Accuracy plot for queuing model accuracy

The mapping accuracy% (100 - $MAPE_{comp}$) is calculated using equation (17) and results are shown in Fig. 3. The above results showed that the estimation of delay using queuing model is highly accurate. On an average accuracy percentage is 90%. We also tested the waiting time distribution derived from the model with actual data of each competency group. The results show that at 95% confidence level, the difference of waiting time distribution between model and actual data is not significant.

The above analysis suggests that the queuing modeling approach can accurately map the resource management problem in IT-service. Therefore, we used this approach to determine the optimal number of resources needed for IT-service industry based on different cost (holding cost of resources, delay cost) and revenue parameters (revenue for each service). This paper considers the cost ratio between idling/holding cost & delay cost is 1: 7 (ID ratio) and average revenue for service per day & idling cost is 1: 10 (RI Ratio). The total cost using equations (14 & 15) are derived for different number of resources (or service rate) for each competency group and the curve for total cost versus service rate (for ERP-Oapps competency) is shown in Fig. 4. The optimal number of resources for each competency group is determined using equations (14, 15 & 16) and the percentage of cost reduction using optimal number of resources for each competency shown in Fig. 5. The results show that the benefit of using optimal resources is on an average 10% reduction in cost.

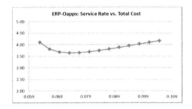  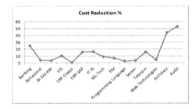

**Fig. 4.** Total cost versus service rate        **Fig. 5.** Cost reduction % different competency

Overall, the performance of queuing model is found very satisfactory. We have also experimented different scenario based on different cost ratio. The results of optimal number of servers using equations (14, 15, & 16) against ID ratio are shown in Fig. 6.

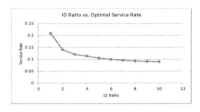

**Fig. 6.** Optimal service rate versus ID ratio

The above results show that the service rate needs to increase exponentially with the decrease of ID cost ratio.

## 4    Conclusions and Future Directions

Overall, this paper provides a queuing modeling approach to find an optimal number of resources for IT services business. An exact mathematical formulation is derived for optimal number of resources determination. The queuing modeling approach is tested in real-life data from IT services business. The model fitness is tested and showed the accuracy of the model for mapping IT services business. The queuing approach provides the optimal number of servers and showed the effectiveness of the mathematical approach using improvement in total cost reduction. Though, this paper considers the issues of lead time and delay in allocation in IT services business, there are other issues, such as, multi-skilling servers, customer priority, need to be considered in queuing modeling. Therefore, the present approach can be extended for multi-skill resources and exact mathematical formulation need to be derived. Based on the cost of multi-skill and single-skill resources, optimal ratio of multi-skill vs. single skill determination can be considered as future directions of research. Also, the changes of resource's shape/skill level due to training need to be considered for future direction of research.

# References

1. Adan, I., Resing, J.: Queuing Theory, Dept. of Mathematics and Computer Science. Eindhoven University of Technology, The Netherlands (2001)
2. Andrews, B., Parsons, H.: Establishing Telephone-Agent Staffing Levels through Economic Optimization. Interfaces 23(2), 14–20 (1993)
3. Artalejo, J.R., Economou, A., Gomez-Corral, A.: Applications of Maximum Queue Lengths to Call Center Management. Computers and Operations Research 34, 983–996 (2007)
4. Bassamboo, A., Michael Harrison, J., Zeevi, A.: Design and Control of a Large Call Center: Asymptotic Analysis of an LP-Based Method. Operations Research 54(3), 419–435 (2006)
5. Borst, S., Mandelbaum, A., Reiman, M.: Dimensioning Large Call Centers. Operations Research 52(1), 17–34 (2004)
6. Grassmann, W.: Finding the Right Number of Servers in Real-World Queuing Systems. Interfaces 18(2), 94–104 (1988)
7. Fazel, F., Fakheri, A.: An Alternative Approach for Determining the Performance of M/M/s Queuing Model. Presented at Decision Sciences Institute Annual Meeting, November 18-21 (2007)
8. Ittig, P.T.: Planning Service Capacity when Demand is Sensitive to Delay. Decision Sciences 25(4), 541–559 (1994)
9. Kolesar, P.J., Rider, K.L., Crabill, T.B., Walker, W.E.: A Queuing-Linear Programming Approach to Scheduling Police Patrol Cars. Operations Research 22(6), 1045–1062 (1975)
10. Radmilovic, Z., Dragovic, B., Mestrovic, R.: Optimal Number and Capacity of Servers in $M^{x = a}/M/c(\infty)$ Queuing Systems. Information and Management Sciences 16(3), 1–16 (2005)
11. White, J.A., Schmidt, J.W., Bennett, G.K.: Analysis of Queuing Systems. Academic Press, New York (1975)
12. Yang, R., Bhulai, S., Mei, R.V.D., Seinstra, F.: Optimal Resource Allocation for Time-Reservation System. Performance Evaluation 6(5), 414–428 (2011)

# Development of Engineering Competencies in Brazil and Innovation Policies, an Overview of the Automotive Sector

Renato Perrotta and Oduvaldo Vendrametto

UNIP – Paulista Universtiy, Post-graduate Program in Production Engineering,
Rua Dr. Bacelar, 1212, São Paulo, Brazil

**Abstract.** As consequence of the economic growth, it is observed the increase of the demand for engineering professionals. The problem of scarcity of engineering manpower is being faced as one of the main obstacles to the continuity of the Brazilian economic growth. The natural demands of infrastructure and industry allied to the fact that engineers are also recruited to occupy non-engineering positions constitute, themselves, already a difficult equation to solve. Besides, along the years, the Brazilian's scientific production in the engineering field has demonstrated to be very shy. Such combination, either in macro or in micro-economy, reflects in the innovation and competitiveness. The objective of this research is to discuss actions to create engineering competencies in micro-economy that could attenuate those structural problems. Additionally, this work aims having an overview of those actions combined with the new regulatory policy for the automotive sector announced in April/12, which integrates the program "Inovar-Auto".

**Keywords:** lack of engineers, engineering competence creation, Brazilian innovation programs, competitiveness in the automotive sector.

## 1 Introduction

Recently, concerns about the scarcity of engineering manpower in Brazil became object of researches as per Gusso and Nascimento [1] and Nascimento et al [2]. World indicators of education appoint that in Brazil less than 5% of the graduates come from engineering areas, which seems to be a very low figure, while, OCDE members, in average, 12% of its graduates come from this field. Moreover, countries like South Korea have 23% of its graduates in engineering; Japan has 19% and Russian Federation 18% [3]. Nowadays, the country contributes with around 2% of the world's scientific production [4] and, more specifically, in the engineering subject area, the Brazilian scientific production shows to be very shy, with a number of publications around 2300 documents (Table 1), far behind countries like the USA with around 45000 documents, Japan with 14000, South Korea with 9000 and other BRIC countries: India with 6000, Russian Federation with 3500 and the impressive number of 63000 from China [5].

C. Emmanouilidis, M. Taisch, D. Kiritsis (Eds.): APMS 2012, Part I, IFIP AICT 397, pp. 716–723, 2013.

**Table 1.** Top 20 World Scientific Production – Year 2010 – Subject Area: Engineering. Adapted from [5]

| Ranking | Country | Documents | Citable documents | Citations | Self-Citations | Citations per Document | H index |
|---------|---------|-----------|-------------------|-----------|----------------|------------------------|---------|
| 1 | China | 63361 | 62857 | 26110 | 18570 | 0,4 | 157,0 |
| 2 | United States | 44983 | 42787 | 40246 | 22501 | 0,9 | 448,0 |
| 3 | Japan | 13716 | 13382 | 7073 | 3516 | 0,5 | 181,0 |
| 4 | Germany | 10270 | 9821 | 9126 | 3920 | 0,9 | 197,0 |
| 5 | United Kingdom | 9956 | 9348 | 9342 | 3621 | 0,9 | 221,0 |
| 6 | South Korea | 8733 | 8550 | 6657 | 2635 | 0,8 | 129,0 |
| 7 | France | 8233 | 7944 | 7221 | 3019 | 0,9 | 180,0 |
| 8 | Canada | 7452 | 7174 | 6527 | 2186 | 0,9 | 180,0 |
| 9 | Taiwan | 6666 | 6501 | 4882 | 2143 | 0,7 | 123,0 |
| 10 | Italy | 6457 | 6188 | 5803 | 2393 | 0,9 | 160,0 |
| 11 | India | 6065 | 5887 | 4316 | 1826 | 0,7 | 115,0 |
| 12 | Spain | 5003 | 4833 | 4992 | 2133 | 1,0 | 127,0 |
| 13 | Australia | 4220 | 4015 | 4235 | 1449 | 1,0 | 137,0 |
| 14 | Iran | 3916 | 3819 | 3737 | 2018 | 1,0 | 63,0 |
| 15 | Russian Federation | 3540 | 3498 | 1102 | 506 | 0,3 | 85,0 |
| 16 | Netherlands | 3021 | 2888 | 4121 | 1294 | 1,4 | 153,0 |
| 17 | Poland | 2588 | 2517 | 1153 | 540 | 0,5 | 75,0 |
| 18 | Turkey | 2480 | 2397 | 1986 | 772 | 0,8 | 83,0 |
| 19 | Singapore | 2430 | 2354 | 3291 | 1036 | 1,4 | 122,0 |
| 20 | Brazil | 2355 | 2298 | 1444 | 577 | 0,61 | 90 |

A wealth of a nation is determined by its internal productiveness, but, principally through its own capacity to create value, besides of the resources available to be applied. So forth, the growth of a country is no longer sustainable while prevail poor or inexistent policies oriented to the productivity. In other terms, a country should prosper if its people have the right and updated capabilities and skills that enable determined specializations, therefore wealth and growth will be limited concomitantly if skills are merely for some [6].

The surplus of US$ 29.8 billion of the Brazilian Trade Balance in 2011, indicates a figure 47.9% higher than 2010 [7], but, a deep analysis shows that 63% of the country exports structure has been based in Food (31%), Agricultural raw material (4%), Fuels (10%), Ores and Metals (18%); whilst Manufactures represents the rest 37%

[8], indication that the nation is losing its competitiveness, once in the year 2000, Manufactures represented 58% of the country's exports structure [8].

Regarding the Automotive sector, in global perspective, Brazil has already secured its position as one of the main players, through an internal market over 3.6 million units and internal production over 3.4 million units, in 2011 [9]. For the internal economy, the sector has expressive importance with nearly 20% share in Industrial GDP [10].

However, in deeper investigation, it is possible to find out that the Brazilian automotive industry competitiveness has been based in premises of weak economic pillars. First, the national production is substantially dependent of the internal market, circa 2.7 million units, which represents 81% of the production share [9]. Second, the imports increased in one year from 18.8% to 23.6% of the market share [9]. Third, the Brazilian trade balance, positive between the years 2002 and 2007, dropped from US$5251 in 2005 to US$(5404) million in 2010 [10]. Finally, the market share of vehicles with engines over 1000cm3, which means, vehicles with higher added value than the ones that the market has been based, have increased contemporarily with the market share of the imports [9].

The consequences of the loss of competitiveness can be observed in the Figure 1, which presents a modest increase in production during the period of 2007 to 2011, compared to other BRIC countries, for instance, China and India. That reflected in the position that Brazil historically has occupied as the 6th major world vehicles producer.

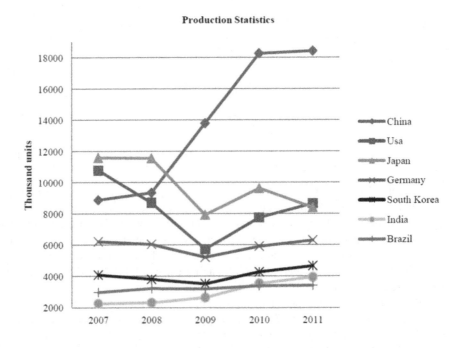

**Fig. 1.** Countries Vehicles Production Statistics. Adapted from [11]

# 2    Objectives

The objective of this research is to present actions oriented to create engineering competencies in micro-economic perspective, face to the present structural scenario. Furthermore, this work aims the combination of such actions with the new regulatory policy announced for the automotive industry, through the program "Inovar-Auto", valid to the period between 2013 – 2017 and that integrates the program "Brasil Maior", which seeks social and economic growth across the mobilization of the productive forces and industrials, focusing the innovation and the competitiveness of the country, both to the internal and to the external markets, through the establishment of a set of industrial, technological, trade and services policies.

# 3    Methodology

The methodology applied for this research is based in bibliographic review, based upon data of the Brazilian automotive sector, that have been obtained through the ANFAVEA annual report (National Association of Auto-motor Vehicles Producer), across the world development indicators - World Bank 2012 , global education figures of 2010 - OCDE (Organization for Economic Co-operation and Development), IPEA (Institute of Applied Economic Research) publications regarding engineering resources in Brazil - 2010 and 2011, ranking of global scientific production and scientific production in the area of knowledge engineering  - SJR (SCImago Journal & Country Rank, by drawing a parallel with other bibliographic references.

In addition, it focuses the analysis and comprehension of program "Inovar-Auto", identifying and determining opportunities for engineering competence creation.

All of this in order to create subsidies that demonstrate the importance to develop engineering competencies, mandatory to foment innovation through researches & developments, innovation one that, enables to create value and differentiation of the country goods.

Notwithstanding, the definition of a model,  proper to enlarge the development of the human capital and competencies, based, for example, in Asian nations, which have supported the rapid growth that have allowed the technological development for innovation [12].

# 4    Results and Discussion

The numbers of the Brazilian automotive industry in the first months of 2012 demonstrate that the model of concentration of its production to supply the internal market is achieving its limit. The number of vehicles produced in Brazil in the period January to May - 2012 is 9.5% lower compared to the same period of 2011, 5.9% lower compared to 2010 and 7.9% lower, when compared with 2008 (Table 2). In fact, the numbers of automobiles produced at this period, surpass only the production achieved in the year 2009, time when the automotive sector experienced the collapse and major automakers like GM and Ford had to go through restructure and very few countries like China and India (Figure 1) had growth in this industry.

**Table 2.** Vehicles Production in Brazil from January to May – years 2008 to 2012. Adapted from [12], [13] [14], [15].

| Period | Vehicles Production | | | | |
|--------|------|------|------|------|------|
|        | JAN  | FEB  | MAR  | APR  | MAY  |
| 2008   | 255,2 | 254,0 | 283,7 | 302,5 | 293,9 |
| 2009   | 184,9 | 204,4 | 275,1 | 253,9 | 269,5 |
| 2010   | 233,4 | 236,6 | 318   | 274,8 | 297,3 |
| 2011   | 238,9 | 294,6 | 295,1 | 282   | 304,2 |
| 2012   | 211,8 | 217,8 | 308,5 | 260,8 | 280,8 |

The strength that allowed the country attenuating the effects of the world economic crisis initiated in 2008 is no longer a fruitful strategy. The internal market sales of the period January to May (Table 3) dropped down to volumes even lower than the ones observed in the first months of 2009 when the country has faced the effects of the world crisis.

**Table 3.** Brazilian Internal Market – Vehicle Sales from Jan to May -years 2008 to 2012. Adapted from [13], [14], [15], [16].

| Period | Sales Volume / Internal Market | | | | |
|--------|------|------|------|------|------|
|        | JAN  | FEB  | MAR  | APR  | MAY  |
| 2008   | 215,0 | 200,8 | 232,1 | 261,2 | 242,0 |
| 2009   | 197,5 | 199,4 | 271,4 | 234,4 | 247,0 |
| 2010   | 170,3 | 180,5 | 295,6 | 228,1 | 206,1 |
| 2011   | 187,3 | 212,2 | 243,8 | 225,1 | 243,8 |
| 2012   | 200,4 | 188,3 | 229,7 | 199,5 | 223,8 |

Moreover, along the years the country did not take the necessary actions to improve its infrastructure, especially the ones with positive impacts over logistics of transportation of goods. Similar inertness can be observed in the internal bureaucracy, so forth, in the amount and in the burden of the taxes that still prevail.

Labor costs, as well as, other direct and indirect costs have increased tremendously. On the other hand, the level of skills, competencies, such as the efficiency have not grown in same levels.

Face to the presented scenario of loss of competitiveness and lack of skilled and competent resources, authorities decided to create the program "Brasil Maior", a set of policies that focus the competitiveness, productivity of the country industry, by supporting and encouraging the increment of the technology of the processes and value chain, all of this, in order to create a proper scenario for investments and for the innovation [17].

In respect to the automotive sector, dedicated attention has been observed, the program "Inovar-Auto", a part of the program "Brasil Maior", provides incentives to the technological innovation and the densification of vehicles productive chain to the period between 2013 and 2017. The aim is to support the technological development, the innovation, the safety, the environmental protection, the efficiency and the quality of automobiles, trucks, busses and auto-parts locally produced. Companies already installed and producing in the country, such as companies that have plans approved to install production plants in the Brazil may take advantage, from January/13, of IPI deduction (VAT over industrial production) based on quarterly outlays made in the country in: researches; technological developments; innovation; strategic inputs; tooling and qualification of suppliers [18].

The technological capacity of a nation is a cluster of abilities, experiences and efforts, allowing companies take benefit and, from this capacity, improving and creating new technologies [12].

By electing strategic areas, Brazilian authorities seek to boost the innovation and R&D initiatives to increment the country competitiveness. Tax reliefs may contribute and force competence creation in micro-economy.

To develop a learning process, the studies appoint to a model based on competence development, as per Kim [12] [19] and Ulrich [21].

According to the model, Knowledge initiates from the Cognitive Perception (Know-what), which is the base knowledge obtained through education and schooling. Despite the fact that this is a pivotal knowledge, other, more advanced ones are required for competitive advantage [21]. That is the kind of knowledge that a nation, at least, should care about.

Advanced Skills (Know-how) are necessary for any productive activity; it is the ability to turn knowledge into practice, the capacity of applying learned disciplines in real and complex problems [12], [19], [21].

Finally, the Systemic Comprehension (Know-why) is the inclination of understanding the principles of a technology. It is the most advanced knowledge that allows professionals thinking beyond the execution, pro-acting in cause-effect analysis [12], [19], [21].

The tax benefits shall contribute to develop competencies, even in face of a scarcity of engineering human resources, they could have important role, and their own history can determine technological efforts across its objectives [19].

The nation can adapt the model adopted in South Korea, that thru its industries, individuals have developed the necessary technological skills [19].

Although individual enterprises are one of the keys for the technological activity, the capacity of a nation is more than a sum its companies' skills and competencies, in individual perspective. It comprehends extra-market systems of networks and the relation between companies, the way of do business and the presence of development institutions [12].

Companies shall handle competencies through methods of competence analysis and management, defining own criteria and steps to achieve know-how / know-why levels.

In any case, technology shall not be obtained uniquely through a radical R&D, the learning process can be developed adjacently to reverse engineering, imitation, licenses, cooperation agreements [19], [20].

The example of innovation of Japan should also be a reference, since, there, the competence is obtained through innovation, incrementally, so that an innovation becomes subsidy to the next [19], [22], [23].

# References

1. Gusso, D.A., Nascimento, P.A.M.N.: IPEA – Radar N. 12 – Tecnologia, Produção e Comércio Exterior - Contexto e dimensionamento da formação de pessoal técnico-científico e de engenheiros, http://www.ipea.gov.br/portal/images/stories/PDFs/radar/110315_radar12.pdf (accessed on April 2012)
2. Nascimento, P.A.M.N., et al.: IPEA – Radar No 6 – Tecnologia, Produção e Comércio Exterior - Escassez de engenheiros: realmente um risco? http://www.ipea.gov.br/sites/000/2/pdf/100223_Radar6.pdf (accessed on April 2012)
3. Education at Glance 2010: OCDE Indicators, http://www.oecd.org/document/52/0,3746,en_2649_39263238_45897844_1_1_1_1,00.html (accessed on: April 2012)
4. SJR – SCImago Journal & Country Rank, http://www.scimagojr.com/countrysearch.php?country=BR&area=0 (accessed on April 2012)
5. SJR – SCImago Journal & Country Rank, http://www.scimagojr.com/countryrank.php?area=2200&category=0&region=all&year=2010&order=it&min=0&min_type=it (accessed on April 2012)
6. Porter, M.E.: The Competitive Advantage of Nations. Free Press, New York (1998)
7. Brazilian Foreign Trade Overview (January-December 2011), http://www.desenvolvimento.gov.br/sitio/interna/interna.php?area=5&menu=571 (accessed on May 2012)
8. The World Bank. World Development Indicators (2012), http://data.worldbank.org/sites/default/files/wdi-2012-ebook.pdf (accessed on May 2012)
9. ANFAVEA. Carta da Anfavea. Indústria Automobilística Brasileira (2010-2011), http://www.anfavea.com.br/cartas/Carta308.pdf (accessed on May 2012)
10. ANFAVEA. Brazilian Automotive Industry Yearbook 2011, p.40 (2011)
11. OICA. Production Statistics, http://oica.net/category/production-statistics/ (accessed on June 2012)
12. Kim, L.: Technology, learning, and innovation: experiences of newly industrializing economies, Cambridge (2000)
13. ANFAVEA. Carta da Anfavea. Resultados de Maio e de Janeiro-Maio de (2012), http://www.anfavea.com.br/cartas/Carta313.pdf (accessed on June 2012)
14. ANFAVEA. Dados Relativos a 2010 – Produção por Tipo, Empresa e Modelo, http://www.anfavea.com.br/tabelas2010.html (accessed on June 2012)
15. ANFAVEA. Dados Relativos a 2009 – Produção por Tipo, Empresa e Modelo, http://www.anfavea.com.br/tabelas2009.html (accessed on June 2012)

16. ANFAVEA. Dados Relativos a 2008 – Produção por Tipo, Empresa e Modelo, http://www.anfavea.com.br/tabelas2008.html (accessed on June 2012)
17. MDIC. Brasil Maior – Inovar para competir. Competir para crescer, http://www.brasilmaior.mdic.gov.br/images/data/ 201204/c29cf558d29f0293eae88bbb2a21fd16.pdf (accessed on June 2012)
18. PRESIDÊNCIA DA REPÚBLICA. Medida Provisória 563, de 3 de Abril de (2012), http://www.planalto.gov.br/ccivil_03/ _Ato2011-2014/2012/Mpv/563.htm (accessed on June 2012)
19. Kim, L.: Imitation to Innovation: the dynamics of Korea's technological learning. Harvard Business School (1997)
20. Andreassi, T.: Gestão da Inovação Tecnológica. Thomson Learning, São Paulo (2006)
21. Ulrich, D.: Recursos Humanos Estratégicos: novas perspectivas para os profissionais de RH. Futura, São Paulo (2003)
22. Nonaka, I., Takeuchi, H.: The knowledge-creating company. Oxford USA Trade (1995)
23. Nonaka, I., Takeuchi, H.: Hitotsubashi on Knowledge Management. John Wiley Trade (2004)

# Holistic Vision of Sustainability in the Production Chain in Oil Exploration Pre-Salt Layer

Alessandro Luiz da Silva[1], Mônica Franchi Carniello[2],
and José Luís Gomes da Silva[3]

[1,2,3] Universidade de Taubaté (UNITAU),
Programa de Pós-Graduação em Administração, Brasil
[1] Mestre em Planejamento e Desenvolvimento Regional, UNITAU, Brasil
ssilengenharia@gmail.com
[2] Doutora em Comunicação e Semiótica, Professor, UNITAU, Brasil
monicafcarniello@gmail.com
[3] Doutor em Engenharia Aeronáutica e Mecânica, Professor, UNITAU, Brasil
gomesdasilvaster@gmail.com

**Abstract.** The current discussions about the future, especially considering the development has been promoting socio-joint policy in favor of sustainable growth, with relevance to the thoughts of Ignacy Sachs, which emphasizes the perspectives, social, economic, geographic, environmental and sustainability cultural. Thus, a holistic view, such perspectives on aspects of sustainability in the supply chain of oil in pre-salt layer, which has been widely discussed, especially in the scientific community. The research methodology is presented as qualitative and descriptive through literature review. Considering the problems wrapped exploration and logistics, and the magnitude in environmental, spatial, cultural, economic and social, we really prepared? As a result, we found basic technological gaps, as since its discovery in 2006, the pre-salt layer of Brazil and, especially, its operation is highly complex, requiring high costs of research and technological development, especially in innovation, since their peak production, is designed for only 12 years since the discovery.

**Keywords:** Productive Chain, Regional Development, Pre-salt, Sustainability Geographic.

## 1    Introduction

The current global scenario, under sustainability aspects, reflects the thinking reflected in the work of the Club of Rome in 1972, which indicated the reality of the scarcity of natural resources, considering the high rate of world population. With the emergence of "environmental crisis" a contemporary line of thought gained political space. Thus, current discussions about the future, considering, especially the development has been promoting joint socio-political in favor of sustainable growth, with relevance to the thoughts of Sachs (1993), which emphasizes the perspectives,

C. Emmanouilidis, M. Taisch, D. Kiritsis (Eds.): APMS 2012, Part I, IFIP AICT 397, pp. 724–733, 2013.

social, economic, environmental, space and cultural sustainability, particularly considering the exploration of the Brazilian pre-salt, particularly considering the exploration of the Brazilian pre-salt, observed by outlays on research and technological development, since there will be high demand for technical training in logistics and risks of exploration.

## 2    Purpose

The objective of the research is in the discussion of the current global scenario, under sustainability aspects, considering a holistic vision of sustainability in the production chain in oil exploration pre-salt layer which in a way reflects the thinking of the work referenced in the Club of Rome in 1972 which indicated the reality of scarcity of natural resources, considering the high rate of world population. With the emergence of "environmental crisis", a contemporary line of thought gained political space.

Thus, the current discussions about the future, considering in particular the development have promoted socio-joint policies for sustainable growth, with relevance to the thoughts of Sachs (1993), which emphasizes the perspectives, social, economic, spatial, environmental and cultural sustainability.

## 3    Methodology

The methodology of the article provides a qualitative approach, based on literature search, design specification, aiming for a holistic supply chain to discuss the pre-salt layer, from the perspective of sustainability, with relevance to the logistics flow. The research was the period between 2005 and 2010, considering scientific publications that give context to the pre-salt exploration, and the relevance of complexity from their extraction and mainly for transport, given that the sustainability aspects refer to the deep thoughts, considering the of environmental events in recent years.

The research was defined as literature, with a descriptive design with a qualitative approach. In addition to scientific publications, to collect data, we also used the database of the Center for Research and Development (CENPES) considering, specially Petrobras's information, relevant to    planning    and exploration    of technological advances in the layer of pre-salt.

## 4    Results and Discussion

As a result, it was found that since its discovery in 2006, the exploration of the pre-salt layer is highly complex, requiring high expenditure on research and technological development, especially in innovation, reaching its fullest designed for 12 years, considering the problems under the aspects of environmental, cultural, economic, and social space.

Considering the extraction of oil in the country, with relevance to the pre-salt layer since its discovery in 2006, provides a holistic view of sustainability and understanding of its complexity, in particular its operation, but is concentrated phase of research and development.

The development maximized and designed for 12 years since its discovery in 2006, certainly, will require further large investments, mainly in Research, Development and Innovation (RD & I), given the problems in aspects of environmental, cultural, economic, spatial and social considering the complexity and magnitude of the pre-salt exploration, surrounded by risks, among which we highlight the sustainability space, reflected mainly by logistical problems, considering the geography of the pre-salt, and environmental impacts involved in this process extraction, these impacts still purely theoretical knowledge, as represented at Table 1, by stages since company foundation.

**Table 1.** Macro view of oil exploration in the country (Source: Authors adapted from Petrobras - Centre for Research and Development - CENPES 2010).

| Years Since Petrobras Foundation (1954) | Goal of Production 1.000.000 barrels of oil per day | Chronology |
|:---:|:---:|:---:|
| 45 | 45 | 1954 |
| 27 | 27 | 1974 |
| 22 | 22 | 1984 |
| 12 | 12 | 2006 |

Thus a holistic view represented in Fig. 1, under a projection of an economic standpoint, the pre-salt will be explored when likely to be high oil prices, yet in a not too distant future, low oil prices, due to the heating global or the development of cleaner sources of energy, can impair the operation of the pre-salt. Considering the array of sustainability, Lima and Fernandes (2009) a holistic view, make an approach on the oil sector, where the exploration and development stages express the relevance of the processes detailed below:

- Exploration and delineation of mineral deposits; Drilling, completion and production activities are concentrated in drilling the well and prepare it to receive the permanent production equipment for oil and gas;
- Refining and transportation back to the transfer of crude oil and gas production units for the derivatives, while the processing and distribution of natural gas cover asset of operations for the transport;
- Distribution and use of natural gas and other hydrocarbon fluids.

| Matrix Sustainable Exploration of Pre-Salt | | | | | |
|---|---|---|---|---|---|
| Sustainabilities | Resources | Industrialization | Product | Market (Internal & External) | Consumer Global |
| Social | Training of human resources, employment generation and income Corporate social responsibility involved intitutions | | | | |
| Economic | Diversification of products: oil and oil products Impact on the country's economic development, contribution of the insertion of the country in the global economy | | | Meet internal demands (self-sustaining) | Export: the international market |
| Environmental | Extraction and Production: High spending on research, considering the magnitude of environmental impacts | | Final Destination | | |
| Cultural | Oil Extraction: Expenditures on Research, Development and Innovation Training of manpower direct local and migratory | | | | |
| Spatial | Exploration, Production and Logistics Distribution considering the final consumers | | | | |

| Segment | Materials and Relevant Equipaments | Main Services |
|---|---|---|
| Exploration | Seismographs, explosives and mainframe computers | Geophysical survey and processing, determining the profile of wells and formation evaluation |
| Drilling, completion and production | Casing, flexible lines, and large turbine generators and compressors | Drilling and cementing wells, chartering of support vessels and submerged launch lines |
| Refining and transportation | Large compressors and pumps, steam turbines, furnaces towers, Vassos pressure control and supervisory systems | Maintenance, installation and assembly of industrial plants, including pipelines and storage systems |

**Fig. 1.** Macro view of the productive chain of the pre-salt (Source: Authors, adapted from Lima and Fernandes (2009, p. 323)

# 5 Development: Holistic Vision of Sustainability in the Production Chain in Oil Exploration Pre-Salt Layer

## 5.1 Geography of the Brazilian Pre-Salt Layer

Geographically the pre-salt layer, covers part of the north coast of São Paulo, with a huge reservoir of oil and natural gas, also present in the Santos, Campos and Espirito Santo,    and presents a macro    view with coverage in    the    coastal region between the states of Santa Catarina and the Espirito Santo.

Above all, the challenges of the pre-salt exploration beyond the technological and environmental aspects,    with    the    geographic relevance    to sustainability,    given the logistical problems of transport, considering the existence of a huge volume of natural gas, inherent in the process.

Variable important, observed    particularly in    the    research    of    Lima (2008) which notes that there is a huge gap in about 350 km the continent almost making it impossible to flow gas through pipelines across the ocean, and thus it is necessary to burn it at the base of production. So the question is:

- Considering sustainability, which the    environmental    impacts of burning  of  these gases, as  it  focuses  on issues related  to the high release of gases?
- The same concept of sustainability with geographical approach, how will the distribution logistics of this production so far inland from the coast?

Thus, this paper discusses the holistic view of sustainability, considering the oil exploration of the pre-salt layer, in particular from the perspective of geography.

## 5.2    Geography of Global Pre-Salt Layer

According to a survey of Lima (2008, p. 4), it is estimated that "the pre-salt layer has an area of 112,000 km².

Of this total, 41.000 km² has been tendered and awarded. This layer is about 800 km long and in some areas, 200 km wide, "considering the reserves in Brazil, located at 350 kilometers of coastline. And also, the pre-salt layer is located between five and seven thousand feet below sea level, it can reach up to two thousand feet thick,

## 5.3    Challenges of Sustainable Development of the Environmental and Cultural Vision of Oil Supply Chain

The concept of sustainable development is concatenated from the emergence of the environmental crisis in mid-1980. Currently, "[...] is closely related to action strategies to implement a set of measures and therefore is not just a theoretical concept, but only instrumental". (BARRETO, 2001 cited in Fernandes et al. 2007, p. 15).

Sachs (1993) describes the cultural sustainability, assumes the role of relevance in the process of regional sustainable development, considering the roots of indigenous models of modernization, especially the regulatory processes of continuous improvement.

Considering the approach of Jacobi (1999), "the issue of sustainability is, in this end of century, a central role in the reflection on the dimensions of development and alternatives that are configured" in a way, "[...] the social and environmental context that characterizes contemporary societies reveals that the impact of humans on the environment "[...] is becoming increasingly complex, both in quantitative and qualitative terms." (JACOBI, 1999, p. 175, emphasis added).

In the same context, recent research by Rodrigues (2010, p. 26) states that no doubt "one of the challenges faced by the Brazilian Petroleum Company (Petrobras), the exploration of oil in the pre-salt is the great amount of associated natural gas."

Rodrigues (2010), this same approach, reveals that the gas transported by pipeline, by the ocean, considering the enormous distance, it would be economically unviable, and also contextualizes, in his research that an alternative would be burning even in the very basis of production, where, however, would encounter another aggravating factor, the production of pollutant gases on a large scale, versus the environmental dimension as defined: "The environmental dimension is focused on a set of actions that aim to prevent or mitigate harm arising from the development process." The solution is not in the suppression of development actions, but the adoption of forms of management that are intended to use not predatory the planet's resources. (CARVALHO, 2005, p. 49).

Considering the magnitude of the complex technological, and as their own definitions of the Brazilian Petroleum (Petrobras), initially for oil exploration in the pre-salt, several alternatives were suggested techniques in relation to excess gas inherent in the process, among which stands out:

- The technologies of the transformation of natural gas for transportation in lieu of using pipelines, which would involve high costs, economically unfeasible;
- Another important variable defined as a challenge to be considered in the process of extracting the pre-salt, is the cultural sustainability with a focus on training of human resources that are necessary for the production. At the same focus, Fraga (2008), estimated that 110 000 professionals will be needed to attend this demand.

But how to meet this demand for human resources?

The technological absorption capacity can be defined by the observations of Cohen and Levinthal (1990), considering that this concept can be understood since it has the ability to recognize the value of new knowledge, which is extremely necessary that assimilation.

This learning process inherent in technological absorptive capacity is of fundamental importance, but there is a learning curve - learning curve, that is, time is a valuable expenditure necessary in the absorption of technological knowledge is considered as another variable in process operation of the pre-salt. In this approach, although innovative capacity of enterprises depends directly from their capital borderline intellectual, and how they are structured, considering a range of variables such as geographic location, its investments in RD & I, this same perspective, Sveiby (1998, p. 24), emphasizes that the so-called "knowledge organizations" are those characterized by having few tangible assets and their intangible assets much more valuable than their tangible assets.

And According to Stewart (1998, cited by ANTUNES; MARTINS, 2007, p. 6), "[...] tangible assets contribute much less to the value of your product or service end of that intangible assets." Whereas the pre-salt extraction requires much more than prior knowledge, and requires investment in large scale research, particularly De Negri (2006, p. 108) in their study identified some factors to measure the ability absorption of the companies, reducing the learning curve.

This requires also was observed by Da Silva; Oliveira; Silva (2011, p. 4), by Factors determining the absorption capacity of technology companies.

Considering the operational know-how, it is clear that Petrobras operates 23% of global production in deep water, being independent of this framework, the exploration of the pre-salt, goes further, and should be considered as new business to a new market, given that alternative fuels increasingly gaining space, not to mention the exploitation of "black gold", the shortage will lead to the same.

Another large and important variable to be considered, without doubt are the environmental challenges and their possible impacts, given recent events, where you can highlight the accident by British Petroleum - BP in mid-2010.

The accident with the Deep-water, the platform operated by British Petroleum (BP) in the Gulf of Mexico undoubtedly produced much more than the leak of five thousand barrels of oil per day. In addition to the environmental consequences, with a spot of more than 50 km in length, the accident did the British company losing $ 25 billion in market value and raised some questions, among which are:

- Considering the magnitude of environmental accident, on an international scale, to what extent the operation of drilling in high seas has been affected?
- While environmentalists around the world to question this type of operation off-shore, pointed to by experts as one of the safest in the production chain of oil black, accidents such as the Gulf of Mexico in 2010, are increasingly rare?

Considering the problems of distribution logistics, with special emphasis on transport, as found in the survey of Rodrigues (2010), it is important to note that other studies reveal that large oil spills at sea occurred more frequently and were more harmful the environment during transport of the product and not on his farm, the scene observed that the representation in Table 2.

**Table 2.** Ranking of the 10 largest oil spill accidents at sea (Source: The International Tanker Owners Pollution Federation – ITOPF 2010)

| Date | Ship | Local | Leak (Ton. x 1000) |
|------|------|-------|--------------------|
| 1979 | Atlantic Empress | Tobago | 278 |
| 1991 | ABT Summer | Angola | 260 |
| 1983 | Castillo de Bellver | África do Sul | 252 |
| 1978 | Amoco Cadiz | França | 223 |
| 1991 | Haven | Itália | 144 |
| 1988 | Odyssey | Canadá | 132 |
| 1967 | Torrey Canyon | Reino Unido | 119 |
| 1976 | Urquiola | Espanha | 100 |
| 1977 | Hawallian Patriot | Honolulu | 95 |
| 1979 | Independenta | Turquia | 95 |

Considering the approach of the problems of distribution logistics, Gouveia (2010, p. 35) also notes that: Two Petrobras projects developed by teachers in the UNESP campus of the North Coast, in San Vicente, and approved by Promimp, seek to ensure rapid and efficient accident associated with extraction and production of oil in the Santos Basin. One proposes the installation of filters made of activated charcoal in the bottom of the sea, for the absorption of oil in case of leaks in vessels or platforms.

The other aims to implement a regional referral center for study control and monitoring of aquatic and terrestrial environments, in order to protect the biodiversity of the regions explored.

The Petrobras itself (2011) states that the challenges are to find ways to provide efficient and especially in finding logistics solutions for this energy source more and more distant. However the flow of production is still a topic in depth discussion, given the risks and costs involved, but is already approaching the reinjection of gas into the soil. Gouveia (2010, p. 33) also reveals that, "[...] the logistics organization is another bottleneck: How to support the transport of people and cargo and supply of diesel for operation of the rigs and production platforms?

The distance of the pre-salt accumulations from the coast is about 300 km, which is the maximum range of flight autonomy of most helicopters.

Petrobras's own research shows that the solution may be the construction of intermediate bases, installed between the point of production and shipment of resources, providing better techno-economic feasibility for the process of extracting the pre-salt. However the search for optimal solution for the scenario of the pre-salt, Petrobras has signed partnerships with institutes and universities stand out among the fifteen Brazilian universities:

- Universidade Estadual Paulista (UNESP),
- São Paulo University (USP),
- State University of Campinas (UNICAMP),
- Universidade Federal de São Carlos (UFSCar),
- Federal University of Rio de Janeiro (UFRJ),
- Universidade Federal da Bahia (UFBA),
- Institute of Technological Research of São Paulo (IPT), among others.

# 6     Practical Implications

This study aims to contribute about thinking in logistics and transportation of petroleum considering the extraction of the same in the pre-salt layer, where large distances must be considered in order to avoid impacts, particularly environmental.

# 7    Value of the Paper

The issue of sustainability, in particular the geographical, directly affects the operation of the pre-salt, considering especially the distances involved, the logistics of transportation and distribution of products, and especially the disposal or reuse of excess natural gas, which is inherent extraction, which somehow has encouraged large-scale surveys in order to obtain effective responses, and provides technical-economic in exploring the viability of the pre-salt layer.

An aggravating factor seen in the research, especially considering the formation of intellectual capital, will be the peak of production that require a highly qualified man power, considering that there will be a learning curve, impacting the absorption curve of technology. How is the timing between research and development, innovation and application themselves of the resources involved?

Considering the presence of foreign corporations in the process of exploitation of the pre-salt layer, as is being conducted to integrate technology, considering the learning curve? Given the magnitude of the project, current events and oil spill at sea.

Considering all the variables considered in this and other research, the question is: Are we truly prepared? Thus, the main result was observed in research that somehow the oil and natural gas should and must have a holistic vision for the future of energy, considering the scarcity of resources and innovation in the search for sustainable alternatives.

In this approach, the coming decades are likely to be the most challenging energy history of the planet, especially considering the recent scientific studies that point to alternative fuels, in a more sustainable world in fact.

# References

1. Carvalho, J.C.A.: Desenvolvimento Sustentável e Turismo: O caso dos Lençóis Maranhenses. Dissertação de Mestrado. Escola Brasileira de Administração Pública e de Empresas– Fundação Getúlio Vargas. Rio de Janeiro (2005)
2. Cohen, W.M., Levinthal, D.A.: Absorptive capacity: a new perspective on learning and innovation. Administrative Science Quarterly 35(1), 128–152 (1990)
3. Fernandes, F.R.C., et al.: Grandes minas e comunidade: algumas questões conceituais. Rio de Janeiro. CETEM/MCT, 58p. (2007)
4. Fraga, C.T.C.: O pré-sal e seus desafios. Audiência Pública no Senado Federal. Out. (2008)
5. Da Silva, A.L., Silva, J.L.G., Oliveira, E.A.A.Q.: Geografia da Inovação Industrial: uma análise da microrregião de são José dos Campos - SP. In: XII Mostra de Pós-Graduação, Internacionalização da Universidade: desafios no cenário global, Taubat (2011)
6. Gouveia, F.: Tecnologia nacional para extrair petróleo e gás do pré-sal. Conhecimento & Inovação 6(1), 30–35 (1984) ISSN 1984-4395
7. Jacobi, P.: Meio Ambiente e Sustentabilidade. In: CEPAM Fundação Professor Faria Lima. O Município no Século XXI: Cenários e Perspectivas, Especial, São Paulo (1999)
8. Lima, J.P.R., Fernandes, A.C.: Demandas e ofertas tecnológicas em economias retardatárias: anotações a partir de dois segmentos econômicos no Nordeste brasileiro. Revista Brasileira de Inovação, Rio de Janeiro 8, 303–340 (2009)

9. Lima, P.C.R.: Os desafios, os impactos e a gestão da exploração do pré-sal. Câmara dos Deputados (2008), Disponível em: http://www.bd.camara.gov.br/bd/handle/bdcamara/984 (acesso em: September 22, 2011)

10. Antunes, M.T.P., Martins, E.: Gerenciando o capital intelectual: uma proposta baseada na controladoria de grandes empresas brasileiras. Revista de Administração Eletrônica da UFRGS (READ), Porto Alegre, edição 3(55) (January/Abr 2007)

11. OSLO MANUAL. Proposed guidelines for collecting and interpreting technological innovation data. Paris: OECD: Statistical Office of the European Communities (1997)

12. PETROBRAS. Disponível em: http://www.petrobras.gov.br/pt/ energia-e-tecnologia/tecnologia-e-pesquisa/ diversificando-os-produtos (acesso em: October 02, 2011)

13. PETROBRAS. Centro de Pesquisas e Desenvolvimento – CENPES (2010)

14. PROVEDOR GOOGLE. Disponível em, http://www.google.com/imagens/pré-sal (acesso em: September 27, 2011)

15. Rodrigues, R.C.: Pré-sal: desafios tecnológicos. Revista: Conhecimento & Inovação 6(1), 26–27 (2010) ISSN 1984-4395

16. Sachs, I.: Estratégias de transição para o século XXI – desenvolvimento e meio ambiente. Studio Nobel/Fundap, São Paulo (1993)

17. Sveiby, K.E.: A Nova Riqueza das Organizações: gerenciando e avaliando patrimônios de conhecimento. Tradução de Luiz Euclides T. F. Filho. Campus, Rio de Janeiro (1998)

# Applicability of Risk Process in Software Projects in Accordance with ISO 31.000:2009

Marcelo Nogueira[1] and Ricardo J. Machado[2]

[1] Software Engineering Research Group, University Paulista, UNIP, Campus of Tatuapé,
São Paulo, Brasil
marcelo@noginfo.com.br
[2] ALGORITMI Center, School of Engineering, University of Minho, Campus of Azurém,
Guimarães, Portugal
rmac@dsi.uminho.pt

**Abstract.** In a progressively competitive global market, software development companies, under the pressure for conquering new market shares, subject themselves to business demands where the inherent risks to these operations are diversified and of exposure not always calculated. Given that a minority of such companies adopt risk management into their business processes, such exposure may affect the participation and success of these projects. To assure the quality of the software risk analysis and risk assessments are required. Among the uncertainties of software design, some risk factors should be treated: timeline, estimated costs and compliance to business requirements, among others, can be mentioned. Through a bibliographical review it was possible to produce a risk roadmap to provide to the professional in the field the understanding of risks process in a friendly way. To contribute to these software projects, this work presents the activities of a risk management process, in order to insert the culture and capacity of professionals who work in such projects, can objectively target to the mitigation of risks into which such projects are exposed. In addition, the adopted approach is in accordance to ISO 31000 standard.

**Keywords:** software engineering, risk management, software crisis, quality software, information systems.

## 1 Introduction

In a competitive environment of increasingly complex change, the appropriate management of information is crucial in the process of decision making in organizations (Nogueira, 2009).

Being this subject both comprehensive and specialized, the adoption of the practices of software engineering as a baseline of information management enables the development and consolidation of knowledge in the production of software.

These practices also prepare professionals to confidently face new challenges in the business world, strengthening their skills and abilities and keeping them up to date on the potential of information systems and new technologies in a globally competitive business perspective.

C. Emmanouilidis, M. Taisch, D. Kiritsis (Eds.): APMS 2012, Part I, IFIP AICT 397, pp. 734–741, 2013.

The objective this paper is present applicability of risk management through the roadmap with critical points the process of software production identified in the literary review.

This literary review consists of a merger between the classical scientific references in the area production software and the recent consolidation the ISO 31000.

## 2    Software Crisis versus Software Quality

Software engineering can be defined as a set of methods, procedures and tools aimed at the production of software with quality, in other words, in accordance with customer requirements (Nogueira, 2009).

Software engineering has as primary objective the quality improvement of software products and the increase of the productivity of software engineers, in addition to meeting the requirements of efficiency and effectiveness (Maffeo, 1992).

In the study of software engineering, author Roger S. Pressman (2006) mentions the "Software Crisis", where numbers are given that express the problem with non-completion of software projects. The same author points out that one of the main factors that cause such "Software Crisis" is the lack of adoption of methods, procedures and tools in building software.

The term "Software Crisis", which began to be used in the 60s, historically alludes to a set of problems recurrently faced in the process of software development (construction, deployment and maintenance) (Maffeo, 1992).

In general terms, the "Software Crisis" occurs when the software does not meet the customers, users, developers or enterprise needs and exceeds cost and time estimates (Nogueira, 2009).

Despite the enormous variety of problems that characterize the software crisis, in computer systems development field, engineers and project managers tend to focus their concerns on the following point: "There is huge uncertainty of estimates of timelines and development costs" (Nogueira, 2009).

Many of these errors could be avoided if organizations could have a software engineering process defined, controlled, measured and improved. However, it is clear that for many IT professionals these concepts are not very clear, which certainly hampers the action of managers in the improvement of their production processes (Blaschek, 2003).

There are several techniques, methodologies and quality standards to contribute to the development of software, including risk management. Professionals who do not embrace them find difficulties in performing software projects which are free of maintenance and re-work, so directly condemning the product quality.

Adoption of software engineering leads the individual to perform the activities related to their professional role through systematic methods throughout the software life cycle, allowing the developed product to represent the company actual processes and to meet in fact the company needs.

Achieving a high quality product or service is the goal of most organizations. It is no longer acceptable to deliver products with low quality and fix the problems and deficiencies after the products were delivered to the customer (Sommerville, 2007).

Quality is a result of processes, people and technology. The relationship between product, quality and each of these factors is complex. Therefore, it is much harder to control the degree of product quality than to control the requirements (Paula Filho, 2009).

When producing software with quality, the real possibility of extracting relevant information from a system is created. This may not only contribute to the decision, but to be a factor of business excellence, enabling new business, retention and survival in an active market. Thus, it is of paramount importance to identify and analyze risks that threaten the success of the project and manage them so that the business objectives may be achieved.

Aiming at quality in the process of software production, risk management has the focus to address the uncertainties inherent to software projects, because many factors that involve technology, people and processes are in conflict and can determine whether the development of the software product will be successful or not.

According to Standish Group (2009), through a study called "Chaos Report", for projects in the area of information technology, the following conclusions were drawn (Table 1):

- 32% of projects finish on time and on budget;
- 44% of projects are challenged;
- 24% are canceled before its deployment.

**Table 1.** Chaos Report (Standish Group, 2009)

| Projects / Year | 1994 | 1996 | 1998 | 2000 | 2002 | 2004 | 2006 | 2009 |
|-----------------|------|------|------|------|------|------|------|------|
| Successful      | 16   | 27   | 26   | 28   | 34   | 29   | 35   | 32   |
| Contested       | 53   | 33   | 46   | 49   | 51   | 53   | 46   | 44   |
| Cancelled       | 31   | 40   | 28   | 23   | 15   | 18   | 19   | 24   |
| Failed          | 84   | 73   | 74   | 72   | 66   | 71   | 65   | 68   |

As for cost and schedule, the following information was obtained:

- Surplus in original estimated cost in 45% of the projects.
- Surplus in original schedule in 63% of the projects.

Other collected data are:

- 94% of the projects have at least one restart (Standish, 2009);
- 9% of projects in large companies come into operation within initially estimated cost and time.
- In software projects only 67% of originally proposed requirements are delivered in the end.

Despite the "Software Crisis" is not a new problem, even nowadays its impact and its negative effects are faced. The scarce use of methodologies and models of quality in Brazil indicates that this reality has to be modified.

According to the Ministry of Science and Technology (2002), only 11.8% of companies in Brazil have adopted risk management in software projects.

Due to the relevance of the theme and its direct impact on the success in producing software, the number presented by the ministry is alarming because the sample used for the research included both the major software companies and the small and medium enterprises in the country (Nogueira, 2009).

The concerning fact is that small and medium enterprises, which hold 65.1% of the software market in Brazil (MCT, 2002), lack a culture of risk management. Besides contributing to the possibility of failure in current projects, this situation undermines the still promising future opportunities that this sector needs to explore in both domestic and foreign markets.

New research in 2005 and 2008 were made by the Ministry of Science and Technology, but the item risk management was not added to the survey.

# 3 Risks and Software Engineering

Risk, such as science, was born in the sixteenth century, during the Renaissance. In an attempt to understand the games of chance, Blaise Pascal, in 1654, discovered the "Theory of Probability" and created the "Pascal Triangle", which determines the likelihood of possible outcomes, given a certain number of attempts (Bernstein, 1997).

Risk in the software area was represented in a systematic manner by Barry Boehm in the 80s through the Spiral Model, which has as its principle be iterative and directed to risks, because for each iteration it is performed an analysis of risk (Boehm, 1988).

Risks in software cannot be mere agenda items. They should be the "heart" of the business, as in other areas (Chadbourne, 1999).

Currently, the area that addresses risks in software engineering has evolved from an analysis within the model of development, as proposed by spiral model, to become a management technique that should permeate all the processes of software life cycle.

Risk management is understood as a general procedure for resolution of risk, ie when it is applied in any instance, the possible consequences are all acceptable, and policies to cope with the worst outcome must be defined in the process.

Risk management, in software design domain, is a defined and systematic process with the purpose of treating risk factors in order to mitigate or minimize its effects, producing a quality software product that meets customer needs, within estimated time and costs (Nogueira, 2009).

According to Robert Charette (1989), the definition of risk is:

First, risk affects future events. Present and past are irrelevant, because what is reaped today was planted by our previous actions. The issue is changing our actions today. Can opportunity be created for a different and possibly better situation tomorrow?

Secondly, this means that risk involves change, such as change of thought, opinion, action or places. Thirdly, risk involves choice and the uncertainty that choice entails itself.

Thus, paradoxically, the risk, like death and taxes, is one of the few certainties of life.

In a simplified way, a risk can be thought as a probability that some adverse circumstance will really occur. The risks may threaten the project, the software being developed or the organization.

Sommerville (2007) has described the types of risks that may affect the project and the organizational environment in which software is being built. However, many risks are considered universal and they include the following areas: Technology, personnel, organizational, tools, requirements and estimation.

The estimation of risks involves the following tasks:

- Identification of possible risks to the project;
- Analysis of these risks, evaluating their probability and likely impact;
- Prediction of corrective or preventive countermeasures;
- Prioritization of risks, organizing them according to likelihood and impact.

Risks do not remain constant during the execution of a project. Some disappear, new ones arise, and others suffer changes of probability and impact, therefore changing the priority. Therefore a monitoring report of the project along with an updated table shall be used for monitoring the risks. The estimation table should be reviewed and updated to reflect the modifications until the risks are realized or completely eliminated (Paula Filho, 2009).

The adoption of risk engineering is part of the critical success factors in software projects. The management of risks throughout the life cycle of development is critical to project success (Nogueira, 2009).

Risk management is particularly important for software projects, due to the inherent uncertainties that most projects face (Sommerville, 2007).

Project managers of information systems should regularly assess the risks during the development process to minimize the chances of failure. In particular, the problems of schedule, budget and functionality of the software can not be totally eliminated but they can be controlled through the implementation of preventive actions (Higuera, 1996).

Risk management has six well-defined activities that are: Risk identification, risk analysis, risk planning, risk monitoring, risk control and risk communication (Higuera, 1996).

The activities of risk identification and risk analysis, critical risk assessment, risk mitigation and contingency plans should be made. The methods of risk assessment should be used to demonstrate and evaluate the risks. Constraint policies of the project must also be determined at the time when discussions with all others involved take place. Aspects inherent to risks of software, such as the tendency of professionals to add features that are difficult to measure or even the risks of intangible nature of software, should influence the risk management of project (SWEBOK, 2004).

The Orange Book (2004), originally developed by the British government, now an international reference handbook, details the guidelines for good risk management, involving the following activities: Identifying risks, assessing risks, risk appetite, addressing risks, reviewing and reporting risks, communication and learning.

The ISO 31000 (2009) standard directs the policy for risk management with the following activities: establishing the context, risk identification, risk analysis, risk assessment, risk treatment, communication and consultation and monitoring and review.

# 4    Roadmap for Risk Management Process

After the literary review, it was possible to identify critical areas in the process of software development.

However, to support risk management in software projects, it is necessary to use a roadmap with activities where the decision maker can use it as an auxiliary instrument in the process of risk management.

Therefore, the following activities make up this roadmap: Communication and consultation; establishing the context; risk identification; risk analysis; risk evaluation; risk treatment and monitoring and review.

These activities are described below according to the complexity of application in accordance with ISO 31000.

## 4.1    Communication and Consultation

Communication and consultation with external and internal stakeholders should take place during all stages of the risk management process. It should take place in the beginning, with the first meeting of sensitization, during activities and in the end, with the presentation of results.

## 4.2    Establishing the Context

By establishing the context, the organization articulates its objectives and defines the external and internal parameters to be taken into account when managing risk, and sets the scope and risk criteria for the remaining process.

## 4.3    Risk Identification

The organization should identify sources of risk, areas of impacts, events (including changes in circumstances) and their causes and their potential consequences. The aim of this step is to generate a comprehensive list of risks based on those events that might create, enhance, prevent, degrade, accelerate or delay the achievement of objectives.

It is important to identify the risks associated to not pursuing an opportunity. Comprehensive identification is critical, because a risk that is not identified at this stage will not be included in further analysis. It is recommended to use a universal framework with risks common to different designs when it is the first iteration.

## 4.4    Risk Analysis

Risk analysis involves developing an understanding of the risk. Risk analysis provides an input to risk evaluation and to decisions on whether risks need to be treated, and on the most appropriate risk treatment strategies and methods.

Risk analysis can also provide an input into making decisions where choices must be made and the options involve different types and levels of risk. A framework can be used with the universal risk weights established from expert opinion, especially when you do not have a knowledge base.

## 4.5    Risk Evaluation

The purpose of risk evaluation is to assist in making decisions, based on the outcomes of risk analysis. It defines which risks need treatment and the priority for treatment implementation.

Risk evaluation involves comparing the level of risk found during the analysis process with risk criteria established when the context was considered. Based on this comparison, the need for treatment can be considered.

## 4.6    Risk Treatment

Risk treatment involves selecting one or more options for modifying risks, and implementing those options. Once implemented, the provision of treatments or modification of controls must be performed.

Risk treatment involves a cyclical process of: Assessing a risk treatment; deciding whether residual risk levels are tolerable; if not tolerable, generating a new risk treatment; and assessing the effectiveness of that treatment.

## 4.7    Monitoring and Review

Both monitoring and review should be a planned part of the risk management process and involve regular checking or surveillance. It can be periodic or ad hoc.

Responsibilities for monitoring and review should be clearly defined. The organization's monitoring and review processes should encompass all aspects of the risk management process for the purposes of: Ensuring that controls are effective and efficient in both design and operation; obtaining further information to improve risk assessment; analyzing and learning lessons from events (including near-misses), changes, trends, successes and failures; detecting changes in the external and internal context, including changes to risk criteria and the risk itself which can require revision of risk treatments and priorities; and identifying emerging risks.

# 5    Conclusion

In this literary review, it was found that the authors recognize the difficulty in the production process of software. It's possible to realize that the scenario of the "software crisis" provides failure to projects. And that the adoption of software engineering and its assumptions are critical to project success. Despite the existence of activities and processes focused on the production of software, its adoption is insufficient, especially in the Brazilian context. However, when teams of software production are guided through a roadmap, it becomes easier to understand "what to do". With the defined scope it is possible to sensitize stakeholders to the adoption of risk management as a common organizational practice. The compliance roadmap in relation to ISO 31000 is essential. As future work, we intend to apply the roadmap on projects that never used the risk management process in software production.

**Acknowledgements.** This work has been supported by FEDER through *Programa Operacional Fatores de Competitividade – COMPETE* and by *Fundos Nacionais* through *FCT – Fundação para a Ciência e Tecnologia* in the scope of the project: FCOMP-01-0124-FEDER-022674 by Portugal and University Paulista - Software Engineering Research Group by Brazil.

# References

1. ISO 31000: Risk management – Principles and guidelines: ISO (2009)
2. Bernstein, P.: Desafio aos deuses: a fascinante história do risco. Campus, RJ (1997)
3. Blaschek, J.R.: O principal problema dos projetos de software. Rio de Janeiro (2003)
4. Boehm, B.: A spiral model of software development and enhancement. IEEE (1988)
5. Chadbourne, B.C.: To the heart of risk management: teaching project teams to combat risk. Pennsylvania (1999)
6. Charette, R.N.: Software Engineering risk analysis and management. McG. Hill (1989)
7. Higuera, R.P., Haimes, Y.Y.: Software risk management technical report: CMU/SEI 96 TR 012. SEI (1996)
8. Maffeo, B.: Engenharia de Software e Especificação de Sistemas. Campus, RJ (1992)
9. MCT. Qualidade e Produtividade do Software Brasileiro. MCT - Secretaria de Política de Informática, Brasília (2002)
10. Nogueira, M.: Engenharia de Software. Um Framework para a Gestão de Riscos. Ciência Moderna, Rio de Janeiro (2009)
11. Orange Book, Management of Risk – Principles, HM Treasury, Crown, London (2004)
12. Paula, F.: Engenharia de Software: fundamentos, métodos e padrões. LTC, RJ (2009)
13. Pressman, R.S.: Engenharia de Software, 2nd edn. McGraw-Hill, São Paulo (2006)
14. Sommerville, I.: Engenharia de Software, 8th edn. Pearson A.Wesley, São Paulo (2007)
15. Standish, CHAOS Summary 1995...2009. Standish Group, Boston (2009)
16. SWEBOK, Guide to the software engineering body of knowledge. IEEE Computer Society, USA (2004)

# Author Index

Printed in the United States
By Bookmasters